PAUL BÉNICHOU

The Consecration ❧ of the Writer, 1750–1830

Le Sacre de l'écrivain

TRANSLATED BY

Mark K. Jensen

University of Nebraska Press

Lincoln & London

Cet ouvrage publié dans le cadre du programme d'aide à la publication bénéficie du soutien du Ministère des Affaires Etrangères et du Service Culturel de l'Ambassade de France représenté aux Etats-Unis.

This work, published as part of the program of aid for publication, received support from the French Ministry of Foreign Affairs and the Cultural Service of the French Embassy in the United States.

Library of Congress Cataloging in Publication Data
Bénichou, Paul.
[Sacre de l'écrivain, 1750–1830. English]
The consecration of the writer, 1750-1830 = Le sacre de l'écrivain, 1750-1830 / Paul Bénichou ; translated by Mark K. Jensen.
p. cm. – (European horizons) Includes bibliographical references and index. ISBN 0-8032-1291-7 (cloth : alk. paper). – ISBN 0-8032-6152-7 (paper : alk. paper)
1. French literature – 18th century – History and criticism. 2. French literature – 19th century – History and criticism. 3. Religion and literature. I. Jensen, Mark K., 1951-. II. Title. III. Series.
PQ265.B4413 1999 840.9′382–dc21 98-42381 CIP

TO *Gina*

CONTENTS

Tzvetan Todorov

Preface

PAUL Bénichou, one of the greatest intellectual figures of this century in France, is the author of an extraordinary body of work. The discipline in which he has distinguished himself is the history of thought. In this discipline one must be both vastly learned and philosophically profound, which doubtless explains why it features so few masters. Bénichou holds a special place among them: he studies, above all, the *thought of poets*. Bénichou does not describe the vicissitudes of abstract ideas; rather, he explores what happens in the singular encounter of an idea with a passion, a narrative, an image, a form. His point of departure is thus a thorough knowledge of literary works, which has no equivalent among other historians of ideas. Poets think, and their thought lives in their works, which are addressed to everyone: such is the simple truth that has served as the point of departure of this exacting labor, embodied today in nearly a dozen volumes.

Bénichou's work, for fifty years now, has remained quite apart from the various fashions that have waxed and waned in the field of literary studies. For he has never been interested in questions of methods, instead going straight to what is most important: the meaning of texts. What separates him as much from traditional historians of literature as from the different formalist or structuralist schools is his passion for what his authors *thought*. A strictly historical inquiry or a formal analysis can be useful preliminaries, but they play a role that is only auxiliary compared to the paramount goal: the search for the meaning of texts, and thus the attempt to understand the dialogue to which these texts, in their time, contributed. If Bénichou must be said to have a method, it consists first in the patient, humble gathering of information, as well as in the conviction that human thought is not entirely determined by the circumstances of its production, being grounded instead in freedom, and therefore in the responsibility of the thinker. This is no doubt the reason that Bénichou's works have aged not at all: twenty-five years after their initial publication, it is possible to read them as if they had been written yesterday.

Paul Bénichou was born in 1908 to a Jewish family in Tlemcen, Algeria. At first he followed the classic path of the brilliant student of that period: secondary school (in Oran), preparatory classes in Paris, the *Ecole normale supérieure*, the *agrégation de lettres* (in 1930). He began to teach at the secondary level while actively participating in French cultural and political life. But in 1940, shortly after the fall of France, he was stripped of the right to teach and also, as a Jew of Algerian origin, of his French citizenship; he succeeded in leaving the country in 1942 and lived in Argentina until 1949. In 1948 his first book appeared, written before the war: *Morales du grand siècle*, a study of the thought of the great French authors of the seventeenth century (Corneille, Pascal, La Roche-foucauld, Racine, and Molière), a study quickly recognized as a classic, whose standing today is still as high as ever. (This volume was translated into English in 1971, and published by Doubleday Anchor under the title *Man and Ethics: Studies in French Classicism*.) From 1958 until his retirement in 1979, he was professor of Romance languages and literature at Harvard University, teaching one semester a year; the free time enabled him to pursue his in-depth researches in Paris libraries.

This free time was indispensable. For upon his return to France in 1949, Bénichou had conceived a project that has occupied him ever since, even to the present day. The problem could be formulated most abstractly thus: what does spiritual power become in a modern democratic state once it is no longer the exclusive affair of ministers of religion? In France, men of letters in general and poets in particular believed from the second half of the eighteenth century on that a new version of this power would be theirs. Several decades later, they were forced to acknowledge that their ambitions had been in vain. It is the history of this hope and of this disappointment that Bénichou undertakes to analyze; through them, he illuminates the political and literary thought of the great movement known as romanticism, which dominated the entire nineteenth century.

To begin, it was necessary to establish as thorough a documentary foundation as possible. Bénichou's approach to this problem was as simple as it was surprising: he devoted the following twenty years to research. He read virtually everything that was published in France in the literary domain from 1760 to 1860: the great authors as well as the minor ones, the poets and the critics, both books and periodicals. The day came when he felt confident that he had mastered the sources; the work of synthesis could begin. The first volume devoted to this theme, *Le Sacre de l'écrivain*, formulating the general problem and exploring the period from 1760 to 1830, appeared in 1973. In 1977, *Le Temps des prophètes* was published, a volume somewhat different in that it is devoted to the doctrines that dominate the beginning of the nineteenth century, rather than to literary works. This was followed by two volumes studying two succesive generations of romantic poets: *Les Mages romantiques* in 1988 (Lamartine, Vigny,

Hugo) and *L'Ecole du désenchantement* in 1992 (Sainte-Beuve, Nodier, Musset, Nerval, Gautier). In 1995 appeared a lengthy work devoted to a poet who can be considered the last romantic: *Selon Mallarmé*. Only Baudelaire has not yet been honored with a study devoted exclusively to him. . . .

It might be said that the romantic poets were simply deluded in their belief that they would be the world's lawgivers, and that, however painful it may have been to become aware of this, it was preferable to maintaining what was an illusion. But in the history that Bénichou's multivolume study of French romanticism unfolds over several thousand pages, it is not simply a question of the past of an illusion. Through the lens of this history, we can get a better view of questions that are decisive for all of modernity—questions that are essential ones for life in a democracy. What can spiritual power be today? Who holds this power? Who has the right to express the ideals of our society? What is the place of common values in a world characterized by the claim of autonomy made by every human being living in it? The time of the prophets is past, but does this mean that the time of the technicians has come? The work of Paul Bénichou prepares us to engage in reflection upon these questions, as well as on many others like them bearing on the identity and the role of intellectuals, scholars, and creators of the present day.[1]

Translated by Mark K. Jensen

1. *Mélanges sur l'oeuvre de Paul Bénichou* (Gallimard, 1995) contains a number of studies and observations devoted to Bénichou; in addition, it brings together the texts of several long interviews he granted. The interview pertaining to literary studies can be read in English in my *Literature and Its Theorists* (Ithaca NY: Cornell University Press, 1987).

Translator's Introduction

WIDELY recognized as a classic, Paul Bénichou's *Le Sacre de l'écrivain, 1750–1830: Essai sur l'avènement d'un pouvoir spirituel laïque dans la France moderne*, first published in 1973, is now in its fourth edition in France and has previously been translated into Italian and Spanish. When the most recent edition appeared, in 1996, the late François Furet wrote: "What is astonishing, indeed, almost miraculous, is that this great work, which seemed old-fashioned when it first appeared, now looks like a work destined to last forever."[1]

The present unabridged translation was undertaken in the conviction that *The Consecration of the Writer* has much to say to those beyond the confines of French literary circles, where Paul Bénichou has long been called "one of the most respected and admired citizens of the Republic of Letters."[2] For this is not merely a specialized work of literary history, as a cursory glance might lead one to believe. It belongs, rather, to a select group of indispensable achievements of twentieth-century literary scholarship on subjects of perennial interest, like M. H. Abrams's *The Mirror and the Lamp* (1952) and Erich Auerbach's *Mimesis* (1946).

The Consecration of the Writer examines with unparalleled depth and subtlety the first stages of a development of enormous importance for modern literature: the process by which writers ceased to speak as representatives of some religious or political power and assumed the mantle of what Bénichou calls "spiritual authority" in their own right, speaking directly to and in the name of all humanity. *The Consecration of the Writer* is important for another reason as well: it controverts the common view according to which romanticism was an irrationalist reaction against the Enlightenment, arguing rather that the romantic movement was founded upon a revised version of the Enlightenment faith in humanity. For Bénichou, romanticism responds to the trauma of the Age of Revolution while better accommodating spiritual experience. His interpretation is grounded in an understanding of the experience of modernity that both accounts for and evaluates the ideological struggles of the past two centuries. Bénichou describes a religiously grounded traditional order faced in the eighteenth century with a decline in the credibility of its doctrinal foundations. The crisis was accompanied by and seems to have been to a considerable extent the result of a new belief in the essential self-sufficiency of human beings. This hallmark Enlightenment belief inspired widespread hope that a regenerating elite would usher in a new order. When the French Revolution arrived, speaking and acting in the name of all humanity, it was seen as an expression of these beliefs. But the traumatic difficulties encountered during and after the French Revolution represented an intellectual and spiritual challenge to the Enlightenment faith. Bénichou recounts in fascinating detail how the revolutionary trauma led to a convergence of the secular tendencies of the Enlightenment philosophy and the religious revival of the early nineteenth century. It is to this deep convergence that Bénichou attributes the romantic consecration of the writer.

Paul Bénichou's work is of much more than historical interest, however, because the spiritual predicament it describes has yet to be resolved. The transition to modernity has meant a new understanding of the status of spirituality, freedom, and belief. Bénichou's analysis of these sheds light on problems that continue to bedevil contemporary societies and the individuals who live in them.

The Consecration of the Writer is also important as an example of what the study of literature can be, of what literary studies can contribute to the understanding of human affairs. Bénichou's remarks on these subjects in the "Final Reflections" of this volume are particularly important. He insists that writers, works, and ideas should be approached on their own terms; he refuses to reduce the intentions of writers to terms foreign to their arguments. Literature is inherently multifaceted; it is irreducible to any single aspect and superior to any effort to explain it. Bénichou's work reminds us that there is no substitute for the exhaustive, respectful study of the work of writers and of the milieu in which they lived.

As Tzvetan Todorov says in his preface to the present translation, *The Consecration of the Writer* is the fruit of immense research. The depth and breadth of Paul Bénichou's literary knowledge is unmatched and inspires awe among his *confrères*. He has consulted all the texts he discusses in their original editions and sounded deeply the immense periodical literature of the period. Yet the reader is never overwhelmed by ponderous erudition. Somehow Bénichou manages to wear his learning lightly. Perhaps this is because these pages attest to a profound belief in human dignity. Paul Bénichou has called his work a "defense of the prerogatives of the creative spirit in literature."[3] Nothing is more fundamental to his approach to literature than the belief that "a work always bears witness . . . to an essential freedom to create. . . . [T]his freedom is one of the mind's essential possessions."[4] Critics and historians who study literature share this essential privilege, and so does the reader. In these pages there is no pretense of strict objectivity, for human beings and the human condition are not and cannot be mere objects. It is in this sense that the present volume both analyzes the modern quest for self-understanding and is itself an important contribution to this quest. The depth of Paul Bénichou's research, the originality of his conclusions, and the importance of his methodological reflections make *The Consecration of the Writer* an essential reference in the contemporary return to literary history.

Mark K. Jensen

1. François Furet, "Le Sacre de Paul Bénichou," *Le Nouvel Observateur* (May 26, 1996), p.116.

2. Marc Fumaroli, ed., *Le Statut de la littérature: Mélanges offerts à Paul Bénichou* (Geneva: Droz, 1982), p.ix.

3. Paul Bénichou, "Réflexions sur la critique littéraire," in Fumaroli, ed., *Le Statut de la litterature*, p.19.

4. Ibid.

A Note on the Translation

With a few exceptions made for the sake of clarity, I have refrained from breaking Bénichou's chains of independent clauses joined by semicolons and colons into independent sentences.

The occasional capitalization of certain abstract nouns (sensibility, being, the poet, etc.) in the original has, in general, been retained here. Minor inconsistencies may be noted. For example, Bénichou is not always consistent on the inclusion of an initial article in a title. In the original, he sometimes italicizes the titles of journal articles and poems; on other occasions he places them *entre guillemets*. The present translation is somewhat more consistent in this regard, placing the titles of poems and articles in periodicals in quotation marks, sometimes translated, sometimes not. In general, when the author has italicized a title, I have left it untranslated; when he has placed it *entre guillemets*, I have translated it. I have almost always followed the rule for the capitalization of French titles used by the *French Review*, according to which the first word and, if the first word is an article, the first substantive and any intervening adjectives are capitalized. I have occasionally provided fuller titles of works for the convenience of readers less familiar with the French literary tradition.

In his extensive notes Bénichou follows no uniform style. Rather than adapt his notes to an American style, I have chosen to adhere as closely as possible to the various forms he employs, since they are clear and always convey the essential information. However, I have generally placed in parentheses (or, if already inside parentheses, in brackets) the city and/or date of publication of cited texts, when these are known to me; I have used "pp." rather than "p." where he cites more than one page; and I have often substituted "ff." for "et suiv." when referring to page numbers. Otherwise, the notes substantially stand as in the original and are given in their entirety. The original edition provides only an index of names; the index at the end of this volume is the work of the translator.

When Bénichou cites poetry, the untranslated verses stand in the body of the text with my fairly literal translation in brackets directly beneath them.

I have occasionally added in brackets a note of my own, followed by *Trans*.

Author's Note

I have reduced the length of the notes as much as I could by sacrificing many remarks and references that could be foregone without excessive loss, in order to make this volume less daunting to the reader. In any case, the body of the text is self-sufficient, and readers may peruse the notes or not, according to their tastes and inclinations.

A methodical bibliography of works consulted for a subject like this one would have been of outlandish proportions; the titles to which I have referred in my notes give what is essential. Readers who so desire can easily find the bibliographical references likely to interest them on any given subject by consulting the table of contents in conjunction with the index.

I wish to thank here all the persons who kindly helped me with their observations and encouragement during the course of this long undertaking. I also wish to express how much I owe to the staff of the Bibliothèque Nationale: during many long years I met with nothing but kindness and valuable assistance at every level of this exemplary organization. I am particularly grateful to Mlle Marguerite-Marie Peyraube, Mme Aline Lattès, Mlle Andrée Lhéritier, and Messrs Roger Pierrot, Jean Bruno, and Francis Peyraube; I was never able to exhaust their courtesy or their competence. I should like to express here how deeply grateful I am to them.

The Consecration of the Writer, 1750–1830

Introduction

A S FAR back as we can go in the history of civilizations, literature has served to instruct humanity, offering to be an interpreter of the human condition and a guide to humanity's views and its choices. But at the beginning of the cultural tradition that has produced us, two different models of this mission of literature can be seen: the Greek model, according to which literature acts with relative independence, in a profane mode, vis-à-vis a religion that imposes only slight spiritual constraints; and the Jewish model, according to which the written word is scarcely conceivable except in strict accord with a sovereign notion of the divine. The authority and the pretensions of literature derive, in the Greek model, from its claim that it alone answers the great questions; in the Jewish model, from the supernatural approval implicit in its literary creations.

The Greeks gave themselves to untrammeled meditation upon the universe and humanity under the name of philosophy; religion and the State were, in principle, outside the purview of philosophers, but if a vision of the whole was desired, they alone could provide it. In Greek culture, philosophy was the highest spiritual authority; it was by virtue of its prestige that the pagan world was able to resist Christianity at first and to influence it later. Literature constituted a worthy companion to philosophy; inspiration, creation, and eloquence had their rights alongside strictly rational thought. Through all of classical Antiquity runs a doctrine of enthusiasm that assimilates poetic inspiration to the gift of prophecy, and attributes poetry, like prophecy, to possession by a god. Poets, though less masters of the truths they teach than sages, hold them from a higher source. The posited divine connection, however, does not constrain the poet's genius; it merely enhances it and, as it were, divinizes the poet. Plato acknowledges the poet's privilege: possessed by the Muses, "the poet glorifies the countless mighty deeds of ancient times, doing this for the instruction of posterity"; the inspired race of poets "grasps many an event in its truth, by the help of the Graces and the Muses"; "fathers and guides in matters of wisdom," such are poets by virtue of a divine influence.[1] It is true that by saying that poets are under the influence of a god, the philosopher intends to depreciate poetry in comparison to philosophy, and to cast some suspicion on minds irresponsible and mimetic by their very nature.[2] But this dispute on the part of the philosopher leaves the homage intact: the poet speaks and teaches with authority.

In these matters the Romans followed the Greeks. They reaffirm the divine source of poetry: "There is a god in us; it is when he moves us that we become animated"; "there is a god in us, and we are in communication with heaven; this afflatus comes to us from the ethereal abode."[3] They consider the educational mission of the poet, attested by the legends of Orpheus and Amphion, to be still alive: "The distinction between public and private and between sacred and profane, the ban on casual couplings and the prescription of the laws of marriage, the construction of cities and the engraving of the law on tablets: by these feats glory and renown redounded to poets and their noble verses." The mind of the poet, "having withdrawn into places pristine and innocent, benefits from holy dwellings where eloquence is born and where it has its sanctuary; and it was thus that eloquence, pouring into innocent hearts exempt from every vice, enabled them to improve our mortal lot."[4] Philosophy, which appeared after poetry, has never dethroned it. In fact, to counterbalance the pretensions of philosophers, an effort was made to reveal the poets as hidden philosophers; Homer was made out to be an allegorist, and, so as to make him the equal of Plato, a profound doctrine was supposed to lie hidden beneath his tales. Thus was born and thus has survived, in the culture of Antiquity itself, an exalted idea of the forces of the human mind as wisdom and inspiration combined.

The triumph of Christianity made literature subject to an orthodoxy guarded by a body of priests. The Jewish heritage, invading in this way a Hellenic culture to which it was so deeply adverse, risked destroying it. Christian sarcasms against the lies and dangers of profane culture have never ceased; an attitude of strict opposition has sometimes prevailed, and for long periods of time; in spite of all this, there has been accommodation as well as conflict. The Fathers of the Church have endeavored to make Plato agree with the God of Sinai and the Trinity. But in thus honoring pagan letters, the door was opened to a Christian literature that was not strictly dogmatic. The philosopher was in danger of being absorbed by the theologian, but the risk for the poet was less. In order to render the Scripture narratives respectable to pagans, allegorical interpretations were offered that were analogous to those with which the pagans themselves had favored their poets. From a certain point of view, the sacred text appeared henceforth as a composition that the Holy Spirit, far from wishing to prohibit literature, had made the divine model of all rhetoric. Thus everything encouraged Christian poets to imitate this example as best they could and to bear witness in their turn and by their works to truth. Throughout the Middle Ages, these views found wide support in theological circles: poetic creation was made respectable by means of a theory of the symbol and "signification," and was even considered in the same light as the truths of the faith, with the poetic books in the Scriptures being invoked as authorities and models and with the Holy Spirit who dictated them standing as the inspiration of poets.

Thus was constituted a doctrine according to which the writer's function, brought into harmony with belief, is defined and esteemed as essential to the glory of God and the edification of men. The renaissance of classical studies did nothing to harm such a conception of things. In the sixteenth and seventeenth centuries, theologians once more take up this apology for literature at the highest spiritual level and modernize it, putting to advantage a renewed knowledge of classical doctrine. Authors do likewise, but from a different point of view: we can observe in their productions a promotion of profane literature to a genuinely higher status. From this point on, everything that can be said to the greater glory of letters is a reminder of their situation in ancient times; literature assumes once again an autonomous role that, while repeating Antiquity, announces something very different: a time when the authority of religion is no longer so complete. The glorious claims of poets establish them high above the status of cantors or harpists of the temple, to which theology, on the whole, assigned them. This prestigious doctrine bursts forth in the works of the poets of the *Pléiade*. Ronsard defines poets as "inspired priests" (*des prestres agités*), glutting themselves with love in the lap of the gods:

> De-là, revolans au monde
> Comblés de segrés divers,
> Ils chantent par l'univers
> D'une vois où dieu abonde,
> Et l'ardeur de leur faconde
> Sert d'oracles, et sont faits
> Les ministres plus parfaits
> De la déité parfonde.[5]

> [Returning whence to the world
> Filled with divers secrets,
> They sing throughout the universe
> With a voice in which God can be heard,
> And the ardor of their speech,
> Free-flowing and oracular, makes them
> The most perfect ministers
> Of the mysterious deity.]

Or again:

Dieu est en nous, et par nous fait miracle,
Si que les vers d'un poëte ecrivant
Ce sont des dieus les secrets et oracles
Que par sa bouche ils poussent en avant.[6]

[God is in us, and through us works miracles,
So that the verses poets write
Are the secrets and oracles of gods
Which they make known through the poets' mouths.]

The great "Ode to Michel de l'Hospital"[7] deploys in French verse a vast synthesis of classical texts and ideas. All the themes are present: the divine spirit breathed into poets, their mission as interpreters of secrets from on high, their authority as judges of kings and conferrers of glory in this world, the stupid hostility and persecution they endure from the vulgar.[8] The strangely exalted character of these professions of faith is surprising; even more so assertions like the one proclaiming poetic enthusiasm to be "the unique staircase by which the soul can find the path that leads it to the source of its sovereign good and last felicity."[9] This absolute preeminence of poets fits into the Christian framework neither as a poetic conceit nor as an abstract idea:

Eulx piquez de la doulce rage,
Dont ces Femmes les tourmentoyent,
D'un demoniacle courage
Les secretz des Dieux racontoyent:
Si que paissant par les Campagnes
Les troupeaux dans les champs herbeux,
Les Démons, et les Soeurs compaignes
La nuict s'apparoissoient à eux:
Et loing sur les eaux solitaires
Carollant en rond dans les prez
Les promovoyent Prestres sacrez
Et leur aprenoyent les mysteres.[10]

[Pricked by the sweet madness
With which these Women torment them,
With a daimonic courage
They tell the secrets of the Gods:
So that when the grazing flocks
Are in the countryside's grassy fields,
The Daimons and the attendant Sisters
Appear at night to them:
And, far over the lonely waters

Dancing and singing in a ring in the meadows,
They promote them to the rank of sacred Priests
And teach them the mysteries.]

The heterodoxy of this poetic doctrine is that of the neoplatonist movement with which it is associated. It is less a question of a synthesis governed by Christian theology than of a sort of syncretism in which theology is outflanked, and in which the poet-*vates*, if taken seriously, risks supplanting the priest.

Was it to be taken seriously? One wonders what sort of reality the sacred delirium of the legendary poets of Greece could possess under the Valois kings. In practical terms, French poets go so far as to claim a role in advising political leaders and in guiding opinion, this being a vestige of the law-giving function of the poets of Antiquity:

Donne-nous que les Seigneurs,
Les Empereurs et les Princes
Soyent veuz Dieux en leurs provinces
S'ilz reverent noz honneurs.
Fay, que les Roys decorez
De nos presentz honorez
Soyent aux hommes admirables
Lors qu'ilz vont par leur cité,
Ou lors que plains d'equité
Donnent les loix venerables.[11]

[Grant us that Lords,
Emperors, and Princes
Be considered gods in their provinces
If they revere our honors.
May Kings adorned
With the honored gifts we bestow
Be admirable to men
When they move about their city,
Or when they equitably
Promulgate venerable laws.]

Ronsard attempted to fulfil this mission, the most exalted one available to the court poet he was obliged to be, when he undertook to write poems about the great national problems of his time. But could such an ambition be accepted in the France of that period?

In one way, the emancipation of literature and its profane flourishing worked against it. The new position of letters was accepted, and a division was finally

instituted according to which dogma reserved to itself the right to decide questions of destiny and salvation, while literature contented itself with adorning life
and teaching worldly virtues — a spiritually limited role, which Boileau's pro-
hibition defines well:

> De la foi d'un chrétien les mystères terribles
> D'ornements égayés ne sont point susceptibles.[12]

> [The terrible mysteries of a Christian's faith
> Are not subject to smiling ornament.]

This axiom, which breaks off communication between literature and religion,
expresses what is perhaps the deepest characteristic of French classicism: a dis-
sociation of the profane and the sacred that is at the same time an equilibrium
and a truce, pending new conflicts. There is, in any case, no more place for
poetic enthusiasm as founder of the human race. This dream vanished, and the
poetic generation of Ronsard fell into disfavor. Every historian of the poetry of
the turn of the sixteenth and seventeenth centuries has noticed this: "For Ronsard," writes one of them, "poetry was a sacred calling; for the 17th century, it is
a profession." Another could say of Malherbe's reform: "It is above all a devalua-
tion, a confession of bankruptcy. . . . In monarchical France one cannot claim to
resuscitate Homer, Pindar, Aeschylus. . . . In the history of thought, the fall
which the victory of the Counter-Reformation represents finds dramatic expression in this abandonment of the high doctrine of the *Pléiade*."[13] The poetic
vocation saw itself repressed at its two extremities, celestial and terrestrial, by
the Church and by absolutism, both triumphant. Malherbe's maxims on the
poetic profession are well known; he judged "that it was silly to make verses and
hope for any other reward than one's own amusement, and that a good poet was
no more useful to the State than a good skittles player."[14] Of the ambitions of
high poetry — and of literature in general — only the idea of a moral usefulness
of letters managed to stay alive throughout the classical era, a modest link
between a degraded tradition and a future renewal. One should not, as some
have done, go so far as to deny this survival, imagining that writers in the age of
classicism were solely preoccupied with giving pleasure and with art: the belief
in the dignity of letters and in their effect on manners and civic life is universal.
But this was precisely the domain conceded to writers by the reigning powers,
and it is exceedingly obvious that the grandiose ambition cherished by literature
during the preceding century had fallen into abeyance.

French society had to be shaken to its foundations during the course of the
following century for literature to be able once again to claim a high mission,
higher this time than ever, and for people to realize that the long development

of a worldly culture had demolished the ancient order of things. In eighteenth-century France, the desuetude of theological certainties and the discredit of traditional sources of authority were proclaimed by a militant secular literature — an altogether unprecedented phenomenon, and one that has made that era and that nation forever memorable. For the first time, literature, finding itself faced with a sort of vacuum or absence of the powers that had governed opinion in the past, saw the opportunity to claim its inheritance. The *philosophe* appeared first — a noteworthy fact, and an important indicator of boldness and conquest — as the theologian's direct competitor and avowed successor: against old dogmas, he brought forth the articles of a new faith; against the books of the Bible, his own. The poet came later, joining his ministry to that of the thinker. In any case, the unprecedented situation that emerged in the course of the eighteenth century and the proclamation of the literary calling in terms never before heard justify the belief that a new subject of study opens with this period. The legacy of earlier periods is not forgotten at this time; but the creations of the present go beyond it and transfigure it.

* * *

Literature, in the following pages, is considered principally as a carrier of ideas, which it quite obviously is; this is not, as some today believe, an inessential characteristic. It is true that it shares this characteristic with philosophy, political science, law, and ethics; but literature handles ideas at a level all its own, in the realm where they are born from deep human causes, speaking in the name of human life and guiding it in its proper pathways. The perfected elaboration of ideas as ideas interests literature less than their self-evidence, their truth-value, their direct applicability. The relation of thought and forms in literature suggests as much: the perceptible matter of literary works distinguishes them from the more rigorous constructions that metaphysics or specialized disciplines have been able to build from similar intuitions. If obliged to define it by some unique characteristic, I would choose that which makes literature the natural expression of thought as well as the place where new values first emerge — the human clamor of question and response on the widest possible scale.

A study like this one has, necessarily, a sociological aspect. Debates about the human condition, such as the ones we find in literary works, respond to situations and concerns that affect an entire society. This is well known, as is the fact that, within a single society, different groups are affected and react differently. Every sociological analysis of works of the mind is led to use the notion of class, which is an indispensable concept, provided that it is handled with a respect for facts. A doctrine held a priori, claiming to derive from Marx, grants real existence as classes only to groups defined by their economic function; everything else can only express relations among these groups. Works of the mind, in particular, are only considered as reflections, rationalizations, or instruments of those classes whose existence the doctrine sees fit to allow. But it ought to be noticed that those whose role it is to express thoughts and to accredit values — philosophers, writers, artists — have every reason to consider themselves a group distinct from others and to think according to their common condition. Their altogether unique role and the special power they wield encourage them to think in these terms; moreover, their autonomy in society is the autonomy of thought in the midst of life. Human beings are so constituted as to stand, as it were, at a distance from themselves in order to consider their own conduct in terms of absolute values. There would be no intellectuals if it were otherwise. It is for this reason that we expect from intellectuals formulas that are universal, that are valid for everyone at all times and are not to be confused with interests and circumstances. The influence of intellectuals depends entirely on this state of affairs, that makes of them, in every period and however organized, whether as a clergy or as a secular corporation, the tribunal as well as the voice of society. This influence is considerable; intellectuals derive it from human nature and from public investiture. It is, on the whole, a legitimate influence: however could they have usurped it? They must therefore exert this influence if they are to be what they are and thus justify the rank that is granted to them. However intimidating those whom they may have to oppose, intellectuals cannot, without harming themselves, limit themselves to serving an established power by expressing thoughts tailored to its needs. If they wish to be anything at all, they are constrained to be something other than a tool of mystification. To see them only in such a light is to misunderstand the essence of a social group of the first importance, necessarily torn between the two opposed forces of conformity and spiritual authority.

And yet all too often a reductionist method, adopted as a principle, has been applied without restraint in order to dismiss as fraudulent any thought that, taking this position, proposes to overcome opposed class interests in human society. The logical consequence of this approach would be to render all literature suspect: such terrorizing is perhaps its chief raison d'être. We would do better to ask why and how nineteenth-century writers were so often able to contest the values of the society and the class from which they came. It will be said that writers can betray their class — knowingly, or in spite of themselves, "objectively." But betrayal would be a case of individuals choosing, contrary to their origins, between two constituted camps: this is what can happen — and often happens — in politics. In literature, things are utterly different; there are not two camps and there is no workers' intelligentsia capable of seducing bourgeois writers. It is the intelligentsia emerging from the bourgeoisie, and it alone, that repudiates the bourgeoisie in works from which the proletariat is generally absent. Rather than a betrayal, this is more of a denial or a retraction; and this denial is a group phenomenon, not an exception that occurs here and there. One could account for this by the influence of the proletariat only through the invocation of a historical unconscious. It is much simpler to allow that thinkers, writers, and artists are to some degree and on account of their role the judges of society as well as its mainstays. In the absence of such a hypothesis, I see no way to describe, in its relation to society, the development of thought and literary creations in nineteenth-century France.

Let us try, then, to capture, at its birth in the philosophic milieu of the eighteenth century, the society or corporation of minds that, dethroning the former spiritual powers and claiming the right to succeed them, elevates itself to the highest level of criticism and edification, laying down laws for a world undergoing renewal. A new legislature of the mind constituted itself at this time, at once both weak and strong in relation to material power, laughable as well as formidable, tormented by its own shortcomings, influenced by its own self-interest, by a desire to assert its own authority and prestige, but in the end dedicated somehow to the ideal as its raison d'être. Granted this reality, we must trace its vicissitudes in the annals of French history, accepting the idea that the quarrels of writers and the ruling class are just as important and as deeply motivated as their agreement. We must also arm ourselves with a spirit of critical fairness. In the presence of this new dispute of the temporal and the spiritual, in the midst of all the various positions they were led to take and the values to which they gave currency, we must not believe too quickly that the new clerics, any more than the earlier ones, were the infallible interpreters of human destiny.

✱ ✱ ✱

The present study extends from the origins of the new spiritual power toward the middle of the eighteenth century to the moment that sees its first serious conflicts with the society it had helped to create; that is, 1830 and the years immediately following. This period forms a whole that can be considered not as closed and finished, but rather as the vast prologue or first important act of a longer history that continues in our own time. The appearance of the philosophic faith in the century of the Enlightenment, followed by the literary creations of the counterrevolution, and, finally, the explosion of romanticism, are on the intellectual plane the three great successive facts of this period.[15] I have attempted to describe these facts by way of the classic works as well as in their echoes — or their sources — deep in the intellectual movements of the time. Above all, in describing them, I have been interested in everything that, in the course of this incessant creation of new values, aimed to invest literature with a high social function. In the literature of the time, this aim accompanies and influences all other aims: far from being a subsidiary theme or a rhetorical fantasy that should be discounted in order to grasp what is essential, the mission of the writer is the vital idea around which the others organize themselves. This accounts for the method I have used and the arrangement of this book. If I consider it to be an essay, even though it may not at first glance appear to have the character of what is ordinarily so described, this is because it aims at a vast synthesis, and also because in this sort of undertaking truth is especially difficult to attain, however carefully pursued. I ask only that the reader believe that I have done all I could to come near.

Chapter 1
In Quest of a Secular Ministry

THE WRITER whose devotion to matters of the intellect contributes to the education of the human race is not unknown as a type in the seventeenth century, which inherits this notion from humanism. Overshadowed by established powers, however, this type of writer cuts a relatively modest figure at this time. It is only the writer's auxiliary moral ministry that is established, a ministry exercised in the domains of *l'honnêteté* or of worldly erudition. But the idea of a vast community including everyone whom we now include in the category of *intellectuals*—scholars, philosophers, and political commentators in general, in addition to *littérateurs*—seems already well established. The word *intellectual* did not then exist in this sense; one spoke, rather, of *gens de lettres*: this is the expression Descartes uses.[1] Controversy is already implicit in such a notion: it can imply a value and rights that not all are prepared to grant. On the one hand are praised the wisdom of the man of letters and the well-balanced nature that keeps the world's strife at a distance; traditional commonplaces are recalled, like that of the excellence of letters compared with martial accomplishments or advantages of birth. Thus Racine, addressing the Académie Française, writes: "Let ignorance demean eloquence and poetry as much as it likes, and treat able writers as useless to the State . . . ; as long as sublime spirits, far surpassing ordinary limits, distinguish and immortalize themselves by masterpieces . . . , whatever strange inequality fortune places between them and the greatest heroes in their own lifetimes, after their deaths this difference no longer exists. Posterity . . . considers the poet of excellence to be on a par with the great soldier."[2] These rhetorical themes seem at times to come to life, judging from the discussions they provoke. It is chiefly the pretension of the *gens de lettres* to play a role in the State that is at issue; the court and officialdom do not easily accept this, refusing to see in the *littérateur* anything other than the traditionally inferior type of the pedant. There is an echo of this debate in Molière's *Les Femmes savantes*, in which the courtier speaks bluntly:

> Que font-ils pour l'Etat, vos habiles héros?
> Qu'est-ce que leurs écrits lui rendent de service,
> Pour accuser la cour d'une horrible injustice
> Et se plaindre en tous lieux que sur leurs doctes noms

Elle manque à verser la faveur de ses dons?
Leur savoir à la France est beaucoup nécessaire!
Et des livres qu'ils font la cour a bien affaire!
Il semble à trois gredins[3] dans leur petit cerveau,
Que, pour être imprimés et reliés en veau,
Les voilà dans l'Etat d'importantes personnes;
Qu'avec leur plume ils font le destin des couronnes;
Qu'au moindre petit bruit de leurs productions,
Ils doivent voir chez eux voler les pensions;
Que sur eux l'univers a la vue attachée.[4]

[What do they do for the State, these heroes you imagine to be so capable?
What good do their writings do for the State
That justifies their accusing the court of a horrible injustice
And complaining everywhere that their learned names
Have been denied favor at court?
Their learning is so essential to France!
And the court is so preoccupied with their books!
The little minds of three poor beggars seem to think
That because they have been printed and bound in calfskin,
They are nothing less than state personages;
That their pens determine the destiny of crowned heads;
That if their productions achieve the slightest renown,
They should see pensions rain down on them;
That all the world is watching them.]

However, the parallel between the man of letters and the powerful officeholder was beginning to be developed just as satirically in the opposite direction; in La Bruyère, the philosopher is gravely ironic:

> What are you doing that is so demanding, Clitophon, in the most remote corner of your dwelling, which keeps you from hearing me? You file away some memoranda, you collate a registry, you sign, you initial. I only had one thing to ask you, and you only had to say one word to me, yes or no. . . . But when you, O important man charged with important business, need my good offices, you may come into the solitude of my study, for the philosopher is accessible; I shall not put you off till another day. You will find me studying the books of Plato dealing with the spirituality of the soul, and with its distinction from the body, or, pen in hand, in the midst of calculating the distance to Saturn and to Jupiter: I admire God in his works, and I seek by knowledge of the truth to order my mind and improve myself. Come in, all doors are open to you. . . . What you bring me is more precious than silver or

gold if it be an opportunity to serve you. . . . The man of letters . . . is seen by all . . . ; he cannot be self-important, and he does not wish to be.[5]

This studious philanthropist, at bottom so confident of his own preeminence, is already a type of the following century.

It is, in fact, in the course of the eighteenth century that the ideal figure of the Man of Letters is described in all his prestige, even while the human group he is supposed to represent is becoming acutely self-conscious: "To the advantage of political and social upheaval, a profound transformation was effected in the character and function of the man of letters, whence issue the magi and prophets of romanticism."[6] This formulation is an accurate abstract of a long history. A famous text from 1743 still shows us the philosopher as a sage and exemplary human being rather than as an apostle of the public good.[7] But the lucidity of this sage, of whom it is said that "civil society is, as it were, the only divinity that he recognizes on earth," is here constantly (and more or less explicitly) contrasted with the harmful fantasies of the zealot, and the gain that would accrue to the human race with his accession to the highest offices is affirmed emphatically: "It is easy to see how much more usefulness society might derive from those who, when raised to high positions, are imbued with notions of good administration and the general welfare and all that is called humaneness, and it would be most desirable to find a way to exclude all those who, because of their mental nature or on account of an unfortunate upbringing, are filled with other sentiments."[8] Thus the philosopher, who still owes much to the *honnête homme*, is already presented as a successor to the powers of heaven and earth. Voltaire, with his customary acuteness, described concisely the progress of *gens de lettres* since the Renaissance. He observes that instead of philologists, they have become philosophers, men of the world, and guides of the human mind: "It is this philosophical spirit that constitutes the character of *gens de lettres*. . . . They were kept at a distance from society until the time of Guez de Balzac and Voiture; since then they have become an essential part of society. . . . Their criticism no longer exhausts itself on Greek and Latin words; sustained instead by a healthy philosophy, it has destroyed the prejudices with which society was infected."[9] Rousseau himself, who began his career around the same time with a diatribe against literature, is no less emphatic: "Let kings no longer disdain to admit into their counsels the people most able to advise them. . . . Let scholars of the first rank find honorable protection in their courts. Let them obtain there the only reward worthy of them, that of contributing by their influence to the happiness of peoples to which they will have taught wisdom. Then and then only shall we see what can be accomplished by virtue, science, and authority, inspired by noble imitation and working together for the felicity of the human race."[10]

The growth and social characteristics of the new intellectual class have not yet been the object of an in-depth study. Several modern authors have, however, assembled a group of interrelated facts: progress in the material condition and legal rights of authors, greater honor and prosperity, access as equals to the upper classes of society;[11] to these should probably be added a notable numerical increase in the secular intellectual community as a result of the growth of knowledge and of technological changes. It is certainly the case that in the period lasting from about 1760 until the Revolution, the apologia of the man of letters becomes a veritable glorification whose exalted tone is associated with a general doctrine of emancipation and progress. There is an effort to trace its ancestry much further back than the humanists of the sixteenth century; the often recalled type of the legendary Legislator-Sages of Greece, Egypt, and the Orient comes to life in the modern Man of Letters.[12] The exaltation of this new power had become a commonplace in the last years of the ancien régime, especially in speeches to the Académie Française: "A tribunal independent of all the powers of the earth and respected by all was raised up, giving every talent its due and pronouncing on every sort of merit; and, in an enlightened age, an age where every citizen can speak to the entire nation by the printed word, the *gens de lettres* are, in short, among a dispersed public what the orators of Rome and of Athens were amidst their assembled peoples."[13] The Académie Française, which was at this time a sort of senate of the new class, prized these speeches: "It was then that there arose among us what we have called *the influence of public opinion*. Men of letters at once conceived the ambition to be its spokespersons, even its judges. A graver taste prevailed in works of the mind; the desire to instruct became more important than the desire to please. *The dignity of the man of letters* — a new and appropriate phrase — soon became an approved expression in common use."[14]

These are relatively restrained homages. Writers of this generation sometimes carried the panegyric much further. In the chorus of voices we find men whose destinies would be as different as Sébastien Mercier, a prolific and uneven author, friend of Rousseau, and Rétif de la Bretonne and future Girondist; Antoine-Léonard Thomas, a generally pontificating academic author who died before the Revolution; La Harpe, at the time an able skirmisher with Voltaire, who would die a Christian and a counterrevolutionary under the Consulate; Chamfort, who was a revolutionary brought by the Revolution to an appalling suicide attempt, already divided between the optimism of the *philosophes* and a sarcastic bitterness. Mercier sketched the following portrait of the man of letters in the sublimity of his calling at the moment when inspiration descends upon him:

> His heart quickens, his imagination takes fire, a delicious shiver runs through his veins; enthusiasm seizes him; on wings of fire his mind takes flight, he passes beyond the confines of this world, he soars on high in the Heavens; there, he meditates, he embraces virtue in its perfection, it sets him afire to the point of ravishment and ecstasy, I see his laughing brow turned toward heaven, tears of joy pour from his eyes, the sacred love of the human race penetrates his heart with a pang of tenderness, his blood courses through his veins; the quickness of his vital spirits gives speed to his thoughts; then it is that he describes with feeling, thunders forth with virile eloquence, creates masterpieces which are the admiration of the ages; everything he touches he animates, he enlivens, or rather he sets on fire. What would he need in order to reestablish the order of the universe? The only thing he lacks is power.[15]

This lyricism supports remarkable claims: "The influence of writers is such that they can today announce their power, and not disguise the legitimate authority they have over minds. Grounded in the public interest and a true knowledge of man, they will direct the ideas of the nation; it is up to them to determine what individual minds will desire."[16] Thomas, too, offered an ecstatic portrait of the Man of Letters:

> I love to think of the man of letters meditating alone in his study: the fatherland is beside him; justice and humanity are before him; visions of those who are unfortunate surround him; pity moves him and tears flow from his eyes. Then he sees from afar the Powerful and the Rich. In his retreat he envies their privilege to be able to mitigate the ills of this world. And I, he says, have nothing with which to succor them; I have only my thought; ah! let it at least be useful to those who are unfortunate. At once his ideas crowd upon him; and his soul shows itself in the world.

There follows a messianic vision of a humanity renewed by the works of thinkers, when "all the power of advanced human understanding will be applied everywhere to the great art of societies."[17]

Such an exaltation of the Man of Letters was in stark contrast to the traditional pettiness and vain quarrels of authors. Thus we often find writers being urged to renounce their bad habits and to show themselves worthy of their role through demonstrations of concord and an awareness of their common interest.[18] And, as a way of redeeming the man of letters from his all-too-well-known sins, the sufferings and persecutions to which the prejudices and envy of the stupid condemn him are often recalled. This theme is everywhere, for there is no apostolate without martyrdom:

If, ungrateful men, you think that vanity alone inspires his pen, observe the persecution he endures, his exile, his wandering life, his misfortunes. What can he hope to gain from all this? What good comes to him? No, I have never seen a man of letters imprisoned for the benefaction his noble writings without myself sharing his chains and misfortunes. Alone, at night, by the light of the lamp that illuminates my nights of study, I felt myself to be there with him, I gave him strength and courage, I urged him to find the fortitude to suffer for a few years and earn thereby centuries of gratitude and glory.[19]

It is obvious that the sort of persecution envisioned is, more and more, that which despotism and the church inflict upon independent thought.

For all these authors, the exercise of philosophic reason is beyond any doubt the principal calling of the Man of Letters; it is the irresistible advance of this reason that confers his ministry upon him. The man of letters, says La Harpe, "is he whose principal profession is to cultivate reason, so as to add his own to that of others," and Chamfort calls writers "those peaceful legislators of reason."[20] But we have seen how much fervor accompanied the use of reason; the ministry of the Man of Letters implies a communion of feeling with men and the universe. According to Mercier, thinkers can disdain actions motivated by envy because "they know by their superior reason that they are supported by men of sensibility, now and in times to come." And as a matter of course La Harpe ends his rational definition by the following evocation: "The vastness of the plains, the somber loneliness of rocks and forests, storms at night, the quiet of the morning, all these nourish enthusiasm and witness genius in its moments of creation"; enthusiasm and truth are the "two immortal torches" that writers and artists hand on to their successors.[21] We should therefore avoid opposing Reason and Sentiment, *Philosophe* and Man of Sensibility. Texts abound that help us overcome this excessively rough distinction. Vauvenargues, who pleads on every occasion for the preeminence of feeling, was already writing:

At bottom, I have never doubted the power of reason. Nature puts in us unthinking inclinations and establishes mysterious relations among all objects; but that proves nothing against the power of the mind; reason is not at all foreign to us; its source is in nature, just like the passions; it is the fruit that is the slowest to grow, the most delicate, the most rare, the easiest to spoil, the most difficult to ripen; but it is also the best, the most powerful in its action on the soul when it is brought to perfection; it cannot be too much cultivated, nor can one exaggerate to oneself what one can hope to gain by cultivating it. Those who limit nature to blind motion know neither its excellence nor its infinite depth.[22]

And Voltaire, whom we usually situate far from the regions of sensibility, writes to Vauvenargues: "Elevation, pathos, feeling, these command me most of all."[23] The notion that Rousseau preached feeling over reason has long ago been abandoned; it is not the understanding he fears so much as the artificial use to which we are tempted to put it, and he trusts the heart only insofar as he sees in it an unwavering commitment to order: "Thus my precept, that I should deliver myself over to feeling, is confirmed by reason itself."[24] In this period it is almost a banality to write: "The amalgam of Reason and Sensibility gives rise to the man of genius, the virtuous man; these qualities lend each other mutual aid."[25]

By making use of reason to criticize the values it believed to be false, the eighteenth century sets up its own in their place. What it calls reason is not just a means to contest and dissolve past beliefs; it is also an argument in favor of humanity, one grounding a belief in the nobility of the human race. If understood in the sense of a pure critical exercise of intelligence, the term *reason* would imply a recognition of facts without connoting any further end or value; it would therefore be useless in the quest for happiness. It is therefore not understood in this way. In the eighteenth century, the term *sensibilité* no doubt tends to be applied to the person seeking happiness as an end in itself, but sensibility itself cannot be understood as a pure impulse, a raw stirring of desire or repugnance. The happiness that sensibility takes as its object is of a sort rationally reconciled both to itself and to the truth of things. This is why the man of sensibility is not at this time a simple psychological type; he incarnates, rather, a way of thinking, since he is a philosopher even in the act of feeling. It is often said that feeling animates reason and reason enlightens feeling, but this is inadequate. At a deeper level, reason reveals an order outside of which no happiness exists, and feeling is the living trace in us of the order that governs us: though different and in some respects rivals, both tend to combine and transmute one into the other. Furthermore, it is purely by means of the unity of human nature that the conflict of reason and feeling resolves itself harmoniously, the supernatural appearing only insofar as this harmony in human beings is made the result of the supposed benevolence of their creator. In other words the harmony of the powers that make up human beings is only possible insofar as they are conceived to exist in the universe, uncontaminated as it were by any fundamental flaw; it is this unmediated legitimation of humanity, this postulate outside of and prior to all debate, that breaks with the traditional perspective and reconciles us with ourselves. The rejection of original sin grounds the new faith; a single impulse inspires what is both a rational repudiation of a myth and a protest that derives from a sensibility that proclaims itself to be innocent and stakes a claim to its own happiness. Such is the evangel of the Man of Letters, the good news that he announces to his century: the glory of God does not humiliate man; better yet, it finds in him its true ground. At the same time that Chamfort was exalting the Man of Letters,[26] he wrote an "Ode on the Greatness of Man" in which God, scanning the universe, pauses to contemplate the human race:

> Il contemple les hommes
> Et dans notre âme enfin va chercher sa grandeur.[27]

> [He contemplates men
> And in our souls will seek his own grandeur at last.]

The credo proclaimed by the Man of Letters is an exaltation of humanity; this credo is the foundation of his ministry.

It is true that even if the theology of the Fall and sin are repudiated, God continues to be generally assumed as the supreme guarantor of order, happiness, and universal meaning. This deism, like all faiths, displays various nuances, according to whether intelligence or heart takes precedence, and is subject to controversies concerning how God governs; its unity, however, is indisputable.[28] Its adepts do not come to God by way of a renunciation of human beings in their natural state, but rather in consideration of their dignity in this state: "You seek to abase yourself in vain!"[29] Such is Rousseau's apostrophe to the atheist, which forms quite a contrast to the traditional reproach to pride. This is why this theology seems so serene and why this God is so benevolent toward a nature for which he is responsible. Such a God, though he is theoretically the source of our being, sometimes seems merely our culmination. Thus an appeal to what humanity finds fitting is often offered as a proof of God's existence. Voltaire famously said: "If God did not exist it would be necessary to invent him."[30] Apparently so theocentric in his metaphysics, in religion he appears as anthropocentric as anyone else. Rousseau says the same thing: "Hearts that feel these sublime truths turn away from petty human passions; and even if the great being with which they concern themselves did not exist, it would be well for them to continue so to concern themselves, so as to be more self-possessed, stronger, happier, and wiser."[31] This "pragmatism," as it has been called,[32] rearranges the relation of human beings to God in a new way, without really altering the conviction of divine reality felt by those who adopt it, but nevertheless admitting that it postulates this reality on the basis of humanity, in relation to humanity, and for the sake of humanity.

The hostile criticism of the end of the nineteenth century and the beginning of the twentieth, which seems to us today so feeble, attacked with gusto this false religion and above all the source from which it sprang: Sensibility with a capital S was reproached both for being coldly abstract and ruinously impulsive. Why do we not also judge the virtues of faith, hope, and charity in the same way? They, too, have their capital letters, and more than one believer, aspiring to them, succeeds only in becoming overexcited, or else ends by losing track of what he meant, just as much as any pilgrim to Rousseau's tomb at Ermenonville. Such are the stumbling blocks of faith. A critique no less hostile explains the religion of feeling as the impotent revolt of a desiccated age against its own desiccation.[33] But the very longing that is being described dismisses this explanation; for this is what we need to take under consideration. Religious souls complained in the same way, long before there were any philosophers of sentiment, of feeling love's springs dry up within them. In the one case as in the other, the desiccation is only momentary; the anguish that characterizes this moment defines a person's permanent yearning and, as a promise, contains within it a plenitude that cannot fail, one that in fact is already abundantly in evidence. From another point of view, of course, it is possible to marvel at a faith in a transcendence that is established above humanity, yet that is destined for humanity's use. Religions, perhaps, exhibit the very same trait, but by definition they affect an attitude that is the very opposite, that of absorbing man into God, and they propose to order the conduct and sentiments of their followers according to this plan. The Man of Sensibility's deism is, let us say, more candid, or perhaps more lucid. But is this lucidity enough to deny it a religious character? Perhaps it is only a terminological question. In any case, the ambiguity of deism with regard to the matter of transcendence is neither more nor less shocking than the contradictions one can observe elsewhere. No doctrine, and in particular no religious doctrine, is free of contradictions, and more than one defines itself in terms of these difficulties.[34]

The doctrine of deism has its strengths like any other; at any rate, it cannot be denied that it marked an era of the human mind. It has its gusts of passion, its temptations, its own experience of the indescribable. In its beginnings it is characterized by a modest emotional affect, but this grew immeasurably, supplanting, finally, traditional religious feeling: simple feelings of moral tenderness and the gift of honest tears overflowed into the infinite, raising themselves to a state of cosmic ecstasy. This endlessly extended crescendo is the spiritual hymn of the time; texts that one could multiply indefinitely mark its stages. Thus: "Delightful repose, agreeable reading, a walk in a cool and lonely place, a conversation in which one opens one's heart, in which one gives oneself over to all of one's sensibility, a strong emotion that brings tears to the edges of one's eyelids, that makes the heart beat, that stills the voice, that ravishes one with ecstasy, whether born of some tale of generous action, a feeling of tenderness, health, gaiety, freedom, idleness, ease, this is true happiness."[35] On a higher level, where virtue attains the divine: "You are hidden, great God! No. Are you not near my soul? When pity makes me weep, when I feel a deep emotion upon hearing of some generous action, that is when I feel you within me. The gracious face of innocence and the gaze of a judge rendering fair judgment reflect your image."[36] With an even more elevated tone: "Have you never experienced those involuntary transports that sometimes grip sensitive souls when they contemplate moral beauty and the intellectual order of things, the devouring ardor that suddenly appears and sets the heart on fire for celestial virtues, the sublime bewilderment that lifts us above our own being and carries us into the empyrean next to God himself?"[37]

Such texts undeniably translate an experience, one that overturns as it were ordinary religious experience: the lightning bolt leaps from earth to heaven. When a person of these times says "celestial" or "divine," it is almost always a question of human things, insofar as they suddenly appear as measureless: one sees oneself as a human being, gifted with a sublimity that embraces the universe. One experiences one's own infinity, surpassing one's own finitude, and calls God or the Great Being whatever there is in one's experience that goes beyond every limit. This discovery one thinks one has made, or this delusion, or whatever one wants to call that which makes humanity participate in the infinite, gives birth to a new sort of exaltation. The engravings of the time have preserved for us the image of these radiant philosophers, demigods in powdered wigs and silk stockings in the ecstasy of their faith; eyes gazing toward the rising sun, arms dramatically lifted toward the crests of towering trees, faces serenely lit, mouths whose eloquence we can imagine, and hearts stammering on the threshold of a reopened Eden: these are images of secular orisons whose spell acted long and well. What historians of letters commonly call the sentiment of nature and that swells up on all sides at this time only makes sense in this context: nature has acquired a spiritual value because the perceptible has taken on an infinite aspect, less with reference to the God who created the universe than with reference to those who inhabit it and to whom God offers a boundless object of contemplation: it is in this theater, now become a temple — whether of God or of humanity — that creatures surpass their own limits. Those who speak of this as pantheism are, I think, mistaken. It is rather a sort of usurpation of the ordinary attributes of divinity by the human subject. In extreme cases, God is no longer even needed. Sylvain Maréchal, a declared atheist, experienced as much as any deist this metaphysical expansion of the "man of virtue": "Even if the universe were infinitely larger, the man of virtue has within him an expansive soul and elevated feelings capable of embracing the entire system of nature."[38]

The type of religious or parareligious experience inaugurated by the deism of sensibility of the eighteenth century demonstrated its vitality in the course of the following generations, even under the auspices of religious revival. In 1794, a walk at sunset suggests to Maine de Biran the following reflections: "Everything that struck my senses imparted to my heart a feeling ineffably sweet and sad. My eyes filled with tears. What a train of charming thoughts ensued! If I could make this state a permanent one, what would be lacking to my own happiness? I would have found on this earth the joys of heaven." About twenty years later, he has been won over to religion, but he feels the same thing: "I felt this evening, in the course of a solitary walk in the most beautiful weather, a few momentary gleams of that ineffable pleasure that I used to taste at this season of the year, gleams of that pure pleasure that seems to tear us away from everything terrestrial and to give us a foretaste of heaven." It is true that he concludes with the idea of "a world superior to phenomena . . . the world that will be connected to God, as to the primary and sole reality."[39] But the lived point of departure matters more than the doctrinal end point; what Christian, before deism, would have thought to approach God in such a way? Doctrine can interpret the experience in the most diverse ways, but it remains fundamentally the same: "I admit," writes Senancour in 1804, "that it is natural for man to think he is less limited, less finite, to believe that he is greater than his present life, when it happens that a sudden perception shows him the contrasts and the equilibrium, the link, the organization of the universe. This feeling seems to him like the discovery of a world that can be known, like the first hint of what may be revealed to him one day."[40] Senancour, albeit an agnostic, leaves the door ajar for a religious explanation; the religious Chênedollé does not even think to raise the question: "It is only during lonely walks when one feels of a sudden tender-hearted, when one feels a sweet need to weep, when one is allowed ineffable revelation. These short moments are revelatory moments of feeling."[41] A mind less easily satisfied will conclude the ecstatic revery with the poison of Christian scruples: "Inwardly I felt inexplicable emotions," writes the marquis de Custine. "I was communicating with a superior being; torrents of happiness sprang from my heart; I was creating the felicity that the world refused me, and this power, increasing my confidence in myself, prolonged my illusions and caused me to find nourishment in a life of fantasy instead of applying myself to my real duties."[42] Custine, like many of his contemporaries who returned or wished to return to the religion of their forefathers, offers an acute critique of these emotions: "One could say," he writes, "that the romanesque is the improper application of what is divine in nature to what is worldly."[43] But the "romanesque," that expansion of what is human that is so suspect to orthodoxy, takes possession of him in spite of himself.

Texts of this kind could make up a rich anthology that would extend well into the nineteenth century, and, while appealing to a variety of doctrinal positions, would attest to the existence of a unique type of emotion and conviction. The young Balzac, in his deism, is still rather close to the *Philosophes*:

> One who from a young age has conceived ideas of love and beauty, whose soul has received as if sown on good earth the seeds of taste and the beautiful proportions of harmony in all of nature, this being, who will weep at the tears of the pauper, who will shudder at the sight of gratuitous barbarism that victimizes an animal suffering in silence, will have the advantage of entering a temple with a shudder of delight, will understand God, and will have a soul that will tend unceasingly toward union with God, as if this eternal principle were its very source. Such creatures never need proofs in order to believe in God. . . . God lives in their sensibility as if he were their sensibility itself.[44]

In the reign of Louis-Philippe, a correspondent of this same Balzac retains as well the tone of the original deism, not without some romantic coloration, when she evokes

> that fire of enthusiasm, that overmastering influence, that need of the infinite, that curious and exalted sentiment, that search for the causes of things, those vivid, pure, and celestial sensations detached from our grosser nature and soaring in space like intangible spirits: dreams at once diaphanous and strong, exhalation of the soul seeking to fly off into the sky, sensations so delicate and fine, every one of them coming from the heart and from the soul! Are you not possessed of an ethereal and immortal nature, are you not the revelation of God![45]

This lady was, by education and past attachments, a supporter of a republic, and was not, apparently, a Christian. At about the same time, however, Lamennais celebrates the rapture of the Christian philosopher building a system for the glory of God in these terms: "From the most secret depths of our bowels wells up I know not what living joy like a torrent of life uniting us to everything that feels, creating in us an expansive feeling in the heart of all creation."[46] It must be allowed that this language was not commonly employed in Christian thought before the arrival of the secular *Philosophes* of sensibility. In this way, literature continued the tradition of the deistic *philosophes* long after the decline of their authority, with the differences of tone and orientation that new times required.

We can thus see that literature has not renounced the ministry with which a memorable era invested it. It has become in its own way a religion and continues to be one. One further suspects that many believers' religion, in its hidden, unconscious sources, has become literature. This is why, finally, the return of traditional religion was unable to put an end to the consecration of the writer.

Let us return to the exercise of this ministry. Writers were quick to identify the superior dignity of Man with their own. Mercier says quite simply: "Most men think only according to the suit of clothes they happen to be wearing; their profession dictates their ideas; only he who has broken the ties that interfere with the progress of reason seems to possess independent judgment."[47] This clearly defines a body of thinkers independent of and superior to every profession. There is hesitation at this time between two apparently contradictory assertions: literature is and is not a social station [*un état*]. "To be an author is a social station today, like being a military officer, a judge, an ecclesiastic, or a banker,"[48] writes one; on the other hand: "Letters do not confer a social station, precisely, but they serve as one for those who have no other."[49] In short, a vague category, till now considered of little account and occupying none of the officially given roles of the old society, imposes itself sufficiently to claim such a role; and yet, while it is impossible to refuse it this role altogether, how can the status of writer be either granted a role among the recognized professions or placed above them in a domain from which the traditional order excludes it? It therefore remains apart, uncertain in the exercise of its newfound power, criticizing and defying traditional authority: "This Voltaire has no social station; granted, but he has that of being a great man; he has, at the least, that of being the equal of kings."[50] In fact, this position outside of ordinary affairs favored writers in the extreme; their prestige and the authority of their judgments was never again as great as during this golden age.

The nineteenth century, at any rate, judging by comparison with itself, felt that this was the case. "The man of letters of former times" had become a legendary figure. Kératry writes: "He practiced a profession and exercised a ministry at the same time."[51] Villemain compares writers of former times to Chinese mandarins: "In the 18th century, men of letters in France had something of the rank of their counterparts in China; they were the leading agency of sociopolitical power [*le grand corps*], the preeminent one; their docility was acknowledged gratefully, their resistance was feared."[52] Tocqueville, seeking to explain such authority held by people lacking any material power, notes that an idle aristocracy, given to pleasures of the mind and troubled neither by doubts concerning its own social superiority nor by fear of real subversion, was able to accept without misgiving reformist speculations while lending its authority to their authors: "Literature had become a sort of neutral ground upon which equality had taken refuge. The man of letters and the great lord met without affectation or fear, and a sort of imaginary democracy reigned there, away as it were from the real world."[53] On the other hand, the markedly routine character of former French society and the fact that the great mass of those possessing special talent was removed from real experience of business left place only for the most theoretical and radical critical views: "It seemed that it was necessary either to tolerate everything or destroy everything in the country's constitution. . . . Political life was violently compressed inside the limits of literature."[54] From this is said to derive one of the characteristics of modern France — the tendency to treat political questions in accordance with "the literary spirit";[55] that is, under the influence of doctrinaire writers. It is to be feared that this analysis, inspired by the uneasiness that the invasion of logical intelligence and the spirit of controversy into the realm of politics induced in a conservative mind, misses the mark. It discredits what it describes by deriving it from the somewhat irresponsible position of writers, which must be dangerous for the social fabric. Tocqueville's analysis places a dangerous spirit of abstraction at the heart of the philosophy of the Enlightenment: a reproach that would come to enjoy surprising popularity, even among serious minds, as if one could criticize or think anything without abstract analysis. The *philosophes* of the eighteenth century, however, said much that was concrete — things for which they would be more reproached than for their utopianism, if critics were to speak frankly. It is really for their audacity and their optimism that they are criticized when they are reproached for the supposed apriority of their thought. A modern analysis, though differently motivated, explains in a similar way what was peculiar about the position of writers before and after the Revolution: "The dealings they had with the sacred caste of priests and nobles," writes Jean-Paul Sartre,

> actually caused them to *lose class*, that is to say, they were torn from the bourgeois class out of which they came, washed of their origins, nursed by the aristocracy without however being able to truly be an essential part of it. . . . They became aware that they didn't belong, that they were suspended in air, rootless, like a Ganymede carried off in the eagle's talons; they constantly felt themselves superior to their milieu. But after the Revolution, the bourgeois class itself takes power. According to logic, it is this class that ought to bestow upon writers their new rank. This would be possible, however, only if writers agreed to enter into the fold of the bourgeoisie. This is out of the question, though: first of all, two hundred years of royal favor have schooled writers to despise the bourgeoisie; but, above all, writers, parasites on a parasitic class,

are used to thinking of themselves as clerics, cultivating pure thought and pure art.[56]

Here the classless position of the writer is clearly endorsed, but apparently to be denounced as a false position, a lie: parasites on a parasitic class, pure thinkers feed on an illusion and lose their way on account of their aloof negativity; literature "identifies with the Mind, that is, with the permanent power of forming and criticizing ideas."[57] Sometimes, however, Sartre says the same things in a somewhat different tone:

> Writers break free with a single wingbeat from their class of origin as well as from the class they adopt; as long as they write they can foster the illusion that they belong neither to one nor the other, that they belong to no milieu and to no class, that they are free-floating, that they are completely untrammeled. Their principal virtue is no longer respect for beliefs and customs; it is, rather, generosity. Writing is giving. The upset affecting their public and the crisis of European consciousness invested writers with a new function. They conceive of literature as the permanent exercise of generosity.[58]

Should we take seriously the word *generosity*? We have been sufficiently instructed how emptiness and poverty can be the substance of a beautiful soul. The meaning of some words resides entirely in the tone with which one uses them. Thus, further on, reading that "the best ones refused"[59] when writers were solicited by bourgeois utilitarianism, one no longer senses the slightest irony: it seems, rather, a case of an honor or an excellence genuinely belonging to writers who are worthy of the name. The other extreme ought perhaps to be nuanced: as with any other body of clerics, it is simply the role of writers that requires them to rise above particular interests and to make their own interest consist in the authority of the values they have defined. This said, it is natural that writers represent this necessity as a state of grace and portray its realization, always difficult and imperfect, as a source of merit.

However perspicacious they may be, the common flaw in such analyses describing the status of eighteenth-century writers is that they take into account neither the content of their precepts nor the position they occupy with respect to the church. The latter defines them better than anything else. What they advocated was not, as is often said (on this point Sartre thinks as Tocqueville does), the application of abstract ideas and pure criticism. Such a definition of the *Philosophes* obsessed the nineteenth century as well as our own, having been propagated both by the counterrevolution and by utopians dedicated to reconstructing society, notably Saint-Simon and Auguste Comte, both of whom were great opponents of negativistic, critical philosophy, and the fathers of Marxism, which inherited from them this legacy, among others.[60] In reality, the *Philosophes* were promulgating a new faith, which they wished to be less dogmatic than the old one, but just as positive, and their critique of the old faith was only an instrument of the new. Before attempting to evaluate their status, then, it is their doctrine and their real system of values that we should try to analyze in relation to contemporary society.

At first sight, the new faith could be taken to be a sort of spiritual *embourgeoisement*. In addition to the fact that Sensibility equalized classes and caused them to mingle, the attitudes it promoted were not in accord with an aristocratic tradition: beneficence, the joy of being useful, respect and feeling for one's neighbor, and the effusions of family life have never figured among the virtues of the noble, for whom every excellence presupposes rarity and command. The man of sensibility judged this proud grandeur to be a revolt against nature and called it false:

> Puisque l'amour et la nature,
> Avec le sens commun, sont tombés en roture,
> J'abdique sans regret la noblesse et les lois
> Qui défendent au coeur l'usage de soi-même.
> Serviteur à la qualité,
> Si, sans se dégrader, on ne peut quand on aime
> Montrer sa sensibilité.[61]

> [Since love and nature,
> Along with common sense, have lost rank and become common,
> I abdicate without regret nobility and the laws
> Which forbid to the heart the exercise of its own virtues.
> Adieu to nobility,
> If, without dishonor, one cannot when one loves
> Show one's sensibility.]

It has often been noticed that it was when plays and novels were flooded with the themes of philosophical sensibility that the bourgeois acceded to literary honors. Traditionally, the bourgeois was only depicted in comedies and realistic (that is, satiric) novels. The novels and dramas that now appear take seriously the perils and grandeurs of bourgeois life. Henceforth every existence has its gravity and can be represented: the literary privilege of birth cannot prevail against the philosophy of sensibility. The new literature, however, only dignified the bourgeoisie by distorting it; so much openness and sublimity denatured considerably its customary ways. Traditionally, the French bourgeoisie was thought to be mean-spirited, narrow-minded, and devoted exclusively to its own interests and undertakings. It is easy to see how the vogue of Rousseau could be taken to imply a "bourgeois conversion experience," and how it could be seen as "a moment in the history of the French bourgeoisie when, inspired by Jean-Jacques, it tried to lift itself up to poetry."[62] The bourgeois had to overcome themselves, to be no longer completely themselves. For the first time an ideal type appeared that, to the benefit of the bourgeoisie, equalized humanity, and in which certain natural bourgeois characteristics were included. But this type was still out of reach, and bore witness to the distance that public opinion placed between bourgeois nature and the lofty regions of life. If the *philosophes* of sensibility, sons of *notaires*, clock makers, or knife manufacturers [Voltaire, Rousseau, and Diderot, respectively. *Trans.*], are unable to wish their spirits to be thought of as bourgeois, this is not due to the company they keep but rather to the nature of the bourgeoisie and especially of the implications of their social role. As a class naturally dedicated to profitmaking, or at best to utility, the bourgeoisie is particularly hard to idealize; every society requires higher values. The *Philosophes*, then, were obeying the logic of their role when they refused to be confused with the bourgeoisie. In fact, the particular case of the bourgeoisie exemplifies a more general law: even the relatively elevated degree of idealization lent to the aristocratic character (despite its drawbacks, especially its braggadocio and its wastefulness) was never enough to legitimate the society of the ancien régime, as we see in its need for a church.

Like the bourgeoisie, the nobility is, in the eighteenth century, in a complex relation to the new literature. The type of the enlightened and sensitively benevolent nobleman has an important place in this literature, and the bourgeois tone is not always prevalent. An atmosphere of noble sensibility reigns at Clarens in the home of M. de Wolmar and Julie d'Etanges; and the influence of Rousseau in aristocratic milieux gives food for thought. It is true that for the nobility it is a sort of abjuration to renounce its own glory in favor of an enthusiasm accessible to all. But in this abjuration something of its habits can be seen to perpetuate itself: the spontaneous union of emotion and virtue reproduces in the modern key the old emotions of generosity. This modulation is already visible in Fénelon, an aristocrat in politics, in whom sensibility hails its initiator; in Vauvenargues, *la gloire* and pure nature are curiously mixed: the cult of great souls and courtly love, reawakened by the philosophers of sensibility, lasts throughout the century; aristocratic pastoral poetry, newly recast in a style of natural simplicity, haunts sensitive imaginations. The nobleman continues to set the tone, though his style has changed; he makes available to all of humanity what was heretofore limited to him by a sort of moral 4 August [when, in 1789, during a famous night of enthusiasm, the Constituent Assembly passed a series of resolutions abolishing feudal privileges in France. *Trans.*] that occurs before the other one.

Thus the nobleman as well as the bourgeois is led to transcend somewhat his own nature, and it is this that brings him closer to the *gens de lettres*. This is not merely the effect of fashion or an imprudent enthusiasm; rather, it could not happen otherwise.

One can, if one prefers, explain differently the creation of a vision of humanity that goes beyond what either the nobility or the bourgeoisie desire while doing violence to the interests of each, and also the creation of an intellectual class that is the vessel of this vision; one can, for instance, explain these as being due to a similar inadequacy of the two great competing social classes: a nobility that is behind the times and a bourgeoisie whose time is yet to come. But the circumstances that give to what happens in France a particular profile are less important than what actually takes place, which is not limited to France and is universal: literature and authors are everywhere finally promoted to a remarkably prestigious role. One can, then, in the case of France, be less struck by the double weakness of the nobility and the bourgeoisie than by the effort these two classes made, with the aid of the new clergy, to unite and harmonize their values. What forced them to this pass was, above all, the weakened state of the old spiritual power: it was here that the true inadequacy was located, one that neither the nobility nor the bourgeoisie could ward off by itself. This was naturally the task of a body of thinkers, which had to conceive of itself not only as hostile to but also as competing with and heir to the church.

There is nothing surprising in the fact that the faith of the *philosophes* laid claim to universal values. This is the nature and aim of all thought, and there is more mystification in claiming to be exempt from this condition than in admitting it. The *Philosophes* naturally formulated a law common to all and valid for humanity as the basis of social existence. This is not their distinguishing characteristic. The novelty of their doctrine is in the emphasis they put on earthly happiness and greatness, in the elimination of the supernatural and the sacred as illusory and inhuman, in a certain treatment of transcendence for the sake of reempowered man, and in the notion of a faith without mystery, going hand in hand with the faculty of independent judgment and its free exercise. These new attitudes on the part of human thought are due more to the general progress of science, wealth, and human relations, which led to a decline in religion's prestige, than to the needs of a special class; even if this progress was mostly linked to the rise of the bourgeoisie, the aristocracy was no less prompt or resolute in seeking something new, once the authority of religion was shaken.[63] The universality of the new faith and the fact that its ministers are at a remove from social classes therefore answers a genuine need. In this regard, the secular ministry found itself in the same position as the Christian ministry that preceded it.

The differences between the two rival types of Priest and *Philosophe* are obvious; as ministers of what is human and of reason, which belongs to everyone, Men of Letters form a corps that is open to all and that mingles with its public; they herald an earthly salvation, scarcely distinguish the spiritual from the temporal, and tend to attribute to themselves a political as well as philosophical competence. These differences could easily be elaborated in greater detail. They do not prevent it from being the case that the elevation of writers to the status of arbiters of value and governors of opinion was a signal event in the history of spiritual authority considered in its basic character as a necessarily distinct element of the social mechanism.

In the new ministry of the spirit, the type of the man of letters was in fact reinforced by more legendary figures, as was fitting. Around the middle of the eighteenth century the Académie Française began to propose, instead of the ordinary topics for essay contests, the theme of praise for great men. The cult of the great figures of humanity began to take form at the beginning of the century; the new genre of *Eloges*, established and popularized thanks to the Academy, which is by common consent one of the centers of the new humanist faith, aims explicitly at celebrating the great man, benefactor, or enlightener, who is more or less consciously substituted for the Saint.[64] But the lay saint is often a man of letters of the past (just as the calendar saint was often a priest of his time); what is venerated in Fénelon, Descartes, or Molière is not transcendent grace but the excellence of human nature in which all participate. The great man, the man of letters who celebrates him, and the public who listens to his eulogy are mingled in the exaltation of their common humanity. The deep meaning of these novelties did not always go unperceived. Abbé Maury remarked, à propos of Thomas's *Eloges*: "The genre which M. Thomas cultivates owes much to that of the pulpit." Villemain, half a century later, said, similarly: "Thomas arose in a time when the Academy was replacing the pulpit."[65]

One variety of Great Man that is cloaked in exceptional prestige is that of the Legislator, the lay equivalent, mutatis mutandis, of the Patriarch. Moses was both; for the traditional faith, he had promulgated laws only as God's spokesman; but in the eighteenth century, Solon, Lycurgus, and Zoroaster accompany him, and their ministry, like his, like that even of Jesus, "the Christians' legislator," is conceived differently: it is doubtless "a special and superior role that has nothing in common with human influence," since it consists of constituting this influence by a sovereign act of the mind. The crowd will only revere this prodigious feat by seeing in it some supernatural operation: "This is what has forced the fathers of nations in all times to have recourse to the intervention of heaven, and to honor the gods by attributing to them their own wisdom." But the prodigious feat is a human accomplishment: "The great soul of the legislator is the true miracle that confirms his mission."[66] This is why the legislator, however prestigious, lives again in the modern Man of Letters. Rousseau, among others, did not hesitate to legislate for Corsica, and a little for Poland. Furthermore, the miracle of lawgiving repeats itself and multiplies itself endlessly, daily, in education: "A governor! oh what a sublime soul! . . . In truth, to make a man, one must either be a father or else oneself more than a man."[67] The legislator, the man of letters, and the educator are admirable in the same way: it is they who bring humanity into being.

✣ The Poet in the Age of Enlightenment

What is called literature in the eighteenth century includes, on the one hand, works of philosophy, politics, economics, history, scientific works written for a general readership—in a word, all the literature of information, ideas, and polemic—and, on the other hand, works of fiction, novels, plays, poems, and criticism. The boundary between these two kinds of work tends to blur in this period, on account of a new and lofty way of looking at things that is thought to be worthy of vitalizing everything. It is accepted as a matter of course that primacy belongs to the new vision rather than to the creations that illustrate it in imaginative literature. Philosophy, which is to all intents and purposes identified with the government of society, uses fiction to work for truth and the happiness of all: "O what a boon it would be to men, if one day all the arts of imitation took as their aim a common object, and competed with laws to make us love virtue and hate vice! It is the philosopher's task to invite them to do so; he should address the poet, the painter, and the musician, and cry aloud to them: Men of genius, to what end has heaven bestowed upon you its gifts?"[68] Literature's status is enhanced by assigning this role to it, along with art, but on the condition that letters be subordinated to philosophy: "It is philosophy that discovers the useful truths of political morality. It is eloquence that makes them popular. It is poetry that makes them, so to speak, proverbial."[69] We find here once again a hierarchy analogous to that which was established in Christianity between theology and poetry. It is true that once the dignity of literary fictions is affirmed, the ability to appeal to the imagination and make beloved higher truths can put the poet or the playwright in competition with the thinker for pride of place: "The poet's job is to arrange precious truths and to make them loved. He will make himself the equal of the philosopher."[70] But how can one believe in a real equality between the end and the means?

A more immediate and more infallible apprehension of truth than that of which reason is capable is often attributed to genius, especially poetic genius.

We find this in Diderot: "Poetry supposes an exaltation of the brain that comes, one could almost say, from divine inspiration. The poet has profound ideas without knowing their cause or their effects. The philosopher, in whom these same ideas are the fruit of long meditation, is amazed at this, and exclaims: Who inspired so much wisdom in that maniac?"[71] Marmontel compares the intuition of the poet to divine intelligence: "In order to conceive of the object of poetry in its full extent, we must dare to consider nature as the supreme intelligence's object of thought. . . . God sees nature. In his weakness the Poet must contemplate it in a similar way."[72] Chénier wrote often in this vein: he makes the acts and metamorphoses of poetic genius equal to the task of understanding the entire universe, giving to the thunderstruck poet access to the truths of science and to the sources of being.[73] Thus we see the age's strong attachment to poetry; but it is the great truths discovered by the Enlightenment that are of the essence, as is the case for any period that founds a faith. Poetry can divine these truths in its own way or translate them into its glorified language; it can emulate the philosophy that proclaims them; but it becomes sterile as soon as it parts company with them. Philosophy does not experience a reciprocal dependence upon poetry.

In fact, the homage to poetry is sometimes opposed by the same minds on account of a grave misgiving: there is doubt whether poetry is still possible in a philosophic age. "Everywhere there is a decline of fiery inspiration and poetry in proportion to the progress of philosophy," notes Diderot. "There is always in poetry something deceitful"; however, "it is no longer possible to tell tales to our people."[74] The age of poetry is pushed back to the beginnings of humanity; all knowledge was then expressed poetically; the hierarchy of the true and the pleasant had not been born: "A sage was formerly a philosopher, a poet, a musician. These talents degenerated by becoming distinct; the sphere of philosophy contracted; poetry came to lack ideas; songs came to lack vigor and energy; and so it was that wisdom, deprived of its voice, no longer made itself heard among the peoples with the same charm."[75] This change is regretted; there is an effort to exhort poetry to recover its greatness. What is needed to accomplish this? That it once again ally itself with wisdom, and that, putting aside the sad futility to which the progress of thought had condemned it, poetry place itself on a par with higher philosophy: "The Language of the Gods, brought back to the nobility of its origins, would in this way serve to instruct men."[76] The circle closes again: poetry has no other recourse, if it is to renew itself, than to bring its special talents into the orbit of triumphant philosophy. The age intends poetry to have a serious calling, a mission that would scarcely have been contemplated before. But this mission is fulfilled, at the same time and in a more essential way, by a rival who has taken the lead.

Thus in France the legendary ministry of the Poet is generally felt to be a thing of the past.[77] But it is curious that this ministry, along with the age in which it was thought to have existed, should be the object of a no less general nostalgia, and that Philosophy should have yielded so often to the temptation of idealizing the origins of the human race. It is well known how the literary criticism of the eighteenth century was interested in what the poetry of the earliest times might have been. Before, hardly anything was known on the subject other than the most ancient Greek poets and the legends concerning their more or less mythical predecessors, who were often discussed. Now, however, curiosity and knowledge extend themselves to the ancient times of every nation, in particular to Scandinavia, Celtic Scotland, and Wales, to the oral poetry (vaguely held to be in its own way primitive) of England, Denmark, Germany, and Spain, to medieval poetry itself, confused with its more distant ancestors. The Bible, meanwhile, takes its place alongside Homer and Ossian.[78] To the knowledge of new texts and the rereading of old ones are added speculative views on times and places scarcely known: ancient Gaul, Egypt, Asia. The result is a body of theory whose documentation is to a large extent fantastical, though incomparably richer and related to more real concerns than the few commonplaces about Homer or Orpheus that had existed before. Henceforth it is thought that one can have access to the primitive poets of the universe, epic poets, Hebrew prophets, bards, scalds, and their counterparts, discovered or imagined in every part of the world. Glimpsed in them is the golden age of poetry and the time of its influence over human society; they are represented as possessed of a high spiritual and civic power. In 1739 a history of French poetry traces its origins to the Gaulish nation: "We know what its *Bards* were. At once theologians and poets, they put into verse the secrets of religion"; but poetry "was not devoted to piety alone; it was still in the habit of honoring merit and virtue, and after using it to sing the blessings of the Gods, it was used to celebrate the fine actions of men."[79] This primitive function of poetry, which was very widely accepted, was variously explained.[80] Attempts to interpret it by virtue of practical considerations abound; Voltaire, who is among those least inclined to get carried away by an enthusiasm for primitive times, invokes mnemonics: verses allowed recitation by heart and song, a mode of transmission common to peoples without writing.[81] Another explanation offered is this: that the metaphoric style now to be found solely within the purview of poets was the only mode of expression used at the time of the earliest human societies, and that it long remained the most apt to persuade minds, even after reason's progress caused it to fall out of fashion in ordinary use; in fact, it is commonly thought that the metaphorical style called "oriental" is the style of primitive humanity in every country.[82] In any case, this primitive style and this poetry that used to spring to everyone's lips is not without prestige among civilized persons in the eighteenth century; they look back to a primitive state with nostalgia, and note with sadness that poetry "is for us no longer anything but a language of artifice."[83] This funeral oration for true poetry is rarely accompanied by an explicit announcement or wish for a resurrection. An attitude of resignation is more common than a hope that current trends may change so as to recreate the conditions of a poetic ministry within civilized society. However, this exaltation of what was thought to be an essential human faculty could not, in such an optimistic age, be purely dirgeful. The editors of the *Journal étranger* and *La Gazette littéraire de l'Europe*, who in the 1760s impart and comment upon everything that pertains to primitive poetry,[84] naturally share an enthusiasm for this lost excellence, and then communicate that enthusiasm to their readers; and by making primitive poetry admired they of course revive it to some extent as a source of contemporary inspiration.

The interest in the figure of the primitive poet was heightened by the interest felt at this time for the allegorical interpretation of pagan myths. Long a preoccupation of the learned and of theologians, and linked as it was to the elevation of the mythologic poet as transmitter of a higher doctrine, this interpretive effort was vastly popular in an eighteenth century keenly interested in retracing the history of the human mind. The idea shared by all is that beneath the manifest content of the fables of paganism is a hidden meaning that enabled them to teach about man and the universe. At the end of the seventeenth century and throughout the eighteenth, both religious and secular writers develop the idea that pagan mythology needs to be interpreted. The diversity of inspiration to be found in the proposed exegeses matters little here — Christian ones presupposed an original revelation that the myths had deformed, others alleged an original deism affected by anthropomorphic representations, still others imagined a development of fables due to the direct contact of ignorant man with the great facts of nature.[85] The fact is that in every case myths signify something more profound than what they seem to recount. Of equally little account here is the diversity of content to be found in these interpretations — agricultural, moral, historical, philosophical — which sometimes clash and sometimes combine; what is of greater interest to us is the close relation that connects this supposed allegorism of fables to the spiritual role attributed to the primitive poet. Poetry was the storehouse of sacred allegories: "This is why the first Poets who excelled in Allegory, Linus, Orpheus, and Musaeus, all of whom studied in Egypt, were called *Théologues*, and to them was attributed the honor of having rendered the habits of men more agreeable, of having civilized them."[86] Court de Gébelin, at the beginning of a treatise entitled *Du génie allégorique et symbolique de l'antiquité*, similarly invokes the "Sages of Memphis, of Babel, of Greece, Orpheus, Homer, Pythagoras, sacred hierophants"; and he celebrates in these terms the poets of primitive times:

> Exalted by the charms of virtue, astonished by the magnificence of the universe, deeply affected by the wonderful laws that govern the physical and moral world, understanding at a glance the immense influences of the Order of things on the happiness of societies and the prosperity of nations, they took up the lyre; and to the sound of its harmonious chords, they sang these admirable virtues: the existence of a Divinity beneficent toward Men, the beauty of virtue, the necessity of order, justice, and peace, the charms and delights of rural life. . . . This is what is known as the Language of the Gods; a language so renowned in antiquity, which Homer often mentions and whose origins we have sought for so long in vain. . . . The Language of the Gods was never the language of a particular people: it was, in the allegorical style of Poetry, Poetry itself, a Language of the Gods and not of Humanity, since it alone spoke worthily of Divinity, and since, at all times, and among all peoples, it was consecrated to divine worship.[87]

Court de Gébelin is a curious figure, on the borderline between natural philosophy and mystical illuminism. This ambiguity was not unusual at this time; he has, in fact, been seen as one of the great exemplars of eighteenth-century thought.[88] He should not, I think, be forced into the theosophic camp; his work as a whole hardly tends in that direction. Besides, a writer as much a naturalist as Dupuis is no less enthusiastic about the august role of the poets of yore: "Poets were the first theologians"; physics, astronomy, agriculture, moral philosophy, politics were all equally the goal of their allegories:

> For all these special aims entered into the general system of the first philosopher-poets who sang the Gods, and who ushered men into the sanctuary of nature, who seemed to have revealed to them its mysteries. . . . This was the veritable golden age of poetry, daughter of heaven and of the gods. Since those ancient times, she has remained well below those sublime heights, which a bold flight enabled her to attain while sustained by all the strength that genius draws from the contemplation of the universe, or of God on high, whose first oracles and first priests poets were.[89]

In the end, this belief in a poetic allegorism of primitive times amounts to supposing the existence at the beginnings of humanity of a moment of spiritual richness, of vital contact with things, of which we are no longer capable today.

Such a supposition is made more or less explicitly, and there can be differences of opinion between those who believe in an ancient science more advanced than our own and those who limit themselves to the idea of a nascent, instinctive intelligence that miraculously deciphers the universe. But all attribute to earliest humanity an affective plenitude and strength of imagination that the development of the race has caused to dry up. There is no common approach to the primitive world; this Edenic house has many mansions: the wilds of America, Egypt, and ancient Greece, the ancient Orient, barbarous Europe. Wherever the primitive world is situated, however, it looks the same. In the novelistic Voyages to past civilizations that become plentiful at the century's end, as well as in commentaries and evocations of every kind, the same traits appear everywhere: handsome old men moved by inspiration, virtuous disciples, modest and fervent virgins. The same scenes recur using the same devices: frugal meals and eloquent speeches, deistic ceremonies, symbolic rites, a language teeming with metaphors, with poetry implicitly reigning over human life. This imaginary universe, which cast its spell over the mind of the time, was not so quickly forgotten: its creatures go on to populate many a romantic epic.

Even the mind of Rousseau, so rigorous, so determined to restrict the primitive type of humanity to the pure mediocrity of natural life, seems to have been tempted at one time by the idea of an age preceding the dispersion of humanity, an age more civilized than the one that followed.[90] Furthermore, whatever doctrine he adopts, Rousseau always associates the idea of a golden age with our origins, declaring this notion to be rooted in his heart.[91] Somber, far-ranging Boulanger, who sees the entire history of humanity as the traumatic consequence of the Flood,[92] cannot keep himself from applying the term "golden age" to the epoch that, after the cataclysm, inaugurates the new history of the human race, though this was, according to his views, a very sorry period indeed.[93] Bailly, better known for his role during the Revolution as mayor of Paris than for his works on early times, was convinced that an earlier era preceding historic times had known advanced science, particularly astronomical science, combined with a sublimely wise philosophy;[94] according to him, this was the period described by the story of the golden age, which was a historical reminiscence for the nations and a law of the heart for individuals: "What happens to the individual in the course of his years and thoughts happens to the race in the succession of generations. Who does not regret the time of youth? . . . The house we lived in was so beautiful, men were so good, friends so reliable, women so sincere and touching: this house was surrounded by a purer air, the sun was as ardent as friendship, the sky as calm as the depths of the heart. This was the veritable Golden Age; every man has had one of his own."[95]

It is perhaps appropriate to ask ourselves what this idealization of the most distant past signifies as the thought of a philosophic century filled with thoughts of the future. Why does philosophical humanism, completely oriented toward a progress of which it is the embodiment, long so for this companion age of aboriginal excellence and poetry? This has sometimes been denounced as a contradiction, and not without reason;[96] logically, Progress and the Golden Age are two irreconcilable hypotheses. But a different sort of logic binds human beliefs together. If the two terms thought to be contradictory coexist and combine constantly, if "the primitivist thesis is never so radical that it does not to some degree embrace its converse,"[97] this is because the faith of the *Philosophes* cannot be satisfied with attributing to man a belated grandeur that is the fruit of time and progress; it needs a greatness that is intrinsic, a title of nobility that is native to humanity, like that which Genesis conferred upon Adam. Their optimism requires a human Eden, whose as it were atemporal primary reality founds their hopes.[98] The philosophic faith secularizes the theological Eden into earthly legend; abolishing the abyss of the Fall, it significantly mingles humanity as it was at first and humanity as it will be one day in humanity as it is now.[99] In doing so and in accordance with its standard procedure, humanity in a state of nature is described as larger than life. Antiquity, felicity, purity: we are these things, though they are also something greater than us, which, having been ours, must be ours again.

It is none the less true that in the eyes of the *Philosophe*, what will be is more important than what was. Under Louis XVI, a new golden age was believed to be at hand. The kingdom of France would give the signal for moral renewal: "May France," writes Court de Gébelin, "bring back that Order of which the Ancients had so sublime an idea that they called it the golden age, the empire of Astraea or of Justice. . . . The time is perhaps not far off: already we are seeing it begin to dawn."[100] And he cites the fourth eclogue, declaring it more appropriate to his time than to Virgil's. Some will say that this is Court de Gébelin, and that this sort of announcement, coming from a mind like his, speaks only for those like him. But a *marquise* whose thinking is strictly royalist and Christian gives us the opinion of "serious people": "France, they said, was undergoing moral renewal. . . . This is what explains how so many people whose morals are honest and pure, among them the king himself, who was the first to share their illusions, were hoping, at that moment, that we were entering into the golden age."[101] In the fervor of such expectation, it is natural that the cohort of philosophical Men of Letters, aglow with the current truths of moral renewal, take precedence over poets, whose spiritual role has only a distant and mostly mythic relation to the present. The Poet has the status of an important memory, one that is needed for the faith in Humanity. But this Poet is not altogether a reality.

In the eighteenth century, a theory of primitive language is inseparable from the generally held idea of poetry's prestigious origins. Poetry was the mode of expression that was natural to nascent humanity. The language of human beings in their beginnings had the strength and savor of life; a spontaneous necessity linked words to things; convention and analysis only came later, as instruments of perfected intelligence seeking an abstract science. How does primitive language represent faithfully and immediately what it expresses? This can be understood in more than one way: it may be believed, for example, that a word relates to a thing according to a metaphysical necessity, situating the intimate relation of the word to what it names on a supernatural level, within divinity itself.[102] Or, taking an opposite tack, it may be believed that the primitive word represents the thing by virtue of a purely natural relation: this is the view that philosophers of language, Condillac and Rousseau in particular, develop in the eighteenth century. For them, language began with expressive cries that were then imitated by the cries with which nature spontaneously accompanies emotions, and that are intelligible by reason of the likeness of these natural effects on all men; to these cries were added onomatopoeic utterances imitating the sounds of objects, these too offering for that reason a meaning that is universally clear; cries and onomatopoeic utterances were reinforced with figurative meanings by way of metaphor — a process that is spontaneous and unequivocal, given the constancy of the fundamental metaphorical relations in the minds of all men; such a language naturally took advantage of action — gestures and mime — and of musical intonation. This theory was developed by Condillac; by abbé Bergier, who arrives logically at the notion of identical primitive radicals for the entire human race and at the project of a dictionary of primitive language;[103] by Jean-Jacques Rousseau; by Charles de Brosses, who affirms the existence of "a primitive language that is organic, physical, and necessary, common to the entire human race," and who in his turn plans a dictionary of primitive roots, which he calls a "universal archeologist";[104] by Court de Gébelin, who is bold enough to demonstrate "that each word had its reason, that this reason was to be found in nature," and who likewise believes that he is able to establish a list of primitive roots.[105] Condillac specifies clearly the purely human and natural meaning of this doctrine: "There are people who have thought that the norms of the primitive language expressed the very nature of things. . . . The cause of their mistake comes from the fact that, having seen that the first names were representative, they assumed that they represented things as they are. This was to gratuitously attribute deep learning to rough-hewn men." In fact, this "deep learning," for a mind so slightly inclined to ontology, amounted to nothing; the earliest men would certainly not have understood any metaphysician who might have told them about it, but "we might add that we would not understand it ourselves."[106] Language therefore emanates from the natural constitution of man at grips with things, not from the secret of being. God gave to man the faculty of creating language, and is the author of the natural laws and causal links according to which this creation takes place: his role goes no further than this.[107] That said, this theory, however purely naturalistic it may be, aims to elevate speech in its origins: while purifying it of any theological opinion, it authorizes the idea of a primitive plenitude of human language and of a poetic faculty aboriginally linked to the practice of living.

For more than one author, the idea of a primitive fusion of the three arts of poetry, song, and dance was added to this conception of primitive language, every means of expression thus being brought into play simultaneously. From this fundamental unity—a sort of vital, aesthetic totality—the arts with which we are familiar emerged by a process of division that was at once a development and a decline. A theory of natural, expressive music whose vogue in the eighteenth century is well known and that informed the long debate on opera was linked to these ideas, which are to be found in diverse forms throughout the entire century, with a growing frequency,[108] and few dissenters.[109] Poetry that sprang from emotions that were sung, represented by gestures, and rendered symbolical by virtue of a faculty of inspiration devoid of artifice—poetry that expressed and put into action everything that was in human nature—had, by virtue of these characteristics, a singular power over human life. One sees how it might have governed society in earliest times. Prior to prose—on this point there is general agreement—it was poetry, possessed by superior gravity and nourished by the needs and vital interests of primitive humanity, that officiated, spontaneously and with universal acceptance, in the name of heaven and earth.[110] "The object of the earliest poems," writes Condillac, "shows us what poetry's character was. It is likely that poems sang of religion, laws, and heroes only to awaken in citizens feelings of admiration and emulation. There were psalms, canticles, odes, and songs."[111] Rousseau agrees:

> In the past all human and divine laws, exhortations to virtue, knowledge concerning gods and heroes, the lives and actions of famous men, were written in verse and sung publicly by choirs to the sound of instruments. . . . No more efficacious way had been found to engrave on the minds of men the principles of morality and the life of virtue; or rather, this was not the effect of a premeditated means, but the effect of noble feelings and elevated ideas seeking in well-wrought measures to forge a language worthy of them.[112]

On the eve of the Revolution, Rabaut-Saint-Etienne, who was a disciple of Court de Gébelin, collects and organizes all the themes we have just reviewed: language that was natural, emotive, active, musical, and allegorical was properly *"the language of the gods,* an expression that we have inherited from ancient peoples, among whom primitive language had kept that sublime name"; "allegories were therefore not the puerile amusement of Homer, Hesiod, and their predecessors, but an ancient, consecrated language, the memory of which they have fortunately saved for us"; "linked with religion and its celebrations, the primitive style was preserved by the Hierophants, the Vates, the Brahmans, the Bards or poets"; poems were not at that time distractions for the idle: "handed down from age to age and embellished by successive generations, they had become sacred, like the religion with which they were intimately linked."[113]

In this way, the future destiny of the mission of poetry is singularly illuminated by a primitivist preface, and this earliest coloring never disappears completely.[114] But when it revives, with romanticism, poetry's tendency will be to define itself in the present and the future. In the eighteenth century, the notion of poetry's mission appears bearing the traits of a myth, like a thought that is both obsessive and far-removed from present applicability. It is as if this idea is latent in a faith upon which it depends, but that keeps it at a distance. The notion of the mission of the poet belongs to the golden legends of philosophical humanism; it has all the strengths and weaknesses of mythical representations in a time of plans, hopes, and actions. It is important for us to be familiar with this point of departure if we are to understand how the situation was later so markedly modified in favor of living poets.[115]

✢ *The Revolutionary Crisis*

The Revolution carries on the thought of the entire century, proposing to realize it in action. Thus the terms in which the question of the writer's social role is posed during the revolutionary crisis are the ones with which we are by now familiar. The only differences are in the emphases now placed on the idea that the time for the task of moral renewal has arrived and on the men who carry it out. Legislators of flesh and blood have replaced those of legend; the great citizens of today overshadow the figures of the past. It is natural that at such a moment a definition of the active role of the writer should appear. And yet, when events are at the highest pitch of intensity, the revolutionary power is seen placing all of literature in a suspect category: "Men of letters," intoned Robespierre, "have in general disgraced themselves in this revolution; and, to the eternal shame of the forces of the mind, it is the People's reason alone that has taken up the slack."[116] This anathema can certainly be explained by the connections writers had with the well-off classes and by the moderantism of many of them. But it is dictated by a deeper logic. The philosophic faith, when constituted as a government, takes on a murderous form; faced with the difficulties every revolution encounters, it fulminates not only against its enemies, but against the very principle on which it was founded and that set it apart from religious dogmatism: that of the free and various activity of the mind. From among the mass of the faithful, a governmental cadre emerges in whom this leading thought becomes frustrated, changes its nature, and finally has no other object than to justify the acts of those in power. Doctrinaire writers are then the victims of choice for the victorious doctrine. It is appropriate to speak of the Calvary of the Man of Letters. Inclined to dream of a society whose essence is an Idea and that is governed by that Idea, his condition is never so unfortunate as when his dream is realized. The free exercise of thought (and any exercise of thought worthy of the name is free) and its incarnation in power—these two natural claims of modern intellectuals are cruelly contradictory. They prosper, in fact, only when governments care little about doctrines or use them only in selective fashion or as rules of thumb. In the French Revolution, it is impossible to say how far the extermination or domestication of men of letters would have gone if the Terror had been indefinitely prolonged. Thermidor, which maintained the Republic while diminishing the doctrinal character of the state, allowed the faith of the *philosophes* to survive and to continue to act. Thus during the ten years of the French Revolution, from 1789 to 1799, the flame of the new faith never ceased to burn.

During this period, the conflict of the new credo and the old broke out into the open. The entire religious politics of the Revolution consists in a constant effort to accredit the new values at the expense of Catholicism. Both the civil constitution [of the clergy] (a sort of alliance of the state with a church reorganized by the state) and the final Separation share this single aim, though they take different approaches. Some, following Rousseau and his *Du contrat social*, demand the union of the Priesthood and the Judiciary, wrongly separated in the past for the benefit of the church.[117] Others, less numerous, make a contrary demand, seeking a more complete separation of Church and State.[118] Both approaches, albeit by opposite means, hope to accelerate the decline of the Catholic religion to the profit of a secular religion supported by new institutions. From the beginning, the revolutionary faith translated itself into various sacred ceremonies and collective practices, which can well be considered a religion, soon to be the rival of the Catholic religion. Long before the dechristianization movement of 1793 and 1794 brought out all the violence inherent in the conflict, there appear altars of the fatherland, trees of liberty, tablets, fascia, civic baptisms, and commemorative celebrations of the great revolutionary dates. After Thermidor and throughout the Directory, the revolutionary cults and the spirit that gave birth to them remain alive.[119] Later, taking advantage of the failure of these forms of worship and of the ebb of the secular faith, Catholics contested their depth and seriousness and were hardly contradicted by adversaries who had become indifferent to this sort of thing. Others acknowledged the continuity and coherence of the phenomenon, but saw therein nothing but an effect of governmental propaganda.[120] To take this point of view is to fail to see the deep roots of the revolutionary faith: in the half century preceding 1789, under Louis XV and Louis XVI, the fervor of what could be called the humanism of moral renewal never ceased to stir up the Man of Sensibility. The ecstasies of 1760 and 1780, which we call preromantic because we are especially interested in their literary character, persist in those of 1789, 1793, or 1795, which are relegated to the category of political rigmarole. It is true that from one era to another the tone and the circumstances have changed; but the fundamental themes — nature, virtue, human sublimity — have remained the same. The preromantic élan took society as its prime object during the Revolution; but in this modification, whose seeds preromanticism already contained, it retained its essential identity.[121]

In this new form, it seems to have reached a wider audience than the ordinary literary public. More than one testimony leads us to suspect that this is so. Half a century after the Revolution, sometimes at an even later date, people were surprised to discover individuals of humble condition whom the revolutionary faith had marked forever, and who never again fit into the world once it resumed its customary ways. Renan in his childhood — that is, in the last years of the Restoration or at the beginning of the July Monarchy — knew in Tréguier a curious character, impoverished, smiling, disdainful of the age, who was known as "Father System" because he used that word when he preached to his interlocutors doctrines they found hard to understand. When he died, after 1830, "in a corner was found a carefully wrapped bouquet of dried flowers, bound by a tricolor ribbon." The origin of the bouquet was made clear to Renan much later, by a news item he read around 1860: "Yesterday in an out-of-the-way street deep in the faubourg Saint-Jacques, there died an old man who provoked the curiosity of his neighborhood as a model of beneficent goodness; but he evaded anything that might have revealed his past. A few books, Volney's catechism, and a broken set of Rousseau were scattered on the table. A trunk contained all his belongings. The *commissaire de police*, summoned to open it, found only a few poor effects among which was a faded bouquet carefully wrapped in a paper on which was written: Bouquet worn by me at the celebration of the Supreme Being, 20

Prairial, Year II."[122] Gabriel Monod tells the story of a Republican veteran from the Vendée who was more than ninety years old when he died during the Second Empire and whose last moments were described to him by the old man's daughter: "At the moment of death, he looked toward the sky with an ecstatic expression and murmured: O sun of '93, I shall die, then, without seeing you dawn again!"[123] Other testimonies evoke other moments of the Revolution and its effect on other social types. During the Restoration, the philosopher Laromiguière, born in 1756, "was unable to hide his emotion when he spoke about the first celebration on the Champ de Mars."[124] In 1833, the princesse de Salm, aged more than sixty years, exclaims as she recalls 1789:

> Qu'ils étaient beaux, les sentiments d'alors!
> Que l'on se trouvait grand, que l'on se sentait libre![125]

> [How fine they were, the feelings we had then!
> How great we thought ourselves, how free we felt!]

Stendhal, whose acquaintance with the Revolution was limited to his youth and adolescence, writes more than forty years later: "In 1794, we had no religion whatsoever; our inner, solemn sentiment was completely summed up in this idea: *to be useful to the fatherland.* . . . There were holidays and many moving ceremonies, which contributed to nourishing the feeling that was foremost in all our hearts. This was our only religion. . . . Later, we were guilty of infidelities toward this religion; but at every great conjuncture it reclaimed its influence over our hearts, just as Catholicism does for its adherents."[126]

The contradictory usage of the word *religion* by Stendhal is apparent, both refusing and then granting it to what he remembers having experienced. The revolutionary religion, like that of the *philosophes* of which it is nothing but a variant, lacks one of the fundamental characteristics of what we call religion: the primacy of the supernatural, the supremacy, not only accepted but experienced, of the divine over the human. The concrete sign of this difference is that the revolutionary cults, like deism, exclude prayer, substituting for it a pure elevation of the mind and spirit toward the sublimity of the universal order. They nevertheless imply going beyond the ordinary limits of human existence; they respond in their own way to a need for the absolute and for plenitude that sets them clearly apart from agnosticism; and we must see in their constant, powerfully emotional reference to the sublime in Nature and in Man more than their immediate political importance. Besides, it is clear that it is only because these cults respond to the same need as religion that they presume to replace it. What they institute in the place of a religion of God is a religion of humanity attaining to God; it is in this sense that Robespierre defends himself from accusations of atheism: "The more a man possesses the gifts of sensibility and genius, the more he is attached to ideas that enlarge his being and lift up his heart; and the doctrine of men of this caliber becomes the doctrine of all." "Man, whoever you may be, you are still able to conceive great thoughts of yourself; you can connect your ephemeral life to God himself and to immortality."[127] Michelet did not hesitate to affirm "the truly religious character of the Revolution," and to explain its hostility to churches by the fact "that it was itself a Church."[128] Mathiez tried to support the same opinion on the basis of a stricter definition, inspired by Durkheim, emphasizing collective attitudes and practices: "It is a religion in which faith and the act of worship refer not to a supernatural object but to the political institution itself, to the Fatherland conceived as the source and instrument of happiness."[129] Such an affirmation falls short of the truth, in that it makes of the revolutionary religion purely a worship of society and neglects the vast movement of thought from which the faith of 1789 emerged and that grounds its entire meaning. Even if this faith does have human society as its principal object, it also has its metaphysics; it enlarges life and illumines the universe.

A religion, then, if you like; and, if you like, a counterreligion; a religion of humanity, if you prefer. It will be objected that such a definition is contradictory. But it is precisely this contradiction that allows us to grasp what we might otherwise misunderstand. It helps us to keep in perspective the disputes among the adepts of the new faith. Carnot, in a speech to the Convention on 27 Floréal year II [after abolishing the monarchy, the revolutionary Convention decreed on September 22, 1792, that year I of the era of the Republic had begun; the revolutionary calendar was used in France until 1806 (year XIV). *Trans.*], identifies the Supreme Being almost explicitly with Nature and exclaims, enumerating all the highest human virtues, friendship, filial piety, and justice: "All these things together, then, make up the Supreme Being; he is the union of all the thoughts that constitute the happiness of man."[130] Some would have us see in this tirade a naturalistic reply to Robespierre's views. This is probably the case, but Robespierre himself had said, precisely in the report arguing for instituting the *fête* that would become a famous object of disagreement: "All sects should of themselves combine in the universal religion of Nature."[131] The Supreme Being does not always seem very transcendent, but nevertheless always maintains this character; as for Nature, it is just as transcendent as the Supreme Being, since in order to equate the two, the qualities of the Supreme Being are attributed to Nature: "Nature" means not blind nature, "but that often intelligent, often wise nature, infinitely powerful, infinitely good, infinitely fertile." We can see, then, how it is possible to say: "Nature and God are incontestably one and the same being."[132] At bottom, what is called Nature is a feminized Supreme Being, an eternal Mother who is more accessible and more benevolent than a Father, in whom transcendence is lessened without disappearing altogether. Those who explicitly exclude the Father are rare, and their faith does not differ essentially from the common faith.[133] Bonneville, "a preromantic and a revolutionary," as he has been defined,[134] thunders forth in 1792 an incredible dithyramb to the exclusive glory of Man: "He is the *universal* image, the first, the last, the only image! He is the great totality, he is the meeting of all thoughts, all minds, all images, all forms, all ages. He is all, everywhere, one. Yes, I shall tear from nature a confession that terrifies her: *Man is god!*"[135] Such a hymn (it takes up ten pages; the preceding lines give only an inadequate impression of it) seems to leave us no place beside divinized humanity for the being who is usually called God. Bonneville nevertheless fulminates against the atheist, "born blind," whom he classes scarcely "above the orangutang."[136] In any case, we know today that there was no absolute opposition between the religion of the Supreme Being and that of Reason. The two were often commingled in practice,[137] and, far from expressing real doctrinal differences, the conflicts that occurred concerning the revolutionary cults were masks for political rivalries or crises in the psychology of the masses and their attitude toward the traditional order. Besides, believers can always split over a credo without renouncing it, even to the point of massacring each other.

The time for action was also a time for propaganda. And propaganda reaches out to literature, not only as a result of calculation on the part of the government, but because the problem of the function of literary creations and the problem of their relation to the humanist faith, which had been the object of reflection throughout the century, became even more pressing when this faith sought to attain power. The idea enjoying the greatest currency at this time is that the peculiar charms of literature and the beaux-arts assist philosophy, or Law, which is its social expression, by bringing about its public acceptance. This idea, which the Revolution inherited from the *philosophes*,[138] implies both the subordination and the elevation of the arts: "Nature has recourse to beauty only to show us what is good or to draw us to it. It has been Nature's intention to direct our attention toward the good and make it dear to us. Such, then, is the sublime property, shared by all arts, of being able to become, through the efforts of an enlightened government, the principal instruments of the happiness of men."[139] "Till now the arts have been considered the decorations of the social edifice: they are part of its foundation"; since the thoughts of men are determined above all by their senses, their imagination, and their passions, "the legislator seized these electrifying motivations and made a chain of them that he stretched around their minds and hearts. The dignity of the Arts is due to this sublime function."[140] Since moral truth depends essentially on feelings, some, without any change in their point of view, go so far as to hold that the fictions that make moral truth beloved approach it, as it were, just as closely as does the thought of the *philosophe*: "What would become of so many social maxims, so many abstract generalizations, if the beaux-arts did not seize them and plunge them again into sensibility, reattaching them to the feelings from which they derive, and thus restoring to them their color and strength?"[141] The same intellectual approach is to be found in the reports on art and on freedom. Art is to serve liberty and show examples of it—this is the function assigned to it, but this is its tendency anyway: art knows that freedom favors it by eliminating obstacles that genius cannot abide, and by providing it with subjects worthy of it in a morally renewed humanity;[142] better still, the artist and the poet are by their nature inclined to thoughts that emancipate man; they can only approve of "a revolution whose cause was that of artists and poets, since it aimed to give luster to the destiny of the human race."[143] This solidarity of art and freedom, which places art at the highest level, is evoked more than once.[144] Genius and Liberty are supposed to proceed from the same source: "Learn that freedom is produced by the same enthusiasm that gives birth to the productions of genius. . . . That sacred instinct which, upon viewing the beauties of the universe, impels the man of genius . . . , is also that which fires the generous man of sensibility with the ardent desire to be free."[145]

The revolutionary period, to a greater extent than the philosophic age that preceded it, had to define the function of poetry in the present. There was an effort to make the type of the primitive Poet current:

> Tant qu'il aima ces jeux et ces pompeuses fêtes,
> Où les vers des grands noms célébraient les honneurs,
> Tant qu'il prit ses devoirs dans les chants des Poètes,
> L'homme fut libre, heureux; il conserva des moeurs.
>
> . . . .
>
> Viens de ces jours de gloire, auguste Poésie,
> Reprendre parmi nous ta puissance et tes droits;
> De la Liberté sainte inséparable amie,
> Sur la base des moeurs tu fonderas ses lois.[146]

> [As long as man loved the games and ceremonial pomp
> Where the honor of great names was celebrated in verse,
> As long as he learned his duties from the songs of Poets,

He remained free and happy in a virtuous way of life.

.   .   .   .

Come back, august Poetry of those glorious days,
Take up once more among us your power and your rights;
As a faithful friend of holy Liberty,
You will give your laws a sound moral foundation .]

Reminiscences of the legendary past or of antiquity, however, led in practice only to the type of the citizen-poet, eloquent accompanist to revolutionary action. Poets, at the time of the Convention, are certainly not legislators; they merely celebrate the virtues and actions upon which is founded the power of laws. In society's earliest days, writes Chénier, "literature was august and sacred, because it was devoted to the interests of society."[147] And the model that comes to mind is Tyrtaeus, the warrior-poet, rather than Orpheus or Pythagoras; hymns suggest themselves even more than religious or moral poems. Leclerc, a member of the Convention, believes that the original poetic genre created by the Revolution is the "hymnic" genre, and he is not mistaken.[148] Whatever can be imagined or said at this time in honor of poetry, it is relegated to the celebration of values whose principal source is elsewhere. Its indwelling power of inspiration and creativity are scarcely glimpsed: this seed did not germinate in the preceding period and it does not develop during the Revolution.

It is the use more than the mission of poets that was a subject of interest during these years. There is a particular explanation for this: the interconnection of philosophy, law, and public awareness was being established during this period through a new institution: the collective celebration [*fête*], which required the participation of poets and artists. Sensibility had always valued shared emotions highly. The natural culmination of a religion of sympathy is spectacle and celebration. The denouement of a comedy or a tragedy is a moving apotheosis of virtue that creates communion among spectators. Already in the ancien régime we can see the first beginnings of secular celebrations in dedications of monuments or inscriptions, assemblies celebrating good works, publicity given to acts of generosity, and local ceremonies at which awards were distributed.[149] But even then the new secular faith is already imagining formal celebrations on a vaster scale. The great assemblies of ancient Greece are recalled; Rousseau exalts the powerful civic efficacy of Greek theater, and of "those imposing spectacles given beneath the sky before an entire nation";[150] he wants a republic to have only open-air spectacles: "Let the sun light up your innocent spectacles: you yourselves will be a spectacle, the most worthy that the sun can shed its light upon."[151] The frequently evoked motif of the people as both spectators and spectacle brings us to the great *fêtes*, meant to be pure celebrations of their embodied ideal by the people gathered together in one place. In a first draft of *Du contrat social*, Rousseau, having laid down the articles of his "civil religion," extols a public profession of faith by all citizens, to be renewed each year, and "accompanied by a ceremony both simple and august."[152] The idea of a simplified ceremony honoring the Supreme Being, preferably celebrated under the open sky and in the midst of nature, a notion common to all deism, including Voltaire's,[153] mingles with and is related to the idea of the *fête*. There is no real distinction between civic sentiment and metaphysical emotion.

Even before the Revolution, then, we see the project of a secular celebration grow in popularity. Such a celebration is foreign to traditional worship and more or less clearly designed to compete with Catholic celebrations, just as the new faith competes with the old. Rousseau advises the Corsicans to fight against superstition "by freely committing resources to the pomp of public festivals."[154] A lay calendar with great men as saints and nonreligious holidays was proposed as early as 1788 by Sylvain Maréchal.[155] From 1789 through the end of the century, these projects become real, hatching from one end of France to the other, multiplying in various shapes and only definitively discontinued after Brumaire. To what extent was public adhesion to the celebrations and rites of revolutionary worship heartfelt? Historians differ on this point, according to the degree of sympathy or antipathy they feel toward the Revolution. Whatever traces it may have left behind, the ultimate failure of the movement inclines most authors to consider it artificial to the core. But this is to confuse two different problems. There can be no doubt that the celebrations respond to a powerful impulse; they display the faith of the thinkers, the leaders, and the militants of the Revolution. This faith has only partially and weakly penetrated the great mass of the population, however. Not only does the credo of the *philosophes* suppose, in order to be understood, a higher than average level of intelligence, but it also disdains to accommodate itself to uncultured individuals, with whom traditional religion has been fraternizing for centuries. The revolutionary celebrations, with their flowering of symbols and rites, were indeed a movement on the part of the philosophic faith in the direction of the masses; but this was more an instinctive movement encouraged by the heat of public sentiment than a calculated tactic. The encounter did not survive the great upheavals that had made it possible. Traditional forms of collective worship recovered their popularity at the same time as the former faith. But the spirit of the new faith and the project of making it public as well as popular endured among both systematizing ideologues and practical reformers—the same grouping that had engendered these phenomena in the first place.

These secular ceremonies, celebrations of a system of beliefs with Humanity at the center, presuppose the collaboration of poets and artists, and just as in 1789 this is so throughout the nineteenth century — as long as they are retained in memory, in fact. Because such rites are the means par excellence of invigorating truths of moral renewal via the senses and the heart, they naturally require the ministry of all those whose profession it is to depict the sublime by means of what is perceptible. Poets and artists exercise this ministry daily in their creations; but the *fête* is a chosen moment, a paroxysm in which all the arts join to produce this shudder, this unforgettable shock that is as it were the state of grace or the ecstasy of the new faith. What the celebrations ought to produce are "these sorts of electrifying shocks that simultaneously transmit to an entire people a single thought — that of virtue; emotional experiences in which all citizens can be identified by the spirit of fraternity, which the common rejoicings inspire in them, moments of happiness for sensitive souls, enjoyed in advance when their recurrence is anticipated, and enjoyed after they have taken place when their memories are perpetuated."[156] Contemporaries characterized *la Fête* as a peak human experience, albeit in different ways. At the beginning of the Revolution, the author of an account of the anniversary celebration of the Oath of the Tennis Court, which was held in Versailles on 20 June 1790, shows us the participants in this celebration on their way back to Paris: "they spoke to each other only of human happiness; it seemed that the Gods themselves were on the march."[157] "Man," writes Robespierre, "is the greatest object nature contains; and the most magnificent of spectacles is that of a great people gathered in one place."[158] De Moy distinguishes the "general celebration," in which everything is part of the scenic stage and all are actors, from public celebrations of special groups, which are like spectacles for nonparticipants; and he desires that all available space at a general celebration be filled with signs and testimonies "that recall constantly the excellence of the day, if I may be permitted to use this expression":[159] this is a notable secular transposition of the holiness that Christianity, following the model of the Sabbath, confers upon the days it sets aside as religious festivals.

One may wonder why so much emotion, which was without any doubt authentic and was shared by an entire generation, produced no notable artistic achievement. Why were Poetry and Art, which were recognized as the legitimate ministers of the common enthusiasm, and which did in fact collaborate in all these celebrations, so poor in what they accomplished? This can always be explained by a fortuitous dearth of talent. It can also be claimed that so new an enthusiasm must have been stifled in the poetic forms of the day, which were inherited from another time and designed for less ambitious objects. But the relative conservatism of canons and of poetic style during an age of such spiritual upheaval itself demands an explanation; it cannot be entirely attributed to the ordinary delay of forms vis-à-vis the thoughts they express; the necessarily subordinate character that philosophy and the Revolution attributed to poetry does a better job accounting for this, perhaps. Poets fashion their language according to the role they believe themselves able to assume; later, they certainly showed that within a few years they were capable of reinvigorating the resources of their art. But in the period of which we are speaking here, the assignment of responsibilities in the corps of thinkers scarcely favored them. However high they might be lifted, others occupied the supreme rank. In 1794 it is Robespierre who is compared to Orpheus, not Marie-Joseph Chénier or Ecouchard-Lebrun.[160]

And there is something else. In its project of renewal, the French Revolution is naively totalitarian. It is by making of them cogs in the workings of the State that it exalts the citizen-poets. Abbé Grégoire says frankly and without shame: "Painting, engraving, poetry, and music will recover among us their original dignity. Among us as among the Ancients, they will be instruments in the hands of the government."[161] We are no longer able to read without concern lines like these: "Celebrations are what impress upon the social mass a single unified character. They are what give to it a single unified spirit. They ground its morals, establish its opinions, and, consequently, combine all the members of the State into a single, unified whole";[162] or these: "It is vital to bring into play everything that can modify, as it were, the substance of man, so as to make him one with the form of government and make the love of freedom his dominant passion."[163] Those who write these things are certainly convinced that giving society total power over humanity is the way to emancipate it. This surprising opinion, which implies an utterly dangerous confusion of the state with the highest values, is a temptation to thinkers, always inclined as they are to imagine in government the incarnation of a doctrine. Rousseau had been in this regard a predecessor of the revolutionary theoreticians of the *Fête*: he is as heedless as they with regard to citizens as individuals: "If," he writes, "they are trained soon enough never to regard their persons otherwise than in relation to the organs of State power, and to perceive, so to speak, their existence as a part of the State's existence, they will be able at last to identify themselves as it were with this great whole."[164] These suggestions, enthusiastic then, have acquired with time a bitter flavor. After all that we have seen, the imprudence or naïveté that explains them can no longer be justified. In any case, they show well enough that in a revolutionary society the apostolate of the poet and the artist is dominated by a social dogma that exists prior to artistic creations. Poets and artists are inter-mediaries rather than guides. The revolutionary state has taken upon itself the august function of the philosophical men of letters. As for poets and artists, they discovered in these events more opportunities for work, but no new definition of their role.[165]

Chapter 2

The Poet Consecrated

W E MUST now transport ourselves into very different regions, putting to one side what occupied center stage in the eighteenth century—the philosophical and revolutionary faith in humanity—in
order to seek among minds faithful to traditional beliefs any new notions concerning the function of literature that may appear there. To do this is all the
more necessary because, although the legacy of the past seemed dull and unin-
teresting throughout the course of this century compared with the philosphical
novelties of the day, this heritage would blossom once more with new ideas and
renewed prestige after Brumaire. The atmosphere has changed, and Chateaubriand and Lamartine triumphantly bring Louis Racine and Lefranc de Pompignan back to life. But what they revive had remained alive, obstinately and
without a break, throughout the age of Enlightenment.

We know that religion had endorsed the idea of a pious poetry, one acquainted
with divine truth and communicating it clothed in symbols. In the poets of
Scripture, singing and prophesying under the inspiration of the Holy Spirit,
poetry was both revelation and salvation. Its excellence, diminished and defaced
elsewhere, shone in the sacred texts. Admiration for the beauties of Holy Scripture, which was ranked above everything else in ancient poetry, as well as the
habit of translating and of paraphrasing the poetic texts of the Bible in French
verse, had long been common. The sixteenth and seventeenth centuries are
replete with these translations, whether Catholic or Protestant, and this tradition continues to be practiced throughout the entire eighteenth century. The
poetic doctrine that accompanies these translations is not devitalized by the
widespread incredulity of the age; in fact, it is strengthened due to the new
interest that the period shows in the origins of poetry. The elements of this
doctrine already appear in Bossuet. According to him, the poetry of the ancient
Hebrews, consisted at first of commemorative hymns: "From these, poetry is
born, later taking on several forms, of which the oldest is still preserved in odes
and songs to be found among all the ancient peoples, found even today among
unlettered peoples, praising divinity and great men";[1] this Hebraic poetry, bold
and imaginative in style, was inspired by God himself, "and indeed, properly
speaking it is only the people of God who have known a poetry that came from

enthusiasm."[2] Of this poetry, several monuments survive that we see included in the Old and New Testaments: Bossuet cites in particular the two songs of Moses, but supposes that still more ancient ones may have existed from the time of the patriarchs. The issue that such a doctrine raises for whoever wishes to understand its implications concerns pagans more than Jews: is the primitive poetry to be found among the peoples of the universe to be considered error merely, a false imitation of true poetry,[3] or does it too derive in some measure from a divine communication? In general, the prerogative is granted to the ancient Hebrews, but speculations about origins remain inconclusive. This vagueness favors a certain ecumenical spirit of accommodation, as the passage by Bossuet shows. Abbé Fleury, who reserves divine inspiration to the Jews, thinks that the Holy Spirit merely made use of the style that they had in common with all ancient peoples: "[W]hat shows . . . that this style was natural is that the style of the oldest profane authors closely resembles it";[4] he observes, however, that primitive poetry was everywhere religious: "Greek poetry in particular constituted a considerable part of Greek religion, and it passed for something holy and divine in its beginnings."[5] Thus in the seventeenth century, well before the great vogue of similar ideas in secular literary circles, we already see a complete theory of the primitive style and original dignity of poetry, linked to an ecclesiastical meditation on sacred poetry. Not even the idea of the primitive union of the three arts is lacking.[6] Another priest, Fénelon, combining the memory of the legislating and civilizing poets of pagan tradition with the evocation of "sacred songs," affirms the high mission of poetry in general: "Poetry is more serious and more useful than the common run of humanity believes. Religion consecrated poetry to its own use from the beginning of the human race. . . . In addition, poetry gave to the world its first laws. . . . Speech enlivened by vivid images, great figures, the exaltation of the passions and the charm of harmony was called the language of the gods."[7] Fénelon is obviously convinced of the superiority of sacred poets,[8] but we see how he inclines at the same time toward the affirmation of the spiritual value of all poetry; *Télémaque* shows us a priest-poet, a new Orpheus, in the pagan Termosiris, who "sang only of the greatness of the gods, the virtue of heroes, and the wisdom of men who prefer glory to pleasure."[9] Dom Calmet, author of a famous *Commentaire* on the books of the Bible, accepts the notion that a "natural poetry," "as ancient as men," spontaneous, rich in metaphors, and inseparable from music, existed among all peoples; he summons up the druids, the bards, Germania.[10] Abbé Massieu, in his "Defense of Poetry,"[11] invokes the religious hymns of the pagans as proof of the earliest aims of the art of poetry. Louis Racine writes:

Ainsi la poésie en toute nation
Doit sa naissance illustre à la religion,

[Thus poetry in every land
Owes its illustrious birth to religion]

or, again: "Even among peoples plunged in idolatry, poetry can still be called
the daughter of religion, since it is born from the exaltation gratitude inspires
at the sight of blessings that we feel can come only from divine power and divine goodness";[12] and he parades before reader Goulish bards, Tacitus's Germans, Goths, Danes, Amerindians, Arabs, and Chinese. At the century's end, La
Harpe, a converted *philosophe* and translator of Psalms, writes: "The poetry of
the Hebrews has generally the characteristics that poetry in its earliest beginnings must have possessed among all the peoples who have cultivated it."[13]

The originality of this Christian school of thought lies in the fact that at
bottom it conceives of the whole of universal primitive poetry according to a
model analogous to the patterns found in Hebraic poetry: it imagines the birth
of poetry as a specifically religious phenomenon. Poetry is, as it were, the original relation of human beings to God: "If one wishes to go back to the first origin
of poetry," writes Rollin, "it seems to me impossible to doubt that its source lies
in the very depths of human nature, or that it was at first a sort of cry or
expression of the heart of man, delighted, ecstatic, enraptured at the sight of an
object alone worthy of being loved, and alone able to make him happy. . . . This
is the origin of poetry, properly speaking. This is what shapes its true character
and its essence."[14] The dawning of poetry in lyric form is tirelessly described by
writers in this tradition. Thus Louis Racine: "Men, after having gathered in the
fruits of the earth . . . , celebrate the blessings of heaven; whence lyric poetry is
born, whose first hymns were dedicated to the praise of the Gods."[15] For abbé
Batteux, man cries out as he emerges from nonentity: "This was at once a cry of
joy, admiration, astonishment, gratitude"; man "wanted all of existence to assist
him in paying the tribute of glory that he owed to the sovereign benefactor. He
inspirited the sun, the stars, the rivers, the mountains, the winds. There was not
a single being that did not raise its voice, joining in the veneration he expressed:
these are the songs of praise, the hymns, the odes, in a word, lyric poetry."[16] All
these authors apparently base their views on the fact that the oldest Hebraic
songs, those collected in the Pentateuch, celebrate promising events and thank
God for them. Based on these hymns of joy, which are historical and national in
intention, our authors go back to even more distant times and imagine a pure
outpouring of gratitude on the part of the creature. But in what times do they
think this took place? Sometimes in what one could call the antiquity of nations,

all of which praise their creator according to the lights granted them, sometimes (and more logically) in Eden itself: the songs of Moses and of Deborah are the echo of what must be the song of Adam, in whom God inspired the first poem to his glory.[17] Everything in this manner of thinking thus implies a fundamental elevation of poetry supported by the authority of religion. All of these authors develop a defense of poetry, following Fénelon: "It is," says Lefranc de Pompignan, "an invariable truth that the writings of the great poets could scarcely have less than they do the character of vain and futile productions. . . . An art whose origin can be traced back to the sovereign Creator is the most beautiful of arts."[18] For this author, it is God himself who established the characteristics of poetic style as distinct from ordinary speech and intended for his glorification. According to another writer, what the ancients called the language of the gods ought properly to be called "the language of God himself."[19]

And, while it is true that this glorification of poetry is associated with the far-off origins of humanity, it remains to a certain extent a present reality for a Christian, whose religion takes itself to be for all time. The songs and prophesies of Scripture are more alive for a Christian than the ancient poetry of Scandinavia for a deistic *philosophe*. This is what explains the astonishing vitality of the genre of paraphrases and versified translations of biblical texts. In the eighteenth century these productions claim to offer a model for a renewed poetry, and they erect a religious poetics to oppose the profane philosophy of the age. A sort of Christian poetic party recognizes itself in them, a lineage of those singing of divine grandeur and earthly virtue, prophesying against the philosophic sect that insults them and supported assiduously by the antiphilosophic party.[20] The principal names are those of Jean-Baptiste Rousseau, Louis Racine, Lefranc de Pompignan, Malfilâtre, Gilbert: these are certainly not the worst poets of the day. A crowd of emulators accompanies them.[21] For us it is chiefly important to get an overall idea of the customs and intentions of this poetry. Its principal object is to transmit in French the poetic texts included in Holy Scripture: an imposing body of work, even if it is limited to the songs inserted in the narrative books of the Old Testament, the psalms, and the books of the prophets, which are mostly made up of poems, including several songs. In this corpus certain texts seem to be the object of a special predilection in the period that interest us, whether because they are translated more often than the others or because a famous translation of one of them is endlessly reproduced and praised. This is the case for the songs of Moses, both the one in which he celebrates crossing the Red Sea (Exodus 15) and the one he delivers before the Promised Land (Deuteronomy 32: "Audite caeli, quae loquor"); Deborah's song of victory (Judges 5); the song of Hezekiah (Isaiah 38: thanksgiving for recovery from an illness); and, finally, the Gospel hymns of Mary (Luke 1:46: the Magnificat) and Simeon (Luke 2:29: "Nunc dimittis servum tuum, Domine"). Among the psalms, the first ("Beatus vir": parallel of the just man and the wicked man); the second ("Quare fremuerunt gentes": the Messiah challenged and triumphant, according to the Christian interpretation of this text); the twenty-second (which begins with the famous cry: "My God, my God, why hast thou forsaken me?"); the hundred and fourth ("Benedic, anima mea, Domino": depiction of the creation of the world); the hundred and fourteenth ("In exitu Israel de Aegypto": the river Jordan is driven back to its source, the hills skip like lambs); the hundred and thirtieth ("De profundis clamavi"); and more than any other, perhaps, the hundred and thirty-seventh ("Super flumina Babylonis"). Also appreciated are some texts of the prophets, especially Isaiah and Ezekiel (notably Isaiah 14: a funeral song on the king of Babylon; Isaiah 38: a song of Hezekiah, already mentioned; Ezekiel 37: the resurrection of dry bones). This group of texts is a sort of florilegium of sacred poetry, a dazzling demonstration of what the spirit of poetry can do when set in movement by the Holy Spirit.

Will poets of today limit themselves to translating and paraphrasing? They do more, often keeping the sacred texts at a distance, combining as they please several texts to achieve a new meaning,[22] taking inspiration from a single episode of Scripture in order to draw an original poem from it,[23] or, with even more license, constructing a meditation or exhortation in verse based on some religious text. The sacred poetry of former times engenders the Christian poetry of today: thus Louis Racine writing an ode on "The Christian Virtues," another on "Tears of Penitence" or on "Christian Death," Lefranc de Pompignan composing "Hymns" for various celebrations and "Christian and Philosophic Odes."[24] There is nothing absolutely new in this, and we could find comparable examples from the sixteenth century or by Malherbe; but the circumstances and the mood of the times confer an uncommon signification to Christian poetry. At a time when "true poetry" is the object of a quest, Christian poetry presents itself as such: a poetry of outpouring and enthusiasm at the spirit's highest pitch, a poetry of unmediated sublimity, which its apologists cannot better characterize than by opposing it to the "poetry of imitation."[25] Christian poetry is poetry renewed, returned to the possession of a lost dignity. The decadence that poetry has undergone since primitive times is explained by a growing forgetfulness of things divine and by an attachment to earthly objects. The explanation suggests the remedy: if the Christian poet's heart is pure enough, God is able to grant something of the grace and spirit granted to the awe-inspiring interpreters of the past. The poetry of olden days has thus a possibility of living again in modern times; all that is necessary is that, instead of limiting oneself to translating sacred poems, one undertake to imitate them: "What is needed," suggests abbé Fleury, "is to try to write similar poetry on subjects that are more familiar to us: on the mysteries of the new Law, on its establishment and progress, on the virtues of our saints; on the benefits that our nation, our region, our city have received from God; and on general subjects pertaining to morals, like the happiness of those who are devoted to goodness, scorn for riches, etc."[26] In order to know of what use poetry can be today, it is necessary, we are told, to consider that use "when it was first established and in its fundamental nature, which consists of treating of the greatest subjects. . . . Through this notion . . . poetry is reestablished in its original dignity."[27] All the authors we are considering make this point: "to recall the art of verse to its holy origin," "to its first intention," "to its first object and to its true moral and harmonic laws"[28] — Christian poetry alone is capable of this, because it alone possesses the legacy of the original creatural enthusiasm.[29]

Such reasoning did not lack pertinence in a century in which all were fascinated by the idea of primitivistic poetics, a century that feared the time of poets had passed forever. To what extent was the argument convincing? Contemporaries outside strictly Christian milieux willingly admired Hebraic poetry and even on occasion granted it a special place in the poetry of primitive peoples;[30] they too, like the religious writers, sometimes imagine man opening his eyes upon the universe for the first time and praising God.[31] What they do not easily accept is that the Christianity of their time might be the depository of this legacy, and that it is capable of keeping it alive. Did the Christian poets justify this pretension? And was a religious poetry possible in the France of that time? The distance that separates the psalms from their French translations under Louis XV and Louis XVI is overwhelming; the pale and diluted paraphrases and their the false periphrastic boldness scarcely do honor to the Holy Spirit, their supposed inspiration. This poetry is surely too much scorned today; it has its beauties, which are sometimes surprising; but in order to enjoy them it is necessary to make an effort to feel our way back into the poetry of those times. Christian odes are in this respect the twins of contemporary secular odes; in these poems an ambitious theory of inspiration is struggling against all-powerful conventions of style, but in vain; the stately solemnity on which their effects finally depend is the very opposite of lyricism. This sacred poetry, whose location and boundaries have long been recognized in the geography of classicism, is no threat to its general order; it is a literary department, a dependency of religion, neighboring a vast realm that was removed from its influence, that of secular literature, which is, according to the spirit of classicism, literature properly so called. The apologists of sacred poetry, by defining it in opposition to ordinary poetry, accept this division despite themselves. The role of the Christian poet, set between the doctrine it serves and a literature flourishing elsewhere, can only be an extremely limited one.

In the Christian eighteenth century the sense of or desire for a complete overhaul of values percolates only obscurely. The possibility of an essentially religious lyricism dominating the entire domain of literature is glimpsed. It is thought that such a lyricism would be the only possible heir in modern times to the poetic mission from time immemorial: "The great, the unique recourse for the ode among us," declares abbé Maury to the academicians, "is the sacred genre, because it is susceptible of a genuine enthusiasm."[32] He was only repeating what J.-B. Rousseau had said at the beginning of the century, based on his experience as a poet: "If I ever felt what enthusiasm is, it was chiefly when working on these *cantiques*."[33] One sometimes has the impression that a wider religious poetics is in the process of being born through the memories of the old quarrel between the sacred and the profane, that an ancient tradition is going to molt in response to a new need. But the renovation is still a long way off. It will be necessary for Christian poetics to free itself of the strict tutelage of doctrine and liturgy, to envisage a field of action and a ministry that are more contemporary, to accept in some degree the contagion of the new faith in humanity.[34] It will also be necessary for it to free itself of the conventional forms of the ode and to renew its efforts in the direction of the sacred poem.[35] The Christian eighteenth century made hardly any progress in these different directions. It only revived an idea of poetry that was latent in the religious tradition and in so doing made its contribution to the future consecration of the poet.

Chapter 3
Illuminism and Poetry

Louis-Claude de Saint-Martin

W E SHALL NOW DISCUSS an important movement of European
thought, whose principal French variant we find in Saint-Martin,
on the borderline between religious literature and literature *tout
court*. The name, the work, and the doctrine of Saint-Martin outlived him a long
time; and though he was never widely read and no great writer was his disciple,
it is nonetheless true that the general influence of his thoughts is to be found far
beyond the limits of his life and work—either because he acted mysteriously by
some sort of osmosis, or because he found a way to express something that
existed around him.[1] Illuminism is, in fact, a diffuse phenomenon. It owed its
strength to the fact that it was one of the most remarkable combinations of
traditional religion and the modern faith in a time of spiritual renewal. Saint-
Martin effected a combination that fit a specifically French context with un-
equaled accuracy. From the very beginning, the eccentricity of his work's outward appearance, with its bizarre claims, radically original style, and impenetra-
ble organization, forbade him any kind of popularity. Yet this work, scarcely
read and—except here and there—scarcely readable, transmits without a doubt
something deep, something intimately linked to the movement affecting the
minds of the time.

What is called illuminism presents itself in forms of such seeming diversity
that it is difficult to formulate an all-embracing definition. But one can at least
discern a majority of doctrines or schools—those of Swedenborg, of Martinez
de Pasqually (to which Saint-Martin is related), of the Waldensian Quietists
with Dutoit-Membrini—that show some common fundamental characteristics; namely, the belief in a universal primitive tradition whose secret meaning
survives among initiates; the essential importance attributed in this tradition to
the doctrine of the primal Fall, with the existence of matter being held to be a
result of that fall; the idea of a moral resurgence to come in the form of man's
reintegration into primal Being; a unitary and analogical conception of the
present universe; the institution of a ladder of intermediate powers between
man and God; the search for manifestations of the supernatural and a penchant
for magic and divination.[2] Such is mystical or theosophical illuminism, the only

variant that is of interest here: on the whole, it remains in the orbit of Christian theology, particularly above all because it conceives the human race as governed by God in its successive phases; in addition, it generally holds the mission of Jesus Christ to have been essential.[3]

Nevertheless, its heterodoxy — that is to say, its originality — is striking. It is true that it maintains the primacy of the divine with vehemence, in opposition to the philosophy of the age: "Nothing can be more false and more ridiculous," writes Dutoit, "than the idea contained in these words, *Natural Religion*. . . . *All religion is supernatural and divine*";[4] secular Sensibility is naturally suspect: "There is a word that human superficiality has brought on stage to give it a value that it did not have in the old dictionaries; this word, so bruited about and so esteemed, is *sensibility*. . . . impiety no longer exists; sensibility ennobles it, or makes it disappear."[5] Illuminist writers implicitly repudiate secular, philosophical humanism on every page, even when they are not being overtly polemical. This does not keep them from taking leave of traditional theology, however, for they, too, effect an enormous magnification of humanity. They obviously adopt with delight the idea of a preexisting God-man, a celestial Christ whom man resembles, the principal object of the Incarnation in history being precisely that of confirming this relationship — in other words of glorifying humanity and completing him triumphantly, as it were.[6] Even this idea, which haunts all of theosophy, is not itself heretical. Illuminism goes further when, taking humanity at its source, it divinizes it already in the man of Eden, a sort of Man-God created with a glorious body and endowed with supernatural powers so as to compensate for the fall of the angels and bring them back to God.[7] Still more simply and more radically, Swedenborgianism, which excludes the Trinity, holds that Jehovah incarnated himself, by virtue of which the human figure defines God, and also defines the universe: both God and the universe are men.[8] In the end this is the vital point of mystical illuminism, its raison d'être, as it were. According to an excellent commentator of illuminist themes, "these themes themselves reproduce a fundamental motif, which is the preoccupation with establishing the sublime origin of man, the eminent dignity of the Minor,[9] the greatness of his past and future role; the cosmological and pneumatological doctrines and the entire apparatus of proofs borrowed from the most unusual modes of demonstrations converge on this point."[10] From this point of view more than from any other it is true to say that the success of illuminism in the eighteenth century is "one of the most characteristic forms of preromanticism."[11]

It is hardly the case that illuminism denounces philosophical humanism's sin of pride; on the contrary, it denounces its penchant to demote humanity metaphysically. Taking advantage of the dimension that religion confers on humanity beyond its earthly existence, it is precisely on the plane of human ambition that it competes with secular philosophy. Whereas humanism often finds it difficult to give an ontological foundation to the pretensions of a mortal being, the theosophists can leave God in the first rank while still triumphantly ensuring humanity a resemblance to and perpetual alliance with the controlling power. The clergy of the existing religions, which had never offered such miracles, paled before such splendid revelationists. Their very manner of speaking, unveiling the secret meaning of texts, announces a direct investiture. The time has come when the voice from on high speaks through new spokespersons, in accordance with a new meaning. Their way of approaching what is mysterious, finding this quality everywhere but only in order to shed light upon it, steeps the spirit in the secret heart of things without making it feel its own inadequacy. It would have been necessary for the age to build a powerful barrier between literature and speculation about humanity to prevent the spirit of poetry from interesting itself in such novelties. In France, it is Saint-Martin who builds a bridge between the two domains.

What has just been said of the constitutive elements of mystical illuminism fits him perfectly. He too sees in the Redeemer "the veritable pattern on which we had been originally formed," and whose advent was meant to permit us to "reestablish our resemblance to him."[12] He believes that man was created in the image of God to bring back the rebellious angels. He expressly refuses to explain by pride the fall of the creature intended by God for the governance of the universe, and who sinned rather from an insufficient consciousness of his dignity and from lowering himself to the level of the physical world.[13] He makes of man, whose thought is "similar to that of the first Being," "the universal cipher, the living sign and the real portrait of an infinite being," "the image and extract of the generative center of everything that exists," and consequently "the point where all the properties and powers of things corresponded."[14] So much so that, in degrading man, the universe is altered and God is effaced: "To extinguish the human soul is to cover as if with a mournful veil Divinity, which this soul alone in all the world has the power to reveal; it is to extinguish the eternal sun from which everything issues and to plunge it, along with the universality of things, into the grief and obscurity of nonexistence."[15] He places man so high that he is tempted to make of him a sort of hidden God for an unworthy universe: "On occasion, the dignity of man has made itself so strongly felt to me that I looked at this *man* as obliged perpetually to wear a mask in the universe, so little worthy was the universe of contemplating him."[16] On the other hand, for man there is nothing hidden; the veils fall before him as soon as he is regenerated: "We are made to bring all mysteries into the full light of day, in our quality as ministers of the eternal source of light."[17] One of Saint-Martin's biographers was doubtless right to observe: "This theory of a spiritualism that is both very subtle and very profound, which places man so high in spite of the dogma of the Fall, and which shows him to be called to so eminent a role despite his powerlessness, was in agreement with the most ambitious rationalism of the day."[18] More precisely, it responded in a different and adverse fashion to the same human ambition as did contemporary "rationalism."

In one way all of Saint-Martin's work is an attack on philosophical deism. He claims that it was his irritation at the *philosophes* that set him to writing and was the cause of his first book: he was indignant to see Boulanger explain religion as the result of a fear of natural catastrophes.[19] Explicitly or not, it is almost always against the *philosophes* that he argues: against those he names the "observers,"[20] refusing to admit their discernment while politely granting their curiosity. He pursues them in every field, attacking in mythology their agricultural or astronomical explanations; in linguistics, the idea of a purely human origin of speech; in political philosophy, speculations on the natural basis of society independent of the relation of man to God.[21] Bernardin de Saint-Pierre and his harmonies find no grace in his eyes: that optimism, however religious in intention, that optimism that forgets so easily the Fall and necessity of moral renewal, is in his eyes a philosophical chimera; after dining with Bernardin, he wonders "how he will go about depicting for us the harmonies of colic, *buhon-upas*, the rattlesnake, and all the noxious insects."[22] He has more respect for Rousseau, although in his opinion he "remained in the lower regions," for lack of any true inspiration; "if Providence," he muses, "had allowed him to receive the tenth part of what it has allowed to come unto me, he would have put it to such good use that he would, I believe, have made God come down to earth." But we should regret nothing; Saint-Martin, with his seraphic calm, concludes: "Apparently the moment had not yet arrived for that."[23]

With its air of a strangely humanistic theology, of an antiphilosophic monument, Saint-Martin's work assumes a tone of self-evidence that can seem arbitrary to us, but that no doubt was for the Unknown Philosopher the result of an experience that produced immediate conviction: real greatness and nostalgia for greatness were all one for him, possessed as he was of a vision that opposed both Christian pessimism and philosophical optimism. Vis-à-vis the *philosophes*, he brandishes what he calls his "divinism," but this divinism is at the same time the conviction of the divine nature of man.[24] Thus our faculty of admiration, which he likes to cite as a proof of divinity, in his eyes simultaneously proves that we are descended from God:[25] this is his *cogito*, as imperious as that of

Descartes. As one might guess, though, he claims no link to Descartes; he is more willing to admit a debt to Pascal, who, he says, "of all those who were not possessed of the secret password, is the one who went the furthest."[26] It is natural that he felt himself related to the author of the *Pensées* and his theistic dialectics, but it is also natural that Saint-Martin believed himself to be infinitely more advanced than he: the Edenic Saint-Martin soars above the trembling disciples of Jansenius; he is sharing with them the discovery of the century; he is experiencing with them, at the antipodes of the spirit of Pascal, what one could call the Communication of the Lost Eden.

As Saint-Martin sees it, the Fall of Adam has obviously not erased man's prerogatives: "Despite the length of time that has elapsed, despite the thickness of the darkness, every time he contemplates his relations with God he will rediscover in himself the indissoluble elements of his original essence as well as the natural signs of his glorious destination."[27] As far as I know, there is no doctrine of grace in Saint-Martin; the divine essence cannot cease enveloping man, "making streams of glory pour down upon him"; nothing would prevent him from uniting with this glory if he were not repeating his original sin every day.[28] This fallen man, so obstinate in his sin, is nevertheless very close to his origin: Saint-Martin's work is steeped in a vivid representation of Eden, present in us and around us at every moment. That which is "immaterial yet perceptible" and anterior to the Fall remains, veiled and at hand, in the "Magianism" of the nature before us:[29] "Is all not symbol in the realm we inhabit?"[30] These views imply in effect a doctrine of "correspondences," not connections between things, but connections of things to the spiritual universe upon which they depend, signs and visible figures of what is hidden: "Matter is only a representation and an image of what it is not. . . . It is like the portrait of an absent person."[31] The correspondences within the sensible world (correlations among the various senses, "synesthesias" in our terminology) seem to him of little interest. He celebrated them at least once, however: "Light gave back sound, melody gave birth to light, the colors were in motion, because the colors were alive; and the objects were all at once sonorous, diaphanous, and mobile enough to interpenetrate each other and traverse all of space in an instant." But this is a portrait of the world at the creation, in which the communication among the senses attests to divine unity: this sort of correspondence can only be of interest to Saint-Martin against a spiritual background.[32] Such a vision of the perceptible world as an analogical figure of Being comes from a great distance, certainly. It is renewed and modernized here by the spiritualism of an unfettered imagination that opens the way to the inventions and the preaching of poets. It would in fact furnish romanticism with the principle of a new poetics and thenceforth establish for generations the metaphysical prerogative of poetry.

In illuminism, the doctrine of correspondences is not peculiar to Saint-Martin; it is found everywhere.[33] But it is accompanied in his writings by a group of ideas on language and poetry that insist upon the notion of a poetic ministry. Like many of his contemporaries, Saint-Martin refuses to allow that convention might be the origin of language; but this is not so that he can ground it in nature, since a natural language, in the sense understood by the *philosophes* — that is, deriving solely from the needs of our earthly condition — would be for him an animal language: he thinks that this is what the idioms spoken by savages are — something very different in this respect from the true primordial language, where words corresponded not to the play of sensation but to the very essence of things, and predated our Fall. These ideas appear in his works from the beginning: it is due to the effect of the Fall that language is what it is; that words, henceforth created by our own feeble means, no longer have any obvious relation to the things they designate and are no longer "analogous to these same things," and can no longer name them "as their natural names unequivocally did" when "every word carried in itself the true meaning of things and designated them so well that it made them appear clearly."[34] It may be seen in what sense Saint-Martin can call the original language natural. In his *Réponse provisoire du psychographe à la question de l'Institut*,[35] the necessary connection between "root signs" and "perfect ideas," which is characterized by self-evidence and absolute equivalence, establishes what he calls "natural relations" between ideas and signs, in opposition to "forced relations" that derive solely from convention: at the level of our original nature, the word is identical to what it signifies; and we of course work our way back from the multiplicity of words as from the multiplicity of ideas to a unique principle, a "mother-idea" expressed by a single word, so that in the last analysis the primordial language depends completely on this word.[36] Saint-Martin recognizes that his readers will with good justification wish to have some idea of this language; he fails, however, to satisfy their curiosity: "I will not be able to gratify them," says he, "having promised myself to name nothing."[37] It is true that elsewhere Saint-Martin reveals to us that the only word that "the fundamental essence of man might pronounce naturally" would be "a tribute to his first cause"; namely, the word SAINT pronounced aloud without interruption: this revelation is an echo of Isaiah,[38] but the announcement of the mystic vocable in the form of a French word can obviously not be taken literally; we would need to know how this word was pronounced in Eden, if indeed the language of Eden was ever spoken.

And Saint-Martin reminds us elsewhere that signs are not always sensations "taken in the ordinary sense": in other words, from what is unintelligible (for how are we to conceive of the word being the necessary figure of what it names?) he refers us to what is indescribable; what is more, he informs us that the idea itself is a sign: it directs us to "a more penetrating life," "a bliss," it "brings us closer to what we could call the mother of all impressions."[39]

These marvels have the defect of passing understanding; it is also true that this is the only thing that recommends them. Similarly, Saint-Martin imagines that at the origin of our music (blighted like us by a declension into temporality) there is a music removed from time, removed even from sound, that is only another effect of our subjection to matter; at the source of ordinary entertainments, he places a show of celestial wonders; at the origin of theater he places what the eyes of the body see not.[40] All these fancies depend closely upon his mystical doctrine of language: a mystical doctrine of exile that nevertheless includes a return and a reuniting. The primordial language of humanity, universal and divinely natural, is the true goal of all spiritual seeking: "It is this that all the nations of the earth long to possess, that secretly motivates men in all their institutions . . . and that they try to express in the works they create. . . . This true language is the only one that can restore to man his rights and confer upon him the enjoyment of his powers."[41] Something of that language survives in our languages, however degenerate they may be,[42] and the path of reintegration is not closed to us: "Man, take heart, since that speech can belong to you. . . . Allow yourself no rest until you have obtained it."[43] In a creation where everything is meaningful, but where every category of beings is testimony only to that particular power from which it emanates, man insofar as he is gifted with speech is utter testimony to God himself; he is "destined to be the sign and articulate expression of the universal faculties of the Supreme First Cause"; or again, "man is like the lyre of God, since in his speech he tends ceaselessly toward the expression of God's divers powers."[44]

It is quite natural that upon such a doctrinal loom should be woven a glorification of poetry.[45] This glorification reproduces certain common themes of the day — notably, those that bear upon sacred poetry; but by being integrated into an innovative spiritualism, these themes stand out in a way not apparent elsewhere. Like many of his contemporaries, Saint-Martin believes in the religious character of primitive poetry; he sees the history of poetry as a long decline, a descent toward earthly subjects and futility.[46] Poetry has degraded itself by making itself a mere translator of the passions or an imitator of things,[47] instead of remaining the pure celebration of the First Cause of our greatness, as in its

beginnings. The hymn of earliest humanity to the Creator, so often evoked at
the time, takes on a cosmic dimension in Saint-Martin's writings: "The primitive poets know that in the truthful praises that man addresses to God, he can
actually be accompanied by the celestial lyre, and he finds therein a proof of his
greatness, for he is beyond all doubt the soul of the concert made up by all
creation to render homage to the Creator."[48] Poetry is more than a divine faculty
of human beings; it is, as it were, the celebration of God by the universe's very
unity. Thus very early on Saint-Martin described poetry as an independent
being, a Virtue in the theosophical sense of the word; that is, an intermediary
acting between God and humanity. This is the doctrine that Saint-Martin developed in "Phanor," a curious "poem on poetry" that, according to what the
editor of his *Oeuvres posthumes* tells us, dates from his youth.[49] The narrator,
who addresses "celestial Poetry" imploringly and offers to wreak vengeance
upon those responsible for profaning her in modern times, feels that his wish is
granted and he is taken up into heaven: he seems to see the divine region where
poetry is born and whence it springs eternal; he contemplates the glory of poets
and lauds Poetry:

> Je vois tous tes élus comme autant de prophètes
> Eclairer l'univers, adoucir ses tourments,
> Oser même imposer des lois aux éléments
> En inclinant sur eux le sacré caducée.
> Que dis-je, la sagesse, à t'instruire empressée,
> Dévoile à tes regards ses plus secrets ressorts;
> Et toi, tu viens m'offrir ces précieux trésors
> Qui ne peuvent germer qu'au sein du sanctuaire.[50]

> [I see all your elect like so many prophets
> Enlightening the universe, mitigating its sufferings,
> Daring even to impose law on the elements
> By passing the sacred caduceus over them.
> Yet more! Wisdom, eager to instruct you,
> Unveils its most secret springs to your eyes;
> And you come to offer me your most precious treasures,
> Which can only come alive within your sanctuary.]

Poetry begins to speak, and instructs Phanor at length about the arrangement of
things divine, and how "Des agents purs, des chefs qui sont autant de Dieux
[Pure agents, leaders who are so many Gods]," surrounding the godhead, each
corresponding to a human faculty or talent, communicate from earth to heaven
the accomplishments or failures of humanity. Poetry is one of these agents, the
greatest of all if truth be told, since the gift of poetry surpasses all other gifts.[51]

In his first published work, Saint-Martin's affirmation of poetry's privileged role in the relation of man to God was similar: of all human products, Poetry is "that which brings him nearest to his First Cause and that, by the raptures it makes him feel, best proves to him the dignity of his origin." Poetry, a surviving echo of the universal language, is animated by the living flame of Truth.[52] The poet takes on the appearance of a miracle worker when the poetic fire ceases to be a metaphor and becomes a real participation in divine power. If it be true that "since we possess speech, we have the power to make things act,"[53] what will the poet not be able to do, since he possesses the faculty of speech par excellence? A poet

> Qui de l'art de parler serait vraiment l'oracle
> Ne ferait pas un vers qu'il ne fît un miracle.[54]
>
> [Who might really be the oracle of the power of speech
> Would not make a single verse that was not a miracle.]

Is this a matter of actual miracles or of edification that is hyberbolically called miraculous? Saint-Martin, citing himself, gives a different version of the first line, and by writing "Qui *du suprême agent* serait vraiment l'oracle,[55] [Who might really be the oracle *of the supreme agent*]," he confirms the properly thaumaturgical interpretation of the text. The reader will have noted, however, his extreme prudence and his decision to couch his thought in the conditional, which protects him from a factual refutation: he seems to say that the fact that such miracles are not observed only proves that no poet (at least today) is really the oracle of the Most High, and that those who speak would be better off keeping silent.

The model Saint-Martin has in view is Scripture, as is the case for the Christian admirers of sacred poetry, so numerous at this time. He exalts biblical authors, defends Lefranc de Pompignan against Voltaire, praises Louis Racine, admires Milton, Young, and Klopstock.[56] He in fact belongs to the school of Christian poets of his time, but with more far-ranging, less traditional views. As is true for the Christian poets, the poetry he desires can call itself lyric because of its effusiveness and its enthusiasm; but in its essence it is not at all subjective; it defines itself in relation to the Being it celebrates, and is grounded ontologically. Understood in this way, lyrical poetry can be descriptive; one can even say that it ought to be so, provided that the object of its descriptions be not things of human or material nature but those that are invisible, and that its descriptions be "depictions of ultimate facts."[57] Thus the earliest poets, guiding men on the path of truth, were acting so marvelously

Qu'ils semblaient dans leurs vers traduire la nature,
De l'univers entier dessiner la structure,
Servir partout d'organe à la vertu des cieux;
Tout leur être était plein de l'image des Dieux.[58]

[That they seemed to translate nature in their verses,
To sketch the structure of the entire universe,
To serve everywhere as a mouthpiece for the heavens' virtue;
Their entire being was filled with the image of the Gods.]

On the level of Truth — that is, of God — poetry is inseparably both representation and the expression of enthusiasm;[59] but it is at the same time historical, since the relation of humanity to God and to things that poetry takes as its material must be thought of in the perspective of the past Fall and the future moral renewal; and it is also, and just as necessarily, predicatory, since the salvation that is its concern is that of the human race. What more beautiful subject is there, asks Saint-Martin, than "the great drama of man, the drama that has never ceased playing since the beginning of things?"[60] It is easy to detect one of the future paths of French romanticism in this ideal of poetry, simultaneously lyrical, metaphysical, narrative, and edifying. The suggestions of Saint-Martin are early harbingers of the romantic epic.

But he dare not count too much on the success of his views concerning the necessary renewal of poetry. Speaking to Phanor, the goddess recounts her history over the centuries, from her "first favorites" till the moderns, whom she has found to be forgetful of the "sublime origin" of their art; they are busy "divinizing the universe" and place the ministry of truth that is their appanage at the service of fictions.[61] How is it possible to doubt, she tells them on a trip to earth during which she has assumed human form,

Que votre mission, mortels, ne soit divine,
Puisque votre seul nom renferme un sens divin.
L'antiquité nommait un Poète un devin.

[That your mission, o mortals, be divine
When your name itself contains within it a divine meaning.
Antiquity called the poet a seer.]

The poet really is a seer, in the most sublime sense, because

le droit des Poètes
Marche d'un pas égal à celui des prophètes.[62]

[Poets
Possess all the prerogatives of prophets.]

But how likely is it that modern poets will recover not only an awareness of their mission but also the will actually to undertake it? "Phanor" ends on a negative note: modern poets, indifferent to the goddess's speech, were not even moved when they saw her reascend into heaven in a sudden and luminous transfiguration; an angry God has plucked her back from earth. But this pessimism is balanced in Saint-Martin's writing by the feeling that the possibility of resurrection is constantly available; all that would be needed is the wish to turn literature toward salvation, and literature would take the helm for the human race: "Illustrious writers, famous men of letters, you have no idea how far your power over us would extend if you thought to apply it more to our genuine interests. We would come and submit to your authority: nothing could please us more than to see you exercise and extend your sweet authority."[63]

"Phanor" was certainly written well before 1789. After that date, ideas of renewal and providential crisis that illuminism always cherished found a new source of sustenance in French political events. Christianity, following Judaism, has always postulated an interpenetration of divine thought and human history: the books of the Bible trace the episodes of this connection; Christian historians, before and after Bossuet, pick up the thread and attempt to continue Scripture in this area. Divine intervention had usually been announced in advance by inspired prophets. But nowhere did religious speculation combine as much with the interpretation of contemporary events and the prediction of the near future as in illuminism in general and in Saint-Martin in particular. More than once he says that true poetry is "prophetic poetry."[64]

In addition to numerous, almost daily notes in *Mon Portrait* or in his correspondence, and various remarks in *Ecce homo* of 1792, Saint-Martin discussed current events in France in two pieces: the *Lettre à un ami* in 1795 and the *Eclair sur l'association humaine* in 1797. He naturally sees the hand of Providence in what has happened. But providentialism is an extremely flexible doctrine, and can lead one to hate revolutionary events because they are thought to be the final crisis before the restoration to its former state of a social system gone awry, just as well as it can lead one to exalt them for being part of a divinely progressive process. The notion of an ordeal that makes suffering the price good must pay in order to triumph specifies no definition of the good, and does not rule out conceiving of this good in two opposite ways: God may be punishing execrable innovations, or he may be extirpating ancient abuses. This accounts for the success of such a notion, which, in the extended crisis from 1800 to 1850 of a French society torn between its past and its future, was able to legitimate an entire spectrum of opinion and inspire Lamartine and Hugo as well as Joseph de

Maistre. The strength of this providentialism resides in the fact that it permits an amalgam of contradictory thoughts both traditional and innovative, whose proportions can be tailored to individual taste, to come under the aegis of divine patronage. The prophet-poets of romanticism would play variations on these themes for a long time and in many different keys.

Saint-Martin never tired of repeating that the French Revolution was part of a providential plan, by which he generally means that in its results it is irreversible: "For my part, I have never doubted that Providence was involved in our revolution, or thought that it was possible to roll it back."[65] One can do away with some details of God's work, but not its essential aspects: "In spite of the shocks that the Revolution has felt and will feel again, it is certain that there was something in it that will never be overturned."[66] On the whole, the work of the Revolution seems to him to be positive; it is overseen by a propitious star;[67] the blows struck at the clergy and the nobility seem to him acts of divine justice. He contests the legitimacy of the Catholic priesthood and applauds its downfall: "the era of Christianity in spirit and truth begins only with the abolition of the power of priests."[68] Himself a noble, he notes with cold satisfaction the humiliation of the nobility and sees in the calamity they are undergoing a means "of cleaning them up and making them more presentable when they appear in the realms of truth."[69] It is God who has destroyed the established powers and convulsed society in order to bring it closer to him;[70] but the divine aid lent to France for its renewal has also something of a punishment about it: an excessively long unmindfulness of God is being expiated by means of a revolution that is "a miniature of the Last Judgment . . . ; it came first and most severely to France because France has been very guilty";[71] innocent lives have been sacrificed, doubtless as "expiatory victims in order to consolidate the edifice": Saint-Martin says he has no fear for their fate in the other world.[72]

This providentialism is in vehement opposition to the ideas of the age's "political writers," who envisage society and its changes as purely human phenomena. Saint-Martin has done in a "divinist" spirit what Rousseau did in the *Discours sur l'inégalité* in order to trace the history of human society from the beginning.[73] According to Saint-Martin, no power could arise whose legitimacy was grounded anywhere but in the divine will; it would be impossible for human beings to be empowered to command other human beings except due to their lesser degree of degeneracy; those who govern must have succeeded in retaining a more extensive participation in the lights we receive from God in our primordial state than the common run of humanity.[74] Saint-Martin calls this doctrine "theocratic." Some pages he wrote, he tells us, "in the time of the Terror," are entitled "On Divine Government or Theocratism," and define this government by "the belief of authorities that they are God's administrators."[75] This is a prudent definition — one that avoids the suggestion of a government of the clergy, which he elsewhere expressly rejects by a call for a "divine, spiritual, and natural theocratic."[76] Even while constantly affirming the union of man with God and the identity of the social bond and the religious bond,[77] he is careful not to deliver society over to a priestly caste, so that his theocratism is limited to wishing that human government tend toward a moral renewal that will return the human race to itself by giving it back to God. If the church is out of the running, who then will guide humanity toward that renewal, if not the thinkers who are the depositories of this hope and this secret knowledge? But we have seen in what rank Saint-Martin places the poet when it comes to intuiting the truth: in fact, he makes the poet the equal of the theosopher himself and merges the two together. But the destiny of society is an integral part of the truth that poets see in God. Which direction will they give to this destiny when they put it into words? Faced with the future, mystical theosophy hesitated. With regard to the Revolution, its reaction was rather hostile. Even while praising the course of events, Saint-Martin remains ambiguous. His friend the duchesse de Bourbon was rather bolder than he; Divonne, less so; but the marquise de la Croix (another friend), Cazotte, Dampierre, and Bergasse were openly counterrevolutionary: Dampierre and Bergasse, still writing under the Restoration, brought to the royalism of the Holy Alliance the contribution of mystical theosophy.[78] Traumatized by events, illuminism adapted itself willingly to the political and religious counterrevolution. When the idea of the consecration of the poet appeared in early romanticism, it kept this coloration for a little — but only a little — while; it flowed from too strong a source to be confined there.

Chapter 4

Counterrevolution and Literature

THE PERIOD in the history of French society that begins with Brumaire and extends to the last years of the Restoration saw successive and equally violent paradoxes: a dictatorship without hereditary title as the heir to the general upheaval of a society, and a subsequent anachronistic restoration. But the political changes did not essentially affect the problems that preoccupied thinkers between the Revolution's ebb at the century's beginning and the nearly total triumph of liberal ideas on the eve of 1830. Thus we see the continual development throughout this entire period of a sort of spiritually counterrevolutionary enterprise, which those in power support from 1800 on, and even more vigorously after 1814 and 1815. Among the general public, the revolutionary trauma shook the secular humanist faith of the eighteenth century; the cooling of this fervor, which was noted by so many in the aftermath of Thermidor, and whose visible symptom is the waning popularity of the republican *fêtes*,[1] was naturally accompanied by a revival of traditional ideas and ways of feeling that became more marked after Brumaire. The disavowal of the Revolution as well as of the principles that inspired it and the refutation of the "sophistries" of the philosophic and revolutionary faith were prime features of the dominant thought of the following period; they gave the Restoration state, in its Napoleonic and then Bourbonian form, the doctrine it needed. The survivors and continuers of the preceding period were for a time put on the defensive by pressure from the state and public opinion. The "*idéologues*" of the Empire and the founders of liberalism kept the legacy of the previous century alive, but at a noticeably lower temperature, and at the expense of more than one alteration of doctrine. The philosophy of the eighteenth century is not dead; it will recover its strength little by little as it adapts to circumstances. Meanwhile, its detractors, too, are led to rethink from a new perspective the old order of things, so as to rehabilitate it in opposition to philosophy; they erect a contrary system of which there was scarcely any idea in Bossuet's time, when it was merely a question of expressing doctrinal values that were generally accepted. The philosophy of the counterrevolution is something new: it is the metamorphosis of an earlier conformism for the purpose of combat. The array of commonly accepted notions had already begun to be modified in the eighteenth century in response to the danger of subversion; but the defenders of the traditional order had remained little known, inferior in talent and success to the prestigious founders of the new faith, and able to mount only a weak opposition to the triumph of Enlightenment and Feeling. The balance of forces is reversed after 1800, when the counterrevolution comes to occupy center stage, deploying its themes and organizing its positions with a conqueror's virulence.

This labor was above all the achievement of two generations.[2] The oldest comprised individuals who were already mature in 1789, sometimes already active enemies of the *Philosophes* in the ancien régime and faithful to their principles throughout the revolutionary crisis, and sometimes having embraced the counterrevolution later under the spur of events, or having chosen to speak out on that occasion. To this generation belong Clément, the "inclement one" of Voltaire; Geoffroy, who was the editor in chief of the antiphilosophic *Année littéraire* after Fréron; Mme de Genlis; Rivarol; La Harpe, who had openly fled the revolutionary camp after Thermidor; and, finally, Joseph de Maistre and Bonald: all were born between 1742 and 1754 and survived the revolutionary period, in some cases by a considerable margin. After them comes the generation of those who, having attained their majority just before 1789, lived through the revolutionary shock at the beginning of their adult lives; whatever their sentiments at the beginning of the crisis, they reached full maturity in the course of the counterrevolution itself. Born around 1770, in the years following 1800 they make up the main body of the army of counterrevolutionary journalists and authors: they include, among others, Fiévée, abbé de Féletz, the Michaud brothers, Dussault, Delalot. This is the generation of Joubert and Chateaubriand; Fontanes precedes it by about a decade; Ballanche follows closely after, Lamennais is still later. Like their elders, these individuals experienced the ordeals of the revolutionary period. Emigration — in 1792 or following Fructidor in 1797 — was for them a decisive experience. In large part it was in Hamburg, London, and Switzerland that the counterrevolutionary contribution developed; it was there that the ways of thinking of the philosophic era were picked apart and disavowed, and that the ancient conservative base, getting the upper hand, was transformed into a militant philosophy. Relations and communication of ideas continued, however, between the émigré authors and those writers still in France who, under the influence of events, had gone through a similar evolution.[3]

The years 1800 to 1802 saw the new party blossom in France: this is the time when the *Journal des débats*, purchased by Bertin, and the *Mercure de France*, resuscitated by Fontanes, along with most of the men whose names we have cited above, undertake a campaign of reaction against the ideas of the preceding century. It is also the time of Chateaubriand's *Génie du christianisme*. It was in these decisive years that the intellectual capital on which the French counterrevolution supported itself during the first quarter of the century was accumulated. The year 1800 and the following few years constituted for this intellectual party a memorable epoch; later, those who lived through it were fond of evoking it.[4] The writers who belonged to the party in opposition felt the importance of this moment, and acknowledged in their fashion the regrettable band of the *Journal des débats* and of the *Mercure*; read the satire "Les Nouveaux Saints" by Marie-Joseph Chénier and his short story "Les Miracles":[5] Clément, Geoffroy, Delille, La Harpe, and Chateaubriand are arrogantly mistreated, sometimes in a Voltairian manner, sometimes in a tone that makes one think of Hugo's *Les Châtiments*. Those whom Chénier attacked prospered nonetheless and believed that they answered the needs of the time better than he. After the return of the Bourbons, their legacy bore fruit in that very youthful generation, born around 1800, whose thoughts were formed under the influence of the Restoration. It was this generation that would inaugurate French romanticism. The early Lamartine, the young Hugo, and the young Vigny in the 1820s are the poetic heirs of the movement that began at the turn of the century. Their history can only be adequately understood with reference to it: the intellectual and emotional themes that the new century thought it could oppose to those of its predecessor are the ones that their work develops first. An inner logic, spurred on by the march of events, later distanced them from their origins; the greatest of their elders accompanied them in this evolution: between 1825 and 1830, Chateaubriand, Ballanche, and Lamennais are similarly on the road to the future. But this occurs when a very different period is beginning.

This is not the place to consider the whole of French counterrevolutionary doctrine, which consisted above all of a sociology founded on the supposed wishes of God and the tradition that reveals them, and more generally on a conception according to which the nature of society is unamenable to human initiatives and the ambitions of perfectibility. A critique of the pretensions of reason and a multifarious rehabilitation of the notion of prejudice as well as of the institutions that rely upon it seemed to be heard on all sides: "Wherever one looks," writes Benjamin Constant under the Directory, "one sees prejudices that we thought were destroyed spring up as if out of the earth."[6] The great doctrinal treatises of the counterrevolution, Bonald's *Théorie du pouvoir* or his *Législation primitive*, Joseph de Maistre's *Considérations sur la France* or his *Essai sur le principe générateur des constitutions politiques* are perhaps less interesting in this regard than the prefaces or articles of an explicitly polemical character, in which are expressed the counterrevolution's outstanding charges against the eighteenth century. Such are, among others, Rivarol's "Recapitulation," Clément's introduction to his *Tableau annuel de la littérature*, Fiévée's essay *Sur l'esprit littéraire au dix-huitième siècle*, or the hostile reviews of Mme de Staël's book *De la littérature*, especially the piece by Fontanes in the *Mercure*.[7] But of the profound efforts that some minds are making we have no better testimony than the notes jotted down by Joubert in his *Carnets*. Having abandoned philosophy and the hope that he had placed in the Revolution,[8] he henceforth writes against the eighteenth century, opposing to philosophical optimism a sort of subtle, solid disenchantment that restores to commonly held beliefs their full value. Since they are widely held, they must be appropriate for man: "It suffices that religion be religion. It is not necessary that it be truth. Some things are good only when they are true. Others need only be thought in order to be good." It is much more appropriate to speak of "pragmatism" here than in the case of Rousseau or Voltaire, who never disposed of truth so offhandedly. But Joubert is not really willing to give up on truth so quickly; he, too, is unwilling to accept the notion that humanity should depend on error pure and simple for reasons of convenience or suitability; this dependence points to a truth, but it is one that is adapted to our weakness: if there are "preformed notions that are necessary, or that inevitably form in the soul unbeknownst to it (natural ideas) . . . then these are truths, or at least they are the only forms by means of which the soul can ordinarily apprehend certain truths." Thus the characteristic anthropocentrism of the period is subtly reworked in a way that tends to dispossess reason; what seems rationally illusory is precisely what indicates to us a deep need and a truth: "Illusion is a component part of reality."[9] This way of thinking leads ultimately to God with his privilege of mysteriousness: "God constantly deceives us and wishes us to be deceived. I mean that he constantly gives us opinions rather than the knowledge for which we are unsuited. . . . He deceives us in order to guide us and save us. . . . He is the *eternal poet*, if I may use that term, on the model of the *eternal geometer*."[10] We see that the forswearing of his faith by a son of the philosophical eighteenth century is tempted to end in poetry.

✣ *The Denunciation of the Man of Letters*

The counterrevolution does not doubt that philosophy is responsible for the Revolution and its horrors. The greatest and most illustrious writers of the eighteenth century are indicted, and the very rights of the Man of Letters, formerly proclaimed so loudly, are contested. The ministry of the writer is one of the counterrevolution's targets; the *littérateurs* who claim to act as guides for the human race are denounced as agents of disorder and subversion; they incarnate the usurping reason that corrupts the social order. In the eighteenth century, the antiphilosophic party had attacked the writers of the enemy camp without questioning the mission of the writer itself, for this notion was accepted by all writers, carried along by a movement that placed them in an honorable position.[11] At the most we can observe on this point some slight skirmishes: for example, on the occasion of Thomas's *discours de réception* at the Academy, it is argued that the man of government takes precedence over the writer, who, it is conceded, is able to serve the State, but "by perfecting the language, by respecting and advancing in written works the taste for Religion, Law, morals, prejudices themselves when they are useful, the Fatherland, our masters, and their government."[12] Not until the period of the Consulate is the chorus of counterrevolutionary men of letters unleashed against the Man of Letters. This attack was inspired by those in power and by the state of contemporary opinion: "There has gradually established itself," notes a contemporary, "even among enlightened persons, a sort of prejudice against men of learning, *littérateurs*, and individuals in general who cultivate or promote the sciences and arts with zeal, as if their sole purpose was to foment public disorder by exciting a spirit of fermentation that is contrary to security and public tranquillity among the different classes of citizens."[13] Political writers [*publicistes*] of the counterrevolution carry this hostility to great lengths: "Our greatest misfortunes," writes Geoffroy, "have come from the ambition of writers, who, in order to seem important, rushed into matters of morality and politics, making a game out of ruining society and the State so as to make themselves admired as *philosophes*."[14] Joseph de Maistre also believes that men of learning have quit their natural social position: "They have everywhere usurped an influence without limit. . . . Prelates, nobles, and the leading officials of the State should be the depositories and guardians of conservative truths, and they should teach to the nations what is wrong and what is right, what is true and what is false in the moral or spiritual order: others have no right to reason on these sorts of questions."[15] No occasion for severely upbraiding those who remain true to the eighteenth century by continuing to exalt the function of the Man of Letters is allowed to pass in silence. To Grétry, who places just below the existence of God that of the "holy family" of writers and artists, the *Mercure* retorts: "Grétry seems to regret most of all that artists are not more important personages in the State; we would point out to him that this is neither appropriate nor possible. In republics as in monarchies the leading place goes to strength or power."[16] The project of creating a literary fund destined to assist men of learning and writers inspires hostile remarks from Féletz,[17] who thinks it inappropriate to favor the interests of a group that already has too many members: "Where did the evils of the Revolution come from? Is it not because every man in France fancied himself a legislator . . . ? Things are so bad that instead of trying to multiply the number of writers, it would perhaps be more useful to write nothing more for a given space of time, fifty years for example, unless it were thought advisable to extend this term."[18]

A similar skepticism and hostility are found among men who are strangers to the counterrevolution properly so called, and for whom the balance sheet of the philosophic eighteenth century is not entirely negative. In 1808, Guizot describes the excessive influence of writers in the preceding century as a characteristic of social decadence: "The public needs masters; those whom their rank designated as such no longer had the strength for this role; the public found them among authors; and, since it adores praising and celebrating those who lead it, the public made of the social condition of *man of letters* the leading rank in the social order."[19] Prosper de Barante, who belongs to the same spiritual family, holding forth relatively serenely about the literature of the eighteenth century, also takes a very dim view of the establishment of this subversive power:

> Little by little the fate of men of letters changed; they became more numerous, they acquired more independence, and their place in society became more important. Their vanity grew correspondingly, and this change showed in their opinions; the token resistance to them was weak and poorly organized; it only served to accentuate their hostile views. Emboldened by public opinion and the flattering reception of all Europe, they joined together and formed a kind of sect whose members did not profess firm and uniform opinions, but who, animated by the same spirit, tended to give the impression of having a common body of opinions.[20]

The same sense of danger is felt even by the writers who are more or less allied with the philosophic camp and who remain convinced that writers have a calling to govern society; it is curious to see by what strange suggestions they try to reconcile their convictions with their fears. One of them recommends an "aristocracy of the enlightened" governing a "nonthinking working class": "I see Ignorance, robust and active, but also submissive, gathering around its directing power and receiving without muttering or suspicion, no, rather with interest, a command given without pride or capriciousness and for the good of both." Between these two classes, a large number of intellectuals would make up a "thinking class, but one that is poor and without social distinction — the class most to be pitied, the most useless, the most corrupted, the most corrupting, which will infect equally the governing and the working classes."[21] To write this is to suggest the same intellectual Malthusianism as the counterrevolution, but for the benefit no longer of the establishment, but of an oligarchy of the learned. Arnault, a liberal, taking China as a model, distinguishes the *lettered*, who pullulate deplorably in France and who prolonged the Revolution, from the *jukiaos*, who are true philosophers and who understood how to put an end to it.[22] Such a degradation of the primary idea among some of those who were most faithful to it allows us to gauge how much the philosophic faith had tottered in the midst of the crisis.

The discredit of the Man of Letters is that of the doctrine he had embodied. The experience of the Revolution's traumatically catastrophic developments caused both the new and old ruling classes to doubt the faith that they had tried to nourish together. They now condemned this faith as a breeder of disasters. The fact that it is not merely those writers who could be held responsible for the course of events but the Man of Letters as a general type that is the victim of this reversal is a striking indication of the extent to which the idea of a clericature had been implicit in the new ideas. It is this clericature that is incriminated; and writers themselves, in order to be listened to and survive, renounce it and dully preach modesty to their fellow writers, who still form a prestigious group.

Not all resign themselves to this state of affairs. The *idéologues*, the Institut, and *La Décade* resist the counterrevolution, and as a matter of course attempt to perpetuate the prestige of the philosophic Man of Letters.[23] It is worth noting how the second class of the Institut, which after 1803 was more or less the equivalent of the old French Academy, acted in the choice of the subjects for competitions that it proposed to young writers. When it proposed a "literary portrait of France in the eighteenth century" as the subject for the prose competition, it was certainly seeking, in the view of its perpetual secretary Suard, to elicit defenses of the century just finished and to counter the counterrevolutionary press's attack; the Institut wanted to see it proclaimed that philosophy, excellent in itself, was not responsible for the excesses of the Revolution; there was an attempt to steer competitors in this direction.[24] We have on this subject the confidential testimony of another academician, Morellet.[25] When the subject had been proposed for the third time,[26] and no competitor had been deemed worthy of the prize, a significant failure was feared. Some proposed doubling the award and conducting the competition yet again; other members, more timid, objected, suggesting "that it might perhaps have been desirable last year not to have proposed any such subject." So the prize money was not doubled, and Morellet writes: "Suard and I, and a very few others, failed to have our way. . . . The movement of opinion among us on these important questions is unfortunately backwards." He writes this to Roederer, who certainly shared his feelings: these letters are a truly sectarian correspondence.[27] Roederer's *Opuscules* of the same period are essential reading; there he defends the philosophy of the eighteenth century from the "Brumairian" (his word) point of view by insisting with a truly remarkable resourcefulness on the terror that the counterrevolution is exercising in the literary world and on its fundamentally royalist goals.[28] In this ongoing underground struggle, each party attempted to make the other suspect in the eyes of the Napoleonic government.

The political writers of the counterrevolution were accustomed to lower the standing of the eighteenth century by comparing it to the seventeenth. "The one sags, the other climbs into the heavens," we read in *Génie du christianisme*.[29] Those who lived through those years noticed the preoccupation: "The dispute over the relative merits of the 17th and 18th centuries . . . seemed to absorb every page of the warring newspapers," remarks a contemporary in 1814;[30] and, half a century later, Delécluze remembers how the royalists profited from this debate: "Louis XIV's *grand siècle* was presented to the public like a new show."[31] The literary excellence of this century was said to be due to its mode of government. Bonald returns incessantly to this theme, laying down the general rule that a period's approach to literary perfection depends on how perfectly the ideal of Catholic monarchy is realized;[32] the eighteenth century, decadent in politics, was also decadent in literature.[33] Old ways of thinking were thus abandoned: in general, the eighteenth century had considered itself as the continuer of the civilization of the preceding century, in a broader and more liberated spirit. Those who remained faithful to this tradition were annoyed to see the two periods opposed to one another: "These sorts of comparisons favor wit more than good sense," says Suard in his 1807 report on the academic competition, thus forbidding candidates from taking such a view of the subject.[34] The prize, finally awarded in 1810, was shared by Antoine Jay and Victorin Fabre, both apologists for the eighteenth century and for philosophy.[35] It is obvious that the type of the Man of Letters haunts these debates: "The first effect of the *Encyclopédie*," writes Jay in his piece, "was to reveal to men of letters the secret of their strength. They showed themselves in the world with greater confidence; and by different roads they all advanced toward the same goal."[36] In fact, the academicians had announced at about the same time a competition to treat the subject of the Man of Letters in verse. The story of this other competition and the public reaction to it well illustrate in what new conditions the problem of the writer presented itself after the Revolution's ebb.

On 5 Nivôse Year XIII (26 December 1804), the Institut's French-language and literature class announced the competition subjects for Year XIV in its public session. For poetry, it proposed as a subject, among others, "The independence of the man of letters." On this occasion, Morellet read different remarks; the subject's greatest difficulty, he observed in particular, "will doubtless be to avoid the exaggeration toward which ardent youth and the sentiment of liberty rushes,[37] and we can put the competitors on notice that one of the greatest merits of the work, in the eyes of the Academy, will be to have remained within the bounds of decency and truth."[38] What was feared was the sensitivity of those in power, for if the competitors gave free rein to their verve, treating the subject in the traditional tone, they would allow its subversive meaning to become apparent, and this would be immediately pointed out by those on the lookout in the enemy camp; hence this counsel of moderation, as well as the choice of the word "independence," which can suggest a serene, detached wisdom even while it reserves the rights of the thinker vis-à-vis civil society. This prudent academic maneuver did not deceive the adversary, who immediately denounced it; in the summer of 1805, a professor friendly to the academicians defended them at length in a speech given in their presence on the occasion of the award-ing of the prizes at a general competition: "The single word *independence* has already alarmed a few worried minds whom the too recent memory of our misfortunes sets against anything that can awaken liberal ideas that, we must admit, have been cruelly misused." Note the circumspect tone of the Enlighten-ment party in these difficult times; they nevertheless preserve the sacred trust: "The man of letters," the orator goes on,

is limited neither in time nor in space; he soars above all centuries, he frater-nizes with all peoples, he brings the past alive, he embellishes the present, he creates the future: the physical world is his theater, the moral world is his domain. Ought we to marvel that his soul should arise at the very thought of these sublime prerogatives, and that from the sentiment of his grandeur should be born the need for his independence? . . . People are wrong, then, to sound the call to arms.[39]

The orator pretends however to pay homage to the vigilance of the censors by comparing them, with heavy professorial humor, to the Capitoline geese.

The goose that cackled first was none other than the viscount Bonald, in the *Mercure*. He had been worrying for a long time about writers as a group and their mischief-making ways. As early as 1796 he remarked that in the preceding period "writers had usurped an enormous influence over society"; this influence was illegitimate, since "the cultivation of letters can make a society more beauti-ful, but it cannot preserve its existence"; it can, alas! destroy it, and in this case, "if arts and letters can do nothing but corrupt men and ruin society, we must destroy arts and letters"; their possible utility as a source of pleasure and moral support can only be ensured by means of a social control; in other words, by subjecting them to censorship.[40] In 1805, as soon as the subjects proposed by the Institut are known, he feels that he must comment upon the one that interests us. The very word *independence* sets his teeth on edge, for this word "makes one suspect something rebellious at work deep in the heart, as M. Bossuet says," and nothing can be independent of the laws of society: "every social role imposes obligations," and literature is obliged to submit to a social truth that does not depend upon it.[41] Bonald was not alone in finding the subject proposed by the Institut shocking. If we can believe Dussault, a less eminent fellow counter-revolutionary, this subject aroused fears in several minds, fears all too justified by "the excesses committed by writers in the past," and the intention of the academicians had been grasped very well.[42]

The examination of the poetic entries lasted three weeks; there were forty-six of them. The minutes of 8 Brumaire Year XIV (31 October 1805) named the laureates. A report by Suard in public session on 2 January 1806 officially announced the results of the competition; as was customary, the winning entries were read aloud in whole or in part.[43] The Academy awarded the prize and an honorable mention to Millevoye and Victorin Fabre, respectively, neither of whom was much over twenty years of age. The winning poems fit the intentions of the academicians admirably with their calculated balance of boldness and moderation. In accordance with the key word of the given subject, both celebrate a spiritual greatness that is somehow self-sufficient and unmilitant, but that excludes neither disdain for power nor a beneficent relation with humanity as a whole. Millevoye's poem, which won first prize, is the better balanced; he represents the Man of Letters as a wise man, a luminous thinker who is superior to the enslaved crowd, incorruptible,

> Libre à la cour, soumis aux rois, mais sans bassesse,

> [Free at court, obedient to kings, but without making himself ignoble,]

defender of the oppressed when need be, preferring silence to the celebration of injustice, capable of heroism in the presence of tyranny

> Tyrans! il vous poursuit de sa franchise austère;
> Et, libre sous le poids de votre autorité,
> En présence du glaive il dit la vérité.

> [Tyrants! his austere frankness pursues you;
> And, free despite the weight of your authority,
> He speaks the truth in the presence of the sword.]

This civic eloquence is less subversive in 1806 than one might think. By making use of ancient commonplaces, it could be taken to refer to kings, the tyrants of the classics, and, if necessary, to the tyrants of 1793; what might be taken as condemnation of imperial mores slipped through under cover of vagueness.[44]

Fabre's hero is bolder and nourishes within himself "that flame," "that fire of liberty," source of virtue and talent; he dominates nature and teaches humanity, and in that way influences kings; he is the minister of reason:

> Il proclame son culte; et vengeant ses outrages,
> Ce génie immortel dans le long cours des âges
> S'avance, encore armé de son flambeau vengeur,
> Et chasse devant lui le faux jour de l'erreur.[45]

> [He proclaims his faith; and avenging acts of unreason,
> This immortal spirit through the long ages
> Marches with his avenging torch,
> And makes the false light of error flee before him.]

This piece was a bit too harsh as well in its scorn for those who are eminent; it received only an honorable mention, and then with the proviso that one passage be deleted.[46] The failing entries that have survived were, on the contrary, too timid or too neutral.[47]

Once the results had been announced and the poems published, the counterrevolutionary critics multiplied their attacks. Dussault, in a second article, deplores "the excessive importance that for the past fifty years has been given to literature and to the social status of man of letters." "The government," he writes,

> lost its authority, social distinctions were derided, morals were degraded, religion was abased and scorned, but literature became a sort of priesthood, and the man of letters a sort of priest who was thought of with a religious veneration: theater was thought to be a sort of school for morals; the Academy a sort of sanctuary; the pronouncements of our writers oracles; algebra and geometry themselves mystical sciences, capable of imparting supernatural knowledge to minds. . . . It angers me to see that the revolution, which at least had the good effect of dissipating many illusions, has not calmed the exalted imagination of writers.[48]

Almost at the same time, a contributor to the *Mercure* doubts whether the very notion of "independence" has a meaning in any profession, and is amused to see Millevoye represent a cell-bound man of letters in a country where writers have imprudently derided everything.[49] Féletz treats in a similar manner the declaiming of the competitors on the "pompous subject" that was proposed to them: the man of letters, properly understood, seems to him more dependent than any other.[50] What all these critics contest is the existence of a function or ministry with regard to the governance of society that is proper to the writer. It is this pretension above all that their sarcasms are intended to deflate; the writer is a member of the community like any other; social or spiritual consecration is to be found elsewhere.

The controversy over the Man of Letters, as a meaningful variant of the general debate, extends well beyond the date of this academic competition. In 1809, an aging Palissot thinks that it would have been better to speak of dignity rather than of independence; in 1817, even, the royalist *Quinzaine littéraire* published an "Unpublished Epistle on the Dignity and Duties of the Man of Letters," which could well be left over from the 1805 competition. The memory of the Man of Letters still haunts extreme reactionary circles devoted to the divine right of kings: in 1822, Eckstein takes up arms once more against this class as it was constituted in France in the eighteenth century: "a scourge of society, a superfluity of the social body, and nothing more."[51] On the other hand, the liberal political writers of the Restoration continue from time to time to evoke the ministry of the man of letters in a moderate tone. Thus, in 1816: "The profession of letters, to which no social rank is assigned in the State, in truth occupies the first rank, due to the influence it has upon public morality, private morals, and national institutions";[52] in 1823: "Thanks to the progress of Enlightenment . . . , every man who exercises his intelligence or his imagination contributes to the instruction of an attentive humanity."[53] But by that time the debate over the Man of Letters, as the eighteenth century framed it, is just about spent.

✤ *Poetry versus Philosophy*

Counterrevolutionary criticism would like to establish that the beliefs of the *philosophes* threaten to wreck not only society but literature itself by drying up its vital springs. Philosophic Sensibility is denounced as artificial and false by this criticism; to the enthusiasm of the reformers it opposes a more instinctive form of sensibility, one to which any doctrinal aim is foreign; and it is in this form of sensibility that it finds the source of true genius, especially in poetry. The literary counterrevolution thus compensates for its negations and refusals by a claim of a positive nature: it believes that it has a better grasp of the secret of true emotion in poetry and art than its adversaries. This position was already clearly marked out in the eighteenth century, and all the more persuasively in that writers in the philosophic camp had often resigned themselves to a possible divorce between intellectual enlightenment and poetry. Speculations on primitive poetry and its excellence presuppose such a divorce. Without going back to the origins of humanity, however, it is possible to contrast the philosophic age and the age that immediately preceded it, in which the exercise of abstract reason had not spoiled the poetic faculty. This is what antiphilosophic polemics aim to do. Abbé de Grainville thinks that philosophy has killed poetry: "While the writer exhausts himself by generalizing ideas and grasping their associations, his heart freezes up, the fire of imagination goes out; the objects that nourish that divine flame awaken what are in him merely reflections. . . . Do not look for the life, the fire, the enthusiasm that animated our first artists in the productions of this century."[54] Another abbé who is professor of humanities at the *collège* of the University of Nancy, writes similarly: "The philosophic spirit can be likened to a slow poison, which tends to cause a fatal chill to spread through all parts of literature."[55] The poet Gilbert takes up the same motif in his antiphilosophic satire "Le Dix-huitième Siècle," dedicated to Fréron:

Maudit soit à jamais le pointilleux sophiste
Qui le premier nous dit en prose d'algébriste:
Vains rimeurs, écoutez mes ordres absolus;
Pour plaire à ma raison, pensez, ne peignez plus.[56]

[Forever cursed be the nitpicking sophist
Who first said to us in algebraic prose:
Futile versifiers, listen to my absolute command:
If you would be pleasing to my faculty of reason, think, but paint no more.]

This polemical motif, together with the system of arguments and the aim assigned to it in antiphilosophic circles, naturally gained strength at the turn of century. The theme came to be so well received that in 1802 Sabatier de Castres, a political writer of the old school, insists on showing that it was he, well before La Harpe and Clément, who first denounced the sterilization of taste by philosophy, since he was already writing in 1790: "You can reason so much about beauty that you become totally insensitive to it."[57] He might have remembered that he had said the same thing almost twenty years earlier: "This corrosive philosophy has dried up talents at their sources, has led them astray with illusions . . . , has weakened their sinews and blasted their charms."[58] He also forgot that others had said it before he did. Around 1800, the idea is found everywhere,[59] and is expanded into a general critique of abstract knowledge and the exact sciences, which are held to be ruinous for poetry and art: "Doubt it not," writes Dussault, "nothing is more to be feared for eloquence and poetry than the excessive ascendancy of the sciences."[60] The simple idea of the preeminence of literature vis-à-vis science becomes one of the passwords of the political writers of the counterrevolution.[61] Only the moral science of man, an ally of belles-lettres, finds favor in Bonald's eyes; he repudiates the purely physical sciences.[62] In 1815, *La Quotidienne* accuses mathematics, chemistry, and botany for the decadence of literature: "*Littérateurs* and poets have only a narrow field left to them, one desiccated by all the fabricators of analyses and nomenclatures. This is how the sacred flame goes out."[63]

These diatribes did not go unanswered. The *Veillées des Muses*, a review that around 1800 grouped writers faithful to the spirit of the preceding century, published a "Dialogue on the Necessity that Writers Know the Theory of the Sciences," whose author asserts that "literature properly so called cannot suffice for the writer."[64] Around the same time, one of Stendhal's masters stated his belief that "harmony and taste do not do away with thinking," and that, in literature, "to succeed one must be as much a philosopher as a man of letters."[65] A moderate *idéologue* explains contemporary denunciations of the sciences by sectarian interest: "I will never be persuaded of the divorce between the true and the beautiful."[66] The partnership of literature and the sciences was an important article of faith for the writers of the philosophic party: otherwise literature would have appeared trivial to them. The old chevalier de Boufflers, in an essay read to the Institut in 1810, exalts literature because of this partnership: "It has thus become the inseparable companion of science, accepted by science itself as sharing the gratitude of the human race."[67] Even more than in the opposing camp, great importance was granted to the moral sciences, though they were understood differently, and in close relation to the natural sciences. Abbé Grégoire, Lacretelle, and Portalis are among the writers of the former generation who continue to argue for the harmony of literature and the sciences, as well as for the eminent dignity of the man of letters, defined as a function of this harmony.[68] These acts of resistance are far from unimportant; they maintain the connection between the spirit of the past century and the various attempts at synthesizing science, the creative arts, and the government of humanity that would flourish in the progressivist nineteenth century.

Meanwhile, contemporary literature was following a path leading in the opposite direction. "Several people have thought," declares Chateaubriand, "that in the hands of man science dries up the heart, disenchants nature, leads weak minds to atheism and from atheism to every crime; whereas the beaux-arts make our days marvelous, sensitize our souls, fill us with faith in the Divinity, and lead from religion to the practice of all the virtues."[69] In the final analysis, it is to turn literary beauty toward religion that it is torn away from the sciences. The century of Louis XIV, whose attractive creations are opposed to the abstractions of the *philosophes*, is seen and advocated as a Christian century. Christianity, not science, is truth; truth with chiaroscuro, and thus lending itself to beauty: "It is in this that it differs essentially from philosophy, which seeks too much to penetrate into the nature of man, and to get to the bottom everywhere. The Christian religion has only raised the folds of the veil as much as is necessary for us to see our path; but it has left in doubt and shadow those things that are useless for our ends. Thus it has charmed the spirit by a ray of light, without destroying the poetic part of the soul."[70] Thus Chateaubriand expresses the full significance of the thinking of his party on the relation of the sciences and literature: the meaning of literary thought, freed from the influence of science, is nothing less than the soul's meaning—that is, religious meaning. And it is a fact that the poetry of the nineteenth century springs from this idea. Lamartine saw his *Méditations* as a challenge to the exact sciences at the time he was writing them; he deplored "the destiny that caused me to be born in a century of mathematics"; and Bonald exalted him for remaining estranged from this influence: "He proves to me," he wrote, "what I have always believed, that the seeds of goodness, beauty, and greatness in the soul of the poet are very different from those in a geometer's soul."[71]

All this goes to show that the discredit of the Man of Letters does not extend to the figure of the poet in the thought of the counterrevolution; on the contrary, the one tends to gain what the other loses. The enemies of the Man of Letters have only good things to say of the poet as an agent of creation and revelation. Poetry is conceived of "as a sublime creation of the spirit insofar as ideas are concerned, and, as for language, as a divine song, and a harmony as powerful as that of Orpheus."[72] The myth of the primitive poet is cultivated more than ever, with a view toward making the Christian poet his modern successor. Orpheus, together with Amphion and Cadmus, are not forgotten in *Génie du christianisme*: "Lutes in hand, golden crowns adorning their white hair, these divine men sat beneath plane trees and dictated their lessons to a rapt people."[73] These privileged qualities of character are easily extended to the poets of every age: "These singers," says René, "are of a divine race."[74] From the Consulate to the Restoration, an extensive movement of conservative thought exalts poetry in order to make of it a support for religion and the salutary mender of philosophic subversion. Publishing in an émigré review in 1797, Fontanes interpolates into a famous poem he wrote around 1785 on "Le Jour des morts"—a heartfelt composition of a religious cast but without any polemical intent in its original version—the following invocation concerning the practice of consulting the dead beside the grave:

> O dogme attendrissant! quel système pervers
> Te rejette, et dément la voix de l'univers?
> Poètes, ramenez ces antiques usages,
> Ces sentiments divins qu'ont proscrits les faux sages;
> Ils ont dégradé l'homme, et vous l'agrandissez.[75]

> [O touching belief! what perverse system
> Rejects you, and flies in the face of universal opinion?
> Poets, bring back these ancient customs,

These divine feelings, which false sages have proscribed;
They have degraded man, and you exalt him.]

Twenty years later the same thing is being said: "Only the Muses can entirely destroy among us this sophistical spirit, a sort of moral illness that is the result of the abuse of reasoning, and of the habit of cold argumentation. . . . Poetry therefore cannot be too much encouraged among us; and for it to be truly useful, it is important to purify it and to recall it to its nobility, to its primitive dignity."[76] Analogous texts abound in counterrevolutionary literature.[77] In 1823 and 1824, youthful Catholic and royalist romanticism in its entirety bases itself on such a conception of poetry.

The restorative power of poetry is also made to reside in its capacity to revive and promote a love of the national past; the poet is made the natural illustrator of monarchical pomp. Chateaubriand's *Génie du christianisme* has a secular pendant in Marchagny's *La Gaule poétique*. A ministry of past time corresponds closely to a ministry that aims at eternity: this composite formula would be that of the first wave of French romanticism. But it is the religious connection that gives to poets their greatest opportunities, and to this intellectual movement its full range and essential significance. This is why the modern consecration of the poet took as its chief point of departure the tradition that relates to the ministry of the poets of Scripture.

❧ The Sacred Poet and the Christian Poet

Chateaubriand, in the chapter of the *Génie* that he devoted to the poetic excellence of sacred texts, does not forget to mention J.-B. Rousseau;[78] and in the *Défense du Génie du christianisme*, he invokes Bossuet, Fleury, and Rollin.[79] The *Mercure*, reviewing a new edition of this same Rollin's *Le Traité des études* in 1805, reprints a page of this old-fashioned author on primitive poetry and its religious source.[80] A legacy of the Christian eighteenth century is thus passing to the nineteenth century and blossoming there. Collections of sacred poems translated into French continue to appear during the Empire and multiply in the Restoration: translations of Scripture both in verse and in prose,[81] collections containing a mixture of poetic paraphrases of the Bible and original Christian poetry, according to a long-established custom.[82] The authors, declared royalists for the most part, add prefaces and dissertations to their works; others hold forth on the sacred lyre without trying their hands at it themselves.[83] In addition, to acquaint themselves with sacred poetry, readers in the Restoration had access to a new prose translation of the Bible, the work of a young royalist, Antoine-Eugène Genoude;[84] in 1839, Genoude published still more *Leçons et modèles de littérature sacrée* with a preface and several critical pieces, attesting at this late date to a still hardy tradition.

This tradition, one of the most important sources upon which the nascent poetic romanticism draws, remained faithful to its themes from one century to another. Translators and commentators are attached to the same scriptural texts, which have become classics of sacred poetry; the translations and paraphrases of their most illustrious predecessors have also become classics and are celebrated everywhere — J.-B. Rousseau, Louis Racine, and Lefranc, and, just as much, the memorable commentaries by Bossuet, Fleury, Fénelon, Rollin, and La Harpe.[85] With this tradition, it is above all a fund of ideas about the origin, dignity, and function of poetry that is being transmitted. If the sacred poet is superior to the profane poet, this is because he is more truly a poet, according to the original and authentic definition of poetry; this definition remains at the root of the royalist writers' religious poetics: "Poetry is born from the spectacle of the universe. As soon as man had considered the marvels of nature, his admiration for its maker burst into transports of gratitude and love. His first songs were hymns." "Poetry never made itself more worthy of its noble origin than when it devoted its songs to celebrating the wonders of God, thanking him for his blessings, and exhorting men to virtue. David, viewed in this light, seems to me superior to the great poets of antiquity."[86] To keep our bearings, we should note the ironical attitude adopted by liberal opinion vis-à-vis the new poetic fervor inspired by the psalms. In *Le Globe* in 1825, at a time when the influence of the strictly counterrevolutionary poetics begins to decline, we read: "When, as we emerged from our turmoil, there occured the religious reaction of which M. de Chateaubriand was the poet . . . , Blair's *Leçons*, Dr Lowth's *Traité*, La Harpe's *Psautier* were read, commented upon, adopted as a rule for taste and for faith. Today the fervor seems to be declining . . . : if this were the proper place, I would be glad to say why."[87] Villemain, in a course given in 1828, notes: "The ode, and lyric inspiration, have been in decline now for thousands of years"; he willingly grants that there was a religious lyricism at the time of humanity's beginnings and that Scripture testifies to this; he doubts that it is possible to revive this kind of poetry in our time.[88] On this point, liberal criticism is doubtless right, if we take things literally. But its skepticism about any resurrection of the past prevents it from understanding the true nature of the event that is taking place and from seeing that a poetic renaissance has begun for the nineteenth century.

What has shown progress in the course of the revolutionary crisis and its aftermath is the enhanced quality of contemporaneity to be found in Christian poetry, which is the modern version of sacred poetry. The very circumstances imposed themes of suffering and prayer, expiation and hope in God, similar to those of the Hebrew poets. A poetic tradition that under Louis XV could seem anachronistic and purely devout could henceforth be reinterpreted more widely and with reference to contemporary experience. A poetry for a time of ordeals, one descended from that of the prophets, is needed to respond to the Revolution and its scourges. Bonald wrote some astonishing lines on this subject: "We need misfortunes, huge misfortunes, in order to achieve what is most beautiful in the most beautiful of arts"; then, in an effort to conceive of the model for the highest beauty, he describes the passion of Christ.[89] And indeed, Louis XVI on the scaffold is for royalists a figure of Christ. A great historical misfortune, the martyrdom of innocents, consolation in faith, providential penances — these will be the subject matter of a fully contemporary sacred poetry. The song of the poet accompanies the impression of ruin and will perhaps have the power of curing it:

> Ne reverrons-nous plus des poètes, des sages
> Sortant de leur retraite, ainsi qu'aux premiers âges
> Pour sauver les humains?[90]

> [Will we no longer see poets and wise men
> Quitting their solitude, as in earliest times
> To save the human race?]

And in fact several poets undertook this work of salvation before Lamartine's *Méditations* and Hugo's *Odes* appeared [1820 and 1822, respectively. *Trans.*].

An example of this is the work of Joseph Treneuil, forgotten, and no doubt justly so. Born in 1763, he was a tutor for different noble families before the Revolution. During the Directory he composed poetic lamentations that were a sort of martyrology of the counterrevolution: "Les Tombeaux de Saint-Denis," a poem about the profaning of the royal sepulchers, "Orpheline du Temple," "Martyre de Louis XVI," "Captivité de Pie VI," whose publication Fructidor prevented. The tolerance during the Empire that allowed the publication of "Les Tombeaux" in 1806 did not extend to the other poems, and the author was almost imprisoned in 1808; however, he wrote works praising the imperial family — while maintaining his dignity, his ultra friends tell us — and in 1810 obtained one of the decennial prizes. During the Restoration he was librarian for the comte d'Artois at the Arsenal, and he reopened his file of royalist writings: a collection of his compositions appeared under the title of *Poèmes élégiaques*.[91] The elegy in the modern European tradition was devoted above all to amorous melancholy and private grief. Treneuil wanted to make public ordeals its object, to make of it a lament for the sufferings of royalty and the church. In general, the poetry of the counterrevolution seeks to be a poetry of suffering. The republican tradition of the nineteenth century as well as our century, which makes us unsympathetic to this approach, keeps us from seeing some of its characteristics; we tend to think of its presumption, its aggressivity, its pitiless harshness; we risk missing the other aspect of royalism, its habits of lamentation and its appeal to the heart for sympathy. Michelet did not miss it; he notes: "The royalist party, defeated in the Vendée and elsewhere, succeeded and spread its influence above all by tears and pitifulness. It was the secret of that weepy party."[92] Whether ultra melancholy was hypocritical, as Michelet implies, or sincere, is difficult to decide, and is in any case moot. Royalism naturally sanctifies its sufferings, which, as we know, were not imaginary, and were the basis, rightly or wrongly, for its good conscience.

Seeking a name for the poetic genre he envisioned, Treneuil called it "heroic elegy," for want of a better term; he theorized about the genre in a long *Discours* that he put at the beginning of his final collection.[93] The epithet "heroic," properly belonging to the epic, indicates what differentiates this poetry with its national scope from ordinary elegies: the term *poèmes* in the title of his collection corresponds to their generally narrative character, something unheard of in pure elegy. In 1816, Mollevault had already entitled the fourth book of his collection of *Elégies* "Elegiac *poèmes*"; this volume, after the first three composed of traditional private elegies, includes among narrations of biblical or historical events a poem on "The Misfortunes of Louis XVI"; and in a contemporary review of this collection we read: "Today the elegy embraces the vast horizon of our public calamities and our private sufferings; it draws sustenance from all the pains, all the hopes, all the fears of the human race."[94] What this really is, under the name of elegy, is a serious form of poetry linked to history and aiming both to convert and to do penance, by which modern poets make themselves the interpreters and guides of their period. Treneuil's "Discourse" faithfully repeats the ideas we have examined concerning the origins of poetry, born from man's original relation to God, and its development among the Hebrews.[95] He cites several of the modern authorities, both ecclesiastical and poetic, who are usually invoked,[96] but he introduces a new note in this tradition by insisting on the fact that the original hymn of love must have been replaced by a song of lamentation since the Fall: it is in this light that he sees sacred poetry. This song of woe, the expression of a great collective lament, one that he is attempting to resuscitate today under the name of heroic elegy, has degenerated in the interval, he says, into private elegy. The high mission of poetic genius, however, has been completely forgotten neither in Greece nor in ancient Europe. But the French above all have just traversed a period in which the spiritual lamentation that is both the soul of poetry and its outstanding role has recovered its full meaning. By dedicating it to the commemoration of our misfortunes in song, one of Treneuil's friends tells us that he "has summoned poetry back to the nobility of its beginning, back to the entire dignity of its earliest functions." "What an august ministry it performs!" adds this admirer, immediately invoking Fénelon's opinion on poetry to legitimize this ministry.[97]

An attempt related to Treneuil's was made at about the same time by Elzéar de Sabran in his poem "Le Repentir."[98] The author, born in 1774, had emigrated with his family while still quite young; he was the brother of Mme de Custine, Chateaubriand's friend, and was one of Mme de Staël's familiars; he returned to France in 1801, and was imprisoned during the Empire on account of his friendships. The subject of Repentance at that time and in those circles naturally implied reflections on the Revolution's crimes and the appropriateness of contrition on a national scale. And in fact these reflections fill the first divisions of the poem; they are illustrated by episodes that recount the conversions and honorable reparations of *philosophes* like Raynal or La Harpe during the crisis. What is peculiar to Sabran is the way in which the traditional themes of national meditation and suffering extend in his work to the supernatural plane; in his poem, the theology of repentance leads to the telling of a sort of sacred epic on the redemption of the rebellious angels; of two angel friends, only one of whom has followed Satan in his rebellion; the other grieves and desires in vain to redeem his companion, who does not repent and is pardoned only at the Last Judgment. As far as I know, this is one of the first attempts in France at what Vigny will call *mystères*, at what will be the epic of redemption so dear to French romanticism. It is significant that the genre, one of those that will establish most resoundingly the ministry of the poet, appears linked in its beginnings to a counterrevolutionary meditation on crime and repentance. This link will not last very long, it is true. But it existed at first, and perhaps too little importance has been attached to the fact — not that it was unknown, however — that poetic romanticism began in France on this terrain.[99]

✺ Sensibility and Religion

We arrive now at the pith of the matter: the counterrevolution condemned Sensibility less often than it attempted to convert it to its own ends, especially by integrating it into religion. A tradition that tended in this direction had existed since the eighteenth century, favored rather than hobbled by analogous tentatives at synthesis undertaken in the philosophic camp. It would be hard to say which side began first to seek to reconcile the two credos, religious and philosophic. The amalgam differs in nuance and intention according to which influence dominates in a given milieu and at a given time. But this matters little: the fact is that an identical impulse drew minds from every quarter, so that a vast area of compromises and alliances between traditional religion and modern humanism grew steadily.[100] Christians rehabilitate sensibility and place the longing for earthly objects on the same sentimental scale (though lower down) as the love of God, the only love that can truly fill the dimensions of the human heart.[101] A theology of sentiment attenuating somewhat the opposition of earth and heaven prospered early and long; this is sufficiently well known[102] to dispense with the need for us to describe this "naturalization of Christianity."[103] This can be considered an abjuration, if you like; what is still more surprising is to see the production of a theology of purely human grandeur that claims to be Catholic. On the eve of the Revolution, an ecclesiastical writer approves of the intimate feeling that "fixes in us the irresistible determination to see the peace and perfection of our existence only in our participation in the *totality of being*"; such a participation belongs to us: "*Homo sum*, spoken by a God, is the sublime and irrevocable expression of the Divinity of Man."[104] "O Man, what then is your grandeur!" — such is the final word of this theology.[105] Ultimately it fraternized with the secular faith in its revolutionary consequences: liberty, equality, and the exalted dignity of the people.[106] The church and the counterrevolution repudiated, of course, this adventurous avant-garde that revolutionized the Gospel in order to justify it.

However, these sorts of accommodations were just as much a danger to the purity of the humanist faith. Sensibility is, by nature, uneasy; its enthusiasms do not prevent it from feeling at every turn what wounds it or what it lacks. Sensibility may be tempted to explain its uneasiness by an infirmity of our nature whose remedy is in God alone: God then becomes the center of faith, and not simply its backer. Secular Sensibility is happy to approach those ill-defined regions that separate it from religious faith, and does not always hesitate to go beyond them. This is how, for example, Bernardin de Saint-Pierre, Jean-Jacques Rousseau's disciple and friend, comes to alter his master's doctrine most curiously when he establishes an absolute opposition between reason and sentiment, whereas humanist philosophy liked to show beneath the conflict of these two terms their profound agreement, endangered only by uncontrolled sentiment or dry, small-minded reason. In reason Bernardin sees systematically the instrument of egoism and special interests, and in sentiment the source of all universal value.[107] And a faculty of sentiment so contrary to reason is necessarily a hidden power that adores mystery and takes delight in the idea of a hidden good. In *Études de la nature* there is much discussion of the "pleasure of mystery," even of the "pleasures of ignorance"; in short, "it is mystery that furnishes one of religion's charms."[108] No doubt, and this is precisely why the deistic *philosophes* exclude mystery so resolutely: "We must," says one of them, "pull the veil of mystery away from religion; mysteries are an insult to the Supreme Being; everything must be obvious in the worship that links us to the deity, as in the laws that bind us to society, and in the principles that lead us to virtue."[109] The worship of mystery is a traditional intellectual tactic, one that serves to put the cause of human happiness and salvation out of human reach. Bernardin flatters himself that he has demonstrated that "everything that seemed delicious and enthralling in our pleasures came from the sentiment of infinity, or from some other attribute of the divinity, who was revealing himself to us at the furthest range of our sight."[110] For "man is an exiled god."[111] And in this exile a vital communication links human beings to God by the faculty of sentiment, just as much and more than to other individuals, since God "has destined for himself alone, as the creator of life, the human heart, which is life's principal organ."[112] It is this communication with God that constitutes humanity: "The only characteristic that essentially distinguishes man from animals is that of being a religious being."[113] Thus a pattern marked by exile and a link to God through the faculty of sensibility reproduces the pattern of the Christian faith; this replaces the primacy of the moral conscience, which distinguishes deism. The movements of conscience are themselves attributed to heaven; this is how Bernardin, describing the enthusiasms of the secular faith in a typical manner, turns them at last into a nostalgia for the divine, just as a Christian apologist would do; a celestial instinct inspires them; this instinct, "as soon as it reveals itself to us in some unanticipated act of virtue, or in one of those events that we call acts of providence, or in some of those indefinably sublime emotions that we so appropriately call pangs of feeling, its first effect is to produce in us an extremely vivid movement of joy, and the second, to cause us to shed tears. Our soul, struck by this divine gleam, both rejoices at glimpsing the country of heaven, and is downcast to be exiled from it."[114] Another of Bernardin's formulas, one that shows clearly his place on the confines of Sensibility and Religion, is that "the feeling of admiration transports us directly to the heart of divinity."[115] Similarly, in his devotion (as a good disciple of the *philosophes*) to men of letters as benefactors of humanity, he presumes that their eloquence derives from the heavenly Word: "Thus," he writes, with reference to Homer, "the word that created the world still governs it."[116]

An example like that of Bernardin, significant in itself and in the response that it evoked, shows us to what extent the new faith was capable of joining forces with the old. Each risked something in this rapprochement. After 1800, circumstances again favored Catholicism and advanced the cause of a predominantly religious synthesis that was one of the great creations of counterrevolutionary literature.

✹ The Génie du Christianisme *or the Conversion of the Man of Sensibility*

This accomplishment was above all Chateaubriand's. It has been aptly noted that *Génie du christianisme* pursues the line taken during the previous century by the apologists for religion who were imbued with Sensibility, or, better still, by Bernardin de Saint-Pierre.[117] The role of Fontanes and his advice in Chateaubriand's conversion are well known; and Fontanes had been in the 1780s a religious poet in Bernardin's vein. His poem "Le Jour des morts dans une campagne" poetically exalted the religion of the cross, but in the person of a village pastor, conforming to Rousseau's ideal, "[u]n prêtre ami des lois et zélé sans abus [a priest who embraces the laws of the civil order and who is zealous without fanaticism]," more concerned with charity than with theology. The poem "La Chartreuse de Paris," published in 1783 in *L'Almanach des Muses*, already praises the consolation of the cloister; but a comparison of the earliest versions of these poems with the text as it was recast after 1800 brings home to us the distance between Bernardin de Saint-Pierre's themes and those of the Christian counterrevolution.[118] Chateaubriand has indeed made use of Bernardin's antithesis of sensibility and reason, and like him has made the value of the faculty of sentiment derive from its mysteriousness. His book begins with a commendation of mystery: "In life, only what is mysterious can be beautiful, sweet, and great";[119] but this thought of Bernardin's leads here to a poetic apology for the *mysteries* of Catholic dogma. More generally, a new foundation for the idea of the hidden God of Scripture and theology is provided by the identification of Sensibility's final object, the infinite, with what is inaccessible and secret: "It is certain that our soul seeks eternally; scarcely has it obtained the object it covets than it seeks anew: the entire universe fails to satisfy it. The infinite is the only field that suits it. . . . It only immerses itself in the heart of the Divinity because that Divinity is shrouded in obscurity, *Deus absconditus*."[120] Another novelty, no less important, is the view that the faculty of sentiment implies the disavowal of life in the here and now and finds in the past the nourishment it prefers: with a certain sadness, its thoughts fly toward childhood and reminiscences of the land of our origins, as well as beyond, toward the celestial homeland from which life separates us.[121] The euphoria characteristic of philosophic Sensibility is condemned: it is of the essence of sentiment to be measured by what is missed.

It is enough to read what preceded the *Génie*; viz. the *Essai sur les révolutions*, to see the deep motive for Sensibility's veering toward melancholy. The faith of the *philosophes* had as its object a moral renewal of human society, and the émigré in London could only hate what was being done in the name of this goal in Paris. "Shining illusion of a durable happiness on earth, adieu!"; and this disciple of Rousseau imagines advising his master to fall silent.[122] "The Revolution," writes his friend Joubert, "has made my mind flee the real world by making it too horrible."[123] Spiritual reversal is, among many men of the time, the fruit of this disappointment. This was still well known in the following generation: "Such was the state of minds at the end of the eighteenth century and at the moment when *René* appeared. Man had hoped greatly, and he had been enormously disappointed."[124] To account for this solely on the psychological plane, and explain the malaise as the century began as a simple shock caused by the violence of events, is to fail utterly to understand this important fact. Psychology and ideology are inseparable in such matters. The disappointed thinkers of 1800 reject hope itself: they think that by doing so they may spare themselves and humanity further disappointments. Disappointment thus turns itself into forswearing and effects an imperious reversal of values: it becomes an irremediable condition. It is this duality that René analyzes in a famous passage: "I am always accused of aiming for more than I can possibly attain: alas, I am only seeking an unknown good that I am unable to renounce. Is it my fault if everywhere I turn I am hemmed in, if what is finite is for me worthless?"[125] This bewitching discontent is at bottom a negative version of the hopes and enthusiasms of philosophic Sensibility.

Sensibility, thus metamorphosed, means to accommodate Christian doctrines, in particular the doctrine of the Fall, which explains the contradictory situation of man, the disproportion between his desires and his nature. The Man of Sensibility was not unaware of this disproportion in the previous century. Rousseau warns him that "limitless desires prepare for him eternal privations."[126] Beneath the euphoria was a doubt against which he struggled and that the irresistible faith helped palliate. It is this doubt that the course of events caused to triumph: one had only to reverse the inner proportions of the mélange to make obvious the proposition that earthly happiness was impossible. The appeal to religion followed naturally. If one charges that contradiction and despair characterize the inmost part of human nature, if one explains the entire human condition by original sin and the Fall, as Chateaubriand does,[127] then one places oneself in the tradition of Pascal.[128] Thus it is hoped that the disenchanted sensibility of the survivors and the victims of the great crisis can be grounded theologically; modern melancholy assumes a Christian identity. This goes so far that a similar state is attributed to the church fathers as a source of their faith: "I feel that I lack something," says the young Jerome in the *Les*

Martyrs. "For a long time now a feeling of restlessness has refused to leave me in peace. . . . Could it not be that the cause of this uneasiness lies in the emptiness of our desires?" And Augustine answers him: "Like you I am tormented by a malaise whose cause I cannot discover."[129] It would be possible, I suppose, to recognize in such a state of discontent an authentic form of religious disposition, if the Christian advocate of melancholy himself seemed more sure of what he is saying. But he is himself considerably embarrassed at the idea of imposing his René as a Christian exemplar, and he arranges to have him quite sternly lectured by a priest. *Atala* and *René*, written before the author's conversion, were probably annexed to the *Génie* only by means of laborious revisions.

Chateaubriand tried several times to establish doctrinally Christians' title to melancholy. First, in 1800, in the *Lettre au citoyen Fontanes sur la 2ᵉ édition de l'ouvrage de Mme de Staël*: the Christian religion as a religion of exile and suffering is "essentially sensitive and melancholy"; persecutions and invasions have accentuated this characteristic in it from the beginning, and have contributed to making the monastery one of its fundamental creations: "a prodigious melancholy must have been the fruit of this monastic life; for melancholy is caused by the *vague des passions*."[130] The *vague des passions* is the subject of a famous passage of the *Génie*,[131] the very one that serves as an introduction to *René*, and where this passage of the *Lettre* to Fontanes is taken up once more and reworked: by contrasting earth and heaven, Christianity "creates in the heart a spring of present suffering and distant hopes from which flow endless reveries." But Chateaubriand commented once more upon the monastic institution in 1803 in his *Défense du Génie*, this time with more prudence, resigning himself to the distinction of reverie from faith, and accepting that there is a difference between the first Christian monks, on the one hand, and the turn-of-the-century traumatized imitators of Rousseauist literary characters, on the other: after the recluses of past times, fulfilled by God and overflowing with virtues, he says, we see today these "kinds of recluses, at once both passionate and philosophic, able neither to renounce the vices of this age nor to love it, who imagine that the hatred of men is a form of the elevation of genius, who renounce every duty human and divine, feed in some secluded place on vain illusions, and descend deeper and deeper into a proud misanthropy, which will lead them before long to madness and death."[132] Sermonizing aside, it is clear that the anthropocentric disposition of modern Sensibility, which remains intact through its various metamorphoses, changes the relation of man to God as it is implied by Christian faith. However much the marriage of melancholy and Christianity is celebrated, it is felt to be discordant. The *Génie du christianisme* no doubt seemed startling to more than one Christian, and the pragmatism that grounded the

truth of Catholic doctrines on their agreement with the charms of a reinterpreted Sensibility could be considered shocking. But circumstances were in
its favor, and the greater part of the literary counterrevolution embraced the
work, Bonald included.[133]

❧ *Ambiguities of the Counterrevolution*

The situation of a class whose privileges have been put to the test and that
desires to survive no doubt explains the movement of thought whose principal
themes we have just reviewed. After 1800, the aristocracy and the upper strata of
the old society as a whole developed a general critique of philosophical humanism, which we can view both as a spontaneous expression of disappointment
and as a judicious instrument in the attempt to retain social power: what better
antidotes to subversion are there than a religion of the beyond and disenchantment? But we risk omitting something essential from this analysis if we do not
add that the return to the past had to be adapted to modernity. In the new
version of Sensibility that includes these revived precedents, the characteristics
of yesterday's and tomorrow's humanist faith are only half effaced; they need
only a change of circumstances in order to reappear. A striking analysis of this
ambiguous and shifting state of affairs was offered at this very time and in a
spirit contrary to that of the counterrevolution by Shelley, when he wrote:

> Many of the most ardent and tender-hearted worshipers of public good have
> been morally ruined by what a partial glimpse of the events they deplored
> appeared to show as the melancholy desolation of all their cherished hopes.
> Hence gloom and misanthropy have become the characteristics of the age in
> which we live, the solace of a disappointment that unconsciously finds relief
> only in the willful exaggeration of its own despair. The influence has tainted
> the literature of the age with the hopelessness of the minds from which it
> flows. Metaphysics, and inquiries into moral and political science, have be-
> come little else than vain attempts to revive exploded superstitions or soph-
> isms . . . , calculated to lull the oppressors of mankind into a security of ever-
> lasting triumph. Our works of fiction and poetry have been overshadowed by
> the same infectious gloom. But mankind appear to me to be emerging from
> their trance. I am aware, methinks, of a slow, gradual, silent change.[134]

This change must indeed have been occurring, deep within these very minds.
Humanitarian romanticism emerged from the melancholia of 1800 and 1820
by a process of metamorphosis and ascent. The butterfly could already be divined in the chrysalis: "Those who went back to the past," writes Sainte-Beuve,
"headed there via unexpected pathways, threw themselves passionately into it,
dazzlingly, as if they were out to conquer the future."[135]

The thematic instability of the ideological counterrevolution and the way in which a will to return to the past led to irresistible borrowing from opposing doctrines are easily explained: the destruction of the old social structures made a return to a previous state of affairs chimerical, both in forms of thought and in institutions. A sort of instinct impelled counterrevolutionary thought toward notions of a precrisis past, but this reaction could be satisfactory only to what remained of the former privileged classes; it supposed that their privileges could be reestablished as they were before, but this was out of the question. Thoughts of a different sort were thus obliged to combine with the reflexive attitudes of the counterrevolution. The ruling class was henceforward composed of aristocrats who had survived the ordeal, accepting out of necessity the new social order, and a bourgeoisie with recently established prerogatives: both more than ever interested in defining a common order that transcended their conflicts and rivalries. In these conditions it is natural that modern values, even the principle of mutability and progress at the heart of the new society, were welcomed, even while arguments continued to be advanced against subversion. The primacy of sociological reality is manifest in imperatives of this sort. We can feel this in the ambiguous form that the Catholic victory cry takes on in the *Génie du christianisme*: "The degenerate world awaits a new preaching of the Gospel; Christianity is renewed, and emerges victorious from the most terrible assault hell has launched against it to date. Who knows whether what we took to be the fall of the Church is not the very thing that sets it back on its feet! It was perishing amidst wealth and peace; it no longer remembered the cross: the cross reappeared, and it will be saved"; or, better yet: "Evangelical genius is eminently favorable to liberty."[136] Everything the author later said about a Christianity reconciled to modern society already has its roots here;[137] the post-1824 Chateaubriand is consistent with the Chateaubriand of 1802, testifying to the same fundamental desire to combine past with future.[138]

The case of Lamennais likewise reveals in a striking fashion the philosophical fragility of the counterrevolution, invaded from the beginning by heterogeneous principles whose logical consequences later take effect as society resumes its course. Lamennais started from the catastrophic feeling that he was living in a ruined society, bereft as it were of its spiritual authority: it is this, visible in his earliest writings, that he essentially suffers from, and his every effort strives for the restoration of such a power in its plenitude, consistent with Catholic orthodoxy.[139] But the practical impossibility that this desire encounters quickly obliged him to come up with new ideas, despite the fact that he wished passionately to restore a former state of affairs. The idea of freedom of instruction—that is, of a Catholic instruction independent of the State, an idea that begins to appear in his writing in 1818[140] — is only a symptom of the necessity that obliges him to accept a modification in the form that spiritual authority takes. The alliance of State and Church according to the formula of prerevolutionary monarchical France seems intolerable as soon as the church's power is seen to be diminished without any visible means of overcoming this diminution. Something else must be founded to restore its ascendency. A theocratic ultramontanism first, and then, later, by a step that is contradictory only in appearance, a doctrine of the separation of Church and State, are announced as heroic remedies;[141] Lamennais goes so far as to propose a liberal password for the Catholic party's flag. Simultaneously, so as to exempt spiritual truths from discussion, the *Essai sur l'indifférence* claims to ground them in an order independent of man's will and critical reason, in accordance with a common practice of the counterrevolution.[142] But this order is embodied in universal tradition: that is, in the last analysis, in the experience of humanity: a dangerous expedient, one that had already tempted the Christian apologists of the previous century and that Bonald himself approved,[143] but by which everything is surrendered to the human race in order to recover an influence over it that has been lost. In this way, by combining the dogmatic sovereignty of the pope with a criterion of human, historic consent, it is suggested that the church imitate the menacing secular ministry and thereby oust it. On this slippery slope, Rome is asked to transform itself in order to conquer.[144] Animated at this time by a completely contrary spirit of immobility and resistance, the papacy condemned Lamennais before allowing itself to be convinced. Lamennais, seeing his suggestions rejected, was naturally led to disqualify the authority of the Roman Catholic Church and, becoming aware of the general movement with which his thought in fact allied him on the ground of fundamental principles, came to conceive of a radical metamorphosis of spiritual authority whose doctrine he spent the rest of his life redefining. This memorable case stands out from all others for its dramatic character and for the abruptness of the positions that were successively taken. But at bottom it reflects a widespread movement, as the broad literary sympathies it evoked testify.

The ideological fragility of the counterrevolution reveals itself in a particularly obvious way through the role that it felt obliged to accord to the new authority of secular intelligence, in areas that until now had been outside its domain. Infiltrated in spite of itself by the modern heresy, the counterrevolution lent an ear to its poorly converted ministers, and authorized their investiture. The God of the *Génie du christianisme* is secretly justified like that of the *Philosophes* — no longer by the moral conscience he sanctions as was generally the case for them, but by the emotions he inspires and the difficulties he renders charming: rediscovered spirituality takes on, significantly, an aesthetic form. All of heaven has become an exalted literature that the idea of God animates. This shows who is God's priest: the man of sensibility whose heart has been molded by his ordeals; the unsatisfied dreamer who sings of his desire; the modern psalmist who can write: "The human heart wants more than it is capable of; above all it longs to admire; it contains within itself an élan toward an unknown beauty, for which it was created from the beginning."[145] An aesthetic defense of religion consecrates the poet, the designated priest of the beautiful. The prudent Joubert escapes from this logic no more than his friend: "What does the poet do? By means of certain gleams, he purges and empties the forms of matter, and makes us see the universe as it is in the thought of God himself."[146] By maintaining and reinforcing the spiritual privilege of the Poet while simultaneously denouncing the philosophic Man of Letters, the counterrevolutionary thought of the beginning of the nineteenth century no doubt bowed to the contemporary in spite of itself. It repressed the greatest danger, but in doing so trusted the defense to a modern power that it was apparently impossible not to acknowledge. Bonald acknowledges: "[L]iterature has become more imposing; it has become the support or the scourge of society." It is therefore necessary to work so that literature uphold society, to subordinate this power whose existence can no longer be denied: writers, he preaches, "are public functionaries in the full meaning of this word"; let literature therefore be "a militia devoted to combatting false doctrines," "a profession within society, and not a plot against society."[147] But literature, whose importance is thus acknowledged, is what is least inclined to resist the seductions of the present, to which it owes its elevation; it is precisely the instrument of renovation and adaptation. Why would it accept the proposed social role, to be passive and subordinated to what belongs to the past? Chateaubriand, even while advising writers to divest themselves "of the vainglory and the exaggerated pretensions that made them unbearable during the last century,"[148] quickly came to understand that something important and irreversible had occurred: "Other times, other ways," he announces:

> heirs to a long sequence of peaceful years, our predecessors could indulge themselves in purely academic discussions, which proved their talent less than they proved their good fortune. But we, pitiful remains of a great shipwreck, we no longer have what is needed to appreciate a calm so complete. Our ideas and our minds have taken a different course. In us the man has replaced the academician: by stripping literature of the futile character it can have, we no longer view it except through our powerful memories and the experience of our adversity. What! after a revolution that made us race through the events of several centuries in a few years, it is proposed to forbid all moral reflection to writers!

New times have elevated the status of literature, and writers, even royalist and Christian writers, now have a grander conception of themselves; their profession is no longer chiefly concerned with the art of pleasing; they will display at the end of their days "a brow furrowed by lengthy labors, by grave thoughts, and, often, those manly sufferings that augment human greatness." Thus he who sings of the ancient beliefs confirms something gloriously new; and the social eminence of the role he proclaims naturally excludes all subjection: "Is liberty not the greatest of goods and the first of man's needs? It sets genius ablaze, it raises up the heart, it is as necessary to a friend of the Muses as the air he breathes. . . . Literature, which speaks a universal language, languishes and dies when put in chains."[149] By a logic as rectilinear as Bonald's and more imperious than his, we are at the antipodes of the writer-functionary that he imagined. The type of the Poet furnishes a compromise: it implies, as is appropriate in a time of peril and apprehension, a grave style, a reference to destinies dictated from on high, whose law humanity must accept, even as it breaks the bonds of servitude. Poets thus take the place of philosophers, which must on all accounts be filled. Poets inherit the attributes of philosophers up to a certain point: their song teaches the great truths of the human condition, as well as the paths that guide humanity through its history. Preaching to achieve the salvation of society, they are necessarily situated above it and in the lead. For a duke and peer just as for a bourgeois, this poetic preachment is without a doubt a strange, but at the same time a convenient thing: it risks, however, overshooting the mark, which indeed it did not fail to do.

❧ Pierre-Simon Ballanche

In this entire intellectual family, no one, perhaps, made himself the interpreter of the common need with as much gravity and depth as did Ballanche. In his work, the ambiguity of the counterrevolutionary ideology does not produce a more or less accentuated or heartfelt hesitation, as it does in other writers. Straightaway he claimed to formulate the law of change at the same time as the law of what endures, the one being inseparable from the other. The poetry of the past and the annunciation of the future are fused in his work, which in this sense we can call the soul of French romanticism.

His point of departure, around 1800, was approximately the same as Chateaubriand's. The similarities between *Du sentiment considéré dans ses rapports avec la littérature et les arts*,[150] his first work, and the *Génie du christianisme*, which appeared about the same time, have often been remarked upon. Bernardin's inheritance can in any case also be seen there. Ballanche acknowledges his influence and presents himself as someone continuing his line of thought.[151] The aim of his book is to demonstrate that sentiment is the origin of the arts and of ethics; but his way of conceptualizing sentiment reflects the experience in Lyons of the siege and the Terror, which he lived through during his adolescence;[152] significantly, he repudiates Rousseau, who, rather than limiting himself to sentiment, "wanted the sanction of prideful reason";[153] and what he, like Chateaubriand, means by pure sentiment is desire divorced from the real, deprived of its object by the Fall[154] and aspiring to regain the celestial homeland.[155] This fateful separation, with, as a response, a sorrowful and hopeless sanctification of suffering, is Ballanche's essential truth and his point of departure: through Greek mythology, the whole of his first great composition, *Antigone*,[156] puts in play these themes of sacrifice, impossible happiness, and eventual consolation. His funereally toned spiritualism thus mingled in a curious fashion the experience of his own sentimental misfortune and the lessons of the recent social cataclysm. When he writes in his *Fragments*, apropos of his unhappy love affair with Bertille d'Avèze: "Only suffering matters in life, and nothing is real except tears," when he sees in the forced refusal of Bertille "a mystery of misfortune," he prefigures his Antigone, and his Antigone herself is in his eyes the type of the Dauphine, survivor of the royal family and symbol of the collective ordeal.[157] All his work reflects this initial discovery: "Social life is a state of suffering, like human life in general."[158] It is not by chance that Orpheus is his second great hero: the myth of Eurydice lost and Orpheus's destiny signifies to us that "happiness is not the goal of the human race."[159] Thus, even more profoundly than Chateaubriand, Ballanche lived through the anxious mutation of sensibility at the point where the France of old becomes *la nouvelle France*. But their tandem careers are parallel in this also, that for both of them literature emerges from the religious metamorphoses of sentiment with enhanced prestige.[160]

According to Ballanche, the proper function of literature — and of the literature of Ballanche — one that official religion does not undertake, consists in a mediation between past and future, a sacerdotal mediation, one could say, or, rather, parasacerdotal, that accompanies and reinforces, with both reverence and independence, the teaching of the traditional priesthood: Ballanche has thought through all the themes of conservation and permanence in the light of change. Thus he based everything on a doctrine of the Fall, but he did so while making it one with a doctrine of the rehabilitation of the human race, implicit according to him in the very advent of Christianity: "Let us not forget that the dogma of fallen humanity must not be separated from that of rehabilitation, and that the Mediator has clothed himself in the human frame so that human nature might consent to rehabilitation."[161] So that "the fertile dogma of fallen humanity and rehabilitation produces the perpetual law of evolution and progress."[162]

Similarly, Ballanche affirmed, in accordance with the counterrevolution, the primacy of society over the individual, but in order to better introduce, beyond individual wills, the inevitability of the palingeneses or successive regenerations of the social body: "The progressive advance of the human spirit is independent of man himself."[163] This advance carries religion with it: Ballanche, who very reverently declares Christianity to be immutable, insists just as much that it realize its potential, or develop progressively; he asks for "a development of Christianity, lest it perish."[164] He does not doubt that "an age of crisis for society, a new era of the human spirit" has arrived; he notes with regret that "priests have not stopped representing the former social order" in the eyes of the French; in religion, he advises against "reerecting what no longer exists" and only believes Christianity to be eternally alive because, in our time, "the genius of Christianity has become the genius of society."[165] He has no objection to wearing mourning for a social order that has been destroyed: "Let us not forget that the entire human race also regrets a lost homeland. Our eyes are still fixed on the angel who guards with a sword of flame the entrance to the land of delights where we once lived, and from which we have been exiled. But it often happens that that great groaning, that general groaning of the human race, makes itself heard more clearly. That is when doctrines end, and when other doctrines begin."[166] Thus for him regret is not a wish for a Restoration; it is a Wait in anguished suspense between two worlds: at the time, this was a frequent formula, repeated on all sides till the reign of Louis-Philippe, and that, in all of Ballanche's work, has the tone of hope in the very heart of distress.

Ballanche adhered from the first to a doctrine that situated truth in universal religious tradition. He often seems to embrace this doctrine — capable of lending itself to every tendency, from the most orthodox to the most open-ended — in the manner of Joseph de Maistre or the early Lamennais. Toward the end of the Restoration, he again declares that these two men "truly advanced genuine discussion more than all the philosophers of our time put together; it was they who laid out the true ground for the lists where the combat must take place."[167] They laid out the problem indeed, but did they solve it? Instead of their apostleship of the past, Ballanche offered the law of palingenetic progress, according to which the tradition is at once fidelity and change;[168] his work is a progressivist version of the basic doctrines of the counterrevolution, one that means to overthrow and inherit their place and that deploys considerable dialectical and inspirational resources to that end. If, in the matter of universal traditions, he prefers a theosophical perspective to one that is in strict accord with Christian theologians, this is because a theosophical perspective allows him greater access to present and future palingeneses. Having gone beyond the traditional Christian framework, Ballanche's theosophy met with great success, and commentators have been quite right to insist upon this aspect of his thought.[169] But because he adhered to no particular school or sect, because he declared himself till the end faithful to Christianity as a definitive revelation (susceptible to progressive realization, but not subject to revocation),[170] because, finally, he is as much a creative writer and poet as a doctrinal writer in his relation to his own ideas, what he arrives at in the end, with however much theosophy, is that vast romantic heterodoxy that few writers of his and the following generation escaped: it grafts onto a Christian trunk a literature of religious synthesis, human progress, and universal redemption, animated by a limitless faith in the destiny of man at the center of the universe.[171] Ballanche certainly adopted the ideas of counterrevolutionary philosophy on the origin and role of language. Divinity, the Word, and Tradition remain closely linked in his eyes. He believes language to have issued originally "from an obscure and mysterious tradition, which goes back to the very origin of the world, but of which society has always been the storehouse."[172] But he specifies at once that thought in its development separated itself from language, whose mission is henceforth accomplished: the time of "traditional language" is over; maintenance of the "magistrature of thought" can henceforth be assured only by an emancipated intelligence:[173] "The new power of opinion, which indeed issues from such a state of affairs . . . , can in any case very well be considered a sort of living language that renews itself constantly without going through the long channels of the various traditions."[174] Ballanche offered an apology for esoteric doctrines and practices in the conduct of peoples, for the "doctrine of ordeals and discretion,"[175] but he believed that the veil was lifting progressively and that the time had come to lift it altogether. He repeats this endlessly, and has his expositor of sacred mysteries say to the visitor in the City of Expiations: "Christianity is the promulgation of every dogma and every truth. You need promise nothing, and you are not secretly bound to any law."[176]

He professed from the beginning the idea that the French Revolution possessed a divine significance. This idea, widespread in counterrevolutionary literature, is of all ideas the most ambiguous. The sufferings caused by the crisis are a factual matter; the notion of an ordeal evokes, beyond matters of fact, the question of meaning — but which meaning? God's design can favor the past just as well as it can favor the future. By evoking such a design, one has merely excluded a purely human philosophy of history; but belief that human events are divinely governed offers to speculation two different directions: tradition, or renewal. The idea is ambiguous in Joseph de Maistre himself, when he says: "If Providence erases, it is doubtless in order to write";[177] it goes from one extreme to the other in the course of Lamennais's career: he first interprets the Revolution as "a great and terrible lesson" given by God to the human race, later evoked a "law of destruction, indispensable for preparing future renewal," and finally saluted the renewal to be found in the revolution that "for the past fifty years has been at work in Europe" and greets it with sympathy as a development of Christianity.[178] For Ballanche, the ordeal is always oriented toward the future; the pain it implies is not a punishment, but the price of an initiation, it being taken for granted that this price must be paid. He interprets the entire crisis of French society since the philosophic eighteenth century and the Revolution[179] as a continual progress in which the Restoration continues the tragic years and develops their fruit: "The sanction that the Restoration brought to the Revolution was for the French people and also for me an immense initiation. The ordeal had not been understood till then; and the genius of the Restoration was in its turn not at first recognized."[180] In practical terms, all Ballanche's dialectics serve to integrate events into a providential vision that excludes the secular doctrine of the sovereignty of the people and also excludes from the social contract all concrete political notions derived from that doctrine: the necessity of the consent of the governed as a condition of legitimate government[181] and, above all, the ever widening enlargement of social rights for the masses, who till now have been held in tutelage or who have been kept away from such questions. Orpheus incarnated one of the stages of the "plebeianism" that is history's formula. The secessions and victories of the Roman plebs constituted another stage.[182] Christianity, given the virtualities that it possesses for a final realization, is to be found at the end of this development, for it is "the eminently plebeian religion, the true religion of humanity."[183]

Ballanche himself tells us that he was the Janus of a progressivist counterrevolution,[184] and this is also corroborated by the reticent evaluations of his work by writers of the two opposing camps; *Le Conservateur* deplores "his affection for the present time," and the *Revue encyclopédique* considers him a reactionary. Joseph de Maistre, who believed he recognized in him one after his own heart, hoped that one day they would laugh together at his errors, but that day would never come.[185] Yet Ballanche's position as a mediator between past and future implies the consciousness of a mission. For it is a mission to teach the filiation of eras, and the link that unites the old forms of the sacred to the new laws of the human community. And this mission has not fallen to the official church, however reverently Ballanche feels toward it, but to an inspired secular writer, at once thinker and poet. The secular ministry conceived of by the writers of the eighteenth century finds its fulfillment in such a figure, metamorphosed by the revolutionary crisis and by the reaction to it. This new figure will dominate the entire romantic era; Ballanche, before anyone else, embodied it.

From his very first publication, his thought, reflecting on the type of the writer as a guide for humanity, focused on the idea of a mission linked to the divine order. The principal suggestions emanate from the image of the primitive poet, whose power we already know: "The founders of the earliest societies," he writes, "were musician-poets."[186] This founding image would persist in all his work, but what is most noteworthy is that it appears at the same time as a legitimating legendary memory and, as it were, an ideal present. It is not without some embarrassment that Ballanche's progressivism embraces this equation of the primitive and the present; he is forced to admit, as inseparable from the growth of the human race and the progress of discursive thought, a certain disenchantment in our vision of the universe: poetry, which formerly entered "into intimacy with things," has ceased to possess this privilege;[187] this art, "which in the beginning was the expression of language as it was handed down," saw itself abandoned by music and reduced to versification; in order to be reborn, it is taking refuge today in prose.[188] In one way or another, however, poetry will return to honor, "for in the end this noble exile must one day recover her heritage."[189] Poetry is eternal, like the secrets of creation that it is her mission to interpret: "Now, I know, poetry seems to be exiled from society: sooner or later she will recover her demesne, sooner or later we shall once again hark to the sounds that fall from the lyre of poets. . . . God and his attributes, man and his faculties will always remain mysterious objects; the foundations of every society too will ever evade the indiscreet light of human reason."[190] Poetry has retained the unique power of causing us to grasp the deeper character of things:

A place, like each individual man, is marked with a distinctive sign, bears what we might call a physiognomic ensemble, which distinguishes it from all others. This is what it is given to poets to see and to make visible to others. . . . Our present languages are like our names; they have conventional meanings only; they lack meanings that are essential and that derive from their peculiar energy. But there always remains a trace, which is nonetheless real for its being worn away by time: without it, our languages would be unsuited for poetry.[191]

In fact, the essential virtue of poetic language subsists in latency, and all that is needed is for this virtue to revive: "Poetry must return to its origins, it must come back to what it was at the beginning."[192] However much Ballanche takes into account the difference of eras, it happens that when speaking of the primitive poet he evokes the eternal Poet, whom the present time summons: "Poetry is primitive speech, revealed to man. It is the history of man, the summary of his relations with God, with higher intelligences, with his peers, in the present, in the past, in the future, in time and outside of time. The poet dominates from on high the era in which he lives, and floods it with light: the future too is in his thought; he embraces in a single viewpoint every human generation, and the intimate cause of events that lies in the secrets of Providence."[193] Such a portrait of the Poet, drawn at a time when poetry had not yet given any noteworthy sign of renewal in France, and yet so strikingly anticipatory of the type that the entire romantic generation would bring to life, may appear surprising. In this, Ballanche was prophetic — that is, he perceived, by a premonitory intuition, the need that his time was preparing to answer.

It is not surprising to find that in Ballanche, as in so many of his predecessors, a theory of language is at the source of his poetics, nor that the ontological privilege of primitive languages tends to appear in his thought as the permanent attribute of human speech: "To name a thing, at the moment when the power that confers the faculty of naming is at its fullness, is to know the essence of that thing. . . . The power to name is thus in some sort a participation in creation."[194] What Ballanche says of the primitive "revelation of speech" can pass for a definition of the gift of poetry, as it exists at all times: it is "the intuition of necessary truths, the faculty of penetrating the essence of beings and things, so as to dictate names: divine insufflation in order to transmit movement to sensation and thought"; it is "the human self awakening in the presence of the outside world"; in brief, "the infinite, or the spontaneous, or intuition, or the primitive form of human intelligence, or speech."[195] Speech and poetry are one for Ballanche's Orpheus because of the symbolic nature of the word:

> Are the objects of nature — trees, flowers, clouds, smells, light, winds — the emblems whose explanation man seeks, after having lost it? And ought he not find that explanation in language, an unending revelation, an eternal chain all of whose interconnected links are indestructible traditions. . . . Is there a universal harmony all of whose chords man can feel, all of whose laws he can divine? . . . One day, as I soared in the upper regions of the spirit, I thought I saw a great light envelop nature in its immensity, and deeply illuminate all things. My sight was not quick enough, my thought was not active enough to be everywhere at once during an indivisible instant. I nevertheless had a genuine feeling, albeit vague and undefinable, of the essence and the connectedness of everything that exists. I heard then a sound, but an intellectual one, and that sound seemed to me to be the speaking of the light. I inquired within myself, and even as I did so the light answered in me, I cannot tell how such a conversation continued, or what was its shape; but everything has remained in the depths of my soul, just as the spark remains hidden in the veins of a stone until the moment when a blow sends if forth. I am certain that every time I need to consult the oracle, I shall find it once again; it will not refuse to answer me, it will not deceive me.[196]

The idea of a universal and analogical harmony in the universe has deep roots, as we have seen. Ballanche often expressed it in its most classical form: "The material world is an emblem, a hieroglyph of the spiritual world,"[197] it being understood that the function of poetry, which is charged with the primordial virtues of language, is to cause us to gain access to this symbolism of the universe; indeed, "our poetry is a symbol, and this is what all true poetry should be."[198] This poetics of the symbol is henceforth inseparable from speculations on the modern ministry of the poet. In fact, it founds this ministry, making of poetry a privileged mode of knowing God and the world. But his familiarity with symbols really only consecrates the poet because it presupposes in him, beyond an understanding of relations with the universe, an additional intuition of the totality of being, which is, as we have seen in Orpheus, his highest title, his highest claim, a capacity for full access at the level of the divine that is the living source of his authority.

Ballanche believed so strongly that the type of the poet of revelation was current that he sought examples in his own society in order to announce them to the age. First, Chateaubriand, "he who, born on the border of two epochs, sums up in himself and reflects utterly this memorable palingenetic age of humanity," "our great poet, our immense poet," "the Orpheus of the new time, the man with two voices that fuse into a single tongue."[199] Lamennais, too, in whom Ballanche sees "a powerfully assimilative genius" — that is to say, embodying in his language a decisive initiation of humanity — or, again, "the priest of the days of transformation."[200] Byron, the type in his eyes of the two great inspirations that have dominated poetry "since poets received the mission of being the peoples' seers": a rebel at first, then redeeming himself by his sacrifice to the Greek cause — doubtless prompted by some "advice from on high" — from the guilt of that initial rebellion, for Ballanche he is "the great poet of expiation."[201] Finally, Lamartine, who understood the movement of the human spirit and the necessary alliance of the genius of the past with the literature of the future: "M. de Lamartine is the poetic expression of this presentiment."[202]

All these canonizations presume a singular authority in him who pronounces them. And, indeed, of all contemporary hierophants, he who deserves to be named first is beyond any doubt Pierre-Simon Ballanche. Behind the poet-priest of earliest times we find his modern advocate officiating; Orpheus, born to unknown parents and promoter of a plebeianist initiation, reflects the thinker who under Louis XVIII interprets providentially the initiations that overwhelmed aristocratic and monarchical France. Thamyris, Orpheus's disciple, charged by the Egyptian priesthood with communicating to Evander the ideas needed for the foundation of the city of Rome, is speaking as much of Ballanche as of his master when he says: "Poets too are the founders of nations; but only those who are instructed in the deep mysteries of moral and political science."[203] And does Eurydice's father, Talaon, who heard Orpheus complain that he owned no land and who consoled him by placing the poet's claim ahead of landed property, define the mind's status in primitive times or in the society in which Ballanche lived, where the feudal rights and obligations of landed property were still recognized? "Orpheus, learn that the lyre is the inalienable sign of property in the celestial domain, which is the type and pledge of property in the earthly realm. Thus you are endowed with the most distinguished property, without which the other kind would not exist."[204] But Ballanche does not always speak by way of an interposed character, whether modern or legendary. "Magna Graecia," he writes from Naples in 1824, "is the primitive homeland of this poetic philosophy, which we can no longer feel but that I have a calling to restore. It now seems to me that I have a destiny to accomplish."[205] He sometimes adopts a haughtier tone: "Perhaps God had great purposes in mind for me, since he inspired me with such ideas."[206] Better yet: "That am I, I am the hermit of Patmos. I know I am the spokesperson of the thoughts and feelings of a tribe dispersed throughout the world, a tribe that is at this moment the elite of the human race, a tribe that is the civilizing power, and that, because the future has been promised to it, excites a thousand hatreds and a thousand suspicions. This is what I know, what I experience, what I see."[207]

On the whole, one may say that Ballanche's profound conviction of being an initiator and seer expressed itself rather discreetly in his work.[208] But the personal mark that distinguishes religious innovators is confirmed there by another sign. His model was Dante, and he believed that he too could name a Beatrice who procured his access to celestial glories. In 1813, Canova, in whose home Mme Récamier had resided during her visit to Italy, "sought in Juliette's features" — it is Chateaubriand who tells us this — "the type of the Beatrice that he dreamed of doing one day."[209] There exists in fact a bust of Mme Récamier as Beatrice by Canova.[210] Ballanche remembers this homage of the sculptor, who rendered visible in the face of the new Beatrice the spirit of the former, and created for poetry and art "a new type of pure and virginal beauty"; then comes a page that is unique in his work, where the lady of his thoughts is mystically transfigured: "I address myself then to the one who has been seen as a vivid apparition of Beatrice. May she encourage me with her smile, with that serious smile of love and grace, expressing at the same time confidence and pity for the painfulness of the ordeal, for the troubles of an exile that must come to an end; sweet, serene omen, where we can already read the certitude of our infinite hopes, the greatness of our final destinies!"[211] In this transfiguration, so oddly fervent, the penchant of the romantic heresy for allying a feminine principle to the sacred is announced; the Juliette of Ballanche, due allowance being made for the peculiar discretion of her adorer, anticipates the Woman of the Saint-Simonians and the Clotilde of Auguste Comte.

Ballanche was not a poet, properly speaking. Like so many royalists, however, he saw in the ordeals of the Revolution a source of renewal for the spirit of poetry. His elegy on the public misfortunes was written in *L'Homme sans nom*, in which he depicts a member of the assembly who had voted for the execution of the king; retired in an Alpine valley, expiating his sins, he redeems himself and to a certain extent justifies himself in conformity with the progressivist doctrine of suffering that is Ballanche's own formula.[212] He gave the title of *Elégie* to a sort of prose poem on the assassination of the duc de Berry that is both a royalist lamentation and a warning to the fanatics of the past.[213] And he planned to conclude his most immense work with an *Elégie* that would have been, he tells us, "the funeral song of a dying society."[214] In one sense his entire work is an ambiguous elegy — a statement of regret and hope — on the destinies of the human race, elaborated in response to the crisis of contemporary French society.

However, he concurrently gave to the same material the form of a mystical, fabulous narration: *Antigone*, then *Orphée*, testify to this. But these partial tales, despite whatever symbolic or contemporary resonance he gives them, do not seem to be enough for him. He tried on several occasions to sketch through his works as a whole a singular construction embracing the history of humanity. In 1827, he imagines under the general title of *Palingénésie sociale* a vast composition including the *Prolégomènes*, *Orphée*, a *Formule générale de l'histoire de tous les peuples appliquée à l'histoire du peuple romain*, the *Ville des expiations*, and the final *Elégie*:[215] it is this philosophico-poetic epic of the past, present, and future that he places under the invocation of Juliette Récamier in the dedication of the *Prolégomènes*. For a long time he had seen in the epics of various peoples "the very history of the eras of the human spirit," and regretted that "the epic cycle of high Antiquity" had not come down to us in its entirety. He also regretted that modern peoples had not "conceived of the epic to its full extent, and . . . achieved an epic cycle enlightened by revelation," thanks to which we would have "the true history of the human race,"[216] and also its spiritual definition, for "the content of this definitive epic is nothing but the very content of universal religion."[217] The work that Ballanche envisions beginning in the first years of the Restoration will be, in its way, that poem of humanity.[218] He imagined it in abbreviated form as a sort of series of inspired tableaux, in his *Vision d'Hébal*, which begins before the creation and concludes with the end of the world. But it is above all his entire corpus that he dreamed of organizing in accordance with this plan: in 1836, he is busy working out a new comprehensive design, of which the *Ville des expiations* seems to have become the framework.[219]

Lyrical meditations born of the collective ordeals of the present and spiritual epics in symbolic form embracing the entire cycle of the ages—these are the two characteristic forms, as we have seen and shall see again, that the poetry of the Restoration adopts. Ballanche assists powerfully in laying out its paths—paths that clearly indicate his fundamental allegiance, but he widens them and is already orienting them toward the future. From the point of view of the re-creation of literary *genres* that are in accord with the movement of society and the new position of writers, his work is richer than Chateaubriand's, which in this respect gives us only a limited and outmoded type of epic in *Les Martyrs*.[220] It is not a question of comparing the two men. Chateaubriand, setting aside the superiority of his genius, brought to the literature of the new times something very different from Ballanche: the magnificent creation of his own personage as an inexhaustible type of the modern literary spirit; his intuition of the vital needs of the public, productive of motifs, evocations, and formulas destined to leave their imprint on the century; and, finally, the invention of a language virtually unknown till him, created with a view to suggestion and symbol and henceforth impossible to forget. But those who choose to read or reread Ballanche will find that in his interminable palingenetic discourse there is lacking neither the modern depth of language nor a certain unique quality of feeling that combines suffering and mystery, regret, waiting, and limitless hope—a quality that was communicated after him to the very breath of the poetic prophets of romanticism.

❧ *First Appearance of the Poet: Lamartine's Beginnings*

The new ideas developed by the counterrevolution appeared first in doctrinal writings or prose creations. It was even believed that poetic prose would from now on be the medium of inspired writers. Chateaubriand began to write at the beginning of the century. Ballanche became known between the First Empire and the Restoration. The *Méditations poétiques* only appeared in 1820. In order for poetry to be reborn, it was not only ideas and feelings that had to be transformed; poetry had to deal with forms, which are more resistant to change, and seemed eternal due to their very emptiness of content: an ode, an elegy, an epistle supposed no particular worldview, rather only a type of subject, a tone, a style, a certain verse form. Now, when Lamartine appeared, it was precisely a question of nourishing poetry with a graver subject matter, continuing the attempts of the eighteenth century to dignify it by allying it with religious and great subjects, and making it participate in the century's sufferings. At first, from 1810 to 1816, Lamartine wrote elegies that were essentially no different from the style and peculiar themes of this genre in the eighteenth century, or so we suspect from what we can read of them;[221] he also wrote, about the same time, odes that were classical in appearance, and epistles like those written during the preceding two hundred years.[222] His originality is not so much in having progressively introduced the thoughts and style of the new religious sensibility into these traditional forms; it is, rather, even while working in the existing poetic genres, to have finally erased the boundaries between them and mixed their tones in the flexible and multiform genre of the *méditation*. The very word tells the nature of the transformation: henceforth, poets think; they are the heirs to the *philosophe* and emulators of the theologian, even while speaking of their love affairs: "he has felt," proclaims his publisher, "that the time of empty fictions is over; that it was in the heart of eternal Truth that poetry should henceforth seek her inspirations."[223] It is understandable that a new poetic instrument was needed to maintain this claim.

Lamartine was neither ignorant nor disdainful of the tradition of sacred poetry handed down by the preceding century. He began around 1812 and finished in 1818 a tragedy about *Saül*, in which appear lyrical songs imitated from several psalms.[224] In 1819/1820 he wrote a dithyramb dedicated to Genoude,[225] which he entitled "La Poésie sacrée" and published in his *Méditations*, and in which, to illustrate the excellence of this poetic formula, he gives several successive examples: A Genesis, free paraphrases of Job, Isaiah, Ezekiel, Jeremiah, and, to conclude, an annunciation of the advent of Christ according to Saint Luke; some of the sacred texts that inspired him are part of that sort of poetic florilegium of Scripture that the religious poets of preceding eras had implicitly constituted.[226] Lamartine used Genoude's translations, which he praised at the same time as the originals; following in the train of a long line of critics, he praises the "character of the poetry of the earlier ages, and especially the sublime poetry of the Hebrews."[227] It is obvious that in Lamartine's work a modern Christian poetry is added to the scriptural paraphrases, as was the case with those who preceded him: "Le Chrétien mourant," "La Semaine sainte à la Roche-Guyon," probably "Le Crucifix" are written at about the same time.

Christian inspiration then went hand in hand with the idea of a general contrition coming after crimes and ordeals. When it wishes to define itself on the spiritual plane, this is how the Restoration sees itself, and the Poet is of some use to it by being able to sketch such a portrait of the period. It is to this endeavor that Lamartine contributed in his beginnings, and sometimes in an immoderate fashion. The themes and the spirit of the counterrevolution can be easily recognized in his first collection. He hymns Genius in the person of Bonald, whom he compares to Moses on Mount Sinai.[228] He shames the French for the decline of their nation from the century of Louis XIV to the following century, and for poetry's ruin, exiled by science:

Où sont-ils, ces jours où la France,
A la tête des nations,
Se levait comme un astre immense
Inondant tout de ses rayons?
Parmi nos siècles, siècle unique,
De quel cortège magnifique
La gloire composait ta cour!

. . . .

Mais, ô déclin! quel souffle aride
De notre âge a séché les fleurs?
Eh quoi! le lourd compas d'Euclide
Etouffe nos arts enchanteurs!
Elans de l'âme et du génie!
Des calculs la froide manie
Chez nos pères vous remplaça:
Ils posèrent sur la nature
Le doigt glacé qui la mesure,
Et la nature se glaça!

Et toi, prêtresse de la terre,
Vierge du Pinde ou de Sion,
Tu fuis ce globe de matière,
Privé de ton dernier rayon.
Ton souffle divin se retire
De ces coeurs flétris, que la lyre
N'émeut plus de ses sons touchants![229]

[Where are they, those days when France,
In the vanguard of the nations,
Rose like an immense star
Flooding everything with her light?
O age unparalleled among all ages,
With what a magnificent cortege
Glory arrayed your court!

. . . .

But, o decline! what arid breath
Of our age has withered the flowers?
What! Euclid's heavy compass
Stifles enchanting arts?
Elans of soul and genius!
The cold craze for calculation
Has replaced you among our fathers:
On nature they laid
An icy measuring finger,
And nature froze!

And you, priestess of the earth,
Virgin of Pindus or of Zion,
You flee this globe of matter,
Stripped of your last ray.
Your divine inspiration recedes
From those withered hearts, which the lyre
No longer moves by its touching sounds!]

But these are merely the harmonics of a more fundamental theme, that of the crime and the necessary expiation of the French:

Peuple! des crimes de tes pères
Le Ciel punissant tes enfants
De châtiments héréditaires
Accablera leurs descendants!
Jusqu'à ce qu'une main propice
Relève l'auguste édifice
Par qui la terre touche aux cieux,
Et que le zèle et la prière
Dissipent l'indigne poussière
Qui couvre l'image des dieux!

. . . .

Pleurons donc, enfants de nos pères!
Pleurons, de deuil couvrons nos fronts![230]

[People! for the crimes of your fathers,
Heaven, punishing your children,
With hereditary punishments
Will overwhelm their descendents!
Until a propitious hand
Builds again the august edifice

By which the earth touches the sky,
Till zeal and prayer
Sweep away the unworthy dust
That covers the image of the gods!

.   .   .   .

Let us weep then, children of our fathers!
Let us weep, let us cover our brows with mourning!]

What we do not perceive in the current version of this poem, entitled "Ode," is the supernatural authority by virtue of which in the original text, entitled "Ode aux Français," the poet dedicated the French to penitence. Gone are three initial stanzas, which painted enthusiasm — that is, inspiration swooping down on the poet from heaven like the eagle upon Ganymede and threatening to strike him down with lightning bolts; he attempts to resist this violent election, but in vain:

Mais en vain . . . déjà fuit la terre,
Mes yeux n'ont plus rien de mortel!
Déjà dans la céleste sphère
J'assiste au conseil éternel!
Aux yeux des Parques étonnées,
J'arrache aux mains des destinées
Les clés du terrible avenir!
Et ce luth, fécond en miracles,
Dont les accents sont des oracles
Entre mes mains va retentir.[231]

[But in vain . . . already the earth disappears,
My eyes no longer have anything mortal about them!
Already in the celestial sphere
I attend the eternal council!
Before the eyes of the astonished Fates,
I snatch from the hands of destiny
The keys of the terrible future!
And the mirific lute
Whose notes are oracles
Will sound in my hands.]

The terrible apostrophe to the French that followed was the prophetic oracle dictated to the poet by the divine council. Thus the philosophy of the counterrevolution allied itself naturally with the idea of poetic ministry.

A contemporary of Lamartine's, who felt himself to be more or less in the same spiritual vicinity, later told how the poet recited his verses at the time of the *Méditations*: "He spoke them like a prophet on his tripod: inspiration gave him some indefinable quality of the supernatural."[232] This inspired attitude was the one engravers gave to poets of the time,[233] who were the successors in their prints to the heroes of sensibility of the preceding century. We have seen how the legacy of Sentiment had changed its character while being handed down during a tragic era. Lamartine continues Chateaubriand in this respect. What distinguishes him is the new place he gives to the love of woman in the alloy of Sensibility and Religion: the poem "L'Immortalité," written in 1817, refutes the atheist by evoking the duos of the poet and his beloved. It is this alliance of heaven and earthly loves that above all defined Lamartine's poetry when it appeared: in "L'Isolement," where the lost beloved and the sovereign good are as it were mingled together ("what I so much wept for," "what I so much searched for," "what I so much dreamed of"—these successive versions make the scale wobble between the feminine side and the celestial side[234]); in "Souvenir," where the lover, transfigured by death, appears as all the symbols of the infinite and the divine. It is hard to decide whether this type of spiritual elegy was entirely the result of a personal experience, whether we owe this decisive invention to the death of Julie Charles, who, almost as soon as she was loved, perished and was inaccessible anywhere but in the beyond. Before her death, Lamartine had at least had an intimation of the genre;[235] it sprang up naturally at this disenchanted and edifying turning point in the development of Sensibility; it leads to the confusion of prayer to God and the fervor of earthly love, with everything "redemptive"—and, from the Christian point of view, dangerous—that there is in this confusion.[236]

More generally, Lamartine's religion resonates with the themes of spiritualized Sensibility. In the poem on *L'Homme*, addressed to Byron in 1819, he communes with the English poet in a moment of discontent; even while catechizing him, he communes with him in an experience of dissatisfaction:

Malheur à qui du fond de l'exil de la vie
Entendit ces concerts d'un monde qu'il envie!
Du nectar idéal sitôt qu'elle a goûté,
La nature répugne à la réalité:
Dans le sein du possible en songe elle s'élance;
Le réel est étroit, le possible est immense;

. . . .

Hélas! tel fut ton sort, telle est ma destinée.
J'ai vidé comme toi la coupe empoisonnée.

[Cursed is he who from the depths of life's exile
Heard the harmonies of a world for which he yearns!
As soon as she has tasted of the ideal nectar,
Nature feels loathing for reality:
In a dream she soars into the heart of what may be;
The real is narrow, the possible is immense;

. . . .

Alas! such was your fate, such is my destiny.
Like you I have drained the poisoned cup.]

A few verses earlier, he had reduced the insoluble conflict to Christian theological terms:

Borné dans sa nature, infini dans ses voeux,
L'homme est un dieu tombé qui se souvient des cieux.

[Limited in his nature, infinite in his desires,
Man is a fallen god who remembers heaven.]

The expression "a god" is only linguistic license; it is more serious to go on to wonder, as he does, whether the Eden that is so strongly desired is a recollection of the past or a presentiment of the future, whether man is fallen (according to the dogma) or imperfect (and perfectible, according to the moderns).[237] Combining tradition and innovations is not always a comfortable process; Lamartine's sort of poetry makes great spiritual leaps. Thus childhood faith is celebrated magnificently:

Notre esprit la reçoit à son premier réveil,
Comme les dons d'en haut, la vie et le soleil;
Comme le lait de l'âme, en ouvrant la paupière,
Elle a coulé pour nous des lèvres d'une mère;
Elle a pénétré l'homme en sa tendre saison;
Son flambeau dans les coeurs précéda la raison.[238]

[Our spirit receives it when we first awaken,
Like those gifts from on high, life and sunlight;
Like milk of the soul when we open our eyelids,
It flowed for us from a mother's lips;
It entered deep into man in his tender youth;
Its torch entered into our hearts before reason did.]

But there is a great distance between this maternal faith and the heterodox fantasies that appear elsewhere: the soul as a particle of solar fire destined to return to its source,[239] metempsychosis, the survival of one star in another.[240]

Even better, *La Mort de Socrate*, seizing the opportunity offered by the pagan philosopher's freedom of speculation, imagines a paradise in which bodies survive with purified senses and new sensual pleasures, and, seeking each other through the infinite, are engendered from universe to universe and people the stars; the same poem welcomes the gods of paganism into the spiritualist gospel as divine names of natural objects, or perhaps even as real beings, rungs on the ladder of creation.[241] An imagination so open-minded concludes nevertheless in an essential monotheism, and banishes the "phantom impostors," whose cohort

> Fera place au dieu saint, unique, universel,
> Le seul dieu que j'adore et qui n'a point d'autel.[242]

> [Will give place to the holy, unique, universal god,
> The only god I adore, a god who has no altar.]

Christians who think they find in this couplet an expression of their faith would have to be unaware of the last six syllables. I say nothing of the doubts and rebellion that Lamartine's poetry allows to appear, nothing about his obsession with a blind, empty universe, nothing about the strange symmetry that he attempts to establish between Destiny and Providence,[243] nothing, finally, of the construction of so many of his poems in the form of debates between faith, which is doubtless his final word, and a marvelously eloquent atheism:[244] the ministry that he attributes to himself supposes that these worries have been overcome. In spite of everything, this ministry is marked by all that transforms the dogmatic tradition in the moderns: to tell the truth, it has no meaning apart from these new modulations; its necessity cannot be distinguished from theirs. For example, when Lamartine writes to one of his friends: "You have found the true word, the *infinite* . . . it is the soul of man in its entirety; and as a consequence everything that should and can act upon his soul, even in the arts, should derive from and converge toward this in some way,"[245] he implicitly justifies a spiritual function that belongs to the new interpreters of this *infinite*.

This spiritual function is even more justified if one conceives of the world as a collection of symbols, if visible things are the language of God. Medieval ideas on the "meaning" of the world and the particular symbolic interpretations consecrated by theological tradition were thoroughly forgotten, and after a long period of rationalism and empirical science they would have appeared puerile in their didacticism. Other meanings had to be found to give life to the universe, meanings more fleeting, less linked to a given order, ones suggesting the divine through the creative freedom of the mind. It is here, in an actual setting, that we see how the poet took the theologian's place. Theosophists had provided the obscure transition; but since from now on belief mattered less than creativity, poets alone were, in their own way, able to make the views of theosophists prosper.[246] The universe is a diffuse and universal representation of the divine that poetic speech alone expresses clearly, but in its own way and according to its own free movement:

> Dieu caché, disais-tu, la nature est ton temple!
> L'esprit te voit partout quand notre oeil la contemple;
> De tes perfections, qu'il cherche à concevoir,
> Ce monde est le reflet, l'image, le miroir;
> Le jour est ton regard, la beauté ton sourire.[247]

> [Hidden God, you said, nature is your temple!
> The spirit sees you everywhere when our eyes behold nature;
> The world is the reflection, the image, the mirror
> Of your perfections, of which it seeks a clear idea;
> The daylight is your gaze, beauty is your smile.]

No doubt Lamartine made of God the key to the meanings of the universe:

> L'étendue à mes yeux révèle ta grandeur,
> La terre ta bonté, les astres ta splendeur.
> Tu t'es produit toi-même en ton brillant ouvrage;
> L'univers tout entier réfléchit ton image,
> Et mon âme à son tour réfléchit l'univers.[248]

> [Space reveals your greatness to my eyes,
> Earth reveals your goodness, the stars your splendor.
> You have copied yourself in your brilliant piece of work;
> The entire universe reflects your image,
> And my soul in its turn reflects the universe.]

But this soul to which the universe speaks of God is a creative source as much as an echo:

> Mais ce temple est sans voix. Où sont les saints concerts?
> D'où s'élèvera l'hymne au roi de l'univers?
> Tout se tait: mon coeur seul parle dans ce silence.
> La voix de l'univers, c'est mon intelligence.
> Sur les rayons du soir, sur les ailes du vent,
> Elle s'élève à Dieu comme un parfum vivant;
> Et, donnant un langage à toute créature,
> Prête pour l'adorer mon âme à la nature.[249]

[But this temple is without a voice. Where are the holy choirs?
Whence will come the hymn to the king of the universe?
All falls silent: my heart alone speaks in this silence.
It is my intelligence that is the voice of the universe.
On the rays of the setting sun, on the wings of the wind,
It rises to God like a living fragrance;
And, giving to every creature a language,
Lends my soul to nature to adore him.]

Lamartine's symbolism, however unemphatic it may seem to us compared with what was seen later, made a considerable impact on contemporaries, who compared this poetry to the poetry that had preceded it. One contemporary commentator wrote: "You will find everywhere in M. de Lamartine this same confusion of nature and the invisible world, each serving the other as explanation or emblem."[250] It is worth emphasizing that this modern poetic symbolism places the human spirit in competition with Being from the very beginning. The human spirit—that is to say in fact the creative privilege of poets as the indispensable facilitators of the double meaning of things and as the modern administrators of the Word. What traditional priesthood would be capable of disputing this claim of theirs? Who could keep them from the temptation to forget Being, and to make all divinity reside in their own discoveries?

This ambiguous attitude between fidelity and innovation, so characteristic of the creations of royalist literature, is everywhere in Lamartine. Proclaiming the eminent dignity of the Poet, he oscillates between two thematic variants, one of which is suggested to him by a modern religiosity that has detached itself from the traditional credo, the other by his desire to resuscitate a sacred poetry in the nineteenth century. Although he attempts to combine these two sorts of thinking in a spiritualism that embraces them both, they can be clearly perceived separately. He writes in 1823 in the notice to *La Mort de Socrate*: "If poetry is not a vain construction of sounds, it is no doubt the most sublime form that can cloak human thought . . . , it takes hold of all of a man at once; it charms him, ravishes him, inebriates him; it exalts the divine principle in him; it makes him feel momentarily that *something more than human* that made it be called the language of the gods. At the least it is the language of philosophers, if philosophy is what it ought to be, the highest degree of elevation of human thought, divinized reason: metaphysics and poetry are thus sisters; or, rather, are only a single thing."[251] He was then under the influence, as he says, of "the admirable translation of Plato by M. Cousin." Plato allows Lamartine to escape from the letter of the various dogmas without having to yield, so he thought, to the spirit of the eighteenth century;[252] and it was possible for Victor Cousin to appear to him in this respect as a contemporary Plato. He hoped, however, that French philosophy would find a reconciliation with Christianity, which he himself makes a dying Socrates presage and announce.[253] But however much this deism would like to take shelter beneath the Christian wing, it still occasionally shows its face openly, and in the most frankly anthropocentric form:

> Muse des derniers temps! divinité sublime,
> Qui des monts fabuleux n'habites plus la cime;
> Toi qui n'as pour séjour, pour temples, pour autels,
> Que le sein frémissant des généreux mortels;
>
> . . . .
> Sentiment plus qu'humain, que l'homme déifie,
> Viens seul! c'est à toi seul que mon coeur sacrifie!
> Les siècles de l'erreur sont passés; l'homme est vieux;
> Ce monde, en grandissant, a détrôné ses dieux,
> Comme l'homme qui touche à son adolescence
> Brise les vains hochets de sa crédule enfance.

> [Muse of latter times! divinity sublime,
> Who no longer inhabits the summit of legendary peaks;
> You who have as temples, as altars, as an abode
> Only the trembling breast of well-meaning mortals;
>
> . . . .
> Feeling more than human, which man deifies,
> Come alone! to you alone does my heart sacrifice!
> The centuries of error are over; man has aged;
> The world, growing up, has dethroned its gods,
> As a man who reaches adolescence
> Shatters the vain rattles of his credulous childhood.]

This invocation of the modern muse opens, in 1825, the *Dernier Chant du pèlerinage d'Harold*. The dead gods are obviously the pagan gods, whose worship has yielded to the "eternal religion": but which one? This verse's resonance is not very Catholic. Poetry is in any case henceforth sacred in its purely human source and because it springs from our excellence; for

> . . . il reste à jamais au fond du coeur de l'homme
> Deux sentiments divins, plus forts que le trépas:
> L'Amour, la Liberté, dieux qui ne mourront pas.[254]

> [. . . there remain forever deep in the human heart
> Two divine sentiments, stronger than death:
> Love and Freedom, gods that shall not die.]

At this time, in 1825, the alliance of modern poetry and freedom is full of meaning. Here, it is true, it is a question of the freedom of the Greeks, and, besides, royalists sometimes celebrated liberty as a favor conferred by the restored monarchy. But Lamartine gave the impression rather early on of transgressing limits; thus as early as 1823, apropos of *La Mort de Socrate* and the *Nouvelles Méditations*, Vigny writes: "I have misgivings about this alliance with the liberals, about this separation from *us*."[255] At the beginning of 1824, in an epistle to the liberal Casimir Delavigne, Lamartine rallies to the cause of Liberty purified of its revolutionary excesses, and proposes that poets devote their songs to moderating and pacifying the parties.[256] We have come a long way, though in only a few years, from the "Ode aux Français." Lamartine did not believe in a pure restoration for long, if he ever really did; he was aware, like so many of his contemporaries, even royalists, of living in a time of transition and waiting: "Our misfortune," he writes as early as 1819, "is to have been born in this accursed time in which everything old is collapsing and in which there is not yet anything new."[257]

Later, Lamartine would take a stand with the idea of a poetry closely linked to modern reason. But another force pulled in a contrary direction this poet of celestial charms, who does not forget the image of the supernaturally inspired poet. He proposes this image to Byron:

> Viens reprendre ton rang dans ta splendeur première,
> Parmi ces purs enfants de gloire et de lumière
> Que d'un souffle choisi Dieu voulut animer,
> Et qu'il fit pour chanter, pour croire et pour aimer.[258]

> [Come and take back your place in your first brilliance,
> Among those unsullied children of glory and light
> Into whom God wished to breathe a choice spirit,
> Because he wanted them to sing, to believe, and to love.]

The Spirit of God, in the poem bearing this title, is the name for inspiration: a Christian version of the Enthusiasm of antiquity to which Lamartine had devoted an ode in 1819; in this poem, all inspiration, from Orpheus to the poet of today, proceeds from the same God, who is that of Scripture, and who requires of his ministers a sacerdotal purity:

> Préparons-lui des lèvres pures,
> Un oeil chaste, un front sans souillures,
> Comme, aux approches du saint lieu,
> Des enfants, des vierges voilées,
> Jonchent de roses effeuillées
> La route où va passer un Dieu![259]

[Prepare for him lips that are pure,
Chaste eyes, an unblemished brow,
Just as, when approaching a holy place,
Children and veiled virgins
Bestrew with rose petals
The path where a God will pass!]

This poetic vein, which can well be called sacred, does not run out after the *Méditations*; on the contrary, it establishes itself more and more broadly in his work up until 1830. In his projected *Visions*, it quickly overflows lyricism into the epic.

Just after the *Méditations* and for several years, Lamartine was busy with an undertaking that would remain that of his entire career as a poet. He imagined a poetic narration of the stages of humanity, a vast Sacred History that would be at the service of the new times. At about the same time that Ballanche conceived of his "general epic"[260] and inspired by a similar impulse, Lamartine felt it was imperative that he compose this great poem. The idea of a composition of this sort thus precedes markedly the humanitarian movement that later produced the most often cited examples of it; it has its roots in the Restoration, and in royalist ground. It is true that the need to rethink the history of humanity had appeared during the Enlightenment as a component of traditional theological views in this area. Historians and thinkers had made attempts, and this ambition had even been taken up by poets toward the end of the century. Sketching the outline of his *Hermès*, Chénier wrote: "The wise magician who will be one of the heroes of this strange poem must have passed through several metempsychoses, ones that are appropriate for showing the history of the human race allegorically."[261] The literary form that interests us, already well defined and taking the place of a religious schema that was becoming less and less popular, was born in this way. Chénier was unable to finish his project, which would doubtless have placed poetry's means at the disposition of philosophy's ends, according to the formula we have observed. In Lamartine's time, something else was the point: to reintegrate the odyssey of humanity into the divine plan, but according to views that were henceforth ones that belonged specifically to poetry. Lamartine's great epic project, mostly known in the form it would take on during the 1830s and of which, as everyone knows, *Jocelyn* and *La Chute d'un ange* have come down to us, thus goes back in reality to 1821. Lamartine, in the epic as elsewhere, had begun with received forms. As early as 1810, at the age of twenty, he planned a *Clovis*, about which he speaks constantly in his letters until 1819, calling it the "great work of my life," and is above all preoccupied with achieving a portrait of the Christian supernatural by combining it with the

"Platonic supernatural."[262] This relatively modest conception was considerably enlarged the day his views on the epic broke with old habits and embraced the general idea he had formed of poetry and its mission. This was the effect of a sort of moment of illumination that Lamartine described in a letter to Virieu written only a few days after it occurred: "Here I am . . . having at last understood the fruit my poetry is to produce; it remains only to bring it forth. Leaving Naples, on Saturday 20 January, a ray from on high illuminated me: I understood. I feel myself a great poet."[263] Thirty-six years later he recounted at length what he evokes here in a few words; he confirms the sudden character of the illumination: "It seemed to me that the curtain of the material world and the moral world had just been suddenly ripped open before the eyes of my intelligence; I felt my spirit undergo a sort of sudden explosion within me and rise high into a moral firmament, like the vapor of a lighter-than-air gas whose crystal vase had just been unstopped, and that rushes into the ether with just a trace of smoke."[264] On one other point this text confirms the letter to Virieu: he evokes "nervous sufferings" during his Neapolitan winter, a terrifying obsession caused by reading Tasso's life and by the thought of his madness.[265] The 1821 letter said: "I thought I was going mad in Naples. I still have my doubts. This is another torture, surpassing them all." It seems that thinking himself to be besieged and, so to speak, impregnated by the Holy Spirit caused Lamartine to experience as much terror as pride.[266]

The 1857 text tells us in detail what vision of the universe offered itself to him in 1821, and upon what great lines he conceived his poem. We have good reason to doubt the veracity of testimony given so long after the fact. The elements of the vision — space, celestial continents, fecundities of stellar couplings and the birth of worlds, peregrinations of souls from sphere to sphere through successive existences — could have been familiar to Lamartine's imagination very early on, along with other analogous themes just as strange;[267] even the Holy Spirit became heterodox when entering into him; but the fact is that what remains to us of the "visions" actually composed after the illumination in the form of fragments or verse episodes and drafts of plans for the whole scarcely corresponds to these retrospective indications.[268] In particular, the 1857 text evokes the successive lives of two souls, male and female, making progress and seeking each other from one level of the universe to another until they meet in God, whereas the 1821 texts, more orthodox, show us the long expiation of an initial sin in a single hero: an angel who has become at his own request a man for the love of a mortal woman, is condemned for this failing by having to go on living again and again through ordeal after ordeal until his final redemption. No attention, therefore, should be paid to the 1857 testimony in its details; it supports, however, the general fact that interests us: the sudden enlargement of Lamartine's epic horizon in 1821 due to an influence experienced as supernatural.

The immense poem sketched out in the course of this and following years began at the creation,[269] and its successive episodes, each devoted to one of the hero's reincarnations, embraced the history of humanity: the eras of the Flood, the patriarchs, the prophets, Socrates or Pythagoras, Christ, the desert hermits, Chivalry, the French Revolution. All these narratives are offered retrospectively by the hero himself, at the end of time, and end with the victorious struggle against the Antichrist, the Last Judgment, and finally the reunion of the redeemed angel and his beloved in the bosom of God. Lamartine was aware that such a project upset the boundaries between genres as they were established by classical poetics. The Epic, by posing the problems of good and evil, of the fallen state and redemption, became a sacred Poem; by embracing every period of human history, it was transformed into symbolic History; by tracing the destiny of a creature taken as a type of humanity, it was an "Epic of the soul."[270] Lamartine cannot better describe his poem than by heaping up adjectives open-endedly: "il grand poema épico, lyrico, metaphysico, etc."[271] He had defined his *Mort de Socrate* similarly, "neither epic, nor lyric, nor didactic, but all three at once";[272] and he repeats the same multiple definition apropos of the *Dernier Chant du pèlerinage d'Harold*, neither didactic, nor descriptive, nor epic, but "belonging to these three genres all at the same time," and in addition representing "the poet himself."[273] Here we are perhaps dealing with something deep: no name, no form suffices where literature goes beyond its proper limits. The Poet undertakes a quest for a work of unheard-of proportions and aspect that will be on the same scale as his ministry. But he then ceases to be an author—that is, a professional of fiction and well-turned speech—so as to become something else: a priest, or a prophet. Laprade, apropos precisely of the *Les Visions*, insists on the difference between an ordinary poet and Lamartine, who is "above all else a religious poet, a philosopher, a magus of nature, the poet of the universal and the divine."[274] Such is the spirit of the romantic epic from its birth: it wishes to be much more than a poetic genre. Therein lies the secret of its vitality and of the exceedingly numerous efforts during the course of a half century to realize it. Therein also lies, perhaps, the reason for its failure, relatively speaking: literature risks perishing when it wishes to outdo itself. Romanticism succeeded and lasted as lyric poetry because this genre could shelter the sacerdotal ambition of the poet without putting it too much to the test. But if one wishes to take this in its full sense, the true monument of this ministry should be something other than language that expresses one soul: it should be a representation of Humanity and its destination through all epochs, a formula of universal belief, a Revelation that is included in the imagination's construction. This is what the romantic epic wanted to be. But the natural situation of poets, between the true and the imaginary, is hardly a qualification for a genuine ministry. Their elevation to the rank of spiritual guide in fact assumes that the time for ministries is past. The poem that for the moderns in the nineteenth century would have replaced sacred texts could not be written. Lamartine did not finish his. We have of the "visions" conceived in 1821 only a few episodes and outlines written between 1823 and 1829. Taken up again in another form after 1830, it would not prove possible to bring the great Poem to a conclusion then, either.

As it was roughed out in the course of the 1820s, it was rather timid both in its style and its lessons. But there was no timidity in the announcement of the poet's celestial mission as the spokesperson of the Holy Spirit, who replaces the Muse in the preliminary invocation of his poem:

> Au nom sacré du Père et du Fils, son image,
> Descends, Esprit des deux, Esprit qui d'âge en âge,
> Des harpes de Jessé chérissant les concerts,
> Par la voix de la lyre instruisis l'univers!
> Soit que, te balançant sur l'aile des tempêtes
> Tu lances tes éclairs dans les yeux des prophètes,
>
> . . . .
>
> Soit qu'en langues de feu, dans les airs suspendu,
> Sur le front de l'apôtre en secret descendu,
> Tu perces tout à coup, comme un jour sans aurore,
> De tes rayons divins son coeur qui doute encore.
> Descends, je dois chanter![275]

> [In the sacred name of the Father and of the Son, his image,
> Come down, Spirit of both, Spirit who from age to age,
> Cherishing the concerts of the harps of Jesse,
> Instructs the universe by the voice of the lyre!
> Whether, rocking on the wing of storms,
> You strike the eyes of prophets with your lightning bolts.
>
> . . . .
>
> Or whether in tongues of flame, in the air suspended,
> Secretly alit on the brow of the apostle,
> You suddenly pierce, like a day without a dawn,
> With your divine rays the heart that still doubts.
> Come down, I must sing!]

The Apostles succeed to the memory of the Psalmist and the Prophets, by an identification of the poetico-prophetic inspiration with the investiture of Pentecost, which is itself meaningful. Lamartine then professes penitence and purity, recommending himself thus to divine election; he asks for the favor that was granted to one of the Prophets:

> Que ce feu dont la flamme éclaire et purifie,
> Ce charbon qui brûla les lèvres d'Isaïe,
> D'une bouche mortelle épure les accents,
> Et que mes chants vers Dieu montent comme l'encens![276]

> [May this fire whose flame illuminates and purifies,
> This ember that burned the lips of Isaiah,
> Purify the utterances of mortal lips,
> And may my songs climb toward God like incense!]

Such ambitious comparisons were unusual, as far as I know, in the tradition that Lamartine thought of himself as continuing. Similarly, he compares himself to Saint John in another invocation, which he thought he would use as the opening of his poem, instead of the one just cited:

> Ah! viens! rouvre pour moi la source des miracles,
> Ange qui de Patmos inspiras les oracles,
> Ange dont le regard tourné vers l'avenir
> Voit comme un jour passé le jour qui doit venir!
>
> . . . .
>
> Récompense en un jour toute une longue vie!
> Jette-moi du grand livre une page ravie,
> La dernière! Et sous toi laisse-moi répéter
> Ce qu'une langue d'homme en pourra supporter!
> Il m'exauce! et j'ai vu![277]

> [Ah! come! open up for me once more the source of miracles,
> Angel who inspired the oracles of Patmos,
> Angel whose gaze, turned toward the future,
> Sees as the day that is past the day that is to come!
>
> . . . .
>
> Reward a long life in a single day!
> Let me see one ravishing page of the great book,
> The last one! And, inspired by you, let me repeat
> Whatever portions a human tongue can bear!
> He hears my prayer! and the vision is mine!]

The lyrical collection of the *Harmonies poétiques et religieuses,* composed beginning in 1826, forms a whole that can be considered as a collection of sacred poetry, conceived according to a formula that was more spacious and free than the traditional attempts in this genre. At first Lamartine wanted to entitle the collection "Modern Psalms" or "Sacred Harmonies."[278] He freed himself from the letter of the Hebrew poets while carrying their spirit over into original poems, "hymns" of varied prosody or "canticles" in stanzas. The *Harmonies* can be judged as the successful flowering at long last of the genre so long dreamed of by his predecessors: for here we find a genuine union of sacred tradition and contemporary lyricism by way of a modern transmutation of the ardent rhetoric of the Hebrews; their symbolism of the unique God, fire, space, breath, and fecundity becomes the poetry of today, according to a formula that the *Méditations*, in a poem like "Dieu," had merely begun to attempt in a timid way. That Lamartine was finally able to succeed in accomplishing what Louis Racine and Lefranc de Pompignan had conceived of and attempted in vain may make one reflect on the relationship of genius to circumstances; much had happened since Louis XV. In any case, Lamartine was very conscious of what he was doing. He expressly offers his poetry as heir to that of the Hebrews: "I conceived," he said later, "the thought of writing at random, in my hours of leisure and inspiration, a few modern canticles, like those that David had written with his tears."[279] Such, then, is the generative idea of the *Harmonies*, with the help of God, whose favor delivers the spiritual meaning of things to the poet:

Et moi, Seigneur, aussi, pour chanter tes merveilles,
Tu m'as donné dans l'âme une seconde voix
Plus pure que la voix qui parle à mes oreilles,
Plus forte que les vents, les ondes et les bois!

Les cieux l'appellent Grâce, et les hommes Génie;
C'est un souffle affaibli des bardes d'Israël,
Un écho dans mon sein, qui change en harmonie
Le retentissement de ce monde mortel.[280]

[And me, too, Lord, to sing of your marvels,
You gave me a second voice in my soul
purer than the voice that speaks to my ears,
Stronger than the winds, the waves and the woods!

The skies call it Grace, men call it Genius;
It is the weakened breath of the bards of Israel.
An echo in my breast, which changes to harmony
The clanging of this mortal world.]

The unusual theology that identifies grace and poetic genius should be noted; it is deep in the heart of the symbolism that figures throughout the entire collection. This theology makes the poet one of the elect:

Non, mon Dieu, non, mon Dieu, grâce à mon saint partage,
Je n'ai point entendu monter jamais vers toi
D'accords plus pénétrants, de plus divin langage
Que ces concerts muets qui s'élèvent en moi.[281]

[No, my God, no, my God, thanks to my blessed portion,
I have never heard rise up to you
Harmonies more penetrating or language more divine
Than these silent concerts that arise in me.]

It is evident that the *Harmonies*, which want to be a song of adoration and faith, reveal in more than one poem Lamartine's uncertainties about dogma, his modernism, his profound doubts. Otherwise Lamartine would no longer be Lamartine, and the *Harmonies* in this regard go further yet than the *Méditations*.[282] The ministry of the modern poet is an uneasy ministry; above all, it is irresistibly turned toward the future, since it justifies itself only by a state of crisis and by a new need. At the moment when the Holy Spirit enters poetry, it blows in an unaccustomed direction: through the mouth of the poet, it commands great changes for humanity. This is the view of the Lamartine of the *Harmonies*; the time is past — that was ten years before — when the Spirit consecrated poets to console martyr-kings and the persecuted church, and to dictate penitence to the godless; the ordeals to which these changes delegate poets are no longer those of an order shaken by crime; rather, they are those of all humanity in the throes of metamorphosis; when people avidly desire a new truth,

Alors tu descends! tu respires
Dans ces sages, flambeaux mortels,
Dans ces mélodieuses lyres
Qui soupirent près des autels!

[You descend, then! you breathe
In these wise men, living torches,
And in these melodious lyres,
Which sigh near the altars!]

When this Spirit, which collaborated in the Creation and governs its human phases, abandons a condemned society, the poets it inspired are the first to die. Angst and apprehension invade the world, which does not understand this mystery:

Mais moi je te comprends, car je baisse la tête!
J'entends venir de loin la céleste tempête,
Et, d'un effroi stupide impassible témoin,

Quand de l'antique jour les clartés s'affaiblissent,
Que des lois et des moeurs les colonnes fléchissent,
Que la terre se trouble et que les cieux pâlissent,
      Je dis: Il n'est pas loin!

[But I, I understand you, for I lower my head!
I hear the celestial storm coming from afar,
And, impassive witness to an uncomprehending panic,
When the brightness of the old day wanes,
When the columns of the law and custom give way,
When the earth shakes and the skies turn pale,
      I say: It is not far off!]

It is then that through sorrows and cataclysms the Holy Spirit opens the way to
the new Sinai:

      Je le vois! mon regard devance
      Le pas des siècles plus heureux!
      La colonne de l'espérance
      Marche et m'éclaire de ces feux!
Tu souffleras plus pur sur des plages nouvelles!

    · · · · · · · ·

      O! puissé-je, souffle suprême,
      Instrument de promission,
      Sous ton ombre frémir moi-même,
      Comme une harpe de Sion![283]

      [I see it! my gaze runs
      Faster than happier ages!
      The column of hope
      Is afoot and lights my way with its fire!
You will breathe a purer air on new shores!

    · · · · · · · ·

      O! may I, supreme spirit,
      Covenantal instrument,
      Myself quiver under your shadow,
      Like a harp of Zion!]

To describe the crisis thus is not at all a commonplace; it is the portrait of a
situation experienced as at present existing in France, in the vacuum caused by
the destruction of the old society; at the end of the reign of Charles X, themes of
restoration no longer seem to furnish a plausible response to the century's
questionings; there is a presentiment of the definitive collapse of the old France,

and there is a sense that there is a need to turn poetic preaching toward other horizons, whence comes a call more imperious than ever. Lamartine convinces himself — he discovers — that his true domain is the future.

Thus the whole of Lamartine's work up to the eve of the revolution of 1830 develops a contemporary idea of the mission of the poet in the light of the tradition of religious poetry inherited from earlier generations. The sacred poet, relegated till then to legendary or biblical times, comes to life in our own age. The Restoration, in the larger sense of a rehabilitation and return to honor on the part of values that had been discredited by philosophical criticism, wishes to be a return to sacred sources, to the first foundations of life and society. It is thus that the types of Orpheus, Ezekiel, and David find new life and are embodied in an inspired gentleman. With what plausibility is another question. It is easy to denounce the role artifice inherently plays in this aspect of the Restoration, as in many others, and to emphasize that this fervor survived only by changing its orientation. But it is precisely this capacity for metamorphosis and renewed relevance that merits reflection. The poetic ministry would eventually be understood in the humanitarian sense; this was without a doubt its final and most important destination. But the spring from which it issued, and whose current extended itself later to other domains, had its own strength; the metamorphosis was not an abjuration. The early Lamartine, of the *Méditations*, *Les Visions*, and the *Harmonies*, would always be a part of who Lamartine was.

In 1851, he had long been separated from the Bourbons and the church. He had presided over the Republic and remained faithful to it. No party nostalgia on his part dictated at that time the following lines, which testify at a distance of thirty years to impressions that are apparently unforgettable: "The Empire had hardly been overthrown when thinking, writing, and singing began anew in France. The century of François I is full of originality; the century of Louis XIV is full of glory. Neither one nor the other displayed more enthusiasm and movement than the first years of the Restoration."[284] Or again: "It was the time of enthusiasm, a time that was poetic as the past was poetic, miraculous, like a resurrection. Old men became young again, women wept, priests prayed, lyres sung, children marveled and hoped. . . . All at the same time, people were living deeply for the past, for the present, for the future. No century will ever again see such a time." There would certainly be no difficulty in citing contrary statements; Lamartine is carried away by the memory of his youth and his first experiences; and one might celebrate the fact that the Restoration inaugurated liberal society in France in a more modest tone, when one considers all that accompanied this blessing. But the fervor of this evocation is not mendacious: it shows us what Lamartine believes was the vital point of departure, the time of public emotion that he lived through and from which his creations were born. It little matters that others disagreed or disapproved. It is difficult not to be struck by the fact that the poetic fountainhead of the nineteenth century sprang up between 1800 and 1820 in the bosom of the counterrevolution. The idea of a spiritual ministry of the poet, which is the soul of modern poetry, germinated in this milieu; it is thence that poets first emerged. We must conclude therefrom that this school of thought had an essential contribution to bring to the ideological recasting that accompanied the destruction of the former society. There can be no doubt that in the thinkers of the nineteenth century, including those who can be considered the most advanced, there is generally a sense of the past and a propensity to religious thought and feeling that the philosophy of the preceding century repudiated. Everything happens as if the conquering humanism of the eighteenth century, elaborated by an elite according to the horizons of that elite, had not been able to resist its own consequences: the violent entry into political society of the human masses that till then had been kept out of the game invalidated the doctrines that had promoted this irruption. The broadening movement continued in social reality, because it could not be cut off, but an uneasiness unknown before took root in society. Those who advocated the view that the present and the future were organically linked to the past, those who affirmed the necessity of some divine foundation for human institutions and professed the belief that human beings belonged to a spiritual order that went beyond simple nature obtained a hearing that they would not have had a half century earlier. Their views were welcomed as answering the need to maintain a social bond in a broader, unstable society. Like the old orthodoxy, they expressed and justified the common condition of a humanity whose earthly desire was not yet near to being satisfied, but in a way that was one step further advanced. The counterrevolution and the church failed in their counteroffensive; but secular thinkers who were exempt from strict dogmatic attachments handled the themes of tradition and faith more freely, in the new way. Such is precisely the larger, continuing fact, appearing in different forms, that we are trying to understand here. It is in this sense that the counterrevolution, apart from its partisan and politically programmatic aspects, contributed an indispensable inspiration to the mind and spirit of the nineteenth century.

Chapter 5

The Liberal Contribution

THE WRITERS who continued during the Empire and the Restoration to identify to some degree with the legacy of the *philosophes* brought to the elevation of letters a contribution that was very different from that of their royalist contemporaries. Faithful to the tradition of the preceding period, the liberal writers (to designate them in a general way with a convenient name), to whatever generation they belonged — whether survivors of the preceding century entrenched in the Institut, or newcomers appearing around 1800 in literary circles, or political writers who emerged in the régime of the Bourbon *Charte*, the French constitution granted by Louis XVIII on his restoration to the throne in 1814 — naturally placed the exercise of thought above the poetic faculty. The counterrevolution found, in its tradition and its instincts, a notion of the sacred through which it could, by a sort of accommodation with the present, honor poetry, which was thus promoted to the first rank. Quite to the contrary, the idea of the sacred — that is, of religious depth and mystery — was in its essence foreign to the philosophic spirit. If it is true that few poets and little confidence in poetry are to be found among liberal writers, nevertheless, given their greater independence with regard to established religions, they were less constrained in their ability to reflect on the conditions of a modern spiritualism than were those in the opposing camp. In doing so, they helped the poetry of their time (though it came from an outlook generally opposed to their own) to constitute itself as an original spiritual power bearing the ideal of the century; they also helped the poet cloak himself in the grave dignity of the thinker. It is chiefly this contribution that we propose to define here.

❧ Senancour

Senancour, born in 1770, was of all the great writers of the period the one who, though feeling profoundly the negative effects of the revolutionary trauma, remained most faithful to the spirit of the eighteenth century — so much so that Sainte-Beuve believed, wrongly, that the Revolution had not affected him, and that he imperturbably continued Jean-Jacques Rousseau's example under Napoleon and Louis XVIII. Modern criticism is of a very different opinion.[1] Even independently of any biographical investigation, one ought to notice that, in Senancour, reverie, faithful to a primitivist ideal but disenchanted by the harshness of an inescapable reality, reproduces the line laid down by Rousseau only by breaking it. The Alpine Eden is only the site of a futile evasion if nothing can pass from there into the society of human beings: "I came back down to earth; there the blind faith in the absolute existence of beings, the chimera of regular relations, of perfections, of positive delights, vanished; a shining hypothesis with which a new heart amuses itself, and at which he whom more depth has cooled, or whom a longer time has matured, smiles sorrowfully."[2] We are certainly obliged to recognize in this the general form of Sensibility frustrated in its object, so characteristic of the aftermath of the Revolution. Senancour's formulas concerning the disproportion of our desires and our faculties echo other similar ones, born in the same period of the same situation; such formulas abound in his work: "I do not know whence come to me these infinite desires, so dissonant with my limited nature"; or else: "By what inconsistency do my wishes surpass my rights, or what injustice deprives me of the rights they attest?"; or again: "When an invincible feeling carries us far from the things we possess and fills us with bliss, then with regrets, because it gives us a presentiment of goods that nothing can bestow upon us, this deep, fleeting sensation is but an inner testimony of the superiority of our faculties to our destiny."[3] The impossibility of happiness is the impossibility of a veritable society; man is similar to the deaf, "he is separated from other beings as a whole, there is no more contact; everything before him exists in vain, he lives alone, he is absent from the living world."[4] In this hollowed-out emptiness, the nullity of all things and the omnipresence of death replace the sublimities of human nature as fundamental themes.[5]

We must not, however, stop at the exterior aspect of formulas. Every generation has its own, to which it returns with predilection; but expressions that are common to the writers of a period can be used in different ways; different experiences cause their tone to vary; in Senancour the most radical dissatisfaction dominates, in which delight itself becomes a cause for despair: "Everything that pleases us and enchants us oppresses us and saddens us. . . . The songs of a distant voice give us a crushing and indefinable feeling of what we have lost";[6] or, better: "I am unable to seek after something in myself without finding there the ghost of what will never be given me."[7] Even more than as confidential asides, though, such formulas have worth as maxims because of what they claim to teach; it is pointless to consider themes and expressive structures apart from the implicit argument that gives them all their meaning. The melancholy of Senancour may resemble that of many others, but it is different in that it does not argue in favor of religion. He himself believes that this sort of uneasiness is philosophical in its essence, and reproaches Chateaubriand for having claimed not to know it.[8] For him, the realization that there is a divorce between desire and reality is not resolved in the bosom of God; on the contrary, the failure of Sensibility causes a simultaneous bankruptcy of the divine sanction with which the Man of Sensibility crowned his euphoria; it implies the danger of a universe without meaning and without God. From his very first writings, he evokes those reasoners, in whose number he seems very tempted to count himself, "who, because they have despaired of their lives, believe that neither providence nor the future exists";[9] and early on, he has an acute vision of the indifferent and inhumane necessity of things.[10]

It is true that his thought oscillates and will always oscillate between this absence of God and the God of the *philosophes* — that of Rousseau, or at the outside that of Bernardin — but he admires these conceptions only with reservations, and does not share the "respectable Bernardin" 's confidence in the providential organization of the world; nor does he admit that preeminence of sentiment over reason that Bernardin believed he had demonstrated.[11] In any case, the God of which he catches a glimpse exists only as a function of a dream of moral renewal here on earth and insofar as this God guarantees the realization of such a dream, without which the very postulate of his existence would vanish. This distant God is the figure of the inaccessible human ideal whereby the writer communes with his readers: "Greetings, young friends of truth sublime, of the truth that is only revealed at a great distance; greetings in the name of that endlessly desirable veiled light."[12] A line of evolution in Senancour's thought has long been sought in a body of work that he ceaselessly reworked, in the inextricable variants and reciprocal borrowings in the *Rêveries sur la nature primitive de l'homme* and in *Oberman* over many years and many editions. He has been judged, to use Sainte-Beuve's hasty word, "more religious as he grows older."[13] It is above all the *Libres Méditations* of 1819, full of spiritualist affirmations, that seemed to authorize such a view: one sees there, for instance, the sadness of man explained by his instinctive sense of an "eternal home."[14] But reserves and doubts abound there,[15] just as much as in the earlier texts of the *Rêveries* and *Oberman* that Senancour republished and largely reworked after 1819, without however modifying their character in this respect. His thought wanders about more than it evolves; it never stops taking on new forms within limits that equally exclude a decided atheism as well as any theocentric faith. Finally, one must remember that the *Libres Méditations* present themselves as a literary fiction: the book claims to reproduce writings found in the care of a hermit in the forest of Fontainebleau, and is preceded by explicit reservations on Senancour's part; these pages, he says, are "not always in conformity with my opinions," "in general it is enough that I think them useful."[16] One has the impression that in it he wanted to present an ideally consoling body of doctrine that would be most susceptible of founding a possible social order: it was well known how great was the preoccupation among those of his time and tradition with basing the social order on beliefs. It is doubtless in this sense that he could consider the *Libres Méditations* to be the great undertaking of his life.[17] He nevertheless makes a religious thought that is "independent of any bold dogma" the main subject of the work.[18] A spiritualism, then? In appearance, perhaps, and for the public; but in the mind of the thinker, his thought has such little assurance, is so distant from Being, is so questioning. In a text that long remained unpublished, we read something that in 1832 specifies the intention of the *Libres Méditations*: "It is in fair-minded conjectures and in hope, it is in bold insights and in philosophic doubts that its depth is to be found."[19]

To tell the truth, the problem of God and religion interests Senancour only because of the problem of happiness. In the beginning is the primitivist dream, the idea of salvation through the return to an elementary plenitude. At first this legacy fills Senancour's works, *Les Premiers Ages*,[20] *Sur les générations actuelles*, *Aldomen*, but with an important difference compared with the eighteenth century and Rousseau: this dream becomes painful due to the feeling of its unreality; an invincible bitterness accompanies it. The agitation we see in the *Rêveries* and *Oberman* proceeds from this fundamental dissatisfaction, which is the kernel of both works, as well as from the ardent refusal to heal it by means of a celestial substitute. Rousseau had severely criticized extending curiosity and needs beyond the horizons of primitive simplicity; but in him this criticism was developed in a climate of optimism; he thought that plenitude was assured at the price of a reduction in human aims. Senancour seems to think as Rousseau does when he attacks the "extension" of desires, which is the typical character of civilized human beings, and according to him a "deviation" from our nature. Humanity, he writes with sarcasm, "gives the name perfectibility to this extension peculiar to our species"; "an extension at once both delightful and deadly," a delirium, a drunkenness "devastating in its aftermath"; the urge for metaphysics and religion, the chimerical audacity of intelligence: "man was demented as soon as he allowed himself to dream in the intellectual realm, unhappy as soon as he gave importance to shapeless fantasies."[21] He calls "*le vague des désirs*" what Chateaubriand a little later will call "*le vague des passions*," but he does so in order to condemn it, judging absurd that this has been presented as the sign of our supernatural destiny: "Our real needs and therefore our felt needs were limited: it is by extending them imprudently into the indefinite that there has arisen this unlimited expectation that now some would have us believe is the proof of a higher destination of life on earth."[22] He is tireless in condemning the "mad grandeur" that makes us abandon the proportions of our nature.[23] The remedy would be to know how to restrict oneself to "the present instant," to "a simple, circumscribed life," to the pure "feeling of one's own existence": "it is by limiting one's being that one possesses fully."[24] Our species must "finally abjure the too extensive desire for what is not yet experienced, and the thirst for extremes, as well as veneration for the unknown, love of the gigantic, the habit of conspicuous passions, pride in austere virtues, the craze for abstractions, the futility of what is intellectual, credulity with regard to what is invisible, and the universal prejudice in favor of perfectibility"; only this renunciation will restore "the primordial man" in ourselves.[25] The usual settings and motifs accompany these intellectual themes: the lonely landscapes where civilized man is morally uplifted by nature (in this case, the high Swiss Alps), a distant, primitively peopled island receptive to the laws of a philosopher of nature: we know that Senancour dreamed briefly of being that Legislator;[26] and he drew, in long enthusiastic pages, the portrait of the "teacher of peoples."[27] But it is hard to understand these themes in a mind like his, which has lost faith in humanity. If one considers every hope chimerical, the exaltation of natural simplicity is itself futile; the opposition of nature to civilization gives way to the opposition of dream to real life: and it is dream that risks attracting all value to itself.

We should note that Senancour always went beyond the purely subhuman representation of a Rousseauist Adam. His primitivism prefers to be of a more magnificent cast. He loves to imagine a primitive science lost to us today, whose "early traces can be discovered by following in Bailly's footsteps, and that can be interpreted by the science of the Gébelins," "a primitive alphabet . . . by which we can read the great book of human thought in all ages."[28] Senancour always accorded much importance to this school of fantastico-erudite primitivists of the eighteenth century; he has read them and cites them frequently.[29] He imagines the earliest science as a "sublime communication between accident and infinity, between the earth's point and celestial immensity, between being and man."[30] Once one has suspected that they are in vain, how can one distinguish such dreams from the "extension" so often condemned? This is the crux of the ambiguities we find in Senancour. Will the very desire for a better world be renounced? Such a renunciation is inconceivable, but in that case one would have to accept living by imagination and hope, which is exactly what was condemned on principle. The logical conclusion is that the extension of desires, ceasing to be the fundamental evil, becomes in a certain sense the very key to human nature.[31] This reversal goes quite far in certain texts, in which self-absorption is described as disastrous: "In our progress backwards, we become attached to abandoning outward things and limiting ourselves when it comes to our absolute needs; a center of sadness, in which the bitterness and silence of so many things do not wait for death to hollow out for our hearts the gaping tomb where everything candid, gracious, desirable, and primitively good that our hearts could contain is consumed and snuffed out."[32] "Primitive goodness" is the survival of a thought that has molted; the primitivist idea has in fact broadened itself and become a metaphysics of universal order. But each new addition to his breadth of vision produces a bitter reaction at its own unreality, and, when this unreality is recognized, it is contradicted by a new desire, since the recognition is never definitive. Senancour understood early on how dear his own error was to him: "Never to suffer again from error would be to exist no longer"; "the infinite is hidden from me: but the infinite is not forgotten; whoever has glimpsed it will forever search for it"; "what I am is infinitely far from what I need to be, . . . I need limitless illusions, which always recede and end by deceiving me."[33] But are we really deceived? "In truth, till now at least, nothing of what exists has fully gained my affection, and an inexpressible emptiness is the constant tendency of my broken soul. But everything I love could exist, the entire earth could be as my heart desires, without anything being changed in nature or in man himself except the ephemeral accidents of the social fabric."[34] To conclude, illusion and truth are indistinguishable: "Sad, futile notion of a better world! Inexpressible extension of love! Regret for eras that pass uselessly by! O universal feeling, sustain and consume my life: what would it be without your sinister beauty?" "But why should these things be purely ideal? Why should what does not exist seem more suited to human nature than what exists? Life according to facts alone, too, is like a dream. . . . The same mixture constitutes both dreams and ordinary feelings. The wisdom of Antiquity has said that the moment of awakening would come last."[35] Such is Senancour's torment, in which doubt about the existence of God and his providence occurs only as an aftereffect, and whose essence is an endless dialectics of the real and the unreal, of the immediate and the infinite, of the near and the inaccessible as objects of human desire.

Nothing expresses these equivalencies and this persistent doubt better than a celebrated passage:

> A daffodil had blossomed. It is the strongest expression of desire: it was the first scent of the year. I felt all the happiness destined for man. That inexpressible harmony of beings, the ghost of the ideal world was entirely within me: never have I experienced anything so lofty, or so instantaneous. I do not know what form, what analogy, what secret relation was able to make me see in that flower an infinite beauty, the expression, elegance, attitude of an uncompli-

cated and happy woman in all the grace and splendor of the season of love. I shall never understand that power, that immensity nothing suffices to express, that form nothing suffices to contain, that idea of a better world one can feel and that nature would not have produced; the celestial gleam we think we seize, that arouses our passion, that carries us away, and that is only an indistinguishable shadow, wandering and lost in the dark abyss. . . . Who will eliminate in our hearts the need for a different order, a different nature? Could this light be only a fantastic glimmer? In the universal night it seduces and subjugates. We are caught, we follow it: if it leads us astray, it also lights our way and sets us afire.[36]

Thus it is a fact that frustrated Sensibility, in Senancour as in so many of his contemporaries, tends to take leave of the earth, but it is not less true that one does not find in him the religious leap or its spiritualist substitutes. The plenitude that is refused to him, and of which he speaks constantly, is, finally, nowhere. His refuge from the poverty of the real is not in Being itself: he never ceased saying that it is out of our reach: "The knowledge of being does not exist"; "I know of no common language between puniness and Infinity, between us who endure not and the unknown Permanence."[37] He constantly mocked those who make of the inexplicable a mode of explanation: Chateaubriand, in particular, who exploits mystery for the benefit of dogma.[38] The universal order that he imagines or that he celebrates is for him merely the possible, the unknown, an intelligence that is suspected in things, a "general melody," sometimes "a first sketch" and sometimes "what ought to be."[39] He willingly conceives of this hypothetical order as grounded in a universal analogy, in accordance with the peculiar symbolism of the theosophists of the preceding century, but it is easy to trace in him the process by which analogy, beginning with its return to honor in the eighteenth century, detached itself more and more from its ontological foundations and increasingly emanated from the spiritual initiative of the subject.[40] It is doubtless true that already in his first published piece he mentions analogy as a method of induction to restore man, who has today deviated from his true nature, to the universal order and to his relationship to other beings; shortly thereafter, Aldomen imagines relations between the inanimate world and "the metaphysical insights of man's destinies."[41] But these views derive from an optimism that we know to be precarious; the anxiety of atheism and mechanistic determinism constantly threatens them: "[T]here are no longer any of those half-shadows, those hidden spaces which are so pleasing to penetrate. There are no more dubious brightnesses where my eyes can rest. Everything is arid and exhausting, like the burning sand under the sky of the Sahara: and all the things of life, stripped of this veneer, reveal in the guise of repulsive truth the complex, sad mechanism of their skeletal frame."[42] Sometimes he makes the perception of hidden analogies the privilege of a few: "We see, for example, that most would not know how to conceive of the relations between the scent a plant exhales and the means to be happy in the world. Should they then consider the feeling of these relations to be an error of the imagination? Are these two perceptions, so estranged one from the other for some minds, foreign to the genius who can follow the chain that unites them?" But immediately he adds: "You must not take all this more seriously than I say it. But I am tired of things that are certain, and seek everywhere for ways to hope."[43] It is in this light that Senancour's theosophic sympathies should be evaluated. He argues for the meaning of numbers, of dreams, of superstitions, for the "magic doctrine" that gives them all their importance, but all these discussions are illuminated by their conclusion: "I am looking for a little craziness, so I can at least laugh at myself: for there is a certain, perhaps bizarre restfulness or pleasure in thinking that everything is a dream."[44] The theosophists' doctrines are not for him a matter of belief; they are the fruits of doubt, and doubt accompanies them: it is thus that Saint-Martin's doctrine on the "redemption" of the universe through the ministry of man is the object in *Oberman* of a commentary that is at the same time favorable and dubious.[45] And as soon as mystical illuminists turn dogmatic, his severity is extreme.[46] In the last analysis, analogy in his eyes is less the law of nature than the tactic of inquiring genius: "Genius is an insatiable need to push back visible limits; to doubt as soon as light fails, but always to hurry onward toward the unknown, following analogy's tracks."[47] Or rather, communication between the human mind and things seems to him to presuppose communication between minds: "Felt nature exists only in human relationships; and the eloquence of things is nothing but the eloquence of man. The fertile earth, the immense skies, the circulating waters are only an expression of the relations that our hearts produce and contain."[48]

This ambiguous, lucid mind moves constantly toward a single goal: what energizes his work is the energy of a humane quest, an approximation that overcomes the perplexities and struggles of mind and spirit. Such is, at bottom, the philosophy of the Enlightenment, to the extent that it repudiates the ambition for a total truth and complete moral renewal — that is, to the extent that it becomes liberalism. Senancour arrived at an equilibrium, but not by the common, facile path taken by spiritualism; that is, by a sharing out between man and God, between this world and the next. By confronting every difficulty and taking it to heart, he maintained the dignity of the modern faith, which underwent a reformation in him without abjuring itself. His path, between illusion and renunciation, is that of hope: "Of a thousand seeds, one alone will germinate. We should like to see what would be the best possible, not exactly in the hope of attaining it, but in order to draw closer to it than we would if we envisaged as the end of our labors only what they will in fact yield."[49] A human perfectibility, which is related to "extension" and rehabilitated to the same extent as it, turns toward the veiled light of hypothetical Being. Senancour's late writings celebrate, in opposition to the dream of a primitive Eden, the "laborious effort of hope,"[50] which defines our condition and is accompanied on the purely human plane by the fruitful experience of suffering: "It is the continuous action of sorrow, it is the fall of that bitter drop that hollows out life, that makes fruitful what truth has sown in the dry soil, and that reveals sublime seeds in the terrestrial manure."[51]

If I have thought it good to trace in such detail the unfolding of Senancour's thought, it is in order to emphasize a unique example of fidelity to the legacy of the eighteenth century in a mind nonetheless overwhelmed by the new worries. His thinking was molded both by a philosophic tradition and his own experience. The way he envisaged the role of thought in society and the spiritual function of the writer will be instructive to us: this mind, open to every pursuit, accessible to every delight, obsessed by the unknown and the possible, knows almost nothing of the Poet. This is not in his eyes the spiritual type destined to guide men, doubtless because he remained, essentially and despite his torments and his openness to mystery, within the terms of thought of the preceding century. The position that he took in the struggles of his time is not ambiguous. If we do not know how he evaluated the events and the leading figures of the Revolution, apart from the obvious fact that he was disappointed, we do at least know with what hostility he greeted the Restoration. In 1814 he successively published three brochures that were hostile to England and the allies, in which Chateaubriand was upbraided for his pamphlet *Du Buonaparte et des Bourbons*; during the Hundred Days, a piece favorable to Napoleon; a liberal tract after Waterloo.[52] He did not like the moderate liberalism of Benjamin Constant any better, and he had, in the *Mercure* of May 1814, treated very roughly Constant's anti-Napoleonic *De l'esprit de conquête et de l'usurpation*, just as he would later comment without enthusiasm upon Mme de Staël's *Considérations sur les principaux événements de la Révolution française*.[53] I suppose it was political animosity that made him publish in 1816 his *Observations critiques sur l'ouvrage intitulé Génie du christianisme*, which were written much earlier. In any case, in 1809 he was already very critical of the literary counterrevolution: "Of the two beautiful centuries in France, the older is vaunted, for it is closer to the time when minds were docile. Those times of docility — it would be difficult to dare to praise them, but it would be so advantageous if our minds could be brought a little closer to them!"[54] We know this theme of the comparison of the two centuries, as well as the theme that he then develops according to which Philosophy is innocent of the Revolution's crimes.[55] All this situates Senancour unambiguously; throughout the entire Restoration, he wrote without exception for the liberal side.[56]

He was convinced of the high mission of the writer, in accordance with the tradition to which he proclaimed allegiance; he did not feel the need to modify its character when reaffirming it under new conditions. He holds the writer to be the modern equivalent of the ancient Legislator, in whom his primitivism and his philosophy naturally sees an exemplary type.[57] He places the beneficent action of the reformer-writer above purely intellectual or literary glory:

> One says to oneself: I shall fight against errors, I shall follow the results of natural laws, I shall say good things, or things that can become good. Then one feels less useless and less alone on earth: the dream of great things is joined to the peace of an obscure life; one takes pleasure in the ideal, one really delights in it, because one thinks one is making it useful. The order of ideal things is like a new world, unrealized, but possible: human genius will seek in the ideal the idea of a harmony that conforms to our own needs, and bring down to earth happier changes that are planned according to this supernatural model.[58]

A mode of progressive, far-reaching action was thus what he envisaged from 1804 on. He came back to this more and more, in accordance with his general view of things. In 1806, in his book *De l'amour*: "Books do not move the world, but they secretly lead it. The effects of violent means are more visible, but less long-lasting";[59] and in 1832: "The present belongs to the man who commands, but the future is the realm of great writers."[60] These great writers, "the legislators for moral man,"[61] form a type that is in the final analysis superior to that of the primitive legislators: "Strong institutions have become almost impossible because of the present difficulty in agreeing to act in concert with the stars or even to clear away the underbrush . . . ; but if the human heart comes to accept the consequences of thought, moderns will be better than the impetuous or credulous men of early times, and we shall see at last what true society is."[62] It will be noticed that Senancour says "writer" rather than "man of letters": this latter designation, so glorious in the preceding century, has become devalued; for some, at least, it was beginning to connote the profession rather than the mission, as it does today: "I don't like savants or great writers to be designated in that way, only hacks, people who *ply the trade*, or at worst, those who are precisely or merely men of letters." To the contrary, "if a sort of authority is inevitable in all the acts of life, it is indispensable for the Writer. Public esteem is one of the most powerful tools of writers: without it, they are merely occupying a social status; and this status loses prestige when it replaces what was a great mission."[63] In any case, this dispute over terms betrays his desire to place in the highest rank whosoever by writing marks out humanity's future path.

In spite of everything, it is strange that Senancour attributed so little eminence to the poet. Not that the nature and function of poetry did not preoccupy him, but it is as if he were reticent on this subject, perhaps in reaction to the alliance of poetic inspiration and religion that was forming before his eyes. In accordance with the most disdainful philosophic tradition, he sees in poetry a frivolous illusion-making power, a "penchant for realizing dreams, for taking literally what in principle is only figurative," an "uneasiness that one can flatteringly attribute to wide-ranging ideas, but whose real source is our weakness"; however, "the truly religious writer, who had become this as a result of his own researches, descends into nature's depths without getting lost in the midst of illusions; without reducing the magnificence of space to the narrow dimensions of the mystical, without shrinking the heavens while peopling them with seraphic beings, without seeing ghosts where there is nothing, he is able to follow the new paths of unknown truth." He also writes: "The ideal is mysterious; but if you refrain from seeking it where it is not, you will see that it cannot be separated from truth."[64] This is to wish that beyond the rational there be a poetry that is reason itself. Such a poetry has the flaw of having existed only as an idea. Furthermore, is Senancour really thinking of poetry? Or is he thinking of a prose text like his own? In any case, reversing a commonplace, he affirmed that prose was the primitive language, and that verse was the result of an artificial institution: "The clever impostor and the wise legislator made use of the same means; in order to captivate, they astonished. Thus the poetry called the language of the Gods was introduced by enthusiastic or frivolous minds."[65] Wherever he sees the slippery slope of poetic mysticism, he prefers to save himself by means of aridity. Not that he is really arid; no, quite to the contrary. But in him abundance flows from a different source: "O primitive men, scattered here and there in this futile age so that a trace of natural things may survive, you recognize each other, you communicate in a language that the crowd does not understand, when the October sun appears in the fog above yellow woods; when a rivulet trickles and falls in a meadow enclosed by trees, at the setting of the moon; when beneath a summer sky, on a cloudless day, a woman's voice sings at four o'clock, in the near distance, amidst the walls and roofs of a great city."[66] This language, which in the soul is awakened by the wildness of nature, is understood by a few, mostly obscure souls, by those lone "adepts" to whom the

Observations placed at the beginning of *Oberman* are addressed, by that "scattered secret society" of which nature had made the supposed author of the book a member.[67] The natural confraternity that embodies the essential excellence of humanity and its future is not that of poets — nor is it that of devotees of beauty, which is another solution, one of which he is almost entirely ignorant. It is made up of those — battered, weakened, but still alive — who, while adapting it to fit new experience, continue philosophic preromanticism.

✣ *The Early Nodier and the Méditateurs*

After Senancour, and in an order of ideas that is closer to his than might be suspected at first, we must say something of Nodier's beginnings, and of a group that has been almost completely erased from memory, having broken up after a few years without producing anything remarkable. Nodier, having come to Paris at the age of twenty, evokes with enthusiasm in his letters to his friend Charles Weiss the discovery that he has just made of this group:

> Have you heard anything of that group of painters and poets whom the common herd had designated by the name of *Illuminati of the arts*, who were more usually called the *Observers of man* and modestly named themselves the *meditators of the Antique?* You had often heard talk of these youths who pride themselves on resuscitating among themselves the beautiful forms, manners, and clothes of the earliest ages; of those artists who wore Phrygian dress, who ate only vegetables, who lived in common, and whose pure and hospitable life was a living painting of the golden age? Well, I have found them. For two months now I have been spending my days among the *méditateurs*, have been living with them, have been drinking their milk and honey, have been sitting on their mats, have been strengthening my being at their school.[68]

If we believe this letter, the reputation of the Méditateurs had previously reached the provinces, and Nodier, who has arrived in Paris only a short time ago, feels it is quite glorious to think that he is among them. The letter gives some of their names: Maurice Quaï, Alexandre Hue, the brothers Jean-Pierre and Joseph Franque — all painters who are students of David[69] — and a writer, Auguste Glaise.[70] Other letters repeat these indications: "Yesterday, I went to the Sainte-Marie monastery, near Passy: it is there that the Méditateurs have their retreat. . . . They were all there. We were dressed in white tunics and our hair was loose on our shoulders. We stretched out on the grass; we talked about the desert, about friendship, about you, we looked at Paris and we wept."[71] Nodier, who, apparently, walked about Paris at this time with a long beard, long, free-flowing hair, and open collar, heard someone behind him whisper: "It's an *observer of man.*"[72] He describes another session, private and nocturnal this time, at the home of one of the group's members: "We sat in a circle on carpets and smoked Eastern tobaccos in bamboo pipes; then we ate oranges and dried figs, and we read Ecclesiastes and the Apocalpyse." Here the leader of the group, Maurice Quaï, appears:

> Maurice got up, unfolded his great red coat and spoke a language so eloquent, so magnificent, that I thought I was still reading the Bible. . . . Try to combine in a single man the genius of Ossian, Job, and Homer in the shapes of Myron's Jupiter, and you will begin to have an idea of this great work of nature. His voice is like a glass harmonica, and his eloquence is like a delicious scent that sweetly flatters the senses and penetrates every faculty. As a painter he frightened David; as a poet, he would be without rivals; and he is twenty-four years old; I'll show him to you, and I'll say to you: There is Apelles, or Pythagoras, take your pick.[73]

And again:

> Maurice Quaï! That man bears within himself a character so great, so sublime, so overwhelming, that you would almost not dare love him; he would have to teach you how to love him first. If you knew how he makes Chateaubriand look like nothing! He is Job, he is Isaiah, he is Klopstock, and think what a man he must be who to everything that is most rare in human genius joins Poussin's brush, Pythagoras's manners, and the Ammon Jupiter's physiognomy. Add to all that the sublime forms of Antiquity and those charming accessories, turban, red coat, buskins and perfumes . . . you'll see that this man is an astonishment, a demigod![74]

This group of young artists with a primitivist aesthetics and a vast spiritual ambition remains in spite of everything extremely obscure to us. We have hints of the exaltation that reigned among them. In 1804, in his *Essais d'un jeune barde*, Nodier again celebrated Maurice Quaï, who had just died, and Lucile Franque, also recently dead.[75] This piece, entitled "Two Beautiful Types," lyrically angelicizes Lucile, but, one can say, almost divinizes Maurice:

> To that beauty, which had something indefinably changeless and eternal, like that of the Gods, to that great character, which made him participate in *Raphaël's Tout-Puissant* and *Myrron's* [*sic*] *Jupiter*, it seemed that we would see shining around his head the lightning flashes of *Olympus* and *Sinai*. . . . It was this aspect that could have lent itself to the founding of a cult, and never did I set eyes upon him without experiencing a holy shudder; never did I hear him call me to his side with that indescribable, melodious way of speaking that he liked to use, without being reminded that the *God made man* also liked to surround himself with the wretched of the earth.[76]

This might be thought to be juvenile rhetoric: in his letters to Weiss, Nodier vehemently protests several times against this interpretation;[77] and almost thirty years later, returning to Quaï and to his 1804 dithyramb with all the perspective one could wish, he writes: "It seems to me that I exaggerated nothing. Age, which has caused the scales to fall from my eyes with regard to so many things and reputations, has enlarged him still more."[78] Gleizes, who was a member of the group, also composed an enigmatic funeral oration for Quaï, under the name of "the man of strength": "Sometimes he strummed Isaiah's harp, and the people listened attentively. . . . Men will not name him, because he traveled in unknown countries, and lifted only heavy eyelids; but in heaven he is seated beside the All-Powerful"; this man of strength, who is both a friend who has recently died and a type of the spiritual guides of humanity, "has carved his mark on the earth, as the sea has carved its mark on the summits. He lives in the heart of men who know nothing of him, as the sun is in the stone and the trees. Everything vanishes away, except what remains of his passage among us."[79] This extraordinary tone reminds one of Bonneville, to whom were dedicated the *Essais d'un jeune barde*. Nodier, who must have met him after his arrival in Paris, could have borrowed from him this facility for seeing the divine in the human. But, given Gleizes's example, it would seem that this disposition held sway in the entire group.

To these contemporary echoes may be added more detailed later reports. Delécluze, who as David's pupil knew the Méditateurs well, remembers Maurice Quaï in 1824, and speaks of the position he took in favor of primitive art as one of the defining events of the beginning of the nineteenth century. Quaï and his friends wanted to "resume art *ab ovo*, with the Greeks"; moreover, they allowed "only works said to be *primitive*, like the vases and Etruscan statues and everything that derives from the earliest style; these young pupils read only Homer and the Bible; their leisure hours were passed in conversations on the most difficult philosophical questions."[80] After 1830, the eccentricities fashionable among the Jeune-France reawakened in Delécluze the memory of the earlier group, whose long beards and Greek outfits he evoked in a detailed article:[81] these youths, who were called, we are told, the "thinkers" or the "primitives," and who were one-upping their master's own cult of Antiquity, wanted to get back to Homer, to the Bible, to Ossian, and spurned the style of classical Antiquity itself as "rococo," "Van Loo," "pompadour." Furthermore, Quaï was aiming for more than an imitation of any artistic style and considered "the most sublime beauty as the only true goal of art." Delécluze, who calls him Agamemnon, describes him thus: "Tall, thin, hair and beard black and bushy, his fiery gaze and his expression had something that was both intimidating and attractive at the same time. People saw in this man something of Mohammed and of Jesus Christ, two figures for whom he had, be it said, a profound veneration." They nicknamed him Don Quixote, and he did not disavow the name, believing that Cervantes' character belonged to the same family of human beings as Jesus. Delécluze, who does not at all share Quaï's enthusiasms, who while discussing him even speaks of a kind of madness, grants that "this sect of *pensive, primitive* artists was the sharpest and most elevated part of that sort of cone in which the society of the day was contained."[82] Delécluze's article provoked another, Nodier's,[83] which in large part aimed to rectify it: it is as much an article by an adept as by a historian, and it must be read with prudence. In it, Nodier insists on the overall aim of the thoughts that animated "that bearded group of men of genius," "hearts quickly wearied, quick, impatient souls who had rushed pell-mell through art and poetry to take refuge in meditation." It is thus their highly exacting spirits that led them to stand apart from the mass of their contemporaries:

> The general feeling that for them before all else took the place of religion . . . was in the beginning love for and fanaticism about art. By their efforts to perfect it, to purify it in the furnace of their souls, they had arrived at nature, the original model of everything, grand, sublime nature, and for them, during that derivative era of artistic institutions far removed from the essence of things and producing art without self-knowledge and without even speaking its own name, art no longer offered them anything more than a point of comparison and a professional resource. In the end, even nature itself shrunk in their thought, because the sphere of ideas had expanded. They intuited that there was something marvelous and incomprehensible behind the last veil of Isis, and they retired from the world, for they went mad, that is the word for it, like the therapeuts and the saints, mad like Pythagoras and Plato.

According to Nodier, the group itself did not take a name, but they accepted that of Méditateurs. Quaï, who was called only Maurice by his friends, was given by some the name of Jesus Christ, "whose divine ideal he evoked by the gravity of his life, as by his clothing and by his beauty." Nodier speaks of his failed mission, yet of a secretly persistent influence; he attributes to him projects for humanity's moral renewal possessing what he implies were miraculous benefits: "This is not the place to delve into this mystery of palingenesis. . . . Would the reader believe what I have still to say? As for that — alas! — will even what I have said be believed?"[84] There is perhaps quite a lot of the 1832 Nodier in these images of 1800 but, overall, putting to one side the personal note, Nodier says pretty much the same thing as Delécluze,[85] both about the behavior and outward appearance of the Méditateurs and Quaï's extraordinary ascendancy as well as about the complex of ideas the group professed: in addition to a certain conception of art, there can be glimpsed the yearning for a doctrine more vast, a preaching of salvation, a virtual apostolate: a natural extension, since the primitivist dream cannot limit itself to an artistic formula. What we have here is a variant, worked out in an artistic milieu, of that dream, or, more precisely, a variant of the failure of that dream in the midst of real society.

David's pupils belonged to the intellectual milieu produced by the philosophic eighteenth century and the Revolution.[86] They were used to not distinguishing the pictorial style of the master from his revolutionary faith, but they could scarcely live that faith in 1800 as David had lived it in 1793. Republican Rome or classical Greece had lost their virtue as primary models of energy and freedom; it was no longer a matter of remaking society along these lines. The idea of moral renewal according to a primitive type, feeling itself cut off from reality, soared higher, pushed further back in time, toward an ur-ideal that was passionately embraced, but also secretly recognized as chimerical. Something similar was experienced by Senancour, and this is what legitimizes placing next to the stern writer the bearded and costumed artists whose paths he may have crossed in Paris around 1800. We know that Nodier, at this time, enthusiastically admired Senancour (the Senancour of the *Rêveries*, the only one of his great works then published); in 1833, in an article on the republication of *Oberman*, he still remembers that enthusiasm, analogous, though in a different key, to the enthusiasm that Quaï inspired in him.[87] Senancour had been the revelation of his youth, the version of Disenchanted Sensibility with which he came in contact. In that article he tells us that a young man who suddenly recognizes himself in an unexpected passage lives through an invaluable moment:

> He is moved, troubled, transformed. . . . It is the finest moment in life, a palingenesis, an apotheosis, adult childhood and Adam's passionate joy amidst the indescribable marvels of the earthly paradise. Before the age of twenty I possessed a shadow of these delights, as much as my weak constitution would allow. It was on a beautiful summer evening that the *Rêveries* of M. de Senancour fell into my hands before the modest stall of the bookseller Cérioux. . . . Chateaubriand and Ballanche had not yet written. Who could tell the hours I spent devouring him, rereading him, learning him by heart?

Never did Nodier speak of Chateaubriand, nor even of Ballanche, in such terms. In 1800 the ardent and hopeless primitivism of the *Rêveries* was much closer to him than the themes of the Christian Restoration.

Whatever Delécluze and later Sainte-Beuve may have imagined,[88] it does not seem that the Méditateurs' — or Senancour's — way of feeling owed anything to the then-powerful return to traditional religion. They derive rather from the vaguely theosophical Pythagoreanism or neopaganism that was fashionable at the beginning of the century, and to which the young Nodier, too, paid homage, writing several years later *Les Apothéoses et imprécations de Pythagore*:[89] this work, a solemn prize-list of names consigned with an account of the reasons to the veneration or execration of men, is given as "a precious, unique monument of primitive society," drawn up according to Pythagoras himself.[90] Some "Prolegomena by the publisher"—that is, by Nodier—propose a modern supplement of apotheoses, where we note, along with the names of Bernardin, Chateaubriand, Ballanche, Senancour, Benjamin Constant,[91] and Bonneville, that of Gleizes and, in a separate category, those of Maurice and Lucile. All this sketches for us, emphatically, a particular moment and milieu, one from which Nodier derives more fundamentally than might have been thought. It is in this "Pythagoricist"[92] sense that the Méditateurs were, if you like, religious, in a way that was completely modern beneath the primitive clothing, and inclined, like the other variants of the same faith, to the hyperbolic magnification of the human figure. The usual ideas on the earliest language and analogy had to have their place there; this is the case at least for Gleizes, the only one who left a written body of work. His *Les Nuits élysiennes*, which appeared in 1800 and which Nodier, more than thirty years later, still admired,[93] praised the Egyptians for having known about "the general harmony of beings," for "the world is not merely what it appears to us to be; something divine is yet hidden beneath its surfaces; and it is this exquisite nourishment that the thirsty soul seeks everywhere, and that the peoples who have been most endowed with this gift from on high have believed they were seeing: all of nature was for them only a succession of representations."[94] This doctrine was taught in the East to the hero of the book by an old hermit, and it is explained to the author by this hero, who has himself become a hermit in the mountains of Occitania, where he has ended up after extended adventures and where he lives according to nature in a sort of oriental costume. He says that his master "had wanted to make a new language whose words would have expressed by their sound as exactly as possible the very things they represented."[95] The work abounds in praises of the natural life, and there are hints of a survival from world to world with a final absorption into divinity, according to a system of natural illuminism that recalls Rétif and Bonneville. As far as primitivist speculations about language are concerned, we know the place they occupied in the young Nodier, in a way that is quite similar. The idea of a primitive natural language presides over the *Dictionnaire des onomatopées* that he published in 1808; and the notion he then had of poetry derived from the same set of ideas.[96]

None of this should be surprising, since it carries on a tradition with which we are acquainted. What is new is to see this tradition, which is henceforth convinced of the fragility of its links with reality, express itself so willingly in themes of mournful nostalgia. Maurice and Lucile, dead in their twenties, are figures to whom the writings of Gleizes and the young Nodier return obsessively. A weird enchantment emanates from these reveries in which the borders of Eden and of death are vague, in which a legendary Orient — nature, poetry, luminous wisdom — inevitably takes on the colors of mourning. In the *Les Nuits élysiennes*, the long-lost daughter of an inconsolable widower is at last found and led by him to her lover's tomb, where she dies; and this father, from whom the author knows the story, inhabits as an eternal ghost his daughter's tomb;[97] a law of expiation is suggested as the principle of individual destinies.[98] Gleizes's symbolism is like a mortuary intuition of things, a disconsolate poetry of the beyond:

> I have heard the lamentation of the dry grass on the hills of the dead, and the oats moaning like reeds. When the moon passes overhead, I have felt the earth shudder, and a release like the sigh of an oppressed soul. . . . Who will be able to describe this nighttime throbbing awakened by a feeble ray of light? Who will depict the majesty of the tomb, so like the majesty of the Eternal One? It is not confined to the limits of the sepulchre. It spills outside; it gives the sky its colors, the sea its murmur, the earth its emotion. Withered rays, dried-up leaves, wandering clouds, stifled voices, winds, waters, storms, suddenly interrupting the silence or blocking the pale light, such is the funeral procession of the dead. Forthwith the spirits take their places on the hills, a stone of the ancient edifices falls, the ages come to an end. A great awakening occurs in nature. Half of the creatures stand up, those who have suffered and are mournful. From which direction will the sun appear? The children of night do not know. Other mysteries are being accomplished.[99]

He is like a Senancour whose despair has converted him to a belief in ghosts. It is the same tone that we find in the stories that Nodier wrote about the same time. Such are *Le Peintre de Salzbourg* in 1803, in which two dead lovers figure, and the stories of the collection entitled *Les Tristes* in 1806, pieces of poetic prose as much as narrations, stories of degenerate consumption, of regret, of cherished ghosts, in an incredibly disconsolate tone.[100] These stories are often called Wertherian, to take note of an influence that Nodier himself emphasized;[101] but this term risks obscuring the originality of their tone: from this source flowed an entire poetic vein throughout the nineteenth century, nourished by post-romantic despair.[102]

We must not see, in such poetic evocation of the supernatural, a culmination of Sensibility in the direction of religion, but rather a point of departure toward something else. In this mournful, nostalgic fervor, the temptation of the beyond is but the form that despair takes. It is even possible to glorify monastic life;[103] this is merely a way of cursing the real world and the ungrateful crowd. Nor should the strangeness of the doctrines and the spirit of community make us think of the utopian sects that followed: here the Pythagorean projects are marked by isolation and impossibility. Nodier, who indeed believed that "language and poetry had in the beginning been one and the same thing,"[104] was also persuaded that the time of poetry was dead: "Now, the aged nations complain that they have no more poets and forget that they no longer have any vitality. If by chance a creative genius like Homer's appeared, it would lack something Homer had available to him: a world capable of hearing him."[105] The sovereignty of art and of poetry is from this point of view not the aim of a doctrine, but a cause for regret. It is one of the forms of the lost Paradise, the Impossible. The disconsolate primitivism of 1800 is several generations ahead of its time, but in a style and according to motifs that are still not distinctly different from those of the preceding century: it prefigures the bitter divorce between the ideal and the real that, after 1830 and after 1848, in the aftermath of new disappointments, will be the negative formula of the priesthood of the spirit.

Secular Spiritualism: Aesthetics

We must now grapple with the current of liberal thought that was born after 1800 from a philosophic revision of the faith of the eighteenth century, effected in a spiritualist direction. The heart of this movement consists in the acceptance of a preeminence of the divine as the source and foundation of human excellence. This doctrine differs from the deism of the preceding century less in the details of its ideas and doctrines, which are often common to both, than in spirit and underlying attitude: from one to the other the share of divine and human has noticeably changed in favor of the former. This spiritualism is sufficiently independent of religions, especially of Catholicism, to remain in conflict with them, but close enough to religions to be able to claim to assist them in the reconstruction of the social order. In the society that emerged from the Revolution, it was the most common way of resolving the degree of conservatism thought to be necessary in the new order of things. A sort of optimism combining faith in God and faith in man characterizes a substantial portion of the literary Left in the Empire and the Restoration. In its idea of the new spiritual power, this Left quite naturally continues to give first place to the philosopher, although the character of its doctrine has changed. Reason defines what transcends humanity without going all the way to the realms of the sacred; it is above all in aesthetics that the Left believes that human thought is capable of communication with the divinity. In this way, liberal spiritualism effects a rapprochement with the ambiguous Christianity of the poetic counterrevolution; but its underlying spirit is utterly different. Though productive of theoreticians of beauty, this school did not in France produce a single notable poet. It is from the outside that it will elaborate its theory of poetry. It will furnish modern doctrinal sustenance to the idea of a poetic ministry, which finds its realization elsewhere; in this sense, royalist poets who are supposedly the offspring of King David and Isaiah will in the final analysis owe much to Mme de Staël and Victor Cousin.

It is not easy to define the intellectual milieu in whose bosom the philosophy of the eighteenth century continued while revising itself and undergoing a partial conversion. Its point of departure is the group of those who are called the *idéologues* — itself an extremely large, varied group in which are included survivors of the preceding century like Cabanis, Destutt de Tracy, or Roederer, born between 1750 and 1760, and men who arrived at adulthood during the Revolution and the Empire like Fauriel or Degérando, born around 1770; in addition, the shared attachment to empirical, nondogmatic forms of thought is accompanied in this ill-defined milieu by such marked differences in moral philosophy and belief that one is tempted to group with the above-named writers all those whose thought, in this dawn of the nineteenth century, is halfway between philosophism and religion: Mme de Staël, her friends in the Coppet circle, and more generally the members of the same generation who introduced philosophic and literary Germanism into France — Frédéric Ancillon, Philippe Albert Stapfer, Charles de Villers, and Vanderbourg, with his *Archives littéraires de l'Europe*;[106] as well as Royer-Collard, the promoter in the university milieu of the critique of philosophic sensationalism, who would later introduce the half-conservative, half-liberal politics of the *doctrinaires*, and his juniors, Prosper de Barante and Guizot.[107] Influence and personal relations doubtless played complicated and diverse roles in this group, whose spiritualist outcome, at the end of a remarkable process of development, contradicts to a considerable degree its point of departure. Nevertheless, it exists as an ensemble, forming a single family of minds in a coherent enough way.

With regard to the Revolution, the men of this family refuse to express a condemnation on principle, even when they have suffered because of it or opposed it after a certain time. The *idéologues*' model is Condorcet, at once victim and spokesman of the Revolution. Among those just mentioned, several had been émigrés during the Terror or after Fructidor; but they believed that a new order was necessary, and the counterrevolution did not treat them kindly. In this milieu, the critical reexamination of the ideas of the eighteenth century is more or less conscious and goes more or less far, notably in what concerns religion: it ranges from a simple wish to understand religion as an element of the human condition all the way to an affirmation of its redemptive role or metaphysical justification. This reexamination does not take place under the direct influence of religious tradition and its dogmas; rather, it is the result of a philosophic undertaking that, faced with religion, is independent of it, even as it pays it homage. It is thus that the revival of metaphysics during the Empire and the Restoration should be explained. A continuous discussion explores and finally rejects sensationalism: starting with a critique of Condillac's psychology, there is a general movement toward the idea of the irreducibility of the ego to sensations and, from this restoration of the subject, toward the reestablishment of a dualism, of the certain existence of divine being or the absolute, outside of the ego and distinct from the world. It is not that the eighteenth century was ignorant of the argument founding transcendence upon the impossibility of reducing active, intelligent being to sensation; Rousseau used it in his *Profession de foi du vicaire savoyard* [in book IV of *Emile. Trans.*]. But circumstances, and consequently the implications of the argument, were now completely transformed; at the beginning of the century, metaphysics is reborn as a power sui generis in a completely new social situation.

There is no point in describing in detail the development we are evoking here: it is well known that it was exemplified in Maine de Biran, and that he continued to search for a "fixed point" until he came very near a sort of mysticism. But this work of spiritual reconstruction, which took place in him by purely philosophic means, makes him more the father of secular spiritualism than of a genuinely religious philosophy.[108] To the extent that he was known in France, Kant was interpreted at this time more or less in the same sense and to the same ends: a legitimate interpretation, taking things as a whole, as is appropriate from the perspective of the public mind that we are adopting. Kantianism seems to have been poorly received by the *idéologues*; but this judgment must be nuanced: there is as much osmosis and communication as opposition.[109] Philosophy is expected to provide a foundation of belief for a revolutionized society. This was Mme de Staël's understanding, for example, even before her trip to Germany, when, wishing to define Kantianism, she writes: "There is something more in our moral being than the ideas that come to us through the senses"; this is an "inner faculty," and "this faculty, if we are immortal, is what must survive us."[110] Villers, who does not much believe in the vitality of Catholicism, counts on the "new philosophy" to uphold society; to the metaphysics of the senses corresponded a disastrous morality of the passions: "Who knows but that Providence has raised up some powerful geniuses to create a philosophy that will renew us morally, restoring the moral order and reestablishing beauty and honesty on more solid foundations?"[111] and Mme de Staël applauds him for this interpretation of Kantianism.[112] In fact, in the later development of French philosophy, and particularly in eclecticism, the concern for the social order will always be present.

The intimate alliance of secular spiritualism with aesthetics was prepared in the 1800s by the specialized writings of theoreticians of art. Reflection on the Beautiful, all the more widespread in that every credo authorized such reflection, but necessarily oriented in a modern direction by the very fact of this liberty, accompanied the progress of *idéologie* toward spiritualism, and confirmed the place of Art in the new spiritual power. In defining the Beautiful, the eighteenth century had hesitated between Nature and the Ideal, and it had disdained to oppose one to the other absolutely. In the period of interest to us, the same repugnance persists, but with a more acute perception of the dilemma. A polemic develops between the adepts of imitation and those of the ideal. Emeric-David, answering a question proposed by the Institut in an essay contest on the perfection of Greek statuary, denies that the model for this perfection is outside of nature, holds that the *"beau idéal"* is an illusion, and pleads for "visible beauty, real beauty, nature's beauty." Quatremère de Quincy immediately replies to him that "the model is only the means, rather than the end of imitation," whose true object is "the type of beauty that the artist carries in the depths of his soul."[113] One's initial impression is that it is the naturalist thesis that is most frequently formulated in contemporary writings on art. "The fogs of an unintelligible metaphysics" are condemned;[114] the view "that there is no *beau idéal* is professed and the "system of idealism" is classed with "errors of the imagination"; it is argued that the Greeks were able to find beauty "solely by a talent for seeing and observing"; that the ideal in art is obtained by uniting traits that are real, but scattered, in nature.[115] But if one looks more closely, one sees that all these authors agree in admitting that the object of art is a type of beauty that no individual natural model realizes: in this sense they are all idealists. To the argument according to which the type of the beautiful is formed of elements borrowed from the real because they are the best, Quatremère de Quincy replies, it seems to me compellingly, that "in order to judge where the best lies, one must be acquainted with it beforehand."[116] And in fact a preliminary idea of a model perfection is supposed by all the theoreticians of the time, even those most desirous of evading the metaphysics of the *beau idéal*. Thus Emeric-David writes: "The beauty of the human body consists in its perfect resemblance to the original exemplar, which nature took as a model, and which she represents in her productions, every time its means are acting with full freedom";[117] elsewhere he has recourse to the notion of an end, a shameful variant of the idea of a model: he thinks it useful, to support the feeling of the beautiful, to invoke "the competition of the superior intelligence that seeks in all beings the end for which they were created, the fit of their means with their object";[118] others who are of his party speak similarly: "[T]he state of beauty for any being is that in which it achieves its destination."[119] In fact, Quatremère de Quincy, declared champion of the *beau idéal*, does not go much beyond this: he assigns as the object of the arts "man as God would have formed him," "as nature or its elementary type wants him to be," "man reduced to a system, in other words man considered according to the universal principles of an organization as close as possible to nature's designs, and to the primeval type that can be revealed by the study of individuals while meditating upon the laws of the creator."[120] It would therefore be futile to try to distinguish at this time, as some have done, two opposed schools of aesthetics, and even more futile to identify idealism and classicism, naturalism and romanticism.[121] The way in which the romantic revolution in painting defined itself as a repudiation, realistic if you like, of academicism, seems to justify such a way of seeing things, and it is true that Quatremère de Quincy never ceased attacking pictorial romanticism once it declared itself. But in fact his aesthetic doctrine, like that of his contemporaries taken as a whole, continues that of the eighteenth century and prepares the way for that of Cousin and Jouffroy, which one cannot separate from what bears the name of romanticism in French literature.[122] A continuous progress led to an aesthetics of the ideal, more and more conscious of itself, but which, because of this, will justify a more and more brutal vision of reality: a more dramatic relation within the bosom of the ideal/real dichotomy, and not a rejection of the ideal for the benefit of the real, is what the novelty of French romanticism will consist of on the aesthetic plane. To confine ourselves to the period of the Empire, it can be said that we can see roughed out with only rather superficial differences an idea of a Beauty that Nature alone would be unable to account for.

The problem neglected by these philosophers of aesthetics, who are at bottom so fundamentally in agreement, is the one that we have already seen arise in connection with the symbol and that modern aesthetics unavoidably raises: that of the very foundations of the Beautiful, a property of Being or else a subjective construction of the human mind. When we examine the various ways our aesthetic philosophers present this type of beauty about which they all agree, we see them sometimes alleging the designs of the creator or the ends of nature, sometimes the peculiar faculty of the mind that imagines and invents. The ambiguity is all the greater in that no one seems aware of it. The adoration of the Beautiful is spontaneously expressed as an apology for human genius: Plato's beautiful is "produced by the faculty of ideation . . . , it belongs more properly to invention than to imitation"; all of art depends on "the action of generalizing";[123] it is in himself that the artist "ceaselessly pursues the types of ideal beauty . . . ; he grasps them, he combines them, he extends their connections, he genuinely invents."[124] It is true that a clear response to this question does not matter much to the glorification of the Artist, which is assured in either case; even ambiguity serves him, by making him both a revealer and a creator at the same time; at bottom, he wishes to renounce neither capacity. In addition, the kinship of the Beautiful and the Good is affirmed: "Genius is the brother of virtue: the destinies of the universe are henceforth dependent upon their indissoluble union"; "the heavenly love of the beautiful and an enthusiasm for virtue," imprinted in us by works of genius, lead the soul to "the contemplation of everything that makes it feel the excellence of its own nature and the greatness of its destiny."[125] But it is clear, in the texts themselves, that art is no longer the simple helpmeet or spur to morality; it has direct access to virtue by attaining the source of the ideal, by its own paths; the relation of the Beautiful and the Good reproduces, in a new way, the ancient connection of faith and morality.

Thus writers do not fail to emphasize that the essence of art is, as it were, religious: "It is by these first fruits of art, as much as by thunderclaps, that religion begins to reveal itself to uncivilized man."[126] "The first steps that man in the state of nature took toward the social state was an homage to the fine arts. . . . Religions in particular owed to the fine arts much of their progress."[127] Formerly, in Egypt, the arts of design "acquired the power of making the divine visible by the discovery of the *beau idéal*"; similarly, Greek artists, by virtue of their "ideal system" of the arts, were the "veritable ministers of a religion whose faith they established or perpetuated."[128] And up to a certain point, these views can be realized. The modern artist has retained the privilege of conferring immortality upon those whom his works represent; in this way his function derives from the divinity: "As ministers of immortality, artists participate in the noble intention that presided over human destinies"; they are "the heirs who succeed to the creative power that acted only once upon the spheres"; "artists do not know the extent of their power; they do not even suspect the influence that they could exert on the destinies of their countries."[129] An entire sociology of art is constructed, valid today as in the past; a harmony of artistic creations "with the positive interest of the nation, with its practical institutions, with its customary points of belief and dogma" is imagined.[130] Here we can grasp how the most ideal notion of art can imply—and not exclude—its grounding in social reality, as opposed to a simplistic conception that has too long dominated discussions of romanticism. We can also see how metaphysical impulses at the beginning of the nineteenth century could be linked to a development of aesthetics and to the promotion of the artist to a higher social status, as implied by this aesthetic. It is in the work of Mme de Staël that this union will be most amply attested.

✸ *Germaine de Staël and Benjamin Constant*

What defines Mme de Staël, perhaps better than anything else, is a certain attitude toward the French Revolution: she was affected by its impact, but her opinions and her general philosophy were not overthrown by it. Even before 1789, the influence of a paternal spiritualism enabled her to avoid an excess of philosophism; and yet the spirit of reform and modernity drawn from the same familial sources survived in her intact, despite the ordeal of the Terror. Spiritually, the Revolution was not traumatic for her. She will never abjure the system of thought that we see already in 1788 in her *Lettres sur les écrits et le caractère de Jean-Jacques Rousseau*, which wishes to reconcile Rousseau's return to natural truth with the development of the civil order. It is, in fact, a synthesis of eighteenth-century thought, in which the deism of the *Profession de foi du vicaire savoyard* takes on the special color of M. Necker's religion.[131] This system implies both moderation and an openness to new things, necessarily making it odious to the two parties: "The Republic exiles me; the counterrevolution hangs me."[132] Revolutionary in the spirit of 1789, and faithful to that moderate line during and after the turmoil, she maintains the system of perfectibility in the face of the reaction of the 1800s: "Will it be said that barbaric monsters made of that opinion the pretext of their crimes? But did Saint-Barthélemy compel atheism? . . . This system has become odious to some people because of the atrocious consequences that have been drawn at several disastrous periods of the revolution; and yet nothing is less related to such consequences than this noble system."[133] We recognize here the usual position of defenders of the eighteenth century during these years. Other intellectual themes that appear in the book *De la littérature* and that belong to the same vein: the unwillingness to see in the seventeenth century the unique and definitive models of literary perfection, the refusal to separate reason from feeling as the source of virtue, to oppose the scientific spirit to the knowledge of man, poetry to philosophy.[134] The book is full of allusions to the counterrevolutionary impulses of the contemporary generation; in one sense, the entire book is a critique of these impulses. There is a hope that supports this defensive polemic: "When the generation that has so cruelly suffered gives way to a generation that no longer seeks to avenge men by attacking ideas, it is impossible that the human mind should not resume its philosophical career."[135] This hope obviously proceeds from a faith in humanity, in its essential dignity that grounds and unifies all value, because "liberty, virtue, glory, and enlightenment, this imposing retinue attending man in his natural dignity, these interlinked ideas with a single origin, would be unable to exist in isolated fashion."[136] And such a faith, human in its object, owes its comprehensibility to reference to a superhuman order: "All disinterested feelings, all elevated ideas, all deep emotions have a religious character; everyone understands this revelation of the soul differently; but there is no compassionate, generous emotion that does not make us desire another world, another life, a purer realm, where virtue recovers its homeland."[137]

That these views coincide with those of Benjamin Constant is well known. A common attitude at the beginning, even before their meeting, had facilitated the harmony that their affair developed. As for their personal motivations, they differed significantly: in him, anguish at death, an obsession with an automatized humanity, and the need for a source of life are no doubt at the root of his faith in man and in God;[138] in her, emotional unhappiness and rebellion against a society dominated by masculine vanity and futility: such a case might help us pose the problem of the convergence in intellectual creations of various individual motifs with a great historic cause. However that might be, Constant, like his friend and more than she, had sympathized with the French Revolution, and the disgust caused by the Terror had not effaced this sympathy. He too maintains through thick and thin a constant view of life and a constant hope;[139] he too formulates the modern synthesis of freedom and civil order;[140] he too opposes to the philosophy of the counterrevolution a faith in man mingled with religion: "Everything that appears limitless to us, and produces in us the notion of immensity, the view of the sky, the silence of the night, the vastness of the seas, everything that leads us to compassion or to enthusiasm, the consciousness of virtuous action, of a generous sacrifice, of a danger courageously confronted, of another's pain succored or mitigated, everything that summons from the depths of our soul the primitive elements of our nature, the scorn for vice, the hatred of tyranny, nourishes religious feeling."[141]

In such a vision of things, what must above all be defined is the way in which philosophism and religion combine, and in what proportion. According to the explicit statements of the writers we are discussing, what is at issue is not a simple deism, but religion properly so called, albeit not subject to particular dogmas: in this sense, they go far beyond Rousseau. Today this attitude appears ambiguous to us, even more so than deism itself, because it places those who adopt it in contradiction with what they hold most dear, on the one side as well as on the other: it is a humanism that constantly transcends man, and a religion that does not dwell sufficiently in heaven. Such a contradictory system could have prospered, as have so many others that are just as contradictory, if circumstances had prolonged its favor long enough. This favor, as we know, hardly extended beyond the middle of the nineteenth century. In sketching the character of her father, Mme de Staël wonderfully defined an intermediate position between philosophism and piety: her father, she says, struggled against irreligion, "not with that hatred for philosophy that is but a change of weapons held by the same hands, but with that noble enthusiasm for religion without which reason has no guide and the imagination no object, without which even virtue itself is without charm, and sensibility without depth."[142] Such an attitude supposes at least a relative break with the eighteenth century: to adopt it, a partial image of that age is raised up by reducing it to the skeptical and negative aspect of its criticism and exaggerating the debate between the *philosophes* and Rousseau in order to pull Rousseau over to one's own side, toward the spiritualism of earth and heaven. This image of a negationist, abasing eighteenth century that reduces man to a material mechanism, and morality to an interplay of interests, will be, for half a century, spiritualism's target and the background against which writers will aim to advance contrasting views.[143] Texts along this line abound in Mme de Staël as in Constant, and are sometimes so virulent that they seem to come from some contemporary counterrevolutionary pen. Thus Constant defines the men of the eighteenth century as "men of the moment who limit their existence and their influence to that moment and write only to push toward egotism and self-abasement the subsequent generation, which indeed paid heed to their counsels."[144] Mme de Staël went very far in this direction, especially in her book *De l'Allemagne*, in which her spiritualism is more pronounced than in her earlier writings. In *De l'Allemagne* she denounces sensationalism, materialism, the ironic spirit, Voltaire, and the deplorable moral influence of mathematics, going so far as to argue that there are good grounds for superstitions and exhorting savants to take into account "the dark side of nature."[145] Benjamin Constant accompanied her into these outer regions,[146] to which neither of them, perhaps, brought much real conviction. But even allowing for the effects of enthusiasm, it remains the case that everything in our two authors that attests the greatness of humanity is given as religious, and the use of this word must certainly correspond to something in their thought.

Unlike their predecessors of the eighteenth century, they postulate two levels of value: that of humanity, and that which, being above man, is the object of his wishes. This dualism, founded on a psychology of dissatisfaction, is sometimes expressed with utter clarity:

> A desire arises ceaselessly in him and seeks something from him. . . . He has
> become the master of visible, limited nature, and he thirsts for an invisible,

limitless nature. He has provided for interests that seem of a more exalted kind, being more complicated and more artificial. He has known everything, calculated everything, and he experiences lassitude because he has only busied himself with interests and calculations. A voice cries out from deep within him, and tells him that all these things are nothing but mechanism, more or less clever, more or less perfected, but that can serve neither as end nor as boundary for his own existence, and that what he took to be an end was only a series of means.[147]

Everything depends in the final analysis on the nature of the soul, irreducible to the world of bodies and its compulsory subjugations: "There are two different principles of life in the creature subject to death and destined for immortality."[148] Man's excellence is thus not in the realization of some nature, but in a going beyond: whence the rehabilitation of prayer and sacrifice, both practices unfamiliar to philosophic deism, even in its most fervent variety, even in Rousseau. They did not insist too much on prayer, although both of them prominently justified it.[149] On sacrifice as a principle of the moral life, both of them are inexhaustible. Mme de Staël exerts herself, beginning in the book *De la littérature*, in rejecting the morality of personal interest; Constant develops the same refutation as early as 1805.[150] With regard to the antinomy of virtue and interest, they exclude every accommodation or synthesis. "What characterizes the veritable moral dignity of man is devotion; . . . admiration is only merited by a sacrifice of the personality, in whatever form this presents itself."[151] Constant even wanted to see in sacrifice, thus understood, a purified form of what this word denotes in its original religious sense: "The idea of sacrifice is inseparable from all religion. One could say that it is inseparable from every vivid, profound emotion. It is pleasing to love to sacrifice to its object everything it holds most dear. . . . We do not think that philosophers have sufficiently noticed this tendency of man to refine sacrifice ever further."[152] It follows naturally that an apologia for sacrifice leads to one for suffering, which "contains the whole secret of the universe"; "one feels that man is impressive by the very infirmity of his nature, which submits his divine soul to so much suffering, and that the religion of sorrow, Christianity, contains the true secret of man's passage on earth."[153] By contrasting so harshly the dignity of man and natural happiness, our authors obviously inflict considerable violence on the faith of the eighteenth century.

In fact, philosophy, while drawing nearer to religion, still keeps its distance. The supreme value that is celebrated under multiple, equivalent names — devotion, enthusiasm, glory, freedom, virtue, religion, genius[154] — derives from a persistent humanism. It is fine to say: "Conscience, love of the morally beautiful, self-esteem, the need for public approval, all the feelings that philosophers contrast with religious ideas are nothing but those very ideas";[155] but this homage to religion is a way of annexing it. The tone of texts of this sort is not that of a conversion, nor does it claim to be: what is involved is an alliance of the revised philosophic faith and religion, a sort of concordat of more far-reaching consequence than that between the first consul and the pope. It brings to religion the reverence even of those who are outside her; but this enthusiasm, which offers to fraternize with charity, eclipses it and in fact leads to losing sight of it, so that religion risks paying an extremely high price for the support offered to her. How little religion possessed a taste for compromises in those times is known; the need was often felt to denounce spiritualism by name as the enemy of faith. In any case, it is understandable that from the beginning there was competition, conflict, and reciprocal denunciation between those who approved of the *Génie du christianisme* and those who approved of *De la littérature*; between, on the one hand, a conversion of the modern sensibility to traditional Christianity that was complete or at least wished to be, and, on the other hand, this sensibility's veering toward a secular spiritualism more or less allied to existing religions. The literary champions of Catholicism saw in Mme de Staël's book a shameful, bastardized product of philosophy; but their adversaries, who felt themselves to be more modern than they and more expressive of the real movement of society, accused them in their turn of guile and utter duplicity. Benjamin Constant, who speaks only with scorn of Chateaubriand's book, considers it a sort of plagiarism of Mme de Staël's, in a derivative Christian mode: "He ransacked the ideas of the work *De la littérature* in everything he says about allegory, descriptive poetry, and the sensibility of the Ancients, with this difference — that what the author attributes to perfectibility, he attributes to Christianity."[156]

The postulate of generous sacrifice as the character of the beautiful soul and foundation of the moral life allows one to oppose both the counterrevolution and revolutionary radicalism. One might even believe that such a postulate is laid down precisely to achieve such an end: enthusiasm, in politics, condemns the despotism implied in these two extreme doctrines of government. In the decade of the 1800s, it also condemned Napoleonic tyranny, concretely and in the present. The political name for enthusiasm is liberty; its contrary is the depression of spirits condemned to egotism while subjected to the whims of an unchecked power. This reasoning recurs constantly in Constant and Mme de Staël: it is one of the cornerstones of their intellectual system.[157] Thus enthusiasm can be neither Robespierrist, nor absolutist, nor caesarist. A narrow and difficult path opens before it; but that path is the only one that can lead to the future, since it is the path of a human dignity that is obvious; in liberty it reconciles new rights and the old ones that have been able to survive; it preserves, with as much equality as possible, the influence of eminent persons and the aristocracy of property; it is thus, in any case, that our two authors describe it,[158] along with the main body of liberal opinion of their time. One can recognize in these views those of M. Necker and the patriots of 1789 — rapidly swept away by the upheaval, but now resuscitated in a time of calm as the formula for salvation.

Indeed, this restorative intent, albeit in a different sense from that of the counterrevolution, appears in a particular intellectual model that was rather widespread at the time: that which compares the revolutionary period that began in Europe in 1789 with the era of barbarian invasions. Mme de Staël develops this in the immediate aftermath of the Revolution: "Men of the lower classes," she writes,

> have, as it were, invaded the upper classes, and everything we have suffered, and everything we condemn in the revolution, is due to the fateful necessity that has often caused the direction of affairs to be placed in the hands of these conquerors of the civil order. They have as goal and banner a philosophical idea; but their education is several centuries behind that of the men they have conquered. . . . The conquerors must be educated, the enlightenment that was limited to a very small number of men must be vastly extended, before those who govern France will be entirely free of vulgarity and barbarism.[159]

Constant has the same perspective: and, according to him, it is "this new irruption of the barbarians" that created the conditions for Napoleonic dictatorship.[160] This interpretation of the revolutionary datum is frequent from 1800 to 1850. Thus Vigny, in the reign of Louis-Philippe, interprets the democratic Christianity of Lamennais as an effort "to carry the cross into the camp of the Barbarians and to plant it there, as did the Christians of the Lower Empire"; and, on the purely literary plane, he favorably compares the romantic movement to the barbarian invasions renewing the Roman world.[161] Stendhal did likewise and gave a positive role to the barbarians of the early Middle Ages as well as to those of today, the revolutionaries of 1793 or the romantics of 1830.[162]

This model is well worth reflecting on, provided that we remove the pejorative intent that seems to be included in the word "barbarians"; this intent is frequent, but we have just seen that it is not necessarily linked to the model. It cannot in any case be attributed to Mme de Staël, who, holding the invasion of the masses to be inevitable and productive of progress in the long run, considers only the problems it creates. In the aftermath of 1830, Saint-Marc Girardin was blamed for having described the workers of the *faubourgs* as modern barbarians, in a clearly hostile spirit.[163] Ballanche was severe when commenting upon this opinion, at the time when he imagined he saw palingenesis being understood by workers.[164] He himself had, without any hostile intent and in a "plebeianist" spirit analogous to that of Mme de Staël, developed the same thought in his *Ville des expiations*; the Revolution, the sudden, unexpected entry of a mass of men into a level of society and civilization from which they had theretofore been excluded, is for him comparable to an invasion from without: "This time the conquering tribe was autochthonous, it emerged from the very soil. . . . Once again the barbarians conquered old Sybaris, the monarchy of Louis XIV, which had become that of Louis XV."[165] In his eyes, this is certainly an irreversible phenomenon, but unfortunately it is one that was unable to be achieved as felicitously as it ought to have been because of the lack of a doctrine capable of welcoming and disciplining the newly arrived masses: neither Voltaire nor Rousseau were fitted to provide it, being ignorant of palingenetic Christianity; Ballanche thinks himself able to deliver what is needed. Mme de Staël, having applied herself long before he did, beginning with the dawn of the century, to the same problem, had resolved it in a somewhat analogous manner. Trying to understand the spiritual influences through which the barbarians of the early Middle Ages were finally integrated into the civilization that they had overthrown, she thought she observed in this historic process the decisive action of Christianity, which fused into a single society the customs of the invaders and those of the ancient world: "We should be happy if we found, as at the time of the invasion by the peoples of the North, a philosophic system, a virtuous enthusiasm, a strong and just system of laws, which might be, as the Christian religion was, the point of view that would permit victors and vanquished to unite."[166] Thus the Christianity of barbarian Europe recommends itself to her eyes above all because it nourished enthusiasm, "the feeling that causes one to find happiness in self-sacrifice":[167] so that in the last analysis, almost the same remedy that succeeded in the fifth century will succeed in the nineteenth; as she understands it, enthusiasm, for which her Christianity is just another name, is the cement and the eternal restorer of societies: it disciplines the passions while allowing them to live; it reveals to them their ultimate object beyond our natural limits, and tempers the spirit of protest even as it justifies it.

We will not be surprised to find modern melancholy occupying a prominent place in what Mme de Staël calls enthusiasm or religion. "In our times," she writes, "imagination, like reason, must be stripped of the illusion of hope. . . . In the period we are living through, melancholy is the true inspiration of talent: whoever is not penetrated by this feeling cannot aspire to eminence as a writer."[168] Liberal spiritualism cannot forgo the ingredient of sadness any more than Catholicism can. Mme de Staël traces its source back to the character of the northern barbarians, rather than to Christianity; but above all she wishes to see in it, unlike counterrevolutionary neo-Catholicism, a spur to action and greatness here on earth: "Man owes the finest things he has done to the painful feeling of the incompleteness of his own destiny."[169] Thus is integrated into liberal philosophy a melancholy that is explicable without recourse to dogma: "We are not seeking to discover," Constant will write, "the origin of this disposition, which makes of man a double, enigmatic being, and sometimes makes him feel that he does not belong on earth. Believers can see in this the memory of a fall, philosophers can recognize therein the seed of future perfection."[170] Mme de Staël, writing on this same dogma of the Fall, offers reflections just as balanced, and wishes to see "the doctrine of perfectibility and that of the golden age joined and commingled."[171] In the concordat of which we were speaking, it is the understanding of our authors that their humanism deals with religion at least as an equal.

The role of secular writers and thinkers as preachers and, as it were, theologians of enthusiasm is obviously implicit in liberal spiritualism. From the first, Mme de Staël affirms this role as an obvious thing: "[T]he *philosophes* made the Revolution, and they will bring it to its conclusion"; after which they will continue their mission in the new society by inspiring its legislation: "Every legislative act should derive from the thought of philosophers adopted by public opinion"; the "thinkers" will occupy "the first rank in a country that wants to found its institutions on the theory of reasoning, because thinkers are the only true adepts of this intellectual politics."[172] We can see how far she is from acquiescing in the disfavor into which "men of letters" have fallen at this time. Benjamin Constant also speculates on how they might influence the government of the Directory,[173] though he is further from the idea of a constituted, officially acting intellectual power than is his friend; in this he is no doubt guided by a surer liberal instinct: for the officialization of intelligence supposes unity of doctrine, which necessarily places liberty, and intelligence itself, at risk. It is expected, in any case, without too much attention being paid to difficulties, that writers will shape opinion through new institutions and through the customs appropriate to them.

Brumaire made these views unrealistic, but our authors continued to maintain them. In the aftermath of the coup d'état, Mme de Staël exalts "independent philosophy, which judges all institutions and opinions before the tribunal of thought."[174] She sees in the philosopher acting for the public good a sort of superman: capable of saving the innocent and overturning tyranny, "he believes that he is endowed with a supernatural inspiration that he actually experiences."[175] Far from renouncing the eighteenth century's idea of the philosopher as benefactor of humanity, she thinks the moment has come to make this idea, which was only illusory in the old social order, real: the philosopher, whose art is "thought itself, that is, the whole of man," will pass from a "subaltern existence," analogous to that which is the natural lot of musicians and painters, to an active, commanding existence, provided a way is found to raise literature to the desired level.[176]

Poetry has little place in all this. Mme de Staël seems to accept poets only by supposing that they are simultaneously philosophers: "Human intelligence has in our century arrived at a level that no longer permits either illusions or the enthusiasm that creates the sort of pictures and fables that impress minds. The genius of the French has never been very remarkable in this genre; and now the only way we can contribute to the effects of poetry is by expressing the new ideas with which time enriches us in that beautiful language."[177] Poetry, condemned to disappear as such in an advanced state of civilization, will inspire more than one funeral oration in liberal circles. In 1794, Constant stated flatly: "I don't like poetry in any language,"[178] and seems to think himself not at all diminished by that confession. The case of Mme de Staël is more complex. She was in fact always tempted by a prestigious idea of poetry in spite of the low esteem she sometimes seems to have for it. This idea is embodied in the figure of the inspired Poetess, undoubtedly an ideal projection of her own personality. One of her juvenile works shows a heroine who sings her own poems: "Never," she comments, "had the men who devote themselves among us to the worship of the gods appeared to be filled with so noble an enthusiasm."[179] This sacerdotal transfiguration is captured in a portrait of her written by one of her friends in the time of her youth in which she is represented as a priestess of Apollo, a favorite of the god, adored by the crowds, similar to and superior to the Pythia of Delphi and the Sibyl of Cumae: she improvises musical poems, then puts down her lyre and "converses with those gathered about the great truths of nature, the immortality of the soul, the love of liberty, the charm and danger of the passions."[180] A similar figure will reappear more than once in the work of Mme de Staël: as Corinne, improvising at the Capitol and crowned "an inspired priestess who devoted herself with joy to the cult of genius" in the presence of the public; as Sappho, improvising in honor of Apollo, also publicly.[181] Such a representation of herself on the part of Mme de Staël is all the more surprising in that she was never a poet, nor, as far as is known, ever attempted to be. But the division of heaven and earth that is proper to spiritualism irresistibly places the lyre in the philosopher's hand by legitimizing an exaltation transcending ordinary reason. Mme de Staël's work attests to this even more in 1810 than in

1800. The acquaintance she has made in the meantime with German idealism, so strongly marked by aestheticism and so inclined to raise the status of poetry, doubtless reinforced the natural tendency of her thinking.[182]

This movement does not constitute a conversion; she remains a philosopher as she advances toward the realms of Beauty. It is enough to listen to Corinne: "I feel myself a poet . . . when my soul rises up and, from above, scorns egoism and baseness — in brief, when a virtuous action would be easier for me to accomplish: it is then that my verses are more noble. I am a poet when I admire, when I disdain, when I hate, not because of personal feelings, not for my own interests, but for the dignity of the human race and the glory of the world."[183] Thus she calls poetry the origin of all the emotions that confirm the spiritualist faith, and in this sense poetry and religion are nearly synonymous in her writings, being properly speaking neither poetry nor religion, but variants of the enthusiasm that is at the heart of her credo, for "enthusiasm gathers together different feelings, enthusiasm is the incense of the earth climbing toward heaven, it joins one to the other."[184] Poetry thus sees itself placed in a very exalted position indeed; it is no longer a pastime or ornament; without any trace of sacrilege, it can deal with the aims of religion, of which it is the soul,[185] or of metaphysics, with which it intuitively harmonizes.[186] But in the philosophic homage thus bestowed, there seems more of an abstract idea than a real sense of poetry. The German poets whom Mme de Staël admired were not persuaded of her competence: "She is," wrote Schiller to Goethe, "completely insensitive to what we call poetry: of works of this kind she succeeds in assimilating only what they contain in the way of impassioned oratory and abstract generality."[187]

Subject to this reservation, there is no question but that poetry and the arts ended up being exalted in her thoughts. In a general way, Enthusiasm could not turn its back on Beauty; quite the contrary, it summons it, it feeds on it; in secular spiritualism, Beauty is the way in which a God who is less frightening, but also less familiar than the God of religion, still communicates with us: "Idealist metaphysics, among the Germans as among the Greeks, has its essential origin in the cult of beauty, which only our soul is capable of understanding and recognizing; this marvelous beauty is a memory of heaven, our former homeland."[188] The feeling of the beautiful is thus in its way a prayer, an intuition of divine presence, a sign of purity: it sums up in the philosophers' spiritualism everything that, in harmony with morality but going beyond it, is called devotion in religion: the Beautiful is held to be the ally and close relation of the Good, though independent of it and excellent in and of itself; the relation of art and morality rehearses the old debate about contemplation and virtue. On this subject, Mme de Staël, following Kant and Schiller, lays down principles that will prevail in France for several generations: "No doubt everything that is beautiful should give birth to generous feelings, and these feelings are an impulse to virtue; but as soon as our object is to reveal clearly a moral precept, the free impression produced by artistic masterpieces is necessarily destroyed."[189] Since the beautiful is, in brief, the divine as it is visible to man, art is endowed with its own excellence, and must endure as long as humanity itself. Because this tenet contradicts the view widely held by the *philosophes* linking poetry to the infancy of the human race, Mme de Staël draws on her reserves of eloquence in an effort to reconcile the two positions: "It may be that the best time for poetry was that of ignorance, and that the youth of the human race is forever over: but . . . the age of Enlightenment has its innocence just as much as the golden age, and if it is true that in the childhood of the human race one heeds only the convictions of one's soul, it is also true that when one has learned everything one comes back to relying only on them."[190] If this were the case, modern spiritualism would be the heir to the poetic virtues of the golden age.

This set of ideas, like so many others, logically rounds itself out with a symbolic conception of the universe. It is by way of the symbol that the poet or the artist (aestheticism combines the two in the priesthood of the Beautiful) lays hold of the spiritual in the realm of the sensible, which is the domain of poets and artists:[191] "To understand the true grandeur of lyric poetry, one must wander in reverie through the ethereal regions, forget the noise of the earth by listening to the celestial harmony, and consider the entire universe as a symbol of the soul's emotions"; "It is this secret alliance of our being with the marvels of the universe that gives to poetry its true greatness. The poet knows how to reestablish the unity of the physical world with the moral world; his imagination forms a link between them."[192] The poet appears here as an inventor rather than as a hierophant. But the correspondence of the universe with the human soul appears elsewhere as real, the consequence of a divine intention that the poet only interprets: "Why would the supreme intelligence, which formed nature and the soul, not have made the one the emblem of the other? These continual metaphors are no futile amusement of the imagination."[193] We are already familiar with this ambiguity, and we shall not be surprised to encounter it here, too. The most modern tendency is naturally to glorify the human subject on account of the correspondences that its imagination and language reveal in nature, even if it means situating in God the source of such a faculty; but the communication of thought with the truth of things is a no less glorious privilege, which cannot really be renounced: so that indecision on this question is powerfully motivated. What is more, deciding in favor of the ontological grounding of the symbol would result in contrasting this mode of knowledge with science; as a result, preference would be given to poetry over science, but this was resisted in France, especially in liberal circles. Mme de Staël certainly admits the high value of symbolic thought as a stimulus to spiritual life, to the arts, to enthusiasm in general; but she has greater reservations, despite a certain movement in that direction, if it is a question of dethroning empirical science on this account, as Schelling and Novalis do.[194] All the more reason to remain in the ambiguity that is characteristic of this intellectual theme, and to make of the symbol both a human invention and a characteristic of being itself. What is essential is that the new poetic ministry be able to build upon this foundation — and it will demonstrate that it most definitely can.

In the idea that she formulated of a modern spiritual power, then, Mme de Staël seems in the course of time to have granted a larger role to the Poet. But in her eyes poetry always remained an eloquent form of enthusiasm, and enthusiasm remained a fervent movement of thought. The way in which she comes to celebrate, even in the book *De l'Allemagne*, the Republic of Letters and the writers who embody it, attests well enough to the permanence in her work of her original philosophy. Those she evokes are doubtless no longer purely philosophic men of letters in the eighteenth-century sense, leaders of opinion and inspirers of laws, but they are always thinkers, albeit at a greater remove from the social body: "It is the association of all thinking men, from one end of Europe to the other. . . . These are really the people of God, these men who have not yet despaired of the human race, and wish to save for humanity the dominion of thought."[195]

❧ Eclecticism: Cousin, Jouffroy

In the course of the Restoration, the development of this secular spiritualism, including, as we have just seen, an implicit metaphysical doctrine of the beautiful and an implicit political doctrine of liberty, clearly reveals an inclination to present itself as an official credo of reconstituted society and a desire to found a new spiritual power. Indeed, this philosophy was felt able to mesh with the state university that Napoleon had substituted for the teaching institutions of the church. For posterity, this combination has been embodied in the person of Victor Cousin: as a professional philosopher, he was responsible for the formalization and triumph of the doctrine in the University (i.e., the body of teachers employed by the state) of which he was for a long time the leader. The spiritualism of the university, with its political ramifications, had already been embodied before Cousin in Royer-Collard: this philosopher, who was a university professor in the Empire and who claimed triumphantly to refute sensationalism and to offer in its place a constructive philosophy, would, as is well known, be the head

of the group of Doctrinaires at the beginning of the Restoration. It is precisely
in this era, during the period of moderate royalist government, which lasted
from 1816 to 1820, between the White Terror and the assassination of the duc de
Berry, that Doctrinairism in the broadest sense of the term, not as the thought of
a small group of politicians but as the alliance of moderate liberalism and spiritualist philosophy, had its golden age. Under the duc Decazes, those adherents whose careers had begun in the imperial era—Royer-Collard, Guizot,
Barante—were able for the first time to believe that they were in harmony with
France's government; those who, following them, were then coming of age, the
initiators of the Eclectic philosophy—Cousin, Jouffroy, and the young members of the staff of *Le Globe* (born between 1790 and 1800)—established in these
years the themes of their thought, in harmony with the movement that seemed
to carry along the most enlightened part of the ruling class. One of them would
later evoke "that earliest age of the Philosophic School, which extends from
1815 to 1820 and was the true incubation period for all the later works and accomplishments."[196] It is appropriate, however, to situate Doctrinairism and its
Eclectic accompaniment in a more extensive spectrum of philosophico-political
thought, embracing, along with the "ministerial" royalism (as it was called at
the time) of Decazes and the whole tradition of tempered *Idéologie* and spiritualism in Mme de Staël's vein, everything in liberalism generally that attempts to
complete the critical mind's work through an effort of spiritual reconstruction.
Sainte-Beuve noted that Royer-Collard did not like to extend the name Doctrinaire to those outside his own group.[197] Such an extension of the meaning of
the term is nevertheless convenient, and corresponds to reality: more than once,
contemporaries were struck by this fact. Hugo, in his *Les Misérables*, defines the
"Doctrinaire party" as follows: "They opposed a conservative liberalism to destructive liberalism, sometimes with a rare intelligence."[198] Such a definition
obviously extends beyond the small group of Royer-Collard and his friends.

A few simple ideas dominated the new doctrine. The *philosophes* of the eighteenth century did not succeed in creating a body of beliefs capable of replacing
those that their criticism discredited. Events showed the rash and finally ruinous
character of their project. Society nearly perished for lack of spiritual support.
The new world needs certainties that it can oppose to the past and to subversion. Only a philosophy that has been returned to its true dignity—that is, only
a restored metaphysics—can procure such certainties. It is not possible to go
into detail here about the sources or procedures of the new philosophy: procedures that were often unconvincing, a sometimes incongruous combination
of thoughts inspired by historically different systems, half-baked constructions
that pretend to be unaware of the difficulties of post-Humean, post-Kantian

ontology. This philosophy, which was known as Eclecticism, was quickly forgotten by philosophers, and was, in fact, never taken very seriously beyond the borders of France.[199] And yet a consistent will animated this intellectual movement. Royer-Collard grounds his metaphysical assertions in what is habitual and acceptable to the human race, and Cousin, in his first class at the Sorbonne, intends philosophy to answer a pressing social need: "Let us," he says, "by means of a system of moral philosophy that will strengthen it once and for all, support French liberty, which still totters, weakly supported, amidst the tombs and debris that surround us; and, Messieurs, let us seek this system from that generous philosophy so honorable to humanity, which, professing the noblest maxims, finds them in its own nature."[200] The very name, Eclecticism, is significant:[201] if one claims to borrow from all, it means one believes in a permanent and salutary philosophic truth scattered among the different systems; it is less one's intention to compose a new system by some anthologizing procedure than to restore the essential basis of which each individual has given a particular version, thus recovering the fundamental certainties without which humanity, and in particular that of 1815 in France, would be unable to subsist.[202] It is in this sense that for Cousin, the history of philosophy, which the *idéologues* had only glimpsed but which he founded in France, is not distinct from philosophy itself.[203] It arrives at assertions bearing on the reality of things and the existence of an infinite being, as well as on the absolute value of the Good, and it claims to provide in its assertions the foundation of political liberty.

The history of philosophy is accompanied from the very start by a philosophy of history, the secular equivalent of Christian historiosophy: lacking the dogmas of the Fall, the Redemption, and the Last Judgment, it retains the notion of the Spirit governing humanity, each historical reality being incarnated in an idea, and the general economy of history reflecting and realizing the "invisible world of ideas." The *philosophes* of the eighteenth century, Turgot and Condorcet especially, already sketched a synthesis of history as a succession of stages of human perfectibility—a notion, according to Cousin, "too neglected today, one that will always be the refuge of every elite soul." Cousin seems to wish to take up this synthesis again with the same fundamental idea, in the new perspective of his spiritualism.[204]

It is easy to detect an ebbing of the humanist faith at the root of Eclecticism, a sort of public apology to religion on the part of philosophy, and Eclecticism is indeed this, in one sense; but the homage is at the same time a renewed declaration of rivalry. The fact that Eclecticism claims to be founded on the common sense and universal tradition of humanity[205] is perhaps due to its philosophical weakness: for our reconstructors, it is a convenient means, borrowed from

Scottish philosophers, to overcome difficulties by peremptory assertions; but more profoundly, it is above all the sign of an ambition to govern spiritually: whoever claims to speak for humanity is in reality legislating for it. It is curious to note in this respect the identity of attitude that we find in Eclecticism and neo-Catholicism, which is hostile to it: Lamennais, too, claimed to base support for the old religion on universal agreement and the tradition of the human race. And in fact, since the authority of scriptural revelation was shaken, there remained no other recourse than having collective belief arise from what is commonly held to be self-evident. Lamennais, too, calls the seat of this self-evidence reason, though unlike Cousin he places therein all the mysteries of Catholicism. For Cousin, moreover, "reason is literally a revelation," in that it reveals God to man, being in some sort "the God of the human race."[206] But we must understand that "philosophy is the light of all lights, the authority of authorities."[207] Cousin reestablishes a hierarchy in the place of the state of war that had reigned in the eighteenth century between philosophy and religion, but one that is the opposite of that which had prevailed before the conflict: henceforth, the supremacy belongs to the philosopher; religion answers the needs of the unreflecting masses; philosophy is the food of minds capable of absolute truth. The arrangements with which Cousin tried to surround this new relation of religion and philosophy should not deceive us: all the family resemblances he suggests between Christian dogma and his own doctrine (for example, between the Word of the theologians and his mediating Reason) only underline the primacy of the philosophic concept over the article of faith. Doctrinally as well as practically, his very position obliges him to handle the church with care; he alternates between accommodation and firmness, because his task is a difficult one: the moderation of the party he represents makes him beholden to the power he opposes, which, however, is neither moved nor deceived by his concessions. The church never thought of him as anything but an enemy; it could not forgive him his philosophy,[208] and even less so given that his philosophy had, in only a few years, become embodied in an institution long held suspect that had stripped the church of its teaching function: through Eclecticism, the University of which Cousin was the head after 1830 took on the appearance of a secular church, with its doctrine, its hierarchy, its prominent individuals, its influence on minds. Cousin defended it as much as he could until the collapse in 1850 and the clerical invasion in education through the Falloux legislation. When the Left was reborn at the end of the Second Empire, it remembered above all the dictatorship that Cousin had wielded over the University, and how it was fatal under his reign to be suspected of holding opinions more advanced than his own. This reaction, albeit legitimate,[209] should not cause us to forget what Cousin's real position was vis-à-vis the church and those who supported it.[210]

Sainte-Beuve, who, at the end of his life, rallied to the support of the Second Empire, looked askance at everything connected to Doctrinairism, and rejoiced in the ruin of the Eclectic philosophy. He attributes this ruin not to the opposition of the "free philosophers" oppressed by the master, but to that of the church: Cousin aspired "to found a great school of intermediary philosophy, that would not offend religion, that would exist side by side with it, that would be independent of it, often appearing to be auxiliary to it but that would be, still more, protective of it, on occasion dominating it, in the expectation perhaps that it would succeed it." Sainte-Beuve, magisterially and with a hypocritically restrained sympathy, describes the great bourgeois panic of 1848 and the almost universal recourse to the church as a last bulwark: in such a state of affairs, "there was no more room for the sort of intermediary philosophy of M. Cousin, and the master himself seems to have understood this when he took refuge in literature properly so called, which now distracts and possesses him more and more."[211] The malignity will be remarked in the allusion to the later Cousin, removed from practical matters and now the historian of the great ladies of the seventeenth century, this being the Cousin who was most known when Eclecticism was forgotten. Ten years earlier, Sainte-Beuve was already characterizing Eclecticism in the same way: Cousin planned to reestablish a second Cartesianism, willing like the first to accommodate the reigning religion; but, circumstances having changed, this church-companion Cartesianism "would only be a sly companion who, with all the respect for his friend in the world, would end by (I sincerely beg your pardon) stripping him bare."[212] At the end of the century, Faguet, too, classifies Victor Cousin among "the men who, from 1820 to 1850, tried to establish a new spiritual power, either to replace the old one, or to live concurrently with it with the title of presumptive heir"; the former University, Faguet continues, "thought of itself as a church, and the word *sacerdoce* [ministry or priesthood] was not then a metaphor to be used when awarding prizes . . . ; the University was wary of the clergy only because it had the pretension of being one."[213] And one can be of the opinion that, of the many attempts of the same kind that occurred in this first half of the nineteenth century, it was Cousin's that came the closest to success: secular spiritualism and the University that taught it had more sociological reality and longevity than the Saint-Simonian family or the phalanstery.

Secular spiritualism offered to the new French society a formula of conservation that was relatively open, in that it was disengaged from institutions and dogmas that belonged to the past and was permeable to reforms, maintaining all the while the spiritual foundations of social discipline. If the antecedents of this philosophy are sought, taking into account milieux and individuals as much as ideas, we find Mme de Staël and her father, the patriotic representatives of the Constituent Assembly and the monarchical emigration, all of them devoted both to reform and conservation, resolved to sacrifice, insofar as this might be necessary, the privileges of the old order so as to maintain in the new the essential institution of property—in brief, a coalition of the old aristocracy prepared to accept change and the bourgeoisie desirous of acceding to the level of power. The leading idea and goal are the recasting of a ruling class, an amalgam of interdependent persons of note who feel loyalty both to the old and the new France. This indeed is the Doctrinaire spirit in politics; the relative failure of the formula in France was due at least in part to aristocratic resistance, which very imprudently divided the establishment; in spite of everything, this spirit triumphed, on the whole, in 1830. This is a simple analysis that has often been made before, and that is very likely accurate, but that does not take enough into account the embodiment of Doctrinairism in a special, distinct body, and of the pretension in higher education of a supremely eminent social mission. Above all, *la Doctrine* was capable of autonomous developments at the highest level, precisely where it became Philosophy. It is remarkable that secular spiritualism was unable to confine itself to a close and strictly obedient adherence to Doctrinaire policies. In romantic humanism, the doctrine of the True, the Good, and the Beautiful irresistibly joined ideas that had come from elsewhere. The intellect had to seek its way outside of the bourgeois order, and, even when it did not condemn that order, place itself above it and judge it. In this sense, the new metaphysicians appropriated from the church a prerogative of which it is obvious that it had not wished to be relieved. It is true that the church was defending the old order; but it would certainly rather recognize the need for change—what happened later at least demonstrated this—than give up its ministry. It does not seem possible to situate properly the spiritualist professors of the Restoration and the July Monarchy without taking into account the degree of autonomy inherent in every body of clerics, and in particular in the body of secular clerics of modern France.

Cousin had the virtues and, to a certain extent, the blithe obliviousness of the leader of a movement. The difficulties of the common enterprise appear more clearly in the case of a disciple who was at once Cousin's contemporary (within a few years), his partisan follower, and his emulator: Jouffroy possessed a sharper intelligence than did his master, and his mind was more all-encompassing, more sensitive to everything in the needs of the new society that went beyond the narrow framework of Eclecticism. At its very origin, Jouffroy's philosophic vocation comes from living through an intense crisis: in a famous account of a December night, he described what the loss of faith in the divinity of Christianity was like for him; as well as how, when he found that after this "nothing was left standing" in him, he resolved to seek in philosophy the answer to the problem of destiny: "My intelligence, spurred on by its needs and broadened by the teachings of Christianity, had lent to philosophy the tremendous interest, the vast background, the sublime importance of a religion."[214] We see here in the intimacy of a spirit the root of a spiritualism that, in Cousin, appears rather as an intellectually and socially necessary construction: in Eclecticism, as in any doctrine, these diverse motivations supported each other. The problem of destiny (which is the soul of philosophy according to Jouffroy) and the necessity of attributing an end (that is, a meaning brought into harmony with a value) to our own existence and to humanity's existence as a whole[215] demote questions of pure metaphysics to secondary importance in his view;[216] with respect to this, he complains of having been disappointed by his first contact with the Ecole Normale and Cousin;[217] this is because, even more than Cousin, he hoped to find in philosophy an answer to what humanity needs. As was the case for all the disappointed progeny of the eighteenth century, his point of departure was an experience of dissatisfaction, of the ordeal of a divorce between what is given to us and what we can conceive: "By our conception," he writes, "we surpass the beauty of everything that exists."[218] Our destiny is therefore superior to our condition: this is what was being said constantly ever since Sensibility's mood darkened and gave itself a spiritual meaning.[219] Just as philosophy, in Jouffroy's eyes, has meaning only insofar as it defines this destiny, so liberal politics for him founds itself on the question of the ends of humanity, arbitrary power being power that denies any meaning to our existence.[220]

We see Jouffroy occupying, then, by way of an original approach, the usual positions of the school to which he belongs. He, too, affirms a faith, and makes the usual leap from desire toward infinite being: "What is lacking exists since we feel its lack."[221] He has acute doubts, however, on more than one occasion, about the validity of this attaining of belief through the need to believe; as early as 1819, he judges Cousin's ontology to be unconvincing: "I'll be damned if I see the slightest reason to believe in the objective, absolute truth of these principles, this destiny, these morals."[222] Or again: "What spoils the affairs of God in our heart is what ruins those of so many lovers, absence."[223] These reservations extend through all his writings;[224] when affirming his faith, he emphasizes philosophically that it should be considered as such: a nuance that well defines the character of this mind.[225] Similarly, it was certainly his (and Cousin's) wish that a permanent philosophic truth, the patrimony of intellectual humanity, be established, with a history of systems as a basis; he, too, sees in such a history of thought the key to history *tout court*, which is "in the last analysis only the history of ideas";[226] the whole of this conception has, for him, too, the consequence of making philosophy the conscience of the human race, it being supposed that there exists an intimate harmony between the spontaneous thought of men, or common sense, and the reflections of the thinker. But it is certain that he, more modestly than Cousin, keeps to an empirically anthropological point of view, according more attention than Cousin to real humanity.[227]

Above all he poses more questions about the credo that should replace traditional faith. Like so many of his contemporaries, he was convinced that the time of Christianity was past; he believed, like the philosophers of his school, that the time of philosophy had come: "Religion is philosophy bending down to pick up children. . . . Philosophy will be the religion of the world grown old, as religion was the philosophy of the world still a child."[228] It was no longer a question any more of refuting religious dogmas, but of taking note of their desuetude and speculating about the beliefs of the future. Eclecticism believes it knows upon what credo society will rest from now on: spiritualistic deism will be the common faith. To what extent is Jouffroy convinced that such a credo can suffice for the humanity of tomorrow? His famous article of 1823, "Comment les dogmes finissent," magisterially depicts the dislike of the old beliefs: he paints the eighteenth century as a time of purely negative criticism, according to the habit of all his contemporaries inclined to reconstruction. But a victory that leads to a vacuum of belief has no future: "We need to believe, because we know that truth exists. . . . What is false destroys, and we want the truth." In this way the adherents of the old faith recover their influence over a demoralized people, and those who triumphed through negation are henceforth powerless; this generation must give way: "Its work was to destroy, it will never be its role to reestablish." But: "A new generation is arising: it has heard and it has understood: for it, the old dogma has no authority; for it, skepticism is right to oppose dogma, but is wrong in itself: when it has destroyed, nothing remains. And already these children have outdistanced their fathers and felt the emptiness of their doctrines. They have had an intimation of a new faith; they attach themselves to this enticing perspective with enthusiasm, with conviction, with resolve. The hope of new days is in them; they are their predestined apostles, and the salvation of the world is in their hands." This generation—that of Jouffroy—knows that its mission is "to discover the new doctrine to which all intelligences aspire without knowing it, in the name of which every hand will arm itself if need be, which will replace the vacuum left by the old doctrine."[229]

The fervent, prophetic tone betrays a mind ill-adapted to be really happy with professorial doctrines and a politics of the *juste-milieu*. Yet such was Eclecticism. Jouffroy adds to this a breath of utopianism, an expectation, which exposes him to suffering the ordeal of events. By bringing Doctrinairism to power, 1830 shrank its dimensions. Jouffroy was the one who had aimed the highest; in the intimation of a faith to come, this subtle, prudent, but vulnerable mind had ventured farther than his companions: thus it is especially of him that explanations will be demanded when faced with the reality of the July Monarchy. The Saint-Simonians, in particular, now without reverence, attacked this inconsistent precursor for being too faithful to his timid school.[230]

Will the philosopher's faith, with neither prayer nor worship, suffice? The Eclectics were not excessively concerned with answering this question. On the other hand, they reflected at length on what takes the place of worship and prayer in secular spiritualism; namely, aesthetic feeling. It is not by chance that the first account of Cousin's philosophy and his most original work is his 1818 course on the ground of absolute ideas, better known under the title *Du vrai, du beau, du bien*,[231] and that one of the two courses by Jouffroy that were able to be published after his death is a voluminous *Cours d'esthétique*.[232] Through these two works, the reflection on the beautiful is integrated into a general vision of man and the world, breaking away from the art criticism to which it had generally been linked in the course of the preceding period. The central step that this aesthetics takes consists in passing from the domain of psychology to the domain of values, from the feeling of the beautiful to the affirmation of an eminent degree of perfection joined to this feeling: this step is arrived at by discovering that the Beautiful in nature is for us different from the agreeable or the useful, and is, in the works of men, independent of imitation.[233] Given this, how can we not see that through the intuition of the beautiful we are in the proximity of an Absolute that is beyond us?[234] This rise in status accorded to the Beautiful naturally frees art from all subjection; morality itself is only connected to it by their common origin in God; this is why, "if art is conducive to the perfecting of moral character, it does not seek this end, it does not propose it as its goal"; "religion is needed for religion's sake, morals for the sake of morals, just art for art's sake."[235] There is something wrong with the triptych Cousin evokes: with morals and art he ought to say, not religion, but metaphysics, and complete in this way the apportionment of the domains of thought, according to Eclecticism; this was certainly Cousin's idea, and it is what the title of the work says, where the "True" certainly does not refer to religious dogmas. It is superfluous to observe that by making the Beautiful its own justification and Art its own master, there is no intent whatsoever to withdraw them from thought. Quite the contrary: the formula of *l'art pour l'art*, which appears here for the first time, has the very same sense it will always have; far from reducing art to sensation and form, it creates in the empyrean of values a sovereign entity, the only one that might rival religion in the intimate apprehension of the divine. We ought not be surprised that Jouffroy, going further, writes: "The moral point of view is . . . only a special case of the aesthetic point of view," and considers himself obliged to prove this: the Beautiful is judged with reference to the absolute, and the Good by adding to this the consideration of circumstances.[236]

Eclecticism offers the first coherent synthesis of the tradition of the *Beau idéal*, which flourished in France in the eighteenth century and during the Empire, and the poetic symbolism favored by the spiritualization of Sensibility. The *Beau idéal* by nature is the occasion for symbols, since it manifests itself to us in perceptible objects, insofar as those objects testify to something else. To define it, as Cousin does, as "a moving plane between nature and infinity" is necessarily to condemn "any school of painting, sculpture, or music that does not conceive of nature as a symbol."[237] How would "the beauty of the invisible . . . , the only sort that we can call by the name of beautiful without logically contradicting ourselves," reveal itself to us if not "through natural symbols that strike the senses?"[238] Jouffroy notes that we naturally attribute a meaning to objects: "Everything we perceive excites in us the idea of some other thing that we do not perceive"; objects thus appear to us as expressive; Jouffroy gives to what they express the names *force* or *soul*, and the effect this expression produces in us, the name *sympathy*, and he reflects at length on the variable degree of expressivity possessed by different sorts of objects in nature.[239]

However, neither Jouffroy nor Cousin stated very clearly whether the meaning that the artist gives to things through the symbol corresponds to their underlying reality — that is to say, to the meaning of the creation according to God — or merely shows a way of being and an endowment of the human mind. We inevitably encounter this question as soon as we come to modern poetic symbolism. Spiritualism would seem to be obliged to profess the former opinion; and yet it hardly ever offers us anything but ambiguous statements. Jouffroy, arguing in favor of the symbol, declares that the perceptible forms are the "intermediaries that alone enable mind to communicate with mind,"[240] but it is not clear whether he is thinking of a communication between human beings and God or between one human being and others, in particular the artist and the public. When he distinguishes "artificial symbols" from "natural symbols," it is not any clearer whether the distinction bears upon the degree of truth in meanings or upon the extent of their suggestive force.[241] Is what he calls expression the manifestation of the true force of things or the mind's inventive way of proceeding when it comes to grips with things?[242] *Expression, meaning, to find, to understand, to discover* — there are double meanings in all these terms that seem to make of the artist-interlocutor a spirit present at the creation: perhaps they refer merely to the human mind itself exploring human talents through the spectacle of the world. Sometimes things seem to have their own immanent, more or less explicit language: "The stone . . . is a poorly written, scribbled word; there are letters there, we know it; but we are unable to decipher them"; elsewhere all meaning is attributed to humanity: "The beautiful is that with which we sympathize in human nature as expressed by the natural symbols that strike the senses."[243] It will be objected that this is an empty distinction, that the meaning of things and the active processing of the mind exhibit both competition and adequation, and that even in the most ontological conception of the symbolism of things, the human mind is at the center of the very notion of meaning: it is for humanity that God makes the objects of the universe speak. But it is precisely the relative proportion of God and humanity that is at issue. The God of the Eclectics, and that of the poets of the nineteenth century, seems scarcely to be the author of meanings: it is artists who engender, who literally create, in whatever way their genius wills, the infinity of possible symbols. All of modern poetry draws its force from its double grounding in the postulate of transcendent being and in the creative freedom of the thinking subject; it supposes both the divinity of the symbol as a reference to the infinite, and its creation by a human being who confers on things the only meaning they are capable of having. This as it were heroic role of the human creator appears clearly in formulae like "to free the ideal from the shackles of the real," "to raise the real up to the ideal, such is the mission of genius";[244] such formulae well express the idea of a transfiguration of the perceptible world of which the artist, acting in the name of humanity, is the author. All romanticism sustained itself on this fertile ambiguity, the reflection of the avowed or implicit essential ambiguity in the domain of poetic creation of the humanistic spiritualism that is romanticism's philosophy.

In this aesthetics of the symbol, poetry is naturally accorded pride of place — that which its medium, language, holds among all sign systems. Poetry "is, so to speak, the center where all the arts meet . . . it is the faculty of expressing everything with a universal symbol"; for "the word is the most vast and clearest symbol . . . it is the simplest and richest manifestation of the absolute."[245] The relation of the Eclectic doctrine of the Beautiful with the romantic works that are coming cannot really be doubted, although in literature and in art the relation of theories to works is always difficult to specify; the ideal and the real, referred to everywhere, is never understood in the same way: Boileau wished to combine them, and so did Victor Hugo; and we have seen that Quatremère de Quincy, who certainly considered himself to be classic, was already thinking in terms that are close to those of Cousin. Here, I think, is the difference: traditional aesthetics willingly merges the *Beau idéal* and the work of art; man in the perfection that we can attribute to him is figured in a Greek statue. The frank dualism of the Eclectics tends to change the result but with scarcely any change in doctrine: the Beautiful in itself withdraws from the real to the point of being called the Infinite, the unrepresentable though always indispensable matrix of every work of art; and the perceptible object that the work represents and by which the reference to the infinite is effected can be any object at all, even an ugly one, since that reference, far-removed and indirect in any case, is the voice of the entire universe. This is how one can say with equal truth that this aesthetics, and the aesthetics of all French romanticism, represents a step toward idealism, or toward realism: it advances at the same time toward the two extremes, which the function of the Poets will always be to join together through the symbolic power of their language. They will repeat it often enough: their domain is henceforth the entire universe, all of whose conditions their genius traverses and embraces. How could it be otherwise? The limits of the Beautiful widened in both directions to the very limits of the world only with the aim of opening to them a realm worthy of them.

Granting all this, we must not forget the obstacles that, right up to the last years of the Restoration, liberal thought, in its efforts to define a new spiritual power, raised against a genuine invasion of poetry. Neither Cousin nor Jouffroy are poets; far from poetry, they follow in the footsteps of Mme de Staël and Constant. And in affirming, with insistence, the primacy of philosophy over religion, they certainly never intended to set up poetry as its equal. Sainte-Beuve, who feared that Jouffroy was getting lost in abstraction, nevertheless only advised him to write a novel.[246] Jouffroy never followed his advice. But what shall we say of these lines in which he compares poetry and philosophy: "Poetry sings the feelings of the period on the good, the beautiful, the true. It expresses with greater animation but not with more clarity the confused thought of the masses, because it feels this thought more intensely without any greater understanding of it. If poetry understood, it would become philosophy and would disappear. This is why poetry is more beautiful and more common in centuries that are not very enlightened, and more rare and colder in centuries of enlightenment."[247] If there are rare poets who have been able to understand pure truth, free of the realm of the senses, they have had to cease being poets in doing so, unless they "found forms to express a thing that had none."[248] We are given to understand that poetry, in revealing the infinite to us, necessarily degrades it, so that the progress of true thought can only be accomplished at its expense. The present time is therefore not called to a great poetic destiny: this is what was already feared in the eighteenth century, and what liberals often repeat in the nineteenth. Besides, poets are concerned only with current, shared beliefs; only philosophers are concerned with ideas on the march and the victories of the mind.[249] In sum, after having raised Poetry so high, we must accept that it is foreign to and inferior to Truth, which is the appanage of philosophers — a condemnation with which we are already familiar.

Chapter 6
The Poetics of the Theosophist

NOTHING in the first quarter of the nineteenth century attests better to general progress toward the unity of every variety of spiritualism, whether linked or not to the reigning religion, than the example of a few theosophists in whom this unification takes place more naturally than elsewhere: it is the function of illuminism to wed traditional religion and independent reflection. After 1800, especially after 1815, the distance between philosophy and religion having decreased, it plays this role in more hospitable conditions than in the eighteenth century. In addition, illuminism is wonderfully suited to the developments that modern spiritualism calls for in the field of aesthetics; it will in particular develop the poetic Word's glorification, which it at least implicitly bore within itself, and identify its own truth with the inspiration of the Poet.

Especially in the work of Fabre d'Olivet, the imperial era saw the prospering of a theosophy with Oriental and Greek predilections, in which Egypt, Orpheus, and Pythagoras took pride of place. The themes of Christian illuminism — the Fall, Redemption, the sacralization of the human figure, theocracy — were considered from a new point of view that the ministry of Jesus Christ ceases to dominate.[1] This sort of secularization certainly had its role in the widening of the illuminist horizon; naturally, it left intact the theosophic views on the divine nature of language[2] and on the original ministry of the poet: in ancient Thrace, according to Fabre, "poetry, revered as the language of the Gods, the product of an eternal Being, descended from its ethereal habitat and propagated itself on earth for the instruction and delight of mortals."[3] The true essence of poetry resides in the symbol: "The essence or spirit of Poetry . . . is nothing else but the allegorical genius, an immediate product of inspiration."[4] Of what degree of realization is poetry, thus conceived, capable? There is hardly any discussion of this. Fabre d'Olivet's only suggestion is to create a high poetry in France by the use of "eumolpic" verses; that is, blank verse with alternating masculine and feminine endings: it is a case if there ever was one of the mountain bringing forth a mouse.[5] It is above all in the following generation that theosophy and literature found that they had drawn closer together. In the Restoration, the works of Fabre d'Olivet (who, born in 1767, lived and wrote until 1825) mingle with those of Saint-Martin's successors, illuminist physicians or naturists, and mesmerists. But, at the same time, under cover of Swedenborgianism, an as it were syncretic widening of the theosophical ideas occurred in some minds, thanks to which these ideas entered into communication with the contemporary literary movement.

The spirit of this synthesis appears as early as 1822 in the *Opuscules théosophiques* of Captain Jean-Jacques Bernard.[6] This military man, still a skeptic in 1818, we are told, came to spiritualism in 1820 through mesmerism, then to Christianity through Saint-Martin, rallying finally to the doctrine of Swedenborg. But this final conversion did not, it seems, cause him to forget any of the earlier stages of his belief. His *Opuscules* invoke the testimony of all the sages of the earth, illuminists, philosophers, and poets, and he names Swedenborg, Plato, and Kant, Klopstock and Lamartine, whose spiritualist verses he cites, Joseph de Maistre, and Saint-Martin.[7] The spiritual history of his friend Edouard Richer, like him from Nantes, resembles his own closely,[8] and likewise combines literary spiritualism and Swedenborgian doctrine. Richer's biographers tell us that his spiritual vocation was born while reading Bernardin de Saint-Pierre: "It was just as if," he often repeated, "I had had a cataract removed from my mind."[9] He never forgot this point of departure; in 1825, already completely converted to Swedenborgianism, he offers another panegyric for Bernardin, praising him for having faithfully developed Rousseau's thought, which he also praises to the skies for "having entered into the profundities of spiritualism":[10] a judgment that is more than doubtful, but proves he first drew upon secular sources for a body of thinking almost immediately imbued with religiosity: in his earliest writings, criticizing Condillac in the way that was common at the time and arguing for the primacy of feeling in accordance with Bernardin's teaching, Richer holds religion to be the foundation of society, and the invisible world to be the foundation of our world.[11] Everything serves the direction he has taken: he applauds Mme de Staël for having, like Rousseau and Bernardin, resisted the ravages of materialism, and he does not hesitate to add Joseph de Maistre to this philosophic list.[12] All his theosophy does not prevent him, in 1826, from showing some hesitation in choosing between Bernardin's optimism and Saint-Martin's harsh views on the present degradation of nature[13] — a hesitation that is all the more remarkable given that the idea of the Fall had the same importance for him that it had had for his masters.[14] The theosophico-philosophical syncretism of Richer, which attests his openness of mind, remains visible in his work *De la nouvelle Jérusalem*, a Swedenborgian summa to which he devoted the last years of his life and whose publication was in part posthumous.[15] As was natural, such a broadness of outlook had led this admirer of Joseph de Maistre to liberal sympathies by the end of the Restoration.[16]

His interest in literary creation and the importance he attributes to it in the spiritual order can also seem to derive from theosophy; but the opposite could be just as true. His very first writing, as far as I know, is an "Ode contre les détracteurs de la poésie" published in 1815.[17] In the same year, he tells us, he conceived a *Poétique générale des beaux-arts*, which he composed in the following years and whose outline has survived.[18] It has been said that Richer had been "one of the only ones, among the French illuminists, who crowned his theology with an aesthetics";[19] it would be better to say that in him the philosophy of art seems to have preceded and—one could say—nourished his theosophy. The outline of his *Poétique générale* sketches an aesthetics of spiritual enthusiasm that is opposed to one of sensation and rules, according to a formula rather in the style of Mme de Staël, but what he aspires to above all is to glorify poetry, the "essence of the beaux-arts," as a privileged mode of access to the spiritual: the misdeed of the philosophers of the preceding century is to have condemned the poet to the futile domain of the imaginary; its hold on the highest truth must once again be acknowledged. Richer's spiritualism is, in its very definition, an exaltation of poetry:

Hors des modes de la matière
Il se lève une autre lumière
Qui nous frappe de ses splendeurs,
Et c'est l'ivresse poétique
Qui jette un coup d'oeil prophétique
Sur le secret de nos grandeurs.

. . . .

Oui, dans cet exil où nous sommes,
La lyre nous élève aux cieux,
Et transmet seule aux fils des hommes
L'héritage de leurs aïeux.[20]

[Beyond material being
Another light arises
That stuns us with its splendors;
This light is poetic ecstasy,
Which casts a prophetic glance
Upon the secret of our greatness.

. . . .

Yes, in this our exile,
The lyre lifts us to heaven,
And alone transmits to the sons of men
The heritage of their elders.]

This mission of poetry makes it consubstantial with even the most traditional religion, which, like it, is only humanity's homage to the infinite.[21] In his eyes, philosophy, poetry, and religion are at bottom only one single, identical thing: what is called the romantic revolution was supposed to consist in establishing this quite new equation, by means of the conjunction and osmosis of diverse spiritual families: Richer — this is the interest and signal value of his work — unifies them naturally in himself.

There is nothing particularly Swedenborgian or theosophical in all this. It is very hard to say at what precise dates Richer became a Martinist, then an adept of Swedenborg. Martinism, which lends itself more to being vaguely adopted, seems to make its entrance rather early; Swedenborgianism, appears after his encounter in Nantes with his compatriot, Captain Bernard, in 1824, we are told; in 1826, he drew up the outline for his *Nouvelle Jérusalem*.[22] The doctrine to which he gave his support at this time did not at all change his views in the area of interest to us. In support of the metaphysical glorification of poetry, it furnished him with a mystical doctrine of communication and the symbol that put him in deeper sympathy with the spontaneous developments of contemporary poetry. Since Swedenborg's doctrine is above all founded on its author's visions, and since Richer, in order to make it acceptable to the public and, no doubt, to himself, had to formulate a plausible theory of ecstasy, he had recourse to the idea that every religion is essentially visionary and founded on "spiritual communications": he sees the proof of this in the books of the Bible, whose style according to him betrays the state of ecstasy in which they were composed. This style reflects the Edenic language, for "man, before his fall, was a poet speaking and writing under the charm of a delightful inspiration." Richer, in a story in dialogue form, makes an unbeliever confess this, who immediately exclaims: "In the few words we have just spoken I glimpse an entire theory of the beautiful in the arts." Thus the visionary ecstasy is only a somewhat sharpened form of poetry, which is always a sight of the nonmaterial world: "What more does ecstasy add to it? The ideas of a poet are real beings and real objects to which he gives a body: when poetry, like love, is carried to the extreme, it succeeds in seeing these same images, along with the body it has given them; then ecstasy begins."[23] In this new perspective, poetry gains a spiritual intensity that it did not have otherwise; literally, "it is indeed the other life that poetry transports into this life"; in this sense, Richer can well say that Swedenborg's doctrine leads to "a new poetics of the arts."[24] In fact, this poetics is only the development of the poetics he had always professed. He himself says: "I prove Swedenborg by the general poetics of the beaux-arts."[25]

Ecstatic—or poetic—language, being made of visions as well as words, is necessarily figurative; it manifests the invisible through the visible: "Among all peoples, the first words have been images, hieroglyphs, symbols"; indeed, "the two worlds, the visible and the invisible, repeat each other: one is the exact type of the other, and just as the sky is completely reflected in the mirror of the waters, the immaterial world is reproduced just as completely in the physical universe"; "all visible things are thus correlatives [*correspondances*] of invisible things."[26] Here once more, then, appears and is developed this doctrine of correspondences, the key to modern speculations on the eminent metaphysical dignity of poetry. The hesitations attached to this doctrine are familiar to us, as well as the difficulties of modern anthropocentrism in pronouncing on the reality of the symbol independently of the thinking subject; to deny it is to cut poetry off from reality; and to admit it is to lessen the creative privilege of the human mind. Illuminism is naturally situated at the more religious pole of this dilemma: the poet does not invent the truth, he *sees* it through symbols; poetry is full of being; what the poet receives is a revelation: "His metaphorical way of speaking is a language formed not by the aid of conventional images; but with the help of substances as it were seen and placed in contact with him"; thus Bernardin de Saint-Pierre, making use of the symbol of the light of truth in his "La Mort de Socrate," divined the spiritual sun that emanates from God and is the creator of the world according to Swedenborg. The great poets "found and saw the true."[27] But such a conception should logically result in a table of meanings that constitutes the fabric of the world, or at the least in an effort to draw up such a table according to the lights we have. Such indeed was the understanding of Swedenborg. He is not thinking of a poetics at all. What preoccupies him is the establishment and distribution of correspondences, the network of ends or "uses" that links the natural world to the spiritual world. This is also the concern of a contemporary of Richer's, Guillaume Oegger:[28] like Richer, very preoccupied with the theory of ecstasy and of the "natural lan-guage" of visions,[29] but caring very little for poetry, he published an *Essai d'un dictionnaire de la langue de la nature*,[30] which is a repertory of symbols. The language of nature or, according to a more strictly Swedenborgian vocabulary, the science of correspondences: this involves an as it were institutional symbol-ism that calls for a doctrinal decipherment. By the simple act of attributing to the poet a privilege in the intuition of symbols, Richer inaugurates, whether he means to or not, a competition between the divine institution and human invention. As far as I know, he never attempted a catalogue of correspondences: that would have been fatal to poetry. Poets receive knowledge of the divine, but, to be sure, do not create it; we know, however, that they multiply and diversify its figures as their imagination sees fit, and that to be a poet is precisely to blur the border between what God creates and what humanity creates.

Richer's illuminism freely embraces its literary consequences; indeed, it may be said to be a sign of the stunning exaltation of literature. It is born of a concern that owes much more to preromanticism in general than to theosophy in particular, and it is delighted to proclaim its harmony with the new literature: "Romantic literature, examined at its true source, is in agreement with these theories that explain man and the end to which he is tending."[31] Richer wrote these lines in a provincial review of which he was the principal staff member, and where spiritualism and the literary revolution were at once identified with one another: "the idealist metaphysicians and the spiritualist moralists will always incur the reproach of vagueness. Poets, especially those of the modern school, will be ranked in the same class."[32] Richer's own literature closely resembles that of royalist romanticism in its forms, its subjects, and its inspiration: he wrote *La Bretagne poétique*,[33] a provincial pendant to *La Gaule poétique* by Marchangy, the latter being, as is well known, a sort of profane and chivalric reply to the *Génie du christianisme*; we owe to him some beautiful texts of prose meditations in the early romantic style;[34] and it is not by chance that the young Victor Hugo collaborated on the *Lycée armoricain*.[35] But from this romanticism of the past, cohabiting, as we have seen, with thoughts that were so open-minded, a modern wind would soon begin to blow. The French character, Richer tells us, has become more serious; poetry is in search of a new tone; "like the Aeolian harp touched by an unexpected breeze," its voice will change so as to respond to what is expected of it.[36]

Chapter 7

The Romantic Revolution

I T HAS been known for a long time now that what is called romanticism[1] was something more than a literary revolution, and it is well known that this movement brought with it a general overthrow of values. However difficult it may be to define the romantic vision of the world by firm characteristics, one can see that a certain mutation of the humanist faith of the preceding century furnished its essentials, and that, although it presented itself as a compromise with religious tradition, the contours of a new spiritual power continued to be apparent at the heart of the mutation. This power was situated in literature, raised to a theretofore unknown eminence. Romantic spiritualism is inclined to invest poetry in particular with this eminence; in this sense, romanticism is a consecration of the poet. It is this not by accident or by an incidental consequence of its nature; romanticism is in its very essence a consecration of the poet. The distinctive trait of romanticism about which there should be the least doubt is surely the exaltation of poetry, now considered to be truth, religion, and the illumination of our destiny, and ranked as the highest value: it is scarcely an exaggeration to say that nothing like this had ever been thought of before. The inspired writer replaced, as the priest's successor, the *philosophe* of the preceding era. Romantic literature proposed a new substitute for religious faith, closer to it: a doubtful substitute, deprived of any official doctrinal sanction, open to doubt and blasphemy, but whose defects, to ways of thinking current then, were so many virtues. Thus the romantic revolution consisted less in the transformation of literature than in its astonishing promotion: the requirements of this promotion are, to a large degree, what drove literary reform. It is not that literature and the arts, and poetry in particular, had in other periods of French literature not been able to enjoy a rather brilliant prestige; but this always took place in a world where pride of place in the sphere of thought was occupied by a power incomparably superior to any literature; the poet then reigned over an auxiliary heaven or over profane Elysian fields; the key to the spiritual world was in the hand of the priest. For romanticism, the Poet is a seeker, an interpreter, a guide, and is at the center of the world of the spirit, of which the priest now holds only one of the possible versions. It is this that is new in romanticism and that makes it the sign of a profound upheaval.

It is remarkable that the idea of a poetic ministry, in the form it finally took, should have been simultaneously dependent on each of the two great currents of thought we have so far tried to describe. Both the counterrevolution and liberalism arrived at this idea, each in its own way and for its own reasons; on this memorable occasion, special and different logics collaborated perfectly with the general logic of circumstances. In the end, each party made the other understand what was lacking in its views, and a sort of romantic unity was born, confirming the ruin of the old spiritual order and inaugurating the new. The properly literary debates that marked the crisis become clearer in this larger perspective. The discussion began in the Empire, limited at first to controversies about the possible reform of the theater and imitation of foreign literary models. It soon extended to a more general review, notably concerning the granting to writers of a freedom of inspiration that called into question the whole of the literary tradition. Little by little these discussions caused the earlier ones to be forgotten, for these had borne almost uniquely on the preference to be accorded, among royalists and liberals, in the context of the classical framework, to the seventeenth or the eighteenth century; that is, ultimately, on the condemnation or approbation to be accorded to the progressivist ministry of the philosophic man of letters. Such a debate, focused on the heritage of the past while being fed in fact by the passion of the present, could be continued as such only with difficulty. A need for new values was felt, but a source of discord was thus introduced within both parties: each aspired but also hesitated to modify its traditional views on literary matters and devise a new approach. The reasons for this temptation to change are grounded in the very philosophies of the two parties, introducing in each of them a division just as marked as that which had been able to separate them one from the other in their differing evaluations of Bossuet and Voltaire. The new ideas that thus appeared separately among the royalists and among the liberals were at first rather different in the two cases. Even the few common ideas appear in a different light, corresponding to the political milieu. As the fall of the Bourbons approached, however, a cross-fertilization occurred, for political conditions were changing, and the unity of romanticism rapidly secured its triumph in active intellectual circles. By what path and in response to what needs did this new set of ideas, which far surpassed the ordinary range of an *ars poetica*, become the object of consensus in post-revolutionary society? To determine this we must first consider how what was novel came into existence in each of the two camps whose points of departure our preceding chapters have sketched.

❧ Royalist Romanticism

The royalist press and the royalist literature of the first ten years of the Restoration offer, with regard to ideas and literary opinions, a spectacle of contradictions very unlike the unanimity of views and passions that usually prevails in this milieu. The royalist dailies pronounce for or against romanticism according to their contributors. *La Quotidienne* is classic with Laurentie, romantic with Nodier;[2] *Le Défenseur* takes a liking to romanticism with Saint-Victor and Nodier, but fights it with Rocher. It is sometimes the same in the periodicals: *Lettres champenoises* (1820–25) oscillates, with regard to romanticism, between being for (Saint-Prosper, Nodier) and against (Mély-Janin, Géraud), not without seeking here and there some formula of compromise; the *Annales de la littérature et des arts* (1820–29), voice of the *bien-pensant* Société des Bonnes Lettres, which so derided the liberals, reprints the ringing diatribes of royalist antiromanticism (Lacretelle, Msgr. Frayssinous), which was also professed by contributors like F. Chéron and Rocher, but the same publication welcomes Nodier and the young writers who embrace the romanticism of the ultra party. Other royalist organs pronounce more clearly for one side or the other: against, the *Journal des débats*, and periodicals like the second *Oriflamme*[3] or the second *Eclair*;[4] for, *Le Réveil* and *La Foudre* (1821–23), the first *Oriflamme*.[5] There is in fact a common problem that is driving the discussion and is felt by all beneath this division of opinion. The counterrevolution needs a militant literature, a concern that the ancien régime at its height did not share: society was at that time sustained in the natural and supernatural order by generally accepted beliefs; it prized literature only as an ornament that called nothing into question and whose function was located at a much lower level: the truth of descriptions, moral advice, pleasure. The writers of the eighteenth century destroyed this disposition of things: their works were raised up to the level of the highest values in order to allow their examination or endorsement; everything was called into question. The simplest remedy for this disaster would no doubt be to make literature return to its old limits. But the evil effected by the sophists could not be repaired in this way; discredited institutions would still be in a weakened state: from now on, in their present danger, they need active defenders. Fortunately, the movement in this direction that had already begun in the eighteenth century, so long inefficacious, finally prevailed; the defenders of faith and monarchy took possession of the literary heights. But, because of this, literature is no longer what it was when faith and monarchy were in power. Neither Chateaubriand's *Génie du christianisme* nor Lamartine's *Méditations* could have been written under Louis XIV. These works are precious, even providential: they attest to the fact that genius and the creative faculty can be on the right side, which people were beginning to doubt; they sow anew a ruined field. Reading them, though, one feels many a strange impression: at times one feels in them a lack of a sense of proportion, an emancipation of the mind and taste that are worrying, that cannot be encouraged without debasing the very order that one wanted to save with their help. These writers who seek to restore ancient beliefs have a troubling air of newness about them, a too haughty way of speaking, a shocking predilection for attitudes that tradition proscribes.

They cannot, however, be disavowed at a time when the need for procuring literature's support for restored institutions is felt so strongly. We have seen Bonald's preoccupation with this question. A young political writer of 1820, in friendly relations with Hugo, notes that the monarchy lacks an "influence on public opinion," that the *Charte* "was like an abstract being," instead of being strengthened by public sentiment by means of an appropriate literature.[6] This repeats, curiously, for the benefit of the monarchy, an idea that was dear to revolutionary philosophers and propagandists: literature making beloved an institution justified by some high political principle. But literature, especially creative literature, does not allow its ends to be so easily dictated, and the role that (it is felt) must be conceded to it confirms its independence: the institution of literature loses its vitality if the public knows that it is under orders, and, in what literature draws from its own fund of ideas, we find that the justification of the social order implies first of all the justification of its own ministry, which colors and affects the rest. The danger was felt more and more as the idea of a Christian, monarchist literature inevitably came into conflict with classicist poetics. The young ultra poets in the society of Louis XVIII assigned themselves the role of redeemers and prophets; how could their preaching accommodate forms that life at court and social mores had given to literature when it was only a distinguished form of entertainment? As the questioning of these forms became more and more aggressive, the debate grew shriller; its tonal range was established, but its underlying principle was the more deeply destabilized: writers, upon whom new times conferred a role in the social mechanism that even from royalism's point of view was unprecedented, could not be limited to preaching the perpetuation of the past; even if they were royalists and Christians, that did not at all alter the fact and the nature of their ministry, which is a fundamentally modern one.

Insofar as it is possible to specify a particular moment, 1820 is when the debate about romanticism in royalist circles becomes obsessive; around 1825 or 1826, the credit that the literary doctrines enjoyed in the bosom of royalism became stronger, less because resistance to them had ceased, for it persisted, than because the innovators became fully self-conscious around that time: they are convinced that a literary revolution is the logical culmination of Christian royalism, and insist on this conviction in their party. They no longer accept the combination of praise for literature as it was understood in the France of old, as a serene and pleasant practice without excessive doctrinal aim, and a call for a literature nourished by healthy doctrines, as does the *bien-pensant* periodical *Annales de la littérature et des arts*: to do so is too obviously to desire two contradictory things; it is necessary to choose between them. But — and this is the problem — the choice puts people in this party on the spot. It is not by chance that Boileau, who however was just as Christian and royalist as Chateaubriand or Lamartine, had looked so askance at the Holy Virgin and Childebrand in literature, who are the double romantic temptation of the ultra thinkers. This temptation risked skewing the old division of values, according to which literary fictions were exempt from religious or national responsibility. Thus there was a long-lasting attempt on the royalist side to define a romanticism free of subversive consequences, a literature that might respond to the need of the times without danger. In 1819, the question that Toulouse's Académie des Jeux Floraux set for a prize-essay competition[7] — "What are the distinctive characteristics of the literature to which the name Romantic has been given, and what resources could it offer to classic literature?" — clearly betrays, by its very wording, an interest that seeks to determine its proper limits. The dissertation that won the prize situated the "resources" of romanticism in melancholy, in the supernatural element in popular beliefs, in the imitation of Scripture; that is, in those romantic aspects that had, in spite of all, worked their way into the literary patrimony of the counterrevolution since the 1800s.[8] Ultra France would indeed have liked a romanticism intended just for it, in which what is flattering to it would be separated from what it found shocking;[9] but it soon appeared that the literary revolution of the nineteenth century would not stop at the revenge of the neo-Christian monarchist imagination upon philosophism, and that writers aimed or were compelled to go farther. The prophetic Ballanche had seen this very early on: already in 1818 he writes: "Soon classic literature will be nothing more than archeology," and he advocates literary recourse to the annals of French history as a means of renewal only insofar as they relate to the history of the human race, marking out in advance, over and beyond the temptations of poetic royalism, the humanitarian destination of French romanticism.[10]

In these conditions, it is understandable that some royalists resisted literary innovations as such, stubbornly condemning them outright and without qualification. A powerful group of critics and feuilletonists multiplied warnings and condemnations in the principal newspapers; academicians and ecclesiastics echoed them, without distinction of age.[11] They attack the romantic temptation at its sensitive point, denouncing specifically the national and Christian pretensions of the new literature: they point out that the innovators, so in love with French subjects, are in fact taking foreigners as models; their sincerity is questioned: "Some others say they are the friends of religion, of morals, and of monarchy: pure charlatanism! pure sentimental hypocrisy!"; the origins of romanticism are situated in "philosophic sensibility," in bourgeois drama, in the movement that, as far back as the time of Diderot and Sébastien Mercier, had attacked the aristocratic Muses.[12] "The period when the philosophic spirit wanted to reform the social contract," one writes, "is also the period when small minds wanted to reform the literary code and establish principles more favorable to mediocrity."[13] Or again: "Romanticism tries to hide what it has in common with the Revolution and seizes with temerity some strange religious feelings fashioned according to its tastes. . . . It has created for itself a sort of new Christianity, which it adapts to its flight of imagination and the frenzy of human passions. . . . Let us not allow religion to be depraved."[14] All these censors, who are not lacking in lucidity, refuse to admit that religion and the monarchy have an interest, as some claim, in the success of the new literature.[15] Quite to the contrary, a bishop equates romanticism with subversion: "Literature has its sophists, just as philosophy does."[16] This is a frequent opinion; we find it in a friend of Lamartine's,[17] and among educated royalists in the provinces: a former *garde du corps* in the service of Louis XVI, made a general at Arcole, then chevalier de Saint-Louis by Louis XVIII, and, having become president of the Academy of Aix, expresses his opinion in public session: "The principles of art are attacked after those of political institutions. . . . The literature of the day has its intriguers, just as politics does: the latter dream of constitutions, the former improvise poetic doctrines in the same spirit."[18] Lamennais's first supporters, too, make of romanticism a variety of heresy by applying to literature the master's theology; in literature, classicism embodies the common reason of the human race, barring secondary local variations; romanticism, which disrupts authority and delivers literature over to independence and what is unclear, derives from the Protestant spirit.[19] At bottom, there is more uneasiness, perhaps, at seeing literature reach out to domains heretofore reserved to graver authorities than at the novelty of romantic themes: "It is politics that is smothering literature":[20] an ultra refrain, which contradicts the so oft repeated wish for a militant literature. Similarly, "the taste for metaphysics that has been introduced into literature and the arts" is deplored.[21] Even the new gravity of poetry alarms the censors, although it is authorized by all of counterrevolutionary sentimentality: "What good to us is all this profusion of melancholy?" we read in a famous antiromantic diatribe read to the Société des Bonnes Lettres.[22] The unaccustomed ostentation of the young poetry is not less shocking: "M. Hugo is a poet, but I dare say he is sometimes too much of one. He seems to think that poetry is so utterly divine that it should never speak the language of men. . . . The *os magna sonaturum* seems to be his guide."[23] We see, in all this, how a profound repugnance at accepting, on the one hand, the new dignity of the Poet and, on the other, the essence of the new doctrines from which this new dignity derives, is all tangled up in purely literary biases.

What makes this resistance anachronistic is not only the need for an active literature in a society threatened with destruction. The new ideas had deep roots in the very sensibility of the counterrevolution as it had been shaped by the emigration, the ruin of noble families, and the guillotine. Lady Morgan, traveling in France at the beginning of the Restoration, noticed with surprise that the ultras for whom Rousseau was anathema imitated nonetheless "his sentimental rhetoric, which is more than ever the idiom adopted by this class of men."[24] There is no doubt a considerable distance from Rousseau's rhetoric to that of the ultras, but the English lady noticed something real. Sensibility was not faked in this party, possessed as it was by interests that were passionately felt. The memory of the tragic scenes of the Temple,[25] the sublimities of the scaffold, the appeal to humanity against the executioners of 1793, all the commonplaces of royalist pathos derive from a collective instinct for self-justification that mixes emotion and practical calculations inextricably, as happens in this sort of creation. The counterrevolution has a claim on the public through misfortune and poetry only insofar as it sees itself invested with impressive attributes: the plea presupposes an inner certitude. The aristocrats of the time of Louis XVIII naturally appealed to widely held values, to the sublimity of tears and inspiration, both to reassure themselves and to convince others. It was no doubt a sign of weakness that people who had been used to prevail by a superiority of force and prestige should come to this; they made themselves dependent upon ambiguous ideas that were, from their point of view, unreliable. But it is certain that the ultra milieu greeted Lamartine's *Méditations* and Hugo's *Odes* with general enthusiasm;[26] it found in this poetic revival a reassuring sign that the Restoration was not the return of an enfeebled past, as liberals kept repeating, but rather a dawning — the beginning of a world accompanying the beginning of a century; the French have survived the ordeals: "let the people of France be reborn, and poetry will be reborn; but poetry will be different on account of its new origin; it is coming back to life in order to oppose the opinions that caused its ruin."[27]

The area where Christian royalism is most naturally led to deny the classic tradition is that of the subjects and figures of pagan mythology. This is, beginning with Chateaubriand, its first step. The legacy of the primitive poet and the sacred poet can be transmitted to the poet of the Restoration and renew itself in him only by means of a denunciation of this intermediate period in which a legend that was alien to national belief made of poetry a futile pastime. Evoking the establishment of poetic paganism in the France of the Renaissance, a royalist, commenting on the *Méditations*, exclaims: "That revolution was fatal to poetry"; he had just described, after so many others, the original function of the poet, hymnist of expressions of thanksgiving to the Creator and institutor of societies; he continues by congratulating himself on seeing the resurgence of true poetry after a long decadence, restored at last by a new generation that he believes "destined to cling more firmly to the good because of the very spectacle of evil and its prodigious effects"; to this generation "it was reserved to reconnect with traditions. . . . It was possible to predict that the poets who would arise in the midst of this society of the children of God would give back to poetry its true character": thus Lamartine causes the religious poet of the earliest times to live again in our time because he repudiates the frivolous poetics that owed its favor to Boileau.[28] The writer expressing this opinion, a friend and adherent of the first Lamennais, would not however have accepted being considered a romantic; he was continuing in the line of the *Génie du christianisme*, but with a still sharper awareness of what opposed modern Christian poetry to the usages of classicism. We can measure by such examples the force of the movement that was impelling royalist criticism toward the new ideas. The historical schema according to which the classical era appears more or less explicitly as the time of an eclipse of true poetry and of the ministry it implies is frequent among writers of this party.[29] More frequent still is the affirmation of a current renewal of this essential ministry. It was in fact royalism that reintegrated into the contemporary scene the image, long confined to myth, of the poet as inspired by God and inspirer of men.[30]

The restoration of the poetic ministry is usually founded on the ordeals of French society: this motif, whose birth we have watched, persists and grows richer. It will be recalled that even in the ancien régime Christian poets had been wanting to accomplish the work of renewal; but "the time was not yet come when the spirit of men would grasp the dangers of sophistry in all its consequences; the finger of God would bring them back to the truth by a bloody road."[31] Today the ordeal has been consummated: "We are quitting a time of revolutions and barbarism, and we need new Orpheuses."[32] "This happy return of poetry to its most noble destination" is hailed, and it is written, magniloquently: "Long, immense sufferings had tried all the powers of the soul, and poetry reappeared bathed in tears and imbued with religion and melancholy."[33] Those who, thinking in this way, accept romanticism by name are not lacking;

Cyprien Desmarais, a royalist and a Catholic, maintains that literature under Louis XIV was not French, that the national sensibility required a new literature, and that romanticism is fundamentally Christian.[34] Ulric Guttinguer thinks the same: "To be romantic in literature is to sing one's country, one's feelings, one's customs, and one's God."[35]

The word *romanticism*, however, matters little in itself; what matters is the feeling of modernity it expresses and that can occur without it, the consciousness of what is new, of something that is not merely recalled from the past and restored, but the image and need of the present. The notion of the romantic as an expression of a modern spirit is doubtless not what seduces royalist writers at first; instead, they are looking to romanticism, as they conceive of it, for an answer to the threat of subversion. But in their very manner of speaking of romanticism, something quite different stands out clearly. One of them points out that, if the ordeals revived religion, "it is *poetically* that Christianity has recovered in French civilization its place of honor"; he recognizes in writers — a new and irrevocable thing — "the supreme magistrates of public thought."[36] Another, who virulently reproaches those of the classic party with having renounced fatherland and religion in their works, accepts romanticism as "the expression of modern society," for "the three great distinctive traits of modern Europe are, it seems to us, its religion, the memories and emotions peculiar to its peoples, and a particular character of exaltation, enthusiasm, and melancholy imprinted on our passions, and principally on the most universal of them all."[37] "Modern" should be understood here, obviously, without any revolutionary connotation, as a broad definition of Europe and of its originality; but it is opposed, not less obviously, to "classic," and suggests, in spite of all, the idea of a recent coming to awareness. One feels here, however, the influence of the intellectual movement that declared itself in 1823 and 1824 around the *La Muse française*, in the aftermath of which it was no longer possible to fool oneself, as Chateaubriand said at the time, about "imitations of the past that are no longer the past," because "new shoots appeared everywhere";[38] royalist, Catholic romanticism was in a favorable situation to free itself from the monarchy and the church, and to announce, independently of them, a modern ministry of the Word.[39]

✵ La Muse Française

During the course of this debate, a group of poets appeared who embodied royalist romanticism, developing everything that it contained *in potentia*. The story of this group and its composition is known, beginning with the meetings at the Deschamps home in the rue Saint-Florentin. Around 1820 these meetings seem to have acquired their air of a coterie; those who participated in them fit

more or less by age within the limits marked by the Deschamps brothers themselves: Emile, born in 1791, was Lamartine's contemporary, and Antoni, born
in 1800, was Hugo's. Soumet, Guiraud, and Rességuier were born between
1786 and 1788; Vigny, Saint-Valry, Gaspard, and Hugo between 1795 and 1802.
Victor Hugo and his brother Eugène founded at the same time *Le Conservateur
littéraire*, a review of royalist inspiration without a clear romantic orientation,
which lasted until the spring of 1821; in 1822 appeared the first works by Vigny
and Hugo. In July 1823, the same group founded and edited, with a few additional collaborators, *La Muse française*, which stayed alive until June of the
following year:[40] it is in this review that royalist romanticism finally declared
itself without qualifications. Something happened there that many testimonials
agree in calling memorable. The ideas of the staff of *La Muse*, envisaged literally,
are not unique to them, and the whole of preromantic royalism already contained them: for example, the rejection of classicist poetics, the abandonment of
the antinomy established by the counterrevolution between the seventeenth
and eighteenth centuries, its replacement by a new antinomy between classicism
as a whole and a renewed literature, the exaltation of the Poet. In *La Muse*, it is
true that from issue to issue these ideas take on an intensity that bothers more
than one kindred thinker: Genoude, Lamartine's friend and admirer, pretends
to laugh at them, as does Lamartine himself.[41] But the true originality of *La
Muse* lies elsewhere. This first *cénacle* bore within it a fervor, a creative hope: it is
marked with the stamp peculiar to those rare and privileged literary moments
when the spirit renews itself. Sainte-Beuve, utterly a stranger to *La Muse*, who
watched it with a liberal's eyes, described in a caricatural mode the special
exalted quality of the little group: "At first there seemed to be something gentle,
scented, caressing, and seductive about these havens for high society; initiation
into them occurred through praise; one was recognized and hailed as a poet
according to I don't know what mysterious sign, I don't know what Masonic
handshake; and from then on, one was coddled, celebrated, and applauded to
death." Sainte-Beuve links this literary phenomenon to a particular era of political history: 1823, he writes, "was the dazzling, Pindaric moment of the Restoration."[42] But even when the Restoration had long been finished, the first *cénacle*,
we are told, still had its faithful adherents, who continued to grieve that time
had marched on and that romanticism had gone down other roads: Rességuier,
Guiraud, Saint-Valry, and others were still meeting at Rességuier's in 1840.[43]
Experiences like the ones these poets had lived through in 1823 are not quickly
forgotten: this one consisted in the feeling of having discovered poetry anew
and of having made it live again in modern France: "Little by little," we read in
the anonymous preamble to the first number of *La Muse*, "the love of poetry,

like any other love, can certainly languish and fail for lack of sustenance. *La Muse française* is founded primarily to revive and maintain this sacred flame."[44] According to Emile Deschamps, the ever so complicated dispute between the defenders of the classic and the romantics is nothing but the eternal war of prose and poetry.[45] Vigny, evoking the *La Muse* group a quarter of a century later, said: "There were a few extremely young men at the time, dispersed and unacquainted with each other, who were contemplating a new poetry. In silence, each of them had felt in his heart a mission."[46] A mission of poetic renewal, but, by virtue of this fact, and because of the dignity that a regenerate poetry claims, a humanizing mission: "Listen for a moment," writes a contemporary, "to these self-proclaimed interpreters of the new muse, and say whether poets speaking so gravely and solemnly ever presented themselves. One can see that the frivolous, modern idea connected with their art has changed; one would almost like to find in the ancient words *vates* and *prophets* a more splendid designation for them, so much does the importance of their words redound to them: it is a duty, a ministry, a mission that they come to fulfill."[47] The missionary side of the poets of *La Muse française* was rather thoroughly forgotten later on; and yet a critic at the end of the century whose attachments to Comte's ideas sensitized him to the ebb and flow of spiritual power among writers, clearly recognized that *La Muse*, in grouping poets together, "united them through the hope of a sort of social mission." "In it they symbolized," he adds, "their semi-priesthood, and, with a sure sense of the times to come, they borrowed from Virgil a famous verse that became their epigraphic motto: 'Here is the Virgin, coming back.'"[48] This mission, which royalism assigned to its poets as psalmodists and maintainers of ancient values, was obscurely felt by them to be oriented toward the future. "Champions of olden times and filled with modern emotions, they were innovators, even when they evoked the past":[49] thus Sainte-Beuve defines them when he is not thinking of making fun of them; and, better still: "Liberals both circumstantially and in essence, even when inclined to reactionary opinions, people governed by whim who were attached to their freedom, they contained in themselves a preexisting, fully formed sympathy for the future movement of society."[50] This "curious example of an historical mirage," to speak like a more recent critic,[51] has its inner logic: the poets of *La Muse* could found their redemptive ministry only on the holiness of Poetry, and this notion, as soon as it was no longer relegated to the legendary past, as soon as they wished to make a present reality of it, necessarily suggested a new order of things.

The judgments of contemporaries on *La Muse française* group and the memories of those involved with it are largely confirmed by the texts published in the

review and by the careers of its principal contributors.[52] The oldest among
them, Alexandre Soumet, was thirty-seven when *La Muse* appeared. He had for
a long time, as early as the Empire, denounced the philosophy of the eighteenth
century, and cited as his masters the prophets, Dante, Young, Klopstock, Chateaubriand; in addition to Saint-Martin, he admired both Joseph de Maistre and
Mme de Staël, only reproaching the latter with not going far enough down the
road of spiritualism and irrationalism that she had taken.[53] Sainte-Beuve describes him thus: "Soumet was unctuous and sly, rather short of ideas, wishing
on occasion to make you believe in some metaphysics that was not in his
possession."[54] These lines are like a malicious birth certificate of the Thinker-
Poet, examples of which the group would furnish in Hugo and Vigny, in addition to Soumet. Since poetry tends to be all of thought and spirit, and at the
highest level, it has to be philosophy as well as religion. The metaphysics to
which Soumet had pretensions is no doubt that which he himself defined by
opposing it to the preceding century's philosophism, and which "tries to grasp
the precious thread that can lead us back to a first language revealed by God
himself," whether it be the case that the spirit contemplated the spheres and
their harmony, "or that it seeks in the moral world the type of the physical world
and in the most hidden phenomena of nature perceives only symbols of the
human soul."[55] It is apparent that this philosophy is not peculiarly his own: this
is the philosophy of the primeval language and of analogies, so often present in
this dawn of modern French poetry. It is more or less explicit everywhere in the
poets of this family, who willingly assign to poetry the task of telling

> Du paisible univers les splendeurs symboliques,
> Et de l'homme et du ciel les merveilleux rapports.[56]

> [The symbolic splendors of the peaceable universe,
> And the marvelous relations of man and heaven.]

In *La Muse*, Soumet again grounds this poetic symbolism in the idea of a primitive language: "Everything is symbolic in the eyes of the poet, and, through a
constant exchange of images and comparisons, he seeks to recover some traces
of that primitive language revealed to man by God himself, and of which our
modern languages are only a feeble trace." It is no surprise to read that poetry so
conceived "explains and finishes, so to speak, the work of the creator."[57] Such
views, which had up till then been commonly applied to the poetry of primitive
times, have taken on a present value for Soumet, who means thereby to set himself apart, seeking in particular what in 1824 might be the equivalent of the original union of poetry and music; of this union nothing but the puny vestige of
rhyme survives; what will fill the void of the lost language will have to be some-

thing very different: a music of the soul, a new song, unknown to the ancient poets, an inner, ineffable religion that Soumet cannot better define than by lending it the traits of the pseudo-Christian melancholy of the moderns: "Let us suffer our poets to seek in their souls the inner harmony that replaces the lyre they have lost, and allow the muse of high Christian thoughts to console us for this loss with her heavenly sadness, her immortal hopes, and her ineffable charms."[58]

The same ideas are found in another contributor to *La Muse* — that Desjardins whose identity is so obscure and whose personality is so poorly known.[59] He seems to have been in intellectual sympathy with Soumet, though in a different mode, not being at all linked — so it would seem — to royalism, and more inclined, even at this time, to the great humanitarian syntheses; his presence alongside the people at *La Muse* says much for the flexibility of their traditionalism. Desjardins reviewed Soumet's *Saül* in *La Muse*: this subject, which Lamartine also took up in a tragedy that long remained unpublished, allowed the newly hatched Christian poets to represent a modern type of more or less frenetic outcast, while remaining faithful to Scripture, which certainly paints Saul in a similar light. Soumet, in his tragedy, had treated the subject with moderation and remained true to the edifying moral of the biblical story. Desjardins is sorry that the drama has not been given more metaphysical reach; according to him, Soumet needs to do more "if he is to fulfill entirely the mission he has received from on high."[60] He speaks, however, of the poetic renewal in terms very similar to those Soumet employs in his articles. He thinks poetry was untrue to its mission when it abandoned music; for a long time the poetry of modern times remained "still to be found." Desjardins believes, though, that in his own time it has at last been born in a few young poets who have substituted a new harmony for the lyres and harps of ancient poetry; already, in David and Isaiah, beneath the audible music of words and sounds, "a great, mysterious, and holy revelation can be heard to resound on all sides." The modern poets have resumed this high tradition: "In those days, it was all of divinity that announced itself; here, it is the entire soul that reveals itself. . . . A new alliance between music and poetry is consummated . . . the lyre and the harps of the poets of old have descended into the depths of the modern poet's soul."[61] What we can call the anthropocentric spiritualism of the moderns is here quite clearly expressed, and in close connection with the poetic ministry.

For Soumet and Desjardins, the renaissance of poetry should culminate in creations of a new kind, much more immense and forceful than the puny productions of the classic age. Soumet, at least as early as 1814, planned a great mystical epic. He returns again and again to Klopstock in 1810 in the notes to his poem "L'Incrédulité."[62] But in the short work on Mme de Staël, it is the entire theory of the supernatural epic that is sketched: "Our epic conceptions," he writes, "must touch in every part the mysteries of another world."[63] Soumet seems to have worked all his life to realize his "epic conception." *La Divine Epopée* that he published only in 1840, a few years before his death, was in the works, he tells us, for twenty-five years.[64] Here is not the place to comment upon this too long deferred poem, one of the monuments of that Romantic Epic, so persistently attempted over a period of a half century and more, and always at an arm's length from Christian orthodoxy. What interests us is that we find in the group around *La Muse* something other than a first timid and refined version of French romanticism; we find, rather, the authentic and already powerful source of its future developments. As for himself, Desjardins, even while considering Milton the only true poet of modern times, was thinking rather of a renewal of drama: he imagined a metaphysical theater, a performance where the meaning of creation would stand revealed: "We are reaching the moment," he writes, "when the spectator, silent and meditative, will leave the performance of a tragedy thinking about the astonishing revelations that the poet has just communicated to him; and, his soul enlarged, full of the solemn and majestic impressions he has received, he will better understand the marvels with which the creation enwraps him on all sides."[65] This is what he later tried to realize with his *Sémiramis-la-Grande*[66] — a work of immense symbolic portent in the author's intention, but of a meaning, so far as I can tell, impossible to grasp, if it even has one.[67]

This poetry inspired from on high presents itself at the same time as militant: the royalist romanticism of 1820 preceded the humanitarian romanticism of the following period in this double ministry of revelation and action. Divine in its origin, poetry is responsible for the conduct of men. Writers, Soumet writes, "will never back down because of consequences, because of the dangers of courageous speech, and they will remember that the god who rendered the oracles at the temple of Delphi was depicted emerging from a struggle." The era itself, a period of crisis and danger, needs this forceful ministry: "The times are past when appealing maxims and sunny precepts sufficed as inspiration. . . . Poetry has here been returned to its original and noble purpose, that of inflaming souls to love virtue through and through."[68] "Here," that is to say in Hugo's militant *Odes*, which are the occasion for these remarks; and what Soumet calls virtue is beyond any doubt conformity to the traditional social and religious order: the mission of poetry is to confound the spirit of subversion and to bind the wounds that the eighteenth century opened. But it was another member of the group, Alexandre Guiraud, who especially developed what could be called a sociology of royalist romanticism. It is not that he is unaware of the heavenly investiture which the poetic ministry can obviously not do without; in a poem dedicated to Soumet, whom he compares to Isaiah, he calls poets

> Cithares du Très-Haut, vivantes et sublimes,
> Hommes de l'esprit saint . . .
>
> [Citharas of the Most High, alive and sublime,
> Men of the holy spirit . . .]

and depicts himself as officiating:

> Eh bien! l'autel est prêt, et j'y monte avec joie.[69]
>
> [Well, then! the altar is ready, and I ascend it with joy.]

But, in a long doctrinal article, he retraces the history of the Poet above all through that of humanity. He begins with the religion of Christ, who, he tells us, "carried over into the soul a part of the worship that the Ancients gave to the divinity," and then discusses the invasions that the West endured for so long[70] — influences that would result in the metamorphosis of literature, but that classical France wanted to avoid. It is true that Guiraud only spares the writer of the century of Louis XIV the better to pour scorn on their "copiers," who, in concert with the sophists of philosophism and affected by the frivolity of a decadent society, consummated the death of poetry in the eighteenth century. The bloody trials of the Revolution gave it a new birth by recalling the primordial truths to man, threatened with annihilation:

> Our revolution came and cut off our withered society at its base . . . ; it was like a new deluge that makes the social world young again. . . . Now, this new world, regenerated by a baptism of blood, is at present still in its youth; and since the energy of the earliest times endowed with an intense poetic coloration the Book of Genesis and the *Iliad*, . . . we do not doubt but that our literature too will feel poetically this new life that animates our society. This life has become more genuine; literature will as well: a seriousness has made a violent entrance into our minds; literature will be serious . . . ; it will finally bestow poetry upon us, for misfortune is the most fertile of all poetic inspirations.[71]

The idea of a Christian poetry that has sprung from the revolutionary ordeals is common in royalism, and we can trace the disavowal of the profane poetics of classicism back to Chateaubriand. But Guiraud and his friends[72] give to these views incomparably more present force and a tone that is deliberately modern.

Thus in a thoroughly royalist milieu the idea of a renovation that is literary and social in the end prevails over that of a restoration. Counterrevolutionary romanticism knew the way to stamp with the mark of youth the prestige of the past; one of the poets of *La Muse* writes these emblematic verses:

Pour former des accords nouveaux
Je viens rajeunir ma pensée
A l'esprit vivant des tombeaux.[73]

[So that I may strike new chords
I come to rejuvenate my thought
At the living spirit of the tombs.]

The Restoration, as a regime, could lend itself to this theme of rejuvenation only through the important novelty and modernity of the *Charte*; royalism's revulsion at this innovation, however strong, could not forget the support that a constitution lent to royalty in the public mind; and it was in the same way, paradoxically, that royalist romanticism benefits from a democratic argument: "Everything is now becoming solemn in literature. . . . Let us realize that this is no longer the time to shut doctrines up in schools and salons: in a government where the entire nation is called on to participate in the rights of counsel and administration, all teachings must be public, especially those of literature, because, if at first it is society that acts upon literature, literature in its turn reacts with an approximately equal influence on society."[74] The old monarchy rejuvenated by the *Charte*, like the old faith rejuvenated by pathos and poetry, such is the natural ground of royalist romanticism; it is with an appeal to truth that these poets embody the movement impelling the spirit of the counterrevolution to transform itself in order to survive; they are, in their way, aware of this, and it is thus that they justify their mission.

Another contributor to *La Muse française*, Saint-Valry,[75] younger than Guiraud, defends romanticism with similar arguments. He refuses the title of romantic to Casimir Delavigne because "when reading him one never remembers that he is writing after so disastrous a revolution."[76] On the contrary, true poetry is the expression of society:[77] Bonald's formula is used to define and legitimate a literature of crisis and suffering. Poetry, "still standing near the steps of the temple, solemnly receives the vow of the nations that have suffered from going far astray to return to the old traditional beliefs whose abandonment alone has been the cause of every evil." The writers who, in the aftermath of the great ordeal, understood the language of ruins, have been committed to action thereby: "For them writing is not the vain desire to shine; no, writing fulfills the most beautiful ministry among men; writing exists to avenge outraged justice, calumniated misfortune, dishonored liberty of the genuine sort, all of humanity, which has been wounded in its dearest and most sacred possessions."[78] Justice, genuine liberty, and humanity can no doubt be understood in the purely ultra sense; but Saint-Valry in *La Foudre* deplores Lamennais's excessive counter-revolutionary violence: "To grapple with an entire century is madness";[79] Chateaubriand was his great man: after his expulsion from the cabinet, he sings his praises to the skies under the name of Augustus in the "Esquisses morales," which he published in *La Muse*, while reproaching Lamennais, under the name of Severus, for rejecting "freedom, daughter of heaven, returned from exile with our kings."[80] However, when Victor Hugo pulled romanticism into paths that were unambiguously liberal, he maintained firmly — and very quickly anachronistically — his earliest position in the *cénacle* and, right up to 1841, multiplied remonstrances to his former friend.[81] The Chateaubriand in opposition of 1824 was the extreme limit of his modernism. In fact, as has often been remarked, *La Muse*, in addition to other more pressing factors, did not survive the royal government's break with Chateaubriand, as if this event had demonstrated the incompatibility of royalist politics with the royalism of the poets: this latter phenomenon, becoming more and more aware after 1824 of its own originality, saw itself driven beyond itself toward what a fair number considered a recantation. But in doing so it was obeying a deep necessity, interpreting with an eye to the future the ambiguity that marked it from the start.

In the meantime, the essential originality of royalist romanticism was to have conceived of and exalted a type of literary character, a poet principally, as the guardian of the vitality of beliefs and institutions. The wish for a literary revolution accompanies, in this movement, the tendency to put Poets themselves at the heart of poetic creations as a central character, at once both type and oracle. And it is not a question merely of restoring personal lyricism to a place of honor; the emotions and thoughts of the poet matter because of their link to the divine order and their application to the destinies of humanity. What the primitivist or Christian eighteenth century had been able to intuit or rough out had in this sense blossomed remarkably in the two royalist generations of the beginning of the nineteenth century. It was then and in that specific milieu that what had long been a whim or mythic commonplace came back to life.

❧ *Liberal Romanticism: Stendhal*

The need for a literary reform was felt very early on in liberal circles, and the poetics of classicism was first called into question in this milieu, rather than on the royalist side. And yet it is also among liberals that resistance was the sharpest and the most tenacious. This contradiction can be explained by existing conditions, which were themselves contradictory: on the one hand, a greater freedom of judgment among minds not bound by any political reverence—just the opposite, in fact—toward the age of Louis XIV; on the other hand, a close attachment to the age of Enlightenment, its literary ideas included: there was a repugnance at the thought of modifying in any field whatsoever a legacy that was so severely criticized in the enemy camp and an unwillingness to think of literature otherwise than as Voltaire and the Academic *philosophes* of 1760 had thought of it. Thus romanticism was long an apple of discord among liberals and ultras alike.

It is certain that the debate on romanticism was begun during the Empire by liberals. It was in liberal circles that the word *romantique* first appeared in the 1810s, with a meaning, new to France, designating a school of literature, in the writings of Villers, Mme de Staël, Sismondi, and Stapfer;[82] and if it is true that the word taken in this sense is borrowed from and applied to Germany by them, it is also the case that the idea of a reform of literature reestablishing its connection to the national past and the earlier literature of classicism was simultaneously applied to France by Prosper de Barante.[83] More importantly, liberal and modernist criticism of classical literary forms goes back to the very first years of the century in Mme de Staël and Stendhal and is prior to the influence of German romanticism. But all this does not prevent more than one contemporary from feeling that the resistance to the new ideas in literature appears most marked among liberals: "This disposition in favor of the status quo with regard to theories of dramatic genres, lyric poetry, and the epic," one writer observes, "pushed many young talents toward the ideas of the aristocracy, where, as we know, a natural indulgence welcomes every fiction";[84] or again: "What is rather curious to observe is that the freethinkers in politics and religion are absolutists in literature, and that those who protest against the Academy almost always belong to the political party that opposes innovations."[85] One may wonder whether such recriminations coming from liberals who argue in their own circles in favor of literary renewal do not exaggerate the evil in order to combat it. The distribution of opinions was in any case complete: "There are classic liberals and romantic liberals," notes one observer, "romantic ultras and classic ultras."[86] And as late as 1830, a foreign visitor, rejoicing that France is getting rid of the debris of classicism, remarks: "These imbecile liberals, in whose interest it would be to encourage this destruction, are opposed to it, and this conduct is an enigma that for ten years I have been trying in vain to understand."[87]

The principal fortress of liberal antiromanticism was *Le Constitutionnel*, a widely read daily newspaper that governed middle-of-the-road liberal opinion, along with the old guard of imperial writers of this tendency—Jay, Jouy,

Etienne, Viennet, and others, forty-five to sixty years old in 1823. But if on the whole the new ideas in literature are mostly the accomplishment of the generation on the rise, whether a critic is romantic or antiromantic is no more essentially a question of age among liberals than it is among ultras. Old and young alike contribute to the small liberal journals that appear from 1815 to 1830 and that usually attack romanticism vigorously.[88] Among the contributors to literary reviews, Tissot, born in 1768, is relatively more open to what is new than Héreau, born in 1791, or than Chauvet, born in 1788—even than Thiessé or Thiers, born in 1793 and 1797, respectively; Benjamin Constant and Senancour, born in the reign of Louis XV, are not more prejudiced than Avenel, born in 1783, or Chasles, born in 1798. It is in the periodicals especially that the diversity of opinions is apparent, against a background of critical mistrust that owes its strength to the polemic against royalist romanticism. Attitudes vary according to the question being discussed, and also according to the times. *Les Lettres normandes* of 1817 to 1820, *La Minerve littéraire* of 1820 to 1822,[89] *L'Album* of 1821 to 1823 are against the new trends or accept from them only what can be reconciled with liberal policies. The *Revue encyclopédique*, an important collection that, begun in 1819, survived beyond 1830, publishes articles favorable to a reform of the theater mixed with the most scathing critiques. The *Mercure du dix-neuvième siècle*, which appeared from 1823 to 1832,[90] more often reserved than sympathetic at first, was converted to the new ideas in 1825–26 under Latouche's influence. Latouche, born in 1785, had, as a friend of the Deschamps brothers, collaborated on *La Muse française*, from which he was separated by his liberalism, and of which he published a cruel satire in 1824—in the *Mercure*.[91] He did not disavow his romantic positions, however, and published in April 1825 *Les Classiques vengés*, an ironically titled pamphlet. His promotion to editor-in-chief of the *Mercure*, a post he occupied from October 1825 to April 1826, was a veritable coup d'état against the influence over this review of the group at *Le Constitutionnel*.[92] Latouche's tenure in this position definitively modified the review's outlook: in 1827, the former contributors of *La Muse* publish there; in 1829, Hugo's friends. The *Mercure* thus played a decisive role in romanticism's conquest of liberal circles, as did its contemporary, *Le Globe*, whose spirit was however quite different: the broad-mindedness in literary matters of this last publication continued the tradition of Mme de Staël and the Doctrinaires; in general, something youthful and original was represented by *Le Globe*, which appeared beginning on 15 September 1824, and whose principal contributors—writers coming from various origins and more or less linked to Doctrinairism or university Eclecticism—were born between 1790 and 1800. In fact, an attitude analogous to that of *Le Globe* with regard to romanticism had already been roughed out in the *Archives philosophiques, politiques, et littéraires* of 1817 to 1818, published by Royer-Collard and Guizot,[93] and this was even truer of the *Tablettes universelles* of 1823.[94] Outside of journalism, the avant-garde group on the liberal side was that which already in 1819 and up until 1830 met at the home of Delécluze: those who became the staff members of *Le Globe*, Jean-Jacques Ampère, Duvergier de Hauranne, Vitet, Rémusat, and Magnin, met there with liberals as sharp-witted as Stendhal and Mérimée. It is in this milieu, more than anywhere else, that was elaborated the idea of a literary revolution of a sort that liberalism could imagine and could wish to desire. How Stendhal judged this moment of French intellectual history is known: "I would not know how to express too much esteem for this group. I have never met anything, I will not say superior to, but even comparable to it."[95]

The liberal objections to romanticism often derive from a simple repugnance for what is new, an attitude common in the ensemble of educated opinion at that as in every time. From that point of view, liberals and royalists, *Le Constitutionnel* and the *Journal des débats*, speak approximately the same language. But the liberal censors of romanticism have their own original tone and their own favorite themes. They are especially shocked by the new literature's vagueness and immateriality, and, to speak like one of them, by "these vaporous images, these ideas of infinity, this secret of melancholy that are the delights of *Messieurs les romantiques*."[96] According to another,

> C'est un monde idéal qu'on voit dans les nuages:
> Tout, jusqu'au sentiment, n'y parle qu'en images.
> C'est la voix du désert ou la voix du torrent,
> Ou le roi des tilleuls, ou le fantôme errant,
> Qui, le soir, au vallon, vient siffler ou se plaindre,
> Des figures enfin qu'un pinceau ne peut peindre;
> C'est un je ne sais quoi dont on est transporté,
> Et moins on le comprend, plus on est enchanté.[97]

> ['Tis an ideal world we see in the clouds:
> There everything speaks in images, even emotion.
> 'Tis the voice of the wilderness or the voice of the rushing stream,
> Or the erlking, or a wandering ghost,
> Who comes to the valley in the evening to whistle or moan,
> Figures in a word that the brush cannot depict;
> 'Tis something undefinable by which we are enraptured,
> And the less we understand it, the more enchanted we are.]

Romantic poetry is reproached for its obscurity, its appeal to the irrational: "An exalted philosophy," writes the young Thiers, "leads the romantic writers to look everywhere for mysterious connections between what they call the moral and physical world, and these connections are usually either false, or confused, or inexplicable."[98] At bottom, romantic literature awakens in the heirs of Voltaire a mistrust of the danger of an extravagant spiritualism prone to mysticism; it is in this sense that they would like to disallow metaphysics in poetry: "It should depict what is most perceptible and most touching in this universe. . . . Final causes, the infinite, and laws of nature are not in its domain; the only philosophy permissible to it is that which reigns in Horace and in a few French poets."[99]

One critic, who reproaches romanticism with being the "poetry of metaphysics,"[100] nevertheless tries in the same work to temper the philosophy of the eighteenth century with some spiritualism. Liberalism's tendencies in this direction were rather general; but the use that royalist poets and their admirers made of an openly religious spiritualism with Catholic trappings gave rise to liberal circumspection; faced with the writers of *La Muse française*, the Voltairian fund of ideas comes to the fore: not altogether unreasonably, the literary revolution seems like a counterrevolution. The material favors and honors that the adherents of royalist romanticism receive from the reestablished monarchy, their supposed thirst for success, the *bien-pensant* ridiculousness of the Société des Bonnes Lettres and its "literary good fellows" [*bonshommes de lettres*], as they are called in the liberal press, are inexhaustible themes for satire.[101] Romanticism is presented as closely united to a state of affairs whose time is past. In 1833, Théophile Gautier, in a narrative whose plot is situated in the Restoration, has a partisan of classicism repeat the proverbial expression according to which the romantics are "regressive innovators."[102] In the aftermath of 1830, more than one liberal believed that romanticism had perished with the Bourbons. "Their Pegasus," we read in the *Gazette littéraire*, "was a Cossack's horse"; and this reminder of the counterrevolutionary invasion of 1814 is followed by a ferocious portrait of *La Muse* group, "veritable Aeolian harps that render no other sounds than those carried to them by the wind from the archbishopric"; to conclude, "romanticism bit the dust on 29 July in the Tuileries, between a Swiss guard and a court page."[103] Such a judgment will appear surprising to a reader today; another article in the same periodical takes the opposite tack: "Romanticism is the expression of the progressive movement of thought."[104]

The reforms of which liberals are capable of thinking imply in any case a condemnation of counterrevolutionary romanticism. This condemnation is just as spirited among those who profess the boldest ideas in literary matters as it is among the most reserved. Stendhal is a testimony to this fact: a champion of liberal *romanticisme*, he has only sarcasm for Chateaubriand. His animosity goes way back; it begins with the *Génie du christianisme* itself and forms the basis for an unbroken link between Stendhal and the *Idéologues* of the Academy of 1800 and Marie-Joseph Chénier. As early as 1802 he planned to write a comedy in which he would ridicule the entire counterrevolutionary school in the type of "the *anti-philosophe*, the Tartuffe of the present day"; he cites Chateaubriand in particular, among others: La Harpe, Geoffroy, Fiévée, Bonald, Mme de Genlis; he was still dreaming of such a project during the Restoration.[105] In 1825 and 1826, Chateaubriand, who has gone over to those opposing Villèle, is still in his eyes a hypocrite, a maker of fine-sounding speeches, a ridiculously bombastic writer.[106] He treats the poets of *La Muse française* no differently, "pygmies," "versifiers," "false bards," who "wrap their sad mystical reveries in pompous verses."[107] He indicts Vigny for his *Eloa*, and Soumet; he links them in his sarcasms to the Société des Bonnes Lettres.[108] In these years, he sees in Hugo the poet of the ultra party, and holds him in low esteem; his great poet at this time is Béranger; he respects Casimir Delavigne; also Lamartine, but putting his thought to one side, and with great reservations concerning his melancholy.[109] This severity makes him feel free to mistreat the group of classicist liberals at *Le Constitutionnel* as a coterie of establishment types closed to every new idea.[110] In the mind of liberal romanticism, the two condemnations go hand in hand; Stendhal also combines them in the *Racine et Shakespeare* of 1825.[111] *Le Globe*, which between 1824 and 1830 worked so actively to make romanticism accessible to the liberal public, is also fighting on these two fronts. It repudiates "that already outdated though still quite young school, which takes what is vague and formless as the basis of its poetry,"[112] those poets for whom novelty consists in counterrevolution, tears, moans, and the return of religion.[113] Lamartine is closely watched in the review, and is often roughed up; Chateaubriand, who is treated more kindly since being expelled from the cabinet, is not highly regarded as a thinker: Jouffroy, speaking of the *Génie du christianisme*, thinks that from now on it takes an effort "to achieve an appreciative understanding of this outdated poetry."[114] But at the same time, *Le Globe* rejects neoclassicism, and its contributors strike a "heavy blow"[115] against *Le Constitutionnel*'s literary influence in liberal circles; *Le Globe* had in fact from the beginning been dedicated to combatting the "Academic anathemas of a school whose time is past,"[116] and it ceaselessly criticizes pure literary conservatism, especially in the person of Viennet, by whom the paper had been attacked.[117]

From a certain point of view, there is a conflict both spontaneous and profound between the classical tradition, in its spirit as well as its form, and liberalism, if we understand liberalism, as we have so far, as the acceptance of the society created by the Revolution in its customs and its spirit. Liberalism's first step toward romanticism was a sociological critique of classicism: this was the very last step taken on the royalist side, as the reader will remember. For a new society, a new literature: when liberals use Bonald's formula according to which literature is the expression of society, they take it in a sense opposite to its author's: it is not used to glorify classicism, as the literary expression of an ideal monarchy, but to relegate it to a dead past, along with Louis XIV and his court. It is indeed a focus of discussion for liberals. Not everyone is convinced that classical literature is linked to a particular era. The Age of Enlightenment's philosophism had integrated classical poetics into a notion of civilized life, regarded as independent, in principle at least, of any particular state of social institutions: classicism's origins, according to this tradition of thought, lay not in the monarchy, but in civilization; what mattered most in classicism was the universal form of literature; what works might owe to particular historical influences was negligible. Thus classical poetics victoriously traversed the Revolution and the Empire; the heirs of philosophism did not at all think themselves obliged to repudiate it. Quite to the contrary, they feared that the entire edifice of the Enlightenment would suffer if it was challenged in the name of historical relativity. When it came to romanticism, which they were told was the historically true and spontaneous expression of the various European nationalities, it was precisely to the specificity of that nature to which they objected, whereas classicism, beneath its antique envelope à la Louis XIV, expressed in their eyes the general character of humanity, upon which they meant to establish their political principles, which according to them were also eternal: "One can be at the same time," says one of them, "both the friend of new political institutions and the partisan of true literary doctrines. It is quite consistent, on the other hand, to show for the invariable rules of taste the same respect we show for those eternal principles of justice and independence that are also found in antiquity, and to wish to conserve religiously the treasure of these twin traditions, which despotism and bad taste have often interrupted, but which they have never been able to destroy."[118] These ideas are almost always linked, as has often been said, to feelings of national pride and French literary preeminence; but the supremacy of the Enlightenment and that of France were not distinct in the minds of these writers, as they have seemed to be in the recent history of Europe.

A liberalism more imbued with historical consciousness, however, more sensitive to the upheaval that the Revolution had effected in the distribution of social values, saw in traditional literary forms the figure of a dead past. This is already apparent in *De la littérature*: in 1800, Mme de Staël criticizes Molière's comedy as linked to the prejudices of the old society, and designed to stamp as ridiculous what contradicts them; she sees in the tragedy of royal personages a form of literature expressing solidarity with the institution of kingship itself; she wonders what might become of the "nature of convention" and the literary genres inherited from the past in the new society.[119] There was no lack of antecedent to this way of thinking: in the eighteenth century, similar considerations accompany the ebb and flow of literary reform in Diderot and others; Rousseau especially, in his *Lettre à d'Alembert sur les spectacles*, had linked classical comedy and tragedy to the customs of a condemned society, from a point of view more moral than historical. Mme de Staël assimilates to her own ends the critique Rousseau had made of Molière's *Le Misanthrope*, in that it ridicules and discourages virtue to the profit of court manners; she praises the publication of Fabre d'Eglantine's counter-*Misanthrope* and imagines as an accompaniment of free institutions a moral comedy where, she says, "ridicule should be oriented in the same direction as scorn."[120] At almost the same time, the young Stendhal is filling his correspondence and his notes with similar thoughts. It must be admitted that he gave them a force and a boldness that were unparalleled; the *Racine et Shakespeare* of 1823–25 resulted less from Stendhal's Italian friendships or English reading than from a long and vigorous meditation begun in his youth. Seeking to define and create in the mind of the *idéologues* a comedy founded on the science of man, and convinced that a "scaffolding" of thoughts on human nature is always the framework of comic construction, he judges that Molière built his notion of the comic on the needs and the maxims of the old society. Furthermore, laughter, which results from the sudden discovery in ourselves of superiority over another,[121] is a tool at the service of egotism that is inseparable from monarchical customs: it punishes variances from the social graces that cloak this egotism.[122] Stendhal repeats, of course, the criticism of Molière's *Le Misanthrope* and the praise for Fabre d'Eglantine.[123] In a society that has ceased to be monarchical and toadying, comedy as Molière conceived it is dead: the triumph of democratic ways renders it anachronistic. What is worth remarking in these analyses, apart from their acuteness, is first of all the originality of the type of criticism they inaugurate, which will have so rich a future; and also the belief they imply in a ministry of the creative writer, held to be an indispensable voice for the social body; it is the genius of the writer that keeps alive and flourishing among the public the axioms and behaviors necessary for the conservation of a society: a simple, down-to-earth view of his function, which is thus considered both ornamental and essential; for, on the one hand, he does nothing but cloak appealingly the "scaffolding" of the social code, of which he is not the author; but on the other hand, the force of this code depends on the attractiveness that he lends it. Thus we see that in their projects for literary reform, Mme de Staël and Stendhal remain faithful to the idea of the role of the creative artist in society that philosophism and the Revolution had fashioned.

In practice, the question toward which all of Stendhal's analyses converge is that of the destiny of comedy in the new society. What will the modern Molière be like, and what sort of ministry will he exercise? What will a comic author be able to do in a world in which personal dignity, the sentiment of equality, and independence from fashion and opinion have replaced the former incentives governing social existence? Old-fashioned ridicule's time is past; Stendhal analyzes it only in order to demonstrate that it is finished in modern France. But can there be another kind, and is comedy not condemned in a republic to taking a sermonizing tone—that is, to self-denial? Stendhal greatly fears so. "The influence of ridicule," he writes, "is thus diminished today, this is the favor that Jean-Jacques has accorded":[124] accorded to society, perhaps, but to comedy? Stendhal, who wants to rescue it, brilliantly imagines a sort of ridicule attached to misguided quests for happiness, the supreme goal that has replaced for us the master's favor or worldly credit. Those who know how to be happy, or at least how to deserve happiness, would laugh at those whom a prejudice or a passion—precisely, perhaps, the toadying or vanity inherited from the old state of affairs—stupidly prevent from being happy: "All my ridiculous characters will be unhappy through their own fault."[125] This is to imagine laughter as the attribute of a sort of philosophic superman, become the inspirer of the ethos of society. Stendhal never really wrote the comedy he planned, and his project bore no fruit after him. What is of interest in him is that the criticism of classical forms is linked to reflection on the social function of the writer, and that this reflection does not break with the tradition of philosophism, even as it transforms it in certain respects. The essence of this tradition is expressly reaffirmed more than once. Whether satire of the counterrevolution or deeper moral instruction, comedy serves genuine social values: "This is the sense in which I must work as a comic poet to be useful to the nation by destroying the tyrants' hold on her, and thereby bring closer *divina libertà*."[126]

As is well known, discussion bore on tragedy much more than on comedy in the 1820s. But liberal partisans of dramatic reform there attested the same spirit of sociological criticism, the same desire to eliminate literary forms that they judged complicit with a former state of affairs: they directed their offensive against the ceremony and social manners of tragedy as the expression of a strictly hierarchical and regimented society that is no longer our own. Before interesting himself in comedy, Stendhal had inclined as he emerged from adolescence toward the tragic and the heroic.[127] He later returned to this, impelled by his natural taste for the grandiose; he had early confessed that the study of the comic — that is, of characters that are essentially low — repelled him.[128] The introduction to his *Histoire de la peinture en Italie*, a text written in 1814–15, he tells us, reproaches the monarchical government with crushing and abasing genius — a timeworn republican theme.[129] From this theme there develops in him the idea of a humanity marked by strong, lofty passions, unacquainted with the straightjacket of courtiers' customs. For him, romanticism will more and more be the representation and exaltation of such a humanity; the criticism of classicism will be that of the "dead souls" of courtiers and slaves, languishing under despotism, that Racine depicted. "It is not a literature devised for a court that we need, but rather a literature for a people."[130] "The generation of *dolls* that began the Revolution in 1788 has been replaced by a generation of strong, somber men who are not yet quite sure by what it is fitting that they be amused."[131] This generation willingly sympathizes with those who in France preceded the triumph of the court civilization, a triumph that Stendhal sometimes dates from the time of François I, sometimes from Richelieu or Louis XIV.[132] The idea of the gravity instilled in the French character by the Revolution and the appeal to an earlier tradition are equally familiar to royalist romanticism. But the same pattern has here a quite different significance: he glorifies revolutionary energy and candor, not the experience of misfortune and the spiritual virtues of poetry: this is a good example of the convergence of divergent purposes toward a single thematic form. Thus, when, for once, approval of the contributors of *La Muse française* is expressly declared in *Le Globe* and their bent seems to be embraced ("the facile, libertine poems of the eighteenth century cannot suit the sons of the revolution"), right away something completely different is asserted: "Those artificial forms of ceremony, that conventional nature where everything is the same, can no longer suit a people that has seen originality and diversities of character produced with an energy at once so artless and so wonderful: our literature needs to become *human*, if I may speak thus, and to get back to reality."[133] The group at *La Muse* did not find the energy of revolutionary France even close to being artless or wonderful, and demanded something completely different from a literature of reality. Similarly, a liberal collaborator of *La Muse*, Lefèvre-Deumier, who like his companions praises the new seriousness of the French character, can only explain it as coming from the practice of freedom.[134] In the *Racine et Shakespeare* that Stendhal published in 1823 and 1825,[135] the evocation of the difference of eras and of societies and the wish for a theater expressing modern energy are complemented by a consideration of the nature of dramatic pleasure, which can only exist if there is correspondence with contemporary conditions of life: "*Romanticisme* is the art of presenting to peoples literary works that, in the present state of their customs and beliefs, are apt to give them the greatest possible pleasure."[136] This definition brings together in a general statement the essence of a liberal contribution to the literary revolution: literature should be, in its object and its forms, something contemporary, and the ministry of the writer should be rethought in accordance with the conditions of postrevolutionary society. What practical consequence is derived from such a principle? It is the foundation, naturally, of a relativist aesthetic, by virtue of which Stendhal rejects the notion of the *beau idéal*,[137] as can be seen in the beginning of his dispute with Lamartine.[138] But we stand here on an unsure and shifting ground: we know how hard it is to draw the line between the real and the ideal in art. Just as the views of royalist romanticism lead to a renewal of the elegy and the sacred epic, what these reflections lead to in the area of concrete literature is a modernization of tragedy, or, more precisely, its disappearance and replacement by modern drama.

Concerning this drama, Stendhal repeats ad nauseam that it should be in prose, last several months, and take place in various places; that it should exclude German "gibberish" and resemble Shakespeare only because our period, like his, has factions, ordeals, and conspiracies.[139] And yet, of all the subjects Stendhal evokes as suitable for this new French tragedy — Clovis and the bishops, Joan of Arc and the English, the assassination of Montereau, the assembly of Blois, the death of Henri III, the death of Henri IV, Louis XIII at the Pass of Susa — not one is a properly modern subject. The new French tragedy is what we call historical drama; it is contemporary only because of the lively interest that the Restoration public is supposed to have in episodes of national history.[140] Stendhal, for all his passion for the contemporary and the real, does not seem to imagine a drama with modern characters succeeding court tragedy.

The set of ideas that we have just gone over and that assume such clarity and force in Stendhal existed in a diffuse state all around him in the 1820s. Paul-Louis Courier mocks the language of French tragedy, which, he says, causes foreigners to burst their sides laughing: "The imitation of the court is the plague of good taste."[141] Guizot, in the introduction to his edition of Shakespeare, justifies the need for a dramatic reform by the new state of society.[142] Reviewing this introduction, Rémusat writes: "Our tragedy is contemporaneous with all the solemnities of absolute power"; and he explains tragic ceremony by the influence of "those strict governments from which the people are excluded."[143] There is no end to such citations. Such views, at first original, became in several years the refrain of whoever wished to draw closer in spirit to the new literature. In 1824 and 1825, the familiars of the Delécluze salon who launched *Le Globe* gave to these ideas an even wider publicity. Duvergier de

Hauranne hopes that "the reign of realities" will come to the theater, and that literature will at last be "vigorous and true, empirical and philosophical."[144] The principle of the need for a specifically modern truth finds its complement in that of the freedom to create, which, since in literature just as in politics modernity and individuality cannot be conceived the one without the other, only apparently contradicts it: "Here as everywhere else, the old régime is struggling against the new, faith against free inquiry."[145] Vitet says, along the same lines: "Taste in France is waiting for its Bastille Day," and he adopts the definition of Lamennais's followers while stripping it of its pejorative intention: romanticism is "Protestantism in literature and art."[146]

The idea of a national historical drama as the successor in the nineteenth century to classical tragedy is very widespread in liberal circles. This idea had, in fact, even more distant origins. The subjects borrowed from French history show up already, and in tragedy itself, in Voltaire; they appear there frequently in the Empire and the Restoration; around 1820 the liberals who are the most hostile to romanticism recommend them; so do, with even more justification, minds that are more open, which pass naturally from the renewal of subjects to the recasting of dramatic forms.[147] At *Le Globe*, the need for this recasting is an article of faith. This near unanimity in wishing for a national renewal of tragic theater is easily explained from the perspective of the writer's civic role, a perspective that is shared by all liberals, romantic or not. One of the most classic among them wishes to see "poetry returned to its noblest goal, that of serving to reveal the secrets of the human heart and apply the great truths of history";[148] that is, liberalism's peculiar philosophy of French history. Indeed, these evocations of the national past, these "historic scenes" that liberal writers of the Restoration made fashionable, are as if naturally a history of the revenge of the Third Estate, a recollection of the painful stages that led to the irreversible emancipation against which the debris of the emigration and the Marsan pavilion can do nothing today. There would appear to be a meeting of minds with Marchangy and royalist romanticism in the cult of the French past, but the aim is utterly different: true history is supposed to dissipate the poetic halo of old, feudal, Christian France and proclaim the present resoundingly. In the mind of liberals, historical drama is a theater that puts history in its place and gives the conquests of the present their due: "Every people," one of them writes à propos of Shakespeare, "that has given some importance to their rights and liberties has given a national character to its literature and dramatic representations."[149] A liberal historian wonders whether it is conceivable that certain persons, the same ones who enclose romanticism in a fuzzy darkness, are dreaming of using the depiction of the past to incline us to regress toward it: "It would be a clever project, but I doubt it will succeed. How can one not see right off that a literature should not conform to the time it is recounting, but to the time when it is produced, in accordance with the minds of the men for whom it is destined? Is it possible to frustrate for long the needs of an age?"[150]

The vogue around 1825 among liberal writers for a historical drama in the form of a chronicle in dialogue, realistic and, as it were, instructive in intention, whose subjects were sometimes taken from recent history, was born from this set of ideas. In 1825 Rémusat read to the Stapfers a drama on *L'Insurrection de Saint-Domingue*, and in 1826 in the home of Delécluze a drama on *La Féodalité*: neither has survived.[151] Mérimée wrote a *Cromwell* around 1823,[152] before publishing *La Jaquerie* in 1828. Though his *Théâtre de Clara Gazul* in 1825 and 1830 does not strictly speaking contain a historical play, it does situate the plots of his dramas in a historical framework: thus *Les Espagnols en Danemarck*. In 1826 Vitet brought out *Les Barricades, scènes historiques, mai 1588*, which he had read at the home of Ampère.[153] In the same year, Ch. d'Outrepont published *La Mort de Henri III ou les Ligueurs*, and *La Saint-Barthélemy*. In 1828 Loeve-Veimars added a *Dix-Huit Brumaire* to his *Scènes contemporaines*, which were only little private dramas situated in recent history, and he added in 1830 a second volume of properly historical scenes touching on the seventeenth and eighteenth centuries. It is curious to note that all these authors had been preceded by a royalist of ancient lineage, the comte de Gain-Montagnac,[154] whose *Théâtre* was published in 1820, including notably a *Charles Ier* in prose in which Cromwell figures, and that is preceded by a remarkable prologue: there he declares the old form of tragedy in verse to be obsolete in our age of revolution, and recommends a tragedy in prose that makes historical characters speak in a simple style.[155] Stendhal, throughout the *Courrier anglais*, or from 1825 on at any rate, enthusiastically approves of all these writings. He himself writes an act of an *Henri III* in 1828.[156] *Les Soirées de Neuilly* by Dittmer and Cavé are often placed in this category: but this is in reality a collection of satirical comedies; only *Malet*, a dramatic chronicle of the 1812 plot against the emperor, is an exception in its subject matter, though hardly in tone.[157] All these works have fallen into oblivion if they have not disappeared altogether. They were in general unstageable; nor were they written to be staged, which is a flaw for dramatic works; they were born of the desire to establish a living connection between the past and the present; each of them attests more to an imaginative, polemical curiosity in its author than to the temperament of a dramatist. The romantic drama, which came from another direction, has obliterated them. It owed much to them, however. They were, between 1820 and 1830, a concrete contribution in the form of real works to the liberal spirit of romanticism.

❧ *The Liberals and Poetry*

At bottom, what really interests this literary reform movement is the invigoration of the role of the writer as the figure in society who describes and instructs an age avid for knowledge. If the poet is to have an important function, it will scarcely be any other than this. There was certainly no shortage of liberal poets. There were many born between 1780 and 1800. In the Empire and at the beginning of the Restoration, they continue the poetry of the preceding century. What is new in what they emphasize is almost uniquely at the level of militant politics: satires of the opposing party, ideologico-political exploitation of the tragic theater, patriotic or national odes, songs about representative types of the day and great events. Their subjects are memories of revolutionary or Napoleonic glory, France's humiliation at being invaded, British iniquity, European revolutionary movements, Greek independence, and Liberty. On their side, royalists proceeded in more or less the same way, but on the liberal side there seems to be less preoccupation with affirming the existence of the poet's special mission. No doubt commonplaces are repeated concerning the benefits of poetry and of the arts conducive to enlightenment; in fact, the poet is only a citizen who is more eloquent, more listened to than another, and thus more useful. Poetry, as echo and exhortation, is the song that accompanies public struggles.

Of the two best-known members of this group, Béranger and Casimir Delavigne, both of whom enjoyed considerable fame during the Restoration (liberal critics usually placed them much higher than Lamartine), neither wrote nor inspired anything before 1830 that exalted his own prerogative as a poet, so far as I know; above all, this poetry is proud to be following the general intellectual movement of the time and to be well received by the public. A liberal critic, reviewing Béranger's poems, declares that he wants "to remind writers, by Béranger's example, that one absolutely must belong to one's own age in order to achieve durable, popular success, and that to wish to cause human reason to go backwards by works stamped with the mark of errors, prejudices, and times that have perished forever would be to compromise all the noble hopes of talent."[158] Another exalts Béranger for having "found the secret of lyric poetry that suits the French"; indeed, "he has become the creator of a genre admirably suited to the genius of his compatriots; as a result, he has been able to become the poet of his age; as a result, it was inevitable that his genre become a national genre, and his works, popular works."[159] These eulogies contain an implicit but obvious condemnation of royalist poetics. Another critic of the same family introduces his praise for Casimir Delavigne by remarking that certain poets "seem to have entered into an agreement to choose only subjects without any relation to the spirit of their age; they lavish the treasures of poetry on some imitations from the Bible, . . . that long-since-exhausted source."[160] Here we see sacred poetry insulted in the name of civic poetry. The prestigious image of the primitive poet is not forgotten on this side either, but this is in order to give it a precise meaning: "Poetry is never more aptly named the language of the Gods than when it is able to speak to men and communicate to them through the double influence of reason and beautiful verses, the duties that go together with their rights, and the interests to which their needs give birth."[161] This is the pure tradition of the preceding century, still alive: the ministry of Orpheus is recalled, but only in order to adapt it to modern, rational proportions. The aged Andrieux, celebrating Casimir Delavigne's entry in the Academy, says to him:

> Possesseur fortuné d'une lyre divine,
> Ramène l'art des vers à leur sainte origine.
> On nous dit qu'autrefois les poètes sacrés,
> Interprètes des Dieux, par le ciel inspirés,
> Donnèrent aux humains des préceptes à suivre.
>
> . . . .
>
> D'Orphée et de Linus rajeunis les merveilles,
> Ou mêle à tes accords, sans remonter si loin,
> Les nombreuses leçons dont notre âge a besoin.
> Guéris des préjugés la lèpre héréditaire.[162]
>
> [Fortunate owner of a divine lyre,
> Bring the art of poetry back to its holy origin.
> We are told that in the past sacred poets,
> Interpreters of the Gods, inspired by heaven,
> Gave to humans precepts to follow.
>
> . . . .
>
> Rejuvenate the miracles of Orpheus and Linus,
> Or, without going so far back, mingle in your harmonies
> The many lessons our age needs.
> Cure the hereditary leprosy of prejudice.]

Sainte-Beuve approved of this effort to link the primitive ministry of poets to their present, militant role, which keeps them in contact with the public: he praises Béranger for being the only one of our time who has really kept up this fruitful rapport. But he is too lucid not to measure the distance separating the original poetic ministry, at least as we imagine it, from modern militancy; with time the function of poetry has been reduced: "The poet ceased to be an indispensable, permanent voice, a social teacher, a guide; his individuality had to carve out a marginal place and limit itself to a more special use of his talent."[163] It is in this diminished perspective that he sets Béranger's success: liberal, national poetry is the residue of a great tradition. Yet who does not see that poetry in the nineteenth century has developed immense ambitions? It is on a different level than that of militant philosophism, however; of Orpheus's ministry, poets have wanted first and foremost to retain as a legacy and revive a spiritual privilege, of which their role as practical guides could only be the corollary; and it was not in a liberal milieu that this claim took shape.

Modern militant poetry has its origins, naturally, in the Revolution. Casimir Delavigne continues in the direction marked out by Chénier and Lebrun, albeit after his own manner. Béranger had the originality to orient in the same direction the old genre of the song, endowing it with more and more substance and public influence in the years between 1815 and 1830. He justifies this alteration in the genre's tradition as due to the accession of the masses to public affairs, the song being unable to do otherwise than to follow in their elevation the popular classes, to which it is tied by its nature.[164] However this may be, the flowering of liberal poetry during the Restoration was robust and interested a vast public. The success of Delavigne and Béranger, neglecting for the moment the less important names, was at least equal and perhaps superior, in the extent of their readership, to that of the royalist poets. Posterity has not ratified this distribution of glory — far from it. The poets it has judged worthy of being remembered are all from the other side; it is they who renewed French poetry, in spirit and in form. It is certain that among the liberal poets there is no anxiety about the real nature of poetry or about the possible conflict between modern inspiration and the conventional genres among which poems were traditionally parceled out: the work effected by Béranger on the genre of the song does not amount to much compared with the work that Lamartine, Hugo, and Vigny began to undertake at the same time with regard to the totality of literary forms. Liberal poetry before 1830 is, in brief, the application of an unchanged traditional rhetoric to militant enthusiasm. This is not much, especially at a time when the apostolate of the Enlightenment has lost much of its fervor and its hopes, and for the most part is limiting itself to the immediate political horizon.

The role that liberalism assigned to the writer is all the more detached from the idea of an inspirational prerogative in that more than one liberal believes that the development of civilization and the development of inspired poetry are incompatible. This doubt, born in the eighteenth century and deeply rooted in the philosophy of the Enlightenment, did not dissipate — far from it — as the poetic beginnings of the European nations and the poetry of the earliest peoples became better known. The idea was grounded in an antinomy of reason and the poetic faculty. Those who believe in the rational development of the human race and who think that European society has entered into adulthood exclude poetry more or less explicitly from the future. It would be difficult to find expressions of such an attitude among royalists; it is common among liberals. "As the human race ages, we become less credulous in everything we do, and consequently, less poetic"; it is Stendhal who says this in 1802.[165] Mignet wrote him the same thing in 1825: "The arts are lost, we can sing their *De profundis*," and Stendhal answers him only weakly.[166] Mignet thought that Stendhal's notion of a prosaic, real theater was the end of theater, and that this end was inevitable. Stendhal resisted admitting this because his temperament was upbeat; but in the case of the poet, he himself had definitely banished him from the stage by his repeated censure of the use of "beautiful verses."[167] Mme de Staël too had begun, as we have seen, by announcing the exhaustion of poetry. Nearly thirty years later one could read in a review, along with objections to the possibility of a Christian poetics, these more radical reflections: "It would doubtless be better to confess that our age, in harmony with our way of life, our habits, our tastes, and the progress of our thinking, rejects every concept of poetry, instead of wearing ourselves out in the vain search for the principles of an art of which all traces are being erased from memory."[168]

Throughout the entire interval between the beginning of the century and 1830, this death knell had never stopped ringing. In 1819, Charles Loyson distinguished three literary ages in the history of civilizations: the primitive age, the only one that is truly poetic, the classic age, a happy combination of natural inclinations and intelligence, and a final period — without a doubt the one in which we have arrived — that is that of the pure diamond and sterility.[169] In 1827, at the time of *La Guzla*, Mérimée only invented Morlach poems because he felt obliged to retreat from modern civilization in order to establish contact with poetry. He later said so: "I can scarcely conceive of poetry other than in a state of half-civilization, or even, not to mince words, of barbarism."[170] Fauriel, discussing the theater with Manzoni around 1823 to 1825, thought poetry destined to yield to history and disappear, and his interlocutor, in order to maintain that "poetry does not wish to perish," felt himself obliged to attack the authenticity of "all contrary appearances and predictions."[171] In the midst of this general declaration of desuetude that writers think themselves able to draw up with regard to the art of poetry, the *Revue encyclopédique* stands out among liberal publications, especially due to the collaboration of Victor Chauvet. This critic[172] was the very one who had, by an 1820 article on Manzoni, provoked in response an Italian writer's famous letter on the dramatic unities. In 1829 he writes: "The more civilization advances, the more poetry loses ground; soon it is nothing more than a noble pastime, and since man ends by putting reasoning and calculation in everything, a time comes when prose alone can communicate completely his sensations and his thoughts"; he repeats exactly Loyson's portraits of three periods, and concludes haughtily: "Romanticism is the poetry of the periods in which poetic feeling slumbers. . . . But it is still the case that it is only a period of transition. It is not classical poetry, but prose, that threatens it."[173] Another contributor to the same review, who resembles Chauvet in his ideas,[174] specifies that poetry, whose characteristic is to combine the physical and the moral, sees its power come to an end as soon as the human mind, through the progress of science, makes an effort to distinguish them;[175] he, too, describes the exhaustion of poetry from an original point of view: this exhaustion begins with the first successes of technology, which depersonalizes and depoeticizes objects; it continues with the progress of industry; today, by a retrograde movement, romanticism could reinstitute barbarism if barbarism were any longer possible; romanticism claims to revive poetry in this way, but it is all in vain: "[T]he period in which the sources of art must at last dry up seems to be a part of the destiny of nations," and we have arrived at that period; the critic ends by prophesying for the European nations a future similar to what already exists, according to him, in the United States of America, whose prosperity, science, morals, and public freedom are experienced by most human beings as constituting a happy era, but one that is felt to be "sterile and painful by those special souls endowed with the needs of poetic genius, whom nature has brought into the wrong epoch by mistake."[176] All these texts seem curious at this late date, after the publication of the first great works of Lamartine, Hugo, and Vigny, but these predictions, so bizarrely false given that a long revival of poetry was destined to accompany the age of science and industry in France, are not without significance. The tradition to which these authors appeal is, in a certain way, contrary to poetry. Since they occur outside their circle of thought, innovations effected in this area seem to them to be forced lucubrations, exercises in false barbarism: it is apparent that this vigorous poetic romanticism is for them lifeless. Yet their confidence is not without melancholy; it is not easy to bury poetry lightheartedly; whence the sometimes afflicted or nostalgic tone of the peremptory prophecies. They help us understand why liberalism was able to play only an indirect role in the movement of rebirth and dignification of poetry that marks in France the period of the Restoration: it reinforced the watchword of a literature of the present and of the future, but this watchword will be followed in a style utterly different from that of liberalism.

There is a curious divorce between the far-ranging, sensitive views of liberal philosophers of aesthetics, who see in the Beautiful a figure of the infinite, and the virtually total absence of poetic power in the poets of the same party. The aesthetic ideal of the philosophers stands empty, unable to find expression in militant poetry. It is tempting to explain this contradiction by the division of intellectual tendencies in the heart of liberalism. To the Doctrinaire, Eclectic tradition deriving from Mme de Staël was opposed the spirit of Voltairianism and the habits of thought characteristic of strict, matter-of-fact *Idéologie*. Stendhal, who is of the latter school, castigates Mme de Staël endlessly, mocking her "turgidity," and accusing her of complicity with the aristocracy,[177] and with her Victor Cousin, whom he reproaches — O irony — for lacking common sense, and for having introduced into France, after the dethronement of Locke, Condillac, and Helvétius, "the mystical and visionary philosophy of sentiment"; he is no more indulgent toward *Le Globe*, founded by "our young fops," whom Cousin has inoculated with German philosophy;[178] Benjamin Constant himself, author of the spiritualist *De la religion*, merely achieved "a Protestant homily"[179] in writing this book. Stendhal believed he saw taking form in the bosom of this family of spirits a new religion, a sort of patchwork of expired beliefs: "[T]he spiritualist party is rising rapidly and will probably be in two or three years the reigning party. . . . The aristocracy hopes to gain some advantage from this and is trying to create a sort of Protestantism."[180] Sometimes Stendhal even imagines a cabal of duchesses (Mme de Broglie, Mme de Sainte-Aulaire, Doctrinaire ladies) undertaking to launch a new sect, as Mme de Staël, he tells us, was planning to do when death overtook her.[181] In *Armance* there are indications of the same sort of role attributed to Mme de Bonnivet, whose "new Protestantism" is tinged with theosophy.[182] Stendhal's hostility unifies everything in the society he is observing that would like to reestablish some form of religiosity in the public mind. It cannot be doubted that in this he is the spokesman of a certain tendency of the liberal mind.[183] Liberal efforts to resist the Eclectic philosophy are well known; the quarrel seems to heat up again at the end of the Restoration.[184] Under Louis-Philippe there will be an anti-Cousin Left, whose spirit will still be alive in the Third Republic. Thus it would be easy enough to distinguish in liberalism a moderate, willingly spiritualist wing, and a more radical wing, critical and down-to-earth in spirit. But such a distinction would risk falsifying reality. We have seen that as early as the Empire the boundaries of *Idéologie* and nascent spiritualism are ill defined. Even with all the bad things he says about the contributors to *Le Globe*, Stendhal counted several of them among his friends; he had met them at Delécluze's and held them in high esteem; he was, in fact, in solidarity with them in the controversy over romanticism. Constant, who was not at all a strict Doctrinaire in politics and who as spokesman of advanced liberalism penned a militant critique of Decazes's doctrines, nevertheless wrote the book *De la religion*, which was not disavowed by his just-as-antiministerial friends on the *La Minerve française* between 1818 and 1820.[185] In its diversity, the liberal milieu was united in the sense that on the whole it remained under the influence of the spirit of the *philosophes*. The spiritualist overture, which was accepted in varying degrees, does not cancel this fundamentally prosaic spirit, which holds its adepts at a distance from the poets of the new generation, born on the opposite side. The acceptance in the wake of Mme de Staël and the Eclectics of the desire for the infinite and of dissatisfaction as fundamental traits of humanity, as well as of the ideal as the object and end of literature, nevertheless helped liberalism to bridge the gap. This acceptance was for the liberal writers in the final process of romantic unification what conversion to the reality of modern France was for Vigny and Hugo.

In fact, in certain liberal critics we see the appearance of a hope that spiritualism will be able to guarantee a new life and future to poetry, whose survival is imperiled by the progress of civilization. Thus Loyson wants to have faith in the future of lyric poetry, even as he announces "a continual retreat of poetry before the advance of reason and science": our spiritual nature is the last enchanted region of the universe; this is why, if "the earliest poets were philosophers, the philosophers will henceforth be poets";[186] in other words, poetry will not only be tinged with spiritualism, it will transform itself completely into spiritualist thought in order to survive: we can see how tenacious a hold the notion of the primacy of philosophy has over these minds; but at any rate poetry will survive. *Le Globe*, which is proud to have inaugurated among liberals an understanding approach toward religions, notes the need to believe that followed upon the incredulity of the eighteenth century, with the resulting literary consequences: "This moral revolution naturally made itself felt in poetry; it is manifested by a religious and melancholy flavor, which was the character of the new school, a character" — adds the anonymous contributor — "that I wish neither to approve nor blame exclusively, but which must be acknowledged."[187] The exclusion of all dogmatic religion does not in any case suppress the need for the supernatural. "But," writes another contributor, "this sentiment takes a different course. In our new situation, the enigma of the universe and of our existence, the secrets of the past and of the future, the unlimited character of passions and virtue give to the religious imagination new sustenance and to poetry a new source of the supernatural."[188] At times spiritualism is even taken to be the essence of romanticism. The religion of Christ has been the dominant fact of modern times; but in our times, the author of a most remarkable article tells us, literature can no longer borrow from it more than its fundamental idea — its principle; now "this principle is spiritualism; romanticism, we may thus say, is spiritualism carried over into literature."[189]

However, what might be ceded to poetry at philosophy's expense remains unclear; more than one member of this intellectual grouping reacts with annoyance at the idea of the poet's mysterious privilege: "I admit that we like to see heavenly inspiration in poetry," writes Rémusat,

> that genius exercises over those who possess it a mysterious power resembling a miraculous gift; that it is a divine voice speaking in them unbeknownst to them; that the true poet is a child lacking reason but sublime by instinct: but I say that the time has passed when it was so, supposing that this time ever existed. No doubt there is still in the poet a special faculty whose source escapes us as does the source of all our natural faculties; he has received a gift, he does not know how, and it is this gift that we call talent. But alongside this talent, reason places itself as a witness, as a judge; reason observes and enlightens talent.[190]

Ampère, as influenced as he is by Ballanche, writes in *Le Globe*: "Poetry in our time is difficult. Our age, so great in so many other ways, is not very favorable to it. . . . A robust faith is needed to believe in poetry." "We must, however," he adds, "believe in it."[191] For we cannot resign ourselves to declaring dead this poetry that has always been indispensable to civilization. Indeed, "great poets are not passive instruments, simple echoes of their age; invested with a double power, they govern it at the same time that they depict it." And they would be unable to carry out this role today by becoming philosophers, as some suggest, even among Ampère's own friends:

> Everything here below has its place, and poetry will hold its own. In us there will always be a certain need of an ideal, a certain élan toward a world superior to our own, that it will certainly become more and more difficult to satisfy, but which neither lofty intellectual abstractions, nor the curious results of science, nor the discoveries of history will be able to replace. After everything we have done, there are still abysses to explore in the imagination and in the heart of man. The progress of the ages is developing new feelings that need to be described. Even these great ideas of science, the elevated views of philosophy and of history have their poetry, and this poetry remains to be written. An ocean of enthusiasm that is not about to dry up lies there before us.[192]

The arguments for poetry that are heard from this critical perspective always seem to be grudging defenses of a cause that has become difficult to defend, appeals to some ultimate emotional reserve on the part of civilized man. Such however is the path liberal philosophy took to encounter poetic romanticism: the idea of a modern lyricism in persistent and creative competition with the contemplation of the philosopher.[193]

It would be easy to demonstrate this in the liberal-inspired writings that try to bring the debate on romanticism to a close by synthesizing opinions. Nicolas Artaud, a liberal professor and translator of Walter Scott's ballads, in a work entitled *Essai littéraire sur le génie poétique au dix-neuvième siècle,* combines praise of inward poetry, melancholy, and dream with the usual liberal arguments in favor of romanticism (a break with an aristocratic academic tradition, recourse to national, popular inspiration).[194] Reviewing in the *Mercure* his royalist colleague Cyprien Desmarais's *Le Temps présent,* he agrees with him in allowing that what liberals especially like in romanticism is a spirit of novelty and liberty, while what royalists like is religious inspiration; but, as for him, he willingly accepts the combination[195] (which obviously presupposes a considerable degree of independence vis-à-vis religion proper). A similar case is that of Junius Castelnau, a young magistrate from Montpellier: the sociological critique of classicism, in which like so many liberals he detects the ceremony and ideals of an absolutist court, and the advocacy of a literature that incarnates the national tradition as expressed in modern times, are only one aspect of his argument for romanticism: he, too, adds to it the idea of a more inward poetry, and the acceptance of melancholy as the defining characteristic of modern Europe.[196]

We are beginning to see that the evolution of opinions, the effect of influences, and efforts at synthesis were the processes by which the final unity of romanticism was able to emerge from a situation that began by being dominated by conflict. It is the whole of the movement of unification that it is now appropriate to consider, for it is this unified romanticism that in France gave definitive form to the idea of the poet's mission.

✍ Romantic Unity, Nodier, the Second Cénacle

The unity of romanticism was already potentially present in its divisions. Pending the coming fusion and sometimes by means of a double-entendre, royalists and liberals who favored a literary revolution already thought alike in more ways than one, as we have been able to see. Such a theme is the one exalting the whole of the army of reformers, with banners mingled. Such is, for example, in the addition to those we have already observed, the theme of the woes of the genius, the popularity of which transcends party differences and applies to the philosopher as well as the poet, whatever be the character of the mission with which they are thought to be invested. The idea of a spiritual mission is everywhere linked to that of an ordeal, a passion. The misfortunes of writers and the great misery of the poet's profession had been commonplaces at least since the Renaissance; the same goes for the disappointments of genius exposed to envy. Compilations in Latin on this subject that had been published in the sixteenth and seventeenth centuries were still known in the nineteenth.[197] The Age of Enlightenment, by raising the thinker to the very heights, gave an unprecedented meaning and impact to these sufferings, and added to them the woes associated with Sensibility. There resulted, as a heroic complement to humanist optimism, a sort of lay version of the Christian cult of suffering: the minister of humanity, whether philosopher or poet, like a secular Christ, establishes his titles through his tribulations. After the Revolution, the general tendency of spiritualism strengthened the theme and favored the poetic variant. Suffering having then been rediscovered as the secret of the universe by Mme de Staël or Chateaubriand, the unique thread running through every human heart, it is quite natural that it also be the preeminent attribute that humanity embodies. To describe in detail the course of this theme and of the various elements that constituted it in 1800 and in 1830, an entire book would be needed, and it would risk being an oversized and monotonous one. A gallery of great persecuted spirits, poets especially, is assembled at this time, and their evocation occurs everywhere: Homer, Dante, Tasso, Camoens, Milton, Gilbert, Byron. Each writer gives a more or less complete list, according to memory or preference, and adds new names to it at will — Socrates, Ossian, Galileo, or moderns of less stature. In 1805, a letter from the young Pichat, the future Pichald of *La Muse française*, joins Malfilâtre to Gilbert alongside Homer and Camoens;[198] around 1816, Lamartine adds Ovid to Homer and Tasso in his ode "La Gloire"; in 1820, Hugo canonizes Chateaubriand in the ode "Le Génie"; Chatterton is mentioned beginning in 1816, before figuring in 1819 in Latouche's preface to his edition of Chénier;[199] in 1824, Frédéric Soulié, in a group of poems, adds Millevoye to Gilbert and Chénier.[200] As for texts where the theme is treated in general, with titles like "Le Poète malheureux," "Génie et malheur," "Le Poète indigent," "Le Poète mourant," they exist in such quantities that we must content ourselves with noting their extreme abundance, as well as the even greater abundance of reflections and allusions that this privileged subject provokes everywhere and on every occasion.

It is through the idea of the misfortunes of genius that there comes into the world, overarching the factions and literary camps, this ideal assembly of the heroes of thought, which the nineteenth century will oppose to the group of kings and eminences of this world, and that by the same token is supposed to compete with the Christian martyrology. The old motif of envy dead set against the brightest and best ascends from the psychological or moral plane to that of metaphysics: the hatred of the common herd pursues the elect and the revealer of truths too high to be understood by the masses. And if the man of genius himself suffers because he is not followed, he also suffers by virtue of his own nature: a soul like his is not proportioned to his body, it is compressed and in pain, trapped in organs unworthy of it; in the man of genius, a feeble being exhausts itself attempting to elucidate Spirit; thus genius attests, gloriously and painfully, to the duality of the universe and the supremacy of the spiritual: "The priestess who gives oracles," writes Mme de Staël in a passage on Tasso, "felt herself animated by a cruel power: some involuntary force pushes genius head-long into misfortune: genius hears the sound of the spheres, which mortal organs are not made to understand; genius penetrates mysteries of feeling un-known to other men, and the soul of a genius has within a God whom it cannot control."[201] The misfortunes of genius are thus no longer explained by reasons deriving from the simple experience of the writer's miseries; they are part of an order where they have their meaning, of the deep nature of things where the good of men is paid for by the sufferings of their guides. The author of the *Génie du christianisme*, parodying unconsciously the title of his masterwork, wrote toward the end of his life: "The genius is a Christ."[202]

The insistence with which this motif recurs and propagates itself during the first half of the nineteenth century and its obsessive repetition among poets both great and minor during the Restoration does not keep it from having a conventional feel throughout the period; one cannot help feeling that the poetic condition at this time, inclining toward syntheses and hopes, is not really per-ceived as tragic. Royalist or liberal poets are trying rather to exalt their role and the fruitfulness of their action, and only make of their supposed unhappiness a halo for their spiritual dignity. In order for writers and poets really to fear that they are victims of a curse, they will have to go through the ordeal of 1830 and the distress born of the definitive embourgeoisement of society. On the whole, poetry will pull through the ordeal, but not without feeling its effects deeply. It is after the still more violent shock and disappointment of 1848 that bitterness will finally be closely associated with the poetic calling. Such is not the situation in 1825. It is all the more remarkable, then, that the motif of the poet con-demned to unhappiness should have constituted itself and prospered as it were in advance, as a possible version of the modern ministry of the poet. Every affirmation of the preeminence of a contemplative aristocracy runs up in prac-tice against the indifference or hostility of the public; the ministry of thought knows it is contested, and it is natural that it should wish to extract additional prestige from anything that makes its exercise heroic. The fact that this attitude was so universally adopted, by men of such widely differing views who con-ceived the role of the poet in such different ways, gives one pause. It is to be explained by the fact that it expresses the relation of the thinkers as a body to society at large. The "misfortunes of writers," transformed into those of the

Genius or the Poet, were a prior, unmediated form—an anticipation—of the common consciousness that was being forged in the diversity of the debate on romanticism.

In the history of literature, it frequently happens that a single theme expresses opposite intentions, as if each period accepted a certain amount of misunderstanding for the sake of an economy of forms. But it is not certain that this economy is solely the result of laziness, or of the difficulty of unlimited invention; unvarying themes, while covering a variety of intentions, can signify some agreement. We must not in this case speak of misunderstanding, but rather ask ourselves where the agreement lies. For the problem before us— namely, the formation of an appropriate new literary doctrine for nineteenth-century France and the role that the writer should have therein—the very nature of the need required a final unity: thus it is not surprising that the initial divergences between royalist romanticism and liberal romanticism were accompanied by common themes in which agreement was prefigured. Byron was another of those themes: this figure, the prestigious realization of the greatness and misfortune of the Poet,[203] was universally celebrated by the poets of the two tendencies. Byron was without any doubt one of the strongest bonds of French romanticism, because Byron's work made visible the image of a romanticism that was independent of factions and superior to them.[204] In France, Byron taught or encouraged what might be called a spirituality without faith. The violence of his tormentedness, so opposed to the self-assured approach of philosophism, was attractive to the Christian poets of 1820. Byron is, in fact, the philosophy of the age, but no longer aggressive and self-satisfied; "he is, rather," writes one of the poets of *La Muse française*, "philosophy sitting on ruins, weeping for its own lack of faith and the mournful results of its knowledge";[205] through Byron the descendants of the *philosophes* will see themselves drawn toward and converted to anxiety. "What then is Lord Byron's atheism? The despair of atheism. . . . There is a doubt that seeks refuge in disbelief—that was the doubt of the encyclopedists; there is a doubt that seeks refuge in faith—that is the doubt of Lord Byron."[206] Such a doubt, which calls for consolation, is in any event less sinister than one that excludes and discourages consolation: "[H]e scourges the soul without withering it," observes the young Vigny, "whereas the *philosophes* of the eighteenth century, with the same fund of ideas, deaden the soul and destroy all of life's hopes."[207] This is indeed what permits the almost brotherly debate of the Christian poet with Byron that occupies so much space in Lamartine's poetry around this time. On their side, the liberals are converted to Byronic perturbedness by means of the freedom of thought and the spirit of rebellion that they find attractive in him; they renounce philo-

sophic wisdom only because of a principle of energy and inquiry that dis-
possesses traditional authority in favor of the poet as a child of the times. This is
also the understanding of Stendhal, a great admirer of Byron, in whom he sees
the true type of the romantic poet.[208] In the end, through Byron, all go together
down the path of modern anxiety, which consists both of dissatisfaction and
audacity, and is as far removed from philosophism as it is from received religion,
and in France was the spirit of romanticism proper.[209]

In the two camps, certain individuals who intuitively possessed a fuller view of
the destination of the movement that was carrying them along contributed
more than others to the triumph of this spirit. For example, liberals of *La Muse
française* like Latouche or Jules Lefèvre possessed such a view. Above all, there is
Nodier, a royalist in name, professing in the aftermath of the return of the
Bourbons a superficial moderation, but in fact profoundly modern and romantic from the Empire on. His orientation had been marked out long before the
flowering of royalist romanticism, with which he sympathized without really
belonging to it. At the time, when the counterrevolution was assembling its
themes, around 1800, he took no part in this intellectual movement; he was
then a Pythagorean, bewailing the loss of our aboriginal excellence much more
than the ruin of France's traditional institutions. There is no sign that he regretted the passage of pre-1789 society; on the contrary, throughout his lifetime
everything he wrote attests to the strong impression made on him by the forceful ways of the Revolutionary and imperial era; so much so that a mythic imagination transformed his childhood and adolescent memories, for which he has
often been derided. The hero of his novel *Jean Sbogar*, roughed out, he tells us,
in 1812,[210] is a modern hero, impassioned by the grandeur of the unspoiled and
therefore in revolt against a decrepit order of things. In the days leading up to
1830, Nodier restrains himself less, and his underlying thought reappears: the
advantage of revolutions, however dearly paid, he tells us, is that they "elevate
the moral character of man by giving him a compelling and solemn destination
that will not be realized, but whose very conception possesses energy and greatness."[211] When compared with his 1804 pages on Quaï and reflections like these,
the ultra, Vendean Nodier of 1815 to 1825 seems quite artificial.[212] Yet it was to
royalist newspapers that he contributed throughout this period, waging in their
pages a circumspect campaign for romanticism, as though he felt himself to be
in foreign territory. This circumspection did not, moreover, prevent him from
cultivating outside their pages an exaggeratedly immoderate literature: the time
of his royalism is that of his vampiric writings, of *Smarra*, of *Infernalia*.

The originality of his conception of romanticism resides in his bringing together a lucid modernism and a deep, vivid feeling for poetry. "One would have," he writes, "an odd notion of poetry if one believed in the possibility of poetry in a language no longer young, that is, one that has passed its classical age. . . . Poetry is in its essence an enchantment, a magic: it needs sensitive, confident hearts, a naturalness of ideas and feelings that belongs only to virgin nature and nascent societies."[213] "What solemnity in the earliest ideas! What power in faculties never before felt! What tenderness in those earliest feelings! . . . Everything had just been born, and most of all society, which has since destroyed everything."[214] This manner of feeling is one that places him above prejudices, royalist as well as liberal: for it is no longer modern sophists alone who threaten poetry, according to the customary counterrevolutionary model, it is civilization itself; but, unlike philosophism and its heirs, who perform more coldly this funeral orison, Nodier suffers in grieving for the death of poetry, and this grief itself is a resurrection. All of Nodier's criticism announces this resurrection, whether he awaits it as an effect of the social upheaval, which has, in a certain way, fractured the civilized order, or whether he imagines the consciousness of disenchantment as a new enchantment. Ultra publications welcome with open arms Nodier's somber melancholy: "It is already time to sit upon the ruins like Jeremiah, and to utter mournful cries like the woman in Rama who had lost her children. It is the situation of our society that has led us to deserve this poetry of grief and regret, whose language speaks to all souls."[215] This is in appearance the refrain of the royalist elegiasts; but Nodier is not thinking only of the recent revolutionary ordeal, but, much more, of the curse upon an old society suffering from inanition: "The poet of Antiquity was the simplest of men. The poetry of peoples who have finished their development will be a work of convulsive despair, the apt expression of their misery."[216] This funereal song lamenting the present state of affairs deceived the ultra public; by it Nodier anticipated, looking well beyond royalist romanticism and even romanticism itself, the poetic pessimism of the following generations. This will appear most of all in the post-1830 Nodier, but in this respect Nodier is already himself as early as *Les Tristes* of 1806, and he continues to be so in 1820 when he celebrates in a royalist novel those souls "condemned to the impossible, as if the supreme power, which cannot without violating its own decrees deprive them of the infinite in the eternal realm, had wished to give them nothingness in the present."[217] Similarly, Nodier was then writing texts marked by a disconsolate apocalypticism in which he tints in his own fashion the themes of the counterrevolution.[218]

We should not, therefore, attach an exaggerated importance to Nodier's variations between the classic and the romantic or to his progress from one to the other; it may be that these episodes have to do with the vicissitudes of politico-literary diplomacy.[219] He never ceased feeling the inevitability of a change. Beginning in the first years of the Restoration, he asserts the existence of new literary needs, and argues both for national subjects and for melodrama: he is seeking means of influencing the masses in an age when literature can no longer be meant for an elite only;[220] yet he hails in romanticism a spiritual promotion of poetry, in that it is linked to "aspects of things that have not yet been perceived. . . , I know not what secrets of the human heart . . . , I know not what mysteries of nature."[221] One can see that in his romanticism he mingles freely the spirit of the two opposite political camps; or rather, this division does not even matter to him; he retains and fuses together everything that seems to him to bear witness to the revolution he proclaims. He does make an effort to give a royalist value to his condemnation of classicism by recalling that the republicanism of 1793 took its models from classical antiquity, but he announces nevertheless that "the romantic could well be nothing but the classic of the moderns; that is, the expression of a new society, which is neither that of the Greeks nor that of the Romans."[222] Is this the new society of chivalry and faith, so often invoked by royalist writers, of which more than one reader of the *Annales* must have dreamed while reading these lines? For Nodier, what matters is the present, and the ministry of literature. In the same year, Nodier writes: "Civilization was about to perish. . . . At that very moment a powerful hand changed the way things were going. . . . The novel acquired I know not what noble, religious authority, which ennobled its character. Christianity and morals, driven from the temples, took refuge in print."[223] Granted, these remarks may be at home in the *La Quotidienne*, where they appeared; but what shall we say of what follows, which is a hymn of death and anguish beyond consolation?

> This immense, painful confusion into which, one after the other, societies descend, in which religious institutions are losing their influence and in which civic institutions no longer have any at all, this vast wasteland of thought in which a fully mature society hurries toward dissolution, this awful hesitation between the false and the true, which is the last faculty remaining to a fallen soul — this is the romantic genre in its entirety. . . . To ask anything else of the present generation and the still more unfortunate generations to come is to ask the storm to be calm.[224]

It is no longer a question here of an edifying affliction that can find the remedy as quickly as the source of the pain, but of an anguish that willingly seeks an outlet in the frenetic, like this word or not: "Peoples that have grown old," says Nodier, "need to be stimulated by what is new and violent."[225] Thus, in his many attempts to define the new literature, Nodier easily forgets the point of view of the Christian, monarchical Restoration; he sees in romanticism rather the response of modern man to the collapse of the entire past: no longer believing in anything, and in particular not in his immortal soul, man today compensates for this loss by spiritualizing matter by means of the supernatural or the horrible: "It is as if a soul has been taken away from civilization, and a deadly genius has suddenly come to teach it about the void. . . . The feeling of a divine destination, which is the characteristic of our noble essence, has been violently driven from the region of intellectual and moral ideas and has taken refuge in physical being, which as if in sport has restored to it the soul that philosophy thought it had banished from nature."[226] What comes through in these lines owes nothing to the past; it is the thoroughly dramatic intuition of a new royalty of the creative spirit grappling with a universe emancipated from dogmas. All this romanticism on Nodier's part, making of literature both the spiritual support and tragic conscience of a humanity henceforth without a church, really answers what was the fundamental problem for writers over and above the opposition of parties and theories of poetry. Once divergent tendencies were overcome, romanticism had to be above all literature's coming to grips with its responsibilities in a world full of doubt.

The part later played by Nodier, in 1823–24, in the open struggle against classicism, alongside *La Muse française*, is perfectly natural. Embracing the group constituted by the young royalist poets, he came to the support of their cause by articulating their views to as great an extent as his own, wedding the "true religion" to the "new society," producing arguments in favor of Christian romanticism and against the frivolous, mythological poetry of the eighteenth century and, in fact, giving free rein to his deep anticlassicism as soon as he saw that he was not alone in the royalist milieu in professing this.[227] In the years that followed, as the ideas of literary revolution gained credit and audacity, he had no hesitation in acting as the godfather for the movement in its new form. In the Arsenal meetings, romantic poetry frees itself from royalist and Christian themes; liberty, which the group at *La Muse française* had made one with religion and the throne, now separated itself from these. While more than one of the young poets of *La Muse* balk at these new ideas, Nodier, who is more than forty years old, presses ahead. Not that he had to be converted, like Hugo and Vigny, to the idea of a literature free of the past; he had always been, at bottom, what the romantics of 1830 had to be: he believed in an entirely modern renewal of the imaginative poetic faculty. In the articles that he writes on the eve of the battle over *Hernani*, which are thoroughly imbued with that historic moment, he sets free his natural boldness.[228] These articles, like those from the time of *La Muse*, are optimistic, sometimes triumphal; Nodier assumes the role of the herald of a poetry at last summoned to give expression to the new society, and to reign over it: "It is thus that poetry appeared, natural and sensitive, when societies were first born, creating them through the word, as God had created the world. It is with such a capacity that it must come back to life in these days of universal renewal, during which, along with all of civilization, it comes to claim its forgotten rights."[229] But this optimism is not confined to Nodier. The unity of French romanticism as it is incarnated in him is not only that of different contemporary tendencies that fused together at the end of the Restoration; it is the unity of the successive, contradictory eras that opened afterwards within victorious romanticism. Nodier experienced the romantic movement both in the optimistic mode of the generation that surrounded him and in the disenchanted, negative version that the ordeal of the real world would impose upon subsequent generations.

We know that Chateaubriand's exclusion from the cabinet in 1824 facilitated the emancipation of the young royalist poets; Chateaubriand's openness to liberal ideas and thoughts of the future encouraged them to orient their poetry similarly. This influence has been observed, and its importance has perhaps been exaggerated, for royalist romanticism was already carrying the seeds of its transformation within itself. But it is significant that the final unity of romanticism is explained by a circumstance that was only likely to affect one of the two camps. This is because in fact the deep impulse toward new creations existed on that side: it was the royalist poets and their conversion that were responsible for the romanticism of 1830. They accepted the France that really existed, according to the instruction of the liberal poets; these latter writers had the present on their side, and in the end the present routed the mythology of the old monarchical, Christian France; in addition, liberal philosophy had elaborated a modern doctrine of the ideal, which prevailed. Hugo was seen to devote the ode "A la colonne de la place Vendôme"[230] to liberal themes, and Lamartine publicly applauded Cousin's texts.[231] From this conversion are born the most influential works of nineteenth-century French poetry. Over on the liberal side, the moment of unification is marked not by works but by a mutation in criticism: their reviews were opened to ideas and sometimes to persons of the group to which they had till now been opposed. More and more they presented romantic inspiration as an emanation from and complement to the spirit of liberty;[232] more and more they allied the mysterious ascendancy of poetry to the emancipatory action of thought.[233] In brief, they broadened their views, while the poets of the other side, moving toward them, broadened their creations. But there was always a gap between the poets' romanticism and the most open-minded liberal criticism: "The romantic school of poets was never able to break into *Le Globe,*" writes Sainte-Beuve;[234] there were only alliances and understandings. They did, for a time at least, in 1825 and 1826, break into the *Mercure du dix-neuvième siècle*, thanks to Latouche, and again in 1827 and 1829.[235] Liberal criticism, by furnishing its contribution to the movement, is only following the new works at a greater or lesser remove.

To describe the romantic victory is above all to show how the royalist poets during the decisive years between 1825 and 1830 transformed their intuitive idea of the ministry of poetry in a resolutely modern direction. This process, the second stage of the romantic revolution in France, was accomplished in a series of works each of which develops a discovery, proposes the final formula of a genre till then in a state of ambiguous gestation, and begins to find a new way for literature to act as the public's spiritual director. This second stage is marked by an influx of new adherents who join those former collaborators and friends of *La Muse* who have remained in the movement; all assemble around the men who had stepped forward as guides: Hugo and Vigny, till then among the youngest of the group, came to the fore; those who joined them were hardly as old as they. With them, the poetic religion that had marked the decisive moment of *La Muse française* continues in a new form, as a religion of free inspiration, bewitching imagination, sovereign art: another memorable moment following the first without effacing it, though it eclipsed it in the memory of posterity. This moment was, for someone like Sainte-Beuve, one of unforgettable fervor, of an all-too-brief poetic possession that fled too quickly: in 1862, he celebrates with emotion those far-off days, enumerating the surviving chaplains of that "ardent church."[236] Vigny too remembers, twenty years later, that "union so innocent and pure," "those élans toward liberty and art, that love of the ideal in its most extensive splendor."[237] The newcomers, familiars of Nodier's salon at the Arsenal or of Hugo's *cénacle*, were named Alexandre Dumas, Fontaney, Victor Pavie, Boulay-Paty; Sainte-Beuve was among them; all were born after 1800. In their literary flowering, there is little or no trace of the royalist themes of 1815 to 1820: the meaning of poetry appears in them in the form of the spontaneous; poetic charm, as multifarious experience of the things that make up life, is born of a free communication with heaven:

Délire inattendu, le charme a sur notre âme
Je ne sais quel pouvoir qui révèle les cieux;[238]

[Unexpected delirium, charm has on our souls
I know not what power, which opens the heavens to them;]

the poet speaks freely, as befits his time, and his ministry of the ideal calls for the rejuvenation of the poetic world as well as that of style:

Ils ne sont plus, les temps où l'indolent poète
Caressait en riant sa lyre toujours prête,
Et d'un futile accord lui dictait les refrains;
Où d'un foyer sans feu remuant l'héritage,
        Des cendres froides d'un autre âge
Son souffle revivait quelques tisons éteints.

A vos chants désormais il faut une patrie,
Poètes, n'allez plus d'une muse flétrie
Mendier plus longtemps les stériles transports.
De ce monde vieilli secouez la poussière.
Montez, montez. Là-haut gravite une autre sphère,
        Là résonnent d'autres accords.[239]

[They are past, the times when the idle poet
Caressed, laughing, a lyre that was always at hand,
And with a futile harmony commanded its refrains;
Or, stirring the legacy of a hearth without fire,
        Revived with his breath
A few dead embers in the cold ashes of another age.

Your songs from now on have need of a homeland,
Poets, go no more to a withered muse
To beg from her those sterile transports.
Shake off the dust of that aged world
Go up, go up. Up there is a different sphere,
        Other harmonies are sounding there.]

The new *cénacle* faithfully preserved the heritage of *La Muse française* in the matter of the poetic ministry; while liberating poetry from the constraints of Catholicism and the monarchy, it left to it the sacred character and celestial stamp with which liberal literature had never marked it so clearly. In becoming the hymnist of the present time, the poet does not cease to be the heir of the prophets: "Like the echo of a loud voice, the poet transmits to men the secrets drawn from the revelation of a nature marked by God."[240] Lamartine undertook to be the spokesperson for this conception of poetry in his *discours de réception* at the Academy in 1830: at once the daughter of religion and the free language of the soul in a time of seriousness and renewal.[241] Romanticism was, in sum, more and more openly an amalgam of the sacred and the modern. The experience of the modern was everywhere; the sacred, which had been so to speak excluded from the universe of the *philosophes* and relegated by them to a church in which they did not believe, had survived to live again, but only at the expense of a literary transposition that had taken place in the poetic imagination of the counter-revolution. We can hardly be surprised that it was those who possessed such a rare ingredient, such an indispensable building-block in the ideological constructions of the new century, who had the leading role in the literary revolution.

It remains to be said that the sanctification of Art constantly recurs as a dominant trait in the enduring memories that these years left in those who lived through them: "The principal traits of this other moment," says Sainte-Beuve (he is speaking of the years 1824 to 1829 and contrasting them with those that preceded), "were the supremacy, the cult of art considered in itself and in a more detached way, a great exertion of the imagination, and the knowledge of how to portray things."[242] Sainte-Beuve, whose special knowledge of romanticism began mostly during this stage, thinks this is its defining aspect: "There existed, during the period from 1819 to 1830, in many young souls . . . a deep, sincere, and impassioned feeling that was all the more disinterested and lofty in that it applied only to what concerned Art, and was all the more holy because of this. There existed the *passion for Art*."[243] We should obviously not suppose this passion to be distinct from that of poetry; the character of the moment that made it original consisted precisely in the communion of poetry and art.[244] Poetry claims to be the soul of the fine arts, and shares with them its new elevation. The artistic coloration that the poetic ministry assumes needs to be explained, no doubt, as do various other metamorphoses or acquisitions of romanticism in the course of these same years. It is best to consider them in the work itself, rich in revivals and creativity, of the principal initiators, Vigny, Hugo, and, to a lesser degree, Sainte-Beuve. But perhaps it is suitable first of all to situate the whole of the romantic movement as it has appeared to this point with respect to the history of French society.

Romanticism and French Society

Romanticism rejects both traditional religion and the *philosophe*'s faith in humanity; but it rejects each faith only to reconcile them in itself. This creative compromise was of a sort to give the new society the general ideas it needed if it was to legitimate itself and endure. The Revolution had been repudiated, but it was equally true that it had prevailed. The ambiguous nature of romanticism doubtless corresponded to this situation. A spiritualism both ancient in its sources and open to human ambition and worldly conquests was to shore up both the permanence and the prestigious development of the newly organized society. What must not be lost sight of is the fact that the elaboration of this new complex of values was entrusted to literature, which was thus invested with a responsibility which it had not hitherto known. What needs were satisfied by royalist romanticism and liberal romanticism, respectively, is hardly worth asking. We know the political milieux to which each of them was linked, their traditions, their ideals; behind them we detect social classes: royalist romanticism seems an attempt at rejuvenating and rehabilitating the aristocracy; liberal romanticism seems to be the victorious bourgeoisie breaking into the domain of literary forms and honors. These analyses would add nothing to what we know through the writers themselves, in both parties. What is much more important is, above all, that in this double movement the unity of its themes and values finally became real. This may be explained up to a certain point by the fact that 1830 integrated the remains of the aristocracy into a society that was definitively bourgeois. But this explanation obscures what is most important: certainly, the romanticism of 1830 is tied only weakly to the aristocracy, but it is not linked to any greater degree to the bourgeoisie. To the romanticism of 1830, the aristocracy appears decrepit, but the bourgeoisie seems inferior by nature. Romanticism defines thought's position as being above classes, the position — *mutatis mutandis* — of a church, that is, a community bearing the highest values and composed of men whose very ministry removes them from any particular class. The poet and the artist, as such, are neither *gentilshommes* nor bourgeois, although they may be so by origin or social status. The period they live in, of which they are the spokespersons, necessarily separates them from what remains of the former society; but why are they so repelled by the idea of identifying with the representatives of the new society? Whence this aversion for the bourgeoisie, which they profess precisely as poets and artists and which henceforth constitutes them as a distinct body?

This resistance has often been dismissed as unimportant, and the aversion that poets and artists claimed to feel for bourgeois society has been denounced as a sort of bourgeois affectation: an alibi, an aesthetic cover-up of the true problems, a mystification thanks to which a class that is conspicuously disparaged but not really called into question is assured its continued reign. Such analyses are not difficult to produce: they signify only that poets and artists do not take the destruction of the bourgeoisie to be their task, which is extremely obvious; thence follows the conclusion that they serve it, by virtue of the totalitarian axiom according to which one can only be either *for* or *against*: an effective means of intimidation, but not of seeking truth. Others, more simply, reduce the entire affair to a grandiloquent grudge of impecunious writers against a society responsible for providing for them which does not feed them well enough. The scorn often felt today for so-called "romantic" attitudes (i.e., of no practical consequence because their generosity is insincere) favors this sort of explanation. But it is necessary to take into account the extent, and, so to speak, the *necessity* of the phenomenon. Stendhal was certainly neither a vain aesthete nor a famished author. He was, apart from his status as a writer, a respectable provincial bourgeois. His biting liberalism, his horror of royalist or religious dupery, are typical of his class as it existed in his own time. But we see him react virulently against a contemporary doctrine in which he thinks he perceives an exaltation of the bourgeois. His ironically entitled brochure, *D'un nouveau complot contre les industriels*, pretends to interpret the glorification of industry as a piece of treachery intended to ruin industrialists by the excessive and overweening character of its praise. Stendhal is annoyed by those writing for the Saint-Simonian *Le Producteur*, but they were more nuanced than he seems to believe, and their thinking about the relation between industry and intellectuals (to use the modern term) was far from superficial. Stendhal takes note only of the fact that they exalt the type of the industrialist, that is, of the entrepreneur or the useful worker; to which he replies: "The profession of industrialists is very estimable; but we do not see what makes it deserve to be more *honored* than any other profession useful to society. Nothing one can do will be able to change the fact that the class charged in France with manufacturing public opinion, to speak like an industrialist, will always be the class of people with investments earning 6000 pounds a year. Only these people *have the leisure* to form for themselves an opinion which is their own, and not their newspaper's." Thus a leisure class of decently but moderately well-off people are invested with the government of opinion. It would be possible to say, and not without some justification, that Stendhal is defending unearned income, the ancient and consecrated form of bourgeois wealth, against industry, another form of the same wealth, which in Stendhal's time has a tendency to develop. But the *rentiers* of whom Stendhal is speaking are not *rentiers* merely. He calls them "the thinking class"; and he gives as representatives of this class, among others, William Tell, Riego, Bolivar, Turgot, Washington, Dupont de l'Eure, that is, men whose action is situated on a higher plane than that of unearned income or of industry: "To attain high esteem, there must, in general, be a sacrifice of interest to some noble goal." Devotion and lofty thought define a sort of special human family whose action may indeed, by Stendhal's own account, tend to establish what we call bourgeois society, but which is marked off from the bourgeoisie by a special distinction. The bourgeois is nothing without heroes and legislators: but Heroes and Legislators are strangers to the bourgeois type and superior to it. Thus the bourgeoisie will cause Greece, emancipated from the Turks, to prosper: "But will they have the wisdom to make the good laws which permit commerce to flourish? But will they have the courage necessary to exterminate the Turks and enforce these good laws?"[245]

Stendhal draws these views on Greek independence from another kind of experience altogether; all his life he was deeply impressed by a historic French figure: the Jacobin, the heroic and legislating *conventionnel*, as the Revolution in France had produced this type. The bourgeoisie had at that time produced, out of necessity, a prodigious race of military and legislative superior beings, quite alien to the spirit of factory, shop counter, and pettifogging, the recollection of which the bourgeoisie found both exalting and terrifying now that it had attained the clearest of its goals and seen itself restored to the ordinary routine of business. We know how enthusiastic Stendhal felt when remembering this: by the light of this memory he imagines the ideal society which he opposes to the aristocracy of the Restoration, enfeebled, inhibited, and governed by fear. But when he thinks of the distance separating this ideal from the real bourgeois world, as it presents itself to him in the aftermath of the revolutionary crisis, he declares an unequivocal hatred and scorn of the bourgeois, and likewise of democracy and "Genevan" morals.[246] He is reduced to seeking examples of energetic life in the manners of the Italian aristocracy of old;[247] his feelings of this sort are so strong that he might even be tempted to rehabilitate the aristocracy, even the legitimist aristocracy, which at least incarnates, in his eyes, in a vestigial state, an unconstrained, exquisite way of life.[248] This ambivalence of Stendhal's is well known. In fact he seeks in his novelistic creations a type of human excellence which ceaselessly repudiates the bourgeois for the aristocratic, the aristocratic for the bourgeois, and thus raises itself above both: the type, finally, of an aristocracy of character, conceived by a free intelligence of the nineteenth century. And in this he is merely continuing an effort which goes back to the very origins of the bourgeois revolution: when the heroic type, born of feudalism, was first forced out of literature, it is not a properly bourgeois type who replaced him, but rather a figure of a sensitive *Philosophe* who possesses traits of both classes, and who is, still more, a precursor of the modern Intellectual. When the old values of the noble and Christian life fell into disuse, it was to make the way for the faith of the thinkers. Everything indicates that the rise of the bourgeoisie to the head of French society coincided with the constitution of a spiritual power relatively distinct from it. This power has accompanied it throughout its reign, and has been sufficiently troublesome to make the bourgeoisie on more than one occasion wish for and realize a reconciliation with the old Church, which was seeking to survive: not without disappointment on that side as well, and the temptation from time to time to curse everything that thinks.

One cannot, then, consider as of little account the distance — real, it would seem, and necessary — separating the victorious bourgeoisie from romantic poets and artists. Is this so strange? The former ruling class, with its prestige, valor, generosity, loyalty, and all the claims to public admiration which it attributed to itself, had never controlled ultimate values: to worldly glory, rooted in the noble *ego*, the Church, in the name of God and of the human race, added — and, if necessary, opposed — love for one's fellow men. Why be surprised that in the time of bourgeois supremacy a modern spiritual corporation should have likewise developed as the interpreter of values that are indispensable to every society, and that cannot merely coincide with the convenience of its directors? To tell the truth, the very nature of the bourgeoisie rendered this complement particularly necessary. This, I think, is the heart of the problem. Profit as a fundamental motivation, the growth of general productivity as a criterion of worth — these traits of the new class offered meager fare for humans needing to feel admiration and experience communion. The bourgeoisie calls itself the bearer of freedom, of prosperity, and of progress, but those over whom it reigns and who have not forgotten its origins know its harshness, its small-minded prudence, its pusillanimity: hence a discussion out of which inevitably arises a type of cleric who, as spokesman for public aspirations, demotes and lectures the bourgeois in the name of an ideal which transcends it. It is true that the relation of clerics to their worldly masters has assumed a new character in bourgeois society. In a sense, clerics have less authority, their supernatural titles having been diluted in the philosophic firmament. But, on the other hand, they believe themselves authorized to feel greater disdain, and they treat as undeserving of respect a class of undistinguished origin, which is only defined by its money; they consider it alien by nature to the sublimities which they make henceforth their exclusive prerogative.

Concerning the precise role of what is called Thought [*Esprit*] in bourgeois society, and the form that the creation of universal values can take in an industrial and mercantile society founded on individual enterprise, there would be much to say. The nature of this society excludes dogma, that is, the subjection of human striving toward happiness to an authoritarian system of values instituted by a church; and it is bourgeois society's great claim to glory, for those who wish to judge it impartially, that the authority of dogmas has been weakened wherever it has developed successfully, and that wherever bourgeois society has been destroyed this authority has returned in new forms. It is thus not difficult to conceive of the existence, in the bourgeois world, of reflection that is free in its movements and ideals and that elaborates, even as it develops the themes necessary to the conservation of economic society, themes that also oblige economic society to transform and broaden itself, a literature at once of edification and criticism, of validation and the overcoming of self: this is more or less what romantic literature has been in France. But one must understand that writers, by assuming the role of mentors of society, separate themselves necessarily from pure conformism: they preach a faith that is at the very source of the new society and which the society accepts as its own, no doubt, but which, like every system of beliefs, transcends society and proposes to it a model. The function of literature in France in this first half of the nineteenth century orients it toward humanitarian values that separate it to a certain extent from the established society. Writers and poets in particular as an integral part of society make themselves its judges and prophets: they are in solidarity and stand apart, apologists and critics; like every spiritual power, they are at the same time recognized and contested by the temporal powers of society. This ambiguous position cannot be understood if in the play of social forces one does not allow a peculiar role and an autonomous activity to the intellectual class, endowed in the nascent bourgeois society with the qualities it had inherited from the eighteenth century and the Revolution. To explain humanitarian romanticism by the aspirations of one or another sector of society achieves nothing. In any case, one would still have to explain why the high literature of the last days of the Restoration and of the entire July Monarchy, especially the poetry, was not conservative instead, why it was attracted to the tendencies we observe. Writers, it will be said, were dragged along by a powerful social movement. They did indeed swell this movement by their patronage; they in large part created it. This movement was not so powerful that it did not finally reveal its weakness in the tragic year 1848; and the failure of democracy, significantly, opened a pessimistic period in literature. The attitude of writers is to be explained by their own promptings, by what one could call their conscience or their governing pretension, by their irresistible tendency to define themselves apart from temporal power and apart from privileged classes, in communion with the whole of mankind. Reflection will show that this stand is their very title to existence, under Louis-Philippe just as under Louis XV. It dominates all the great creations that, after the return of the Bourbons, founded the literature of modern France.

Chapter 8
The Beginnings of the Great Generation

❧ *Alfred de Vigny*

TODAY WE too often tend to forget the importance that authors and the public once attached to the distinctive character of each poetic genre. The way that statements of poetic doctrine strictly distinguished the ode, the elegy, the idyll, or the dithyramb seems in our time a futile prejudice; poetic language seems to us to be situated above such labels. This was not the case in 1820, and the work of the innovators was at first thought to be a new definition of the genres, before finding its culmination in the fluidity of their boundaries. We have seen the role that the metamorphosis of the elegy plays in Lamartine's beginnings. Emile Deschamps, in 1828, still thinks that the signal accomplishment of modern poets has been to do justice to certain genres that had until then remained undistinguished: "The lyric, the elegiac, and the epic were the weak parts of our former poetry. It is therefore upon these areas that the vitality of contemporary poetry had to bring itself to bear. Thus M. Victor Hugo made himself known in the Ode, M. de Lamartine in the Elegy, and M. Alfred de Vigny in the Poem."[1] This genre of the *poème* whose renewal motivates Deschamps's exaltation of Vigny, is, in the logic of his text, the modern form of the epic, disencumbered of "all the trappings of the supernatural," and enclosed "in compositions of moderate length not copied from any other sources."[2] This modernization of a genre that had in France in its traditional form produced only a series of failures or half-failures, from Ronsard's *La Franciade* to Chateaubriand's *Les Martyrs* [published in 1572 and 1809, respectively. *Trans.*], had been in the works for a long time. The short narration in verse, free in its choice of subject matter and stripped of fabulation, does not date from Vigny: various stories from the Bible or from antiquity are related in verse, and narrative romances with medieval or modern subjects are published from the eighteenth century on and are in vogue during the Empire, clearly attesting to efforts in this direction. In 1729 there is an anonymous "Fille de Jephté, poème,"[3] with which Vigny was perhaps acquainted before writing his own, and his poem on the love between Emma and Eginhard, "La Neige," is in the tradition of troubadour romances. In an 1823 article, Deschamps was already pointing out to the new generation as a field to cultivate "the *poème* proper, from the Homeric epic to the Scottish ballad": by "the *poème* proper" he means, of course, the narrative poem, and he praises Chénier for having reduced it to "moderate proportions" in his compositions from antiquity,[4] which were, as is well known, among Vigny's models.

The *poèmes* published by Vigny in the 1820s were the first sign of the astonishing romantic revival of narrative poetry. What this poetry might turn out to be was uncertain in such novel conditions. The former epic poet, singing in a long poem of a nation's or a civilization's origins, such as Homer, Virgil, and the moderns who had imitated them, by their very subject assumed the position of teachers and edifiers of the public. The author of short, freely imagined narratives or of historico-legendary romances ran a serious risk of proving unworthy of this high post. But this is not part of Vigny's conception. It is true, of course, that he was not at first conscious of the dignity with which he was going to invest the *poème*; he came to this little by little. His first poems are mostly genre paintings of classical, Jewish, medieval, or Spanish inspiration, in which he attends as much to the setting as to the narration; and as for the subject matter, these poems aim more at an emotional effect than at a philosophical lesson. The oldest, between 1815 and 1817, are not yet *poèmes*: "La Dryade" is an idyll; "Symétha," is an elegy; "Le Bain d'une dame romaine," a pure portrait without fabulation. Those that follow, from 1819 to 1821, "Le Somnambule," the fragments of the poem "Suzanne," "La Neige," even "La Femme adultère," show no thought that belongs especially to the poet. In the course of this period, Vigny allows an original teaching to appear only in "La Fille de Jephté" and in "La Prison," which illustrate the inhumanity of God. But to define the spirit of these poems, he thinks only of their moving, intimate character, which places them outside of any sort of public interest: "Everyone complains of the misfortunes due to heartache." This is what he writes in the introduction to his first collection of *Poèmes*, in 1822, where virtually all the pieces we have just mentioned are gathered together. In the same year, "Le Trappiste" appears, a narration full of a pointed meaning; "Moïse," the most famous *poème* in this genre, also dates from 1822, according to Vigny.[5]

In these first creations, then, two different series are intermingled: one, above all picturesque and sensitive, first appears around 1815 in Vigny's earliest writings, and will last until 1823 and 1825 with "Dolorida" and "Le Cor"; the other, the philosophic series, which begins in 1820 and coexists with the preceding one, shows, despite the briefness of the poems, a desire for a spiritual ministry that goes beyond the ambitions of the epic of old. The combining of a narrative that is historical in the broad, poetic sense of the word with a teaching that concerns the human condition, a formula that Vigny inaugurates here, will in fact be one of the solutions that romanticism will try to give to the still unresolved problem of the French epic. No doubt it was after the fact that Vigny realized what he was contributing; it is only in 1829, in the preface to the second edition of his *Poèmes*, that he writes: "The only merit that no one has ever denied to these compositions is to have preceded in France all those of the same genre, in which a philosophical thought is almost always adapted to a form that is epic or dramatic."[6] Around the same time, and in reference to this same edition, he notes in his *Journal*: "To originate and meditate a philosophical thought; to find in human actions the one that is most obvious *proof* of it; to reduce it to a simple action that can be engraved on the memory and represent, as it were, a statue and an impressive monument for the imagination of men, it is in this direction that poetry that is both epic and dramatic at the same time must proceed."[7] In his preface to the third edition of the *Poèmes*, written two months later, he returns to the question of his role as a predecessor and develops on this subject the theme of the precursor striding at the forefront of a human army:[8] this proves that his conception of the *poème* seemed to him to go further than simple literary invention. Vigny's accomplishment, in placing a thought conceived according to the free meditation of modernity—that is, promoted to the status of the universal on the basis of personal experience—in parallel with epic narration, freed from the strict conventions of former times, amounted to the creation of an instrument similar to what the sacred narrative had been for the priest, for the use of the poet as teacher of peoples. The odyssey and destination of the human race, formerly mapped out in Scripture, will be found from now on in the symbolic narratives of poets.

The idea of an epic of humanity made of a collection of short poems about different epochs and subjects, the seed of which we see in Vigny as early as the 1820s, was destined to have a magnificent future: Hugo's *La Légende des siècles* is in fact the fulfillment by a genius more fruitful and powerful than his own of what Vigny was the first to rough out. It is true that this sort of epic was not the generally preferred one during the course of the romantic era, even if it was the only one that produced completely successful works before the new eclipse—which still endures—of the epic genre. The secular prestige of the great epic architectures and the ambition to imitate or surpass them dominates the history of the romantic epic, whose first attempts aim chiefly at a modernization of the traditional "sacred poem," a religious variant of the classical epic. This variant, which had sometimes been attempted in France, with even less success, if that is possible, than was the case with the profane epic, seemed to some to be undergoing a renaissance at the beginning of the nineteenth century; knowledge of Milton, Klopstock, Dante, and the growing ambition of a poetic ministry favor this renaissance; Chateaubriand's *Les Martyrs* already goes in this direction, even if the setting of this work is on earth. And, finally, there was the dream of a great poem in which the adventures of heaven should play as great a part as earthly life, a poem of the totality of the destinies of the human race and of creation. The supernatural parts of the epic, which were inevitable as long as this genre took the place of the old sacred history, seemed to dictate not only the strengthening of the supernatural elements traditionally linked to the genre, but also keeping a unitary structure of vast dimensions. Lamartine, in the course of the same decade of the 1820s, conceived his poem *Les Visions* in this spirit. Vigny, on the other hand, faithful to his formula, imagined the mystical epic itself as a collection of different "mysteries," the unity of the epic project as a whole being guaranteed by the fact that the line between the "poem" and the "mystery" is as uncertain as can be: heaven and earth are as effectively in contact in a collection of episodes as in a unitary epic. "Moïse," a *poème,* and "Le Déluge," a *mystère,* are both earthbound narratives (except that the hero of *Le Déluge* is the son of an angel); "Eloa," a *mystère,* takes place entirely in heaven; the three poems will be joined in the 1837 edition of the *Poèmes antiques et modernes* under the title "Mystical Book"; "La Fille de Jephté" is excluded from this book and joined to the "Livre antique," no doubt as a purely human subject; but "La Femme adultère," in which Jesus appears, suffers the same fate; and later "La Colère de Samson" and "Le Mont des oliviers" will be called merely "philosophical poems." Historical, mystical, or philosophical is all the same in the new perspective of the epic genre, as is the teaching that through his various narrations the poet gives to humanity about its condition and its destiny.

Vigny nowhere defined the *mystère.* This word, borrowed perhaps from Byron,[9] if not directly from medieval dramaturgy, and that in its two sources designated dramatic works, is only applied by him to narrative poems, as soon as they include, like the dramas of the Middle Ages or Byron's poems, a plot and supernatural characters. Vigny's mysteries are a landmark in the romantic recreation of the epic because they are the first pieces to prove in their relative brevity that sacred narration could live once more unencumbered by classical conventions and emancipated from theological control. Heterodoxy peeks out everywhere in "Eloa": the ministry of the modern hierophant implies this independence; his anxious faith treats tradition with a free hand. Vigny's first try at the genre of the *mystère,* however, was a poem, "Le Jugement dernier," of which some fragments have survived, and that certainly seems to have respected the Catholic conception of the subject, for all the imaginative liberties taken here and indeed always taken in works of this genre.[10] This doctrinal conformism did not exclude a clear consciousness of the prerogatives of the poet, revived from

Dante: "In the middle of a frightening tale, interject like Dante . . . : Sages of every land who attend to my words, it is for you that the truth shines in my mysterious songs."[11] An invocation to the Holy Spirit appears again at the beginning of "L'Ange tombée," no doubt a prior version of "Eloa":

> Esprit venu du ciel, où portez-vous mon âme?
> Pour soutenir l'éclat de ces astres de flamme,
> Qui suis-je? Ai-je reçu comme un don précieux
> L'oeil de l'aigle inspiré que saint Jean vit aux cieux?
> Dans les ravissements d'une extase imprévue,
> Pourrai-je voir le ciel sans mourir de sa vue?

> [Spirit come from heaven, where are you taking my soul?
> To bear the brilliance of these fiery stars, who am I?
> Have I received like some precious gift
> The eye of the inspired eagle that Saint John saw in the heavens?
> In the ravishment of an unanticipated ecstasy,
> Will I be able to see heaven without perishing from the sight?]

Till then the poet had been satisfied to evoke figures from the human past, chiefly those whose misfortunes resembled his own:

> Je demandais alors à leur foule éplorée
> L'aventure par moi le plus souvent pleurée,
> Et j'écoutais surtout, par mon coeur emporté,
> Ceux dont le coeur saignait par le même côté.[12]

> [I used to ask to hear from this weeping crowd
> The story that had made me weep most often,
> And, moved by my heart, I especially listened
> To those whose hearts' suffering resembled my own.]

By thus distinguishing personal from sacred inspiration, Vigny helps us to understand in what sense, perhaps without fully realizing it, he was affirming in 1822 the intimate character of his poems: Moses and the Man in the Iron Mask, metaphysical heroes, were at the same time symbols of his personal misfortune. No doubt in the romantic perspective an outpouring of the self and philosophical meaning always go together; it is in this way, much more than by a psychological communion, that the poet's personality is exemplary. Yet sacred poetry tears Vigny away from his human condition, or makes him discover its meaning, among heavenly beings, at a level so high and so far from that to which one is accustomed that his ministry frightens him, and he makes his own the terrors of the face-to-face confrontation with God, formerly the province of the prophet or the apostle in the theophanies of Scripture. It is on this note of fear that the fragment concludes. Vigny later published "Eloa," in 1824, without any liminal invocation, whether because such an adornment already seemed too Catholic to him, or because he had been won over in the interval to a more sober view of poetry.

In any case, "Eloa," in which Satan deplorably and miraculously seduces an Angel-Woman who wants to redeem him, presents from the Catholic point of view a scabrous aspect that was immediately pointed out. It was criticized as having "an adulterous mixture of religious ideas and profane sentiments" — which is to define all of romanticism, albeit imprecisely, for it is more a transposition and a recreation than a mixture; critics denounced "a sort of sacrilege in this delirium of the imagination."[13] But it was precisely what shocked tradition in this poem that revealed its merit. *La Muse française* and Lamartine at this time were moving vaguely toward the summit where the poet receives a glimpse of the supernatural world so as to communicate it to men. Vigny is the first to have successfully attained this in what Gautier called forty years later "the most beautiful, perhaps the most perfect poem in the French language."[14] Vigny was never more conscious than during the nocturnal hours when he wrote "Eloa" of intensely experiencing the fervor that was, according to every testimony, the soul of the first *cénacle* — the religion of poetry, signifying its own resurrection: "The feeling of solitude, of silence, and of dream that the night awakens is poetry itself for me, as well as the revelation of the future angelic existence of man. I never had this feeling as completely as when I wrote 'Eloa.' "[15] Vigny did not rise so high in "Le Déluge," the second of the *mystères* retained in the body of his work. This poem, nearly contemporary with "Eloa," is a sort of biblical episode in a gigantic setting, shot through with primitivist recollections, and which, like "Moïse," is a precursor of similar compositions by Hugo; the supernatural world appears there as background, and heterodoxy manifests itself in an embittered feeling of celestial injustice: two lovers, engulfed in the deluge because they wanted to remain together, are the innocent victims of the divine order, like Jephthah's daughter, like Moses, like Eloa.

Vigny, in the genre of the mystery as in others, accomplished less than he planned: his correspondence evokes, in addition to "Eloa" and "Le Déluge," a mystery of Satan, linked beyond any doubt to the story of the fallen Angel, but by a link about which it is impossible to be precise, especially chronologically; in any event, he was working on it after the publication of "Eloa."[16] Already in 1823 his journal, enumerating titles of mysteries finished or planned, noted between "Eloa" and "Le Déluge" a "Satan racheté," which must be the same poem,[17] and adds to it "Anté-Christ," "Homme-Dieu," and others: nothing of these last works has survived, if they were ever anything more than titles. Projects of this kind never stopped haunting Vigny: in the very year of the *mystères*, he was dreaming of a "poem to make," reproducing "three lost works" (holy books resuscitated, I think, by the poet): "the book of the Lord's wars," including "the history of humanity"; "the book of the just," evoking "the illustrious men of the Orient and all civilizations up to Christ"; finally, "the book of prophecies," announcing "the future of the earth."[18] This vast project was not pursued. It is the destiny of the romantic epic to surpass the limits of the possible and, new Bible *in potentia* as well as poem, to exist more as a giant, multiform project than as completed work. But the ambition to create such a work, necessarily unfulfilled, animates French romanticism from its birth; the ambition ceases only when the movement ceases, after having marked the careers of its greatest poets. In one sense, all of romanticism's successes in France, the lyrical successes in particular, which are particularly celebrated, can appear to the historian as literary accomplishments on the margins of a great unfinished spiritual enterprise. We can agree that French romanticism is lyrical in nature, if we understand by lyricism an effusion transmuted into a profession of faith — in other words, a thought that a subject lives. Lyricism thus understood was only the raw material of the poetic ministry; the work in which this ministry would be fully exercised would be that in which poets took upon themselves, along with their own experience, that of all of humanity. Epic, theogonic poetry holds the first rank because it is not only the voice of the poet expressing his being, but the Word of humanity affirming itself as the center of the universe.

The lyrical alteration of the epic, so often remarked upon, is no more remarkable, in the experiments by trial and error of romantic invention in the matter of genres, than is the opposite proceeding: that which, in Vigny, propels the lyrical genre toward a narrative form. At the beginning of his career, Vigny was almost indifferent to the tradition of lyrical poetry to which the first works of Lamartine and Hugo belong. "Le Bal," which dates from 1818, is a sort of elegy, a melancholy exhortation to young girls dancing;[19] "Le Malheur," which he dates from 1820 and which he dropped from several editions of his poems, is an ode in the old style. But Vigny did not persist in these directions; more than once he composed more or less circumstantial poems of love or sentimental outpouring; he included none of these pieces in his collections.[20]

On the other hand, it seems that around 1826 he conceived of an original lyric formula: he planned to write *élévations*. The poems or sketches for poems that he left under this name are not very homogeneous and it is with difficulty that we extract from these a definition of the genre. At first glance, an "elevation" ought to be a meditative poem in the form of a prayer or a hymn; and indeed the oldest of Vigny's poems that is known under this label is the soul's speech to God as it quits life.[21] The *Journal*, in 1830, offers three projects for poems of the same type, all three entitled *Elévation*, in which the soul also addresses God, in different tones: anger, doubt, prayer.[22] It would certainly seem that this was the original formula of the elevation as Vigny conceived of it, in conformity with the sense of the word itself.[23] But as early as 1827, a projected "elevation" noted in the journal is of an altogether different sort: a comparison of the millet seeds that Tom Thumb throws behind him with the days God assigns us and that we "sow carelessly on our way without any fear at seeing their number diminish."[24] We recognize clearly here the liberty with which Vigny changes the sense of traditional tales;[25] but what is important is that he gives the name *élévations* to the symbolic use of some well-known, preexisting scene or episode. In 1838, he again plans an "elevation" of a related kind: the comparison of life to a mountain whose ascent workers undertake only to find at the summit the rich, groaning from boredom.[26] The same year, he attempted a definition of the elevation that, at the price of the word's interpretation, consecrates the genre's slippage and substitutes the symbol that bears a spiritual lesson for pure lyricism: "I named these poems *Elevations* because each is supposed to take an altogether earthly image as a point of departure and rise to views of a more divine nature, depositing (insofar as I can achieve this) the soul who follows me in higher regions; to pick it up on earth and deposit it at the feet of God."[27] Vigny is here speaking only of the elevations he had published, to a correspondent who was translating them: of these two poems, "Les Amants de Montmorency" and "Paris," respectively dated 1830 and 1831, the former is a poetico-philosophical commentary on a recent news item (the suicide of two young lovers), the latter a meditation on Paris, organized according to the symbols of the Wheel and the Furnace.[28] At this period, Vigny was thinking of composing a collection of elevations in which these two poems were supposed to take their place.[29]

As we see, the elevation, apparently born of a desire to escape from the narrative form of the *poème* in favor of a more subjective sort of meditation, tends toward a new form of objective poetry: that which evokes situations or objects of ordinary life rather than characters in human or divine history. What Vigny ended up adding to the epic or sacred material in his work was contemporary life, treated in like manner as significant material. In fact the *Journal* sketches poems of this type quite early on, as early as 1824, without Vigny calling them elevations; all his life he continued to plan additional ones,[30] and they make up a fair portion of his later work. His lyrical project found itself absorbed into this current of symbolic fabulation, which was much more powerful in him; the elevation, both the thing and the word, was fused into this; it was unable to prosper as such, perhaps because Vigny's fervor lacked the necessary dose of optimism.[31] What one could call the modern fable is the equivalent of the sacred Parable, adapted to the nineteenth century; it has its spirit, and often its form; it complements the new sacred History with a contemporary Gospel. These two modes of poetic language were not, in Vigny's view, in the final analysis so incompatible that the latter needed a separate collection and a special name. In Vigny's later career, the book of *Les Destinées* will gather together "La Mort du loup" and "La Colère de Samson," "La Bouteille à la mer" or "La Flûte" alongside "Le Mont des oliviers," just as the *Poèmes antiques et modernes* of 1837 had placed "Moïse" and "Le Déluge" alongside "Les Amants de Mont-morency." The choices made by Vigny's imagination with regard to poetic genres take advantage of a single formula sufficiently varied in its originality to be of use to the apostolate of the modern poet.

This apostolate tried other approaches to the public than poetry proper. The time of *poèmes* and elevations is also that of novels. Novelistic projects take the place of projects for mysteries in Vigny's *Journal* beginning in 1824. "Historical" or "epic" novels, according to his own terms: a novel on the Knights Templar; another whose setting would have been Judea and Rome at the time of the Passion of Jesus; another would have been situated in the period when priests married; another on Louis XIV; finally, a prose poem or a novel — Vigny designates it in both ways — recounting the life of a contemporary of Jesus in this world and the other, as well as his encounter with him in hell.[32] The subjects of these sometimes semimystical projects derive from the spiritual preoccupations of Vigny at this time; the novel, the modern narrative form par excellence, will grow in large part from the same soil as the poem; it will be conceived with the same symbolic structure. The lines in the *Journal* that come just after the sketches cited above, defining the character of "every imaginative work," state this clearly: "Imagination bodies forth ideas and creates living types and symbols that are like the palpable form and proof of an abstract truth."[33] The only novel that Vigny published in this period was *Cinq-Mars*, an episode of the nation's history lacking in metaphysical resonances, following the formula made popular by Walter Scott, and equally dear to royalist and liberal romanticism. But, within this limited horizon, *Cinq-Mars* fits Vigny's conception of creation: a profession of faith in the form of a narrative.

Thus as soon as it is a question of history, he feels obligated to explain how the novelist differs from the historian. *Cinq-Mars*, considered from the point of view of strict historical truth, is indefensible, and contemporaries did not refrain from saying so. Vigny himself is perfectly conscious of having recourse to history without following it exactly. It is not that he intends to manipulate it in favor of the counterrevolution or to argue for the Restoration by appealing to French history; on the contrary, the fact that he turns to this history betrays his plan for a work in which royalty will be judged. What matters to him is what he considers to be the very function of the writer: the interpretation of the events of the real world according to a higher inspiration. His whole theory of the historical novel has as its object to justify this prerogative in the face of the liberals' veristic conception in the domain of historical portraits: "In art, truth is nothing, probability is all; bad historical novels have been made in which chronicles and the dialogues of unknown people have been copied down. Everything was true, but readers didn't believe it."[34] The rights of the novel with regard to history are, for Vigny, the same as those of poetry, which liberal prosaicness fails to appreciate adequately: "Vitet once wrote a preface to prove that historical reality was preferable to Poetry"; Vigny refuses on principle that the two be opposed: "the Poetry of character, raised to the unity and stature of figures of the past, can be wrapped in the most precise reality. . . . This is the summit of art."[35] In fact, the harmony of poetry and history is assured only because he believes in the primacy of the idea over the event: "History laying its proofs at the feet of the idea. The idea rules."[36] To the extent that he doubted the possibility of a harmony thus formulated, he concluded from this that it was necessary to renounce the so-called historical novel: "If I did not write a second *historical* novel, this is because I recognized that it is vulnerable on one point: *the real truth of facts*. This is why I wrote two . . . *philosophical novels*."[37] Philosophical novels — that is to say, meaningful fictions. Yet *Stello*, and even *Servitude et grandeur militaires*, the two novels to which he is alluding here, are full of freely handled historical characters. Vigny promulgated the theory of this treatment in his "Réflexions sur la vérité dans l'art," which is, he tells us, from 1827, and in which the reduction of historical reality to the idea appears as the natural approach of the historian-poet. If the poet, in our period, cannot avoid history, this is because the "study of the common destiny of societies is not less needed in literature today than the analysis of the human heart"; history has forced itself on art because of the crisis that French society has just lived through: "In recent years (and it is perhaps due to our political movements), Art has been marked by history more deeply than ever. We all have our eyes glued to our Chronicles, as if, having attained to manhood while striding toward greater matters, we were pausing for a moment to take stock of our youth and its errors. So it has been necessary to reinforce INTEREST by adding MEMORY to it." Thus is aban-

doned the classic postulate of a literature with fixed values linked to a civilization that is the best one possible; the human race exists only with reference to a
past and a destination. And the understanding of that destination, which traditional theology no longer illuminates, is the function of the novelist-poet, distinct from the historian in that he has the power of intuiting the ideal sense that
exists beyond facts and their material causality. Whence his right "sometimes to
make the reality of facts yield to the IDEA that each of them should represent in
the eyes of posterity." In the final analysis, with Fable being the poet's proper
domain, this amounts to claiming for the poet the right to develop History in
the form of a Fable. But in doing so he is responding to the need of men, whose
collective work Fable always was: which is a proof that it is necessary for them,
and that it is true in its fashion, possessing a special truth that is "completely
beautiful, completely intellectual," which is, precisely, "the soul of all the arts."
Thus the intuition of the artist revealing and proclaiming the truth meets the
needs of the human race, for "ALL HUMANITY needs its destinies to be a series of
lessons for it; more indifferent than is commonly thought as to the REALITY OF
FACTS, humanity seeks to perfect the event so as to give it a great moral significance, sensing that the succession of scenes it plays here on earth is no mere
dramatic spectacle, but that, since it is advancing, it is moving toward a goal
whose explanation must be sought beyond what can be seen."[38] In itself, the
aesthetics of the ideal truer than the true was not new; beginning in the eighteenth century, debates on art had made it familiar; it was an article of faith at *La
Muse française*.[39] Vigny's originality lies in his making this aesthetic into a philosophy of history in the hands of the thinker-poet.

Vigny, in these same "Réflexions," assigns to Drama the mission of representing
"the particular fate of the INDIVIDUAL";[40] no doubt he means that the theater
does not go beyond the plane of individual destinies in its depictions. Around
1828 and 1829 he was drawn into the movement that carried the poets of the
cénacle toward drama and led them to adopt the liberals' critical views on classical tragedy. The "Lettre à Lord *** sur la soirée du 24 octobre 1829" that Vigny
placed at the beginning of his translation of *Othello*,[41] a veritable declaration of
war on tragedy, adopts against it the modernist sociological critique of the
liberals, Stendhal's in particular. These pages are among those where one can see
most clearly the depth of the break with classicism. But on this point, Hugo had
preceded and eclipsed him; Vigny's share in the explosion of poetic romanticism against the rules and literary traditions remained modest. His poetry was
hardly changed by it;[42] and in his search for literary forms that might harbor his
essential inspiration, he scarcely paused at drama. He wrote in 1830 and had

performed in 1831 a historical drama, *La Maréchale d'Ancre*: it is curious that this prose work looks more like an "historical scene" in the liberal style than a romantic drama; one finds therein an apology for the Third Estate, incarnated in a character named Picard; Vigny wanted to claim that the "mother-idea" of this drama was the abolition of the death penalty in political matters,[43] whereas this idea, of current concern due to the trial of the ministers of Charles X, only appears in a few passing lines. In reality, he believed that the theater imprisoned an idea in a framework too narrow in space and time — that it turned the poet's thought over to the interpretation of actors;[44] he thought the "big novel" more propitious to the epic genius as he conceived it: "Epic genius has room to open its wings in the big novel; in drama, it has to reduce itself to too small a size."[45] Only much later, with *Chatterton*, would he find a formula for a drama with spiritual meaning; even there, the play was drawn from a preexisting narrative. In the period we are discussing, he hardly thinks of such a formula. On the other hand, he expresses no reservations about the genre of the novel, which he considered throughout his entire career to be an appropriate vehicle for the Idea.

Up to this point we have limited ourselves to discussing Vigny's innovations in the recasting of literary genres: it is clear that all his labors tend to make it possible to proclaim the truth by way of narrative. At the beginning of his career, Vigny paves the way for the ministry of the poet by modifying the high secular mode of narration to this end. There is no doubt that from this time on he had a clear enough idea of what he was about. In 1824, his *Journal* sketches the following parable: "Poetic comparison: Iceland. In the course of six-month nights, the long polar nights, a traveler climbs a mountain and, from there, sees far off the sun and daybreak, while night is at his feet: thus the poet sees a sun, a sublime world, and utters cries of ecstasy about a world that has been saved, while men are plunged in night."[46] This glorious consciousness of the poet's mission implies an identification of the poet with the thinker. In this way, in Vigny more than in any other writer, romanticism takes upon itself the claims of the Philosophy it supplants: he integrates the Philosopher and the Poet, reason and myth: "If there is something that has prevented society from perishing in its continual shipwrecks, it is the sovereignty of the most intelligent of each epoch. These kings, chosen *by themselves*, have repaired its bonds as well as possible with artful fictions."[47] It is in this poetic light that one should read the texts where Vigny affirms the right of superior minds to govern humanity. Thus: "To submit the world to the unlimited domination of superior minds in whom resides the greatest part of divine intelligence must be my goal — and that of every contemporary man of strength."[48] Such a domination is in conformity with the deep order of things, which makes of History the development of the Idea, and of the great man the place where the two meet: "Humanity constitutes an endless discourse, of which each illustrious man is one idea."[49] This conception of history is perfect for founding the higher truth of the symbolic epic as Vigny conceives of it in the form of the poem or the novel. The soberness of the *Journal* and the impersonality of the narrative mode can mask Vigny's secret sacerdotal fervor, which would become so obvious after *Chatterton*, if we are to believe Sainte-Beuve's ironies.[50] This fervor, a cult of poetry and the conviction that it has the power to teach and to reveal the truth, is at the very source and origin of his work.

What remains is to define the content of the preaching that Vigny's poetry contains. It is remarkable that as soon as these poems display a philosophical meaning, they contain a disavowal of Providence, a complaint concerning humanity's relation to God. The spiritualism of Vigny is from the first affected by a doubt about the harmony of human values and the divine order. If we can speak of spiritualism with regard to Vigny, it is due to the value he attributes to suffering and sacrifice, and also because God remains an indispensable character in his universe; but the relation of man to God is not that taught by the spiritualist tradition, unless one limits oneself to the accusatory part of the book of Job. God is indifferent to the human misery of which he is the author, and the prayer that ascends to him is a reproach. Already in his first biblical poem, and by the choice of the subject itself, Vigny takes this direction: Jephthah, trapped by his vow and obliged to sacrifice his daughter, testifies bitterly to this:

> Seigneur, vous êtes bien le Dieu de la vengeance;
> En échange du crime il vous faut l'innocence.

> [Lord, you are indeed the God of vengeance;
> In return for crime you demand innocence.]

Neither the Bible, nor Byron had given such a twist to this subject.[51] It is a common practice for Vigny to make use of Scripture while transforming it, imposing the new meaning at the expense of the old. He succeeded in this up to a certain point: who among us is not tempted to imagine Moses as he recreated him? There is, in the nineteenth century, scattered through the work of poets, the draft of a Scripture revised along the lines of the romantic credo, one that has sometimes caused the original to be forgotten; Hugo's Cain, his Booz, are today vastly better known in France than those of the Bible.

The meaning of "Moïse" has been much discussed; it was very quickly taken as a figure for the solitude of genius: thus Magnin understood it in 1829, and also Sainte-Beuve in 1834, David d'Angers in 1836, Balzac in 1839;[52] this is also how the lines are generally read where Vigny, in 1838, explains Moses to his translator: "This great name only serves as a mask for a man who exists in every century, and who is more modern than ancient; the man of genius, weary of his eternal widowerhood and in despair at seeing his solitude grow ever more immense and arid as his grandeur grows."[53] It was later noticed that such a symbol does not appear so clearly in the poem; and Sainte-Beuve specified that the idea "of the literary and poetic pontificate . . . only appeared in a roundabout way" in "Moïse." Ordinarily the solitude of genius is understood as an effect of the crowd's ignorance and ingratitude. However, neither in "Moïse," unless we arbitrarily impose this model on the text,[54] nor, if we look closely, in the lines cited above where Vigny explains the poem, do we find any such thing. Jews are not presented as guilty toward Moses, though it would have been an easy matter for Vigny to develop this motif from the biblical text itself; rather, they are struck with respectful terror when faced with the divine investiture that renders Moses a stranger to humanity:

> Et quand j'ouvre les bras, on tombe à mes genoux.

> [And when I open my arms, they fall at my feet.]

The solitude of Moses does not come to him from the ill will of men, then, but from the election of God. Thus it is to him, and of him, that he complains. This is why it has been possible to find possible sources of Vigny's poem in the complaints of Job, whose situation is however utterly different, much more than in the books of Moses,[55] and to see in the divorce that separates the prophet from his God the real subject of the poem. The theme of the solitude of genius in Vigny is a variant of a more general theme, that of divine abandonment, which defines the entire human condition. Moses denounces the deceptive favor by which God claims to exempt his elected one from the general wretchedness, and that deprives him, in fact, of the supreme consolation of man: the fraternity of his creatures. Thus the ministry of thought in Vigny is developed against a background of enmity between priest and god. Shall we say that to suppose the god inhumane is a way of denying him? But Vigny never uttered this negation, and this was not only because of propriety, but because his universe is not a godless one; his implicit doctrine might be said to be a spiritualism of separation, however strange this expression may seem. A gap has opened up between the God who obsesses him and the moral values that are supposed to belong to this God; power and goodness are not in the same place; but what Vigny does not find in God, he reverences in man, and at this level devotes to Thought a worship that atheism would seem to exclude.

The condition of humanity ignored and oppressed by God is the subject of the poem "La Prison," more or less contemporary with "Moïse":[56] the Man in the Iron Mask, at the moment of death, refuses the sacraments of the God who permitted his martyrdom. When one is aware of the use that Vigny later made of the symbol of the prison to represent human life, this poem takes on its full meaning, over and above the historical incident he is evoking. It is remarkable that the Man in the Iron Mask neglects his human persecutor and wants to acknowledge divine responsibility only: the explanation is that Vigny is less aggrieved by the injury itself than by the omnipotent indifference that allows it to triumph. Louis XIV as his prisoner's executioner does not interest him. But Ferdinand VII of Spain, turning his back on his faithful subjects to make a deal with liberal rebels, is a good poetic subject: the royalist abandoned by the king is the theme of "Le Trappiste,"[57] as the creature abandoned by the creator was that of "La Prison."[58] There is a reciprocal correspondence between the royal type and the divine type. An inhuman Power is the dark, vacuous background against which the ministry of Thought stands out. In this the majority of his contemporaries, who are attracted to a spiritualism of harmony and salvation, seem to be pulling ahead of Vigny. But in reality he is ahead of them: he had a sort of premonition of the bitterness that would be born in the next generation from the general collapse of hopes.

Not that he was not tempted. He was of his time, and he glimpsed, like so many others, the end of Evil and the great reconciliation. It is true that the "mysteries" he published do not much give this impression; "Eloa" and "Le Déluge" show souls that are too pure, too loving, victims of a higher law: Eloa, who intends to glorify love in heaven and who thinks she is obeying this divine exhortation when she tries to save Satan, sees herself helplessly abandoned to the Seducer; Emmanuel and Sara perish in the waters of the flood because each refused to be saved alone if it meant renouncing the other. It is certainly not by chance that the only two "mystical" narratives that he finished and included in his collections confirm the dominant thought of the "poems" as a whole. But his drafts and sketches of "mysteries" betray a thought that is more complex. We have seen that he was planning a "Satan," of which numerous fragments and sketches have survived, and from which "Eloa" as it was printed seems to have been taken. As a project it preceded "Eloa"; and if on occasion it became identical with the latter poem in Vigny's mind, the project nevertheless outlived "Eloa."[59] The fragments of it that remain[60] contain "Les Reproches de Satan," in which the Devil no longer appears as the tempter of innocence arguing for obscure and marvelous delights but as an accuser of the tyrant-God; he refuses to submit to the Almighty's arbitrariness and preaches a sort of heroic pride of the creature. Other fragments show the Rebel, redeemed at the end of time,

and, with Evil abolished, recovering his place in heaven: this is the future romantic outline of more than one End of Satan; thanks to the character of Eloa,
who reappears in these fragments, not even the theological promotion of the
Feminine as agent of redemption, which was the obsession of the heresiarchs of
these times, is lacking. Much has been written about Vigny's thought in this
group of texts. At bottom, the three types of Satan — seducer, rebel, redeemer —
are not irreducible one to the other; they reproduce, with a positive value, the
traits that orthodoxy combines to create the single figure of the demon: perver-
sity, pride, and guilty conscience. The sympathetic interpretation of these traits
obviously signifies an identification of the satanic and the human; that is, a refusal, if not of God, at least of the traditional representation of the divine order.
The redemption of Satan puts an end to this representation; but it is a great
scandal to proclaim the Evil One to be innocent, and one may quail at taking so
bold a step. This is what Vigny seems to have done in only publishing, out of his
entire project, this "Eloa," a poem of demonic seduction, whose argument con-
forms to dogma. He knew very well that by concluding the poem with Eloa's
perdition, and in showing by this end all the preceding seductions of the demon
in their true light, he rejoined orthodoxy: "I have just written accursed verses,"
he writes to Emile Deschamps; ". . . they make me fear excommunication. . . .
You will guess that I am speaking of 'Satan,' which is almost finished. I am going
to blacken the ending in order to save myself."[61] To blacken the ending — that is,
to ruin Eloa — is to avoid the heresy of rehabilitating Satan; but by the same
stroke, Vigny also avoided the characteristic optimism of this heresy, which
went quite against the grain of his nature. The pieces describing the End of
Satan are made to rehabilitate, along with Satan, God himself, He who damns,
along with his Damned: the dark side of Christianity disappears entirely in such
a euphoric light. Vigny preferred, then, the impenitent Hell of orthodoxy; not
because of fidelity to this orthodoxy, but in order to conceal another heresy,
more secret and more grave: that of a God who is absent and a humanity for
whom there is no help. An apparently Catholic portrait of sin and damnation
masks a bitter set of questions about God's presence, goodness, and justice.

It is here, in this mistrust of the sovereign Power, and in the inability of man to
conceive of it in his own image, that we find, present from the beginning, the
vital center of Vigny's thought.[62] For social power wears for Vigny the same
features as divine power; Thought does not recognize itself in it, either. *Cinq-
Mars* repeats in a different mode what is said in "Le Trappiste." It is true that the
novel betrays other concerns in addition to that of expressing a political morality: melodramatic plotting with horrible or violent episodes on the one hand,

and on the other historical scenes aiming to reproduce lived experience, attest to the search for a modern novelistic form. But the Idea is not forgotten. Cinq-Mars's defeat is a significant episode in the long conflict between royalty and nobility; victorious royalty does not realize that it has undermined its own base; the Revolution is prophesied in the novel as the consequence and expiation of absolutism, but according to an aristocratic view of things. Richelieu himself wonders whether he is not destroying the foundations of the monarchy; the duc de Bouillon warns Anne of Austria and the young dauphin of this danger; the rioters conclude from the ruin of the great lords and the Parliament that there is no longer in France any other power than their own; Milton predicts to Corneille, after the execution of Cinq-Mars, the coming of a republic or the dictatorship of a parvenu, and the novel ends with the name of Cromwell.[63] Vigny is only putting the traditional arguments of the aristocracy's political apologists in the form of a novel: "No nobility, no monarchy," said Montesquieu. Vigny accepted this old feudalist maxim, as well as the theory (spruced up in his time by Montlosier, and in a contrary sense by Augustin Thierry) according to which the conflict of the nobility and the Third Estate was based on a racial opposition between the conquering Franks and the autochthonous Gauls.[64] We see that the distance between "Le Trappiste" and *Cinq-Mars* is not as great as it seems: Ferdinand VII abandons the Catalan Vendée just as the kings of France abandoned and ruined their nobility over the centuries.

The fact that the destiny of the nobility was at the center of Vigny's historico-philosophical meditations, and more particularly of the historical novel as he envisioned it, is sufficiently attested by the novelistic outlines that mark the pages of the *Journal*: in 1836 he was again planning a "historical series" of novels on this subject.[65] Shortly after *Cinq-Mars*, the unfinished novel *L'Almeh*, which was set in Egypt during Bonaparte's campaign, was supposed to depict, in this memorable period of French military history, the dramatic situation of the émigré nobility's consciousness.[66] If this is not its secret, it is in any case one of the most keenly felt forms of Vigny's bitterness: the aggression of the kings against the nobility has produced a disaster for which there is no help; the royal victory has caused the divorce between Power and Right to break out openly: "When you want to remain pure, you should not get involved in exercising power over men," says Father Joseph,[67] defining thus the political world in its essence. But absolutism could not really be a step backward. Vigny accuses the kings, but at bottom thinks that their conduct was in conformity with the real nature of things. Vigny turns toward the future: but what future will break the baneful law of Power? Vigny was certainly not converted to the bourgeoisie in 1826, nor will he be converted to bourgeois royalty in 1830: neither one nor the other possesses the sacred character that distinguishes the honor of old; this character trait, lost along with the old world, has taken refuge on the margins of active society, in those who take on the ministry of Thought, in the new aristocracy of thinkers. Vigny's "liberal" evolution — that is, his conversion to a modern view of things — consists above all in such an affirmation: an ambiguous affirmation, reactionary in that it implies a fundamental scorn for the society of commoners, and innovative in the authority it attributes to thought in the government of human matters.

The prestige and credit that *Cinq-Mars* denies to absolute power is certainly not transferred in the novel to the traditional church, which is rather mistreated, notably in the episode of the martyrdom of the curé Grandier in Loudun. Lofty consciousness is embodied in de Thou, magistrate and thinker, in whom the old law of honor takes on a philosophical dimension. Cinq-Mars himself, more subject to human passions, is an aristocrat in revolt, and has caught the contagion of thought; in a draft of the novel, Richelieu said of him: "That pensive brow worries me."[68] And even if the lawyer Fournier, Grandier's defender, represents to some degree the honest and courageous Third Estate, he acts more by virtue of his thoroughly spiritual role as defender of the oppressed than by virtue of his class. Thus on all sides the novel of aristocratic breakdown suggests the social investiture of thought: it is not by chance that chapter 20, which in the home of Ninon de Lenclos brings together de Thou, Descartes, Milton, Corneille, and Molière, bears as epigraph a text by Lamennais that speaks of "the royalty of genius, last resource of exhausted peoples."[69]

It is clear that in Vigny's conception the mission of the poet could not be an active mission, directly interceding in the struggles of his time. But his entire work, both in the forms he chose and the faith he professed, attests his interest and faith in this mission. The world he describes does not seem ready to conform to the lessons of Thought, but this does not cause him to despair; the world's curse is not the last word. In this, Vigny, despite his pessimism, belongs to the generation of Lamartine and Hugo. He merely situated the Thinker-Poet's mission at a greater remove from real society than they did. Every ministry combines active fervor and solitude, and he oriented his more in the latter direction, but without breaking the connection with men. The refusal of metaphysical hope and his obsessive consciousness of belonging to a socially condemned class rendered all the more necessary in his eyes a ministry of thought among men that would restore an order whose absence caused everything to lose direction and meaning. It is a question of heroically reestablishing a notion of a value that would be misunderstood, but that would also, inevitably, reign, it being the only one possible. He repeated for himself, in his *Journal*, the sentence he had attributed to Father Joseph in *Cinq-Mars*: "When you want to remain pure, you should not get involved in exercising power over men"; here he adds: "The application of ideas to things is only a waste of time for the creators of thoughts"[70] (by this we should understand the immediate application, for a more long-term relation unites the thinker to the public); "the common man can no more do without people he doesn't know than one of those persons, even if he is a genius, can do without the common man."[71] Thus Vigny can just as easily affirm the close connection of the genius with the public as their divorce: "The public consciousness judges everything. There is a power in a people assembled. An ignorant public is worth as much as a genius. Why? Because the genius divines the secret of public consciousness. Consciousness, *knowing with*, seems collective"; and, around the same time: "The man of thought should esteem his work only to the extent that it does not enjoy popular success and insofar as he is conscious of its being ahead of the movement of the crowd."[72] This is not a contradiction: this polarity is the very law of the poetic ministry as he conceives it, both reserved and fruitful. How could an individual in advance of others not be isolated, even if he knows that he is being followed at a distance?

The reconciliation takes place in history and according to a manner of advancing according to which the crowd, learning to disregard the advice of today, becomes open to that of yesterday: "Your pages," he writes to a poet, "will one day be the guides of a public better prepared to receive the word from on high and more docile to the divine yoke of the only Aristocracy that ought to reign forever over the world as it has always done in spite of the world's resistance; that is, the Aristocracy of higher minds who will be the pontiffs and kings of the earth as it unites the world's societies into a single family."[73] The parables that he conceives on the eve of the 1830 revolution say the same thing: "Never, no, never have I observed the second hand, that arrow at once so quick, so nervous, so bold and so agitated, which rushes ahead and shudders as if from a sense of its own audacity or as if from the pleasure of its conquest of time; never have I observed it without thinking that the poet has always had and must have this same quick way of walking in anticipation of the centuries to come, ahead of the general thought of his nation, farther on than even its most enlightened segment."[74] Or else, joining the suffering that is inevitable to the destiny of the prophetic Spirit: "Thought is like the compass needle, which pierces the point on which it turns, although the extremity of its legs describes a distant circle. — Man succumbs to his work and is pierced by the compass; but the line that the other leg has traced remains engraved forever for the good of future races"; immediately after this, linking the torment of the Precursor and Humanity's lag, which are one and the same thing, to a heroic humanism against the background of divine abandonment: "You have left us in uncertainty, Lord. Your son begged you in vain on the Mount of Olives. Forgive us then for having seized the compass."[75]

Thus the idea of the poetic ministry, which would oscillate during the crises of the nineteenth century between spirited self-assurance and withdrawal, found in Vigny, in the first years of his career, a definition that was, so to speak, permanent and had a prepared response for every vicissitude. It turned out that the embittered nobleman, transformed in order to survive into the intellectual herald of progress, protected better than anyone else the sacerdotal type of the Poet from being swept away under the influence of adverse events. His austere, somewhat gloomy formula made less of an impression than others; yet it is the one that stood up best through the necessarily varying circumstances of a society still in its birth pangs. There is in Vigny both an activist poet and a poet in exile, a Hugo and a Baudelaire, but the rigor of his thinking about the condition of the poet excluded his being as dazzling as either one or the other.

❧ *Victor Hugo*

Hugo is the poet who was long believed to have invented the idea of the modern poetic ministry. It was thought, moreover, that this idea took shape above all in the visionary Hugo of his exile, in the poem *Les Mages* and in *William Shakespeare*, whereas it is in fact present throughout his entire career from its beginnings. Only a lack of attention to what was with a certain disdain long held to be the ideology of romanticism, but that was in fact its substance, kept his missionary professions of faith from being perceived as part of their rich environment. "It was a strange undertaking," people used to write, "to wish to establish the supremacy of poetic genius."[76] As if Hugo had been the only one to undertake this, and as if one could so quickly accuse of strangeness the persistent project of several generations. Besides, people define themselves as much by their illusions as by their real condition. This truth, which applies to all of us, applies also to a society or a period. It is not that the importance in Hugo of his faith in "the supremacy of poetic genius" has not been felt; this faith has even seemed to some to be the very affirmation of his personal essence: "The role of the poet, the mission of genius, which he defines and whose acceptance he wants to effect, is his role, his mission."[77] But the *I* of Victor Hugo was not always taken seriously; it was thought that taking what was an act of deep faith to be a gloriously imposing rhetorical device was being fair to him. A strange idea admirably deployed in a language that was, at bottom, a little hollow: such was for a long-time criticism's dominant judgment concerning the ministry of the poet according to Hugo. In the last generation, an attention newly alert to the religious or prophetic aspects of romanticism has, by putting the visionary Hugo back at the heart of a vast historical landscape in which his sacerdotal impulses recover their milieu and their affiliations, made possible a review of this judgment.

> He was a very young man with a frank, innocent smile, bearing a blossoming genius stamped on his expansive brow; something forceful, powerful, and inspired could be felt even in his most casual remarks; his upraised eyes shone like those of an archangel. . . . Like every man of strength, he felt a call to fulfill a mission . . . ; love, poetry, inspiration, even reason were in him like the great wings of an iron will that nothing could turn aside from its goal. He had marked out this goal for himself from the very beginning; he had stretched out his hand, and he had said to himself: I will go there; what Christopher Columbus accomplished in the physical world, Luther in the sphere of religious ideas, Mirabeau in the world of politics, I shall accomplish in the literature of my century, and once he had said something to himself, he regarded it as done.

It is thus that an intimate friend of the 1820s depicted Hugo fifteen years later;[78] and the sentiment of a purely literary mission hardly suffices to explain a character so described, unless we first suppose, as we must, a promotion of literature itself. In any case, we perceive in Hugo, still almost an adolescent, something that betrays the feeling of a personal election. This feeling certainly does not go as far in him as it does in many of his contemporaries who founded sects. He did not see himself as the Messiah, but as the consecrated Poet of modern times. However, the history of his works up to 1830 can hardly be written except in relation to the vicissitudes of a fundamental missionary impulse. Little by little critics have become convinced of this.[79] Today it is hard to speak better concerning the deep motivations of his youth than the most recent spiritual biographer of the young Hugo:

> If the soul of the immense edifice that is Hugo's oeuvre was, finally, his messianic role, he could flatter himself with having had a premonition of this in his earliest writings. . . . There was a contradiction in thus wanting to institute in Christian terms a prophetic and sacerdotal spiritual power through a direct election of genius by God alongside the institutional spiritual power. This matters little. Victor-Marie Hugo will only later become aware of the contradiction. For the moment, he is contented to live this contradiction, and to lend the Christian language of his current poetic theory to this notion of the poet as mediator between God and men. He does this with a glow of

sincerity and faith that obliges us to situate at this point the nerve center and, even more, the motor center of his opinions, his activity, and his life.[80]

The mission of the poet appears in Hugo's juvenile poetry at the moment when, around 1820, his royalism became Catholic, according to the formula prevalent at the time. It would not be quite right to say that his faith in the role of poetry clothed itself in Christian royalism due to circumstances and in order to equip itself for action. For sufficiently deep reasons, Christian royalism implied an exaltation of poetry, as we have seen — and not only in the Restoration, but from the earliest origins of the counterrevolution.[81] So the young Hugo was able to shape his prophetic vocation under the influence of these doctrines just as much as use them as the instrument of a prior intuition. Nor is it certain that Hugo, at the time of his Christian royalism, must have felt the frustration and uneasiness that comes from a faith secretly recognized as having no future. It is true that the counterrevolution was troubled, but emotions unknown elsewhere were cultivated there with conviction; and when the hope of conserving the past in the future was recognized to be illusory, it was abandoned only at the cost of a veritable crisis.

However this may be, Hugo inaugurated his mission as an ultra poet, showing more resolution in doing so than any of his comrades. The 1822 preface to his *Odes* boldly declares that "the history of men has a poetic aspect only when seen from the lofty point of view of monarchical ideas and religious beliefs." In the same year, he defines liberalism as "a faction that is antipoetic because it is antireligious and antisocial."[82] Between 1819 and 1826 he specializes in the ode, traditionally devoted to great public celebrations, and there he deploys the annals of the counterrevolution, so moving in their depiction of ordeals and triumphs: "La Vendée," "Les Vierges de Verdun," "Louis XVII," "Quiberon," "La Mort du duc de Berry," "Buonaparte," "La Naissance du duc de Bordeaux," "Le Baptême du duc de Bordeaux," "La Guerre d'Espagne" — such are the subjects of his poems. Sacred annals, in which the historical and the supernatural tend to get mixed up, in which the little Louis XVII is welcomed by God like a new Christ:

> Viens, ton Seigneur lui-même eut ses douleurs divines,
> Et mon fils, comme toi, roi couronné d'épines,
> Porta le sceptre de roseau,

> [Come, your Lord himself had his pains divine,
> And my son, like you a king crowned with thorns,
> Carried a reed for a scepter,]

in which the duchesse de Berry, pregnant with an heir who will be the savior of the dynasty, replicates the Salvific Virgin:

Ainsi, quand le Serpent, auteur de tous les crimes,
　　Vouait d'avance aux noirs abîmes
　　L'homme que son forfait perdit,
Le seigneur abaissa sa farouche arrogance;
Une femme apparut, qui, faible et sans défense,
　　Brisa du pied son front maudit,

[Thus, when the Serpent, the author of all these iniquities,
　　Was plotting to send to blackest hell
　　Man, whom his heinous crime had doomed,
The Lord humbled his wild arrogance:
A woman appeared who, weak and defenseless,
　　Crushed his accursed brow beneath her foot,]

in which the duc de Bordeaux, being born, reproduces the baby Jesus sent to men by God for their salvation:

Par un autre berceau sa main nous sauve encore.
Le monde du bonheur n'ose entrevoir l'aurore,
Quoique Dieu des méchants ait puni les défis,
Et, troublant leurs conseils, dispersant leurs phalanges
　　Nous ait donné l'un de ses anges,
Comme aux antiques jours il nous donna son fils.[83]

[By another cradle his hand saves us again.
The world does not dare glimpse the dawn of happiness,
Though God has punished the challenge of the evil ones,
And, confusing their councils, scattering their armies,
　　Has given us one of his angels,
As in the old days he gave us his son.]

These comparisons, whose insistent repetition abolishes the distance between the profane and the sacred, were familiar in royalist literature; their archetype is the theme of the King-Christ at the Golgotha of 21 January 1793. They signify, in fact, a sort of actualization and prolongation of sacred history in the pages of the modern historian: the destinies of French royalty are treated there like those of the kingdom of Judah in the Old Testament. Sacred poetry lives again as a supernatural narration of contemporary events.

Hugo's political ode is, beneath a similar exterior, something quite different from the official court ode of old, which celebrated the actions of a king and the memorable feats of his reign. It is now an inspired commentary on events, the sign of the poet's communion with history; and if this communion is as it were made inevitable due to an obsession with the recent cataclysm, its chief object is to overcome the disaster, and to reestablish the course of human destiny by a referral to the divine order:

> Le sort des nations comme une mer profonde,
> A ses écueils cachés et ses gouffres mouvants.
> Aveugle qui ne voit dans les destins du monde
> Que le combat des flots sous la lutte des vents!
>
> Un souffle immense et fort domine ces tempêtes.
> Un rayon du ciel plonge à travers cette nuit.
> Quand l'homme aux cris de mort mêle le cri des fêtes
> Une secrète voix parle dans ce vain bruit.
>
> . . . .
>
> Muse, il n'est point de temps que tes regards n'embrassent,
> Tu suis dans l'avenir leur cercle solennel;
> Car les jours, et les ans, et les siècles ne tracent
> Qu'un sillon passager dans le fleuve éternel.[84]

> [The fate of nations, like the ocean depths,
> Has its hidden reefs and shifting vortices.
> He is blind who in the destinies of the world
> Sees only the struggle of the waves beneath the contending winds!
>
> A vast and powerful suspiration dominates these tempests.
> A beam from heaven plunges through this night.
> When man mingles cries of celebration with the moans of the dying,
> There is a secret voice speaking in the midst of this noise.
>
> . . . .
>
> Muse, your glance embraces all the ages,
> You follow into the future their solemn round;
> For the days, and the years, and the centuries trace
> But a fleeting wake in the eternal stream.]

Poets become historians in order that their visions and their language may fit into the providential vision of history that belongs to the Judeo-Christian tradition; they become the revelators of the bond formed by God between the human generations and the ages they inhabit. They do this in their own era, in the nineteenth century, commemorating and proclaiming human affairs in the name of God. It is no longer a question of referring nostalgically to the Poet of the earliest times, as had so often been done: here these poets are, among us, reinvested with their mission, and full "of that naive conviction that the poets of earliest times bore in their souls when at the same time they acted as prophets and legislators."[85] And if, of all the poets of the earliest ages, it is definitely the Hebrew poet who lives again in the young romantic poet, the reason is that the poets of Scripture are the only ones to offer to a society imbued with Christian tradition something more than the abstract, legendary memory of their ministry; an example of fervent intervention in the lives of kings and peoples whose legacy is waiting to be claimed. The explanation of tragic events according to the spirit and themes of Scripture was a very natural temptation for the counter-revolution; but in addition it was perhaps necessary that poets who were the sons of the eighteenth century should feel less intimidated than their predecessors by the supernatural prestige of the ancient prophets, if sacred poetry was to become current once again and the time come when a modern voice could be raised to their pitch. The *Odes* attest to this pretension on every page. Deploring that the poet, who formerly "Parlait au ciel en prêtre, à la terre en prophète [Spoke to heaven as a priest and to earth as a prophet]" should have been stripped of his ancient ministry, Hugo imagines Moses or Isaiah coming back among us and prophesying without being listened to; he develops their supposed prophecy, he prophesies in their place, he proclaims the Last Judgment on the heels of the turmoil of revolutions, and through this voluntary confusion of sacred voices with his own he manifests the modern prophetism, of the Poet.[86]

This prophetism soon felt itself ill at ease in the consecrated poetic forms. Hugo chose the ode as others seeking the same end had chosen the heroic elegy or the *poème*; in fact, since the new poetry was as willing to be a lament or a narrative as it was to be an inspired outpouring, it erased the boundaries of the ancient genres, which had been conceived for ends that were incomparably more modest; it seeks a more expansive and more supple instrument, whatever it may be. Hugo's choice of the Ode merely marks a particularly acute consciousness of the poetic ministry, in the sense that primitive poetry, the origin of this ministry, was commonly imagined as a sort of eloquent lyricism: Hugo said he had adopted the ode "because it was in this form that the inspirations of the earliest poets formerly appeared to the earliest peoples."[87] But he also feels authorized because of this illustrious origin to criticize immediately after the above remark the French ode of his own time, and to justify a renovation of the genre. And in fact Hugo's odes, which seem to us today so classical in form, on the contrary struck readers with their novelty and their boldness when they first appeared. The critic of the *Gazette de France* found mingled there sacred eloquence, drama, and elegy; that of the *La Quotidienne* saw therein dialogue and narrative, rather than the ode according to the received definition.[88] In general, the young Hugo lives more intensely than anyone else the adventure of royalist poetry, led by an inner logic to rebel against classical forms. In the same ode to Lamartine in which he prophesies through the mouths of Moses and Isaiah, the false sages who disdain this prophecy are represented as blinded by classical poetics:

> Nos sages répondront: Que nous veulent ces hommes?
> Ils ne sont pas du monde et du temps dont nous sommes.
> Ces poètes sont-ils nés au sacré vallon?
> Où donc est leur Olympe? où donc est leur Parnasse?
>   Quel est le Dieu qui nous menace?
> A-t-il le char de Mars? A-t-il l'arc d'Apollon?[89]

> [Our sages reply: What do these men want with us?
> They are not of our world and time.
> Were these poets born in the sacred vale?
> Where then is their Olympus? Where then is their Parnassus?
>   Who is this God who threatens us?
> Does he have the chariot of Mars? Does he have Apollo's bow?]

One would be tempted to consider this literary diatribe frivolous, after inspirations of such gravity, if one were not aware that the prejudices of traditional poetics were at this time the principal obstacle to the advent of a modern prophetic poetry, and that this poetry was unthinkable without the overthrow of the Parnassus of old.

Hugo's growing interest in formal literary questions betrays a deeper concern. He wrote in the first preface of his book: "Poetry is not in the form of ideas, but in the ideas themselves. Poetry is all that is inward in everything."[90] The inwardness of everything is the spiritual meaning that is hidden there—that through which, Hugo himself tells us, there is "more than things in things"; namely, the signals of an "ideal world" that is latent beneath the real world.[91] This ideal world, which he evokes again in a review of "Eloa," is the proper realm of the poet: "It is only when the physical world has completely disappeared from his eyes that the ideal world can appear to him. . . . One is sometimes a stranger as a man to what one has written as a poet."[92] What is more, this review began with a long diatribe on questions of form, repudiating the mythological accessories of traditional poetry, "Tartarus, Pindus, Io the cow, Silenus the god." Hugo's battles against the poetic forms inherited from the past derive from the lofty role he attributes to poetry, as the means derive from the end. He notes that as classicism has fashioned it, French poetry could only be a feeble interpreter of the spirit of the sacred poets;[93] according to him, the grave archetypes of the poetic ministry are responsible for making classical models lose their luster in the eyes of the young generations: "There are now coming up," he writes, "young heads full of fresh vigor that have meditated on the Bible, Homer, and Dante, who have drunk at the primitive sources of inspiration, and in those heads is the glory of our century."[94] In brief, it is the spirit of gravity that condemns in poetry an apparatus designed for literature as a pastime.

The great crisis that society has been through and has not yet overcome invalidates the literary games of the past. And the gravity of the poet is not thought of as merely a psychological effect of events; it is due to the role that events assign to him, and is the mark of a spiritual ministry: "On all sides a calmly serious generation is arising, full of memories and hopes . . . ; it demands more of the poet than the generations of old got from him, it asks him for beliefs."[95] Here we have the poet in possession of the symbol of faith and charged with communicating it to the public mind: poetry is henceforth "what the shared thought of a great nation must be after great calamities — sad, proud, religious. When it is necessary, it does not hesitate to get involved in public disputes to judge them or to calm them."[96] It is clear that Hugo claims to define this necessary novelty as an effect, not as a legacy of the Revolution: "The literature of the present day could be in part the result of the revolution, without being an expression of it." In history's great upheavals, events speak; it is then that "all those marvelous voices proclaiming God" are heard; poets are said to receive them, as in Isaiah 62:6-7: "And it is thus that heavenly teachings continue in song. Such is the mission of genius; its elected ones are *those watchmen left by the Lord upon the walls of Jerusalem, and who shall not hold their peace day nor night.*" What do these watchmen announce? The advent of that renewal of the past as future that is the new Jerusalem of royalist romanticism: the literature of the present day is "the anticipatory expression of the religious, monarchical society that will doubtless rise from the midst of so much ancient rubble, from so much recent destruction." In order to take on this role, literature has transformed itself too late, moreover; an investiture accomplished sooner might perhaps have avoided the crisis instead of having to provide a remedy: "If the literature of the century of Louis XIV had invoked Christianity instead of adoring pagan gods, if its poets had been what those of primitive times were, priests singing the great things of their religion and their country, the triumph of the sophistical doctrines of the last century would have been much more difficult, perhaps impossible." The remarkable preface to *Les Nouvelles Odes* from which the preceding texts are taken ends neither with an apology for romanticism nor with an apology for the Restoration, but with what unites them and dominates them both in the mind of Hugo during this period — the portrait of the poet who is humanity's guide: "He must go before the peoples like a light and show them the way. . . . He will never be the echo of any word, unless it be that of God."

After all that we have seen so far, we may expect to find in the young Hugo a militant conception of the poetic ministry, since the word of the poet is linked by way of an imperious sense of vocation to the active work of restoration and renewal. And indeed he envisaged all the vicissitudes of a struggle between the poetic word and human powers in crisis. He envisioned the poet thundering victoriously against the forces of evil:

> Dieu, par qui tout forfait s'expie,
> Marche avec celui qui le sert.
> Apparais dans la foule impie,
> Tel que Jean, qui vint du désert.
> Va donc, parle aux peuples du monde;
> Dis-leur la tempête qui gronde,
> Révèle le juge irrité;
> Et pour mieux frapper leur oreille,
> Que ta voix s'élève, pareille
> A la rumeur d'une cité![97]

> [God, by whom every crime is expiated,
> Accompanies whoever serves him.
> Appear before the impious crowd,
> As did John, who came out of the wilderness.
> Go then, speak to the peoples of the world;
> Tell them of the storm that is brewing,
> Reveal the exasperated judge;
> And to better get their ear, let your voice be raised,
> Like the murmur of a city!]

This image of the poet obsessed him to the point that he applied it, paradoxically, to the Lamartine of the *Méditations*, whom he calls "the *os magna sonaturum, the mouth capable of saying great things, ferrea vox, the voice of iron*, the man who will not flinch before a tyrant's whims or a faction's furies."[98] Sometimes it is enough for the poet to make himself heard in order to calm social unrest: "And who then will sacrifice himself if not the poet? What voice will be raised in the storm if not that of the lyre that can calm it? and who will defy the venoms of anarchy and the stings of despotism if not he to whom ancient wisdom attributed the power of reconciling peoples and kings, and to whom modern wisdom has given the power of dividing them?"⁹⁹ At other times the poet despairs of being listened to and affects to renounce his mission:

> Je vous rapporte, ô Dieu, le rameau d'espérance.
> Voici le divin glaive et la céleste lance;
> J'ai mal atteint le but où j'étais envoyé.¹⁰⁰

> [I am returning to you, O God, the branch of hope.
> Here is the sword divine and the heavenly lance;
> I have not done well at reaching the goal where I was sent.]

Sometimes he will have to offer himself as a victim to cruel tormentors in order to bear witness to the truth he brings and in order to redeem those who persecute him:

> Le mortel qu'un Dieu même anime
> Marche à l'avenir plein d'ardeur;
> C'est en s'élançant dans l'abîme
> Qu'il en sonde la profondeur.
> Il se prépare au sacrifice;
> Il sait que le bonheur du vice
> Par l'innocent est expié;
> Prophète à son jour mortuaire,
> La prison est son sanctuaire
> Et l'échafaud est son trépied.¹⁰¹

> [The mortal moved by God
> Marches on full of faith;
> It is by throwing himself into the abyss
> That he sounds its depth.
> He prepares himself for the sacrifice;
> He knows that the pleasure of sin
> Is expiated by the innocent;
> A prophet on the day of his death,
> Prison is his sanctuary
> And the scaffold is his tripod.]

The traditional misfortune of the poet is thus changed into an expiatory sacrifice whose type is, here again, all too obviously, that of Christ.

It was less a properly Christian or religious poetry like that created by Lamartine in the *Méditations* (and especially later in the *Harmonies*) that Hugo intended than a sort of "prophetic" poetry accompanying the perils of humanity.¹⁰² It is not that the objection that any militant poetry raises did not occur to him: the danger of a degradation or abasement of the Muse. The risk of being tainted by action was particularly great for a heavenly muse. Noting that Vigny's "Héléna," a philhellenic poem, is the least good of his collection, Hugo wonders whether the Muse has not wished to "punish the poet for having pinned the flag to his lyre in order to attract the crowd."[103] And it is sometimes regretfully that he himself plunges into the strife.[104] But in him the dilemma is quickly and spontaneously resolved: for the investiture from on high consecrates the poet only in order to guide men. For Hugo, a duty of apostolic presence derives from the divine definition of the poet, indeed from the very distance that it places between him and humans. But it is necessary that men be aware of his august position and not importune him with appeals for frivolous activity:

> Pourquoi traîner ce roi si loin de ses royaumes?
> . . . .
> Laissez donc loin de vous, ô mortels téméraires,
> Celui que le Seigneur marqua, parmi ses frères,
>   De ce signe funeste et beau,
> Et dont l'oeil entrevoit plus de mystères sombres
> Que les morts effrayés n'en lisent dans les ombres,
>   Sous la pierre de leur tombeau!

> [Why drag this king so far from his kingdom?
> . . . .
> Let him remain far from you, O you bold mortals,
> He whom the Lord has marked among his brothers
>   With this fateful, beautiful sign,
> And whose eye glimpses darker mysteries
> Than do the fearful dead in their shadows
>   Beneath their tombstones!]

But this prayer to men to leave the poet in peace immediately changes into an evocation of a startlingly and dramatically self-evident ministry:

> Un jour vient dans sa vie, où la Muse elle-même,
> D'un sacerdoce auguste armant son luth suprême,
>   L'envoie au monde ivre de sang,
> Afin que, nous sauvant de notre propre audace,
> Il apporte d'en haut à l'homme qui menace
>   La prière du Tout-Puissant.

> Un formidable esprit descend dans sa pensée.
> Il paraît, et soudain en éclairs élancée,
>   Sa parole luit comme un feu.

Les peuples prosternés en foule l'environnent;
Sina mystérieux, les foudres le couronnent,
      Et son front porte tout un Dieu![105]

[A day comes in his life when the Muse herself,
Arming his exalted lute with a majestic mission,
      Sends him into the bloodthirsty world
So that, saving us from our own rashness,
He may bring to the baleful man
      The prayer of the Almighty.

It is through his thought that a tremendous spirit comes down to earth.
He appears, and suddenly, flashing out in lightning bolts,
      His words shine like a flame.
The people surround him, prostrate and en masse;
Mysterious Sinai and its thunderbolts crown him
      And on his brow one can see a very God!]

Very early on, Hugo thought himself the confidant of the beyond: "Mon esprit de Pathmos connut le saint délire [My spirit knew the holy delirium of Patmos]," he writes in 1823;[106] and Sainte-Beuve, reminding him in 1829 of the ordeals of his youth, says to him: "When you had wept enough, you withdrew to Patmos with your eagle, and your clear sight expressed itself in the most terrible symbols. There is no longer anything that can make you turn pale; you are able to sound every depth, hear every voice; you are familiar with the Infinite."[107] Sainte-Beuve was at this time entirely in sympathy with Hugo, and here paints him as Hugo liked to see himself. And this positioning of poetry at such a distant height is not a withdrawal, it is a sacred summit from which the law descends for the good of men. It is thus that, from the beginnings of his career, Hugo conceived of the poetic ministry in accordance with two supreme, linked terms: Patmos and the tribune. It is surely because he embodied, from one pole to the other, the conquering aspect of the poetic ministry in all its amplitude that he has remained its symbol in the eyes of subsequent generations.

Around 1825, Hugo's work changes tone: every reader notices this without difficulty. The pomp of sanctified French royalty and the spiritual, militant ministry of the poet give way to new formal and tonal experiments. From the European Middle Ages through Spain to the Orient, it seems as if the poet, instead of seeking that which gives him authority as a spirit, is now solely in search of visible, sensuous material for his art. This invasion of the sensory, which asserts itself in the *Ballades* and *Les Orientales*, defines a second Hugo: it is the first to which many of his contemporaries paid any heed, the one that so many articles and reviews define with greater or lesser sympathy in the days leading up to 1830 as the poet par excellence of the material world. Criticism has long held the *Odes* to be unimportant, and has been accustomed to make Hugo begin with the *Orientales* and the preface to *Cromwell*, making the metaphysical, prophetic Hugo date from maturity and old age. A more just appreciation of his first work, in which the source of Hugolian prophetism has become so visible for us, obliges us today to ask ourselves about the significance of the sensuous, imaginative eruption of 1825–30 in the poet's career, as well as about the at least apparent ebbing during these years of the inspiration that dominates his entire work.

It is extremely obvious that this change of orientation coincides in the young Hugo with the decline of his royalism. Chateaubriand's dismissal in 1824 and his going over to a sort of liberal opposition helped disillusion the younger poetic generation with royalism. Furthermore, the idea of a Restoration capable of moral renewal opening the way for a new century was sapped by the long, dreary experience of the Villèle ministry; under Charles X, this hope breathed its last. Shall we believe that the missionary poet, disenchanted with what he had made the very substance of his mission and suddenly cast upon a spiritual void, for lack of any other matter had to give himself over to exercises in sensuous fantasy in order to continue to sing? In fact, the period in question is also for Hugo a time of decisive spiritual maturation. This is when the Christian critique of classicism changes into a more and more categorical disavowal of the age of Louis XIV on his part: "Its wealth is only in its ceremonial splendor, its grandeur is only in its imposing majesty": he rejects pell-mell "classical rags, philosophical tatters, metaphysical finery."[108] This is when the slogan of liberty in art appears in his writings, along with the vehement denunciation of traditional rules and proprieties. The preface to the *Odes et ballades* in 1826, that of the same collection in 1828, that of *Les Orientales* in 1829, and, on the eve of 1830, the *Lettre aux éditeurs* of Ch. Dovalle's poems and the preface to *Hernani* tirelessly repeat this theme, which in the end makes of the revolution in literature not the reaction to and reparation for the revolution in society, but, now, the social revolution's complement: an obvious conversion to the views of liberal criticism on this subject. "It is the principle of freedom," writes Hugo, "that . . . comes to breathe new life into art as it has breathed new life into society."[109] The old royalist motif of a new literature that is the daughter of the ordeals is present, but in an unexpected variation: it is the entire revolutionary tragedy, with all its pains and its glory, that poetry is going to take to itself; whence its sense of "a profound grief mixed with dignity and pride."[110] The younger poetic generation, formerly hailed as grave and serious, is this still, but now with a different justification: strength has replaced its suffering: "A strong school is arising, a strong generation is quietly growing up to support it."[111] The change in poetic manner in Hugo, then, clearly accompanies an ideological molting: in brief, a swing toward liberalism. But the project of a poetic ministry has neither been sacrificed nor forgotten in this mutation: far from it, it is this that drives Hugo's conversion in the presence of a new state of affairs.

It was indeed difficult for the mission of the Poet, which had grown up on the themes of the monarchical, Christian counterrevolution, to exchange this commitment for another without transition, as one puts an end to a chance affair. For as we have seen, this one was anything but. What sources could have been drawn upon to consecrate the poet? Liberalism hardly tended in that direction. Humanitarian democracy did not yet exist. Hugo, then, who more than any other had based his life on the notion of this consecration, indeed found himself, when he ceased to believe in the Restoration, in possession of an ambition without an aim, or more precisely without any leverage on reality. It seemed to him that the world was failing to live up to his desire. "Ubi defuit orbis" [when the world failed] is the epigraph of an ode he entitles "Fin": he wants, he says, to close the book of brass wherein he has read, with lute in hand, the history of the troubles of his time; he no longer possesses the key to this book; the enigma of the sphinx is too difficult for him; he renounces the quest for its secret. But he justifies his former way of thinking as being at one with poetic genius:

> C'est qu'il fallait à ma pensée
> Tout un grand peuple à remuer.

Des révolutions j'ouvrais le gouffre immonde?
C'est qu'il faut un chaos à qui veut faire un monde.
C'est qu'une grande voix dans ma nuit m'a parlé.
C'est qu'enfin je voulais, menant au but la foule,
> Avec le siècle qui s'écoule
> Confronter le siècle écoulé.

Le génie a besoin d'un peuple que sa flamme
Anime, éclaire, échauffe, embrase comme une âme.[112]

> [It was because my thought required
> The whole of a great people to stir up.

I was opening up the horrible abyss of revolutions?
It was because whoever would make a world needs a chaos.
And then, there was a great voice speaking to me in my darkness.

And, finally, I wanted, leading the people to the goal,
    With the present age
    To juxtapose the age that was finished.

Genius needs a people for its flame
    To awaken, enlighten, warm, and inflame like a soul.]

Hugo's ambition, detesting a vacuum, sought a way to get a grip on things, to be intensely saturated with the visible and the imaginable, as these might be perceived without restraint. It was not a question of renouncing the poetic ministry, but more than ever of making it current. Now this living world, which henceforward rejects that of the Restoration as unreal, is in Hugo's eyes a world with a broader conception of society, that has broken the old code of ceremony, a world ruled over by what is concrete and brightly colored, where the frightful and the supernatural have revealed their truth. During the years when the missionary-poet no longer knows how to apply his mission to the universe around him, his first instinct is to adapt himself to this universe, to capture without preconceptions of propriety all its truth. Not in vain did the researches that occupied these years bear upon sensation and style; they were not merely preparing a new instrument; they were the beginning, in thought itself, of the metamorphosis of the poetic ministry, the still unconsummated marriage of missionary poetry and the modern world.

From 1820 to 1825, the *Odes* already bear witness here and there to the need Hugo felt to renew literary forms. As early as 1822 there are a few pieces that incline toward the fantastic element that would be one of the principal ingredients of nineteenth-century poetics: thus "La Chauve-souris" and "Le Cauchemar";[113] others, in 1823 and 1824, are so marked by this tone that although they were first published among the *Odes*, in 1828 they will go over to the *Ballades*, whose character they already possess.[114] The Middle Ages of the *Ballades*, from 1825 to 1828, repudiated the neoclassical gracefulness of the troubadour style in order to embrace the imaginative spontaneity and formal boldness of the new school. The appeal to the traditional superstitions of Europe had since the beginning of the century been one of the most constant themes of anticlassical criticism. The Middle Ages in the *Ballades* is sometimes still lords of manors, shepherd girls, gallant knights, and squires; but it is above all witches' sabbaths, sorceresses, and satanic spells, that were more shocking to the established poetic;[115] with this world is mingled that of non-Christian mythology, sylphs, fairies, and goblins, presented in a terrifying poetic light.[116] This irruption of the supernatural into a poetry that has been emancipated from classicism is a European event; the very name of *ballade* designating this genre was English and then German before being adopted in France. This literary phenomenon does not necessarily have the same significance everywhere and always. We are here pointing out the moment when, in Hugo, Christian romanticism is converted to this mythology, and we may well ask ourselves how it is that such a conversion can be a part, and, it would seem, so essential a part, in a process of poetic modernization. Why does an imagination that calls itself and desires to be modern, in freeing itself from memories of antiquity, attach itself to the fabulous representations of another past epoch? Why does the elimination of the last vestiges of the feudal world, which will occur precisely in France, send minds scurrying toward the belief and legends of the Middle Ages?

We should notice that this fashion also affected liberal writers: the medieval temptation is present in Mme de Staël, in Nodier, in all those who, whatever their credo, wished to give new life to poetic imagery. The authors of verse ballads and prose legends before and after 1830 are not necessarily ideologues advocating the past. Their works, whose function is to supplant the fictions of pagan mythology in a new imaginative style, do not presuppose a real adhesion to the beliefs they pretend to adopt. By substituting the legendary traditions of Europe for the images of classical mythology, it is hoped that the wishes of a broader public than that of the salons and courts may be satisfied. The new fable democratizes literature: these are not really reinstated beliefs, but rather a vernacular mythology, less aristocratic than the one that had peopled the poetry of monarchical times with the gods and goddesses of Olympus. This romantic mythology is also less serene: it appeals more to reverie and to fear, and it has deeper roots in simple humanity than the legends of antiquity, as the literature of antiquity and classicism had elaborated them for an elite public. To counter the classical tradition, the supernatural element in medievalism appeals not to an ancient faith but to imagination and to a capacity for feeling that is judged to be more alive. It is no longer a question of sacrificing Greco-Roman legends to the Christianity of the writer and his public, as was the case at the time of the *Génie du christianisme* or of *La Muse française*; it is a question rather of giving the poetic spiritualism of the moderns a language of its own. The legends of folklore or of what is given as folklore constitute this language. The Christian supernatural, despite a long and futile effort, was never able to take shape; now comes the modern supernatural in the shape of fictions whose origins are lost in the mists of European time and that have sustained our imaginations since childhood. If today they are less objects of belief than a literature, then they are all the better adapted to our view of the world, for it is also a literature, but in the sense in which literature is a focus of spiritual life, maintained by writers in the name of and for the sake of everyone. It is difficult to deny the modernity of this new supernatural element if we recognize how important it has been to the revival of the epic genre: the formula is that of a supernatural to which we grant total control in emotional terms by means of a simulated belief. At bottom, it is the definition of the Legendary: an admirable way to resuscitate epic naïveté in the nineteenth century. The sacred supernatural itself, from Vigny's *Moïse* on, made itself over based on such a formula: in that poem it is in fact the aura of legend that makes the figure of the wonder-working prophet plausible. The first rumblings of a tremendous epic grandeur — a particularly Hugolian variant of the Legendary — can already be heard:

> Ma tête ainsi qu'un mont arrêtait les nuages;
> Et souvent dans les cieux épiant leurs passages
>   J'ai pris des aigles dans mes mains![117]

> [Like a mountain peak my head thus stopped the clouds;
> And often, espying their passing in the skies,
>   I grasped eagles in my hands!]

Almost simultaneously with this new supernatural, a supposedly oriental coloring floods Hugo's work (light, brilliant tones, azure, luxurious splendor, life given over to the senses), evoking not so much the depths of the imagination as its deployment in an exciting, inwardly motivated poetry. Philhellenism was the occasion for the blossoming of *Les Orientales*, which are sometimes militant odes in favor of the Greek cause, but are always poems of dazzling color — Greek, Turkish, Muslim, even Hispano-Moorish, or quite simply Spanish. Almost all written in 1828, *Les Orientales* echo the *Ballades* of the preceding years in that their exoticism accompanies the resurrection of the past and its legends as another form of romanticism's conquests. These peregrinations and discoveries in the realm of the senses are another aspect of poetry's invasion by the richness of things: here too the visible and the imaginary join in an irresistible movement that is taken to be the very face of truth. The poet, opening himself to the world of the senses, is not at all betraying the world of the spirit. The dazzling, fabulous imagery of *Les Orientales* shimmers in the spirit's secret heart; it awakens reverie and memory according to a formula of which Baudelaire will be the most significant legatee.[118] In its richness, it also offers itself as an instrument of epic creation: it helps us understand the work of these years to consider that Hugo chose to place at the beginning of his collection the poem entitled "Le Feu du ciel," a recounting of the punishment of Sodom and Gomorrah, though it is connected only by the pretext of the Orient. The Hugo who is learning to brilliantly depict sultanas and pashas is at the same time employing masterfully his new resources to rework Scripture for the use of modern readers. And it is not by chance that in the same collection an affirmation of the poetic ministry appears recast in a new world of imagery in accordance with a thought that is more militant than ever: the romantic universe extends the domain and tribulations of the creative spirit to infinity, and seems to give it, as a reward for its ordeals, a universal royalty. The symbol is that of Mazeppa, the Cossack tied to his galloping horse, bleeding and humiliated, who would become the ruler of the Ukraine; a royal consecration is similarly awaiting the one whom Genius is impelling and torturing:

Il traverse d'un vol, sur tes ailes de flamme,
Tous les champs du possible, et les mondes de l'âme,
      Boit au fleuve éternel;
Dans la nuit orageuse ou la nuit étoilée,
Sa chevelure, aux crins des comètes mêlée,
      Flamboie au front du ciel.

. . . .

Il voit tout; et pour lui, ton vol que rien ne lasse,
De ce monde sans borne à chaque instant déplace
      L'horizon idéal.
. . . .

Il crie épouvanté, tu poursuis implacable.
Pâle, épuisé, béant, sous ton vol qui l'accable,
      Il ploie avec effroi;
Chaque pas que tu fais semble creuser sa tombe.
Enfin le terme arrive . . . il court, il vole, il tombe
      Et se relève roi![119]

[In a flash he traverses on your wings of flame
All the domains of the possible and the worlds of the soul,
      Drinks of the eternal stream;
In the stormy night or the starry night
His crown of hair mingled with the manes of comets
      Shines before the brow of heaven.

. . . .

He sees everything; and for him, your tireless flight
Constantly displaces this boundless world's
      Ideal horizon.
. . . .

He cries in dismay, you implacably go on.
Pale, exhausted, gasping, at your overwhelming flight,
      He doubles up in fright;

Every step you take seems to dig his grave.
Finally he reaches the end . . . he runs, he flies, he falls —
Then rises, a king!]

In the same period and in the same order of ideas, a new intellectual theme appears in French romanticism: the sovereignty of Art takes the place of the purely poetic cult that we saw in the years of *La Muse française*: this is clearly visible in the preface to *Les Orientales*. An entire romantic and postromantic lineage will profess this religion of art. Not that art has dethroned poetry; they are held equally in honor, and the latter is like the soul of the former. We should nonetheless take note of the appearance of this new watchword, and speculate about its significance. The union with art annexes a world of forms and sensations to poetry, thereby making it better able to carry out its mission. The romantic religion of art has with great superficiality sometimes been mixed up with what is rather unintelligibly called the cult of form, and it has been contrasted with the human ambitions of poetic spiritualism. It is appropriate to point out this error when we deal with the years in which the problem arises, when even Hugo says he is proud to have written a "useless book of pure poetry."[120] Useless here means: having value only in what it is in itself, in relation to nothing else, and thus all the more valuable. This sort of proclamation, which proclaims the highest value to be inherent, is a characteristic of every religion. By placing themselves under the sign of Art, poets established it as a principle sovereign in itself, free of all dependence on other consecrated values, whether of knowledge or morality: Art, which does not claim to strive against them, is ascribable to a special inspiration that is beyond them. The poetic ministry was definitively constituted and instituted only by this step. Here, we are merely pointing out the moment when it becomes definite in France; but European aestheticism laid the foundation for and accomplished this feat everywhere. We can see that more is involved than a glorification of form at the expense of thought or inspiration — an absurd profession of faith by which romanticism, if it had understood itself thus, would have proclaimed its own insignificance.

Furthermore, during this same period Hugo was also making efforts toward an intense representation of individuals and things by means other than poetry. It is in the novel that he first broke with a conventional representation of the universe and cultivated sensation in all its violence: *Han d'Islande*, from 1823, preceded the *Ballades*; theatrical works followed. But in these creations, in which according to many contemporaries matter and sensuousness dominate, Hugo continued to effect the reign of the symbol; that is, of thought. *Han d'Islande, Bug-Jargal* reworked in 1826, *Le Dernier jour d'un condamné* in 1829, then *Notre-Dame de Paris*, and, in these same years, the plays *Cromwell, Marion de Lorme*, and *Hernani* — in all these works, Hugo believed he was transmitting a spiritual message to the public as well as a reality seen according to art. He never distinguished between these two things. For him characters and events mean more than they are; they establish a symbolic link between reality and the preaching of a creative spirit. This is equally true of his novels and plays. We can wonder about the reasons for Hugo's failing, at least relatively, in these areas, and explain this by the inconsistency of the symbols and the values they suggest. The novels are perhaps of greater worth in this regard than the plays, and *Notre-Dame de Paris* has worn better than *Hernani*. But this is not what interests us here. We are only following the course of the work as a whole, and through its variations and different degrees of success we see it dominated by a continuous design.

The passage from the missionary lyricism of 1820 to the post-1825 creations was so little a break for Hugo that during the very period when this transition was taking place, he attempted a doctrinal synthesis of his recent past and his present. It is from this perspective that we should read the preface to *Cromwell*, in which he undertakes to graft all the discoveries of the romantic revolution onto the Christian trunk of his earlier poetics: the supernatural elements from the Middle Ages, brilliancy, picturesque representation of evil and ugliness. First of all, Hugo's personal evolution as he understands it in 1827, from lyricism to drama, becomes a law of human history. He repeats the idea, so current in Europe for at least a century, according to which lyricism is the spontaneous language of the first men giving thanks to the Creator at the birth of the world: "In primitive times, when man awakens in a world that has just been born, poetry awakens with it. In the presence of miracles that dazzle and exhilarate him, his first word is only a hymn. His existence is still so close to God that all his meditations are ecstasies, all his dreams are visions. He unbosoms himself, he sings as he breathes. . . . This is the first man, and also the first poet. He is young, he is lyrical. Prayer is all his religion, the ode is all his poetry."[121] If, on the level of the contemporary and the modern, Hugo glorifies drama at the expense of lyricism, this is because at this date he sees in it the means for a more effective influence over a wider public. Lyricism springs from what humanity has inherited from the earliest ages, and by virtue of this Hugo would doubtless admit that it should be considered eternally human; he well knows that in his own time, and in part thanks to him, lyrical poetry has been returned to its first dignity, to use the expression so often used at this time. But drama seems to him to be fundamentally modern. As is well known, in trying to organize as a theory of universal literary evolution the choice toward which he is currently moving during these years, Hugo multiplied interpretations and dicta of the most arbitrary nature. After a fanciful age of earliest spontaneity, he imagined an intermediate theocratic and military age that is the age of the epic, into which he crams all of antiquity. In themselves, these bold constructions hold no interest.[122] It is the intention that engenders them that matters to us: it is a question of making the entire literary history of humanity culminate in the romantic drama, in the very manner that Hugo is in the process of inventing.[123]

Wishing to make of drama the literary expression of modern times, Hugo also desired to give it a Christian origin; thus is affirmed in him the continuity of the romanticism of 1820 with that of 1830, so different in so many ways. In the poetic renewal that took place beginning with the counterrevolution, we have seen that the link between present and past is not completely broken. Chateaubriand had made modern melancholy flow from a Christian source; Hugo, in his preface to *Cromwell,* picks up this thread, and going back to the origin of Christianity sees in it "a spiritualist religion" that opposes heaven and earth, shows man that he is double, separates breath from matter, and in doing so engenders melancholy and unease. But to this legacy of Chateaubriand,[124] to which it is significant that he remains constantly faithful throughout the modernizing metamorphosis of his poetry, Hugo adds something new that was unsuspected in 1800 and that is the raison d'être for the whole exposé: Christianity, he says, necessarily produces an aesthetic of contrasts, in which ugliness has its place. The idea of the mixture of the beautiful and the ugly as a law of life had struck Hugo as early as 1823;[125] but here it enters into an ensemble that gives it its entire import: "Christianity," Hugo writes,

> brings poetry to truth. Like Christianity, the modern Muse will see things with a loftier and more all-embracing eye. Poetry will feel that not everything in creation is humanly *beautiful*, that the ugly exists there beside the beautiful, the deformed near the gracious, the grotesque on the flip side of the sublime, the evil with the good, the shadow with the light. . . . Religion's point of departure is always poetry's point of departure. . . . The modern genre is born of the fruitful union of the grotesque type and the sublime type. . . . From the day when Christianity said to man: You are double, you are composed of two beings, one perishable, the other immortal, one carnal, the other ethereal . . . , on that day, drama was created.[126]

One can rightly be amused by this notion of affiliation that makes Christianity responsible for the new *cénacle*'s taste for violently contrasted images; but it is true that all this vividness abounds in connection with a dualist metaphysics — soul and body, good and evil — that, if it is not strictly Christian, at least repre-

sents the most essential modern survival of Christianity. At this level the affiliation really exists. Nor is it absolutely gratuitous to attribute to the advent of
Christianity a new accent on ugliness, the negative ugliness of vice and filth, as
well as ugliness dignified by suffering and humility. For a long time now art
historians have been describing this irruption as an effect of the Christian vision
of the world.[127] It is in this way that Christianity belongs to everyone, and
embraces the entire truth of the human condition, its wretchedness included.
The aristocratic aesthetic of classicism tended to obscure this, although it was
situated in a Christian milieu. Hugo is not wrong to say that in this sense this
romanticism resumes the tradition of medieval Christianity; the theory of the
contrast between the sublime and the grotesque does the same in its humanly
comprehensive and potentially plebeian aspects. We ought to add that this
imitation deforms the original considerably, and that the legacy that is being
claimed has been profoundly modified in accordance with a modern situation.

The aesthetics of the sublime and the grotesque appears at the moment when
an essentially democratic society implicitly valorizing the people rises up and
imposes itself on the consciousness of young royalist poets. Under this influence, the romantic lyre changes its tone; the position of vulgarity and propriety
in literature is upset; style and imagination assign themselves a new task: writers
must speak to a society in which all classes are estimable, where the hierarchy of
status and the hierarchy of values do not coincide, and where diversity and
contrast are everywhere and affect every spiritual itinerary. The old Christian
dualism was already very freely interpreted in romantic melancholy; in the
preface to *Cromwell* it underwent an even more unexpected transformation: the
sublime/grotesque dichotomy as Hugo understands it attests an acceptance of
humanity in all aspects of its nature. The Christian spirit recognizes itself only
with difficulty in this dichotomy, and for it is the birthmark of the society that
was born of the eighteenth century and the Revolution. The supremacy of the
ideal is only established on the basis of a sort of broader rehabilitation of humanity of which the promotion of the People to importance is doubtless the
principal determinant. In these new conditions, the ministry of poets could not
take second place to the church, which was made for a society in which the
People and Man were valorized only within the limits of a strict theology and by
means of a renunciation of this world. From now on, feeling that they alone are
in tune with the modern world, poets claim as their prerogative the intuitive
knowledge and preaching of spiritual truths.

Hugo relies on a theory of total truth that is one of the principal ingredients
of his preface to *Cromwell*. It is all too obvious that theories of truth are different in different literary schools: all of them advance claims to truth, but each

understands truth in its own way. Romanticism, in the eyes of many of its adversaries, was a literature of the unreal. A contributor to the *Journal des débats* reproached it for being acquainted only with the imaginary world and for scorning reality, a charge that astonished the young Hugo and inspired him to deny it vehemently.[128] Another contributor imagined Romanticism pronouncing this oracle:

> Pour un fils d'Apollon le véritable monde
>   Est celui qui n'existe pas.[129]

> [For a son of Apollo the real world
>   Is the one that does not exist.]

We could cite, by way of comparison, a host of texts that make of romanticism a literature of sensation, and of Hugo a poet of materiality. Sometimes, with more penetration, we perceive the attributions conjoined and we see romanticism defined as "the shocking mixture of a measureless exaltation and an ignoble familiarity";[130] this is to subscribe to the very doctrine of the preface to *Cromwell* in pejorative terms. As early as 1822 a more objective critic grasped the considerable spiritual conquest effected by romantic contrasts: "The harmonies of reality and ideality, of the senses and the spirit, of the natural and the possible that the romantic creates have not been sufficiently noticed: these harmonies extend the space in which the poet deploys the wonders of his art."[131] In fact, the necessity of uniting the ideal and the real is just as much an article of faith in classicism, but in a different sense: in classicism it is a narrow border that separates ideal beauty from the best of nature, but for the romantics the distance between things and spiritual intuitions can be infinite. For classicism, the belief that the true is being represented depends on a moderate and controlled use of the imagination; in romanticism, on the contrary, this conviction is born of an imagination that does not accept any limit and claims to embrace the totality of the universe and of humanity. This difference is the difference between two societies; but it also indicates the spectacular promotion of the figure of the creative writer from one society to the other.

Romanticism in this new form does not appear to have immediately gained the assent of its liberal faction. Hugo's theory of the grotesque was doubtless subject on this score to less hostility and irony than the monarchico-Christian preaching of *La Muse française*; but it was on the whole poorly received. Already, apropos of the *Odes et ballades* of 1826, it was possible to read in *Le Globe* the review (famous especially for the praises it contains) in which Sainte-Beuve deplored in the poet "I know not what warp of imagination, against which French taste protests."[132] Sainte-Beuve had in view at that time the first fantastic poems and, while he is at it, *Han d'Islande*. In 1827, apropos of the preface to *Cromwell* itself, another article in *Le Globe*, also said to be by Sainte-Beuve, sees in the theory of the grotesque the most unquestionably original of Hugo's contributions, but expresses considerable reservations concerning its validity.[133] More than two years later, again in *Le Globe*, Duvergier de Hauranne expressed the same reservations concerning the excessive realism in Sainte-Beuve's poems: "Reality was summoned; it came, and by a natural usurpation, it has invaded everything. . . . Expression was summoned, and it soon introduced ugliness."[134] Similarly, the *Revue française*, which in part spun off from the contributors to *Le Globe*, denounces the "poetic materialism" of the new school.[135] Hugo's aesthetics of contrasts, which plays on extremes and mixes together the immaterial with the sordid, the royal with the plebeian, worried the moderate reformers of doctrinaire romanticism. Here once again we put our finger on what separates the romanticism of poets—of sacred poets—from that of critics who spring from bourgeois liberal stock. Even when poets ceased to be royalists, even when a Hugo undertakes to create the instrument of a literature for new times, they retained from their origins a lyrical or religious sense (in romanticism, it is all the same) that separates them from the liberal bourgeoisie. The romanticism of 1825–30, the modern mutation of the royalist brood, reconciles itself to the new society only by going beyond it: an essential prophetic vocation makes it conceive of extreme ideals for the bourgeois world—lofty illusions relating to the essence of life and justifying the bourgeois world's existence, but that also snatch the bourgeois world away from the bourgeois, who at the outset resist adopting these ideals. The seeds of all the humanitarian romanticism of the future are present in these years: it is not by chance that *Le Dernier jour du condamné* is contemporary with *Les Orientales* and *Hernani*. Thus, in the genesis of the ideals of the nineteenth century, a sensibility that was at first foreign to liberalism furnished a contribution that it alone was able to provide. It did so by broadening itself and by undergoing a metamorphosis, but without denying its fundamental inspiration: the theme of the poetic ministry, maintained and strengthened from one *cénacle* to another, clearly attests to this continuity in change.

It is understandable that the preface to *Cromwell* emphasizes as much as it does the proclamation of liberty in art. This liberty is not understood simply in relation to a system of conventions whose rejection is the initial condition for a new poetics; it signifies the sovereignty of genius and its inspirations. In fact, this sovereignty is always limited by group tastes and obsessions: romanticism fixed, as much as any preceding school did, types, characters, situations, combinations of thoughts and images; its universe is as conventional as any other literary universe, and originality is as difficult to achieve there as it is anywhere else. But in principle — and it is the principle that matters here — romantic liberty invests the poet with a boundless power, a power of moving about in and of connection with the universe that equals that of the Creator himself; art is liberty insofar as it is royalty, choosing at will and illuminating everything it touches: "Like God, the true poet is present everywhere at once in his work. Genius resembles the coining press that stamps the royal likeness on copper coins and on gold crowns alike."[136] The extended defense of art over against brute reality that Hugo develops in his preface, and the defense of verse over against prose as well, should be understood in the same spirit. It is not just a question of the basic protest of an artist against the threat of vulgarity, of the "common"; in any case, this artist, who is jealous of his art's prerogatives, has no intention of enclosing himself in his profession and cultivating forms and colors for themselves; this conception, if indeed it has ever existed, was never Hugo's at any time. The exaltation of art, which he contrasts by more than one obvious allusion to the prosaic and veristic doctrines of liberal romanticism,[137] is for him the exaltation of the artist, who should be something other than a recorder of the real. Art is the seal of the poetic ministry, distinguishing the poet's teaching from any other by an inimitable mark, one that is outside the common order. This is, in the nineteenth century, the only more-than-natural light that can accompany human speech and give it a sort of oracular value. In exalting art, Hugo and his friends do not renounce poetry's power of edification and illumination; very much to the contrary, it is by means of these that they liberate it from fealty to any heterogeneous power, be it theological or social; in a word, they give to the Poet, as a poet, a special prerogative in the world of thought.

❧ Sainte-Beuve

The beginning of Sainte-Beuve's career is distinctive in that it allows us to see, in an unmediated, natural state, the combination of religiosity and outright modernism that was, for the poets of his generation, both the result of the way things were developing and a conquest of their own. How real Sainte-Beuve's original Catholicism was is often discussed, and doubt is often cast, justifiably, upon his denials late in life concerning his childhood religion. It is probable that these religious feelings were real, and that his first awakening to adult life under the influence of *idéologie* and physiologism repressed them. The religious Sainte-Beuve can be deduced from his later temptations; but this religion owes nothing to the spirit of the counterrevolution, which is not where Sainte-Beuve came from. In the complex history of the romantic revolution, he is — like Nodier, though for different reasons and at a different moment — a unifying element: a willingly religious and disenchanted interpretation of the themes of Sensibility does not prevent him from belonging entirely to the new society.

We do not really know, then, whether he was telling the truth when, much later, speaking of "the most advanced eighteenth century," he asserted: "that is my true foundation."[138] At *Le Globe*, where he made his début at the age of twenty, a different spirit held sway: that of Victor Cousin's spiritualism. It is certain that Sainte-Beuve never adhered to this doctrine: at first no doubt due to fidelity to the eighteenth century and *idéologie*, later for different reasons; namely, the fervent worship of art and the cult of poetry. In 1825, however, with respect to poetry, he was still thinking as many liberals did. The idea of a poetry with religious resonances, in the genre of that of the Lake poets of England, inspires a certain irony in him: "These vague outpourings of enthusiasm have been reduced by them to a theory: every fuzzy thought, every fleeting impression has been noted down or, more accurately, consecrated: they have made of poetry a religion of which their books are the oracles,"[139] he wrote, thinking in this connection of "the incomprehensible harmonies" of Bernardin de Saint-Pierre; "Rousseau's and Bernardin's school," he adds, "is beginning to appear in poetry: the history of the Lake poets might well reveal to them the dangers against which it should take precautions."[140] This warning, which he expressly addresses to Lamartine, is certainly ascribable to the typical spirit of liberal criticism. At this time (in 1825 and 1826) Sainte-Beuve conceived of poetic gravity only along the lines of the civic spirit then touted by this sector of public opinion. If, in order to condemn the colorless poetry of the eighteenth century, he invokes "something imperishable, stamped by adversity" that the revolutionary tragedy has left deep in peoples' hearts, he borrows this royalist theme only to conclude with a call for civic gravity; we have become "serious, and, if you will, a little sad, worried both about ourselves and about people other than ourselves as well, citizens above all"; and on this score he exalts Béranger.[141] In 1827 he still thinks that Casimir Delavigne shows modern poetry its true direction, and that the modern generation needs "a prophet who shows it the future of science and freedom to which it aspires."[142] One of the oldest pieces in *Vie, poésies et pensées de Joseph Delorme* contains a supposed speech by Milton to the young Joseph, exhorting him to civic poetry and offering himself as an example in this direction; thus the author of *Paradise Lost*, the sacred poem of the moderns, so often invoked and exalted as such, appears unexpectedly as the patron of the patriotic lyre:

Ainsi parlait Milton; et ma voix plus sévère,
Par degrés élevant son accent jusqu'au sien,

Après lui murmurait: "Oui, la France est ma mère,
   Et le poète est citoyen."[143]

[Thus Milton spoke; and my sterner voice,
By degrees coming to emulate his tone,
Murmured after him: "Yes, France is my mother,
   And the poet is a citizen."]

On the other hand, in this same period, his adhesion to the *cénacle* is announced by the sort of spiritual unease that Sainte-Beuve incarnated in his hero
(the very feeling that Milton is trying to dislodge), as well as the notion that the
form of poetry must be revolutionized (which Sainte-Beuve regrets not finding
in Delavigne). Sainte-Beuve met Hugo at the beginning of 1827, which marks
what he calls his transition to "poetic romanticism": an adhesion more whole-
hearted than any other in the course of his long and varied career; "I seemed," he
confesses, "to fuse with it utterly."[144] The emergence in him of a romantic
sensibility doubtless developed old tendencies that had till then been stifled by
his mistrust of the counterrevolutionary school. Everything points to the failure
of poetic royalism and the liberation in him of old reserves of sentimental
speculation due to the new orientation of the leaders of the group at *La Muse
française*. The review of the *Odes et ballades* that he wrote in *Le Globe*, which in
fact would lead to his rapprochement with Hugo, begins with a funeral oration
for *La Muse*, exalting nevertheless the possible legacy of its poets: a religion of
poetry in harmony with the modern world. "After the collapse of their theory,"
he writes, "a rather fine role may remain for young talents who, disillusioned by
their vain attempt and abjuring jargon and systems, may feel themselves strong
enough to head down better paths and to make poetry with their souls. This
time, they may achieve glory and deserve the gratitude of the public; for let
there be no mistaking, despite its down-to-earth tastes and its apparent disdain,
the public needs and above all will soon need poetry."[145] As a contribution to
this poetic future, Sainte-Beuve brings a Wertherism free of Catholic or monarchist attachments, whose roots in France can be traced at least as far back as
René. He noticed that Chateaubriand, in his *Essai sur les révolutions*, had sometimes spoken as "a Werther and a René of the working class," and he placed his
Joseph Delorme under this prestigious aegis.[146] He introduced into poetry,
draped in a romantic aura, the humble, introspective muse of the urban run-of-
the-mill, and the image of the Poet in daily struggle with social surroundings
totally devoid of sympathy for him. In this he was ahead of the poets of the
group to which he attached himself, going further than they in the consecration
of the real through art and in the experience of the embittering aspects of the
modern poetic ministry. In this sense he was an early Baudelaire in the bosom of

the romantic generation; the two poets, otherwise so different, were conscious of this relationship,[147] which would have been noticed without their confession simply by lending an ear to their poetry.

Joseph Delorme, in 1829, concludes with a collection of *Pensées*, mostly concerned with the reform of the art of poetry. In this domain, Sainte-Beuve had evolved progressively. His *Tableau historique et critique de la poésie française et du théâtre français au seizième siècle*, on which he worked from 1826 to 1828,[148] attests to this evolution, which led him to a more and more direct critique of the poetics of the seventeenth century: since classicism broke the continuity of the national tradition, this tradition with all its freedoms must be reestablished, as Chénier began to do, and after him Hugo and the new school;[149] a critique of absolutist France and its court culture accompanies these views, in accordance with the liberal tradition, that of Stendhal in particular.[150] There is less originality in this set of ideas than in the underlying doctrine of a poetry of art: it is above all in this that he agrees with the Hugo of the same years; it is in this exaltation of Art, and of poetry as the supreme art, that he saw in Hugo, and that attracted him to the *Cénacle*: for he lived this moment of his life essentially as a conversion to Art; he said this again and again, evoking the "charm" that bound him to this new milieu;[151] therein lay, for him, the exciting novelty. This indeed is why, rather paradoxically, the thoughts of the melancholy Joseph Delorme have as their unique object the glorification of brilliancy, power, and freedom in the matter of style; this is what gives to the dazzling poem "A la rime" such a different tone in this collection.[152] Sainte-Beuve's contribution to romanticism was certainly not a small one; what interests us here especially is the sort of necessity by which the search for modern subjects and a modern audience, or if you like the inclusion in poetry of what had been held to be vulgar or aesthetically plebeian, converges with the cult of Art to form on the eve of 1830 the doctrine of triumphant romanticism.

Sainte-Beuve's attitude with regard to *Le Globe*, which is in the midst of an evolution that has already been described, poses the problem of his spiritualism, which continues to have a curious cast. Sainte-Beuve attributes to his strong attachment to the eighteenth century the fact that he never fully subscribed to the doctrines of *Le Globe*, even when he was writing for it; and we know that this explanation was still valid in 1827.[153] But two years later, when he wrote the poems of *Les Consolations*,[154] his spiritualism was not in doubt: his poetry there appears transfigured by the use of the symbol and the constant reference to the divine, even to prayer. How is it that the period in which he took this course, between 1828 and 1830, did not bring him closer to *Le Globe*? He does applaud Cousin for undertaking a supreme struggle "against Broussais, Daunou, and that tough, hardy philosophy known as *sensationalism*,"[155] which attests to an open reversal of position on his part. But at the same time we see that he disavows the thought of *Le Globe* and comes up with the term "Genevan school"[156] for its contributors, an ironic label that accompanies the imputation of artistic impotence: "This was the weak side of the talent of Mme de Staël and her disciples. They felt deeply and even gave new life to art by means of their reinvigorating beliefs, but they did not achieve any work of their own."[157] Such is the difference between the spiritualism of the liberal philosophers and that of the poets who come from royalism, who, "isolated by special circumstances of birth, social condition, and, if you like, prejudices, and raised in the bosom of ideas that were perhaps narrow but were also lofty and strong, withdrawing early on from political discussions and distractions into which an initial chivalric enthusiasm had thrown them . . . , came to art as artists and lovingly set themselves to creating."[158] Thus an apparently paradoxical fact — that Sainte-Beuve distanced himself further from the people at *Le Globe* while being converted to the spiritualism for which he had at first reproached them — reveals to us one of the conditions of the renewal of poetry at that time; the romantic flowering supposed the experience of a religion of poetry and art, whose springs did not flow in philosophic regions. The philosophers had the idea of it, but the fervor came from elsewhere, having first been born from a critique of philosophy. In the preface dedicated to Victor Hugo in *Les Consolations*, Sainte-Beuve again pays homage to Cousin, whose genius "reconciled philosophy to the noblest faculties of human nature," but he nonetheless says of his disciples that "they are minds more than souls."[159] It is completely otherwise for the poet and the artist:

> The feeling of art implies an acute, inward feeling for things. Whereas the majority of men do not go further than surfaces and appearances; whereas philosophers properly so called recognize and take note of a *je ne sais quoi* without being able to determine the nature of this *je ne sais quoi*; the artist, as if he were endowed with an extra sense, calmly busies himself with feeling beneath the perceptible world that other thoroughly inward world that most never know and of which philosophers limit themselves to noting the existence; he is in the presence of invisible forces at work, and sympathizes with them as with souls; he has received at birth the key to symbols and the understanding of faces: what seems incoherent and contradictory to others is for him only a harmonic contrast, a chord on the universal lyre heard from afar. He soon joins in this great concert and, like the brass jars in the theaters of antiquity, he joins the echo of his voice to the music of the world.[160]

We have here a perfect image of romantic spirituality, and we understand that, if its ideas derive from contemporary philosophy, it subordinates these concepts to the characteristic experience of the artistic creator. We perceive at the center of this universe the gift of poetry and art posited as an overarching value and pathway to the divine, and the figure of the Artist-Poet as spiritual revelator. In short, Sainte-Beuve, in order to make the transition from Daunou and the *idéologues* to Hugo and Lamartine, implies that Victor Cousin did not suffice for him, and we can well believe it.

However this may be, as soon as he was linked to the *Cénacle* and in the grip of the "charm" of Hugo and his friends, Sainte-Beuve participated in the romantic consecration of the poet: otherwise, what would his conversion to a religion of which this consecration was the essence have amounted to?

> Tous réunis, s'entendre, et s'aimer, et se dire:
> Ne désespérons point, poètes, de la lyre,
>   Car le siècle est à nous.
> Il est à vous; chantez, ô voix harmonieuses,
> Et des humains bientôt les foules envieuses
>   Tomberont à genoux.[161]

> [All gathered together, to understand one another,
>   to love one another, and to say to one another:
> Let us not give up our hope, poets, in the lyre,
>   For this century is ours.
> It is yours; sing, O harmonious voices,
> And soon the envious crowds of humans
>   Will fall on their knees.]

Around the same time, he was devising a history of lyricism from humanity's earliest beginnings, following the example of so many contemporaries and of Hugo himself; he concludes this history with a double portrait of modern lyricism; lyrical poets will be those "in every time of troubles and renewal, who, as witnesses to political storms, grasp the deeper meaning or sublime law of some aspect of them and respond to every blind accident with an intelligent, resounding echo; or those who, in these days of revolution and destruction, withdraw within themselves and make themselves there a world apart, a poetic world of feelings and ideas."[162] We should not be surprised to see Sainte-Beuve envisage with equal favor a missionary lyricism and a poetry of solitary withdrawal; there was no fundamental opposition in his mind between the two formulas, any more than there was in the Christian mind between action and contemplation. Criticism was a little too hasty later, imagining this incompatibility and thinking that it had found a sign of contradiction in the necessary duality of aspects possessed by the poetic ministry; but every ministry implies both communication and withdrawal.

Les Consolations, a collection of introspective poetry and spiritual experience, amply affirms the divine investiture of the poet. Celebrating Milton and Shakespeare, Sainte-Beuve takes them to be prophets, with Rubens, Rembrandt, and Mozart alongside of them; it is God who

> A des temps inégaux suscite par endroits
> Quelques rares mortels, grands, plus grands que les rois,
> Avec un sceau brillant sur leurs têtes sublimes,
> Comme il fit au désert les hauts lieux et les cimes,

> [When one least expects it calls into being in various places
> A few rare mortals who are great, greater than kings,
> Marked out with a shining seal on their sublime heads,
> As in a wilderness he creates the uplands and the peaks,]

with this difference, that the night obscures the uplands,

> Tandis que sur ces fronts, hauts comme des sommets,
> Le mystique Soleil ne se couche jamais.
> Ces mortels ont des nuits brillantes et sans voiles;
> Ils comprennent les flots, entendent les étoiles,
> Savent les noms des fleurs, et pour eux l'univers
> N'est qu'une seule idée en symboles divers.

> . . . .

> Tous, ouvriers divins, sous l'oeil qui les contemple,
> Bâtissent du Très-Haut et décorent le temple.[163]

> [But on these brows, as high as summits,
> The mystic Sun never sets.
> These mortals have nights that are brilliant and unveiled;
> They understand the waves, they understand the stars,
> They know the names of the flowers, and for them the universe
> Is but a single idea in different symbols.

> . . . .

> They are all divine workmen, beneath the eye that contemplates them,
> Building and decorating the temple of the Almighty.]

But the priests in charge of this temple are not necessarily retired from the world. The period in which Sainte-Beuve was writing the *Consolations* was that in which the poets of the *Cénacle* were turning toward drama to attain a wider public. Sainte-Beuve saw this orientation clearly, and his approval was such that when Vigny's adaptation of *Othello* was staged he devoted an entire piece to encouraging the poet in his new career; those who were urging him to write pure heavenly poetry were motivated by a secret malevolence:

> . . . De peur qu'un éclatant spectacle
> De l'art régénéré n'achève le miracle,
> Et ne montre en son plein l'astre puissant et doux,
> On veut s'interposer entre la foule et vous.
> On veut vous confiner dans ces régions hautes
> D'où vous êtes venu.

> [. . . For fear that the dazzling spectacle
> Of the renewal of art should complete the miracle
> And reveal to its full extent that strong sweet star,
> They want to come between the crowd and you,
> They want to confine you in those lofty regions
> From which you came.]

But the poet, quitting communion with angels, has entered the fray:

> Afin de mieux remplir le message divin,
> Vous avez dépouillé l'aile du Séraphin,
> Et, laissant pour un temps le paradis des âmes,
> Vous abordez la vie, et le monde, et les drames.
>
> .   .   .   .
>
> Là, des plaisirs trompeurs et mortels au génie;
> Là, le combat douteux et la longue agonie,
> Mais aussi le triomphe immense, universel,
> Et tout un peuple ému qui voit s'ouvrir le Ciel.
> Et le Poète saint, puisant au Jourdain même,
> De poésie et d'art verse à tous le baptême,
> Et partage à la foule, affamée à ses pieds,
> Des pains, comme autrefois, nombreux, multipliés.
> Oh! ne désertez pas cette belle espérance;
> Sans vous laisser dompter, souffrez votre souffrance;
> Les pieds meurtris, noyés d'une sueur de sang,
> Gagnez votre couronne, et, toujours gravissant,
> Surmontez les langueurs dont votre âme est saisie;
> Méritez qu'on vous dise Apôtre en poésie.[164]

> [In order better to fulfill the message divine,
> You have taken off the Seraph's wings,
> And, leaving for a time the paradise of souls,

You confront life, the world, and drama.

. . . .

There, deceptive pleasures are to be found that are fatal to genius;
There, the uncertain combat and the long agony,
But also the immense, universal triumph,
And the emotion of an entire people at the opening of the Heavens.
And the holy Poet, drawing on the Jordan itself,
Baptizes everyone with poetry and art,
Sharing with the famished crowd at his feet
Many a loaf, multiplied like those of old.
Oh! do not abandon this sweet hope;
Suffer your pain without letting yourself be subdued;
With bruised feet drowned in a bloody sweat
Earn your crown, and, climbing ever higher,
Overcome the exhaustion that grips your soul;
Earn the name of Apostle of poetry.]

We see that the religion of Art as it was understood around 1830 does not hold men at a distance; we also see that the sort of engagement to which it leads is not peculiarly political, but concerns the government and edification of minds: the figures of the poet are the Baptist, Christ, the Apostle, and — later in the same poem — the Angel of Purgatory and the member of the Elect who intercedes for others.

These views presuppose Sainte-Beuve's hope for a coming renewal of humanity led by poets. He is the first of the romantic group to have grasped the intimate connections among the poetic ministry, literary reform, and the palingenetic faith; knowledge of Ballanche perhaps helped him in this overall view of the Age:

Il est malade, hélas! il soupire, il espère:
Il sort de servitude, implorant d'autres cieux;
Vers les lieux inconnus que lui marqua son Père,
Il s'avance à pas lents et comme un fils pieux.

Il garde du passé la mémoire fidèle
Et l'emporte au désert; — dès qu'on lui montrera
Un temple où poser l'arche, une enceinte nouvelle,
Tombant la face en terre, il se prosternera![165]

[Alas, he is sick! he sighs, he hopes;
Freed from bondage, he longs for other skies;
Toward unknown places that his Father has marked out for him
He advances slowly, like a pious son.

Of the past he retains a faithful memory
And has taken it with him to the wilderness; — as soon as he is shown
A temple where he can place the ark of the covenant, a new tabernacle,
He will prostrate himself, falling with his face in the dirt!]

What distinguishes Sainte-Beuve even more is, in the midst of so much fervor and poetic élan for the future of the human race, a certain note of desolation, a doubt, what may be called a pleasure in humility, inherent in a personality that is well known to us, but that, when seen in the context of the poetic generations of the nineteenth century, anticipates the themes of future disenchantment. The spiritualism of *Joseph Delorme* and of *Les Consolations* is haunted by an obsession with failure and impotence when faced with the inaccessibility of the ideal; the voice of the infinite is heard in vain:

Parle, que nous veux-tu, voix puissante et bizarre?

. . . .

Cette onde dans sa source est comme du bitume
Elle brûle et dévore, et toujours elle écume
    Et bouillonne toujours.[166]

[Speak, what do you want of us, strange and powerful voice?

. . . .

This water at its source is like hot tar,
It burns and devours, and still it froths,
    And still it boils.]

This is already the lament about the gnawing, devouring Ideal, the Ideal as enemy, that we will hear so often in the poets of the two following generations. This theme, summoned to so great a future in the aftermath of romanticism, is however only in a state of annunciation or germination: all around Sainte-Beuve it is hope and faith that are dominant.

Chapter 9
1830 and the Jeune-France

T HE YEAR 1830, which marked the definitive victory of the new society over the old, was nevertheless the date of a great and bitter disappointment. The republicans and the democrats, who had thought they were gloriously attaining their goal during these three days, saw themselves kept from power by the moderate bourgeoisie; and the uncertain aftermath of July quickly became the triumph of the new monarchy and the *juste-milieu*. Whence came new problems for the old liberalism, henceforth divided, as well as the beginning of a long history of conflicts for the now completely established bourgeois society, in which we still find ourselves today. So much for the general state of affairs. What is especially interesting to us is the reaction to this crisis on the part of writers and poets, especially those who on the eve of the July Revolution felt themselves to be the bearers of the values of their time and the heralds of the future. Now we find them, too, worried and disappointed, like the far Left, to which however they do not in general belong. Sainte-Beuve evokes their earlier illusions, describing in 1833 the recent experience of his friends: they thought the rising intellectual movement of recent years was leading to a summit; then "they would complete the last half of the task, they would apply truth and justice, they would rejuvenate the world; the fathers had to die in the wilderness, but they would be the generation that succeeded in reaching the goal." After 1830, however, they saw "a plain that opened again before them, wider than the one before the last hill, and already covered with muck"; the most vulgar rushed to get jobs; meanwhile, "it became clear, to those who had hoped for more, that it would not be this generation . . . that would reach the goal."[1] Romanticism did not recognize the regime of the July Monarchy as the future of whose spirit it had believed itself the herald; the history of romanticism under Louis-Philippe is that of the various responses given to this disappointment. The precursors and leaders of the movement, Lamartine, Hugo, Vigny, Sainte-Beuve, already in positions of responsibility and endowed with considerable spiritual experience, tried to overcome the difficulty: they claimed to define, beyond the present reality and without condemning it absolutely, an ideal horizon, a salvific prolongation that was delayed, but not refused. Even in their moderation, they all celebrate something other than the world of Casimir Périer, Thiers, or Guizot. Their efforts will continue through all the length of the regime. But in the younger generation and beginning in the immediate aftermath of the July Revolution, the conflict is very openly declared: this is when the incompatibility of romanticism and bourgeois values becomes shockingly obvious.

✸ *Youthful Romanticism and the Bourgeoisie*

The youths who had joined the *Cénacle* on the eve of 1830, the artists and poets who made up Hugo's staff in the battle of *Hernani* and in the struggles of the following years, were distinctly younger than their master. Born around 1810,[2] they had been able to know the Restoration as adults only in its final moment, and they had lived this moment while despising the existing state of affairs and burning with a desire for revolution. Given the limited perspective that their age gave them, the disappointment was more brutal for them. Between ideally sovereign Art and actually triumphant Commerce they saw no possible accommodation, and they greeted the advent of the bourgeoisie with anger and despair. Isolated in an extreme position, they nevertheless bear witness to a profound truth: the truth of rebellion, the ascertainment of a divorce and an impotence that June 1848 and December 1851 would confirm, definitively and in a more overpowering way, for the intellectual generation that followed them.

The fact is that the exaltation of Poetry and Art, taken by the *Cénacle* as supreme values, became exacerbated in youth, who began to assert themselves as explicitly antibourgeois at the moment when the bourgeoisie acceded for the first time to the complete domination of society. This fact is well known, and has often been discussed. The hostility to the bourgeoisie of these young artists and poets, strangers for the most part to political action and themselves participating in the bourgeois condition, has often been considered a sort of hypocrisy: it is said that they place the bourgeoisie out of reach, that they immunize it as it were by means of a futile aesthetic opposition, distracting from the real struggle. But if it was their function to serve the established order thus, indirectly, how much more support poets who affirmatively exalted it would have provided! Why were there none of these? The unfortunate ones who attempted this have remained on the mediocre outskirts of literature; all the brilliant writers fulminated against them. Was a high bourgeois literature impossible, then? We must believe so; that is, we must recognize as authentic and deep the divorce of which we are taking note, and that has obstinately persisted for several generations.

The origins of this divorce go rather far back. The glorification of art and of the artist had developed progressively. In the middle of the eighteenth century, the word *artiste* only designated a workman skilled in some delicate technique.[3] From this modest beginning, the meaning of the word grows in dignity to the point of designating those who practice the beaux-arts: already in 1762, "a painter, an architect, are artists" because genius competes with mastery in their professions; in 1798, they are artists because they cultivate the liberal arts.[4] In the meantime, the Revolution had appealed to poets, musicians, painters, and sculptors for its propaganda by calling them artists; in 1803, Saint-Simon, continuing this tradition, addresses them by this name at the same time as savants.[5] The word's elevation of meaning made it a desirable label for a host of various professionals; as early as 1801, artist-actors, artist-dancers, artist-ventriloquists, and artist-poulterers are made fun of;[6] in 1808 it is written: "Stage actors and the vilest jugglers . . . have for some time been taking the title of Artists in Paris";[7] and in 1814: "Today it is used by courtesy to designate the condition of a crowd of people who do not really have any."[8] This title was so widely claimed only because it had become flattering. Its democratization accompanied a contrary semantic evolution: the artist had become a rare and privileged being. Of all those to whom common usage accorded this name, intellectual opinion reserves it to creators of beauty, and to those who are capable of appreciating their creations. Mme de Staël, as early as 1811, speaks of the "artistic spirit" of the ancient Greeks, in which their entire lives were steeped;[9] similarly, in 1839, "[a]rtist is said, in a figurative sense, of a person who, without being an artist, according to the proper acceptation of the word, has a feeling for the arts."[10]

The influence of aesthetics and of the religion of the Beautiful may, of course, be perceived beneath this evolution. The chroniclers of those times duly noted the advent of this religion, before which they are obliged to bow even as they mock it: "The despot of the day," writes one of them, "is the word *artiste*. . . . Art is almost a cult, a new religion, which arrives just in time, when the gods are leaving and the kings, too. Even money, that power of our times, is forced to recognize an opposing force. The bankers want to be artists. . . . It was often said of the good artists of the old days that they had beliefs. . . . But art itself is a belief. The true artist is the priest of this eternal religion."[11] Or again: "From the attic to the mezzanine, from the stable to the porter's lodge, from the concierge to the hall porter, art reigns in every conversation."[12] *Art* had indeed evolved at the same time as *artiste*. At first designating any technique, this word only evoked the techniques of the beautiful by specifying beaux-arts; then, beginning at the end of the eighteenth century, this meaning was conserved in the plural by doing without the adjective.[13] The singular, which has kept up to the present day the old meaning, since we can speak of the art of the mason, and denominate *"homme de l'art"* whoever is competent in a given technique, has nevertheless taken on a higher meaning: that for which it is usually adorned with a capital letter. "Instead of the beaux-arts, all of which we know either by their family names or by their given names, we have Art, the new king that the century has carried in on its shields, governing like a gloomy despot."[14] The arts are henceforth only secondary manifestations of Art. This radiant singular had imposed itself from the earliest days of romanticism. Cousin, among others, uses it in 1818, in a text we have already encountered.[15] Several years before 1830, Art is the *Cénacle*'s banner; Sainte-Beuve in 1828 feels worthy of entering the romantic group only if he pledges allegiance to this flag: "I owe to you," he writes to Hugo, "and it is sweet to me that it should be so, an understanding and feeling for art, because before I was a barbarian."[16]

The divinization of Art inspired many objections. Thus Andrieux, ever an antiromantic, expostulated on the eve of July 1830 in his course at the Collège de France "on this word *Art* that is used so frequently, that is *vociferated* today."[17] The debate has a social aspect, which is more apparent when it bears on the Artist, for here it is a question of a category of men who are being raised to an unwonted eminence. A strong prejudice opposes this, which Hugo himself at first shared: in 1821, he is worried that his fiancée is frequenting an artist who is a painter, and fears that she herself is intending to enter this profession — "incompatible," he says, "with the rank you should hold in society" and that "certainly discredits women, since it discredits men."[18] But the principal source of his prestige is precisely the fact that as soon as this type emerges, the Artist seems to testify against received notions. The young Lamartine writes to his friend Virieu: "Artists above all, my dear friend, artists, that's what I like, people who are not sure whether they'll be dining tomorrow, but who would not exchange their philosophic hovel, brush, or pen for heaps of gold! I tell them about you, I tell them that you are worthy of appreciating them, of enjoying them, of being their emulator, that you are like me, a universal artist, an artist to the soul, an artist by natural bent!"[19]

In a few years, the theme of Art and the Artist became, in the circles of the youthful literature, the object of unlimited enthusiasm. In 1831, romanticism is dated from the day when painting allied itself with poetry.[20] In fact, these two concepts, art and poetry, are equivalent; the two words have equal force. Balzac and Vigny say as much when the first declares that people have thought to "organize all works, paintings, statues, books, buildings, under the single banner of Art," the second that "the name of poet applies to any artist whose works are poetic."[21] Scandalized contemporaries tell us of the habit that then became established of saying about morally or humanly horrible things like disease, parricide, or the guillotine: "There is poetry in that."[22] This is a proof that poetry shared art's metaphysical privilege of being above morality and its ability to scandalize. But between this aesthetic religion and society as it actually existed a sign of contradiction was emerging. The fact must be recognized, and it cannot be better described than by saying that relations between the spiritual powers born of the bourgeois revolution and the bourgeoisie were strained from the beginning.

In the old society of nobles and clerics, it was natural to hold the bourgeois in low esteem. The literature "of Sensibility" of the eighteenth century rehabilitated its virtues up to a certain point, by means of a generous, philanthropic transfiguration of a kind of person till then held to be mediocre. But the Academy's dictionary continues throughout the entire length of the century to note the pejorative nuance that attaches to this word.[23] Even in 1835, at the time of the bourgeois triumph, the sixth edition of this dictionary keeps the entry for *bourgeois* unchanged, apart from some formal changes, and adds only one new acceptation: that of *bourgeois* opposed to *militaire*, in which a new layer of scorn can be felt handed down by the soldiers of the Empire. Better still, the eighth edition, published in 1932, notes, as it reproduces the earlier editions, the scorn of artists and bold young people for "bourgeois ideas" and "bourgeois tastes." Ill-fated among the ruling classes of history, who have generally been able to make their name stand for the highest values,[24] the bourgeoisie has not been able to achieve for itself a similar privilege. This is so much the case that at a certain level of wealth it denies its own name in order to appear to be something else. A little newspaper writes during Guizot's reign: "It is not our lords the bankers, who only proceed by millions, who will ever consent to resign themselves to the paltry denomination of bourgeois. Artists and writers consider this title as the expression of the most vulgar thing there is. At the very most there are only the eternal grocers, backed up by all the shopkeepers and a few courtiers of the civic court, who would still be able to condescend to allow themselves to be saddled with this label."[25] Is this phenomenon peculiar to France? To this degree, probably so. An English writer of the time is convinced that the bourgeoisie is the antipode of French character — that is, of the values traditionally esteemed in France: "What does the history of France show us? The reign of the court, the reign of the *philosophes*, rabble, army, priests and poor nobles; a revolution effected by the lower classes, soldiers, and journalists. Is there in any of these eras the seed of a government of the bourgeoisie?"; whence the conclusion: "a government of shopkeepers, which is the personification of the feelings, wishes, and prejudices of commerce, cannot be popular in France."[26] These are naive remarks, for they do not take enough into account the victorious influence of the bourgeoisie in French society, and of the changes that would thereby result in the character and the ideas of the nation. It is nonetheless true that all these changes would never go so far as to render the bourgeoisie prestigious in the eyes of thinking people, nor, consequently, in public opinion in general. This fact is well worth emphasizing, but cannot be surprising to one who thinks of the difficulty, rooted it would seem in humanity itself, of idealizing money, and of the particularly strong impress that an unproductive, glorious aristocracy had left on the French mind. The bourgeoisie, of course, rebelled against such a situation; but what could it offer to counter the prestige of the new spiritual power that was taking shape outside of and against it? The bourgeois literature that had already flourished in the Restoration—light comedies, moralizing drama, and liberal poetry—remained on a lower floor of literature; nothing changed in this regard after July 1830. Dramatic censorship came down hard on romanticism; the bourgeoisie fulminated, denouncing the new literature no longer as extravagant or strange but as antisocial and destructive of the moral order.[27] All to no good: the spirit, obviously, was blowing in a different direction. The bourgeoisie seemed to produce its own caricature as soon as it expressed itself. There was no shortage of caricaturists, moreover: from the eve of 1830 on, they were the artistic army's tireless light infantry, deployed on the widest front vis-à-vis the public.[28]

✣ The "*Jeune-France*," *or* Petit Cénacle

In the years that immediately followed the July Revolution, there emerged a new romantic group, younger and more aggressive than its forerunners. Already at the end of 1829, Hugo's *cénacle* seemed to recede into the past. Sainte-Beuve says so, and to Hugo himself: "What has happened to those friends all the same age, those brothers in poetry, who grew up together, united, not yet well-known, who all seemed destined for glory?"[29] In 1833 he composes the funeral oration of the *Cénacle*:

> Et maintenant, un soir, si le hasard rassemble
> Quelques amis encor du groupe dispersé,
> Qui donc reconnaîtrait ce que de loin il semble
>   Sur la foi du passé?[30]

> [And if now, of an evening, chance gathers together
> A few friends from the scattered group,
> Who could recognize what testimonies from long ago
>   Made it out to be?]

Around the same time he hailed the new youthful group in his bittersweet style:

> Two or three years ago, a group of young painters, sculptors, and poets was formed. . . . They thought they could pursue on a grander scale the reorgani-

zation of the *cénacle* roughed out by their elders in 1829; but like all imitators, they fell into the most serious difficulties. The result among some of them has been a precocious self-satisfaction, a scorn of the larger public, strange, mannered forms that are not understood outside the circle, a sort of Masonic jargon that often interferes with their thinking. We have too high a regard for the hearts and minds of these young artists not to speak with them frankly.[31]

Gautier later described the group to which he himself had belonged; he calls it the "little *cénacle*" and informs us about its meetings and its members: Nerval, O'Neddy (really named Dondy), Borel, McKeat (that is, Maquet), Bouchardy, Gautier himself; the last two were respectively an engraver and a painter as well as writers; in the way of pure artists, Gautier names Célestin Nanteuil, Napoléon Tom (Thomas) and the statuary sculptor Jehan Du Seigneur, in whose home they met.[32] Nerval, too, speaks of this "*petit cénacle*," which seems to have been formed in 1830.[33] Gautier gives many picturesque details concerning the members of the group, whose "program" he celebrates: lyricism, passion, unrestrained intellectual whimsy, scorn for ordinary taste and proprieties, hatred of the "unholy vulgar," of "what mustachioed long-haired art students call shopkeepers, whether Philistine or bourgeois," the cult of love and art that it is imperative to "sanctify and deify . . . like a second creator."[34] The "*petit cénacle*" was thus named in deference to the great one that had preceded it and whose recent memory it venerated. Its members also accepted being called the Jeune-France,[35] although this name was not of their own invention, apparently, but was applied to them by *Le Figaro*.[36] However, the name *Bousingo* or *Bousingot* (as a collective singular or in the plural form, and sometimes written with a *z*), which criticism often uses in our day to evoke them, does not seem ever to have designated them as a literary group.[37] A *bousingot* was a republican with extreme opinions and a provocative air; the *petit cénacle* can only be considered *bousingot* insofar as it was persuaded by revolutionary political ideas; and to this extent it shared the label *bousingot* with a much larger, extraliterary part of the youth of the day.

The sway of the republicanism of the 1830s over the *petit cénacle* can be variously evaluated; but in any case the deepest concern of its members was not politics; it is not politics that was indelibly engraved on the memories of the Jeune-France. In the Second Empire, when, old or getting old, they remembered their early days, they evoked a common worship of Art, a fervor unmatched since, a state of holy fury against the bourgeois and the vulgarity of life. It is thus that the *petit cénacle* marked a new season in the life of romanticism. This season, like its predecessors, remained unique in the memory of those who lived through it; 1830, like 1827 and 1824, was a *moment*, in the strong sense of the word: an experience lived through briefly, with intensity, to then become — forever — a lost paradise. This is what Gautier tells us as he nears the age of fifty:

> Twenty-seven years already separate the present day from 1830. The memory has the freshness of a memory from yesterday: the impression of enchantment still survives. From the land of exile where we pursue our way, earning glory by the sweat of our brow, through brambles, stones, and roads bristling with snares, we turn our eyes longingly back toward the lost paradise. . . . To be young and intelligent, to feel mutual affection, to understand and commune under the aegis of art — a more beautiful way of living cannot be conceived and all those who practiced this have kept a sense of bedazzlement that does not diminish. . . . See how an allusion to this congenial past in a newspaper article can tickle the good, brave, sensitive Bouchardy, see how he remembers everything![38]

Gautier had just published — this was in 1857 — a critical article on *Le Secret des cavaliers* by Bouchardy (whose specialty had become melodrama), and his old friend had written him in thanks the sort of letter that only a member of the unforgettable "camaraderie" could send. "Camaraderie" is in fact the name by which the members of the group generally designated it, in a proud reprise of a word pejoratively applied by Latouche to Hugo's *cénacle*. The use of this word by Borel, Nerval, Bouchardy, and Du Seigneur reflects the desire to set the little republic of Poetry and Art apart from general society. The camaraderie is like a new chivalry; it certainly meant more than a bond of sympathy; one feels in it a sort of echo of the "association" that was so celebrated in this time of religious and human searching. If romanticism in its essence is an effort to found a new credo upon art and poetry, we should not be surprised that the fraternity of the adepts should have played so important a role. The romantic *cénacles* were sufficiently mocked from this point of view; but for those involved it is no joke: "Holy, beautiful union, my dear Théo," writes Bouchardy to Gautier. "We formed a family in which no one came last and no one came first. While the Fourierists formed phalansteries and Saint-Simonians formed new social contracts and democrats formed plans, we were deaf to all this humming activity of the time and heard only the whisper of art that was in labor with the birth throes of progress."[39] From time to time during the course of the century, the spark rekindles when two comrades meet. Gautier, at a banquet where several of them find themselves together, already almost sixty years of age, meets O'Neddy, who, he says, "emerged from the catacombs of the mysterious life where he had disappeared," and asks him: "When's your next book of poems?" O'Neddy, recounts Gautier, "looked at us with his blue eyes, wild and disconcerted, and answered us with a sigh: "Oh! when the bourgeois are all gone."[40]

There is in this entire group, along with exacerbation and defiance, a discouraging feeling of impossibility, of high ambition aborted or reduced to solitude: a seed that we have seen appear first in the young Nodier — one that will develop at the heart even of the most prestigious literary achievements of the properly postromantic generation, that of Baudelaire and Flaubert. Poetry and art become a curse, more or less thoroughgoing, at the same time as a vocation. For the poets of the *petit cénacle*, failure was often a personal reality: Gautier, the one among them who "succeeded" the most, was great only in the high poetry of his youth, his later life being consumed in crushing journalistic chores of which almost nothing has really endured. Nerval, for all his genius, to the end was held to be and believed himself to be a sort of minor writer. What can we say of the others? Gautier, imaginatively reviving "the brave ones of 1830" in a Castle of Memory, cannot forget the despairing note that marks, at bottom, all these destinies:

> Celui-ci me conte ses rêves,
> Hélas! jamais réalisés,
> Icare tombé sur les grèves
> Où gisent les essors brisés.[41]

> [This one tells me his dreams,
> Alas! never realized,
> Icarus fallen on the shore
> Where all broken flights lie.]

We cannot doubt that the brief existence of the *petit cénacle* marked a culminating moment — a supreme exaltation and sense of failure — of the romantic revolution. At the moment when the victory of July 1830 unexpectedly but unequivocally inaugurates a society quite contrary to the dreams of its poets, these dreams become frenzied; a natural movement causes romanticism to affirm its essential nature more than ever in frustration. If the attitude of those whom we call the little romantics "betrays an attempt to conquer, a will to transcend the status of artist and man,"[42] if they embody "an experience and not an aesthetic" and if we can evoke with regard to them "a sort of existentialist romanticism,"[43] if sometimes they expressed through words of art and poetry an unlimited and imperious commitment of all their being, this is because romanticism, from its beginnings, bore in itself such an ambition. But it is also true that this ambition, becoming self-conscious in adverse circumstances, is tragically formulated in them as a longing for the impossible, a gloriously outsized and scandalous passion, a limitless defiance, a wild rush to disaster. Neither the lyricism of the passions nor the importance accorded to the self are the essence of romanticism, rather, the infinite scope given to desire and the impossibility of humanly satisfying it; and it is the sense of this impossibility, attenuated when the human condition seems susceptible of expansion, that makes itself cruelly felt at a moment like that which followed July 1830: humiliated and ridiculed, the religion of man exalts itself, curses itself, and despairs. It is thus that Byron, the object of preachment for the first French romantics even as he was revered, like a frightening double kept at a distance, now coincides with romantic consciousness itself, by reason of his very virulence and pessimism.[44]

The attitude of the Jeune-France was that of an entire class of youth, of which the *petit cénacle* was the expression as much as the inspiration. Not only did a spirit similar to that of its members exist in many young writers who did not belong to the group, but poems and unpublished confidings of little-known young people have since come to light attesting a wide diffusion after 1830 of Jeune-France themes — the frenzy of passion, the attraction of nothingness, rebellion, hatred of the bourgeois, the religion of art, the divinization of the poet.[45] What occurred during these years was sufficiently deeply motivated to prolong itself: throughout the nineteenth century, and in a newly dazzling way in the twentieth century, after World War I, poetry and revolt were more or less continuously allied: whence the temptation that appeared in the 1920s to describe 1830 in terms of 1925, to the neglect of significant differences. The Jeune-France, who seemed like the ancestors of the surrealists, were returned to honor and treated with a fruitful sympathy; but they were seen in an anachronistic light, as more determined and consistent than they were. It was thought that a name, that of *bousingots*, which was not theirs, had consecrated their existence as a coherent politico-literary group. The ephemeral character of the group — by 1833, we are told, it had ceased to exist[46] — was forgotten. Preconceived formulas borrowed from the language and movements of our century have been applied to the vivid but confused aspirations of the Jeune-France.[47]

No doubt they felt that as writers they were pursuing something other than success alone; rather, their wish was to fling in the teeth of the society that was consolidating itself before their eyes a fervently humane exigency. They wanted the creative spirit to be preeminent, and their wish appeared to them to be hopeless. They did not put much stock in beliefs, and saw the world neither according to the doctrines of militant Revolution nor according to the dogma of Sin. Although now and then a wistful regret for the great communion of Catholicism enters into their love of the Middle Ages, it cannot be said that this is a central theme in their work. It is quite obvious that the pleasure of a powerful set of images, the idea of a life devoted to adventure and legend, an obsession with fantastic and tormented architectures make of their medievalism something quite different from a religious nostalgia. The period of the Middle Ages in the romantic universe is what the time of the patriarchs is in the Christian world: a period that precedes modern norms, a sacred stock of themes and figures endowed with a primordial authority. As for the Jacobinism of these poets, which was inconstant and in any case very atypical, it was from the first the object of contemporary mockery. *Le Figaro*, which notes their republican sympathies, and their romantico-Jacobin cry against "the Carlist Racine,"[48] is convinced that the Jeune-France group expresses love of country "for the sake of strangeness"; that it defends the people "because the people are spontaneous, crude, dramatic, blunt, highly picturesque, bearded";[49] this is to reduce the Jeune-France rebellion to a partiality for certain forms and colors, perhaps without seeing that for the Jeune-France group these tastes and political views have the same source. There is widespread doubt about the possibility of such a synthesis of imagination and action; especially in times in which empirical reality seems to be triumphing, one has to be either a poet or a man of action; they are suspected of really being more one than the other, and their desire for an active poetry and for total renewal is laughed at. The Jeune-France themselves were acutely aware of their weakness; in the history of the poetic ministry, they herald, at the moment of the greatest exaltation, the depression to come. Their special character is in this ambiguity, which later was no longer understood. Asselineau, who during the time of the Parnassian movement undertook to revive their memory, treats them hardly any better than *Le Figaro* did in their own time: "[T]he love of the young heads of the day went all to poetry and art. The July Revolution forced them to think about politics; they remade politics in their image, and wanted to speak romantically about the king and the chambers."[50] "It was a matter of literature rather than of real political conviction."[51] Baudelaire, who calls them *bousingots* and takes their conflict with society seriously, can nevertheless do no more than attribute to them, on this conceptual plane, an "aristocratic hatred" of established society[52] — a benevolent interpretation, since it depicts them so as to resemble Baudelaire himself, but one that disqualifies them as republicans. In Baudelaire's day the fever had abated, and only execration, distance, and scorn were any longer thought of as responses to society's hostility. The burning ambition to transform life that still accompanies the first disenchantment in the aftermath of 1830 is, under the second Bonaparte, a thing of the past.

𝕹 *Pétrus Borel*

Pétrus Borel was, according to Gautier, the "pivotal individuality" of the *petit cénacle*; he was, Gautier tells us, the object of a sort of respectful admiration on the part of the other members of the group;[53] Asselineau, like Baudelaire, makes himself the echo of this tradition, which contradicts O'Neddy: according to him, the group was a republic, in which each member played an influential role.[54] It matters little; Borel was without a doubt the one in whom romanticism and neo-Jacobinism were most closely united, so that if the group is considered from the perspective of this combination of ideas, he was incontestably its principal member. In any case, his reputation is established as the representative type of a certain variant of the romanticism of 1830.[55] The horizon of his work is limited; the poetic act is presented there without any metaphysical character; the ministry of the infinite, the powers of the symbolic imagination, and everything that constitutes the religion of romanticism proper are more or less absent. A sort of devouring pessimism and the rhetoric of a measureless, aggressive despair absorb all his inspiration and exclude from his consciousness the marvels of the new poetic universe. One might think that he was altogether ignorant of them — that in him it is not romanticism that has become republican but political passion that has assumed the language of exaggeration and accursedness. What prevents us from believing this is what fundamentally distinguishes him from the ordinary republican: the idolatry of art, a taste for moral scandal and for death, the dream of a privileged position among men for creative artists.

The great poems of his *Rhapsodies*[56] are the bitter complaint of a man who sees himself frustrated everywhere, a pariah cursing the rich, those who are happy in love, the poets of high society, the well-off of every sort. These are poems of hunger in the most general sense of the word — of a hunger not sublime but virulent. This is not dissatisfaction experienced in the insufficiency of every object, as it had been for at least a century in the delicate experience of elite thinkers and poets; it is felt in privation: a plebeian rage, described as such, that feeds a tireless accusation of society, reveries of tyrannicide, and fine hymns to insurrection.[57] Desire expresses itself in him with voluntary exaggeration and a furious defiance that anticipates failure: it issues in the idea of suicide, a frenetic suicide meant to express the shameful abjection of the world.[58] Such a chain of paroxysms obviously overflows the limits of a political position. Borel certainly makes use of the traditional revolutionary moralism, exerting himself in denouncing vice in power and social iniquity;[59] but the catastrophic orientation of his fancy and the often horrifying character of his heroes themselves, into whom he projects himself, give to his rages a meaning that is something more than moral. At bottom, it is a question of a disdained religion whose priests adopt the metaphysical program of disaster and cursing: life ought to be atrocious and impossible, given the fact that they are not being heeded. If they do not proclaim a punitive God, this is because in their faith God is not in the highest position; they themselves are the wrathful god who sees the world as degraded and curses it. In these conditions, optimism in any area whatever is the chief crime: "Let the impostors come, so I can strangle them! the hypocrites singing of love, *garlanding* it and *poetastering* it, who make it some chubby-cheeked child, puffed up with pleasure, let them come, then, the impostors, so I can strangle them!"[60]

The simplicity that this subversive pessimism takes on in Pétrus Borel springs directly from privation and is what gives him his revolutionary appearance in the social sense of the word. To become Jacobin, romanticism needed this dagger-carrying, Phrygian-bonnet-wearing Diogenes. But these accessories of a member of the Jeune-France group converted to the *bousingots* do not alter his deeper nature. Borel's anger goes further than the social goal: "I am for a republic the way a lynx would be; my republicanism is lycanthropism! If I talk about the republic, it is because this word represents for me the widest independence that society and civilization can allow. I am a republican because I can't be an Indian [*caraïbe*]."[61] And his hatred of society no longer finds a sufficient remedy in the wilderness idealized by Molière's Alceste, Rousseau, or Senancour. Champavert, who once dreamed this rustic dream along with his friend Jean-Louis, now an agricultural laborer, henceforth renounces it: "It is no longer the exhaustion of hard labor that I need, it is nothingness."[62] Pessimistic suicide is certainly not a Jacobin solution; still less the provocative dilettantism with which the preface to the *Rhapsodies*, for example, ends: "Fortunately, to console ourselves for all this, we still have adultery! Maryland tobacco! and *papel espaol por cigaritos.*"[63] Thus it is clear that Pétrus would not have had the prestige among his comrades that Gautier attributes to him if he had been only a republican poet; the source of this prestige lies far from the political struggles of the period: "The presence of Pétrus Borel," writes Gautier, "produced an indefinable impression whose cause we finally discovered. He was not a contemporary; nothing in him made you think of modern man, and he always seemed to come from the distant past, and you would have said that he had left his ancestors only the day before. We never saw that expression on anyone; it was hard to believe that he was French and born in this century. But a Spaniard, an Arab, an Italian of the fifteenth century, certainly."[64] And the language that his friend O'Neddy attributes to Pétrus during a Jeune-France soirée is an ardent defense of the old days as violent, superstitious, and adventurous.[65]

What is certain is that Pétrus Borel, however Robespierrist and *sans-culotte* he wanted to be, professes ideas more specifically romantic than republican on the role of the poet and the artist. Like all his friends, he places the priesthood of poetry and art above everything. He makes the privilege of creative genius consist in enthusiasm and lofty thoughts, in the vision of the ends and not in the handling of the means of art. It is the greatness of humanity that makes the artist; the report that someone saw "Viva el hombre" engraved on a boulder in Spain makes him exclaim: "God! what artists could be made from such hearts!"[66] Some think "that since modern artists, unlike the great masters, live in an age of faith, belief, love, and enthusiasm — far from it, since they live in a time of doubt and scorn — it is inevitable that their works be unable to contain or express more than society itself contains and expresses."[67] This is what the Saint-Simonians said, refusing to romanticism the ability to carry out its mission and wishing to base the mission of the artist on a modern dogmatics. Borel, too, professes the belief that one cannot be an artist without faith, but the principal article of this faith is for him the principle of liberty, which is the soul of romanticism. From 1832 to 1833 he published with Du Seigneur *La Liberté, revue des arts*, whose title well expresses its spirit, and situates Borel and his friends vis-à-vis contemporary neodogmatic and utopian tendencies. It would be impossible to overemphasize this point, for what distinguishes romanticism, in France at least, from so many other attempts to define a modern spiritual power is that even while aspiring to a communion of spirits, it excludes the idea of a church. Borel certainly admits the human mission, and in this sense, the utility of art and its synthetic function: "Art," he writes, "will always be on the decline as long as people insist on not regarding it as an element of society and on denying its mission to express the relationships of all beings, the relationships of the created to the creator, of men to men, of man to the universe. . . . For no one will deny that the artist is a veritable apostle; that is, a man of the crowd, who emerges from the crowd in order to speak to the crowd from which he emerges."[68] Having said that, which excludes formal futility and "empty" art, he repudiates just as forcefully the utilitarianism that submits art to a system of strictly defined ends: "I also humbly beg not to be confused with the *utilitarians*."[69] This position is that of all romanticism: it defines both a commitment and an irreducible spiritual prerogative. The most Jacobin romanticism fits it without any difficulty, rejecting the confused debate in which art for art's sake is opposed to social art; art's essentially free and sovereign irresponsibility and its salvific mission are inseparable, according to romanticism; these are two aspects of a single thought, never contradictory, but one or the other can, according to the occasion, counter the various objections of the vulgar.

❧ *Philothée O'Neddy*

O'Neddy is another representative of the Jeune-France spirit—less violent though in his way just as tragic; endowed with a deeper, more genuine poetic vocation and a thought capable of far-ranging fancy, even in the absence of hope. Poetry, love, the moral renewal of society are in him the object of a single wish, embittered by the certainty of its powerlessness, but fervent to the end. He published only a single volume of verse, *Feu et flamme*, in 1833, then over the course of the years a few poetic fragments, tales, and articles of dramatic criticism,[70] which gained scarcely any notice. But he did not stop writing until 1846, and then, beginning in 1856 (he died in 1875, at the age of sixty-four), resumed writing verses that were published some time after his death.[71] And his correspondence reveals that he was faithful to the end to the republicanism of his youth.[72] His destiny was a sad one; he was lost from sight almost at the same moment that the *cénacle* fell apart, lived through a long, fruitless love affair, eked out a miserable existence among the clerks of the Ministry of Finance, and savored till the end the bitterness of "the disharmony of the real and the ideal."[73] His friend Havet captures him well as he was in his beginning when he writes: "He enrolled in a sort of avant-garde of the future, which was claiming to restore, first, art, remaking it from top to bottom, and then, by means of art, society."[74] "Was claiming" is too strong; we should speak rather of desire, hope, and doubt mixed together. "Faith is alive beneath *idéologie* and utopia," wrote a twentieth-century critic apropos of O'Neddy;[75] we should add that despair is latent beneath the faith. A dream, constantly exalted and constantly disappointed, of human synthesis under the sign of poetry makes O'Neddy a representative type of the Jeune-France spirit, different, but just as essential, as that of Pétrus.

The foreword to *Feu et flamme* clearly announces the moral renewal both of literature and of society. "The artistic and moral Babel that the elite intellects of our age have undertaken to construct" is not merely a *cénacle*; it is the human community transfigured by poetry. Addressing himself to the "strong, muscular workmen" of this Babel—that is, to the elders of the great *cénacle*—whom he asks to smile upon his collaboration, he sketches a program much more ambitious and radical than theirs: "Like you, I scorn utterly from the height of my soul the social order and above all the political order that is its excrement; like you, I mock reactionaries and the Academy; like you, I stand incredulous and unmoved before the magniloquence and finery of the religions of the earth; like you, I feel pious transports only for Poetry, that twin sister of God, who gives to the physical world harmony, light, and sweet scents; to the moral world love, intelligence, and will!" He expressly assigns as a mission to the new literature "a

metaphysical crusade against society." Now that this literature "has completed
all its fine reforms of the apparel of *art*, it is devoting itself exclusively to the ruin
of what it calls the *social lie*." How does one go from art to revolution? Beyond
the slightest doubt, by virtue of the sovereign vocation of poetry, which extends
well beyond its visible frontiers; in the new Babel, Poetry "can freely deploy its
two natures: its human nature, which is *art* — its divine nature, which is *passion*."[76] By proclaiming the sacred principle that inspires the agitations of romanticism, these last words illuminate O'Neddy's revolutionary logic: a principle as divine as that with which he feels animated could not limit its influence; it
makes the poet break through the limits of art: it contains *in potentia*, like a
divine revelation, a social order and a body of laws,

> . . . l'immense ambition
> D'unir à l'action la contemplation[77]

> [. . . the immense ambition
> Of uniting contemplation and action]

— this injunction to totality heard by the poet does not enjoin him to embrace
any particular program; if he suggests a profound moral renewal of society,
this is due to a sort of absolute poetic theocratism. The hostility toward the
ruling bourgeoisie creates a union with the political far Left, which is both an
understanding and a misunderstanding. But at bottom the revolutionary Jeune-
France group, in its deep motivations, is closer to any of the romantic elders,
however moderate in politics, than to the neo-Jacobins with whom it fraternizes. Its revolution is the one whose idea was born with romanticism itself: the
revolution that makes of poetry the heir of religion and the source of all value.
"We dreamed the dream of Art, it is true," writes O'Neddy thirty years later. "It
seemed to us that one day religion would in its conditions of *externality* have to
be replaced by *Aesthetics*. But we also wanted something else. The preface to *Feu
et flamme* expresses wishes for a social revolution."[78] This is because the social
revolution under the sign of art is the only way for art to affirm itself as a value
and a universal power; aesthetics would otherwise be nothing but a special
discipline, instead of being a faith and an imperative.[79] A ministry of the Poet is
obviously implied in the sanctification of Poetry:

> Longtemps à deux genoux le populaire effroi
> A dit: laissons passer la justice du roi.
> Ensuite on a crié, l'on crie encore: Place!
> La justice du peuple et de la raison passe.
> Est-ce qu'épris enfin d'un plus sublime amour,
> L'homme régénéré ne crîra pas un jour:

Devant l'Art-Dieu que tout pouvoir s'anéantisse.
Le poète s'en vient; place pour sa justice?[80]

[For a long time a frightened people fell on its knees,
Saying: make way for the king's justice.
Later they cried, and they are crying still: Make way
For the justice of the people and of reason!
Will it not be that, enamored of a love more sublime,
Regenerate man will one day cry:
Every power must be as nothing before the god Art.
The poet is coming; make way for his justice?]

Such verses appeared, like a sort of chimera, in the reign of the bourgeois *"juste-milieu."* We have seen how tenacious was O'Neddy's hatred of the bourgeois. In 1833 he swore with his friends to "skewer the stomachs of the calculators";[81] in 1862, commenting on Lincoln's politics, he hopes to see him assume an outright dictatorship, like the Convention, and for similar ends; and why, he asks, "should I in my nothingness take so strong an interest in those affairs? You old idiot, what does that get you, and what can you do about it?" There is an answer: "Dear bourgeois! may I see you *bled white* before I die!"[82] This hatred, properly considered, is that which the spiritual opposes to the temporal: an eternally rancorous pretension sharpened by the special baseness that is attributed to the new kings of the world, who are more inclined than their predecessors to believe that material prosperity fully satisfies the needs of man. To the revolutionaries' way of feeling, 1830 was the story of a fraudulent inheritance: the bourgeoisie had cheated the people out of the succession to the prerogatives of the former ruling classes, and the underhanded elevation of Philippe d'Orléans to the throne of France was the symbol of this fraud. But for our poets, what mattered was a different fraudulent inheritance, less visible but more loftily outrageous: the class of poets, artists, and inspired thinkers, which had believed itself the natural heir of the old prerogatives as well as the depository of the hopes of the human race, saw itself condemned to uselessness by triumphant, self-satisfied Commerce.

This disappointment coincides with, but should be distinguished from, the disappointment that affects the political far Left. It is enough to read the "Pandémonium" that opens O'Neddy's collection of poems to appreciate how little the portrait of a Jeune-France soirée resembles a meeting of militants or republican conspirators. O'Neddy was conscious of the difference — more than Borel, who pretended to be unaware of it. Although a republican (a Girondist, he says),[83] he sometimes seems to reproach political republicanism with its narrowness of outlook and to oppose it to the need for a more thorough recasting of society: "Every day," he writes, "many young people with patriotic convictions come to perceive that if the political state of affairs has the nature of Caliban, the social state of affairs, which is the mother of politics, is to blame; they then abandon republican fanaticism, and rush to enroll in the squadrons of our Babel."[84] The Jeune-France Babel offers, then, its own synthesis — one that is wider than ordinary republican ideology. Later, O'Neddy tried to give an idea of it by imagining a modern Chivalry, in which would be united the spirit of romanticism and the ideal of the Republic.[85] But the fusion between the Revolution of the poets and that of the politically minded was never accomplished. Surrealism attempted it in our time with more insistence than in 1830, but without more success. In both cases, there is a wish for a thorough overhaul of society, but based on principles so different as to make disagreement inevitable. Both lineages, however, are persistent in bourgeois society, which defends itself against both as much as it can.

We have just considered in the case of O'Neddy the positive, triumphal aspects of the Jeune-France ambition. But to stop there would leave a false impression. For even in its enthusiasm this ambition is conscious of the obstacles that reality presents to it; its feeling of failure and exile is just as present and just as fundamental as its affirmation of its conquest. Total romanticism gives all too many signs of its secret weakness. The foreword to *Feu et flamme*, so triumphal, ends with an odd recantation: "It would be a mistake," writes the author, "to take these outbursts literally, since for the most part they are only enthusiastic whims. It would be a mistake to consider them to be the absolute expression of my true feelings."[86] Even short of this disavowal, which validates the mockery of the bourgeois, the feeling of the impossible surfaces in midst of the enthusiasm itself: it is thus that, by a paradox that is merely apparent, a nihilist temptation accompanies the most outlandish hopes:

> Les plus divins élans de morale énergie,
> Les extases de gloire et d'immortalité,
> Les voeux pour la patrie et pour la liberté,
> Se noyaient, s'abîmaient dans le rire et le spasme
> D'un scepticisme nu, tout lépré de sarcasme.[87]

> [The most divine transports of moral energy,
> The ecstasies of glory and immortality,
> The hopes for country and for freedom
> Drowned and sunk in the convulsive laughter
> Of naked skepticism, all crusted over with sarcasm.]

This note is clearly that of 1830: conflict, furor, aggressive despair. But a more bitter sentiment appears in the intervals of this fever. The young French Byrons have a cruelly depressing idea of their condition; they know that they are inferior to the ideal type they are dreaming of; as early as 1833, poor O'Neddy sees himself in a dream banned from the three temples of his ideal: Liberty, Glory, and Love reject him.[88] And already in a piece dated 1829 (he was eighteen years old) he gave to his enthusiasm a lugubrious conclusion:

> Que faire, dites-moi, de ce culte funeste
> Pour tout ce qui dans l'homme est grand, noble, céleste,
> De ces fougues d'amour, de ces élans d'orgueil,
> De ces bouillonnements, de cet intime orage,
> Qui, de mes nerfs brûlés dévorant le courage,
> Me font déjà rêver le repos du cercueil?

> [What should I do, tell me, with this sinister cult
> Of everything in man that is great, noble, celestial,
> With these transports of love, these proud enthusiasms,
> These exaltations, this inner storm,
> Which, as they devour the courage of my frazzled nerves,
> Make me dream already of a restful coffin?]

More moderately, he foresaw his own poverty:

> Adieu l'enthousiasme. — En des travaux serviles
> On t'ensevelira comme en un froid linceul.[89]

> [Adieu enthusiasm. — In servile labors
> You will be buried, as if in a cold winding sheet.]

A more and more mournful depression tends to replace his old exaltations during the course of the lonely poetic career that followed the publication of *Feu et flamme*. The "Epilogue général" with which O'Neddy ended in 1863 his *Mistica Biblion*, a collection of poems composed between 1834 and 1846, depicts the Poet by way of the grating symbol of the "legless cripple":[90] powerless, ashamed of himself, and prideful, pathetically clinging to the imagined victory of the "true knights" of his dream. Poetic bitterness has never gone so far in its choice of images: the legless cripple already goes farther than the clown or the rope-dancer of the postromantics and symbolists. To the poem is added a disconsolate note: "August 1863. Exactly thirty years, alas! after the printing of *Feu et flamme*, whose preface bears the date 10 August 1833." O'Neddy was very naturally conscious, like all the poets of the time, of the relation between the dramas of thought and those of society. In a poem in which he recapitulates his career, he mingles grief for poetry and love with the defeats of the republican party; the disappointment of the 1830s and the disaster of 1848 (a return of unlimited hope and total collapse) are, in this recollection of his life, episodes that affect the Poet as such, at the same time that they affect France.[91]

In a case like this one, we clearly glimpse how the Jeune-France, despite their enthusiastic ardor, were able to carry the seed, a generation early, of postromantic poetry's pessimism. Moreover, Philothée's posthumous work allows us to see already in the 1830s and 1840s the forms that this pessimism would take, as well as, for example, the transformation of despair into scorn, and anger into impassivity. Thus an 1837 poem, typically Jeune-France in the violent oscillation it shows between fervor and profound apathy, concludes in Parnassian style:

> Frères, nous avons tort! Frères, il n'est pas chaste
> De laisser voir ainsi notre âme en nudité.
>
> . . . .
>
> Toujours, autour de vous, Muses de notre caste,
> Du bourgeois contempteur rôde l'hostilité.
>
> . . . .
>
> Quel que soit notre mal, il faut savoir se taire.[92]

> [Brothers, we are wrong! Brothers, it is not modest
> To let our souls be seen naked like this.
>
> . . . .
>
> Muses of our caste, the hostility
> Of the contemptuous bourgeois is always prowling around you.
>
> . . . .
>
> Whatever you are suffering, you must be able to keep silent.]

The silence is a prestigious one, being the silence of a priesthood that withdraws into itself without ever doubting its own metaphysical qualifications: the Poet, excluded from the communication of men, is sure that he has the key to the universe:

> Les rêveurs qu'amour illumine
> Ne contemplent jamais en vain.
> Leur esprit volontiers devine
> Les choses d'essence divine
> Parce que lui-même est divin.[93]

> [Dreamers whom love illuminates
> Never contemplate in vain.
> Their willing spirits divine

Things in their essence divine
Because they themselves are divine.]

The *poètes maudits* of the period after 1848, whom O'Neddy anticipates, dispossessed of the active ministry dreamed of by their elders, will not renounce this foundational claim of their ministry. On the contrary, they will take refuge in their symbolic intuition into the secret meaning of things, cultivating this as their prerogative, their unalterable raison d'être and, even if they be misunderstood, their claim to preeminence among men.

Gérard de Nerval

Nerval was never Jeune-France in the same sense that Borel or O'Neddy were; at least his youthful writings do not have the convulsive character that marks those of his friends. He nevertheless belongs to the same group,[94] and like them he is a witness to a moment of crisis in young, post-1830 romanticism. In his very first beginnings, he was far indeed from the new literature. At the age of eighteen, and in the years that followed, he is a liberal poet, in the sense of Béranger or Delavigne, the author of patriotic Napoleonic odes and satires against Villèle and the Jesuits.[95] He is then at the antipodes of the revolution in poetry, to which he would not really rally before 1829. These youthful poems by Nerval are so far from what we like today that the good recent editions of his works think they can omit them. He himself disowned them: "Gérard de Nerval," O'Neddy tells us, "had during the Restoration published national and Napoleonic poems that he did not want read, being the first to declare them trite."[96] He continued, however, to write them in 1830 and 1831 on the occasion of the July events and their aftermath: "Le Peuple" (an ode), "Les Doctrinaires" (a virulent poem), "En avant, marche!" (an exhortation to Europe, still enthusiastic and already disillusioned).[97] These pieces, superior in their style to those that had preceded them, continue their spirit. But romanticism, meanwhile, by changing its politics, had willingly annexed to itself the themes and rhetoric of liberal poetry. After July 1830, Nerval's political poems coincide with those of Hugo.

This romanticism of the three revolutionary days rarely had an extremist, or, as was said, *bousingot* character; nor does it have this character to any great degree in Nerval, who merely adjusts his former Napoleonic enthusiasm in favor of liberty and the people. Did he take part in the combats of July? The poem "Les Doctrinaires" implies this: its "us" designating the combatants should leave no room for doubt. A recently rediscovered fragment tells how "the squad at the place Saint-Michel surrendered to us," but shows us a Gérard who is as much a stroller as a combatant, busy with various visits.[98] Another fragment, published in 1841, pertaining to a stay by Nerval in the prison of Sainte-Pélagie, attributes this imprisonment to a misunderstanding and represents Nerval and his friends as dilettantes, emulators of those who supped together during the Regency and of the epicureans of Alexandria, far removed from any political passion.[99] The indices that we possess do not allow us to imagine a militant Gérard around 1830. Nor does politics appear to have preoccupied him during all the remaining years of his life. He once protested against an article that represented him as entirely indifferent in this domain: "I am not a skeptic," he writes, "concerning myself neither with politics nor socialism"; and he implies that he was a *bousingot*.[100] But Nerval's socialism, if it existed, is like his illuminism: conviction has less to do with it than the spirit of illusion and poetry: it can go hand in hand with a very weak inclination to action. Pétrus Borel reproduced, as an epigraph to the piece entitled *Champavert*,[101] a few verses signed "Gérard," taken from a poem that had appeared in 1831 above the signature "M. Personne,"[102] with the title "Poème extra-romantique, profession de foi."[103] This poem is a skeptical proclamation, whose author declares that he would prefer any fate whatsoever

> que de m'entendre appeler Philippiste,
> Républicain, Carliste, Henriquiste, — Chrétien,
> Païen, Mahométan ou Saint-Simonien,
> Blanc ou noir, tricolore, ou gris, ou vert, ou rose;
> Enfin quoi que ce soit qui croie à quelque chose.

> [rather than hear myself called Philippist,
> Republican, Carlist, Henriquiste — Christian,
> Pagan, Mohammedan, or Saint-Simonian,
> White or black, tricolor, or gray, or green, or pink;
> In fact, anything at all that believes in something.]

But there is skepticism and there is skepticism; this skepticism is impassioned, and it is the son of anger: society is nothing but a swamp, fetid on the surface,[104] whose purer depths rarely bubble up; when the crisis is over, the swamp reconstitutes itself and reigns once again. It is the very recent experience of this sad law that has killed the poet's faith, obliging him to believe in nothing, perhaps, but himself:

> C'est bien triste! et, sans doute,
> En venir à ce point est chose qui me coûte;
> J'ai fait ce que j'ai pu, pour qu'errant au hasard
> Mon âme autour de moi s'attachât quelque part,
> Mais comme la colombe hors de l'arche envoyée,

Elle m'est revenue à chaque fois mouillée,
Traînant l'aile, sentant ses forces s'épuiser,
Et n'ayant pu trouver au monde où se poser!

    [It is very sad! and, no doubt,
To come to this takes its toll on me;
I have done what I could to try to enable
My wandering soul to settle somewhere,
But like the dove sent forth from the ark,
It always came back to me drenched,
Dragging its wings, feeling its strength giving out,
Unable to find anywhere in the world to land!]

These lines give us a clear glimpse of the mechanism of withdrawal that the encounter of the poetic ministry and bourgeois society can trigger. They allow us to gauge the angry bitterness burning beneath the affected disdain. They show us a poetry of solitude being born of a historic disappointment. They situate the debate between the poet and society elsewhere than in politics proper: whereas any disappointed political project tends to modify itself and persevere by adapting to circumstances, what we see here is radical discord between, on the one hand, the spiritual and intellectual realm (and those who think they embody it), and, on the other hand, social reality. Every spiritual or intellectual demand is apt to feel the effects of such discord. This falling-out between the spiritual and intellectual realm and the world as it exists is the distinctive character of the Jeune-France, much more than the adhesion of some of them to the political revolution. And it is in Nerval, more than in any of his friends, that this characteristic appears.

Nerval did not distinguish himself by a revolutionary attitude in literature any more than he did in politics. As a critic, he develops the discoveries of the 1827 *Cénacle*. His contribution to romantic literary criticism, a little late, it is true, but outstanding in its finesse and lucidity, deserves to be better known, especially the remarkable introduction that he wrote for his anthology of poets of the sixteenth century.[105] But when he argues for the reestablishment of a national continuity in literature, for a reconnecting of the nineteenth century with the Middle Ages and the Pléiade, passing over the historical excrescence of classicism, he continues Sainte-Beuve, Nodier, and Hugo, and he goes no further than they do. We can say the same for his introduction to the anthology of German poets, in February of the same year.[106] It is quite clear that it is not through the boldness of his poetics or his style that Nerval is situated at this time in the avant-garde of romanticism, but by the extreme distance that he instinctively places between the life of the poet and the real. He had not yet become aware of this essential aspect of his nature, but he does not leave us unaware of it: "What generous soul has not experienced something of this human spiritual state, constantly aspiring to divine revelations, straining as it were at the length of its chain, until the moment when cold reality comes to disenchant the audacity of its illusions or hopes."[107] Here then is the experience of the impossible placed at the heart of the spirit, in him as in his friends. But his peculiar tone is not that of rage, but rather a half-silent introversion marked by nostalgia and solitude. His poetry of these years is a poetry of lost or unattained happiness, which he modulates with a fading voice, evoking a woman who has died, or who is absent, or who is imaginary.[108] An 1831 text, which he gave as a translation from Jean-Paul Richter and is of his own creation, sees no other remedy for the departure of the beloved than to "surround his soul with a grave, to cut off the world all around, and, like the fallen archangel, to cover his eyes with his wings."[109] Already at this time grieving and dreaming are but a single thing for Nerval. The exaltation of the imaginary world is his response to disappointment. Paradoxically, but quite naturally, the distance placed between the imaginary and the real engenders the confusion of one with the other: the mind avenges itself on reality, which banishes it by invading its creations. Nerval learned this from Hoffmann, whose enthusiastic Traveler "is so far from keeping his inner life visibly apart from his outward life that it would be difficult to indicate precisely the limits of each."[110] Gérard makes this characteristic his own; like one of his characters, "he peopled the earth with his visions; fusing himself with them, he ends by no longer distinguishing the possible from the impossible, the true from the false."[111]

What sets Nerval's imagination apart from that which ordinarily takes flight in the Jeune-France genre is that in him it is essentially nostalgia, not defiance or tumult. Whether it expresses itself in terms of personal experience, producing frustration and regret, or of metaphysical religion, as a desire for an inaccessible ideal, it opens a new path that will be taken by many of the wounded romantics of the subsequent generations. In this path, the ministry of poetry is no longer felt as a solitary pact with the divine, a privilege of the initiated. Literature loses nothing of its sacred character or of its potential powers: "Literary people were never graver than at this time. . . . They were all lined up, as if by magnetism, so they could have dreams of the future."[112] While waiting for this hypothetical future, the poet prefers to practice his ministry in that realm of obscure, marvelous enthusiasm that is his province alone, where he continues his ministry in a time of misfortune.[113] Twenty years later, Nerval remembered in the same terms what 1830 had been for him and his friends: "We were living then in a strange period . . . ; it was a mixture of activity, hesitation, and laziness, of brilliant utopias, of philosophic or religious aspirations, of vague enthusiasms, mixed with certain instincts for rebirth — something like the era of Peregrinus and Apuleius." But disgust at the aftermath of July 1830 and at the "greedy scramble" for posts and honors that had followed the return of order discouraged the Jeune-France: "The only remaining place of refuge for us was the poets' ivory tower, where we climbed ever higher in order to isolate ourselves from the crowd. Our masters guided us to these lofty elevations, where we breathed at last the pure air of lonely places, drank oblivion in the golden cup of legends, and were drunk with poetry and love."[114]

✳ *Théophile Gautier*

Of all the Jeune-France, Gautier is by universal consent the one who most influenced the postromantic generation, and even the following one as well. Of the group, he is the only one who, for the rest of the century at least — beyond that, values are no longer the same — was regarded as a master. This is because his work, more clearly than any other, fixed the lines of a new poetic philosophy, in response to shock and disillusion. It is in the years of crisis that his work should be considered, in the dramatic period in which the dismay of 1830 is struggling with an aesthetic and a wisdom that claim to go beyond it. It is in light of this conflict that we must understand Gautier's work and even his person. It ends in results some of which, linked to the title and contents of his late *Emaux et camées*, have falsified the idea that we have today of this writer, who passes in the eyes of most for a goldsmith of rhyme, a hollow epigone of romanticism, and the deplorable apologist of form without content. The truth is that he, too, in his way, went to the limit of the experiment according to which Art, taken to be a supreme value, discovers that it has been divested of its former function and is alone in a hostile universe. Since rage cannot be a definitive attitude, he wanted to color it with disdain, to invest the poet-priest with an irresponsibility that is above insults. We must not forget that this attitude, of superiority against a background of bitterness, whose formula he was the first to perfect, was one that was handed on to all of French poetry for a half-century, and that, among his most important successors, in Baudelaire, in Mallarmé, it was the very foundation of the poetic temperament. Not that such a situation for poetry was not highly inconvenient: haughty scorn risks sounding a false note among beings as destitute as poets, who are for the most part materially restricted to a social status and tasks that are in fact mediocre, and whose spiritual preeminence itself is not always taken seriously. Poetry is public speech, and the public is not listening to him. What is more, poets claimed to make of poetry the Word—the Supreme Message and the Guide of the human race; and there is no question of renouncing this promotion. Whence the deep-rootedness of the difficulty: poetry would not be a state of solitude if it did not dream of being a form of instruction and an immense communion. This ambition inevitably adopts a new language when faced with failure. Gautier is at the birth of a long poetic ascesis, which will resolutely attempt to transmute a devastating feeling of powerlessness into an increase of grandeur. Others succeeded at this better than he, being better endowed with pride and profundity, and also less inclined to flee into a provocative futility of limited scope, which is what he is constantly tempted to do. Nevertheless, he is at the origin of what we could call the ministry of *Dépit*, taking this word in its gravest sense: a bitter disappointment of the Spirit, which, seeing that the values it claims to carry within are given no real credit, claims to be superior to the anger that this engenders.

Gautier is, among the Jeune-France, the one who attended the least to politics. In his mature years he maintained that politics had never preoccupied him, retrospectively denying even the republican whims of the Jeune-France: "We were merely *sham medievalists*. And this applies to everyone. . . . A republican— we didn't know what one was. Pétrus Borel was the only republican. We were all against the liberals and for Marchangy. We represented the machicolation party, that's all it amounted to."[115] Gautier's denial goes too far; we are not likely to be convinced that his friends in the *petit cénacle*, in 1830, were generally antiliberal. Marchangy was not only the author of the *La Gaule poétique*, and as such one of the leaders of royalist romanticism; he was one of the most virulent ultra magistrates, one of the bêtes noires of the liberals: in 1822 he had (did Gautier know this?) sought and obtained the execution of the four sergeants of La Rochelle. This allusion should be compared with another statement by Gautier, who, we are told, "refused absolutely to remember that Sainte-Beuve met him, after 1830, at a commemorative march for the four sergeants of La Rochelle."[116] We are more inclined to trust Sainte-Beuve's memory than the settled prejudices of Gautier's later years. Perhaps he remembered his first education, which was Catholic and royalist; or rather, remembering what had always distinguished a Jeune-France from a republican, he exaggerated disproportionately in this direction, on account of the desire to place oneself at a distance that was the refuge or excuse of writers during the Second Empire. We have, in any case, testimony from Gautier himself very close to July 1830 about his political feelings in the "Sonnet VII" that appeared in 1832 with *Albertus*. This poem, which proclaims the necessity of breaking with the century and the universal dupery that kings and peoples are imposing upon the poet, well expresses the drama of July 1830 and its aftermath as the cause of this detachment:

Avec ce siècle infâme il est temps que l'on rompe;
Car à son front damné le doigt fatal a mis
Comme aux portes d'enfer: Plus d'espérance! Amis,
Ennemis, peuples, rois, tout nous joue et nous trompe.

Un budget éléphant boit notre or par sa trompe.
Dans leur trône d'hier encor mal affermis,
De leurs aînés déchus ils gardent tout, hormis
La main prompte à s'ouvrir, et la royale pompe.

Cependant en juillet, sous le ciel indigo,
Sur les pavés mouvants ils ont fait des promesses
Autant que Charles X avait ouï de messes!

Seule la poésie incarnée en Hugo
Ne nous a pas déçus, et de palmes divines
Vers l'avenir tournée ombrage nos ruines.[117]

[It is time we broke with this squalid age;
For on its damnèd brow a fatal hand has written,
As on the gates of hell: No more hope! Friends,
Enemies, peoples, kings, everyone fools and deceives us.

An elephantine budget drinks our money with its trunk.
On the nearly new, still shaky throne
Of their fallen ancestors they possess everything except
The generous hand of fellowship and royal ceremony.

And yet, in July, beneath a sky of indigo,
When the very paving stones rose in revolt,
They gave as many promises as Charles X did masses!

Only poetry incarnate in the person of Hugo
Has not let us down, and with divine palms
Turned toward the future shelters our ruins.]

At bottom, all of Gautier is here: the religion of pure art born of a dramatic retreat; in brief, the very opposite of dilettantism.

The romantic dyad Real-Ideal appears henceforth as an antinomy, an essential divorce. The Desires of the soul and Prison of the body, Heaven and Earth, these are the terms of the divorce, borrowed from the spiritualist tradition. But — and this is new and important — to these must be added Poet and Society:

Car elle manque d'air, mon âme, dans ce monde,
Où la presse en tous sens de son étreinte immonde
Une société qui retombe au chaos,
Du rouge sur la joue et la gangrène aux os![118]

[For my soul lacks air in this world,
In which, pressing it on all sides in its horrible embrace,
A society is returning to chaos,
With rouge on its cheek and gangrene in its bones!]

This evocation of the chaos of modern society refers to a dream of harmony and social health, which around 1830 was common to several families of thought. Saint-Simonians and Catholics, with different intentions, were in agreement in opposing the ideal of a community unified by dogmas to the divided society that issued from the eighteenth century. Gautier had grown up in Catholicism, and these ideas had existed in a diffuse state in Catholic literature since the beginnings of the counterrevolution. Furthermore, he was perhaps tempted at one point by Saint-Simonianism,[119] which gave form and consistency to this opposition of two types of society, "critical and organic." In any case, as early as 1831 his poetry develops the dichotomous theme of a social Faith in moral renewal leading to great art, and a spiritual decadence linked to the triumph of the spirit of inquiry. His originality is first of all to be neither entirely Catholic nor Saint-Simonian, but something else; for, above all, he explains the ruin of art by the triumph of a completely dry form of knowledge, and in this he is faithful to a properly romantic inspiration.[120] Thus architecture dies in a matter-of-fact world:

O vous, maçons du siècle, architectes athées,
Cervelles dans un moule uniforme jetées,
          Gens de la règle et du compas,
Bâtissez des boudoirs pour des agents de change,
Et des huttes de plâtre à des hommes de fange,
          Mais des maisons pour Dieu, non pas!

[O you masons of the century, atheistic architects,
Brains cast in a uniform mold,
          People of the compass and rule,
Build boudoirs for stockbrokers,
And plaster huts for men of the mire,
          But houses for God, no!]

The poem where these lines are found, *Notre-Dame*,[121] echoes, of course, Hugo's novel. These are the arguments of the romantic battle expanding into anathemas against the century, as in these lines from another poem:

L'on cherche, l'on raisonne; au fond de chaque chose
On fouille avidement, jusqu'à trouver la prose.[122]

[They seek, they reason; to the bottom of each thing
They eagerly grub, till they find prose.]

The decrepitude of our world is understood in relation to the old dream, henceforth hopeless, of a full, primitive affectivity, of vitality, and of character. In an article on "originality in France," the denunciation of politeness and the spirit of imitation, inherited from Rousseau and Mme de Staël, become the death song of the modern world: "Our decrepit world is in its death pangs: it is time for its *De Profundis*."[123] To this world at death's door, Gautier opposes some past era, the Renaissance, the Middle Ages, always conceived as a sort of golden age when spiritual sanctity and that of art were intimately united.[124]

What above all keeps us from associating Gautier with either of the two schools, Catholic or Saint-Simonian, that were then exalting the organic virtues of the former Christian society, each from its point of view, is that these schools were proposing in one form or another the modern resurrection of these virtues. In him, however, the evocation of the past has no other object than to discredit the present. In him is articulated not a new faith but the ruin of the romantic faith:

L'avenir menaçant, dans ses noires ténèbres,
Ne présente à nos yeux que visions funèbres;
Un aveugle destin au gouffre nous conduit:
Pour guider notre esquif dans cette mer profonde,
Dont tous les vents ligués fouettent en grondant l'onde,
        Pas une étoile dans la nuit![125]

[The threatening future, with its black shadows,
Presents only funereal visions to our eyes;
A blind destiny is taking us to the abyss:
To guide our little boat over this deep sea,
All of whose winds are moaning and whipping up the waves,
        There is not a single star in the night sky!]

No hope of resurrection for this dead century:

Rien ne vit plus en nous: nos amours et nos haines
Sont de pâles vieillards sans force et sans vigueur,
Chez qui la tête semble avoir pompé le coeur.
La passion est morte avec la foi; la terre
Accomplit dans le ciel sa ronde solitaire,

Et se suspend encore aux lèvres du soleil.
Mais le soleil vieillit; son baiser moins vermeil
Glisse sans les chauffer sur nos fronts, et ses flammes,
Comme sur les glaciers, s'éteignent sur nos âmes

. . . .

De nos cieux dépeuplés il ne descendra pas
Un ange aux ailes d'or pour nous prendre en ses bras,
Et le siècle futur, s'asseyant sur la pierre
De notre siècle à nous, et la voyant entière,
Joyeux, ne dira pas, ainsi qu'au temps du Christ:
Il est ressuscité comme il était écrit.[126]

[Nothing lives in us any more: our loves and our hates
Are pale old men without strength and vigor,
In whom the head seems to have drained the heart dry.
Passion has died along with faith; the earth
Makes its solitary round in the heavens,
And is still hung above the lips of the sun.
But the sun is getting old; its kiss, less pink,
Slides over our brows without warming them, and its flames
Are extinguished on our souls, as if on glaciers.

. . . .

From our depopulated skies there will not descend
Some angel with wings of gold to take us in his arms,
And the century to come, sitting on the stone
Of our own century and seeing it entire,
Will not as in the time of Christ say with joy:
He is risen from the dead, as it is written.]

Such are the basic thoughts from which sprang what is called the doctrine of art for art's sake. This basis is unhealthy, due to the temptation toward sterility and renunciation that it implies. To conclude that the harm comes from examining things too closely, from knowing too much, and from exhausting the sources of creation, is to disavow the very disquiet for which the modern faith — and romanticism, a variant of this faith — glorified humanity:

Et puis l'âge est venu qui donne la science,
J'ai lu Werther, René, son frère d'alliance
            Ces livres, vrais poisons du coeur,
Qui déflorent la vie et nous dégoûtent d'elle,
Dont chaque mot vous porte une atteinte mortelle,
            Byron et son don Juan moqueur.

Ce fut un dur réveil: ayant vu que les songes
Dont je m'étais bercé n'étaient que des mensonges,
      Les croyances, des hochets creux,
Je cherchai la gangrène au fond de tout, et, comme
Je la trouvai toujours, je pris en haine l'homme,
      Et je devins bien malheureux.[127]

[And then came the age that gives knowledge,
I read Werther, René, so closely akin,
      Those books, veritable poisons of the heart,
That deflower life and make us lose our taste for it,
Whose every word causes you a mortal wound,
      Byron and his mocking Don Juan.
It was a hard awakening: having seen that the dreams
With which I had rocked myself to sleep were nothing but lies,
      That beliefs are nothing but empty baubles,
I sought the gangrene at the root of everything, and since
I found it without fail, I began to hate man,
      And I became most miserable.]

Albertus's case is the same:

Notre héros avait, comme Eve sa grand'mère,
Poussé par le serpent, mordu la pomme amère;
Il voulait être Dieu. — Quand il se vit tout nu,
Et possédant à fond la science de l'homme,
Il désira mourir. — Il n'osa pas, mais, comme
On s'ennuie à marcher dans un sentier connu,
Il tenta de s'ouvrir une nouvelle route.
Le monde qu'il rêvait, le trouva-t-il? J'en doute.
En cherchant il avait usé les passions,
Levé le coin du voile et regardé derrière.
—A vingt ans l'on pouvait le clouer dans sa bière,
      Cadavre sans illusions.

[Our hero had, like Eve his grandmother,
Impelled by the serpent, bitten the bitter apple;
He wanted to be God. — When he saw himself all naked,
And in possession of all the science of man,
He wanted to die. — He did not dare, but, since
It is boring to walk on a well-known path,
He tried to open a new road.
The world he was dreaming of, did he find it? I doubt it.

In looking he had worn out the passions,
Had lifted the veil and looked behind.
—At twenty he could be nailed in the coffin,
  A cadaver without illusions.]

And Gautier, echoing his hero:

Malheur, malheur à qui dans cette mer profonde
Du coeur de l'homme jette imprudemment la sonde!

. . . .

—Oh! si je pouvais vivre une autre vie encor!
Certes, je n'irais pas fouiller dans chaque chose
Comme j'ai fait. —Qu'importe après tout que la cause
Soit triste, si l'effet qu'elle produit est doux?
—Jouissons, faisons-nous un bonheur de surface.[128]

[Woe, woe to whoever in this deep sea
Sounds imprudently the human heart!

. . . .

—Oh! if I could relive my life!
I would certainly not dig into every last thing,
As I have done. —After all, what does it matter that the cause
Is sad, if the effect it produces is sweet?
—Let us enjoy, let us make a happiness of the surface.]

By such texts we see how the highest degree of fervor can be close to apostasy. The cult of the absolute and the impossible is tempted to resolve itself into a prudent art of living. To have anathematized the bourgeois so much in order to rally finally to its own wisdom!

This ambiguity prevented Gautier from being taken too seriously; in his most provocative moments, he seems to take pleasure in his own verve, to defy received ideas for the pure pleasure of scandal, and to exalt novelties only with the hidden motive of deriding them. Alongside the tragic verses that he was writing at this time, we must not forget to put *Les Jeunes-France*, which is from these same years.[129] Gautier did not write what this title seems to announce— the memorial of the little *cénacle*, the book of young romanticism's ideals and types. He presented only a sequence of "jeering novels," ironic portraits borrowed from the real or imaginary world that he enjoyed with his friends. Two of the texts that make up the collection had appeared earlier in periodicals: the story of the painter Onuphrius Wphly, an imaginary victim of Satan, and that of Elias Wilmanstadius, the man obsessed with the Middle Ages. The Jeune-France, in the first versions of these texts, are not yet named.[130] Let us say that their spirit, for want of the right word, is already there; but let us above all note that neither of these two hyperromantic types is treated with respect or gravity: a gentle mockery envelops the figure of Elias, the maniacal medievalist; if Onuphrius's misadventure with the devil is told with more seriousness, it still concludes with a sermon on the deadly effects of the imagination.[131] The later pieces that expressly mention romanticism and the Jeune-France contain the caricature of the new school at the same time as that of its adversaries in the classical camp.[132] A satirical treatment of romanticism and a conclusion with a down-to-earth moral combine in the longest of the pieces in the collection, "Celle-ci et celle-là ou la Jeune-France passionnée," whose hero, Rodolphe — who is Jeune-France and, like Dumas's protagonist in *Antony*, in quest of a frenetic passion — finds in the end only a banal adultery with a society matron, and confesses: "I most definitely see that I am cut out to be a candle merchant and not volume two of Byron. This is painful, but it is the truth." Following which he resolves to find happiness in a comfortable affair with his servant Mariette: "Mariette is poetry without a corset and without make-up, the muse as compliant girl," et cetera. We are here far from the desperate idealism of the poems. While drawing the moral at the end of the story, Gautier informs us that the friend who advises and convinces his hero, "Albert, who returns Rodolphe to the right path, is true reason, the intimate friend of the true poetry, which is fine and delicate prose, a prose that, with the tip of a finger, restrains poetry, which is always wanting to quit the solid earth of reality to fly into the nebulous regions of dreams and illusions."[133]

Reading these texts one has the feeling of an abdication, a renunciation. The case of Gautier testifies to the difficult position of avant-garde romanticism engaged in a struggle with real society, and henceforth torn between heroic fidelity to an illusion and an accommodation that lacked sublimity. These two extremes are capable of meeting. The generation of Gautier, Nerval, Houssaye, and the unconsoled army of whimsical poets of the reign of Louis-Philippe combines conformism with disenchantment and poetic depth: an involuntarily ironic conjunction that parallels and attempts to thwart a voluntary irony. Gautier mocks the ideal and the real at the same time; the Jeune-France style in him aims to scandalize the bourgeois even while asserting that the poet is not taken in by the futility of his dreams or the insignificance of the figure he cuts. Gautier prides himself, in the preface to his collection, on being ordinary, without an opinion of any sort, not worth mentioning; he asserts there that art "is pure fraud"; he declares that he is only Jeune-France because of a few friends who wanted to shape him according to that type. Why this predilection for quips that go directly against articles of faith professed elsewhere with such gravity?

This can be explained by the desire to avoid clichés, or by the decision to deny everything rather than furnish the Vulgar with ideas that it will trivialize. But there is something more: in the negative poetic religion born of the falling-out of romanticism and society, there is and will long continue to be a mark of powerlessness, a sign of and a yearning for nothingness. The poet is nothing, at the very moment when he is tempted to believe that he is everything: "As a result of my concentration within my *ego*," we read in the preface to *Les Jeunes-France*, "the idea came to me many times that I was alone in creation; that the sky, the stars, the earth, the seasons, the forests were only decorations, hurriedly worked-up backdrops that the mysterious scene-shifter placed around me to keep me from seeing the dusty, cobwebbed walls of this theater they call the world; that the men moving around me are only there like the confidants of tragedies, to say: *My lord*, and to break up with a few replies my interminable monologues."[134] These lines well express both the keenness and the deficiency of the poetic doctrine that they portend.

As we have been able to see, the members of the "*petit cénacle*" are quite different one from the other, to a greater extent, no doubt, than was the case for their illustrious elders. A bond unites them, however: the feeling that society poses an obstacle to their wish, and, in the still intact fever of the romantic religion, the fear that this religion is futile and powerless vis-à-vis reality. This character marks them all, and justifies placing them at the conclusion of a study like this one. It is remarkable that this little group, ardent and embittered, should emerge at the moment when the long transformation of the old France into the new is finally accomplished — that it accompanies with a message of disapproval and disillusionment the achievement of a historic mutation whose beginning had been marked by the triumphal cohort of humanist *philosophes*. The juxtaposition will be thought strange; it will be said that there is nothing in common between the two groups, and that, for a parallel with the Jeune-France, we should consider rather what the minor poets of 1760 may have been. But — and this is the point — the minor poets of 1760 were of no particular significance in their time; it was the philosophic literature that bore within it the spirit and problems of the century; it was romanticism that played the same role under Charles X, and in romanticism, the Jeune-France marked, after July 1830, a crucial moment. The most enthusiastic and the youngest of them lived through this moment of urgency and disappointment with a peculiar intensity that in fact foreshadowed the future destiny of the entire movement. They were then the advanced spokespersons of the class of thinkers, relatively out of harmony with the great generation of older writers who remained on the scene, continuing their work of hope and instruction. For the malaise they showed corresponded to a problem whose danger was felt by all of romanticism, and that would become perniciously obvious after 1848: society's resistance to the promises glimpsed by the Spirit come down to earth amid the ruins of the old order and the advent of the new.

This is why, in the odyssey of the new spiritual power born in the eighteenth century from the disrepute of the old church, the youthful romanticism of 1830 can be seen as the outcome of a great first phase, which has been the subject of this book. At that time there appears a conflict, previously unforeseen and henceforth deep-seated, between this spiritual power and the society from whose birth it arose. It was then that two powers, both newly promoted, found themselves for the first time facing each other, and that it was necessary to ask what relations could be established between them, it being obvious that they were not reducible one to the other. The romanticism of the older writers, which had organized itself in the 1820s for just such a task, long sought to work out an agreement by adding to real society a future horizon of hope and progress, and by keeping the door open in spirit between institutions and the desired moral renewal. The history of French "high romanticism" after 1830 is that of this apostolate of the time to come, an effort to respond positively to the problem that emerged in 1830; the vicissitudes and ordeals, the persistence or retreat of this apostolate will be another phase of the history of which we have seen the first unfolding. The thought that worked for the advent of a new world would henceforth have to judge it; they were now at cross-purposes. The cry of defiance and anguish from the Jeune-France is still remembered because it inaugurated this new period.

Final Reflections

I HAVE attempted in the preceding pages to see how the history of society and the history of literature were linked in the dramatic period during which the France of old gave way to modern France. Much has been written — before as well as after Marx — about the link that connects society and literature, and about the precise nature of that link. These discussions are already of long standing, and they have shed little light. It is nevertheless clear that they presuppose a place and a role peculiar to literature that cannot be denied without suppressing the debate itself. For to imagine thought — the place of ideas and values, as they manifest themselves in literary works — to be entirely dependent on infrastructural and especially economic forces that are alien to it is to render it superfluous and to renounce any understanding of its role. We must accept as a self-evident truth that the writer is on a different plane than the producer of consumer goods, of any kind whatsoever; if we want to attribute to the writer a social existence, we ought to make up our minds to define this existence and the function that is associated with it separately, in a manner that does not depend on preconceived ideas. No aspect of production, no economic or social process in itself discredits or glorifies anything at all. By definition, no infrastructural phenomenon is endowed with this capacity, which is that of thought without any mediation whatsoever, and which cannot be contested by any means I can see other than words. In brief, one can really inquire about the relation that links works of the mind to the social substratum only if one first presupposes what can be called the mind or spirit acting according to its peculiar nature, which is to lay down laws — whether well or badly is not at issue, but inevitably — concerning values that are irreducible to facts and that are universal.

Such remarks have been made many times, but especially by those who, in the examination of literary works, hold the action of collective interests upon writers to be negligible, and wish literature as such to depend only on their own choices. This sort of criticism is obviously contrary to the sociological point of view that has generally been adopted in this work, but one can neither be unaware of it nor refuse to respond to its objections. It is not untrue that the stumbling block of sociological criticism, which makes it so dangerous from a literary point of view, is the difficulty of maintaining a sense of the inherent life of works, as they are felt by authors and readers, in the models that sociological criticism inevitably ends by producing. This irreplaceable life risks being absent from the formulas by which historical analysis claims to express what is essential, and in fact it often happens that literary sociology possesses self-assurance only to the extent that it mutilates that for which it claims to account. The method is only justifiable if one can achieve a point of view from which the visible content of the work and its historical justification are so close as to be indistinguishable. If there were no such point of view, the sociology of literary works would be pure illusion. But this point of view does exist: it identifies a social need that emerges from a decisive moment of the historical drama as well as its issue in new dispositions of thought: there, the creator is on the same ground as the mass of his contemporaries, who welcome in him the instrument of their salvation. This dynamic relation supposes that works exist as ends, as answers to a specific call, as well as in their aspect as necessary maneuvers in the realm of the universal, to which aspect alone is due their power to persuade human minds. If our analyses are to be valid, the social conjuncture and the work, the call and the response, must appear to be so close that the two voices merge, and what results from this must amount to a sort of self-evidence for us, which is the echo of what contemporaries experienced. If this condition is satisfied, a literary work retains for us its literary character: it loses neither its tonality nor its life; we succeed in discovering the human perspective to which the work of literature gives expression, which we cannot lose sight of without impoverishing it. Such is the goal — the ideal goal, at any rate — of the undertaking that has been pursued here.

Sociological criticism has often gone astray in its attempts to situate this meeting ground of the social and the literary, with which its investigations ought to have been concerned as their natural object. It is a waste of time for it to calculate the influence of economic realities over literature. It is obviously not on this imaginary ground that it could establish its influence and its truth. It is the passions of human beings living in society and of the groups they make up that furnish literature with its tasks and its material. Statistics referring to the economy can doubtless explain collective emotions up to a point, but literature is oblivious of economics and can feel its effects only in a mediated, distant manner, through the movements of social psychology that alone affect it directly. What carries writers along is this psychology, which at the same time is irresistibly an ideology; that is, a constellation of values and a structure of judgments concerning things: it is this powerful but confused inspiration that they interpret, that they anticipate, that they guide. As far as statistics are concerned, we should like to have some for what the public or publics thought about every important moment of the past concerning the types, situations, expressions of values, and axioms that furnish contemporary literary works with their material. But what will such statistics give us? Those of the fluctuations of business or the oscillations in the revenues of royal officers at the periods that interest us, however precious they may be in their way for the historian, cannot replace those that we lack in our domain. We are thus obliged for the foreseeable future to restrict ourselves to what has been written and published in this order of things; that is, to take literature itself as the principal witness concerning the suggestions it has received from the public mind, and to form our intuitions based on the greatest possible number of these testimonies.

This is to say that the indisputable relation that links works of the mind to the society that is contemporary with them is not accessible to us by procedures that are comparable to those of the natural sciences, and that in this domain as perhaps in several others we can speak only of a science of humanity if we take the word science in its broadest denotation. It is in any case better for us to try to use properly what means to knowledge we possess and to go as deeply into them as we can than to delude ourselves by thinking up others that do not exist. Even so, these means enable literary criticism to teach historians of society at least as much as if not more than it can learn from them. Any history is insufficient if it claims to render an account of life while turning its back on representations, imaginings, and affirmations of value, without which human beings and the societies they constitute could neither live nor form an idea of themselves. So far, with a few exceptions, social history has made only a deplorably impoverished use of the teachings of literature. The connection between the two disciplines has mistakenly been imagined to go in one direction only.

What is usually called method in criticism is, once the common obligation of accuracy and plausibility is acknowledged, really nothing but the choice of one perspective among many, none of which is excluded a priori. The point of view I have chosen seems above all to look to the ideas that literature conveys. Now ideas, it may be said, are not works, although they necessarily enter into their composition; it could even be objected that they are only a common, undifferentiated raw material that literature shares with various other reflective activities, being properly literary only in the peculiar use that literature makes of ideas when integrating them into representative, expressive ensembles appropriate to its own ends. But it is precisely our point that, in a study grounded as this one is, the distinction between ideas and forms has less meaning than ever: ideas answer human needs only when they present themselves in the concrete forms that literature gives them: structured genres with a view to a certain effect, human types adopting a variable sign of prestige or low status, situations and ways of behaving that are more or less exemplary, constellations of inter-related axioms, stylistic orientations, verbal patterns established through their variants. It is futile to wonder whether ideas in literature come before form or whether the opposite is the case, for literature is precisely the place where ideas meet form. Though it may be true that speaking literarily there is no pure idea, pure literary form is even less conceivable. In fact, at the hypothetical moment when a concern of thought or of form isolates itself and exists separately, literature ceases to exist.

All literary criticism must submit to this law, whether it will or no, through a natural accommodation to its object. Sociological criticism can escape this constraint less than any other, for it is supposed to seek in the heart of literary works a living desire that is from the beginning both idea and configuration, both a way of seeing things and a way of expressing this — in other words, literature at the source. A study like the one attempted here necessarily implies, despite its generality, the consideration of particular literary problems, genres or forms, discernible themes, poetics, style — all of which are raised by the way literary works come into being. In this respect, an attempt at a synthesis covering such a long period is subject to the same necessity as the study of an author or a page; the only difference is that what appears as a tangential development or sidelight in specialized studies must here occupy an essential and central position.

* * *

This book has attempted to describe the ways in which in the eighteenth and nineteenth centuries the old religious system entered into competition with or was supplanted by a faith in which human beings, and not God, tended to occupy the primary position. We have noted, along the way, the traumatic influence of the revolutionary years. The new faith had expressed the hopes of an elite emancipated from religion and prejudices; it had proclaimed a moral renewal adapted to the level of this elite, but of which society at large was far from capable — one, moreover, that this elite itself could endorse only theoretically. The dream was severely mutilated when it collided with reality, and the humanist faith abandoned much of its optimism in order to conform to this reality, groping toward traditional religious concepts and merging with them. Those who claimed to restore the old beliefs were in fact just as deeply penetrated with the new beliefs: Chateaubriand, Ballanche, and Lamennais bear witness to this. Those who wanted on the contrary to remain outside of the old society's system of values were nevertheless invaded to different degrees by the religious spirit, the renunciation of excessively imminent hopes, and the worship of a distant ideal: thus Senancour, Mme de Staël, and Cousin. All contributed to the common enterprise, which, by its very nature, required contributions from all sides. From this profound convergence was born the thought of the nineteenth century: the new society established its belief upon a spiritualized recasting of ideas that had established themselves violently. This obvious retreat was also, in a way, an advance, because from that point on writers seeking to define values considered the general state of society, the real character of which the revolutionary crisis and its sequel had made them feel: the nineteenth-century spiritualism of effort, suffering, and hope may not conform to the truth of things and the final definition of humanity, but at least it recognizes more adequately than did the philosophy of the Enlightenment some important problems; namely, the limitations to which a march of progress that had been too quickly envisaged as coming to a successful conclusion had been seen to be subject. The spiritualizing transposition of ideas inherited from the previous century was to a considerable degree a "plebeianization," to use Ballanche's terminology — an adaptation of ideals earlier conceived by a privileged elite to the level and language of the suffering multitude.

Romanticism, due to the very modalities of its arrival, well reflects this movement. Born in various forms in the two opposed realms of the counterrevolution and liberalism, it only really declared itself as a new and victorious literature after the conjunction and fusion of the two currents. It borrowed from the counterrevolution a revivified sense of the spiritual and the sacred as well as the idea of a flavor of things for which reason cannot account. From liberalism it borrowed the philosophic theory of the beautiful and the promotion of the real, the current, and the popular to a higher status, at the expense of the conventions inherited from the old society. The unity of romanticism could not have been accomplished if a common vision of the world had not finally animated the movement as a whole. The essence of this vision is in the polarity and correspondences of the entire realm of the ideal with the entire realm of the real, as these are experienced intensely and unconstrainedly by human consciousness beyond the confines of any dogma whatsoever, so as to provide a way to redeem and justify every phase of the human condition, just as the old religion had done.[1]

This view of the world, sometimes weakly elaborated and in more than one instance the occasion for naive creations, may seem to pull back from the adult humanism of the preceding era. The exaltation of the symbol as an essential part of the activity of thought allows the irrational to win back terrain that the Enlightenment philosophy had deliberately stinted. The analogical representation of the world, through the very variety of works and tendencies by which this expresses itself and upon which the ministry of thought is henceforth grounded, involves a regressive tendency: it makes of analogy a cognitive mode and diverts thought toward an ontology of the symbol. But romantic irrationalism, to at least as great an extent as it was a doctrine concerning the symbolic nature of being, was also a pure exaltation of the mind's powers of invention, a poetics of the human subject. In this way it reconquered from religion the powers of imagination still alive in human hearts as well as the memory of the spiritual infancy of the human race, returning them to humanity. Here again literature, with however much ambiguity, achieved a step forward toward a broader consciousness of the human condition. It is only in these circumstances that literature was able to transform itself in its very substance, and that it undertook — as it had not done in the eighteenth century, in the initial moment of integral faith and triumphant enthusiasm — the quest to find new instruments appropriate to the greatness of its role and the expansion of its public. It was during the Restoration that the first great romantic works by Lamartine, Vigny, and Hugo bear witness to this effort. It is then that the new dignity of literature creates, or indicates in outline, in a form free of the old shackles, the reflective lyricism of modern times, the epic of humanity, the symbolic novel, and the symbolic drama.

This literature, which was the bearer of a new way of seeing the world, was also a new way of seeing the writer. In this respect, the revolutionary years also marked a critical juncture. The Enlightenment philosophy had consecrated the Man of Letters, both thinker and political writer. The spiritualism of the nineteenth century consecrates the Poet. This latter type, presupposing an inspiration from on high rather than the deployment of purely human lights and to some degree appealing to the mystery of things and to their ineffable nature, was first celebrated in a counterrevolutionary mode, in opposition to the *Philosophes* and in order to supplant them: it seems to imply the supremacy of the divine, in harmony with the religious tradition, and to favor somber, conservative preaching. But the antithesis of the Poet and the *Philosophe* did not prevent the advent of a wider spiritualism that, instead of opposing the two types, and even while maintaining the prerogative of poetry, caused the one to be absorbed into the other. The dominant type was then the Thinker-Poet: an inspired bearer of modern Enlightenment as well as of mystery, showing human beings a pure, distant goal while accompanying their progress toward it. All progressive or emancipatory thought at this time found itself wrapped in a halo of the ideal, and poetry reigned over prose itself. Thinker-Poets guaranteed both the final moral renewal and its accomplishment without violence or hatred. They seemed to preside with dignity over a new society, whose recognized law was progress. This type, which would especially dominate the years between 1830 and 1848, had constituted itself, as we have already been able to see, at the end of the Restoration, when the fundamental contributions of the counterrevolution and liberal thought fused in romanticism.

* * *

If we now ask ourselves more precisely what agent, what human medium effected this renovation of values, begun in the old society and pursued dramatically during and after the revolutionary crisis, we are obliged to recognize — and this is the other object of this book — the rise of an intellectual corps possessing new prestige and a new social make-up, which assumes the role of a spiritual guide for society, in competition with the old church.

In the vision of the world that it proposes, this group is obviously dependent on the needs of society as a whole and on the different classes that compose it. In this sense, others have been able to see what it was in the humanism of Enlightenment and feeling that was able to respond to the situation of the contemporary aristocracy and bourgeoisie. It remains no less true that this humanism developed further than such motivations could carry it, and that the group that was its bearer constituted itself in a state of relative autonomy in the bosom of society, situating its mission above any special interests. Not that this group — or any comparable group, even if it is a church or a clergy — was in a position to exist or to survive by itself outside of all social pressures. When the revolutionary events modified the situation and the state of mind of the aristocrats as well as of the bourgeois, this newly formed intellectual corps saw itself in danger of being repudiated and quashed by society before having been able to conquer it. There was no choice but to acknowledge that it could not then go on as it had. Around 1800, the intellectual champions of the old order invaded it with their influence, flouting its pretensions and prestige from within: men of letters, born within the ranks of this new secular clergy, could be seen using the very influence that they owed to its rise to bring it into disrepute; an army of intellectuals proclaimed the misdeeds of intelligence. But, once the initial moment of reaction is past, we do not see a serious threat either to the existence of this corps, or to its fundamentally original views in regard to the theological tradition that its role was to supplant. In the final analysis, the type incarnated in eighteenth-century Men of Letters survived and prospered in the nineteenth century thanks to an adaptation of their faith to new circumstances. The romantic vision of the world, as it was popularized in France, is the result of that adaptation.

It is true that this was at least as much the result of society's need as the result of the new intellectual corps's will to survive and attain influence. But it is also true that it would be very difficult to relate the sort of credo to which this evolution sensitized public consciousness to the interests of a particular class. What is remarkable in the nineteenth century is that the ideological differences are spread over a continuous line between two opposite poles, reaction and revolution, rather than being constituted in truly heterogeneous formations (which had existed, for example, under Louis XIII and Louis XIV). This disposition can no doubt be explained by the very structure of society, where class barriers were weakened, and the passage from one class to another was increasingly fluid. So that, even if the events that stirred up French society during the course of this century can be explained by the clash of classes, the ideas that accompany these events are all situated in a continuous ideological rainbow dominating the whole of society, whose extreme points—pure reaction and total revolution—remain somewhat unreal. Romanticism deploys the colors of this rainbow, and Victor Hugo was the embodiment of this period in that his life itself as well as his work were deployed according to these colors: Tradition, Progress, future Renascence.

It would be convenient to suppose that each color corresponds to a class: traditionalist romanticism to the aristocracy, the romanticism of temperate progress to the bourgeoisie, humanitarian romanticism to the petite bourgeoisie and the emerging proletariat. But these conjectures neglect something essential: romanticism, in the broad sense in which we have taken it, is the spiritual space in which an entire society moves—one henceforth not so much fragmented into classes as it is organized into gradations less strictly divided one from another than the social conditions of old. This society discusses itself, continuously and on every occasion, through the intellectual class whose raison d'être this debate is. We can easily grasp the importance that the community of writers and thinkers takes on in such conditions, especially if we add that, by its natural instinct to assume prerogatives and oppose those who exercise temporal power, this humane group favors the imagination of what might exist more willingly than it favors the approval of what actually does exist. From this point on, writers and thinkers play the role of a causative force in society, pushing and urging the social body to transform and reform itself according to their ideas. They want to be, and they do indeed become, the embodiment of what they call the Ideal.

We have proof that this is indeed so at the moment when, in a decisive episode of the social drama, this ideal is brutally disavowed by the real society or the powers that dominate it. In such crises, while some repudiate their convictions or fall silent, others, more imbued with the group's sense of vocation, maintain it by the very consciousness of their solitude: they still worship the Ideal, even if in their eyes it has become a symbol of powerlessness. From the beginning, the nineteenth century bears the seeds of this pessimism of modern intellectuals, this idea of a priesthood far removed from human society, and this testifies to the reaction of an autonomous group to the overthrow of what it held to be its own prerogative: we have been able to see this around 1800 in Nodier and the Méditateurs, and around 1830 in the Jeune-France; after 1848, what till then was only anxiety and disquiet will turn into a long, crushing wretchedness: writers in this period establish the authority of the mind and spirit upon a revulsion for reality and human beings as well as upon an embittered contemplation of the inaccessible. At least, all those who matter adopt such an attitude at this time; none of them embraces the disavowal of the ideal, though this disavowal is triumphing around them; they all denounce this as the supreme degradation; they constitute themselves vis-à-vis society as a humiliated and distant clergy. It is easy to denounce the futility and ineffectiveness of their pessimism: it is all too certain that a spiritual power is not of much account when what it preaches no longer has any influence. But this negative ministry is still a spiritual ministry: by standing thus apart, writers show clearly that even if they are dependent upon the present social conjuncture, they judge it and bear witness to it.

* * *

The history of the secular spiritual power that issued from the France of the eighteenth century certainly does not end in 1830, nor in 1848. What has been attempted here is only the preface to this history. An indication of the point of view from which this could be undertaken in its entirety, even up to its current phase, is perhaps to be found here. The power whose birth this book tries to describe took on increasingly important proportions and influence in France and in all of the liberal West, simultaneously and spontaneously showing a trend toward choices that call for further reflection. Indeed, we must not forget that this power, from its origin, is critical in its essence, and that, as we have been able to see, it takes pleasure in contentiously laying down laws; this means that it is itself subject to the law of examination and debate.

The sort of transmission of powers that is the subject of this book, and that tended to dispossess the traditional church to the benefit of secular authority, can in the final analysis be considered to be a dispossession of religion by literature. But we must ask ourselves how it is that literature, promoted from the usual role of entertainment and intellectual or sensual pleasure to a ministry of lofty edification, can be capable of assuming such a role. The consecration of the writer risks striking a false note to the extent that literature, which despite its promotion retains the marks of its earlier irresponsibility, finds itself unable to exercise a genuine vocation. It is, to tell the truth, the consecration of a time that no longer believes in priests, that accepts the divine only on the condition that one still be allowed to doubt and criticize freely: therein lies its true nature and the underlying form of its action. The new loftiness of its pretensions and the imitation of the traditional characteristics of the priesthood has sometimes inclined it to proclaim its mission with excessive grandiloquence. This tone, which is so often heard in romanticism, rings hollow. The age, which knows where the real priests are and no longer counts much on them for its salvation, is not ready to grant to newcomers a kind of authority that it denies to their predecessors. Indeed, it goes so far as to wonder whether a writer or a poet is qualified to guide human beings: as soon as such a pretension takes too peremptory or too precise a form, it can appear absurd to the average person. It was precisely because there was no longer room in the spiritual domain for authority properly so called that the writer and the poet were promoted.

Moreover, the newcomers, having brought heaven and earth closer together, necessarily communicate a message that is more down-to-earth than that of the old church. If dogmatic views were favored with authority in this domain, they would in fact amount to tyranny, and would result in a servitude of which the new clerics would end by being themselves the victims. The soul of the new spiritual power is liberty of thought and belief; in order for this liberty to exist and influence society, it must actually be exercised. Dogma in any form whatever is its ruin. Even granting all this, the role of the new spiritual power, within the limits to the action of ideas created by the nature of things, institutions, and events, can be considerable. This was clearly seen in the past; it is even more visible today. Literature, ideas, and the values literature sanctions in an orbit of society that is more and more vast, have for two centuries been responsible for a considerable part of humanity's destiny. One of the objects of this book is to point out this responsibility, and to encourage reflection upon it.

Notes

INTRODUCTION

1. Plato, *Phaedrus*, §245a; *Laws*, III, §682a; *Lysis*, §214a.

2. This intention is explicit in *Ion*, §§533–36; also in the *Apology*, §22b, and in the *Laws*, IV §719c.

3. Ovid, *Fastes*, VI, 5; *Art of Love*, III, 549–50: the famous "Est deus in nobis" is repeated from one text to another.

4. Horace, *Ars Poetica*, 391ff; Tacitus, *Dialogue on Orators*, XII.

5. Ronsard, *Odes*, I, 16 (*Oeuvres*, ed. Laumonier, vol.1, p.145).

6. *Odes*, II, 2 (*Oeuvres*, ed. Laumonier, vol.1, p.176).

7. Ronsard, *Odes*, V, 8 (*Oeuvres*, ed. Laumonier, vol.3, pp.118ff.)

8. The same themes may be seen in the "élégie" to Jacques Grevin, as well as in the "Hymne de l'Automne," and the *Abrégé de l'art poétique français*.

9. Pontus de Tyard, "Solitaire premier," cited by Henri Chamard, *Histoire de la Pléiade* (Paris, 1939–40), vol.3, p.145.

10. "Ode à Michel de L'Hospital," Antistrophe XVII (Ronsard, *Oeuvres*, vol.3, pp.149–50). The nocturnal chorus of the Muses in the prairie, borrowed from classical poetry, is to be found everywhere.

11. Ibid., Epode XI (*Oeuvres*, vol.3, pp.139–40): this is the prayer that Calliope addresses to her father Jupiter in the name of the Muses.

12. Boileau, *Art poétique*, III, 199–200. The idea of a Christian literature has always had its partisans, and, from the sixteenth to the eighteenth century, sacred lyrics, heroic-Christian epics, biblical or hagiographical tragedies continued to be produced with varying success — but always on the margins of the main tradition and in the background of the great works.

13. René Bray, *La Formation de la doctrine classique en France* (Paris, 1927), p.25; Antoine Adam, *Histoire de la littérature française au dix-septième siècle*, vol.1 (Paris, 1948), p.32.

14. Racan, *Vie de Malherbe*, in *Oeuvres*, ed. Tenant de Latour, vol.1 (Paris, 1857), p.271.

15. To these should be added the beginnings of Utopia, which was born at this time and which is marked with particular clarity by the quest for a new spiritual power that was the chief undertaking of the minds of the period. If Utopia does not figure here, this is because it scarcely affected public opinion and literature until after 1830. I hope to return to this in a subsequent work [*Le Temps des prophètes* (1977). Trans.].

I. IN QUEST OF A SECULAR MINISTRY

1. Descartes, *Discours de la méthode* (1637), 3rd part (end of the penultimate paragraph): "to read books or frequent *gens de lettres*."

2. Racine, *Oeuvres*, ed. Mesnard, vol.4, p.360 (*Discours* on the occasion of

Thomas Corneille's *réception*, 2 January 1685); see also the comments of Raymond Picard, *La Carrière de Racine* (Paris, 1956), pp.376ff.

3. *Gredin* at this time means *beggar, wretch*.

4. Molière, *Les Femmes savantes*, IV, 3.

5. La Bruyère, *Caractères*, ch."Des ouvrages de l'esprit," ed. Garapon (Paris, 1962), pp.182–83.

6. André Monglond, *Histoire intérieure du préromantisme français*, vol.2 (Grenoble, 1929), p.159.

7. That which formed the article "Philosophe" in the *Encyclopédie*, and whose first known version dates from 1743; Herbert Dieckmann has given a critical edition with notes (*"Le Philosophe," Texts and Interpretation* [St. Louis MO: Washington University Studies, 1948]); see especially his comment on pp.91–92.

8. "Le Philosophe," ed. Dieckmann, pp.46, 58.

9. Voltaire, s.v. "Gens de lettres," in the *Encyclopédie* (1757).

10. Rousseau, *Discours sur les sciences et les arts*, ed. G. R. Havens (New York, 1946), p.160.

11. See Maurice Pellisson, *Les Hommes de lettres au dix-huitième siècle* (Paris, 1911); Louis Ducros, *La Société française au dix-huitième siècle* (Paris, 1922), pp.358ff.; Paul Hazard, *La Pensée européenne au dix-huitième siècle de Montesquieu à Lessing*, 3 vols. (Paris, 1946), vol.1, pp.352ff., and vol.3, pp.103–4; Suzanne Fiette, "La Correspondance de Grimm et la condition des écrivains dans la seconde moitié du dix-huitième siècle," in *Revue d'histoire économique et sociale* 47 (1969), esp. pp.500–502, 505.

12. See, for example, J.-J. Garnier, *L'Homme de lettres* (Paris, 1764), especially the second part, "Inquiry into the status of the man of letters in ancient governments." Garnier, born in 1729, was professor at the Collège de France and member of the Académie des Inscriptions.

13. Malesherbes, *discours de réception* to the Académie Française (1775), cited by Pellisson, op.cit., p.247.

14. Rulhière, *discours de réception* to the Académie Française (1787), cited by Pellisson, op.cit., p.247.

15. Sébastien Mercier, *Le Bonheur des gens de lettres* (Paris, 1766), p.42.

16. Mercier, *De la littérature et des littérateurs*, ("A Yverdon," 1778), p.9. Similarly, abbé Raynal, in book XIX of his *Histoire philosophique et politique des établissements et du commerce des Européens dans les deux Indes* (vol.10, p.94 of the ten-volume Geneva edition [Pellet, 1781]; this entire book XIX was, we are told, really written by Deleyre): "Every writer of genius is naturally a magistrate of his country. He should enlighten it if he can. His talent gives him the right. . . . The entire nation is his tribunal, the public is his judge, not the despot who does not hear him or the minister who does not wish to listen."

17. A.-L. Thomas in his *discours de réception* to the Académie Française (*Discours prononcés dans l'Académie Française le jeudi 22 janvier 1767 à la réception de M. Thomas* [Paris, 1767], Bibl. Nat. Zz 4156, pp.5–6, 12).

18. Thus, among others, Mercier, *Le Bonheur*, p.52; *De la littérature*, p.62.

19. Mercier, *Le Bonheur*, p.17; the second part of the passage (act of communion with the martyr, from "Non, je n'ai jamais vu") was added by Mercier as a note when he republished the pamphlet in 1776 (*Eloges et discours philosophiques*, p.18, note a).

20. La Harpe in his *discours de réception* (*Discours prononcés dans l'Académie Française le jeudi 20 juin 1776 à la réception de M. de La Harpe* [Paris, 1776], Bibl. Nat. Z 5053[145], p.5); Chamfort, *Combien le génie des grands écrivains influe sur l'esprit de leur siècle?* (1768 text), in *Oeuvres complètes*, ed. Auguis (Paris, 1824–25), vol.1, pp.219–20.

21. Mercier, *De la littérature*, p.4; La Harpe, *discours de réception*, p.12.

22. Vauvenargues, *Oeuvres posthumes et oeuvres inédites*, ed. D. L. Gilbert (Paris, 1857), pp.176–77 (letter of 3 March 1740 to the marquis de Mirabeau).

23. Voltaire, *Correspondance*, ed. Bestermann, vol.12 (letter of 5 April [1744] to Vauvenargues).

24. Rousseau, *La Profession de foi du vicaire savoyard*, ed. P.-M. Masson (Freiburg-Paris, 1914), p.91. [The *Profession de foi du vicaire savoyard* appears in book IV of *Emile. Trans.*]

25. Mistelet, *De la sensibilité par rapport aux drames, aux romans et à l'éducation* (Amsterdam, 1777), p.6. The conclusions of today's critics tend in this direction: "The view that opposes the sensibility of Rousseau to the rationalism of Voltaire is too schematic" (René Pomeau, *La Religion de Voltaire* [Paris, 1956], p.224); "Nothing is more disappointing than the prejudice of historians that considers separately what belongs to *philosophy* or *the Enlightenment* and what is abandoned, not without irony, to *sensibility*" (Robert Mauzi, *L'Idée du bonheur dans la littérature et la pensée française au dix-huitième siècle* [Paris, 1960], p.10). Pierre Trahard (*Les Maîtres de la sensibilité française au dix-huitième siècle*, 4 vols. [Paris, 1931–33]) had already evoked this problem several times. (See especially his conclusions, vol.4, pp.270, 275).

26. Chamfort, *L'Homme de lettres, discours philosophique en vers* (Amsterdam and Paris, 1766); see also *Combien le génie* (1768).

27. Chamfort, Ode on *La Grandeur de l'Homme* (1767), in his *Oeuvres complètes*, ed. Auguis, vol.5, pp.123–26.

28. Voltaire's profession of faith in his poem on *La Loi naturelle* (1752) was much admired by Rousseau (see his letter to Voltaire of 18 August 1756, *Correspondance générale*, ed. Dufour, vol.2, p.323); Pomeau, op.cit., p.279, emphasizes this agreement and the probable influence of the poem on Rousseau's religious views.

29. Rousseau, *Profession de foi*, ed. Masson, p.161.

30. Voltaire, *Epître à l'auteur du livre des trois imposteurs* (*Oeuvres*, ed. Garnier, vol.10, p.403). It is well known that Robespierre, whose deism can seem so different from that of Voltaire, repeated this saying word for word (speech of 1 Frimaire year II, Bibl. Nat., Lb40 2322, p.5).

31. Rousseau, *La Nouvelle Héloïse*, 3rd part, letter 18 (vol.3, p.68 of the Mornet edition).

32. See Pierre-Maurice Masson, *La Religion de J.-J. Rousseau*, 3 vols. (Paris, 1916), vol.2, pp.258ff., vol.3, pp.125ff.; and the introduction, pp.19–21, by Beaulavon to his edition of *La Profession de foi* (Paris, 1937).

33. See, for example, Gustave Lanson, *Nivelle de la Chaussée et la comédie larmoyante* (Paris, 1887), pp.257–58; André Monglond, *Histoire intérieure du préromantisme français*, vol.1, pp.9, 15.

34. Eighteenth-century aesthetics reflects religion in this regard: there is hesitation between the two poles of Nature and the *Beau idéal*; an unending discussion analyzes these two concepts, it being rare for one to be clearly preferred over the other. The ideal is sometimes the summary of nature, sometimes something that surpasses it. Diderot did not overcome this difficulty, which has occupied all the commentators of his aesthetics: see especially Lester G. Crocker, *Two Diderot Studies* (Baltimore: Johns Hopkins University Press, 1952), pp.67ff., and H. Dieckmann, *Cinq Leçons sur Diderot* (Paris, 1959), 4th lesson, esp.p.118. The beginnings of German idealist aesthetics (Mendelssohn, Mengs, Winckelmann) were not unknown in France.

35. Diderot, letter of 2 October 1761 to Mlle Volland (*Oeuvres*, ed. Assézat-Tourneux, vol.19, p.61).

36. Sébastien Mercier, *Mon Bonnet de nuit*, vol.4 (Lausanne, 1786), p.47.

37. Rousseau, *Lettres morales* (written for Mme d'Houdetot, 1757–58), 4th letter (in *Correspondance générale*, ed. Dufour, vol.3, p.360).

38. Sylvain Maréchal, *De la vertu* (Paris, 1804), p.87: a posthumous work, a moral testament of this writer who lived from 1750 to 1803; see Maurice Dommanget, *Sylvain Maréchal* (Paris, 1950), p.398.

39. Maine de Biran, *Journal intime*, ed. Lavalette-Monbrun (Paris, 1927), vol.1, pp.37–38 (27 May 1794) and p.153 (17 May 1815).

40. Senancour, *Oberman*, letter 61 (ed. Monglond [Grenoble-Paris, 1947], vol.3, p.80).

41. *Extraits du journal de Chênedollé*, ed. Mme Paul de Samie (Caen, 1922), p.41, text of [1808].

42. Astolphe de Custine, *Lettres au marquis de La Grange*, ed. Luppé (Paris, 1925), letter of 7 August [1818], pp.39–40. Custine recalled, perhaps, the reproaches of Father Souël to René.

43. Ibid., p.38.

44. Balzac, *Notes philosophiques* (1818–19), cited by H. Evans, *Louis Lambert et la philosophie de Balzac* (Paris, 1951), p.35.

45. *Lettres de femmes adressées à M. de Balzac*, 1st series, 1832–36, edited by Marcel Bouteron (*Les Cahiers balzaciens* 2 [1924], p.38). This correspondent, who has not been identified with certainty, seems to have been born around 1795.

46. Lamennais, letter of 9 March 1835 to Montalembert, in *Lettres inédites à*

Montalembert, ed. Eug. Forgues (Paris, 1898), p.355. I stop my citations here; it would be possible to multiply them in drawing on romantic literature; artists, too, experienced these "illuminations" (see for example David d'Angers, *Carnets*, ed. Bruel, vol.1 [Paris, 1958], p.215). An in-depth study of this theme, its usual or occasional elements, the formulae or expressions that identify it, and in brief of this literary constellation as a whole, would be of great interest.

47. Mercier, *Le Bonheur*, p.27.

48. Rémond de Saint-Sauveur, *Agenda des auteurs* (n.p., 1755), cited by Pellisson, *Les Hommes de Lettres*, p.245.

49. Duclos, *Considérations sur les moeurs de ce siècle* (Paris, 1751), p.231.

50. Letter by Thomas dated 8 May 1760, cited by E. Micard, *Un Ecrivain académique au dix-huitième siècle: Antoine-Léonard Thomas (1732–1785)* (Paris, 1924), p.209.

51. Kératry, *Les Gens de lettres d'autrefois*, in *Le Livre des Cent-et-un*, vol.2 (1831), p.416. Kératry, who was rather well known at the time, was a gentleman of Chateaubriand's generation; he was moderately liberal and a mystic.

52. Villemain, *Cours de littérature française, Tableau du dix-huitième siècle*, part II (Paris, 1828), p.14 of the first lesson.

53. Tocqueville, *Etat social et politique de la France avant et depuis 1789* (*Oeuvres*, ed. Mayer, vol.II-1 [Paris, 1952], pp.48–49).

54. Tocqueville, *L'Ancien Régime et la Révolution* (*Oeuvres*, ed. Mayer, p.196).

55. Ibid., p.201.

56. Jean-Paul Sartre, *Baudelaire* (Paris, 1947), pp.158–59 (text first published in 1946).

57. Jean-Paul Sartre, "Qu'est-ce que la littérature?" in *Les Temps modernes* (March 1947), p.984.

58. Ibid., p.988.

59. Ibid. (April 1947), p.1199.

60. In this school of thought the idea takes on an unexpected form, borrowed from Hegel's metaphysics: the *philosophes* of the Enlightenment are reproached with not knowing about "dialectics." It is certainly true that they knew nothing about it.

61. La Chaussée, *Le Retour imprévu* (1756), cited by Trahard, op.cit., vol.2, p.21.

62. Monglond, *Histoire intérieure*, vol.2, ch.4, title and p.280; on the traditional French bourgeoisie, ibid., pp.211–18.

63. This can already by seen in Montesquieu, as early as the *Lettres persanes*, whose political doctrine is that of an aristocratic opposition to absolutism that also treats harshly the church, orthodoxy, and Christian morality itself.

64. See on this subject Albert Chérel, *Fénelon au dix-huitième siècle en France* (Paris, 1947), pp.289, 359; Léon Béclard, *Sébastien Mercier* (Paris, 1903), p.41. Thomas especially excelled at this kind of *Eloges*; he wrote in addition an *Essai sur les Eloges* (1773; see *Oeuvres complètes* [Paris, 1802 – year X], vols 3–4). The texts of the period on great men and the worship that is due to them (proposals for monuments, *élysées*, etc.) are beyond counting.

65. Maury, "Discours sur l'éloquence de la chaire," in *Discours choisis sur divers sujets de religion et de littérature* (Paris, 1777), p.146; Villemain, op.cit., 3rd part (Paris, 1829), p.73. Monglond, *Histoire intérieure*, vol.2, pp.21–22: "With Jean-Jacques, the man of letters tends to replace the spiritual director."

66. Rousseau, *Du contrat social*, book II, chap.7.

67. Rousseau, *Emile*, edn. Furne of the *Oeuvres*, vol.2, p.409.

68. Diderot, *De la poésie dramatique* (1758), in *Oeuvres*, ed. Assézat-Tourneux, vol.7, p.313.

69. Chamfort, *Maximes et anecdotes*, edn. Incidences (Monaco, 1944), maxim 444.

70. Mercier, *De la littérature*, p.66 n.31.

71. Diderot, *Réfutation suivie de l'ouvrage d'Helvétius intitulé L'Homme* (around 1775), in *Oeuvres*, ed. A.-T., vol.2, p.342.

72. Marmontel, *Poétique française*, 2 vols. (Paris, 1763), vol.1, pp.316–17.

73. See *Oeuvres*, ed. Dimoff, 3 vols., vol.2 (Paris, 1911), pp.18ff., 28–29, 124.

74. Diderot, *Salon de 1767* (*Oeuvres*, ed. A.-T., vol.11, pp.131, 136, 137).

75. Diderot, "Entretiens sur le Fils naturel" (1757), 3rd *entretien* (*Oeuvres*, ed. A.-T., vol.7, p.157).

76. Roucher, *Les Mois*, 2 vols. (Paris, 1779), vol.2, p.57, in the notes to chant VII.

77. The search for a currently possible "true poetry" is less discouraged outside of France (see Van Tieghem, "The Notion of True Poetry in European Preromanticism," in *Le Préromantisme*, vol.1 [Paris, 1927], pp.17ff.).

78. The bibliography of collections and works that are milestones of these discoveries is well enough known; on this subject see Van Tieghem, *Le Préromantisme*, vol.1, pp.34–43; and, by the same author, *Ossian en France* (Paris, 1917), vol.1, pp.197ff.

79. Abbé Massieu, *Histoire de la poésie française* (Paris, 1739), pp.69–70 (the author of this posthumous work had died in 1722; he had been professor of Greek at the Collège de France and an academician).

80. See, for example, the *Journal étranger* (December 1761), p.48; the *Gazette littéraire de l'Europe*, vol.8 (1766), pp.237–38 (article by Suard); Thomas, *Essai sur les Eloges*, in the chapter on "Elegies among the earliest men" (1773), in *Oeuvres complètes* (Paris, 1802), vol.3, pp.20ff. Marmontel, s.v. "Lyrique" in *Supplément à l'Encyclopédie*, vol.3 (1777).

81. Voltaire, *Essai sur la poésie épique* (1733), in *Oeuvres*, ed. Garnier, vol.8, pp.314–15 (cf. the earlier preface to *Oedipe* [1730], ibid., vol.2, pp.54–55); similar explanation, from the ignorance of writing, in the *Année littéraire* (1767), vol.3, p.106.

82. *Journal étranger* (September 1760), pp.4ff.; ibid. (January 1761), pp.3–7; *Gazette littéraire de l'Europe*, vol.1 (1764), pp.88–92, 238–39 (article by Suard). Saint-Lambert, in his *Principes des moeurs chez toutes les nations ou Cathéchisme uni-

versel, vol.3 (Paris, year VI — 1798), pp.234–35, invokes at the same time mnemonics and the virtues of poetic style.

83. *Journal étranger* (December 1761), p.42.

84. See notes 80, 82, and 83 above; in addition, *Gazette littéraire de l'Europe*, vol.6 (July–August 1765), pp.102–16, 234–51: excerpts from the *Critical Dissertation* of Hugh Blair on the poems of Ossian (1763); ibid., vol.1 (1764), p.11, a review that had appeared of the *Dissertation on the Rise, Union and Power of Poetry and Music* by John Brown (1763); a second edition, abridged, of this book, published in 1764, was translated into French in 1768.

85. In recent years many authors have devoted themselves to very diverse studies of this intellectual movement: thus John Hampton, *N. A. Boulanger* (Lille-Geneva, 1955), pp.93ff.; René Pomeau, op.cit. (1956), p.59; L. J. Austin, *L'Univers poétique de Baudelaire* (Paris, 1956), pp.63ff.; Roger Mercier, *La Réhabilitation de la nature humaine, 1700–1750* (Villemomble, 1960), pp.107ff.; Pierre Albouy, *La Création mythologique chez Victor Hugo* (Paris, 1963), pp.36ff.; Louis Le Guillou, *L'Evolution de la pensée religieuse de F. Lamennais* (Paris, 1966), pp.17ff.

86. Blackwell, *Lettres sur la mythologie*, 2 vols. (Paris, 1771), vol.2, p.91 (original English edition, London, 1748).

87. The treatise is part of the *Monde primitif* of Court de Gébelin, in 9 vols.; it appears in vol.1 (Paris, 1773), with a separate pagination; the texts cited above are pp.9, 149–50.

88. Baldensperger, *Mélanges Huguet* (1940), pp.315ff.

89. Ch.-F. Dupuis, *Abrégé de l'Origine de tous les cultes* (year VI), ed. Garnier (Paris, 1895), pp.45, 77–78.

90. Rousseau, *Essai sur l'origine des langues*, *Oeuvres*, ed. Furne, vol.3, pp.504, 506–7.

91. See *Oeuvres*, ed. Furne, vol.3, p.369: "Stanzas added to those making up Gresset's idyll, *Le Siècle pastoral*"; also, *Emile*, ibid., vol.2, p.718.

92. N.-A. Boulanger, *Recherches sur l'origine du despotisme oriental* (Geneva, 1761).

93. Boulanger, *L'Antiquité dévoilée* (Amsterdam, 1766), pp.396ff.

94. J.-S. Bailly, *Histoire de l'astronomie ancienne* (Paris, 1775); he places the time of primitive astronomy before the Flood, p.90; see also his *Lettres sur l'origine des sciences et sur celle des peuples de l'Asie* (London-Paris, 1777), p.205: the letters were addressed to Voltaire, who corresponded with Bailly on these subjects. Bailly, who often invokes Court de Gébelin, seems at first to have hesitated to attribute primitive science to any known people; he finally decides in favor of the imaginary Atlantides, who, he affirms, formerly inhabited Greenland and Spitzberg, then migrated to Tartary (see his *Lettres sur l'Atlantide* [London-Paris, 1779]). Voltaire did not follow him on this point: he made everything come from the Brahmans.

95. Bailly, *Lettres sur l'origine des sciences*, pp.98–99.

96. See Sainte-Beuve, article on Bailly (1854) in *Causeries du lundi*, vol.10, p.352.

97. J. Ehrard, *L'Idée de nature en France dans la première moitié du dix-huitième siècle* (Paris, 1963), p.747.

98. Sainte-Beuve, ibid., p.753, again with reference to Bailly, shows great insight in noting "this need for a full-blown golden age that was one of the optimistic traits of his time."

99. Diderot applied this Edenic postulate to the theory of fine arts by assuming that the Beautiful was the representation of an unaltered human body, pristine, or, as he says, not having "suffered": see *Salon de 1767* (ed. A.-T. of the *Oeuvres*, vol.11, p.12); *Salon de 1769* (ibid., pp.412–13).

100. Court de Gébelin, *Monde primitif*, vol.8, pp.lxvii, lxix.

101. Marquise de la Tour du Pin, *Journal d'une femme de cinquante ans, 1778–1815*, 2 vols. (Paris, 1913), vol.1, p.160. These remarks refer to the spring of 1789.

102. Plato inaugurated the debate in his *Cratylus*: Cratylus believes that there exists one term that is fitting for each thing and that primitive names were established by a power higher than man (*Cratylus*, 383a & b, 438c). Furthermore, within the supernaturalist conception, the name's bond to the thing can be related to God in several ways, depending on whether the source of a mystical analogy of signifier and signified is placed in him, or whether the necessary fit of the lexicon instituted by God is inferred from the excellence of his reason, or whether some other related or intermediary hypothesis is adopted.

103. Condillac, *Essai sur l'origine des connaissances humaines*, 2 vols. (Amsterdam, 1746), vol.2, chap.I and II; *Grammaire* (Parma, 1775); abbé Bergier, *Les Eléments primitifs des langues* (1764).

104. Rousseau, *Essai sur l'origine des langues* (composed, it is believed, in 1754), especially ch.4; de Brosses, *Traité de la formation mécanique des langues et des principes physiques de l'étymologie*, 2 vols. (Paris, 1765), vol.1, pp.xv, xlviii.

105. Court de Gébelin, "Natural History of Speech," vols. 2–3 (1774–75) of the *Monde primitif*, vol.2, p.ix; see also abbé Copineau, *Essai synthétique sur la formation des langues* (Paris, 1774).

106. Condillac, *Grammaire*, p.21.

107. See Bergier, op.cit., p.8, note a; Copineau, op.cit., pp.254ff.; Condillac, *Grammaire*, p.24n. As is well known, Rousseau, who sometimes seems to be of the same opinion, declared himself, in his *Discours sur l'inégalité* (*Oeuvres*, ed. Furne, vol.1, pp.543, 545), to be incapable of understanding how language could have been instituted by human means; it is often to Rousseau that authors are responding.

108. See abbé Dubos, *Réflexions critiques sur la poésie et la peinture*, 2 vols. (Paris, 1719), vol.1, pp.398–596 (taken up and developed in vol.3 of the edition of 1733), also p.634; Rousseau, *Essai sur l'origine des langues*, ch.19, and his various writings on music; Morellet, *De l'expression en musique et de l'imitation dans les arts*, in *Mercure de France* (November 1771), pp.113–42 (a rather remarkable text, dated from Milan, 1759); reproduced in 1818 in vol.4, pp.360ff. of the *Mélanges de littérature et de philosophie du dix-huitième siècle* by this author); *Journal étranger* (October 1761),

pp.5ff. (review of a dissertation on Chinese dances; republished in 1768 by Arnaud and Suard in vol.1, pp.472ff., of their *Variétés littéraires*); Diderot, *Le Neveu de Rameau*, ed. A.-T. of the *Oeuvres*, pp.458–59; Lacépède, *La Poétique de la Musique*, 2 vols. (Paris, 1785), book 1 and pp.51ff.; abbé Barthélemy, *Voyage du jeune Anacharsis en Grèce* (1788), ed. Hachette (1860), vol.1, p.421 (ch.27); Grétry, *Mémoires ou Essais sur la musique*, 3 vols. (Paris, year V), vol.2.

109. The theory of imitative and expressive music did not, however, convince everyone, as can be imagined; see, for example, Chastellux, *Essai sur l'union de la poésie et de la musique* (The Hague-Paris, 1765); Chabanon, *Observations sur la musique et principalement sur la métaphysique de l'art* (Paris, 1779).

110. See Condillac, *Essai*, p.104; Rousseau, *Essai sur l'origine des langues*, ch.3.

111. Condillac, *Essai*, p.113.

112. Rousseau, *Dictionnaire de musique* (1768), s.v. "Musique" (*Oeuvres*, ed. Furne, vol.3, p.742); this article had already appeared in vol.10 of the *Encyclopédie* (according to Rousseau's preface to the *Dictionnaire de musique*, he wrote it before 1750); the text changed somewhat from 1750 to 1768; the last lines of the passage cited, insisting on the spontaneity of poetry and the ministry of poetry in primitive times, are absent in the *Encyclopédie*; they are the fruit of further reflection on Rousseau's part.

113. Rabaut-Saint-Etienne, *Lettres à M. Bailly sur l'histoire primitive de la Grèce* (Paris, 1787), pp.59, 65–66, 76, 367. Rabaut was a pastor from Nîmes mostly known for his activity in the Constituent Assembly, and who died on the scaffold in 1793; in 1784 he had published some *Lettres sur la vie et les écrits de M. Court de Gébelin*.

114. The complex of ideas that can be grouped under the global name of poetic primitivism survived into the Restoration and beyond. One could cite a host of examples.

115. I say nothing about the European-wide vogue of ideas similar but not prior to those we observe in France. I have noted contacts with English writers. On the whole, it seems to me that the ideas in French thought on this subject are well-developed and mostly autonomous.

116. Robespierre, *Rapport du 18 floréal an II sur les fêtes nationales* (Bibl. Nat. Lb41 3914), p.39.

117. See, for example, *Le Magistrat-Prêtre* (n. d. [1790]), which has been attributed to Boissy d'Anglas, p.1: "I propose that order be reestablished by reuniting the Spiritual Authority [*le Pontificat*] and national sovereignty, the Priesthood [*le Sacerdoce*] with the Judiciary."

118. Thus De Moy, *Accord de la religion et des cultes chez une nation libre* (Paris, An IV de la Liberté [1792]), p.29: "The civil and the religious power have been too long and too closely linked together."

119. See A. Mathiez, *Les Origines des cultes révolutionnaires (1789–1792)* (Paris,

1904), pp.29ff.; and, by the same author, *La Théophilanthropie et le culte décadaire (1796–1801)* (Paris, 1903).

120. Thus abbé Sicard (*A la recherche d'une religion civile* [Paris, 1895]). The well-documented and extremely informative studies by David Lloyd Dowd scarcely modify that point of view (*Jacques-Louis David and the French Revolution* [Lincoln: University of Nebraska Press, 1948]; *L'Art comme moyen de propagande pendant la Révolution française* [Paris, 1953], from the acts of the Seventy-seventh Congress of Learned Societies [Grenoble, 1953]).

121. This was clear to André Monglond; preromantic heroes and "apostles of equality" rub shoulders in his book; he stresses (*Histoire intérieure*, vol.2, p.408) the "extraordinary, unheard-of heat" of the Revolution's beginnings. P. Trahard completed his studies on eighteenth-century French Sensibility with *La Sensibilité révolutionnaire* (Paris, 1936).

122. Renan, *Souvenirs d'enfance et de jeunesse* (Paris, 1883), pp.110–11.

123. G. Monod, preface to Mathiez, *Contributions à l'histoire religieuse de la Révolution française* (Paris, 1907), p.1.

124. A.-F. Rio, *Epilogue à l'Art chrétien*, 2 vols. (Freiburg im Breisgau, 1870), vol.1, pp.221–22. [This was the Festival of Federation held in Paris on the first anniversary of the fall of the Bastille, July 14, 1790. *Trans.*]

125. Princess of Salm, *Mes Soixante Ans* (Paris, 1883), p.5. Constance-Marie de Theis, who became Mme Pipelet, then princess of Salm-Dyck, was born, according to biographies, in 1767.

126. Stendhal, *Mémoires sur Napoléon* (written in 1836–38), p.31 of the volume devoted to them in the Martineau edition of the *Oeuvres*.

127. Robespierre, *Rapport du 18 floréal*, p.29; second speech to the Festival of Supreme Reason, 20 Prairial year II (same collection, Bibl. Nat., p.72).

128. See Monglond, *Histoire intérieure*, vol.2, pp.155–56, and G. Monod, preface, pp.ii–iii.

129. Mathiez, *Contributions*, p.33; same views in *Les Origines*, pp.10–12, and also in *Robespierre et la déchristianisation* (*Annales révolutionnaires* [1909], p.324).

130. Cited in Aulard, *Le Culte de la Raison et le culte de l'Etre suprême (1793–1794)* (Paris, 1892), p.293.

131. *Rapport du 18 floréal*, p.42.

132. Ch.-Alex. de Moy, *Des Fêtes*, (Paris, year VII), note 3, p.152, p.149. De Moy, born in 1750, *député-suppléant* in the National Assembly, was a curé of Saint-Laurent in Paris who accepted the Civil Constitution of the Clergy in 1790; later, we are told, he taught in the Imperial University and died only in 1834.

133. Mathiez holds the "godless men" of those times to have been "religious souls" (*Contributions*, p.27), and Dommanget (op.cit., p.438) thinks it best to define Sylvain Maréchal as "a religious atheist."

134. This is the title of the book by Ph. Le Harivel, *Nicolas de Bonneville, préromantique et révolutionnaire, 1760–1828* (Strasburg-Paris, 1923).

135. Bonneville, *Appendices de la seconde édition de l'"Esprit des religions"* (Paris, 1792), p.95.

136. Bonneville, *De l'esprit des religions*, one volume in two parts (Paris, 1791), I, p.25, II, p.65.

137. See Aulard, op.cit., passim; Mathiez, *Contributions*, pp.122–24; *Robespierre et le culte de l'Etre suprême*, in *Annales révolutionnaires* (1910), pp.209ff.

138. It already appears in the debates of the Constituent Assembly: thus Talleyrand, *Rapport sur l'instruction publique* (September 10, 11, and 19, 1791) (Angers, 1791), pp.120–21. See also Mirabeau, *Travail sur l'éducation publique* (found in his papers after his death) (Paris, 1791), second speech.

139. *Considérations sur l'état actuel des Arts . . . publiées et présentées à la Convention Nationale* (neither place nor date of publication; Bibl. Nat. Vp.19292): this brochure, according to its text, dates from the days following Thermidor; the *Société républicaine des arts*, led by David until the fall of Robespierre, had survived that event and was following the line of the new régime.

140. Chaussard, *Essai philosophique sur la dignité des arts* (Paris, Ventôse year VI), pp.3, 7. Pierre-Jean-Baptiste (called Publicola) Chaussard, born in 1766, was a revolutionary and a theophilanthropist, later professor during the Empire.

141. Daunou, opening speech to the first public session at the opening of the *Institut*, 4 April 1796, cited by Sainte-Beuve, *Portraits contemporains*, vol.4, p.314. See also La Revellière-Lépeaux, *Réflexions sur le culte . . . lues à l'Institut le 12 floréal an V* (Paris, year V), pp.18, 20.

142. These ideas are to be found everywhere at this time. See Talleyrand, *Rapport*, p.121; *La Décade* of 10 Floréal year II (vol.1, pp.8–9), etc.

143. Chaussard, *Essai*, p.19.

144. See for example André Chénier, *Le Jeu de Paume* (ed. Dimoff of the *Oeuvres*, vol.3, pp.230–32); Grétry, *Mémoires ou Essais sur la musique* (Paris, year V), vol.3, pp.4–6.

145. Boissy d'Anglas, *Quelques Idées sur les arts* (Paris, year II), Bibl. Nat. Lb41 1127 A, p.128.

146. "Du pouvoir de la poésie," ode that won the prize proposed by the Lycée des Arts, *Magazin encyclopédique*, vol.16 (1797), pp.88ff.

147. André Chénier, *Essai sur les causes et les effets de la perfection et de la décadence des lettres et les arts* (text from the 1780s), *Oeuvres*, ed. G. Walter (Bibliothèque de la Pléiade), p.591.

148. J.-B. Leclerc, "Essai sur la propagation de la musique en France" (dated Prairial year IV), in *Opuscules moraux* (anthology by La Revellière-Lépeaux and Leclerc) (Paris, year VI); in another short work in the same collection, entitled "On Poetry Considered in Its Relation to National Education" (speech of 10 January 1792), he cited "La Marseillaise" as an example. The comparison of Tyrtaeus and Rouget de Lisle is found in the ode "Du pouvoir de la poésie," cited above, in the ninth stanza; also in abbé Grégoire, *Rapport sur les encouragements, récompenses et*

pensions à accorder aux savants, aux gens de lettres et aux artistes (Paris, Vendémiaire year III), p.11; and probably in many other places.

149. See Mornet, *Les Origines intellectuelles de la Révolution française* (Paris, 1939), pp.258–66.

150. Rousseau, *Lettre à d'Alembert*, ed. Fuchs (Lille-Geneva, 1948), p.105. To the same effect, see in Diderot an encomium of the Greek theater, said to unite "an entire nation on its holy days" ("Entretiens sur le Fils naturel," 2nd *entretien*, *Oeuvres*, ed. A.-T., vol.7, p.123; also abbé Barthélemy, *Voyage du jeune Anacharsis en Grèce* (1788), passim and notably ch.77.

151. Rousseau, *Lettre à d'Alembert*, p.168. Rousseau remembers Swiss civic festivals (see the letter to J.-L. Mollet [1761] in vol.6, p.145 of the *Correspondance*, ed. Dufour).

152. Text included in Vaughan, *The Political Writings of J.-J. Rousseau*, 2 vols. (Cambridge, 1915), vol.1, p.507.

153. See the Garnier edition of the *Oeuvres*, vol.18, p.378 (passage of the *Dictionnaire philosophique*, s.v. "Dieu," borrowed from the *Questions sur l'Encyclopédie* [1771]).

154. Rousseau, *Projet de constitution pour la Corse* (1765), in Vaughan, vol.2, p.351.

155. Sylvain Maréchal, *Almanach des honnêtes gens* (n.d. but the date of 1788 is well established as the latest possible by a dated republication: see Dommanget, op.cit., p.453); Maréchal, in this idea of a calendar, had in fact had several precursors in the course of the 1780s; see ibid., pp.121–23.

156. *Le Rédacteur* (23 Fructidor year IV) (cited by Mathiez, *La Théophilanthropie*, p.30; the author is perhaps La Revellière-Lépeaux).

157. Cited by Mathiez, *Les Origines*, p.48.

158. Robespierre, *Rapport du 18 floréal*, p.46.

159. De Moy, *Des fêtes*, pp.8. 18–19.

160. "Robespierre, speaking of the Supreme Being to the most enlightened people in the world, reminds me of Orpheus teaching the first principles of civilization and morals." These lines are by Boissy d'Anglas (*Essai sur les fêtes nationales* [Paris, 12 Messidor year II], p.23), who certainly was not being sincere; what he thought it fitting to write is meaningful nonetheless.

161. Abbé Grégoire, Report, p.11.

162. De Moy, *Des fêtes*, p.2.

163. La Revellière-Lépeaux, *Essai sur les moyens de faire participer l'universalité des spectateurs à tout ce qui se pratique dans les fêtes nationales* (Paris, year VI), p.5.

164. Rousseau, *De l'économie politique* (*Oeuvres*, ed. Furne, vol.1, p.595); this text appeared in 1755 in vol.5 of the *Encyclopédie* (s.v. "Economie").

165. This holds generally. There exist occasional special cases, but they are too complex to recount in detail in a work like this one, which tries above all to describe the main lines of force. Thus Bonneville, in his *Poésies* (Paris, 1793 — year II), went a

long way toward the idea of a specifically poetic ministry: see especially the group of pieces entitled "The Poet" at the end of the collection. But these poems date from a time when the September massacres had horrified him: the great figure of the Poet rises up in him, not because of his revolutionary faith, but because he is revising this faith — which, as we shall see, is in the nature of things.

2. THE POET CONSECRATED

1. Bossuet, *Discours sur l'histoire universelle* (1681), in *Oeuvres*, ed. Migne, vol.10, col. 790; see also the "Dissertation on Psalms," at the beginning of the *Liber Psalmorum*, ibid., vol.5, col. 405–8, 420ff.

2. Bossuet, *Discours*, cited edition, col. 791.

3. Thus Frain du Tremblay, (*Discours sur l'origine de la poésie, sur son usage et sur le bon goût* [Paris, 1713]) holds that the Greeks could only be poets by imitating what they were able to know (?) of Hebraic poetry. Huet (*Demonstratio evangelica* [1679]) had similarly explained Fable as a plagiarism of Scripture. These theses were not without authority at this time.

4. Abbé Cl. Fleury, *Moeurs des Israëlites* (Paris, 1681), p.166.

5. Abbé Fleury, "Discourse on Poetry and Particularly on That of the Ancient Hebrews," in *Opuscules de M. l'abbé Fleury*, vol.2 (Nîmes, 1780), p.645; this text first appeared in 1713 in the *Commentaire littéral sur tous les livres de l'Ancien et du Nouveau Testament* de Dom Calmet, at the beginning of the second volume on the psalms.

6. Ibid., p.650.

7. Fénelon, *Lettre à l'Académie* (1716), ch.5.

8. Fénelon, *Dialogues sur l'éloquence* (1718; composed in the 1680s), 2nd and 3rd dialogues.

9. Fénelon, *Les Aventures de Télémaque*, ed. Cahen (Collection des Grands Ecrivains) (Paris, 1920), vol.1, p.75.

10. Don Calmet, "Dissertation on the Poetry of the Ancient Hebrews," in *Commentaire*, vol.2 (1708), pp.xlix–l; see also "Dissertation on the Music of the Ancients and Particularly of the Hebrews," *Commentaire*, vol.10 (1713), pp.lv–lix.

11. Abbé Massieu, *Histoire* (1739), p.27.

12. Louis Racine, *Epître sur l'abus que les poètes font de la poésie, à M. de Valincour* (1720), in *Oeuvres* (Paris, 1747), vol.2, p.181; *Réflexions sur la poésie*, ibid., vol.3, p.21.

13. La Harpe, *Le Pseautier en français* (Paris, year VI), p.xxv.

14. Rollin, *De la manière d'enseigner et d'étudier les belles-lettres*, vol.2 (Paris, 1740), p.210 (original edition in 1726); this primitive poetry was sung and danced.

15. Louis Racine, *Réflexions*, vol.3, p.63.

16. Abbé Batteux, *Cours de belles-lettres*, vol.2 (Paris, 1748), p.27. One could go on forever giving citations; see, for example, Laurent Garcin, *Odes sacrées* (Bern, n.d. [1764]), p.vi.

17. See Frain du Tremblay, *Discours*, pp.6ff.

18. Lefranc de Pompignan, "Preliminary Discourse" to the *Poésies sacrées* (Paris, 1751), p.vi.

19. Gabriel-Henri Gaillard, *Poétique française à l'usage des dames*, 2 vols. (Paris, 1749), vol.1, p.vi.

20. See in particular the reviews in *L'Année littéraire* (1764, vol.3, p.168; 1770, vol.5, p.241; 1771, vol.8, p.3; 1775, vol.6, p.145).

21. In Roger Mercier, op.cit., p.38, will be found a list of collections that appeared from 1700 to 1735. I give here summary references of those that I have seen, especially in the second half of the century: J.-B. Rousseau (about twenty sacred odes, almost all of which are already to be found in the editions of his works in 1712); abbé Desfontaines, *Poésies sacrées* (1717); Louis Racine (about twenty biblical odes in his *Oeuvres* [1747]); abbé Batteux (op.cit., vol.2 [1748], one psalm); Lefranc de Pompignan, *Poésies sacrées* (1751); abbé Séguy, *Nouvel essai de poésies sacrées* (1756); P.-T. Masson, *Elégies sacrées* (1754); Baculard d'Arnaud, *Lamentations de Jérémie, odes* (1757); Pierre de Bologne, *Odes sacrées* (1758); Malfilâtre (died in 1767; one psalm in *Oeuvres* [1825], p.205); abbé de Reyrac, *Poésies tirées des saintes Ecritures* (1770); Gilbert (died in 1780, "Ode Imitated from Several Psalms": these are the famous "Adieux to Life"); cardinal de Boisgelin, *Le Psalmiste* (1799). This production is marked now and then by the publication of anthologies: thus that of E.-J. Monchablon (*Les Psaumes et les principaux cantiques mis en vers par nos meilleurs poètes* [1762]), that by Garcin (*Odes sacrées* [1764], an anthology combined with original pieces), that of Couret de Villeneuve (*Les Lyriques sacrés ou chefs-d'oeuvre poétiques en ce genre* [1774]).

22. See such amalgams in J.-B. Rousseau, Bologne, Gilbert, Reyrac.

23. Thus in Malfilâtre "The Prophet Elijah Taken up into Heaven."

24. Bologne and Reyrac did the same, and the other anthologized authors collect and mingle poems of these two genres.

25. Fleury, *Opuscules*, vol.2, p.651; Louis Racine, *Réflexions*, vol.3, pp.24ff.

26. Fleury, *Opuscules*, vol.2, p.659.

27. Frain du Tremblay, *Discours*, p.67.

28. Louis Racine, *Epître*, p.188; Lefranc de Pompignan, "Preliminary Discourse," p.xvi; Reyrac, *Poésies tirées*, p.xlvi. See also Couret de Villeneuve, *Les Lyriques*, p.vi.

29. This entire intellectual movement, to judge from its dates, developed in France independent of foreign influences. The Englishman Robert Lowth's book, *De sacra poesi Hebraeorum*, which develops all the themes we have mentioned, is often cited: see the *Gazette littéraire de l'Europe*, vol.3 (1764), p.65; Roucher, *Les Mois*, vol.1 (1779), p.138; La Harpe, *Le Pseautier* (year VI), p.xv; but it appeared, in Oxford, only in 1753. Hugh Blair's *Dissertation on the Poetry of the Hebrews* is from 1783; I see it published in French only in 1785 (Millin, *Mélanges de littérature étrangère*, vol.4) and 1789 (second edition of Couret de Villeneuve's *Lyriques*). It is in 1777 that the *Supplément à l'Encyclopédie* (vol.4, s.v. "Ode") makes known a fragment of the Theory of Beaux-Arts of a German, Sulzer, which exalts Hebraic po-

etry and refers to Lowth. As for Herder's remarkable work, *Vom Geist der ebräischen Poesie*, it appears in 1782/83, and was translated into French only in 1844: it is scarcely mentioned in France in the last years of the eighteenth century (*Magazine encyclopédique*, vol.18, p.563).

30. Thus Boulanger, s.v. "Langue hébraïque" in the *Encyclopédie*, vol.8 (1765); see J. Hampton, op.cit., p.48; Marmontel, s.v. "Lyrique" in the *Supplément a l'Encyclopédie*, vol.3 (1777); Roucher, *Les Mois* (1779), vol.1, pp.276ff.

31. See, for example, s.v. "Poésie lyrique" in the *Encyclopédie*, vol.12 (1765) signed Jaucourt; also Louis de Cahusac, *La Danse ancienne et moderne*, 3 vols. (The Hague, 1754), vol.1, pp.18–19; G. Legouvé, *La Mort d'Abel* (Paris, 1793), p.x.

32. Abbé Maury, *Discours prononcé à sa réception à l'Académie française le 27 janvier 1785*, in *Discours prononcés*, etc. (Avignon, 1807) (Bibl. Nat. 80 Z. 1836), p.19. Abbé Maury succeeded Lefranc de Pompignan as academician.

33. *Oeuvres diverses du Sieur R*[ousseau] (Soleure, 1712), p.xxi.

34. This is what happens in an isolated case that resembles a caricature: Jean-Marie Chassaignon, an unrestrained preromantic, a deviant Catholic, counterrevolutionary and half mad, published in 1779 the *Cataractes de l'imagination*, 4 vols.: one can read therein (vol.4, pp.213ff.) a "Paraphrase of the Poems of Ezekiel, etc., Visions, Hells, New Apocalypse, an Offering to the Clergy," in which the Poet makes himself the Messiah in order to exercise a contemporaneous ministry that is a sort of Last Judgment of miscreant *philosophes*.

35. The "sacred poem," the Christian form of the epic, had not met with much success in the previous century. In the 18th century Milton was known and admired, and his *Paradise Lost* was translated several times (notably in 1755 by Louis Racine). Klopstock was admired rather early (thus Fréron in the *Année littéraire* in 1755: see the *Revue d'histoire littéraire de la France* [1895], p.183); *Der Messias* was translated into French as early as 1769; however, if his piece *Von der heilige Poesie* (1755), in which he argues above all for a high modern religious poetry, was not unknown in France (see *Journal étranger* [October 1760], pp.174ff.), it does not seem to have had much influence at this time; it was only completely translated into French in 1825, in the translation by M.-J. d'Horrer of *Der Messias*. Interest in Klopstock will only grow around 1800, and hardly any sacred poems inspired by these novelties will be written before the Restoration.

3. ILLUMINISM AND POETRY

1. There has been a renewal of interest in Saint-Martin in our time due to the development of research on illuminism. See the works of Aug. Viatte, mainly *Les Sources occultes du romantisme*, 2 vols. (Paris, 1928) and, on Saint-Martin in particular, those by Robert Amadou. An article by Robert Kanters (*Revue de Paris* [August 1953]) brought "the Unknown Philosopher" once more before the public; and Léon Cellier (*Revue des sciences humaines* [1964], pp.25–35) summarized the state of

Saint-Martin studies at that time. Finally, an overview recently appeared in Poland (M. Secrecka, *Louis-Claude de Saint-Martin le philosophe inconnu* [Breslau, 1968]).

2. See Viatte, op.cit., vol.1, in particular pp.25ff., 37ff., and Léon Cellier, *L'Epopée préromantique* (Paris, 1954), pp.43–46. Even neopagan or syncretic illuminism sometimes keeps the Fall-Redemption pattern: thus in the *Thréicie* (Paris, year VI) by Quintus Aucler (see on pp.284–85 an explicit homage to Saint-Martin), to whom Nerval dedicated a chapter of his *Les Illuminés*.

3. What is called illuminism in figures like Dupont de Nemours or Rétif de la Bretonne, or occasionally in those like Court de Gébelin or Bonneville, is to be distinguished by a fundamental naturalism which, in fact, turns its back on theosophy, though it is true that it embraces some of the beliefs or tendencies evoked here.

4. Dutoit-Membrini, *La Philosophie divine par Keleph Ben Nathan*, 3 vols. (n. p., 1793), vol.1, p.112 n.2. The duchesse de Bourbon, a high-born lady with theosophical tendencies, having read Dutoit, repeats these formulas with conviction (*Correspondance entre Mme de B... et M. R... sur leurs opinions religieuses*, 2 vols. [Barcelona, 1812–13], vol.1, p.45).

5. Dutoit-Membrini, *La Philosophie*, vol.2, p.76.

6. Thus Swedenborg, according to Martin Lamm, *Swedenborg* (Paris, 1936), pp.228, 232; see also Antoine-Joseph Pernéty (a Swedenborgian alchemist from Avignon), *Les Vertus, le pouvoir, la clémence et la gloire de Marie, mère de Dieu* (Paris, 1790), pp.329–30. Dutoit, op.cit., vol.1, p.20: the object of the incarnation is to "divinize" human nature and to raise it to the level of the celestial prototype; to the same effect Dampierre (a magistrate, friend of the Waldensian Quietists, an acquaintance of Mme de Krudener and Mme de Staël), *Vérités divines pour le coeur et pour l'esprit*, 2 vols. (Lausanne, 1824), vol.1, p.74; vol.2, pp.49–50, p.305: Incarnation resuscitated the Man-God in us (Dampierre was born in 1743; 1824 is the date of his death); the count of Divonne, *La Voie de la science divine* (Paris, 1805), p.5 (dialogues of the English illuminist William Law, freely translated; Divonne knew Saint-Martin and was also a familiar of Mme de Staël's circle at Coppet; L. Bonifas-Laroque (Protestant minister and a Swedenborgian), *L'Elève de l'Evangile*, 2 vols. (Toulouse, 1812), vol.1, pp.286, 314, 316, 320. The same theology can be seen in a French translation of Eckartshausen, *La Nuée sur le sanctuaire* (Paris, 1819), pp.121, 160.

7. Thus Martinez de Pasqually, *Traité de la réintégration* (composed in 1771–72) according to R. Le Forestier, *La Franc-Maçonnerie occultiste au dix-huitième siècle et l'ordre de Elus Coëns* (Paris, 1928), p.21 (in Martinez, Adam seems to participate in the divine nature more than Jesus); Dutoit, op.cit., vol.1, pp.43, 219 ("microtheotic" Adam); Divonne, op.cit., p.109 (Jesus Christ a "second Adam"; orthodox theology would only be able to say that Adam is the figure of Jesus, which is very different).

8. See Lamm, op.cit., pp.228, 238–39; also the Swedenborgian Devismes, *Essai sur l'homme ou l'homme microcosme* (Rouen-Paris, 1805), p.4 ("Heaven, considered

as a whole, represents a man"); p.13 ("God is man, properly speaking he is the only Man"). These are essential articles of faith in Swedenborgianism: see also, in 1835, Edouard Richer, *De la nouvelle Jérusalem*, vol.6, p.402: "What is God? He is uncreated Man."

9. This is the name of man for Martinez, who however magnifies as much as he can this "minority."

10. Le Forestier, op.cit., p.70; he is speaking only of Martinez, but the observation applies, I believe, to all of illuminism.

11. Viatte, op.cit., vol.2, p.269.

12. Saint-Martin, Letter to his German translator (1784) (cited by R. Amadou, p.xiv of his edition of Saint-Martin, *Mon Portrait historique et philosophique* [Paris, 1961]).

13. Saint-Martin, *De l'esprit des choses*, 2 vols. (Paris, year VIII [1800]), vol.1, p.56.

14. Saint-Martin, *Des erreurs et de la vérité* (Edinburgh [Lyons], 1775), p.235; *Tableau naturel des rapports qui existent entre Dieu, l'Homme et l'Univers*, 2 vols. (Edinburgh, 1782), vol.1, p.73; *Le Ministère de l'Homme-Esprit* (Paris, year XI [1802]), p.285 (this last text refers to the past since it deals with man at his creation; but the Fall has not radically changed things for Saint-Martin).

15. Saint-Martin, *Lettre à un ami ou Considérations politiques, philosophiques et religieuses sur la Révolution Française* (Paris, year III [1795]), p.4.

16. Saint-Martin, *Mon Portrait*, ed. Amadou, no.656. No. 503 is even more curious: "In my childish ideas, and in reflecting, in my way, on the unknown being that was presented to me as the Divinity, it sometimes happened that I asked myself why this bountiful God should not be myself." Why indeed? Saint-Martin calmly attributes this thought to childhood ignorance.

17. Saint-Martin, *Le Ministère de l'Homme-Esprit*, p.280 (on the Eucharist, which the church is wrong to call *mysterium fidei*, an expression not to be found in the Gospels); see ibid., pp.47, 371; and already *Des erreurs et de la vérité*, p.227.

18. Matter, *Saint-Martin le philosophe inconnu* (Paris, 1862), p.113.

19. Saint-Martin, *Mon Portrait*, no.165.

20. Saint-Martin, *Des erreurs et de la vérité*, passim.

21. Saint-Martin, *Tableau naturel*, vol.1, p.204; *Des erreurs et de la vérité*, pp.460ff.; also *De l'esprit des choses*, vol.2, pp.126ff., and *Cahier des langues*, published by R. Amadou in the *Cahiers de la Tour Saint-Jacques*, no.7 (1961), p.183; *Lettre à un ami*, passim, and *Eclair sur l'association humaine* (Paris, 1797 [year V]), passim. These works belong to different periods of Saint-Martin's career. To them can be added the satirical and often enigmatic *Crocodile* of year VII (republished by Amadou [Paris, 1962]), which is essentially a diatribe against false sciences, philosophism, the academies that shelter these doctrines, and so forth.

22. Saint-Martin, *Mon Portrait*, no.1007; see also *L'Homme de désir* (Lyons, 1790), no.210, and *Le Ministère de l'Homme-Esprit*, pp.395–96. *Buhon-upas* is an Asian vegetable poison.

23. *Mon Portrait*, no.497; he compared himself elsewhere to Rousseau with the same blend of modesty and superiority (see ibid., no.577).

24. See on "divinism" *Mon Portrait*, no.576.

25. See *Lettre à un ami*, p.6; "Fragments of a Treatise on Admiration," in *Oeuvres posthumes*, 2 vols. (Tours, 1807), vol.2, pp.353–403; *De l'esprit des choses*, vol.1, beginning; *Mon Portrait*, no.72.

26. *Oeuvres posthumes*, vol.1, pp.319–20; and see Viatte, op.cit., vol.1, p.190.

27. Saint-Martin, *Ecce homo* (Paris, year IV of Liberty [1792]), p.30; also *Lettre à un ami*, p.10.

28. *Tableau naturel*, vol.1, p.38; *De l'esprit des choses*, vol.2, p.343.

29. See especially *De l'esprit des choses*, vol.1, pp.88ff., 128ff.

30. *L'Homme de désir*, no.295, p.404.

31. *Le Ministère de l'Homme-Esprit*, p.82; see also *Le Crocodile*, song 23, p.42 of the Amadou edition; *De l'esprit des choses*, vol.1, pp.256ff.; *Oeuvres posthumes*, vol.2, pp.247, 291.

32. *De l'esprit des choses*, vol.1, pp.259–60; *L'Homme de désir*, no.46, p.80.

33. Allegorism, which contemporaries generally made an intellectual characteristic of primitive man, is for the illuminists a doctrine of being and a key to truth: thus Swedenborg (see Lamm, op.cit., pp.88ff.) and the Swedenborgians (Pernéty, *Les Fables égyptiennes et grecques*, 2 vols. [Paris], vol.1, pp.50–51; Devismes, *Essai*, p.19). Similarly, Dutoit (op.cit., vol.1, p.346, vol.2, pp.264, 272–73); these views are often linked to an affirmation of the allegorical meaning of Scripture. See also Q. Aucler, op.cit., p.281. On this matter of correspondences, naturalistic illuminism is no less affirmative than theosophy, though without the same metaphysical perspectives; see Dupont de Nemours, *Philosophe de l'univers* (n.d., written in 1792–93), p.136; and especially Rétif de la Bretonne, who proclaims "the great and majestic idea of universal polytypism" (*Philosophie de M. Nicolas*, 3 vols. [Paris, year V — 1796], vol.1, p.262) and never tires of repeating that "everything in nature is image and type" (ibid., vol.2, p.271; also in *Les Posthumes*, 4 vols. [Paris, 1802], vol.1, p.205; vol.3, p.301).

34. *Des erreurs et de la vérité*, pp.457, 485.

35. First published separately, the *Réponse* was annexed to *Le Crocodile*, where it appears as song 70.

36. *Le Crocodile*, ed. Amadou, pp.144, 146, 159–60.

37. *Des erreurs et de la vérité*, p.485.

38. *Le Ministère de l'Homme-Esprit*, p.310; see Isaiah 6:3: a passage used in the Jewish liturgy as well as in the Roman Catholic liturgy, where it is *Sanctus*.

39. *Le Crocodile*, pp.160, 172–73; see similarly *De l'esprit des choses*, vol.2, pp.228–30.

40. *De l'esprit des choses*, vol.1, pp.174, 182–83, 185.

41. *Des erreurs et de la vérité*, pp.485, 506.

42. *De l'esprit des choses*, vol.2, pp.212ff., especially p.217.

43. Ibid., vol.2, p.223. For Saint-Martin, "reintegration," the "longing for God," and the "root of all languages" are connected expressions and notions; see ibid., vol.2, pp.343–44.

44. *Tableau naturel*, vol.1, p.65; *De l'esprit des choses*, vol.1, p.179.

45. The exaltation of poetry as knowledge of the divine and a key to an analogical world is, in the eighteenth century, more common in Germany than in France. But as far as I know, Saint-Martin was familiar neither with Hamann nor with the young Herder; we know only that he was partial to Klopstock (see Viatte, op.cit., vol.1, pp.189, 193).

46. Saint-Martin, "Question proposed by the Academy of Berlin," in *Oeuvres posthumes*, vol.2, pp.34ff.: primitive poetry is an intuition of the supernatural, and the first poets are the first wise men.

47. See, among other passages, *L'Homme de désir*, no.149, p.122; no.192, p.277; "On Prophetic, Epic, and Lyric Poetry," in *Oeuvres posthumes*, vol.2, pp.274–75.

48. "On Prophetic Poetry," p.273.

49. *Oeuvres posthumes*, vol.2, p.282; "Phanor" takes up pp.284–313.

50. "Phanor," p.289.

51. Ibid., p.291.

52. *Des erreurs et de la vérité*, pp.492–93.

53. *Cahier des langues*, p.159.

54. "The Cemetery of Amboise," in *Oeuvres posthumes*, vol.1, pp.352–53; the poem was finished in February 1801 (see *Mon Portrait*, no.1022); it was published the same year in an edition that I have been unable to consult.

55. *Le Ministère de l'Homme-Esprit*, p.389. Cf., *Oeuvres posthumes*, vol.1, p.199 — these lines, which are to be found among the miscellaneous thoughts: "One should only write verse after having accomplished a miracle, since verses ought to have no other object than to celebrate this."

56. *L'Homme de désir*, no.131; *Oeuvres posthumes*, vol.2, p.343; ibid., p.314; *Mon portrait*, no.422; and see Viatte, op.cit., vol.1, p.189.

57. "On Prophetic Poetry," p.276.

58. "Phanor," p.293.

59. Saint-Martin has not the least hesitation about the *reality* of the ideal; he reproaches artists for presenting it as imaginary when it is merely beyond their ken: see *De l'esprit des choses*, vol.1, p.54; and similarly "Phanor," pp.304–5; also a remarkable page in Saint-Martin's *Pensées mythologiques*, published by R. Amadou (*Cahiers de la Tour Saint-Jacques*, no.VII [1961], pp.22–23).

60. *Le Ministère de l'Homme-Esprit*, p.365.

61. "Phanor," pp.297, 303, 306, 307.

62. Ibid., p.307.

63. *Le Ministère de l'Homme-Esprit*, p.362.

64. See *L'Homme de désir*, no.273, pp.376–78, and the piece entitled "On Prophetic, Epic, and Lyric Poetry," already cited several times.

65. *Correspondance inédite*, p.115 (letter of January 1794).

66. *Mon Portrait*, no.559.

67. See ibid., no.653; *Correspondance inédite*, p.193 (May 1795); *Lettre à un ami*, p.18.

68. *Mon Portrait*, no.707; also ibid., no.596: already in 1787, he tells us, upon seeing the pope sweating profusely under his tiara, he sarcastically applied to him the biblical saying: "You shall gain your bread by the sweat of your brow."

69. Ibid., no.969; see also no.839.

70. Ibid., no.594 and no.846.

71. *Correspondance inédite*, p.199 (June 1795).

72. *Mon Portrait*, no.679.

73. See *Lettre à un ami*, pp.20ff.; *Eclair sur l'association humaine*, pp.49–51; the same ideas are already to be found in a text dated 1778 (*Oeuvres posthumes*, vol.1, pp.388–95).

74. See *Des erreurs et de la vérité*, pp.282–83; *Lettre à un ami*, pp.28–29.

75. *Oeuvres posthumes*, vol.1, pp.395–98.

76. *Lettre à un ami*, pp.28–29.

77. For example, *Eclair sur l'association humaine*, pp.34–35.

78. See the *Correspondance entre Mme de B. . . et M. R. . .*, passim; Divonne, *La Voix qui crie dans le désert* (Paris, year XIII — 1805) (at the beginning of *La Voie de la science divine*, translated from the English of William Law), pp.28ff.; Cazotte, *Oeuvres*, 4 vols. (Paris, 1817) (posthumous edition: he had died in 1792), vol.1, passim; Dampierre, *Vérités divines*, vol.1, pp.349ff., by the same author, *Historique de la Révolution tiré des saintes écritures* (Dijon, 1824); Louis Bergasse, *Nicolas Bergasse, 1750–1832* (Paris, 1910).

4. COUNTERREVOLUTION AND LITERATURE

1. They were finally officially abandoned in Nivôse year VIII (the beginning of the year 1800).

2. This notion of generations, so controversial in itself as well as in its applications (see Jean Pommier, *L'Idée des générations*, in *Conférences de Franz Cumont et J. Pommier*, Publications de l'E. N. S., section des lettres, II [Paris, 1945], pp.3–43, and the bibliography mentioned in this study; also Henri Peyre, *Les Générations littéraires* [Paris, 1948]), appears artificial when placed in the light of the continuous succession of births, which does not seem susceptible of compartmentalization. It would seem that its only justification is the relation of human beings to great events. These events, in their discontinuous succession, cut out distinct groups from the human tide and influence them spasmodically. This is how the notion will be used here. Those who were twenty, or fifteen, or thirty years old in 1789 could have been affected similarly; the Revolution dominated their experience, even if they reacted to it differently: in this sense, Senancour or Mme de Staël are indeed of Chateaubriand's generation. Those who were even forty years old at the same moment

had been formed according to other impressions, while those who were only ten did not experience the ordeal. In France the generations that we can call, on the whole, romantic arrange themselves according to the events of 1789, 1815, 1830, and 1848. Vigny and Hugo, born approximately at the turn of the century, only five years apart, and ten years after Lamartine, are closer to Lamartine than to Gautier, Musset, or Nerval, who were born about ten years after Vigny and Hugo (Nerval only six years after Hugo), but too late to have experienced the return of the monarchy and the church; Vigny and Hugo become thinking beings in 1815–20 and are men of the Restoration; Gautier, Musset, and Nerval belong to the generation of 1830: their basic problems are not the same. And those who in 1830 were children — Baudelaire, Leconte de Lisle, Flaubert — belong to the generation of 1848 (of the eve and the aftermath of 1848). In any case, all this can only be global and approximate: the irregularities and exceptions would be easy to point out, they do not, in my opinion, affect the overall pattern.

3. See F. Baldensperger, *Le Mouvement des idées dans l'émigration française*, 2 vols. (Paris, 1925), especially the second volume. The best-known literary periodicals of the emigration are *Le Spectateur du Nord*, which appeared in Hamburg from 1797 to 1802: Barbier (*Dictionnaire des ouvrages anonymes*, vol.4, col.559) indicates that this periodical was at first (until September 1797 and the coup d'état of Fructidor) reprinted in France.

4. See for example the letter from Dussault to the editor in chief of his *Annales littéraires*, vol.1 (1818), pp.xivff.; the article that Chateaubriand devoted to this work in 1819, and reproduced in his *Mélanges littéraires* (Ladvocat edition of his *Oeuvres*, vol.21 [1826], pp.335ff.); the short piece by Féletz on Dussault collected in his *Jugements historiques et littéraires* (Paris-Lyons, 1840), pp.158–60.

5. M.-J. Chénier, *Oeuvres*, 5 vols. (Paris, 1826), vol.3.

6. Benjamin Constant, *Des réactions politiques* (n.p., year V), p.30.

7. Rivarol, *Oeuvres*, ed. Fayolle-Chênedollé, 5 vols. (Paris, 1808), vol.1, pp.298–380 (original date: 1800); J.-M. B. Clément, vol.1 of the *Tableau*, 3 vols. (Paris, year IX [1801]); Joseph Fiévée, five articles in the *Mercure de France*, vols. 15 and 16, from 28 Pluviôse to 8 Floréal year XII (February-April 1804); Fontanes, two articles in *Mercure*, vol.1, pp.13 and 171 of 13 Messidor and 1 Thermidor year VIII (July 1800).

8. See André Beaunier, *La Jeunesse de Joseph Joubert* (Paris, 1918).

9. *Les Carnets de Joseph Joubert*, ed. A. Beaunier, 2 vols. (Paris, 1938) (continuous pagination), pp.626, 453, 127.

10. Letter from Joubert to Molé (30 March 1804) reproduced by R. Tessonneau (*Joseph Joubert éducateur* [Paris, 1944], pp.497–98).

11. See especially in *L'Année littéraire* (1764), vol.3, pp.3ff. a very favorable review of a work by Garnier; ibid. (1766), vol.6, pp.156ff., a review of *Le Bonheur des gens de lettres* by Mercier, scarcely skeptical, and a laudatory commentary on the same work: ibid. (1776), vol.2, p.154.

12. *L'Année littéraire* (1767), vol.2, p.20; and p.27, mention of reservations in his response by the cardinal de Rohan.

13. Ch.-Théod. Dalberg, *De l'influence des sciences et des beaux-arts sur la tranquillité publique* (Parma, 1802), p.43. Dalberg (1744–1817) was, among other things, archbishop of Regensburg and grand duke of Frankfurt; this prince of the church, who was a friend of the Enlightenment, was a notable personage in Napoleonic Europe.

14. Geoffroy, notice in the *Journal des débats* (17 September 1803) (collected in his *Cours de littérature dramatique*, vol.1, p.70).

15. Joseph de Maistre, *Soirées de Saint-Pétersbourg*, 8th conversation, in *Oeuvres complètes* (Lyons, 1884–86), vol.5, pp.107–8.

16. *Mercure*, vol.6, pp.174–78 (October 23, 1801), review signed O (?) 12 of A.-E.-M. Grétry, *De la vérité*, 3 vols. (Paris, year IX [1801]) (see ibid., vol.1, p.74).

17. *Réclamation de la littérature . . ., ouvrage traduit de l'anglais de M. David Williams par le citoyen Blondet du Jura* (Nantes-Paris, year XI) (Bibl. Nat. Z 34364). A society was founded whose president was François de Neufchâteau, former minister in the Directory, member of the *Institut* and senator: see his *Discours pour l'ouverture de la société au faveur des savants et des hommes de lettres* (Paris, year XI) (Bibl. Nat. Rp.1385).

18. *Journal des débats* (20–21 September 1803), article signed A., collected in the *Jugements historiques et littéraires* of Fiévée, pp.279ff.

19. Guizot, *Tableau philosophique et littéraire de l'an 1807*, in *Archives littéraires de l'Europe*, vol.17 (1808), pp.247–48; see also his review of *Mélanges de littérature et de philosophie* by Ancillon (1809) in the *Mercure* of 13 January 1810; and also Ancillon himself in his *Essais philosophiques* of 1817, vol.1, pp.169–70.

20. Barante, *De la littérature française pendant le dix-huitième siècle* (Paris, 1809), pp.262–63; this work was inspired by an essay competition sponsored by the Academy (see below), and did not receive the prize (see *Souvenirs du baron de Barante*, ed. Cl. de Barante, 8 vols. [Paris, 1890–91], vol.1, pp.259, 268).

21. L.-G. Petitain, *Quelques Vues sur ce qu'on appelle la propagation des lumières . . .*, vol.1, no.5 of the *Mémoires d'économie publique, de morale et de politique par Roederer* (year VIII), pp.285, 310, 297. And see a most sarcastic royalist commentary in Colnet's *Journal d'opposition littéraire ou Mémoires secrets de la République des Lettres*, vol.1 (Floréal year VIII), pp.193–94.

22. A.-V. Arnault, "Des hommes ou gens de lettres," in the *Veillées des Muses*, vol.7 (Vendémiaire year VIII), pp.8ff.

23. *La Décade* had been founded in Floréal year II (spring 1794); the *Mercure*, founded in 1800, was in fact an anti-*Décade*.

24. See Monglond, *La France révolutionnaire et impériale*, vol.8, introduction, pp.xvi, xxx.

25. Morellet was born in 1727, Suard in 1734; they were veterans of the literature and philosophy of the eighteenth century. Suard controlled *Le Publiciste*, which

was one of the breeding grounds of doctrinaire liberalism. Guizot and Pauline de Meulan wrote in it; Rémusat (article at the beginning of the collection of pieces by Guizot and Mme Guizot entitled *Le Temps passé* [Paris, 1887], p.20) writes delectably of *Le Publiciste*: "The philosophy of the eighteenth century, illuminated or intimidated by the Revolution, such was the spirit of this collection."

26. *Recueil des discours, rapports, et pièces diverses lus dans les séances publiques et particulières de l'Académie française*, volume pertaining to the period 1803–19 (Paris, 1847), p.767 (Bibl. Nat. 4° Z 47).

27. Abbé Morellet, *Lettres inédites sur l'histoire politique et littéraire des années 1806 et 1807* (Paris, 1822), pp.41, 42, 49 (letter of March 1807, addressed to count Roederer, *procureur-général syndic* of the Seine department during the Revolution, a moderate revolutionary, involved in Brumaire and then serving as Joseph Bonaparte's minister of finance in Naples.

28. Roederer, *Opuscules* (Paris, year XII) (collection of articles published from 1802 to 1804): see especially the *Observations morales et politiques sur les journaux détracteurs du dix-huitième siècle, de la Philosophie et de la Révolution*, added at the end of the volume. Two other collections of *Opuscules* by Roederer had appeared in year VIII and year X.

29. Part III, book IV, ch.5 in the definitive edition. Chateaubriand even made the contrast between the two centuries the subject of a conversation between René and Chactas (*René*, ed. Weil [Lille-Geneva, 1947], pp.33–34).

30. Malte-Brun, *Coup d'oeil sur les intrigues littéraires pendant la domination du général Bonaparte*, in *Le Spectateur*, vol.1 (1814), p.54.

31. E.-J. Delécluze, *Souvenirs de soixante années* (Paris, 1862), p.84.

32. See Bonald, *Du style et de la littérature* (1806) in *Oeuvres complètes*, ed. Migne, 3 vols. (1859), vol.3, p.975, and his article in the *Mercure*, vol.21, pp.75–76 (29 June 1805). It is in this sense that his remark that literature is the expression of society, so often repeated in his work and later stretched in every direction, should be taken: see *Oeuvres complètes*, vol.1, p.1195; vol.3, p.1173, etc. Bonald does not give this formula the slightest relativist meaning and does not at all mean to justify all literature as the expression of a given society.

33. Thus Fiévée, in the *Mercure*, vol.15, p.395 (18 February 1804).

34. *Recueil des discours*, p.763.

35. The former was born in 1770, the latter in 1785; both were liberal political writers under the Restoration. The two pieces were published by Baudouin, printer for the *Institut*, in 1810.

36. Jay, *Tableau littéraire de la France au dix-huitième siècle* (Paris, 1810), p.21.

37. This clause seems confusedly constructed; the periodicals of the time sometimes give it without *and*, which does not improve it.

38. Text graciously communicated to me by Mlle A.-M. Laffitte, the Academy's archivist, whom I thank very sincerely for her kindness.

39. *Discours sur l'indépendance des gens de lettres prononcé à la distribution des prix du*

concours général des Lycées le 29 thermidor an XIII [17 August 1805], *par M. Luce de Lancival, professeur de Belles-Lettres au Lycée impérial* (Paris, 1805), pp.4–5, 8, 14; a little later, p.27, there is a vitriolic note against the inquisitorial and defamatory dictatorship of the counterrevolutionary party in literature. Luce de Lancival, born in 1764, was one of those ecclesiastics defrocked in the Revolution who were so common then in the professorial ranks; he was a great flatterer of those in power and a sworn enemy of Geoffroy. In 1803, at another prize ceremony, he had given a *Discours* on the question: "By what means can writers preserve their dignity?" ([Paris, year XI — 1803], Bibl. Nat. Rp.3132).

40. Bonald, *Théorie du pouvoir*, in *Oeuvres*, ed. Migne, vol.1, pp.844ff.

41. Bonald, *Réflexions sur les questions*, in the *Mercure*, vol.21, pp.51ff. (29 June 1805).

42. Article signed Y. (Dussault's usual initial) in the *Journal de l'Empire* (new name of the *Journal des débats*) (7 January 1806) just after the awarding of prizes. *Le Publiciste*, on the other hand, on 24 January applauds the success of the competition and mocks the "officious censor" who was scandalized by the choice of subject "in I can't remember which paper."

43. Archives of the Academy, *Procès verbaux des séances* (graciously communicated by Mlle A.-M. Laffitte).

44. Millevoye's poem can be read in the original 1806 edition; also in vol.2 of the *Oeuvres complètes* (Paris, 1880). The principal literary reviews (*La Décade philosophique, Magasin encyclopédique, Mercure*) reproduced it in 1806.

45. Fabre's piece too was published in the reviews of the time; it can be found in his *Oeuvres*, ed. J. Sabbatier (Paris, 1844), vol.1, pp.373ff.

46. This involved fourteen virulent lines against intrigue and favoritism; they are reproduced in the *Oeuvres*, vol.1, p.376.

47. To my knowledge, four of them were printed; the Academy's archives have not preserved the manuscripts.

48. Dussault's review of Millevoye's poem in the *Journal de l'Empire* (31 January 1806) (signed Y and collected by the author in vol.2, p.18 of his *Annales littéraires*: 5 vols. [1818–24]).

49. Review of the prize poems signed C., *Mercure*, vol.23, pp.21ff. (1 February 1806); C. appears frequently in the *Mercure* between 1805 and 1807 but who this represents remains unknown.

50. Review of Millevoye's poem by Féletz in the *Journal de l'Empire* (9 March 1806) (article signed A., collected in Féletz, *Jugements*, pp.285ff.); the same paper publishes on the following 24 March an *Epître sur la dépendance des gens de lettres* by Hyacinthe Gaston, former émigré and royalist in good standing.

51. Palissot, *Mémoires pour servir à l'histoire de notre littérature*, in *Oeuvres complètes*, 6 vols. (Paris, 1809), vol.5, article "Millevoye," p.109; *La Quinzaine littéraire*, vol.3, pp.214ff.; Eckstein, *De Voltaire*, in *Annales de la littérature et des arts*, vol.8 (1822), p.105.

52. E. Jouy, *L'Hermite de la Guyane*, 3 vols. (Paris, 1817), vol.2, p.20 (dated 17 January 1816).

53. P.-F. Tissot, prospectus of the *Mercure du dix-neuvième siècle*, vol.1, p.14 (April 1823).

54. Abbé de Grainville, *Discours qui a remporté le prix d'éloquence de l'Académie de Besançon en l'année 1772 sur ce sujet: Quelle a été l'influence de la philosophie sur ce siècle?* (Paris, 1772), pp.15, 23. This is the same Grainville who, after having sworn an oath of loyalty to the republic and marrying under the Revolution, composed a fantastic-poetic narration in ten stanzas on *Le Dernier Homme* that was published in 1805 after his suicide, and that Nodier republished in 1811. In 1772, at the age of twenty-six, he seems like any other *bien-pensant* priest, and places Bossuet's *Discours sur l'histoire* above Voltaire's *La Henriade* as an epic.

55. Abbé Ferlet, *De l'abus de la philosophie par rapport à la littérature* (work presented to a competition conducted by the Academy of Nancy) (Nancy, 1773), pp.4, 10–11. In his ideas and examples, Ferlet follows closely the just mentioned work by Grainville: both are praised to the skies in the *Année littéraire* (year 1772, vol.6, p.313, and year 1773, vol.4, p.112). The same review devotes yet another article to the same subject, and along the same lines, in 1779, vol.1, pp.3ff.: "Discourse on the influence of philosophy on letters"; and *Le Spectateur français au dix-neuvième siècle* (12 vols., 1805–12), a collection of articles that appeared in the counterrevolutionary press under Napoleon, reprinted this old "Discourse" (vol.5, pp.412ff.): this testifies to the continuity of the tradition from one century to another.

56. Gilbert, *Oeuvres*, ed. Nodier (Paris, 1817), pp.36–37.

57. Sabatier de Castres, *Lettres critiques, morales et politiques sur l'esprit, les erreurs et les travers de notre temps* (Erfurt, 1802), p.7; a note reminds us that the first publication of "Letter I," which contains this passage, was written in 1790.

58. Sabatier de Castres, *Les Trois Siècles de la littérature française* (Amsterdam, 1774), 3 vols., p.11 of the preface.

59. See, for example, *Le Spectateur du Nord*, vol.1, p.242 (February 1797); F.-B. Hoffman, *Oeuvres*, 10 vols. (Paris, 1829), vol.9, p.18 (1808 article); etc.

60. Dussault, article signed Y. in the *Journal des débats* (24 October 1801), collected in his *Annales littéraires*, vol.1, p.217; another article on 11 June 1802 (reproduced in the *Spectateur du Nord* [November 1801 and October 1802]).

61. See in particular the articles by Michaud in the *Journal des débats* of 11 September 1902 and the *Mercure* of 7 May 1803, and a notice by Féletz in the *Journal des débats* of 24 November 1803.

62. Bonald, "On Literature, Science, and Art," May 1807 article, reprinted in the *Oeuvres complètes*, ed. Migne, vol.3, pp.1135ff.

63. "On Some Causes of the Decadence of Letters," *La Quotidienne* (13 May 1815) (cited by Eggli & Martino, *Le Débat romantique*, vol.1 [1933], p.296).

64. The *Veillées des Muses*, Ventôse year VIII (1800), p.252. The author is Cadet-Gassicourt, a pharmacist and a writer, born in 1769.

65. Dubois-Fontanelle, *Cours de belles-lettres* (Paris, 1813), vol.1, p.30 (cited by V. del Litto, *La Vie intellectuelle de Stendhal* [Paris, 1959], p.14). Dubois-Fontanelle's course at the *Ecole centrale* of Grenoble dates from 1798 (ibid., p.13 n.18).

66. Degérando, "On the Influence of the Spirit of Meditation on Literature," in *Archives littéraires de l'Europe* (September 1805), p.356.

67. S.-J. de Boufflers, *Essai sur les gens de lettres* (Paris, 1811), p.12.

68. Abbé Grégoire, *Plan d'association générale entre les savants, gens de lettres et artistes, pour accélérer le progrès des bonnes moeurs et des lumières* (n.p., n.d. [certainly between 1814 and 1817]); articles by P.-L. Lacretelle (the elder) in *La Minerve française* (1818), vol.3, pp.204ff., 392ff. (in particular, p.392, against the desire of some to return literature "to its old powerlessness"); these remarkable articles are reproduced in part in the author's *Oeuvres*, vol.6 (Paris, 1824), pp.378ff.; he had already written on these subjects in 1808: see *La Minerve française*, ibid., pp.64–72, an article that, according to the *Oeuvres*, vol.5, p.210n., dates from that year; J.-E.-M. Portalis, *De l'usage et de l'abus de l'esprit philosophique durant le dix-huitième siècle*, 2nd edn., 2. vols. (Paris, 1827), vol.1, p.216 (the Fructidorized author had written this work abroad, between Fructidor and Brumaire, before being one of the authors of the Code Napoléon; his son published the work in 1820: see Sainte-Beuve, *Causeries du lundi*, vol.5, pp.440ff.).

69. Chateaubriand, *Génie du christianisme*, vol.3, p.37 of the original edition, from which I am quoting (part III, book II, ch.1 in the definitive edition; see also the beginning of the chapter on mathematics, and ch.2).

70. Ibid., original edition, vol.2, p.119 (in the definitive edition, part III, book III, ch.1).

71. Lamartine, letter of 24 December 1818 to Mlle de Canonge (*Correspondance*, sextodecimo edition, vol.1 [1881], p.365); Bonald, letter to Mme Charles, 24 September 1817, reproduced in Doumic, *Lettres d'Elvire à Lamartine* (Paris, 1905), appendix, p.78.

72. Notice in the *Journal des débats* on Thomson's *The Seasons* (25 October 1801), signed Z. (probably Delalot); see also Féletz, article of 14 September 1805, collected in the *Spectateur français au dix-neuvième siècle*, vol 3, pp.366ff.

73. Part I, book I, ch.8.

74. *René*, ed. Weil, p.28.

75. *Le Spectateur du Nord*, vol.4, pp.414ff. (December 1797). The poem appeared for the first time without these lines in *Le Magasin encyclopédique* in 1795 (vol.3, p.549; the date of 1785–86 for the composition of the poem is given in a note).

76. *La Quinzaine littéraire*, vol.2 (1817), pp.255 and 257; anonymous article, probably by Amar du Rivier (see, to the same effect, an article by him, ibid., pp.1–2.) This royalist collection congratulated itself for carrying on in the tradition of Fréron's *L'Année littéraire*, of illustrious antiphilosophic memory.

77. See, among others, in Malte-Brun's *Le Spectateur*, vol.1 (1814), the "Discourse on the Place of the Sciences and of Letters in the Moral and Religious Order,"

pp.24–25; an article signed X in *Le Spectateur religieux et politique*, vol.1 (1818), pp.78ff.; an anonymous article entitled "Literature" in *Le Réveil* of 28 October 1822, etc.

78. *Génie du christianisme*, part II, book V, ch.1 and ff.

79. This *Défense* dates from 1803; see paragraph 12 of the "Explanations on the subject of this work."

80. *Mercure de France*, vol.22, pp.70–71 (5 October 1805); the review is by Petitot.

81. Among others, A. Ripert (parish priest in the Grenoble diocese), *Odes sacrées* (Lyons-Paris, year XII — 1804); Sapinaud de Boishuguet (knight of Saint-Louis and a participant in the Vendean insurrection), *Les Psaumes traduits en vers français*, 2 vols. (Paris, 1818) (dedication to the Duchesse d'Angoulême; according to *Le Conservateur* of 16 October 1818, vol.1, p.142, "collection written in the midst of our civil troubles" — so admired that Laurentie, in *Le Spectateur politique et religieux*, vol.1 (1818), pp.73ff., does not hesitate to rank the author ahead of Lefranc de Pompignan; G. de Grandval, *Traduction complète des psaumes en vers français* (Paris, 1819).

82. Thus the *Odes choisies* of the comte de Valori (Paris, 1819) (Henri Zozime, count then marquis of Valori, born in 1786 and taken abroad as a child in the emigration, was from a fiercely royalist family and was imprisoned by order of Bonaparte after the execution of the duc d'Enghien); 2nd expanded edition in 1830; Cl.-L. Mollevault (born in 1776 or 1777), *Chants sacrés* (Paris, 1824) (the author, in his earlier collections beginning in 1816, had begun to cultivate the same genre and had composed in particular narrative "poèmes" on biblical episodes that make one think of Vigny's); B.-M.-F. Levasseur (born in 1775), *Le Livre de Job traduit en vers français* (Paris, 1826) (review by Chênedollé in the royalist *Annales de la littérature et des arts*, vol.27 (1827), p.413; comte de Marcellus, *Odes sacrées* (Paris, 1825); *Cantates sacrées* (Paris, 1829) (born in 1776; this is the father of the diplomat who served under Chateaubriand).

83. For example, J. Chérade de Montbrun (born in 1766, a volunteer in Condé's army, took part in the landing at Quiberon), *Essai sur la littérature des Hébreux*, 4 vol.(Paris, 1819); Jacques-Barthélemy Salgues (born in 1760, a royalist, object of a decree of accusation in Fructidor, a collaborator on the virulently royalist *L'Oriflamme* of 1824), *De la littérature des Hébreux* (Paris, 1825).

84. Lamartine knew Genoude well (see the commentary on the poem "Sacred poetry" in the 1849 edn. of the *Oeuvres*, with *Les Méditations*). Genoude, born in 1792, would play an important role in the history of the royalist party until after 1848.

85. The foreign authorities who are widely evoked also remain the same: above all Lowth, whose treatise, Chateaubriand tells us, "is in every writer's hands" (*Génie* and *Défense*, at the places already cited); Lowth was translated twice into French during the Empire (Lowth, *Leçons sur la poésie sacrée des Hébreux*, trans. and ed.

Ballanche, 2 vols. (Lyons, 1812); Lowth, *Cours de poésie sacrée*, trans F. Roger, 2 vols. bound in one (Paris, 1813). After 1800 Herder's book on Hebrew poetry begins to be more widely discussed: see an article by Michel Berr in *Le Magazin encyclopédique* (1806), vol.5., p.305, and some lines by Mme de Staël in *De l'Allemagne*, part II, ch.30; Treneuil, in 1817, does seem to have read Herder (*Poèmes élégiaques*, p.43n., p.46n., p.52n.).

86. Sapinaud de Boishuguet, op.cit., preface, p.v; Genoude, *Leçons*, p.255n. ("On Hebraic Poetry and on Isaiah," text very likely predating 1820).

87. *Le Globe* (12 March 1825), announcement of the book by Salgues mentioned in our note 83; and see ibid., (12 April 1825), a review of the same book signed H. R. (probably Hippolyte Rolle, liberal journalist). Similarly see a review of the *Chants sacrés* by Mollevault in *La Revue encyclopédique*, vol.32, p.449 (August 1824), signed E. H. (Héreau).

88. Villemain, *Cours de littérature française*, 4 vols., vol.1 (Paris, 1838), p.43.

89. Bonald, *Pensées sur divers sujets et Discours politiques*, 2 vols. (Paris, 1817), vol.1, p.368.

90. These lines are by Fontanes, in an ode on "Society without Religion" that appears in his *Oeuvres* (vol.1 [1839], p.147), dated 1813.

91. (Paris, 1817). What we know of Treneuil comes from the notes he appends to his poems and from the reviews and articles that were written about him at the time; see the *Le Moniteur* of 16 May 1814, review of *L'Orpheline du Temple*; ibid. (27 May 1814), on the sixth edition of *Les Tombeaux*; *La Quinzaine littéraire* (1817), vol.2, p.312, and vol.3, p.165, on the *Poèmes élégiaques*; ibid. (1818), vol.5, p.209, obituary notice (all these articles are probably by his friend Amar du Rivier, who signed some of them; also the notice on Treneuil in the *Biographie Michaud*, which is signed A. D.-R.

92. Michelet, *Histoire du dix-neuvième siècle*, vol.2 (1873), p.131.

93. "Discourse on the Heroic Elegy," pp.5–155 of *Poèmes élégiaques*.

94. Malte-Brun, review of Mollevault's *Elégies* in the *Quotidienne* of 10 June 1816, cited by Helen Maxwell King (*Les Doctrines littéraires de la Quotidienne, 1814–1830* [Northhampton-Paris, 1919–20], p.53), who points out a review on 16 June 1817 by the same author on Treneuil, where he expresses the same ideas.

95. Among Treneuil's poems is a "Chant funèbre sur la mort du roi Josias," a sort of biblical cento that claims to recreate the lost song that Jeremiah dedicated to the death of Josias, following II Chronicles 34:20–24 and Josephus, *Antiquities*, X, 6.

96. See above, n.85 and text.

97. Amar du Rivier, review of *Les Tombeaux de l'abbaye royale de Saint-Denis*, in *Le Moniteur universel* of 27 May 1814.

98. Elzéar de Sabran, *Le Repentir, poème en sept chants, achevé en 1815* (Paris, 1817).

99. Sabran is certainly influenced by Klopstock, and as early as the first division of his poem, p.22, he evokes the episode of Abbadonnah (*sic*), the repenting angel of the *Messias*. Treneuil, too, mentions Klopstock in his "Discourse," p.134. In the

period we are examining, it is certain that knowledge of Klopstock progressed among the French, and that he was seen as a model of the contemporaneous sacred poetry that was trying to be born in France. A connection between the French émigrés who published *Le Spectateur du Nord* and the German poet had been formed in Hamburg. Chateaubriand, Ballanche, Mme de Staël cite Klopstock, who had been the first to effect the "happy union of Christian religion and poetry," (*De l'Allemagne*, part II, ch.5 [vol.2, p.57 in the De Pange-Balayé edition]).

100. See on this subject R. Mauzi, op.cit., pp.180–82 and p.208, end of passage.

101. Despite appearances and whatever may be said to the contrary, we are a long way here from the "heart" and the "God whom the heart can feel" of Pascal; in this case the reference to sentiment grounds a humanistic optimism that aims to bring "natural man" to God.

102. See Pomeau, op.cit., pp.47–70, for the end of the seventeenth century and the beginning of the eighteenth; Mauzi, op.cit., pp.185–97 (various treatises on Christian morals between 1760 and 1766); P.-M. Masson, *La Religion*, vol.1, ch.7 and vol.3, ch.4 (religious writers before and after Rousseau); Albert Monod, *De Pascal à Chateaubriand* (Paris, 1916), particularly pp.475ff. (Rousseau's Christian posterity).

103. This is Masson's expression (op.cit., vol.1, p.279); he also noted (vol.1, p.233) among the Christian apologists the same "pragmatism" as in Rousseau; i.e., the same demonstration of God by his human utility.

104. Abbé Lamourette, *Pensées sur la philosophie de la foi* (Paris, 1789) (sole right to print granted 7 July), pp.196, 212. These ideas are based on a doctrine of the incarnation according to which Jesus is less an expiatory victim or redeemer of Adam's sin than glorious witness as God-man of the divine privilege of humanity (see Lamourette, ibid., pp.10, 130–32, 161–63, etc.; also *Les Délices de la religion* [Paris, 1788], pp.57ff.); this doctrine, dear to illuminism, as we have seen, is not in itself heretical; everything depends on degree and tone.

105. Lamourette, *Pensées sur la philosophie de la foi*, p.132.

106. See Lamourette, *Prônes civiques ou Le Pasteur patriote* (Paris, n.d. [1790]), passim; and, in the same register, abbé Fauchet, *Sermon sur l'accord de la religion et de la liberté, prononcé dans la métropole de Paris, le 4 février 1791*: Fauchet and Lamourette, both made bishops in 1791 after having sworn allegiance to the Civil Constitution of the Clergy, perished under the guillotine in 1793 and 1794.

107. See *Etudes de la nature* (1784), ed. Didot, 5 vols. (Paris, 1792), vol.3, pp.8–17, where the antinomy is developed at length.

108. Ibid., vol.3, pp.96ff.; p.101 and note et seq.

109. Delisle de Sales, *De la philosophie de la nature* (1769), 3rd edn., 6 vols. (London, 1777), vol.6, pp.470–71.

110. Bernardin de Saint-Pierre, *Etudes*, vol.3, p.509.

111. Ibid., vol.1, p.638.

112. *Paul et Virginie* (1788), ed. Souriau (Paris, 1930), p.170.

113. *Etudes*, vol.3, p.74.

114. Ibid., vol.3, p.189.

115. Ibid., vol.3, p.94. The interpretation of the faculty of admiration as linked to the divine naturally recalls Saint-Martin; I do not know whether Bernardin had read him in 1784; it is certain that they met (see Saint-Martin, *Mon Portrait*, ed. Amadou, no.1007), but this took place at a later date.

116. Ibid., vol.3, p.523. Passing from Homer to Jesus, he continues: "But when it [the word] came down itself from heaven," etc. This whole passage makes of Rousseau's disciple a definite precursor, in 1784, of Chateaubriand. To what extent Bernardin really believed in the incarnation of the Word, I would really be at a loss to say.

117. See V. Giraud, *Le Christianisme de Chateaubriand*, vol.1 (Paris, 1925), pp.129ff.

118. We have already seen something of this in the case of the *Jour des morts*; the final text of the *Chartreuse* may be seen in the *Génie*, part III, book V, ch.2, where Chateaubriand gives it in its entirety.

119. *Génie du christianisme*, part I, book I, ch.2.

120. Ibid, part I, book VI, ch.1 (I am quoting from the original edition, vol.1, pp.245–46). The apology for what is obscure leads naturally in this school of thought to the rehabilitation of the superstitions of the people (ibid., III, V, 6).

121. Ibid., respectively III, IV, 5; I, V, 14; I, V, 7.

122. *Essai sur les révolutions*, in the Garnier edition of the *Oeuvres*, p.457, 557.

123. Joubert, *Carnets*, ed. Beaunier, p.326 (25 March 1802).

124. Saint-Marc Girardin, *Cours de littérature dramatique*, vol.4 (published in 1860), p.93.

125. Chateaubriand, *René*, ed. Weil, pp.40–41.

126. Rousseau, *La Nouvelle Héloïse*, part I, letter 25.

127. See *Génie du christianisme*, part I, book I, ch.4.

128. There is no need to emphasize again all that separates the Man of Sensibility who feels the lack of religion from Pascal, despite several analogous formulas; the tone, the impulse, the intention are all different.

129. Chateaubriand, *Les Martyres*, ed. Giraud (Paris: Garnier, 1936), p.86.

130. *Mercure de France*, vol.3, pp.14–38 (22 December 1800).

131. *Génie du christianisme*, part II, book III, ch.9.

132. *Défense du Génie du christianisme*, paragraph 8 (reprinted on p.127 of Weil's edition of *René*). The final version of the chapter "On the *vague des passions*" in the *Génie*, II, III, 9, included at the end a new version of this passage of the *Défense* that condemns contemporary "guilty melancholy"; see also in the same place the harsh passage added in 1803 (Weil edn. of *René*, pp.119–20).

133. Bonald's review appeared in *Le Publiciste* of 24 April 1802; see also Delalot's in the *Mercure* (vol.21, pp.103ff. [6 July 1805]) and Bertin's in the *Journal des débats* (26 May 1802), and the collection of contemporary reviews in vol.15 of the Lad-

vocat edn. of the *Oeuvres complètes* of Chateaubriand; also Delalot's review on *Atala* and *René* in the *Mercure*, vol.21, pp.207–8 (20 July 1805).

134. Percy B. Shelley, *Laon and Cydna* (London, 1818 [1817]), preface, pp.x–xii, a work also published under the title *The Revolt of Islam* and that was known in France only much later. The pages that Shelley wrote at about the same time on the role of the poet, the perpetual recreator of language and thus a religious intermediary between man and beauty, were only published in 1840 (*A Defence of Poetry*, in *Essays and Letters from Abroad*, see pp.5–7, 55, 57) and were long unknown in France.

135. Sainte-Beuve, 1845 article on Fauriel in *Portraits contemporains*, vol.4, p.125.

136. *Génie du christianisme*, part IV, book VI, ch.6 (I am quoting from the original edition of 1802, vol.4, p.281); ibid., ch.11.

137. Texts abound after 1825: see the references in the Levaillant edition (centenary edition) of *Mémoires d'outre-tombe*, vol.2, p.5 n.3, and in Derré, *Le Renouvellement de la pensée religieuse en France de 1824 à 1834* (Paris, 1962), pp.597ff. The pages written last are the best known, in particular the famous conclusion of the *Mémoires* (a text used before in the article "L'Avenir du monde," *Revue des deux mondes* of 15 April 1834), but Chateaubriand had taken this position much earlier.

138. This is what Pierre Clarac demonstrated convincingly (see *Chateaubriand, le livre du centenaire* [Paris, 1949], pp.135ff.).

139. See his article "On the Clergy" (1816) in the *Mélanges religieux et philosophiques* of 1819, collected in the *Oeuvres*, ed. Daubrée-Cailleux (1836–37), vol.6, pp.196–97; also "On the People's Education" (1818), same vol.6, p.330; "Diverse Thoughts" (1819), ibid., p.423, etc.

140. "On Education Considered in its Relation to Liberty," ibid., pp.369ff.

141. This thought is perfectly formulated as early as the book *De la religion considérée dans ses rapports avec l'ordre politique et civil* (1825); see *Oeuvres*, vol.7, p.280.

142. In vol.2 of this work (1820).

143. See Lamennais, *Défense de l'essai sur l'indifférence* (1823), pieces relating to the aforementioned vol.2 (*Oeuvres*, vol.5).

144. See Lamennais, *Des progrès de la révolution et de la guerre contre l'Eglise* (1829) (*Oeuvres*, vol.9, pp.73, 85).

145. *Génie du christianisme*, part II, book II, ch.8.

146. Joubert, *Oeuvres*, ed. P. de Raynal (5th edn., Paris, 1869), in vol.2, title XXI, *pensée* 2; see also for this whole complex of ideas, XXI, 17 and XX, 3, as well as the Beaunier edn. of the *Carnets*, p.607.

147. Bonald, *Oeuvres*, ed. Migne, vol.2, pp.1463, 1466 (1822); vol.3, p.1114 (1810); *Mercure*, vol.21, p.55 (29 June 1805).

148. Chateaubriand, *Des lettres et des gens de lettres*, in the *Mercure* of 3 May 1806; reprinted in the Garnier edition of the *Oeuvres*, vol.6, p.510.

149. Chateaubriand, *Discours de réception* to the Académie Française (1811) reprinted in the *Mémoires d'outre-tombe* (centenary edn., vol.2, pp.269–70, 276).

150. *Du sentiment considéré dans ses rapports avec la littérature et les arts* (Paris and Lyons, 1801).

151. *Du sentiment*, p.21.

152. Ballanche was born in 1776. The events of 1793 in Lyons are evoked at length in his book, pp.104–7, 284; see also the *Chant funèbre sur les héros de Lyon*, p.286; he had, he says, composed a long poem on the dramatic events in Lyons.

153. *Du sentiment*, pp.57–58.

154. Ibid., p.71, where Plato is interpreted according to this doctrine; also p.75.

155. Ibid., pp.111–12.

156. Original edition (Paris, 1814); republished in vol.1 of the edition of the *Oeuvres* in six volumes in-12 (Paris: Bureau de l'Encyclopédie des connaissances utiles, 1833).

157. The *Fragments* appeared in the *Bulletin de Lyon* in 1808–9; they are reprinted in the already cited edition of the *Oeuvres*, vol.1, pp.338ff.; the passages I am citing are pp.343 and 380. The comparison of Antigone and the Dauphine is at the end of the epilogue of *Antigone* (vol.1 of the *Oeuvres*, pp.330–31).

158. Ballanche, *Essai sur les institutions sociales dans leurs rapports avec les idées nouvelles* (1818), in *Oeuvres*, in-12, vol.2, p.295.

159. Ballanche, *Orphée*, in *Oeuvres*, vol.5, p.261. *Orphée* was published in 1829 (it is vol.2 of the *Essais de palingénésie sociale*, whose *Prolégomènes* in 1827 are the first volume); but it was already begun in 1818: see Viatte, *Un Ami de Ballanche, Cl.-J. Bredin* (Paris, 1928), pp.39ff., 111.

160. See *Du sentiment*, pp.154ff.

161. *Prolégomènes* (1827), in *Oeuvres*, vol.4, p.247.

162. *Oeuvres*, vol.3, p.357 (passage incorporated into the *Réflexions diverses*, no.37, which concludes vol.3 in the earlier octavo edition of the *Oeuvres*, 4 vols. [Paris-Geneva, 1830]; these reflections seem to be contemporaneous with the *Prolégomènes*). See also *La Ville des expiations*, in the edition by Les Entretiens idéalistes (Paris, 1907), pp.4, 22.

163. *Essai*, in *Oeuvres*, vol.2, p.91; see also ibid., p.43.

164. *Prolégomènes*, in *Oeuvres*, vol.4, p.347; see also pp.236, 338.

165. *Le Vieillard et le jeune homme*, in vol.3 of the *Oeuvres*, pp.19, 91, 85, 92. The Old Man preaches to a disillusioned young man, a sort of René inclined toward an unadulterated return to the past; in fact, a similar figure appears already in 1804 in *La Grande Chartreuse*, fragment collected in vol.1 of the *Oeuvres*, pp.18ff.

166. *Essai*, in *Oeuvres*, vol.2, pp.168–69. Same idea in the *Elégie* (composed around 1820), *Oeuvres*, vol.3, p.310; in the *Formule générale* (*Revue de Paris* [May 1829], p.147); and until the end of his life in a projected reworking of his dedication to the *Palingénésie sociale*, *Prolégomènes* (text published by Ch. Dédéyan in *Les Lettres romaines* [1953], p.229; another manuscript with variants in Oscar A. Haac, *La Théodicée et la Virginie romaine*, collection of texts by Ballanche [Geneva-Paris, 1959], pp.40–41); this reworking, according to Haac, dates from around 1840.

167. *Réflexions diverses*, no.18, in *Oeuvres*, vol.6, p.301.

168. *Prolégomènes*, the entire third part (*Oeuvres*, vol.4, pp.289ff.).

169. See on this subject Viatte, *Les Sources*, vol.2, ch.7; also Léon Cellier, *Fabre d'Olivet* (Paris, 1953), pp.337ff. (on Ballanche and Fabre d'Olivet).

170. See *Prolégomènes*, in *Oeuvres*, vol.4, p.57, and in 1832 *Palingénésie sociale, Epilogue*, in *La France littéraire* of February, pp.237, 242.

171. Ballanche, though inclined more than anyone else to the spirit of mortification, wonders, with respect to man: "Who knows what he is called upon to become, since rehabilitation must sooner or later place him in the state that was destined for him?" (*Prolégomènes*, in *Oeuvres*, vol.4, p.126), and again: "Will regenerate man regenerate the earth?" (*Orphée*, in *Oeuvres*, vol.6, p.164).

172. *Essai*, in *Oeuvres*, vol.2, p.183.

173. Ibid., pp.199, 209, 349ff.

174. Ibid., p.360; and the entire third part of chapter 11 is devoted to "the consequences of the emancipation of thought in the sphere of political ideas"; these consequences are far-reaching: duelling, war, the death penalty, nationalities, and colonization are condemned.

175. Ibid., p.212.

176. *La Ville des Expiations*, ed. Rastoul (Paris, 1926), p.96.

177. J. de Maistre, *Considérations sur la France* (1797), ed. Johannet-Vermale (Paris, 1936), p.28.

178. Lamennais, *Essai sur l'indifférence*, vol.1 (1817), in *Oeuvres*, vol.1, p.333; *Des progrès de la Révolution* (1829), in *Oeuvres*, vol.9, p.73; *De l'absolutisme*, in *Revue des deux mondes* (1 August 1834) (collected in *Oeuvres*, vol.11, pp.166–67).

179. See, for example, in *L'Homme sans nom* (1820), *Oeuvres*, vol.3, pp.277–79, a eulogy of "the sentiment of humanity" as a modern conquest, which extends to the *philosophes* of the eighteenth century despite their excesses, and to the Revolution despite its bloodshed and atrocities.

180. An 1830 note added to *Les Adieux à Rome* of 1813, in *Oeuvres*, vol.1, pp.37–38; and see also ibid., pp.380ff., the ninth of the *Fragments*, dated 31 March 1830.

181. See *Le Vieillard et le jeune homme*, in *Oeuvres*, vol.3, p.30, and his theory of the "assimilation" by which man voluntarily integrates into his own substance what he is ordered to do (*Prolégomènes*, in *Oeuvres*, vol.4, p.334).

182. Ballanche never finished or published in a book this *Formule générale de tous les peuples appliquée à l'histoire du peuple romain*. Fragments appeared in the *Revue de Paris* (1829), vol.2, pp.138–54; vol.4, pp.129–50; vol.6, pp.70–98 (history of the first secession, in 493 B.C., on the Aventine); in the *Revue des deux mondes* (May 1831), pp.221ff.; and in *L'Echo de la Jeune France*, vol.1 (November 1833), pp.284ff.; (December 1833), pp.328ff.; (January 1834), pp.358ff. (Second secession, 449 B.C. and the story of Virginia: of this second secession, O. A. Haac has given a more complete version, pp.75ff. of his already cited collection, but he is unaware, p.13

[like M. Levaillant in the preface of this collection, p.1], of the earlier publications of 1831 and 1833–34.)

183. *Prolégomènes*, in *Oeuvres*, vol.4, p.156.

184. It is in the *Essai* (*Oeuvres*, vol.2, p.20) that he compares himself, "on the edge of two eras," "to the Janus of legend."

185. All these reactions were produced apropos of the *Essai*, his first great doctrinal work: see *Le Conservateur*, vol.6 (1820), p.69 (review by Genoude); the *Revue encyclopédique* (February 1819), p.388 (review by Lanjuinais); and a letter from Joseph de Maistre to Ballanche in C. Huit, *La Vie et les oeuvres de Ballanche* (Lyons-Paris, 1904), pp.151–52.

186. *Du sentiment*, p.61; and see *Essai*, in *Oeuvres*, vol.2, pp.51, 203.

187. *Prolégomènes*, in *Oeuvres*, vol.4, p.374.

188. *Essai*, in *Oeuvres*, vol.2, pp.205–6; and see also pp.315–17.

189. Ibid., p.206; see also p.383.

190. Ibid., pp.109–10.

191. Ibid., pp.313–14.

192. Ibid., p.391.

193. Ibid., p.312.

194. *Prolégomènes*, in *Oeuvres*, vol.4, pp.124–25.

195. *Essai*, in *Oeuvres*, vol.2, pp.420–21, 425–36 ("Addition to chapter 10"). These definitions of speech were first found in *Orphée* (original edition of 1829), as "Postscript" to the "Continuation of the Preface."

196. *Orphée*, in *Oeuvres*, vol.5, p.168: it is Orpheus who is speaking.

197. *Prolégomènes*, in *Oeuvres*, vol.4, p.212; also ibid., p.248; and see a letter from Bredin to Ballanche in Viatte, *Un Ami*, p.54. On the related idea of correspondences among the senses, see *La Ville des expiations*, ed. Rastoul, p.72.

198. *Orphée*, in *Oeuvres*, vol.6, p.82. Ballanche shared this idea with his friend Bredin writes to him apropos of the manuscript of *Orphée* (1818) that poetry is the daughter of heaven and the sister of truth because it is "the interpreter of the great apologia that the world offers to the eyes of man"; "the word of the priest and the poet . . . is truth's most efficacious means of entering into us"; and this speech always hides more than it says openly, but it is more transparent in the poet, because of the magic of music and poetry, than in the priest, who has no recourse to these (Viatte, *Un Ami*, pp.42, 64–65).

199. Article by Ballanche on Les Mémoires de M. de Chateaubriand, in the *Revue européenne*, vol.8 (1834), pp.231–32 (given as an extract from *La Ville des expiations*, and as far as I know collected nowhere else).

200. Article on *Paroles d'un croyant*, ibid., pp.347–49.

201. Article entitled *L'Avenir* in *Le Polonais*, vol.2, p.212 (May 1834).

202. Article entitled *Le Dix-Neuvième Siècle* in *La France catholique*, 1st year, vol.2 (17 May 1834), p.3.

203. *Orphée*, in *Oeuvres*, vol.5, p.100.

204. Ibid., p.150.

205. Letter from Ballanche to Mme Récamier, in *Souvenirs et Correspondance tirée des papiers de Madame Récamier*, by Mlle Lenormand (Paris, 1859), vol.2, p.65. Magna Graecia was the birthplace of Pythagoreanism.

206. Remark by Ballanche reported around 1833 by Th. de Ferrières in a letter to Mme d'Agoult (see Jacques Vier, *Marie d'Agoult, son mari, ses amis* [Paris, 1950], p.50).

207. *La Ville des expiations*, ed. Rastoul, p.87.

208. The word "seer" is his (ibid., p.90); but he means by it a function that is more modest than that of prophet, one that concerns the present, not the future. He considers himself "assimilative"; that is, bearer of a feeling common to his time, and not "intuitive" like the legislators of old who anticipated the future; it is true that since initiation is now available to all, "intuitives" are no longer needed (*Orphée*, in *Oeuvres*, vol.6, p.276).

209. *Mémoires d'outre-tombe*, centenary edn., vol.3, p.357.

210. It is in the Lyons museum: see Edouard Herriot, *Madame Récamier et ses amis* (Paris, 1904), Iconography, p.1.

211. *Prolégomènes*, dedication, in *Oeuvres*, vol.4, pp.7 and 8.

212. Original edition in 1820; collected in vol.3 of the *Oeuvres*.

213. Appeared for the first time in vol.1 of the octavo edn. of the *Oeuvres*; figures in vol.3 of the in-12 *Oeuvres* that we usually cite.

214. See *Prolégomènes*, in *Oeuvres*, vol.4, p.13, and the epilogue of the *Palingénésie sociale* in *La France littéraire* (February 1832), p.243. This projected *Elégie* was supposed to be absolutely distinct from that of 1820 on the death of the duc de Berry, contrary to what Rastoul states (op.cit., p.lxi), seeming to confuse the two.

215. See *Prolégomènes*, in *Oeuvres*, vol.4, pp.13, 18–19. Only the *Prolégomènes* and *Orphée* were completed and published and figure in the *Oeuvres*; the *Formule générale* and *La Ville des expiations* were only partially realized in periodicals, and have been the object of incomplete modern publications; the *Elégie* does not seem to have been written.

216. *Essai*, in *Oeuvres*, vol.2, pp.326, 332–33.

217. *Vision d'Hébal* (Paris, 1830), p.53; see also *Formule générale*, in *Revue de Paris* (May 1829), p.154.

218. The *Essai*, already so explicit, is from 1818; but he confesses (preface of 1830 to *Antigone*, in *Oeuvres*, vol.1, p.47) that at the time of *Antigone* (1814) he had not yet "conceived of the general epic."

219. See Marquiset, *Ballanche et Mme d'Hautefeuille* (Paris, 1912), p.71, and Rastoul, op.cit., p.lxxii and note.

220. Ballanche, too, had between 1801 and 1810 thought of writing a narrative relative to the advent of Christianity, "The Faith Promised to the Gentiles": see *Oeuvres*, vol.1, p.10, n.1.

221. See my collection *L'Ecrivain et ses travaux* (Paris, 1968), pp.120ff.

222. See in M.-F. Guyard's edition of Lamartine's *Oeuvres Poétiques complètes* (Paris: Bibliothèque de la Pléiade, 1963) the youthful poems, pp.1636–37, 1717ff.

223. "Publisher's Notice," at the beginning of the ninth edition (1823) of the *Méditations poétiques*.

224. These are the "Chants lyriques de Saül" that figure in the *Méditations*.

225. Such was the name of a sort of irregular, varied ode.

226. The Genesis is inspired by Psalm 103; from Ezekiel he takes the famous vision of the resuscitated bones (Ezekiel 37) of which Lefranc de Pompignan had made a famous paraphrase; for the rest, his choice is rather original: Job and Jeremiah had been relatively little used by poets.

227. Review signed A. de la Martine of Genoude's translations in *Le Défenseur* of August 1820 (vol.2, 20th installment, p.317). See also, for this complex of ideas, the poem entitled "Dieu" in the *Méditations* (lines 95ff.), an evocation of the primitive world, where everything speaks of God to man.

228. "Le Génie," dedicated to Bonald (ode, 1817).

229. "Ode" (poem entitled "Ode aux Français" in manuscript and in the letter to Virieu of October 1817: *Correspondance*, in-16 edn., 4 vols. (Paris, 1881–82), vol.1, p.275.

230. Ibid.

231. *Méditations*, ed. Lanson (Paris, 1915), vol.2, pp.313–14; the poem in its original form contained four additional stanzas on the horrors of the Revolution, and concluded by demanding the destruction of the Vendôme column.

232. Ch. Brifaut, *Souvenirs d'un académicien* (Paris: Albin Michel, n.d. [1920]), vol.1, p.278.

233. See M. Souriau, *Histoire du romantisme en France*, tome 1, vol.2 (Paris, 1927), p.79.

234. See *Méditations*, ed. Lanson, vol.1, p.15.

235. In "Le Temple"; also in "Invocation," written no doubt very soon after meeting Julie Charles, and without any anticipation of her death.

236. See "Dieu," lines 33–34: the language of heaven and that of love participate in a single "living word heard in the heart."

237. "L'Homme," lines 91ff., 69–70, and see 71–75. Some hesitation concerning the Fall in *La Mort de Socrate* (p.97 in the Guyard edition of the *Oeuvres Poétiques*).

238. "La Foi" (summer 1818, lines 143ff.).

239. "La Foi" (lines 92ff.).

240. "Les Etoiles" (*Nouvelles Méditations poétiques* [1823]), lines 99–100; see also *Philosophie* (1821 poem, *Méditations*, 9th edn. [1823], lines 61–64). This belief, or reverie, was very widespread among writers, not just theosophists, and earlier than is ordinarily thought: we find something similar in the *Essai sur l'astronomie* by Fontanes, which dates from 1788; see also, in Lamartine himself, the poem in *Les Harmonies poétiques et religieuses* entitled "Pensées des morts" (*Harmonies*, II, 1, 7th decasyllabic stanza).

241. *La Mort de Socrate*, Guyard edn. of the *Oeuvres Poétiques*, pp.99–100, 96.

242. Ibid., p.105.

243. See in the *Méditations*, the poem *Le Désespoir* (1818), stanza 6, lines 1–2; also the letter to Virieu of 8 August 1818 published by Father du Lac (*Jésuites* [Paris, 1901], p.384), that to Cl. Vacher of 25 December 1818 published by Jean Richer (*Archives des lettres modernes*, no.50 [1963], p.62), and various 1819 letters (in the *Correspondance*, cited edn., vol.2, pp.13, 42, 92).

244. This contrasted composition appears as early as 1813 in an epistle on "Les Sépultures" (*Correspondance*, vol.1, p.211); we find it several times in the *Méditations* (in "L'Immortalité," "L'Homme," "Le Désespoir," and "La Providence à l'homme," "La Foi"), in *La Mort de Socrate*, in *Le Dernier Chant du pèlerinage d'Harold*, in *Les Visions* (ed. Guillemin [Paris, 1936], pp.152ff., 1824 text): the model is the book of *Job* (see Claudius Grillet, *Job dans les Méditations de Lamartine*, in *Le Correspondant* [December 25, 1922], pp.1023ff.).

245. Letter to Virieu of October 21, 1818 (*Correspondance*, vol.1, pp.341–42).

246. Sainte-Beuve clearly perceived this historic filiation: see his remarks on Lamartine and Saint-Martin in his *Portraits contemporains*, vol.1, pp.275ff. (1 October 1832 article in the *Revue des deux mondes*).

247. "L'Immortalité" (1817), lines 113ff.

248. "La Prière" (autumn 1819), lines 47ff.

249. Ibid., lines 27ff.

250. H. Patin, review of the *Harmonies* in the *Revue encyclopédique*, vol.47 (July 1830), p.128. Patin, born in 1793, was of the same generation as Lamartine; he had studied at the Ecole Normale Supérieure and was a university professor of liberal tendencies.

251. *La Mort de Socrate* (Paris, 1823), pp.13–14, and for the following citations, pp.22, 23, 24.

252. Lamartine had doubtless been acquainted with Plato since 1811, through Fréminville (see Lamartine, *Correspondance générale de 1830 à 1848*, published by the students of the Ecole Normale Supérieure under the direction of Maurice Levaillant [Lille-Geneva, vol.1, 1943], p.107, note 1).

253. *La Mort de Socrate*, Guyard edn. of the *Oeuvres Poétiques*, pp.105–6: Socrates announces the incarnation of the Word, which turns out to be none other than his familiar daimon!

254. *Le Dernier Chant du pèlerinage d'Harold*, 1.

255. Vigny, *Correspondance*, ed. Baldensperger (Paris, vol.1 [1933]), p.46 (letter to V. Hugo of 3 October 1823).

256. "Epître à M. Casimir Delavigne," in the Guyard edn. of the *Oeuvres Poétiques*, pp.283ff.

257. Letter to Mme de Raigecourt of 19 August 1823 (*Correspondance*, vol.2, pp.62–63).

258. "L'Homme," lines 283ff.

259. "L'Esprit de Dieu," 1822 poem, appeared in the *Nouvelles Méditations* of 1823.

260. See above, pp.169–70.

261. Chénier, Dimoff edn. of the *Oeuvres*, vol.2, p.52; text mentioned and discussed by H. J. Hunt, *The Epic in 19th-Century France* (Oxford, 1941), p.4, n.3.

262. Letter of 28 June 1816 to Fortuné de Vaugelas (*Correspondance*, vol.1, p.264); December 1818 letter to Virieu (*Correspondance*, vol.1, p.358); he says Platonic where we would say Platonist. A fragment of this *Clovis* went into the *Nouvelles Méditations* in 1823: this is "L'Ange, fragment épique."

263. Letter of 25 January 1821 to Virieu, (*Correspondance*, vol.2, p.147).

264. Lamartine, *Cours familier de littérature*, vol 3, pp.359–60 (Entretien XVII, May 1857).

265. Ibid., pp.355–56.

266. This would give some real foundation to the poems in the *Méditations* that, like "L'Enthousiasme" or "L'Esprit de Dieu," depict, with a rhetoric that can sometimes seem conventional, the pains of poetic parturition. The style of older poetry sometimes disguises emptiness, but it also sometimes makes us prejudge it too quickly.

267. We have already seen something of this; notably, (see our note 240) the idea of survival among stars. Henri de Lacretelle, *Lamartine et ses amis* (Paris, 1878), p.62, evokes confidences that Lamartine made to him on this subject in 1845; but, p.270, it is he who preaches to Lamartine the "theory of the spheres," without definite success; Lacretelle doubtless derived this belief from his father, who had tried to persuade Mme de Staël of it (see Charles Lacretelle, *Testament philosophique et littéraire*, 2 vols. [Paris, 1840], vol.1, ch.19).

268. Lamartine, *Les Visions*, critical edition with an introduction and notes, by Henri Guillemin (Paris, 1936); several of these fragments had already been inserted here and there in various works published by Lamartine after 1830.

269. See the plans that were kept, Guillemin edn., pp.77–87. These plans hardly differ in respect to the essential idea; I am describing them as a whole.

270. *Cours familier de littérature*, vol.3, p.355.

271. Letter to Virieu of 6 August [1823] (*Correspondance*, vol.2, p.244).

272. Letter to Virieu of 15 February 1823 (ibid., vol.2, p.238); according to contemporary testimony (Falconnet, Boulay-Paty), *La Mort de Socrate* was supposed to be part of the great poem (see the Guillemin edn. of *Les Visions*, p.75).

273. *Le Dernier Chant du pèlerinage d'Harold*, Foreword.

274. Victor de Laprade, preface to Lamartine's *Poésies inédites* published by his niece Valentine ([Paris, 1873], p.v). Laprade rightly judges Lamartine's undertaking to be more vast than Dante's or Milton's.

275. *Les Visions*, cited edition, p.91.

276. Ibid., p.92; this "Invocation" dates from December 1823.

277. Ibid., p.239 ("Chant lyrique du jugement dernier": text of March 1829 according to the editor, ibid., p.21).

278. See Ch. Alexandre, *Souvenirs sur Lamartine* (Paris, 1884), pp.290ff., and the article by Bernès in the *Revue d'histoire littéraire de la France* (1931), pp.387ff. In his old age, Lamartine still subtitled "modern psalm" the poem "La Vigne et la maison," and planned a collection of similar "psalms." See H. de Lacretelle, op.cit., p.33, and Guillemin, *Lamartine* (Paris, 1940), p.159.

279. Commentary on the first *Harmonie* ("Invocation") in the edition of the Works called that of the Subscribers (1849–50).

280. "Invocation" (in *Harmonies*, I, 1): 1826–27 poem.

281. "Invocation."

282. See for example the poems entitled "Pensée des morts" (1826), "Pourquoi mon âme est-elle triste?" (1826–27), and especially "Novissima verba" (1829), where the act of faith is preceded by more or less insistent questions and doubts.

283. "À l'Esprit-saint" (*Harmonies*, IV, 12): this poem is believed to date from 1829–30.

284. Lamartine, *Histoire de la Restauration*, vol.2 (1851), p.394.

5. THE LIBERAL CONTRIBUTION

1. Saint-Beuve, article on *Oberman*, in *Revue de Paris* (21 January 1832), p.218 (collected in vol.1 of the *Portraits contemporains*); and compare Monglond, *Le Journal intime d'Oberman* (vol.1 of his edition of *Oberman*) (Paris-Grenoble, 1947), pp.340–41; also, Béatrice Le Gall, *L'Imaginaire chez Senancour* (Paris, 1966), vol.1, pp.128–30, 180.

2. Senancour, *Oberman*, letter 75 (ed. Monglond, vol.3, p.168; I always cite the 1804 text, which is the basis of this edition).

3. Senancour, *Sur les générations actuelles* (1793), ed. Marcel Raymond (Geneva-Paris, 1963), p.3; *Rêveries sur la nature primitive de l'homme*, vol.1 (Paris, 1910), p.17 (1799 text; I cite the *Rêveries* in their 1799 and 1809 texts, as given by the Merlant-Saintville edn., 2 vols. (Paris, 1910–40); *Oberman*, letter 13 (vol.2, p.73).

4. *Oberman*, letter 22 (vol.2, p.101).

5. See, on these themes, the admirable pages in *Oberman*, letters 48 (vol.3, pp.21–22), 85 (vol.3, p.219), and in the *Rêveries* (1809 text), vol.2, p.122 of the cited edition.

6. *Rêveries* (1799), vol.1, p.57.

7. *Oberman*, letter 89 (vol.3, p.249).

8. Senancour, *Observations critiques sur l'ouvrage intitulé Génie du christianisme* (Paris, 1816), p.142.

9. *Sur les générations actuelles*, p.164.

10. See, for example, *Rêveries* (1799), vol.1, p.20; texts of this sort abound in the whole body of his work.

11. See his article on the *Harmonies de la nature* in the *Mercure du dix-neuvième*

siècle of 1823 (vol.2, p.604); *Rêveries* (Paris: Librairie A. Ledoux, 1833), p.364, note J.

12. *Rêveries* (1833 edn.), p.17.

13. Sainte-Beuve, *Chateaubriand et son groupe* (1872 edn.), vol.1, p.358.

14. Senancour, *Libres Méditations d'un solitaire inconnu* (Paris, 1819), pp.99–199; see also p.104.

15. Notably pp.90, 130, etc., and in Merlant, *Bibliographie des oeuvres de Senancour* (Paris, 1905), p.39 (Törnudd manuscript; see B. Le Gall, op.cit., vol.2, p.489).

16. *Libres Méditations*, p.x.

17. See his letter to Ferdinand Denis (1837) published by Merlant in the *Revue latine* (1906), p.251.

18. Letter to Sainte-Beuve, dictated to his daughter in 1845 according to Merlant, ibid., p.381.

19. Törnudd manuscript, in Merlant, *Bibliographie*, p.48.

20. Senancour, *Les Premiers Ages. Incertitudes humaines. Rêveur des Alpes* (n.p., 1792).

21. *Sur les générations*, p.57; *Rêveries* (1799 text), vol.1, pp.58, 19; *Sur les générations*, p.102.

22. *Rêveries* (1799), vol.1, pp.73, 126. It is apparent that the dialectics of the *Génie du christianisme* were already in the air in 1799.

23. *Oberman*, letter 59 (vol.3, p.70).

24. *Aldomen*, ed. Monglond (Paris, 1925), p.44; *Rêveries* (1799), vol.1, p.69; p.137.

25. *Rêveries* (1799), vol.1, pp.8–9.

26. See the 1797 and 1798 texts on this subject in the introduction by Marcel Raymond to his edition of *Sur les générations actuelles*.

27. *Rêveries* (1799), vol.1, pp.209–17.

28. Ibid., p.215 and note 5.

29. See in B. Le Gall, op.cit., vol.2, in the text of the *Annotations encyclopédiques* (Senancour's reading notes) the mention of their works. In 1821, Senancour again evokes "the vast and useful researches of Court de Gébelin and Rabaut Saint-Etienne" (review of the *Lettres à M. Bailly sur l'histoire primitive de la Grèce* by Rabaut, which had just been republished, in *L'Abeille*, vol.5 (1821), pp.445.

30. *Rêveries* (1809), vol.2, p.4.

31. See on this subject a remarkable page by Marcel Raymond, *Senancour* (Paris, 1965), p.143.

32. *Oberman*, letter 21 (vol.2, p.95).

33. *Aldomen*, p.14; *Rêveries* (1809), vol.2, p.124; *Oberman*, letter 18 (vol.2, p.82; see also letter 21, ibid., p.88).

34. *Oberman*, letter 4 (vol.2, p.27).

35. Ibid., letters 12 and 13 (vol.1, pp.71–72, 74).

36. Ibid., letter 30 (vol.2, pp.113–14).

37. *Rêverie* (1799), vol.1, p.26, note 10; letter to Mme Dupin (1837), paragraph 6 (letter cited at length by Sainte-Beuve [*Chateaubriand et son groupe*], vol.1, pp.362–63: see p.363 n.2) and by G. Michaut (*Senancour, ses amis et ses ennemis* [Paris, 1909], pp.363–67): note the dates at the extremities of his career; and for the intervening period, see *Oberman*, letter 63 (vol.3, p.85), *Rêveries* (1809), vol.2, pp.9–10.

38. See *Rêveries* (1799), vol.1, p.164; *Oberman*, letter 44, vol.2, p.214, note); and on Chateaubriand the *Observations critiques* already cited, pp.22–23.

39. *Rêveries* (1799); and see *Oberman*, letter 81 (vol.3, pp.202–3: text incorporated in the *Rêveries*, 4th reverie, 1809 and 1833 editions; *Rêveries* (1809), vol.2, p.120.

40. See on this subject an interesting discussion in B. Le Gall, op.cit., vol.1, pp.351–87; my feeling is that Senancour does indeed valorize the imagination, but on the human plane, not the ontological plane.

41. *Les Premiers Ages*, p.v; *Aldomen*, p.8. Man's relations with the inanimate are again mentioned in the *Observations* at the beginning of *Oberman*, p.xvii; and in 1821 in an article, "Du génie" (*La Minerve littéraire*, vol.2, pp.303–4).

42. *Oberman*, letter 39 (vol.2, p.167).

43. Ibid., letter 46 (vol.2, pp.244–45).

44. Ibid., letter 47 (vol.3, p.20).

45. See *Oberman*, letters 42 (vol.2, p.196) and 85 (vol.3, pp.220–21). Same attitude in a review of *Les Vers dorés* by Fabre d'Olivet (*Mercure de France* [28 August and 4 September 1813]).

46. Thus on Eckartshausen (in *L'Abeille*, vol.3 [1821], pp.70–75); on the whole of mystical theosophy, in his *Résumé de l'histoire des traditions morales et religieuses chez les divers peuples* (Paris, 1825), pp.404–5, and in the *Extraits d'une digression sur les dispositions de l'esprit humain en Europe* (*Mercure du dix-neuvième siècle*, vol.15 [1826], especially p.177); on Eckstein and neo-Catholicism's appeal to universal traditions, in the same *Mercure du dix-neuvième siècle*, vol.13 [1826], pp.396ff., 576ff. (especially 580).

47. Article already cited, "Du génie," p.296.

48. *Oberman*, letter 36 (vol.2, p.148).

49. Ibid., letter 46 (vol.2, p.233).

50. *Rêveries* ([1833], p.307); Marcel Raymond made this phrase the title of one of the chapters of his book; see an analogous phrase, ibid., p.164 — also in the *Petit vocabulaire de simple vérité* (Paris, 1833), s.v. "Avenir" and in the already cited letter to Mme Dupin, first paragraph, p.363 of the *Senancour* of G. Michaut.

51. *Rêverie* (1809), vol.2, p.21; see also the *Libres Méditations*, p.20; the *Rêveries* of 1833, pp.79ff.; and *Isabelle* (Paris, 1833), p.255. I do not believe that there is in Senancour any religious attachment to suffering, whatever may have been said on this subject; see how he rejects the sanctification of suffering: *Sur les générations,*

pp.80–81 and *Oberman*, letter 63 (vol.3, p.85): "If we do not seek pleasure, what will be our goal?"

52. *Lettre d'un habitant des Vosges*, then *Seconde et dernière lettre d'un habitant des Vosges* (Paris, May 1814); *Simples observations soumises au congrès de Vienne et au gouvernement français par un habitant des Vosges* (Paris, [October 1814]); *De Napoléon* (Paris, n.d. [1815, during the Hundred Days]); *Quatorze juillet 1815* (Paris, n.d. [1815]).

53. See the *Mercure de France* of May 1814, pp.248–53, and *L'Abeille*, vol.3 (1821), pp.99ff.

54. *Rêveries* (1809), vol.2, p.165.

55. Ibid., pp.169–70.

56. He collaborated on the *La Minerve littéraire*, then on *L'Abeille*, then on *Mercure du dix-neuvième siècle*, and also on *Le Constitutionnel*, which was then the great daily of the Left.

57. See especially *Oberman*, letter 84 (vol.3, pp.212–13); and recall the important text mentioned in our note 27.

58. *Oberman*, letter 78 (vol.3, pp.177–78).

59. *De l'amour*, 1st edn. (1806), p.x.

60. *Du prince sous le rapport moral et politique*, in *La France littéraire* (August 1832) (I cite from Merlant, *Bibliographie*, p.73).

61. *De l'amour*, reworking of the passage cited above in the 1808 edition, p.248, and in that of 1829, p.370.

62. Ibid., 3rd edn. (1829), p.86.

63. *Oberman*, letter 79 (vol.3, p.184, note); ibid., p.186.

64. Senancour, *Du style dans ses rapports avec les principes, le caractère et les opinions de l'Ecrivain ou de l'Orateur*, in the *Mercure de France* of 14 and 21 August 1813, pp.319–21; *De la justesse en littérature*, in *La Minerve littéraire* (1820) (vol.1, p.342).

65. Senancour, *De la prose au dix-neuvième siècle*, in the *Mercure du dix-neuvième siècle*, vol.4 (1824), p.421.

66. *Oberman*, third fragment: *De l'expression romantique et du ranz des vaches* (vol.2, pp.161–62).

67. *Oberman*, vol.2, p.xv.

68. Undated letter, cited from the original at the Bibliothèque de Besançon by Jean Larat, *La Tradition et l'exotisme dans l'oeuvre de Ch. Nodier, 1780–1844* (Paris, 1923), p.23. Nodier's stays in Paris extend from 1800 to 1803. According to Delécluze, *Louis David, son école et son temps* (Paris, 1855), p.73, the Méditateurs lasted from 1797 to 1803.

69. See these names in the *Dictionnaire des peintres, sculpteurs, dessinateurs et graveurs* by E. Bénézit, 8 vols. (Paris, 1948 et seq.).

70. His real name was Gleizes, or Gleïzès according to the southern pronunciation (see below). Nodier, in the same letter, names Chateaubriand as coming "to

study poetry in the desert" among the Méditateurs. Could *Atala* owe something to the tastes and tone of this milieu?

71. A. Estignard, *Correspondance inédite de Charles Nodier, 1796–1844* (Paris, 1876), letter 11, p.22.

72. Ibid., letter 12, pp.24–25.

73. Ibid., pp.25–26.

74. Ibid., letter 13, pp.28–29.

75. Quaï and Lucile Franque were born in 1780, like Nodier. Lucile Messageot, wife of the painter J.-P. Franque and herself a painter, was by her mother the sister of Désirée Charve, Nodier's future wife; on this subject see P.-G. Castex, p.5 of his edition of Nodier's *Contes* (Paris, 1961).

76. Nodier, *Essais d'un jeune barde* (Paris, year XII [1804]), pp.90–91 (the piece is signed, bizarrely, UNZER).

77. See the Estignard collection, pp.13, 22.

78. Nodier, *Les Barbus* (article in *Le Temps* [5 October 1832], reprinted by Delécluze, op.cit., p.444).

79. *Les Agrestes, par l'auteur des Nuits Elysiennes* (Paris, year XIII [1804]), "First Elegy," pp.25–27.

80. E.-J. Delécluze, *Carnet de route d'Italie, 1823–1824*, ed. Robert Baschet (Paris, 1942), p.115; and see ibid., note, a hint about Quaï's works preserved in Aix.

81. *Les Barbus d'à présent et les barbus de 1800*, in *Le Livre des Cent-et-un*, vol.7 (1832), pp.61–86 (article reprinted by Delécluze in his *Louis David*, pp.421ff.).

82. Delécluze, *Louis David*, pp.422–29.

83. Article in *Le Temps*, already cited. These articles revived a little the memory of the forgotten group. Jal, who was five years old in 1800, evoked in 1833 as something well known "the pupils of David who disguised themselves as Greeks or as Romans" (A. Jal, *Salon de 1833, les causeries du Louvre* [Paris, 1833], p.87). Let us also mention in the *Histoire de la peinture en Italie* by Stendhal, which appeared in 1817 (ch.89, at the end), a few lines on "some young painters who had worn special clothing"; but Stendhal places this fact "at the beginning of the Revolution": a misdating? Or a reference to something altogether different?

84. Text reprinted in Delécluze, *Louis David*; the cited passages are pp.440–46.

85. In his book on *Louis David*, pp.71ff., Delécluze later returned to the thinkers or primitives, as he persists in calling them. He offers petty criticisms of Nodier in his turn, but offers practically nothing new, except the anecdote according to which Quaï, in David's studio, once indignantly stopped one of his comrades from mocking Jesus. Quaï is evoked again by Delécluze in his *Souvenirs de soixante années* (Paris, 1862), p.48.

86. This is also the case for Gleizes, beyond any doubt: see J.-C. Demarquette, *J.-A. Gleizes et son influence sur le mouvement naturiste* (Paris, 1928), p.19. Gleizes was born in 1773.

87. Article in *Le Temps* (21 June 1833), never reprinted, as far as I know.

88. Delécluze, *Louis David*, pp.419–20; Sainte-Beuve, *Nouveaux Lundis*, vol.3, pp.94–96. They rely solely on the studio incident when Quaï intervened in favor of Jesus.

89. "In Crotona," no place or date of publication (Besançon, 1808).

90. More precisely, Nodier himself tells us, according to the biographers of Pythagoras—namely,"Sylvain Maréchal in particular."

91. Nodier had met him at Dôle in 1806.

92. The vegetarianism of the Méditateurs and of Gleizes and of Nodier himself (see *Apothéoses*, p.xxvi) must certainly be connected to Pythagoreanism. This vegetarianism is the central idea of the later works of Gleizes; it is by these that he was mostly known (see Esquiros's article on him, *Revue des deux mondes* [1 September 1846], pp.837ff.).

93. Nodier, "New Preface," to *Trilby*, in vol.3 of the *Oeuvres complètes*, ed. Renduel (Paris, 1832), p.176.

94. Gleizes, *Les Nuits élysiennes* (Paris, year IX), pp.43–44.

95. Ibid., p.117.

96. See his *Précis de l'introduction à la connaissance des langues*, unpublished till its publication in the *Notes d'un curieux* by Boyer de Sainte-Suzanne (Monaco, 1878), pp.411–17. Nodier as a linguist (in that time's sense of the word) deserves an entire study, for which this is not the place.

97. This last motif was supressed in the new version Gleizes produced in 1838 of his *Nuits élysiennes* under the title of *Séléna ou la famille samanéenne*.

98. *Nuits élyséennes*, fifth night; taken up again in *Séléna*, p.147, note.

99. Gleizes, *Les Agrestes*, pp.103–4. This beautiful text has already been noted by A. Viatte (*Les Sources*, vol.2, p.158 n.7).

100. Nodier, *Les Tristes ou Mélanges tirés des tablettes d'un suicide* (Paris: Demonville, 1806). The stories of which I am thinking are entitled "La Nouvelle Werthérie" (also entitled "La Filleule du seigneur"), "Les Jardins d'Oberheim," "Le Tombeau des grèves du lac," "Une Heure ou la vision," "Sanchette ou le laurier rose." For the most part Nodier reprinted them in his *Romans, nouvelles et mélanges*, vol.1 (Paris: Gide, 1820) and in vol.3 (1832) of his *Oeuvres complètes* published by Renduel.

101. See the "New Preface" to *Trilby*, in *Oeuvres*, vol.3 (1832), p.181.

102. In 1821 and 1822, *La Foudre*, a royalist review on which Nodier collaborated, published under various signatures several stories in the same vein (see vol.4, p.388; vol.5, pp.11, 122; vol.6, pp.59, 81, 88, 234, 398); two others, "La Fièvre" (vol.6, p.365) and "Une Heure" (vol.7, p.321; this story is different from "Une Heure ou la vision"), are signed respectively "Ch. N." and "C. N." but are attributed to the prolific royalist Brisset in the table of contents. Later, some of Aloysius Bertrand's pieces, and later still Mallarmé's first prose poems, will continue this lineage.

103. Nodier did so in *Les Méditations du cloître*, which appeared for the first time in *Les Tristes* in 1806 (see p.90), but that may have been written as an 1803 sequel to

Le Peintre de Salzbourg, to which Nodier appended *Les Méditations du cloître* with this date in the *Romans, nouvelles et mélanges* of 1820, vol.2, and in the *Oeuvres complètes*, vol.2 (1832). See a similar development in Senancour's *Libres Méditations*, pp.252ff. in the 1819 edition.

104. Nodier, *Précis de l'introduction* in Boyer de Sainte-Suzanne, op.cit., p.412.

105. Nodier, third article on the *Poésies illyriennes* in *Le Télégraphe officiel* of Laibach (April 25, 1813) (reprinted in *Statistique illyrienne*, a collection of Nodier's articles published in Ljubljana by F. Dobrovoljc, see p.49).

106. Frédéric Ancillon (1766–1837), of the Prussian Royal Academy, a Protestant minister and son of a Protestant minister, published several collections of miscellanies and essays in French beginning in 1801. Philippe Albert Stapfer (1766–1840), a Protestant minister and Swiss plenipotentiary in Paris during the Consulate, and author of an article on Kant, is the father of Albert, the translator of *Faust*. Charles de Villers is rather well known. On Vanderbourg, see Roland Mortier, *Un Précurseur de Mme de Staël, Charles Vanderbourg, 1765–1827* (Paris-Brussels, 1955).

107. Royer-Collard was born in 1763; Barante in 1782; Guizot in 1787.

108. In politics, however, Maine de Biran, who lived from 1766 to 1821, was an outright counterrevolutionary, as we can see in his *Journal* (ed. Gouhier [Neuchâtel, 1954], vol.1: the 1814–16 period, passim).

109. On this subject, see a remark by Pierre Deguise (*Benjamin Constant méconnu* [Geneva, 1966], p.82).

110. *Lettres inédites et souvenirs de Mme de Récamier et de Mme de Staël publiés par M. le baron de Gérando* (Paris-Metz, 1868), letter of 31 October 1802, pp.52–53.

111. Charles Villers, *Philosophie de Kant ou principes fondamentaux de la philosophie transcendentale* (Metz, 1801), pp.159–63, 168–69.

112. Mme de Staël, 1 August 1802 letter to Villers, in Isler, *Briefe von . . . Madame de Staël auswahl aus dem handschriften Nachlasse des Charles de Villers* (Hamburg, 1879), p.269. Same approval in the letter cited above to the Degérandos.

113. T.-B. Emeric-David, *Recherches sur l'art statuaire* (Paris, year XIII – 1805), pp.276–78, 280, 285; A.-C. Quatremère de Quincy, *Sur l'idéal dans les arts du dessin*, pamphlet with neither place nor date of publication, pp.11 and 12 (= articles that appeared in the *Archives littéraires de l'Europe*, vol.6–7 [1805]).

114. N. Ponce, *Dissertation sur le beau idéal considéré sous le rapport des arts du dessin* (collected in his *Mélanges sur les beaux-arts* [Paris, 1826], p.177); it assuredly dates from 1806: see in *Le Magazin encyclopédique* (1806), vol.6, p.168, the review of a reading at the Institut of a work whose title is almost identical. The authors cited so far were born around 1750.

115. Kératry, *Du beau dans les arts d'imitation* (Paris, 1822), vol.2, book II, ch.12, title page; vol.2, pp.79, 98; Girodet, *Oeuvres posthumes*, ed. P.-A. Coupin, 2 vols. (Paris, 1829), vol.1, p.409; Joseph Droz, *Etudes sur le beau idéal dans les arts* (Paris, 1815), p.39. All these authors were born around 1770.

116. Quatremère de Quincy, *Sur l'idéal*, p.39.

117. Emeric-David, op.cit., p.223; see also p.305.

118. Ibid., p.144.

119. Kératry, op.cit., vol.2, p.11.

120. *Sur l'idéal*, pp.34–35.

121. This is what R. Schneider does (*L'Esthétique classique chez Quatremère de Quincy, 1805–1823* [Paris, 1910]).

122. Those who, like Hoffman, defined and struggled against romanticism as an abuse of the ideal did not spare Quatremère: see in Hoffmann's *Oeuvres*, vol.10 (Paris), pp.1–36, a review of Quatremère de Quincy, *Essai sur la nature, le but et les moyens de l'imitation dans les beaux-arts* (1823), very significant with regard to this point.

123. Quatremère de Quincy, *Sur l'idéal*, pp.17, 34; *Essai sur la nature*, p.288.

124. Girodet, *Oeuvres posthumes*, vol.2, p.117.

125. Ibid., vol.2, pp.124, 125, 204. Similar texts in Droz, op.cit., pp.118, 128.

126. J.-F. Sobry, *Poétique des arts* (Paris, 1810), p.35. Sobry, born in 1743, was a theophilanthropist; see the article on him, doubtless by Beuchot, in Michaud's *Biographie*.

127. Ponce, *De l'influence de la peinture chez les anciens peuples*, in the already cited *Mélanges*, pp.140, 142 (speech given in year x).

128. Quatremère de Quincy, *Considérations sur les arts du dessin en France* (Paris, 1791), p.30; *Sur l'idéal*, p.101.

129. Kératry, op.cit., vol.3, p.141–42.

130. Quatremère de Quincy, *Considérations morales sur la destination des ouvrages de l'art* (Paris, 1815), p.14; in reality the work dates from 1806 (see *Le Magazin encyclopédique* [1806], vol.6, p.163).

131. Necker's book, *De l'importance des idées religieuses*, appeared in the very same year, 1788.

132. *Lettres inédites de Mme de Staël à Henri Meister*, ed. Usteri and Ritter (Paris, 1903), p.147 (letter of 22 April 1797).

133. Mme de Staël, *De la littérature* (1800), ed. Paul Van Tieghem (Paris-Geneva, 1959) (2 vols., continuous pagination), pp.13, 43.

134. Ibid., pp.9, 23 and 368–69, 15.

135. Ibid., p.371.

136. Ibid., p.30.

137. *Delphine* (1803), in *Oeuvres complètes* (Paris, 1820–21), in-16 edn., vol.7, p.257.

138. See on this subject my study on B. Constant in *L'Ecrivain et ses travaux* (Paris, 1967), pp.6off.

139. See G. Rudler, *La Jeunesse de Benjamin Constant* (Paris, 1909), book v, ch.2, and especially on p.487 the letter of 9 September 1794 to Mme de Charrière; also the letters to his family (years 1792 et seq.) added to the Melegari edition of the *Journal intime* (Paris, 1895); and for the period that followed his return to Paris in 1795, the

excellent study by Béatrice W. Jasinski, *L'Engagement de Benjamin Constant* (Paris, 1971).

140. B. Constant, *De l'esprit de conquête et de l'usurpation* (1814), 3rd edn. (Paris, 1814), p.107.

141. B. Constant, *Principes de politique*, in the *Cours de politique constitutionnelle*, ed. Laboulaye (Paris, 1861), vol.1, p.131. The original edition of the *Principes de politique* is from 1815, but one can wonder whether this work was not composed beginning in 1806: see B. Constant's *Journaux intimes*, ed. Roulin-Roth (Paris, 1952) under the date of 4 February 1806, and passim up to October.

142. Mme de Staël, *Du caractère de M. Necker et de sa vie privée* (1804), in *Oeuvres complètes* (Paris, 1820–21), octavo edn., vol.17, p.37.

143. The practice was denounced from the very beginning: see Jay's protest in his review of the first volume of B. Constant's book *De la religion*, in the *Mercure du dix-neuvième siècle*, vol.5 (2nd trimester 1824), p.575, and vol.6, pp.55ff.

144. B. Constant, *Journaux intimes* (21 November 1804); see also his letter to Hochet of 9 August 1812 in B. Constant–Mme de Staël, *Lettres à un ami*, ed. Mistler (Neuchâtel, 1949), pp.218–19.

145. See Mme de Staël, *De l'Allemagne*, part III, especially ch.3 and 4 (pp.66ff. of vol.4 (Paris, 1959) of the Pange-Balayé edition; on mathematics, ibid., part I, ch.18 (vol.1, p.251); on superstitions, part III, ch.10 (vol.4, pp.264–65). It would be a mistake to attribute all this to the German influence: the editors of the *Journal des débats* and the *Mercure*, and the author of *Génie du christianisme* had spread similar themes among the French public.

146. See in particular B. Constant's letters to Prosper de Barante (especially that of 27 July 1808, *Revue des deux mondes* [15 July 1906], p.262), and Constant's preface to his *Wallstein* (Paris-Geneva, 1809), p.xli.

147. B. Constant, *De la religion*, vol.1 (Paris, 1824), p.29.

148. Mme de Staël, *De l'Allemagne*, part III, ch.2 (vol.4, p.19); see also Constant, *De la religion*, vol.1, p.37.

149. See *De l'Allemagne*, vol.4, p.34, note (manuscript version); and *De la religion*, vol.1, p.40: definition of religious feeling by the "need that man experiences to put himself in communication with the invisible powers." Whether they themselves made use of prayer in their own lives is another question. I do not think we need take too seriously the, in the terms they use, "mystical crisis" that they are supposed to have passed through in 1807–8 (see in Deguise, op.cit., the pages devoted to this crisis).

150. *De la littérature*, pp.384ff.; see also *De l'Allemagne*, part III, ch.12 (an entire chapter on this subject); for Constant in 1805, see Deguise, op.cit., pp.137–38.

151. Mme de Staël, *Réflexions sur le suicide* (1818), in *Oeuvres complètes*, octavo edn., vol.3, pp.347–48. "Personality" then meant something like "egocentrism," an exclusive preoccupation with the self in every domain.

152. *De la religion*, vol.1, p.253; see also the preface, p.xxxviii. It need scarcely be

said that the interpretation of sacrifice in ancient religions as a gift to the beloved divinity is very subject to caution, and hardly valid even partially.

153. Mme de Staël, *Delphine*, part II, letter 5 (in-16 edn. of the *Oeuvres*, vol.5, p.258); *Corinne* (1807), book IV, ch.3 (p.80 of the Charpentier edition [1841]). See also *De l'Allemagne*, part IV, ch.6. For B. Constant: *De la religion*, vol.5 (Paris, 1831), in particular p.268. For more details and all the nuances needed on this subject, see Deguise's excellent chapter, op.cit., pp.135ff.

154. Texts abound: for Mme de Staël, *Delphine*, cited edn., vol.6, p.148; *De l'Allemagne*, part III, ch.12 and 14 (vol.4, pp.289, 327) and part IV in its entirety; for B. Constant, *De l'esprit de conquête*, 3rd edn., p.140; *Principes de politique*, p.133; *De la religion*, *Préface*, pp.xxii ff.; vol.1, pp.88–89.

155. Mme de Staël, *Des circonstances actuelles qui peuvent terminer la Révolution et des principes qui doivent fonder la République en France* (manuscript that its editor, John Viénot, dates from 1799) (Paris, 1906), pp.215–16.

156. B. Constant, letter to Fauriel (probably of 1802), cited in Galley, *Cl. Fauriel* (Paris, 1909), p.126.

157. See Mme de Staël, *De la littérature*, p.45; *De l'Allemagne*, part III, ch.12 (vol.4, pp.293–94); *Dix Années d'exil*, ed. P. Gautier (Paris, 1904), p.4; etc. B. Constant, *De l'esprit de conquête*, 4th edn. (1815), added chapter, p.279; *Mémoires sur les Cent-Jours*, part I, (Paris, 1820), pp.83–84.

158. See Mme de Staël, *Réflexions sur la paix adressées à M. Pitt et aux Français* (1794 or 1795), in *Oeuvres complètes*, octavo edn., vol.2, pp.35–94, especially p.59; also the *Réflexions sur la paix intérieure* (1795), ibid., pp.95–172, especially p.104. Same thought in the pamphlets by Constant during the Directory: *De la force du gouvernement* (1796); *Des réactions politiques* (1797); *Des effets de la terreur* (1797). Their policy (acceptance of the effects of the Revolution, political liberty, property) never changed; under the Restoration they speak and act in the same way, taking circumstances into account.

159. *De la littérature*, p.138; see also pp.292–93, 366.

160. *De l'esprit de conquête*, 3rd edn. (Paris, 1814), p.96.

161. Vigny, *Journal d'un poète*, in *Oeuvres*, ed. Baldensperger (Bibl. de la Pléiade), vol.2, p.1033 (7 November [1835]); ibid., p.1233 [1845].

162. Stendhal, *Mémoires d'un touriste* (1838), Le Divan edn., vol.1, pp.128–29.

163. In an article in the *Journal des débats* of 8 December 1831, reprinted in the *Souvenirs et réflexions d'un journaliste* (Paris, 1859), p.144, with a preamble in which the author attempts, very unsuccessfully, to exonerate himself of any injurious intent (see also, ibid., p.151, the text of an article in the *Journal des débats* of 18 April 1832, in which he had already attempted to answer this reproach).

164. See Ballanche's letter to Mme Récamier of 1 September 1832, cited in L. Séché, *Le Cénacle de La Muse française* (Paris, 1909), p.266.

165. Ballanche, *La Ville des expiations* (1907 edn.), p.42; these pages are not dated, but the context shows they predate 1830. This is obviously not the place to

discuss the validity of this model. It consists in explaining history by the progressive extension of a dominant civilization to human masses previously excluded from it. This explanatory principle includes the class struggle and the interior "invasions" that result from it as a variety or special case of a fundamental phenomenon. In our time, in which the problem of underdeveloped peoples and of their entry into the universal civilization built by the West tends to occupy the limelight, eclipsing the internal class struggle in the course of events, it would be legitimate to seek a more comprehensive explanatory principle than that which is solely inspired by the internal antagonistic aspects of a society.

166. Mme de Staël, *De la littérature*, p.139.

167. Ibid., pp.132–33.

168. Ibid., p.365.

169. Ibid., p.183.

170. B. Constant, *De la religion*, vol.1, pp.33–34.

171. Mme de Staël, *De l'Allemagne*, part IV, ch.5 (vol.5, p.76): "the golden age," signifying the biblical Eden, is an expression of the *philosophes*, very meaningful in this context.

172. Mme de Staël, *Des circonstances actuelles*, pp.187, 191, 206.

173. See his pamphlet *Des réactions*, chs. 5 and 6.

174. *De la littérature*, p.35.

175. Ibid., p.289.

176. Ibid., pp.322ff.

177. Ibid., pp.359–60.

178. Letter to Mme de Charrière of 7 June 1794, cited in Ph. Godet, *Madame de Charrière et ses amis*, vol.2 (Geneva, 1906), p.124.

179. Mme de Staël, *Mirza*, in *Oeuvres complètes*, in 8, vol.2, p.229. This narrative, which appeared for the first time in the *Recueil de morceaux détachés, par Mme la Baronne Staël de Holstein* (Lausanne-Paris, 1795), was already written, we are told, before her marriage, which took place in 1786.

180. This portrait is cited in the *Notice* that Mme Necker de Saussure placed at the head of Mme de Staël's *Oeuvres complètes*, vol.1, pp.xxix ff. It is believed that this portrait is the work of Guibert, who is chiefly known for having been loved by Mlle de Lespinasse, and whose eulogy Mme de Staël wrote (*Oeuvres complètes.*, vol.17, p.275). If the portrait is by him, it cannot postdate 1790, which is the year he died.

181. *Corinne*, book II, ch.4, p.49 of the cited edition; *Sapho*, prose drama in five acts, in *Oeuvres complètes*, vol.16 (this drama dates, we are told, from 1811).

182. The question of Germany's actual influence on Mme de Staël has not been resolved. In general, we can say the same of the foreign influence on French literature between 1800 and 1850, that is, on its deep, underlying causes, not on some particular theme or orientation: see on this subject Sainte-Beuve's famous pages (2 November 1863 letter to W. Reymond, in the *Correspondance*, Bonnerot edition, vol.13, pp.326–30). Of German aesthetics in particular, the knowledge possessed by the

French in general, and even by Mme de Staël, was paltry. Neither Kant's *Critique of Judgment* nor Schiller's aesthetic opuscules nor Hegel's *Lectures on Fine Art*, to cite the most important works, were translated before 1840; some of these were only translated during the Second Empire. What a few translations of poems during the Empire and the Restoration could reveal of German ideas concerning the spiritual privilege of poetry was not new even in France. It is certainly true that among European nations Germany's contribution to aesthetics and to the doctrine of the ministry of poetry and art was capital; but it is a fact that this contribution was very little known in France, and more often by rumor and reinterpreted hearsay than by real communication. As much perhaps as the difference in languages, it is the difference of circumstances, crises, and conflicts peculiar to each national society that limits the influence of a literature beyond its borders. A European literature has existed only to the extent to which situations and problems have existed here and there that were similar, though experienced differently: thus, in the example of interest to us, the theory of the Beautiful as a sign of the divine was able to prosper everywhere at once, because everywhere the tottering of religious dogmas made it necessary to define a new, more "natural," sort of communication between man and God, so as to provide a foundation for values and social order. One can explain in the same way the universal character that the promotion of the writer and the poet takes on.

183. *Corinne*, book III, ch.3, p.65 of the cited edition.

184. *De l'Allemagne*, part II, ch.10 (vol.2, p.114).

185. Ibid., part II, ch.18 (vol.2, pp.344–45). Mme de Staël defends Chateaubriand from the reproaches that he incurred on this subject (part IV, ch.4: vol.5, pp.79–80).

186. Ibid., vol.2, p.118, p.124 (manuscript variant).

187. 21 December 1803 letter cited in the Pange-Balayé edition of the book *De l'Allemagne*, vol.2, p.92, note, according to the Herr edition of the Schiller-Goethe correspondence (Paris, 1923), p.290.

188. *De l'Allemagne*, part II, ch.6 (vol.2, p.74: approval of Winckelmann's aesthetics).

189. Ibid., part III, ch.9 (vol.4, p.223: the passage is an homage to Kant).

190. Ibid., vol.4, pp.232–33.

191. Before Mme de Staël, the French had scarcely been able to learn of the spread of this idea in Germany except through Ancillon, who develops it in his *Mélanges de littérature et de philosophie*, 2 vols. (Paris, 1809), vol.1, pp.23–24, pp.156–57 (on Ancillon, see *De l'Allemagne*, part IV, ch.1 [vol.5, pp.17–18]).

192. *De l'Allemagne*, part II, ch.10 (vol.2, p.118); ibid., ch.13 (vol.2, p.191; and p.190 a manuscript variant evokes "this analogy between man and the universe").

193. Ibid., part III, ch.10 (vol.4, p.246).

194. See *De l'Allemagne*, part III, ch.10; part IV, ch.9; and, similarly, the both sympathetic and measured way in which Benjamin Constant speaks of Tieck (*Journaux intimes*, 24 October 1804).

195. *De l'Allemagne*, part III, ch.21 (vol.4, pp.402–3).

196. Paul Dubois, *Cousin, Jouffroy, Damiron: Souvenirs*, ed. Ad. Lair (Paris, 1902), p.15. For what concerns Cousin, we should add that after about fifteen years he ceased to create, limiting himself to revising his philosophic oeuvre and making it palatable. For this reason we shall confine ourselves almost exclusively to this first period in what follows.

197. See Sainte-Beuve, *Portraits littéraires*, vol.3, p.329, in an article on Rémusat.

198. *Les Misérables*, part III, book III, ch.3. This definition, which the context renders rather pejorative, was not pejorative in the first state of the manuscript (that of *Les Misères*): the Doctrinaires were not named there, and Hugo argued there on his own account in favor of this kind of liberalism; after 1848, having moved significantly to the left and embarrassed by what he had thought before, he dumped onto the narrow back of the Doctrinaires a point of view that—as his own example proves—had enjoyed appreciably wider favor.

199. In 1895, however, Barthélemy Saint-Hilaire was still writing fearlessly: "M. Cousin was the greatest philosopher of his time in France, and, one could even add, in Europe." (*M. Victor Cousin, sa vie et sa correspondance*, 3 vols. [Paris, 1895], vol.2, p.526).

200. Cousin, *Discours prononcé à l'ouverture de l'histoire de la philosophie* (Paris, January 1816), p.33.

201. It was used (also by Cousin himself) in competition with "spiritualism" to designate the new French philosophy. Sainte-Beuve regretted that usage did not limit itself to this latter term (see *Portraits littéraires*, vol.3, p.468). Paul Janet (*V. Cousin et son oeuvre* [Paris, 1885], p.97) finds "spiritualism" inaccurate because Cousin hardly dealt with the soul, and preferred "idealism," but this word, which evokes above all the primacy of the knowing subject, is even further removed from what is essential in Cousinism: the axiomatic affirmation of a two-tiered reality, infinite being communicating with finite minds through mediating reason and by means of enthusiasm. Latouche, who had been acquainted with Saint-Martin, who also called himself a spiritualist, calls him "the ambitionless precursor of your Platos of the Chambre des pairs" (*La Vallée-aux-loups* [1833], p.129): a transparent allusion to Cousin, but "precursor" is inexact: Saint-Martin's spiritualism, which keeps the notions of the Fall and rebirth as fundamentals, is a variety of Christianity; that of Cousin, a semireligious variety of philosophism.

202. We recognize in all this the legacy of Mme de Staël; for precise points of derivation, see, for example, the *Cours de philosophie professé à la Faculté des Lettres pendant l'année 1818*, pp.79, 319.

203. See P. Janet, op.cit., p.453: "The history of philosophy itself, in other words, the Eclectic method."

204. V. Cousin, *De la philosophie de l'histoire*, text published by Buchon as an appendix to his translation of the *Histoire des sciences métaphysiques, morales et politiques* by Dugald Stewart, vol.3 (Paris, 1823), pp.333 and 335; it is Buchon who dates

this text from 1816, the work, he says, of one of his friends; Cousin is this friend: see G. Monod, *La Vie et la pensée de Jules Michelet* (Paris, 1923), vol.1, p.51. The idea of perfectibility as the motor of history supposes a mind judging events and appreciating their advance toward what is better; if it is not God, it must be man who is this judge and this guide. The system no longer works if one wishes to attribute progress to an immanent force in things, and if, substituting History, not man, for God, one advocates events themselves while refusing to judge them. This affected faith in the course of events is convenient for excusing the triumph of force from condemnation when one applauds it oneself, and in a general way, to justify a victorious party to which one belongs. This is what it fell to the unfortunate Cousin to attempt one day, under the influence, it is supposed, of Hegel. His philosophy of history caused a scandal when, in 1828, he undertook to identify might with right, "to demonstrate the morality of success," and "that the vanquished is always he who ought to be vanquished," that "to accuse the victor and take a position against victory is to take a position against humanity and complain about the progress of civilization" (*Introduction à l'histoire de la philosophie* [Paris, 1828], 9th lecture, p.37): a bizarre avatar of spiritualism, which ends by confusing force and justice, when the raison d'être of the doctrine was to distinguish them; Mme de Staël, in 1828, must have turned in her grave. But as early as 1824, if we are to believe Charles de Rémusat, Cousin had communicated this manner of thinking to Thiers and Mignet, and held meetings with them on this subject (see Ch. de Rémusat, *Mémoires de ma vie*, vol.2 [1959], pp.145–46; Rémusat prides himself, along with the youthful contributors to *Le Globe*, in having resisted Cousin's influence on this point). In Cousin, these views were intended to justify the Revolution, the Empire, and the imminent accession of Doctrinairism to power, over against the Bourbons. There is no need to evoke here the later, and current, career of this sort of reasoning.

205. See Cousin, *Cours d'histoire de la philosophie morale au dix-huitième siècle* (given in 1820), ed. Vacherot (Paris, 1841), pp.74–75; foreword to the *Fragments philosophiques*, 3rd edn. (Paris, 1838), p.xvi.

206. Cousin, *Fragments philosophiques*, 1826 preface, reprinted in the 2nd edn. (1833), pp.42–43.

207. Cousin, *Introduction à l'histoire de la philosophie* (1828 course, already cited), 1st lecture, p.29.

208. The most weighty accusation was that of pantheism. Without wishing to discuss this or to consider Cousin's wavering on this subject, we may make the following observation: what in the speculations of romantic spiritualism is merely the idea or the feeling of divine omnipresence is too often accused of pantheism. These often inconsequential speculations remain fundamentally dualist in the special, transcendent value that they always reserve to Spirit, even when they see it everywhere.

209. There is a good example in the article that Larousse's *Grand Dictionnaire universel du XIXe siècle* devotes to Cousin.

210. This is what Paul Janet is right to emphasize, though he is well aware of the

flaws of the person he is describing (op.cit., pp.270ff.). See also Jules Simon, *Victor Cousin* (Paris, 1887), pp.114ff.; and among other texts by V. Cousin, the *Discours prononcé à la Chambre des Pairs dans la séance du 26 décembre 1838 sur la renaissance de la domination ecclésiastique* (Paris, 1839), also the *Défense de l'Université et de la philosophie* (Paris, 1844) (April and May speeches to the Chambre des pairs).

211. Sainte-Beuve, *Causeries du lundi*, vol.6, pp.151–52, 153–54 (24 May 1852 article in the *Le Constitutionnel* "On the Retirement of MM. Villemain and Cousin").

212. Sainte-Beuve, letter to Mme Juste Olivier of October 3, 1843 (*Correspondance*, ed. Bonnerot, vol.5, pp.334–35).

213. E. Faguet, *Politiques et moralistes du dix-neuvième siècle*, 2nd series (Paris, 1898), pp.229, 280. Faguet himself, we should remember, taught in the University.

214. Jouffroy, "On the Organization of the Philosophical Sciences," in *Nouveaux Mélanges philosophiques* (Paris, 1842), pp.115, 119 (this text probably dates from 1836).

215. Ibid., p.146.

216. See in particular, on this notion of destiny (understood in the sense of destination, and linked to the notion of value or order), the piece entitled "On Good and Evil" (1824) in the *Mélanges philosophiques* (1838 edn.), pp.363ff.; and, in the same collection, "On the Problem of Human Destiny" (an 1830 lecture), in particular pp.387ff.; also the *Cours de droit naturel* (lectures from 1833–34), 2nd edn. (Paris, 1843), vol.2, pp.373, 390, etc.

217. See "On the Organization of the Philosophic Sciences," *Nouveaux Mélanges*, pp.121ff. The text had been altered in this first (posthumous) edition, here and in other places, through Cousin's intervention; G. Gazier made known the authentic text of the manuscript (*Revue d'histoire littéraire de la France* [1925], pp.588ff.).

218. Letter of 17 February 1822, to Dubois, in *Correspondance*, ed. Ad. Lair (Paris, 1901), p.324.

219. An anthology of analogous formulae appearing between 1800 and 1825 could be made. See, in Jouffroy himself, the *Cours d'esthétique* (given in 1826), ed. Damiron (Paris, 1843), pp.35–36 (he has just exalted, p.34, the character René); in *Le Cahier vert*, ed. P. Roux (Paris, 1924), pp.47–48, a gloriously spiritualist definition of the *vague des passions*; also "On the Problem of Human Destiny" (text already cited), pp.399ff.

220. Letter of 8 August 1818 to Damiron in *Correspondance*, pp.219–20.

221. *Le Cahier vert*, p.47.

222. Letter to Damiron of 4 June 1819. See also the letter of 19 January 1819, to the same person, and the letter to Dubois of 10 July 1819.

223. *Le Cahier vert*, p.45.

224. See, in particular, "The Object, Certitude, Point of Departure, and Delimitation of Psychology," in the *Mélanges philosophiques* of 1838, pp.258–59 (1823 text); "On Skepticism," ibid., pp.211–19 (1830 text); preface to vol.1 of the translation of the complete works of Thomas Reid (Paris, 1836), in particular p.clxxxix;

"On the Legitimacy of the Distinction between Psychology and Physiology," in *Nouveaux Mélanges*, pp.276–77 (1838 text).

225. We see again, at the end of this line of minds that issue from the eighteenth century, what we saw there at the beginning, and what in them is most subtle and refined: by the remarkable acuity of his intelligence, Jouffroy sometimes makes one think, albeit with all sorts of differences, of Senancour.

226. Jouffroy, "Reflections on the Philosophy of History," in the *Mélanges* of 1838, p.50, and see pp.58–61 (1825 text).

227. See, for example, "On Philosophy and Common Sense," ibid., pp.145ff. (1824 text).

228. *Le Cahier vert*, p.34.

229. *Comment les dogmes finissent* first appeared in *Le Globe* of 24 May 1825; the article is reprinted at the beginning of the *Mélanges philosophiques* with the note "1823" as the date of composition (I am citing according to this collection, the 1838 edition: pp.12, 18–19, 21–22); P. Poux republished it in 1924 following *Le Cahier vert*.

230. It will have been remarked to what an extent the succession of historic moments described in *Comment les dogmes finissent* (era of established beliefs, era of inquiry and negation, establishment of a more modern faith) resembles, except for the vocabulary, the Saint-Simonian model, which has "organic eras" alternate with "critical eras." This model appeared between 1820 and 1822 in the writings of Saint-Simon and Auguste Comte, who was then his disciple. It is difficult to say whether Jouffroy, in 1823, knew of those writings and could have been inspired by them. The idea of a necessary reconstruction after negation was, in any case, widely current.

231. This course was first edited according to auditors' notes by Adolphe Garnier in 1836, and was published by Hachette. Later editions were extensively revised and toned down.

232. Course given in his home in 1826, edited by Damiron and published by Hachette in 1843, according to an auditor's notes.

233. Cousin, *Du vrai, du beau, du bien*, pp.106ff., 218–22; Jouffroy, *Cours d'esthétique*, Lectures I to VI, and especially pp.21–29.

234. Cousin, ibid., p.182; Jouffroy, ibid., pp.76–77, 245.

235. Cousin, ibid., pp.223, 224 (see also p.230).

236. Jouffroy, ibid., pp.291–92.

237. Cousin, ibid., pp.210, 268.

238. Jouffroy, ibid., pp.245, 184.

239. Jouffroy, ibid., pp.133, 148, 154, 157.

240. Jouffroy, ibid., p.154.

241. Jouffroy, ibid., pp.154, 155.

242. Jouffroy, ibid., p.167.

243. Jouffroy, ibid., p.184.

244. Cousin, ibid., pp.301, 267.

245. Cousin, ibid., pp.290, 281.

246. Sainte-Beuve, *Portraits littéraires*, vol.1, pp.296–324 (article in the *Revue des deux mondes* of 1 December 1833, see pp.531–32).

247. Jouffroy, "Reflections on the Philosophy of History," in *Mélanges philosophiques* (1838), p.71.

248. Ibid., p.75.

249. Ibid., pp.72–73.

6. THE POETICS OF THE THEOSOPHIST

1. On Fabre d'Olivet, a primitivist philosopher in Gébelin's line, later a theosophist, see the excellent work by Léon Cellier, *Fabre d'Olivet, contribution à l'étude des aspects religieux du romantisme* (Paris, 1953). No doubt the success in the second half of the century, especially in the time of symbolism, is due to his independence in relation to Christianity. However, his syntheses change constantly, and his philology is particularly disconcerting.

2. See Fabre d'Olivet, *La Langue hébraïque restituée*, vol.1 (Paris, 1815), p.45 ("There is nothing conventional in speech"), p.95 ("The sign derives directly from the eternal principle of the Word, which emanated from the divinity"). The work was finished as early as 1811.

3. Fabre d'Olivet, *Les Vers dorés de Pythagore expliqués et traduits en vers eumolpiques français* (Paris, 1813), p.20.

4. Ibid., p.12.

5. Ibid., pp.137ff.

6. See on him an obituary article by Richer in the *Lycée armoricain* of March 1828, p.176; a few pages by the same author in *Les guérisons opérées par Mme de Saint-Amour* (Nantes, 1828), pp.17ff.; and an anonymous account in the review *La Nouvelle Jérusalem*, vol.2 (1839), pp.204–19.

7. Bernard, *Opuscules théosophiques*, pp.22ff., 81ff., 41, 169. He remains deeply marked by Saint-Martin and by the writers of his school (see pp.125–26, 138ff., 159ff.).

8. He was born in 1792, Bernard in 1791: both are almost exactly the contemporaries of Lamartine and Cousin. On Richer, see an article by Emile Souvestre in the *Revue de Paris* (June 1837), pp.40–59, reprinted in vol.1 of Richer's *Oeuvres littéraires* (Nantes, 1838); and the *Mémoires sur la vie et les ouvrages d'Ed. Richer*, published by Piet in this same volume.

9. Souvestre, cited article, p.41; Piet reports the same thing.

10. Article in the *Le Lycée armoricain*, vol.6 (1825), p.558; vol.8 (1826), p.38; also vol.12 (1828), pp.17ff.

11. Richer, *De la philosophie religieuse et morale dans ses rapports avec les lumières* (Paris-Nantes, 1821) (work written in 1819 according to Piet, op.cit., p.135); *L'Immortalité de l'âme*, ode (Nantes-Paris, 1821).

12. *De la philosophie idéaliste*, in *Lycée armoricain*, vol.4 (1824), pp.313–21. In

letters in 1827, sketching a Swedenborgian analysis, he also invokes, besides Saint-Martin and Joseph de Maistre, the German philosophers, Cousin, Degérando, Mme de Staël, Constant, etc. (posthumous *Mélanges*, ed. Le Boys des Guays [Saint-Amand-Paris-London-New York, 1861], vol.2, pp.192ff.).

13. *De l'état actuel de l'esprit théosophique en Europe*, in *Lycée armoricain*, vol.7 (1826), p.144.

14. See *Le Mot de l'énigme* (Paris, 1826) (a work he composed in 1822 according to Piet, op.cit., p.115, and in which he draws on Saint-Martin and Law for this subject); also the already cited *Mélanges*, vol.1, pp.139–62.

15. Richer, *De la nouvelle Jérusalem*, 8 vols. (Paris-Nantes, 1832–35); see in particular references to Saint-Martin (vol.4, p.242; vol.5, p.214; vol.6, p.226), to Ballanche (vol.4, p.362), to Chateaubriand (vol.5, p.515), to Mme de Staël (vol.4, book II, ch.5 "On Correspondences").

16. See Richer, *Des guérisons*, pp.82–84, where Royer-Collard, Benjamin Constant, Victor Cousin, and *Le Globe* are invoked sympathetically from a point of view of liberal spiritualism.

17. *Mercure de France* in September 1815.

18. Richer also intended to entitle this work *Essai sur la poétique naturelle*; the almost finished manuscript was burned by robbers in 1821 (see Souvestre, cited article, p.43; and Piet, p.146). The outline that has survived (today Ms. 527 in the public library of the city of Nantes) was known to Piet, who mentions it, ibid., p.348, in his bibliography; there is no doubt about the attribution. I have been able to examine it: it is entitled *Théorie philosophique de la poétique générale des beaux-arts*.

19. Viatte, *Victor Hugo et les illuminés de son temps* (Montreal, 1942), p.38.

20. *Epître à M. L. [impost]* (Nantes, 1821); epigraph: "Ante omnia Musae" (see Piet, p.145).

21. See for example Richer, *Mes Pensées* (Nantes-Paris, 1825), pp.224, 277–78.

22. See Piet, pp.185, 236.

23. Richer, *La Visite de Gustave* (following *Le Livre de l'homme de bien ou le Testament du Docteur Cramer* [Paris-Nantes, 1832], pp.86–89, 96, 101. On the primitive language identified with that of the ecstatics, see also *De la nouvelle Jérusalem*, vol.4, p.376 (text reprinted, no doubt by mistake, in vol.5, p.384).

24. *De la nouvelle Jérusalem*, vol.6, pp.313, 331.

25. *Mélanges*, vol.2, p.256 (1827 letter).

26. *La Visite de Gustave*, pp.110 and 111; *De la nouvelle Jérusalem*, vol.3, p.424.

27. *De la nouvelle Jérusalem*, vol.4, pp.371, 373; vol.6, p.324.

28. See on him the article by Viatte, *Les Swedenborgiens en France de 1820 à 1830*, in the *Revue de littérature comparée* (1931), pp.416ff., also *V. Hugo et les illuminés de son temps*, pp.40ff.; and an article by R. Michaud (*Revue de littérature comparée* [1921], pp.388ff.). Oegger was born in 1789.

29. See Oegger, *Le Vrai Messie ou l'Ancien et le Nouveau Testamens examinés d'après les principes de la langue de la nature* (Paris, 1829).

30. (Paris, 1831). *Le Vrai Messie* already had a chapter "On Hieroglyphic Keys."

31. Richer, *Du romantique* in the *Lycée armoricain*, vol.1 (1823), p.56.

32. Richer, *Du vague en littérature*, in the *Lycée armoricain*, vol.3 (1824), p.371.

33. Richer's *La Bretagne Poétique* occupies volumes 5 and 6 of his *Oeuvres littéraires* (Nantes, 1838); it had first appeared in the *Lycée armoricain* in the years 1823 to 1825.

34. Piet has collected these in his article, already frequently cited, pp.89ff.

35. He published there in 1823, in volume 1, pp.106 and 258, and volume 2, p.302, extracts from an unpublished translation he had made of the *Aeneid*.

36. Richer, *De la nouvelle Jérusalem*, vol.4, p.128.

7. THE ROMANTIC REVOLUTION

1. I mean by romanticism what is usually called by that name in French literature and which does indeed exist there as a characteristic ensemble. The degree of appropriateness of the term and the fact that in other literatures it has been able to designate realities that were markedly different does not interest me here.

2. See the previously cited work by Helen Maxwell King, *Les Doctrines littéraires de la "Quotidienne."*

3. This is the *L'Oriflamme* of 1824–25, founded by the bookseller Dentu and on which Salgues collaborated.

4. See on this periodical the article by G. van Welkenhuysen, "L'Anti-romantisme de *L'Eclair*, 1827–1829," in the *Revue d'histoire littéraire de la France* (1931), pp.367ff., 518ff.

5. On this *Oriflamme* of 1823–24, whose principal contributor was Saint-Prosper, see Michel Vivier, *Victor Hugo et Charles Nodier collaborateurs de l'"Oriflamme,"* *Revue d'histoire littéraire de la France* (1958), pp.297–323.

6. Armand Malitourne, *De l'influence politique de la littérature*, in *Annales de la littérature et des arts*, vol.3 (1821), pp.353ff. (lecture to the Société des Bonnes Lettres).

7. *Recueil de l'Académie des Jeux Floraux*, year 1821, pp.lxiii ff.

8. See F. Ségu, *L'Académie des Jeux Floraux et le romantisme*, vol.1 (1935), p.121, and the collection in the Academy's *Recueil* beginning in 1812 (especially 1821: Report of the perpetual secretary on the competition of interest to us; this report is reprinted in Ségu, op.cit., vol.1, pp.108ff.). The speech of the laureate, La Servière, is in the *Recueil* (1821), pp.xxxi–lxi.

9. See a remarkable effort in this direction by Auger, in his memorable Academic harangue (*Recueil des discours prononcés dans la séance publique annuelle de l'Institut royal de France le samedi 24 avril 1824* [Paris, 1824]).

10. Ballanche, *Essai sur les institutions sociales* (1818), in vol.2 of the duodecimo *Oeuvres*, pp.103, 380–383.

11. At the very most we can note a stronger tendency toward antiromanticism among the oldest; among those who strike hard at what is new, Hoffman, Duviquet, Lacretelle, Auger, Géraud, and Msgr. Frayssinous were born between 1765

and 1775; but Laurentie, Rocher, and the members of the staff of the *Mémorial catholique* are younger than Lamartine (born from 1793 to 1800).

12. "Du romantisme" in the second *L'Oriflamme*, vol.3 (1825), pp.354, 358, 361; the article is signed J. (?)

13. Article signed Z. (Hoffman) in the *Journal des débats* of 23 November 1820, cited by abbé Pierre Dubois (*V. Hugo, ses idées religieuses de 1802 à 1825* [Paris, 1913], p.309).

14. Laurentie, *Du romantisme*, in *La Quotidienne* of 21 January 1824 (cited by H. M. King, op.cit., pp.116 and 117; see also ibid., pp.121–22).

15. See, in the same vein, the review signed Z. (Hoffman) of Hugo's *Nouvelles Odes* in the *Journal des débats* of 14 June 1824.

16. Msgr. Frayssinous, *Discours pour la distribution des prix au Concours général*, read on 16 August 1824, in the *Collection intégrale et universelle des orateurs sacrés*, ed. Migne, vol.77 (Complete oratorical works of Msgr. Frayssinous) (Paris, 1856), column 997.

17. See Joseph Rocher, *De la décadence des lettres*, in *Le Défenseur*, vol.3 (December 1820), pp.599, 602. In 1816 Joseph Rocher de la Côte appears frequently in the correspondence of Lamartine, who dedicates to him his ode on "L'Enthousiasme"; in the Second Empire he was a magistrat and rector of Toulouse. There is an article about him by Gustave Vallier (1878).

18. Speech by General Pascalis, in *Séance publique de la Société des Amis des sciences, des lettres, de l'agriculture et des arts d'Aix tenue le 15 juin 1822* (Aix, 1822), pp.5–6. On the figure of General Pascalis, see the *Discours de réception à l'Académie delphinale prononcé par M. Georges Gariel . . . séance du 16 février 1935* (Grenoble, 1935).

19. These are Salinis's theses in the *Mémorial catholique* (see especially vol.1 [January 1824], pp.49–60, *Du principe d'autorité dans la littérature*). The romanticism-Protestantism equation is already found in 1821 in Joseph-Théophile Foisset, magistrate in Dijon (born in 1800), who would later follow Lamennais's group on the path to liberal Catholicism: in his article "Du genre romantique" *(Mémoires de l'Académie des sciences, arts, et belles-lettres de Dijon*, [1821], pp.230–31), he puts this equation forward as new. Salinas, in the continuation of his study (*Mémorial catholique*, vol.1 [March 1824], p.162), refers to Foisset's article with praise.

20. *De la politique par rapport à la littérature*, anonymous article in the very royalist newspaper *Le Spectateur religieux et politique*, vol.1 (1818), p.268.

21. Edmond Géraud, in *Annales de la littérature et des arts*, vol.28 (1827), p.367.

22. Lacretelle, *Discours du 4 décembre 1823 à la Société des Bonnes Lettres*, in *Annales de la littérature et des arts*, vol.13 (1823), p.420.

23. Hoffman, review of V. Hugo's *Odes*, in the *Journal des débats* of 17 November 1822.

24. Lady Morgan, *La France*, 3rd edn. (Paris, 1818), vol.1, p.155 (orig. edn., 1817).

25. See, for example, Jarrin, "The Youth of Edgar Quinet," in *Inauguration de la*

statue d'Edgar Quinet à Bourg le 14 mai 1883 (Bourg, 1883), p.12: Jarrin, who was a child under Louis XVIII, remembers having learned to read in prayer books illustrated by episodes of the royal martyrdom placed in parallel with the Passion.

26. See Lanson's edition of the *Méditations*, vol.1, pp.xciii ff.

27. Jules Janin, introduction to *Choix de poésies contemporaines*, part of a "Bibliothèque choisie" directed by Laurentie (Paris, 1829), p.xv. Jules Janin, who after liberal beginnings was collaborating at this time on *La Quotidienne*, is imitating a little belatedly the early fervors of royalist romanticism.

28. J. Bins de Saint-Victor, *De la poésie en général et des "Méditations" de M. de La Martine*, in *Le Défenseur*, vol.1 (May 1820), pp.345ff., 352; vol.2 (July 1820), p.112.

29. See, for example, in *La Foudre* of June 15, 1823, vol.9, pp.56–57, an anonymous review of the *Odes et poésies diverses* of Antoine Cunyngham.

30. See among others Genoude, reviewing the *Méditations* in the *Le Conservateur*, vol.6 (1820), p.509; *Le Conservateur littéraire* (June 1820) (vol.2, part 1, of the republication of this periodical by Jules Marsan, p.242); J. M. V. Audin, "On the Romantic," preceding his novel *Florence ou La Religieuse* (Paris, 1822), pp.xlvii–xlviii. The writers cited here and in what follows are either of the former generation, like Saint-Victor, born in 1772, or of that of Lamartine, like Guttinguer, born in 1785, Le Prévost in 1787, Saint-Prosper and Desmarais in 1790, Genoude in 1792, Audin in 1793; the younger generation, born around 1800, is especially represented in *La Muse française*, of which we shall speak later on.

31. Article signed P. Y. T. (review of Mollevault's *Chants sacrés*) in the *Lettres champenoises*, vol.18 (1824), p.147.

32. Article already cited in *La Foudre* (15 June 1823), p.57.

33. Article signed P. in the *Lettres champenoises*, vol.17 (1824), p.29.

34. See Cyprien Desmarais, *Essai sur les classiques et les romantiques* (Paris, 1824), pp.22, 70, 105; same ideas in his *Considérations sur la littérature et sur la société en France au dix-neuvième siècle*, which are from the same year; also in *Le Temps présent* (Paris, 1826), especially p.120.

35. See the review, in the *Annales de la littérature et des arts*, vol.24 (1826), pp.419ff., a speech given by Guttinguer to the Academy of Rouen; and the *Précis analytique des travaux de l'Académie royale des sciences, belles-lettres et arts de Rouen pendant l'Année 1824* (Rouen, 1825), pp.123ff. Ulric Guttinguer, the author of *Arthur*, is well enough known.

36. Saint-Prosper, 17 February 1824 article, in *L'Oriflamme*, collected in his *Mélanges politiques, littéraires et biographiques* (Paris, 1828), p.78. Saint-Prosper is thinking especially of Chateaubriand; he is a very strict royalist, who calls himself classic to boot, but with an openness to the changes that have affected France.

37. Auguste le Prévost, *Sur la poésie romantique* (Rouen, 1825), pp.17–18. This essay is a speech given in 1824 to the Academy of Rouen in the course of the debate on romanticism (see the *Précis analytique* already cited); excerpts appeared under the title "Des différents âges de la poésie" in the *Mercure du dix-neuvième siècle*,

vol.12 (1826), pp.7ff. Le Prévost, a Norman "antiquarian," was a prefect in the first Restoration.

38. Chateaubriand, general preface to the edition of the *Oeuvres complètes* (Ladvocat, 1826) (p.vi of the Pourrat edn. of the *Oeuvres*, vol.1 [1832]).

39. In this attempt at a synthesis of royalist opinion concerning romanticism, I have said nothing of the baron d'Eckstein, whose articles in the *Annales de la littérature et des arts* (beginning in 1822), in the *Le Drapeau blanc* (from 1823 to 1827), and in *Le Catholique*, which he composed almost entirely from 1826 to 1829, clearly suggest a modern renewal of literature from a royalist, religious perspective. But it is nothing to Eckstein if he considers French classicism defunct, since he is thoroughly Germanic in culture; his testimony to this effect is thus not important in the present context.

40. *Le Conservateur littéraire* formed three volumes, of which the first two have been republished, each in two volumes, by Jules Marsan (Paris, 1922–38); *La Muse française* had been republished in its entirety in two volumes (Paris, 1907 and 1909), also by Jules Marsan. Only two or three liberals belonged to the group: Latouche, linked to the Deschamps brothers, and Lefèvre-Deumier; their writings, of a different character, are not considered here.

41. Lamartine, letter to Genoude of 23 March 1824 (*Correspondance*, vol.2, p.265: "I occasionally receive this French muse that amuses you so: it is indeed quite amusing. It is delirium instead of genius").

42. Sainte-Beuve, *Portraits contemporains*, vol.1, pp.409–10 (article on V. Hugo, of 1 August 1831).

43. See Jules Bertaut, *L'Epoque romantique* (Paris, 1947), p.39; and Antoni Deschamps's regrets, in his *Dernières Paroles* (1835); see Sainte-Beuve, *Portraits contemporains*, vol.2, pp.58ff.

44. *La Muse française* (July 1823) (vol.1, p.4 of the Marsan edn.: "Foreword," which reprints the prospectus).

45. Emile Deschamps, *La Guerre en temps de paix*, in *La Muse française* (May 1824) (pp.263–79 of vol.2 of the Marsan edition.).

46. Vigny, *Discours de réception* to the Académie Française (26 January 1846), Pléiade edn. of the *Oeuvres*, vol.1, p.968.

47. Brizeux, review of *Eloa*, in the *Mercure de France au dix-neuvième siècle*, vol.25 (1829), p.308.

48. Dorison, *Alfred de Vigny et la poésie politique* (Paris, 1894), p.viii. Virgil's hemistich, Eclogue IV, "Jam redit et Virgo" and the following verse, "Jam nova progenies caelo demittitur alto," were indeed the motto inscribed at the beginning of *La Muse française*.

49. Sainte-Beuve, review of Hugo's *Odes* in *Le Globe* of 2 January 1827 (*Portraits littéraires*: vol.1, pp.164ff.).

50. Sainte-Beuve, *Du mouvement littéraire et politique après la révolution de 1830*, in *Le Globe* of 11 October 1830 (article reprinted in the *Premiers lundis*, vol.1, pp.394ff.).

51. H. Girard, *Emile Deschamps, 1791–1871* (Paris, 1921), p.63.

52. Hugo and Vigny will be discussed later.

53. See: against the eighteenth century, Soumet's poem on *L'Incrédulité* (Paris, 1810); on Mme de Staël, his short work on *Les Scruples littéraires de Mme la baronne de Staël* (Paris, 1814); on Saint-Martin, one of his articles in *La Muse française* (November 1823) (ed. Marsan, vol.1, pp.240–41); on Joseph de Maistre, his review of *Les Soirées de Saint-Pétersbourg*, ibid. (October 1823) (ed. Marsan, vol.1, pp.189ff.); on his other admirations, the texts we cite, passim.

54. Sainte-Beuve, *Portraits littéraires*, vol.3, p.418, note (1846 article on the Academic *réception* of Vitet, who succeeded Soumet, who died in 1845).

55. Soumet, review of Portalis's book on the eighteenth century in the *Conservateur littéraire* (December 1820), vol.3, p.217.

56. Durangel, *Le Détachement de la terre*, in *Annales romantiques*, year 1831, p.209. This Durangel, who was a contributor to *La Muse*, has confused criticism and the compilers of the catalogue of the Bibliothèque Nationale with his multiple alliterative pseudonyms (Durand, Holmondurand, de Modurange, etc.). See L. Séché, *Le Cénacle de la Muse française* (Paris, 1908), pp.159–61.

57. Soumet, review of *La Jérusalem délivrée traduite en vers français* by Baour-Lormian in *La Muse française* (December 1823) (ed. Marsan, vol.1, p.296).

58. Soumet, review of Hugo's *Nouvelle Odes*, ibid. (March 1824) (ed. Marsan, vol.2, p.146).

59. He signs G. Desjardins in *La Muse*, and we have up to 1858 various socio-political or aesthetic writings under this name, as well as a drama of *Sémiramis-la-Grande* (1832) dedicated to Jules Lefèvre (who also contributed to *La Muse*), to Buchez, and to the English biblical painter John Martin. Without wishing to enter into this discussion, where so many have blundered, it seems completely certain that the author of these works with mystico-humanitarian tendencies is indeed the same person as the Desjardins of *La Muse*, whose tone is already approximately the same. A letter from Desjardins to Soumet of November 22, 1843, reprinted by Anna Beffort, *Alexandre Soumet, sa vie et ses oeuvres* (Luxembourg, 1908), p.95, containing comments on Soumet's recent *Divine Epopée* that are utterly analogous to those by Desjardins in *La Muse* on the *Saül* by this same Soumet, should eliminate any remaining doubts. We know almost nothing of the biography or the person of Desjardins, except what Jules Lefèvre tells us while reviewing *Sémiramis* in the *Revue républicaine* of September 1834 (vol.2, p.407); namely, that he had been "an officer of Napoleon's," which obliges us to place the year of his birth around 1785 at the latest.

60. Desjardins, review of Soumet's *Saül*, *La Muse française* (September 1823) (ed. Marsan, vol.1, p.138).

61. Ibid., pp.130–32.

62. Soumet, *L'Incrédulité* (Paris, 1810) (2nd edn., pp.167ff.).

63. Soumet, *Les Scrupules*, p.11. Soumet goes further than Chateaubriand, who

wanted religion to be only a secondary element in a poem (*Génie du christianisme*, part II, book I, ch.2).

64. See A. Beffort, op.cit., pp.8, 19.

65. Desjardins, already cited review of Soumet's *Saül*, p.132.

66. Desjardins, *Première Babylone, Sémiramis-la-Grande, traduit d'un manuscrit hiéroglyphique égyptien* (Paris, 1832).

67. Durangel himself, forty years after the period of *La Muse*, in 1863, published the beginning at least of a *Christodie*, which begins inevitably with an invocation of the "Harp of olden days." The prospectus announced eight songs; I have only found the first installment — the only one, it is thought, that ever appeared; the poem opens — in medias res, I suppose — with the resurrection of Lazarus.

68. Soumet, already cited review of the *Nouvelles Odes*, pp.143, 145, 151.

69. Alex. Guiraud, *Le Poète*, in *Poèmes et chants élégiaques* (3rd edn. [Paris, 1825], pp.129ff.) (1st edn., 1824).

70. Guiraud, *Nos Doctrines*, in *La Muse française* of January 1824 (ed. Marsan, vol.2, pp.7–8). This article answered Lacretelle's diatribe to the Bonnes Lettres in December 1823.

71. Ibid., pp.20–21.

72. See, for example, on the gravity of letters as a consequence of the Revolution, the article by Jules de Rességuier in *La Muse* of February 1824 (vol.2, p.86), where it is in fact Guiraud's *Poèmes* that he is reviewing.

73. Nestor de Lamarque, *La Gloire, ode, suivie de deux élégies* (Paris, 1825), p.23.

74. Guiraud, *Nos Doctrines*, pp.25–26.

75. See on Saint-Valry, in particular, G. Charlier, *Une Amitié romantique: Saint-Valry et V. Hugo* (Brussels, 1927) (excerpts from *Le Flambeau* of 1 February 1927). Various allusions in his *Napoléones* (Paris, 1867) make it impossible to place his date of birth before 1795. Son of a soldier of the Empire, Adolphe Souillard de Saint-Valry, a royalist during the Restoration and a Legitimist under Louis-Philippe, supported Napoleon III's Empire (whence his collection of *Napoléones*). Séché (*Le Cénacle*, p.137) is thus mistaken in having him die a royalist, and Charlier is wrong to give 1862 as the date of his death (op.cit., p.20): the dedication of his *Napoléones* attests that he was still alive on 14 July 1866.

76. Saint-Valry, review of the *Tablettes romantiques* in the *Annales de la littérature et des arts*, vol.10 (1823), p.4.

77. Saint-Valry, review of Lefèvre's *Le Parricide*, ibid., vol 10, p.257.

78. Saint-Valry, review of Hugo's *Odes et poésies diverses*, ibid., vol.8 (1822), pp.66–67.

79. Saint-Valry, in *La Foudre*, vol.10 (1823), p.201.

80. Saint-Valry, "Esquisses morales," in *La Muse française* (June 1824) (ed. Marsan, vol.2, pp.346, 333).

81. See Charlier, op.cit.

82. See Ch. Villers, Letter to M. Millin, in the *Magazin encyclopédique*, vol.5

(1810), pp.5–24; the well-known pages by Mme de Staël in *De l'Allemagne*; Sismondi, *De la littérature du midi de l'Europe*, 4 vols. (Paris, 1813), passim; Philippe Albert Stapfer, preface to the translation of the *Histoire de la littérature espagnole* by Bouterwek (Paris, 1812), vol.1, pp.48ff.

83. Prosper de Barante, *Tableau de la littérature française du dix-huitième siècle* (Paris, 1809), pp.37ff. Barante, born in 1784, was, as is well known, a friend of Mme de Staël's and had frequented Coppet and those who went there. He applies the question to France because he is writing for an essay competition held by the Institut and he must keep to the proposed subject.

84. *Tablettes universelles* (18 October 1823), p.80.

85. Dubois, review of Guiraud's *Chants hellènes*, in the *Globe* of 12 October 1824.

86. A. Pictet, in the *Bibliothèque universelle des sciences, belles-lettres et arts* of Geneva (November 1826), p.219.

87. L. Boerne, *Lettres écrites de Paris pendant les années 1830 et 1831*, trans. F. Guiran (Paris, 1832), pp.51–52 (letter of 30 October 1830).

88. For example, *Le Nain jaune* of 1814–15 or *L'Homme gris* of 1817–18, continued respectively by *Le Nain jaune réfugié* (Brussels) in 1816 and *Le Nouvel Homme gris*, 1818–19; *Le Miroir*, 1821–23, and *La Pandore*, which succeeded it up to 1828 and reappeared again in 1829–30; *Le Corsaire*, which appeared without interruption beginning in 1823, and the *Don Quichotte* of 1830.

89. It changes its name in April 1822 to *L'Abeille*.

90. Beginning in October 1827 its title was *Mercure de France au dix-neuvième siècle*.

91. *Mercure du dix-neuvième siècle*, vol.4, p.378.

92. On this subject see Stendhal, *Courrier anglais*, vol.3, p.36, in the edition of the *Oeuvres* published by Le Divan; and *Le Globe* of 14 March 1826 (anonymous note on the recent history of the *Mercure*).

93. See especially *Archives*, vol.1, pp.17ff.

94. The *Tablettes universelles*, which had existed since 1820, became Doctrinaire (or Eclectic) in spirit only in 1823, after being purchased by Coste in January and before Villèle gained control of this publication at the beginning of the following year. To this group of publications we can add *Le Lycée français* of 1819–20 (which was principally Decazist), more hesitant with regard to romanticism; Charles Loyson, a former Normalien and a friend of Cousin's, was a notable contributor.

95. Stendhal, *Souvenirs d'égotisme*, cited edn., p.1514.

96. *Lettres normandes* (February 1820) (vol.10, p.55, in the "Literary Mosaic," very probably by Léon Thiessé). See similarly Jouy, *L'Hermite de la Guyane*, vol.3 (Paris, 1817), p.229.

97. Viennet, *Épître aux Muses sur les Romantiques*, in the *Mercure du dix-neuvième siècle*, vol.5, p.1 (14 April 1824).

98. Thiers, *Des littératures classique et romantique*, 3rd article (25 September 1822), in *L'Album*, vol.6, pp.104–5.

99. Thiers, ibid., p.106.

100. Baron Massias, *Traité du beau et du sublime* (Paris, 1824), p.240. This baron of the Empire, an Oratorian under Louis XVI, a colonel in the Revolution and diplomat under Napoleon, lived till 1848.

101. See, among others, Evariste Dumoulin, in the *Mercure du dix-neuvième siècle*, vol.2 (1823), p.45; and, in the same periodical, the articles by Sylvain Dumon (vol.5 [1824], p.10; etc.), and by Latouche (vol.9 [1825], p.536).

102. Th. Gautier, *Les Jeunes-France*, ed. Charpentier (1878), "Daniel Jovard," pp.116–17; and ibid., "Celle-ci et celle-là," p.248: "Come, come, I know them well, all the subversive principles of your regressive innovators, to use M. de Jouy's fine phrase"; but later the parties speaking cannot decide whether the expression comes from Jouy, or Etienne, or Arnault, or Baour-Lormian.

103. Anonymous article in the *Gazette littéraire* of 2 September 1830 (vol.1, pp.622–23); this review had been founded by the bookseller Sautelet, a friend and publisher of Mérimée and Stendhal.

104. *Gazette littéraire* of 24 February 1831 (vol.2, p.305): another anonymous article.

105. See *Oeuvres*, ed. Martineau (Le Divan), *Théâtre*, vol.2, pp.57ff., especially 91; vol.3, introduction and pp.18–19, 27–28, 33); *Pensées*, vol.1, p.207; vol.2, p.167; *Correspondance*, vol.1, p.252.

106. *Oeuvres*, same edn., *Courrier anglais*, vol.2, p.354; vol.4, pp.156–333; vol.5, p.61.

107. Ibid., vol.2, p.162; vol.4, p.334 (1825 articles).

108. Ibid., pp.230ff., 299.

109. Ibid., vol.1, pp.71, 133, 163–64; vol.2, p.421; vol.5, pp.41ff., 65–66, 101ff.

110. Ibid., vol.2, pp.358–60; vol.3, pp.38–39.

111. *Racine et Shakespeare*, ed. Martino (Paris, 1925), vol.1, pp.72–73, 106ff.

112. *Le Globe*, 22 February 1825 (anonymous article).

113. See for example the advertisement for Cyprien Desmarais's *Essai* on 16 April 1825; the review of Duvergier de Hauranne on 11 June; and a more virulent criticism of the same work in an "Editor's Note" on 6 December of the same year.

114. Article on Walter Scott in *Le Globe* of 4 November 1826.

115. This is the expression Stendhal uses (*Courrier anglais*, vol.4, p.386: article dated 18 February 1825).

116. "Profession of Faith" dated 14 September 1824.

117. See in particular in *Le Globe* of 29 January 1825 an anonymous review of Viennet's *Epîtres et dialogues*; also *Le Globe* of 15 October 1825.

118. Article signed E. (very probably Etienne) in *L'Abeille*, vol.3 (1821), p.493. Same ideas in a review of Stendhal's *Racine et Shakespeare*, signed F., in the *Revue encyclopédique*, vol.17 (March 1823), p.623, and in Jay, *La Conversion d'un romantique* (Paris, 1830), pp.236ff., especially pp.255–62.

119. *De la littérature*, ch.5 (especially, in the Van Tieghem edition., pp.346, 352, 357).

120. Ibid., p.350.

121. This is Hobbes's definition, to which Stendhal recurs constantly: thus *Pensées*, vol.1, pp.93 and 417 (1803), etc.; *Correspondance*, same edition, vol.1, pp.121–22 (1803), 204 (1804): also ch.2 of the *Racine et Shakespeare* of 1823, etc.

122. See for example Stendhal's letter to his sister, *Correspondance* (ed. Divan), vol.1, p.206; *Pensées*, vol.1, pp.271–72: these texts are from summer 1804; similarly, *Racine et Shakespeare*, ch.2 (1823) and notes to the Martino edition, vol.2, pp.164–72, 193–207.

123. See *Journal* (vol. *Ecrits intimes* of the Pléiade edition, p.514, text of July 1804, and passim); also an 1823–25 text, reprinted in vol.2, pp.175–78 of the Martino edition of *Racine et Shakespeare*.

124. *Pensées*, vol.2, p.9 (August 1804).

125. Ibid., vol.2, p.41 (6 December 1804); same ideas in 1822 (*Courrier anglais*, vol.1, p.331), in 1823 in *Racine et Shakespeare* (vol.1, p.38 of the Martino edn.), and in a text of the same period (ibid., vol.2, p.172).

126. *Pensées*, vol.2, p.9.

127. See Del Litto, *La Vie intellectuelle de Stendhal (1802–1821)* (Paris, 1959), pp.96ff.

128. *Pensées*, vol.2, p.217 (23 July 1804).

129. *Histoire de la peinture en Italie*, ed. Martineau (Paris, 1929), vol.1, pp.63–64.

130. 1818 text, published in the Martino edition of *Racine et Shakespeare*, vol.2, pp.26 and 32.

131. *Courrier anglais*, vol.1, pp.74–75, letter of 3 January 1823.

132. See *Courrier anglais*, vol.1, p.111 (30 April 1824), p.159 (21 April 1825), etc.

133. Dubois, review already cited of Guiraud, *Chants hellènes*, in *Le Globe* of 12 October 1824 (the article is unsigned, but was collected in the *Fragments littéraires de Dubois* by Vacherot, 2 vols. [Paris, 1879]).

134. See Jules Lefèvre-Deumier, "On Poetic Literature in France since 1814" (undated article, which can be placed with confidence in the 1820s, published in his posthumous *Critique littéraire* [Paris, 1896], pp.40–43).

135. As is well known, these were two successive pamphlets published under the same title.

136. *Racine et Shakespeare*, ed. Martino, vol.1, p.39.

137. See his *Histoire de la peinture en Italie* (1817), books IV–V–VI, passim (passages considered original, not borrowed from other sources); also his *Vie de Haydn* (1814), ed. Le Divan, pp.210ff.

138. See in the Martino edition of *Racine et Shakespeare*, vol.2, the letter that Lamartine wrote on 19 March 1823 to M. de Mareste, their common friend (pp.265–67), and the plan of a response by Stendhal (pp.229–63).

139. *Racine et Shakespeare*, ed. Martino, vol.1, pp.46ff., 80, 95, 99.

140. Stendhal does mention a modern subject, the Return from the Isle of Elba, but to be treated in 1864 (ibid., p.151).

141. Paul-Louis Courier, *Prospectus d'une traduction nouvelle d'Hérodote* (Paris, 1822), p.xviii.

142. *Oeuvres complètes de Shakespeare, traduites de l'anglais par Letourneur*, new edition revised by Guizot and Amédée Pichot, vol.1 (Paris, 1821), p.clii. This introduction is a "Life of Shakespeare."

143. *Tablettes universelles*, vol.10 (March 1823), p.343. The same review had published in January (p.116 of the same volume) analogous reflections by Sylvain Dumon.

144. Duvergier de Hauranne, *Remarques sur les bonnes et les mauvaises innovations dramatiques*, in *Le Globe* of 28 May 1825; review of Desmarais's *Essai*, ibid. (11 June 1825); see also his articles on the theater on 18 March 1826 and 6 and 10 May of the same year; he signs all these articles O., according to his custom.

145. Duvergier de Hauranne, *Du romantique*, in *Le Globe* of 24 March 1825.

146. Vitet, *De l'indépendance en matière de goût*, in *Le Globe* of 2 April 1825; and see the remarkable article (anonymous) of 29 October 1825 entitled *Situation du romantisme au 1er 1825*.

147. See, among others, an anonymous article in the extremely classicist *Lettres normandes* in 1820 (vol.10, pp.104–6); Tissot, in the *Mercure du dix-neuvième siècle*, vol.12 (1826), pp.335ff., goes over to the reform party; Thiessé alone (*Revue encyclopédique*, vol.31 (August 1826), pp.388–89, and p.657 (September 1826) holds absolutely firm for subjects from antiquity, which according to him have become national by being adopted by French taste. Avenel, who signs A. in *Le Lycée français*, speaks only about subjects (vol.3 [1820], p.340), but his reviews in the *Revue encyclopédique* (around 1824 and following years), usually signed M. A., go further; and see also in the *Mercure du dix-neuvième siècle* (vol.9 [1825], p.494), a thoroughly radical article, signed A., but I know of no indication that Avenel (Martial Avenel, 1783–1875, critic, historian, and librarian) collaborated on the *Mercure*.

148. Edme Héreau, in the *Revue encyclopédique*, vol.29 (March 1826), p.731.

149. Ph. Chasles, *Revue encyclopédique*, vol.1 (March 1820), p.522 (cited by Cl. Pichois, *Philarète Chasles et la vie littéraire au temps du romantisme* [Paris, 1965], vol.1, p.109).

150. Félix Bodin, *Considérations sur la littérature romantique appliquée à l'histoire, aux Antiquités et aux moeurs nationales*, in the *Revue encyclopédique*, vol.17 (February 1823), p.240. Bodin, born in 1795, who also published in 1823 a *Histoire de la Révolution française*, was Thiers's friend.

151. On these dramas see Ch. de Rémusat's *Mémoires de ma vie*, ed. Pouthas, vol.2, p.148, and Delécluze's journal, cited by Trahard in his edition of Mérimée's *Théâtre de Clara Gazul* (Paris, 1927), p.xi.

152. Trahard, ibid., p.viii.

153. Ibid., p.xxxix.

154. Gain-Montagnac recounts in his *Journal d'un Français depuis le 9 mars jusqu'au 13 avril 1814* the active role he played in the Restoration of the Bourbons.

155. Comte J.-R. de Gain-Montagnac, governor of the royal château at Pau, *Théâtre* (Paris, 1820) (posthumous publication: the author lived from 1778 to 1819).

156. Published in 1952 by J.-F. Marshall (Urbana: University of Illinois Press).

157. M. de Fongeray (pseudonym of Dittmer and Cavé), *Les Soirées de Neuilly, esquisses dramatiques et historiques* (Paris, 1827) (in the same year, there were three editions of the work; I have seen the third, in two volumes; the introduction explains that the pieces were composed by a group of friends at "the château de Neuilly, in the department of the Ardèche" (?): whence the title.

158. Tissot, in *Mercure du dix-neuvième siècle*, vol.1 (April 1823), p.113.

159. Berville, in the *Revue encyclopédique*, vol.30 (May 1826), p.385.

160. Léon Thiessé, in the *Revue encyclopédique*, vol.16 (1822), p.305.

161. Villenave, in the *Revue encyclopédique*, vol.38 (1828), p.94.

162. Andrieux, *Discours en vers sur la perfectibilité de l'homme*, read to the Académie Française on 7 July 1825, in *Almanach des Muses*, vol.62 (1826), p.266.

163. Sainte-Beuve, article on Béranger (*National*, 4 March 1833), collected in the *Portraits contemporains*, vol.1, p.120.

164. Béranger, "1821 Postscript" to his 1815 preface, reprinted in the Perrotin edition of the *Oeuvres complètes* (1847), vol.2, pp.348–49.

165. *Pensées*, vol.1, p.21, in a notebook dated December 1802.

166. *Correspondance*, vol.6, p.123.

167. See *Racine et Shakespeare*, ed. Martino, pp.18–19, 146.

168. Anonymous article apropos of *Eloa*, entitled "Incompatibilité de la religion chrétienne avec la poésie," in the *Revue trimestrielle*, vol.1 (April 1828), pp.431ff.; this periodical was directed by the liberal historian Buchon.

169. Ch. Loyson, in *Le Lycée français*, vol.1 (summer 1819), p.297.

170. Mérimée, review of a collection of popular Romanian songs in the *Moniteur universel* of 17 January 1856 (cited by Jovanovitch, *La "Guzla" de Prosper Mérimée* [Paris, 1911], pp.205–6). *La Guzla*, "selection of Illyrian poems collected in Dalmatia, Bosnia, Croatia, and Herzogovina" (in reality, poems fabricated by Mérimée himself, with rare exceptions), appeared in 1827.

171. See Sainte-Beuve, 1845 article, collected in the *Portraits contemporains*, vol.4, p.221.

172. See on him the works of Carlo Cordié (*Romanticismo e classicismo nell'opera di Victor Chauvet* [Messina-Florence, 1958]; and a collection of Chauvet's texts published under the title *Manzoni-Stendhal-Hugo e altri saggi* (Università di Catania, 1958).

173. Chauvet, review of Hugo's *Odes et ballades* and *Les Orientales* in the *Revue encyclopédique*, vol.42 (April 1829), pp.128, 133.

174. I have not been able to identify him; he signs with a θ. Could it be Chauvet himself under another signature?

175. Review of Chateaubriand's *Oeuvres complètes* (third article, on the *Génie* especially), in the *Revue encyclopédique*, vol.39 (July 1828), p.117.

176. *Des causes du romantisme ou de l'influence de la civilisation sur la poésie et les arts*, in the *Revue encyclopédique*, vol.45 (January 1830), pp.27, 28, 32, 33.

177. "Turgidity" is for Stendhal the true name for spiritualism. For his pronouncements on Mme de Staël, see the texts collected by Martineau in his edition of the *Oeuvres*, vol.3 of the *Mélanges de littérature*, pp.169ff.

178. On Cousin, I cite the *Courrier anglais*, vol.2, p.29 (1813) and vol.3, pp.62–63 (1826); there is a mass of other texts, especially in this same *Courrier anglais*, up to 1828 at least. On the *Le Globe, Courrier anglais*, vol.3, pp.41 and 213 (1826).

179. Ibid., vol.2, p.224; also, p.192, etc.

180. Ibid., vol.4, pp.336–37 (1825).

181. Ibid., vol.4, p.13 (1824), in a long article on Constant.

182. *Armance*, ed. Martineau, pp.45, 66–67, 73–74. The novel is from 1827.

183. See, for example, in the *Revue encyclopédique*, vol.16 (December 1822), a review, signed A., of the *Oeuvres* of Mme de Staël.

184. See the Doctrinaire periodical *Revue française* (March 1829), pp.291ff.: polemic with Marrast, who wanted the Left to return to Laromiguière and sensationalism.

185. See on this subject Ephraïm Harpaz, *L'Ecole libérale sous la Restauration* (Geneva, 1968), pp.53ff., 333.

186. Ch. Loyson, in *Le Lycée français*, vol.3 (1820), pp.310, 317–18; see also, by the same writer, ibid, vol.4, pp.51ff., on Lamartine's *Méditations*, vol.4, pp.241–45, a spiritualist ode on poetic enthusiasm.

187. *Le Globe* (10 September 1825), review of the *Elégies rémoises* by Cyprien Anot.

188. Ibid. (4 February 1826), review of Parseval-Grandmaison's *Philippe-Auguste*.

189. Ibid. (1 October 1825), *Du romantisme considéré historiquement*. The author, who signs M. D., is difficult to identify, and a complete discussion of the question would occupy more space than it merits. The Desprès of whom some speak seems to be a myth. The most probable answer is that this is by a certain Desloges, of the Ecole Polytechnique, who was a Saint-Simonian. Eight articles in *Le Globe* between 1824 and 1826 are signed M. D.; one of them is mentioned on p.ciii of the note on *Le Globe* in the Vacherot edition of Dubois's articles, already cited, as having as author "perhaps M. Desloges." Sainte-Beuve names this Desloges in a letter to Hugo on December 8, 1832 (*Correspondance*, ed. Bonnerot, vol.1, p.326) and in *Ma Biographie* (posthumous fragment, published at the beginning of vol.13 of the *Nouveaux lundis*). Delécluze (*Souvenirs de soixante années* [Paris, 1862], p.464, note) places Desloges on a list of Saint-Simonians. Moreover, this name often appears in the unpublished papers of Saint-Simonianism (see D'Allemagne, *Les Saint-Simoniens*

[Paris, 1930], and Charléty, *Histoire du saint-simonisme* [Paris, 1931], passim), but it would seem that this is someone else.

190. Rémusat, review of Hugo's *Cromwell*, in *Le Globe* of 26 January 1828.

191. J.-J. Ampère, review of Pierre Lebrun's *Voyage en Grèce*, in *Le Globe* of 26 March 1828.

192. J.-J. Ampère, *De l'histoire de la poésie*, speech given to the Athénée of Marseille for the opening of the course in literature (12 March 1830), in *Mélanges d'histoire littéraire et de littérature*, 2 vols. (Paris, 1867), vol.1, pp.32, 49–50.

193. See, for example, H. Patin, review of Lamartine's *Harmonies* in the *Revue encyclopédique*, vol.47 (July 1830), p.128; and another, anonymous review of the same volume in the *Gazette littéraire* of 17 June 1830 (vol.1, p.477).

194. N. Artaud, *Essai littéraire sur le génie poétique au dix-neuvième siècle, lu le 2 décembre 1824 à l'Athénée* (Paris, 1825), pp. 9, 13, 18–19. See also, in his *Etudes sur la littérature* (collected and published after his death by his son Paris, 1863), the study entitled *Origine et développement des littératures modernes*, a reworking of two articles from the *Mercure du dix-neuvième siècle* (vol. 12 [1826], pp.415ff., 479ff.). Artaud (1794–1861) was *inspecteur général de l'enseignement* and argued against the *loi Falloux*.

195. *Mercure du dix-neuvième siècle*, vol.13 (1826), pp.110ff.

196. J. Castelnau, *Essai sur la littérature romantique* (Paris, 1825) (a foreword indicates that the work was composed in 1820 for the Jeux Floraux competition). On Castelnau, see Pierre Jourda, "Junius Castelnau," in the *Revue d'histoire littéraire de la France* (1932), pp.355ff.

197. The classics are, to my knowledge, Pierius Valerianus, *De litteratorum infelicitate libri II* (Venice, 1620; posthumous, the author had died in 1558), and the *Appendix* that Cornelius Tollius added to it in the Amsterdam edition (1647) (the theme of the work is "fortunae erga literatos odium," and nothing more; that is, the animosity toward writers of fate, illnesses, bad luck, and premature death); Josephus Barberius, *De miseria poetarum graecorum, liber* (Naples, 1686) (also a catalogue of mishaps). These works were published together in Leipzig in 1707; the first is cited in 1766 by Sébastien Mercier in his *Bonheur des gens de lettres*; in 1821 it was again republished in Geneva. The custom of drawing up lists of men of letters who endured martyrdom was still alive at the beginning of the nineteenth century: thus a "List of Authors Who Died of Hunger" figures in the *Art de dîner en ville* by Colnet (3rd edn. [1813], pp.105ff; see *Revue d'histoire littéraire de la France* [1936], pp.102ff.); Bins de Saint-Victor had published in 1802 *Les Grands Poètes malheureux*, which I have been unable to examine. On the other hand the theme of the mud-bespattered poet, either a parasite or ending his days in the poorhouse, is frequent in the satiric poetry of the sixteenth and seventeenth centuries (thus Boileau, Satire 1); also that of the misdeeds of envy, which is handled more gravely (Boileau, Epître VII).

198. Letter from Michel Pichat to his father (1805), cited by Camille Latreille in the *Revue d'histoire littéraire de la France* (1901), p.410.

199. See La Servière, "Des gens de lettres," in the *Mercure de France* (December 1816), pp.343–48; F. Ségu, *H. de Latouche* (Paris, 1931), p.238 and n.4.

200. Frédéric Soulié, *Les Amours françaises, poèmes suivis de trois chants élégiaques* (Paris, 1824).

201. Mme de Staël, *Corinne*, cited edn., p.304.

202. Chateaubriand, *Mémoires d'outre-tombe*, part IV, book VIII, ch.3 (centenary edn., vol.4, p.426).

203. He himself eloquently developed the theme in *The Prophecy of Dante*, which dates from 1819 and figures in the Pichot-Salle translation of the *Oeuvres*, vol.10 (1821), pp.127ff.

204. The influence of Byron in France has been the object of a remarkable work by Edmond Estève (*Byron et le romantisme français* [Paris, 1907]: see especially pp.102ff., 164ff.; also pp.477–79 on the theme of the *poète maudit*; and the remarkable conclusion, in particular pp.516–17 and note).

205. Saint-Valry, review of *Le Parricide* (Byronic poem by Jules Lefèvre) in the *Annales de la littérature et des arts*, vol.10 (1823), p.264.

206. Cyprien Desmarais, *Le Temps présent* (Paris, 1826), pp.116–17.

207. Vigny, review of Byron's *Oeuvres*, in *Le Conservateur littéraire* of December 1820, vol.3, p.214.

208. See his *Correspondance*, ed. Martineau (Le Divan), vol.4, p.369 (letter of 28 September 1816). The *Revue encyclopédique*, a liberal review not much inclined toward romanticism in general, is consistently favorable to Byron; also the *Mercure du dix-neuvième siècle*, even before its romantic turn.

209. What we say of the universal influence of Byron in France is also true of the influence of Shakespeare and Walter Scott, though these are less important from the point of view that interests us. In what concerns the ideas of a dramatic revolution or of a recourse to national sources in the theater or the novel, the potential for the unity of romanticism is visible from the beginning.

210. See the preliminary matter to this novel in volume 1 of the edition of the *Oeuvres complètes* (Paris, 1832); *Jean Sbogar* appeared for the first time in 1818.

211. "Sociétés populaires," *Revue de Paris* (1829), collected in *Souvenirs, épisodes et portraits pour servir à l'histoire de la Révolution et de l'Empire*, vol.1, p.86.

212. See especially the articles collected in his *Mémoires de littérature et de critique* (Paris, 1820); also *Thérèse Aubert* and *Adèle*, novels of 1819 and 1820.

213. Nodier, review of Ballanche's *Antigone*, *Journal des débats* of 4 April 1815, reprinted in the 1820 *Mélanges*, vol.1, pp.270–71.

214. Nodier, review of Legrand d'Aussy, *Histoire de la vie privée des Français*, in the *Journal des débats* of 23 November 1816; similar ideas in his review of Ballanche, *Essai sur les institutions sociales*, ibid. (16 December 1818).

215. Nodier, review of Chênedollé, *Etudes Poétiques*, in *Le Défenseur*, vol.3 (1820), pp.606–7.

216. Ibid., pp.608–9.

217. Nodier, *Adèle*, in *Oeuvres complètes*, vol.2 (Paris, 1832), p.161.

218. Thus the text entitled "Méditations" in *Le Conservateur*, vol.4 (1819), p.600, or "Apocalypse du solitaire," which appeared in *Le Défenseur*, vol.4 (1821), pp.145ff., and in *La Quotidienne* of 29 January 1821 (reprinted in the *Souvenirs de la Révolution et de l'Empire* [Paris: Charpentier, 1850], vol.2, p.365ff.).

219. For example, when he argues for the romantic by distinguishing it from the frenetic, to which so many of his own pieces so obviously belong: see this distinction in Nodier's article on Spiess's *Petit Pierre* (*Annales de la littérature et des arts*, vol.2 [1821], pp.77ff., reprinted under the title "Du Génie romantique" in the *Tablettes romantiques* [Paris, 1823], pp.6ff.); same distinction in other texts of the same year.

220. See, on melodrama and its social mission, Nodier's article in the *Journal des débats* (8 November 1818) (first article on Mme de Staël, *De l'Allemagne*); his review of Marchangy's *La Gaule Poétique* in the *Journal des débats* of 27 November 1817 (*Mélanges* of 1820, vol.2, pp.317ff.). In 1835, Nodier is still arguing for melodrama, which came into existence to "take the place of instructions from the vacant pulpit" ("Du mouvement intellectuel sous le Directoire et le Consulat," in the *Revue de Paris* of 5 July 1835); see also, in 1841, his introduction to Pixérécourt's *Théâtre choisi*, pp.vi–viii.

221. Nodier, *Journal des débats* (16 November 1818) (2nd article on Mme de Staël, reprinted in the *Mélanges* of 1820, vol.2, p.344–45).

222. Already cited article on *Le Petit Pierre*.

223. Articles on Walter Scott in *La Quotidienne* of December 1821 (H. M. King, op.cit., p.96).

224. Ibid., p.98.

225. Foreword to *Bertram* (French version of Maturin's work [Paris, 1821], p.vi). Similar ideas in *La Quotidienne* of 12 March 1823, review of *Han d'Islande*, cited by H. M. King, op.cit., p.101; it is still more remarkable to find them in embryo as early as 1808, in the literature course that Nodier gave at that time in Dôle (see Eunice Morgan Schenck, *La Part de Nodier dans la formation des idées romantiques de Victor Hugo* [Paris, 1914], p.8).

226. Preliminary matter by Nodier at the beginning of Lord Byron's *Oeuvres complètes*, vol. 1 (1822), pp.1–16.

227. See his articles in *La Quotidienne* between March 1823 and March 1824, and in *L'Oriflamme* in January–March 1824 (notably "Impromptu classique" [2 February 1824]); in *La Muse française* of April 1824, the aggressive article entitled "De quelques logomachies classiques" (ed. Marsan, vol.2, pp.193ff.); also (ibid., p.239), the ironic "Adieux aux romantiques."

228. Articles in the *Revue de Paris* (September 1829), p.241 ("Du style topographique"); (October 1829), p.141 ("Quelques observations pour servir à l'histoire de la nouvelle école littéraire"); (June 1830), p.226 ("De la prose française et de Diderot"). The October article can also be read, in the form of a note, at the

beginning of the republication of Ramond de Charbonnières's *Dernières aventures du jeune d'Olban* (Paris, 1829). See also the preliminary matter by Nodier to an edition of *La Philomèle*, a Latin poem (Paris, 1829); and in the *Album littéraire*, a collection that appeared in 1831, pp.224ff., the text entitled "Du style et surtout de celui des chroniques."

229. Nodier, review of Alcide de Beauchesne's *Souvenirs Poétiques*, *Journal des débats* (30 June 1830) (cited in the 2nd edition [1830], p.x of these *Souvenirs*).

230. V. Hugo, *Odes*, III, 7 (1827).

231. In the foreword to *La Mort de Socrate*; Casimir Delavigne, in an "Epître à Lamartine" (1824), comments rather sympathetically on Lamartine's poem (*Oeuvres complètes* [1833], vol.1, pp.291ff.).

232. See, for example, *Mercure de France au dix-neuvième siècle*, vol.25 (1829), p.500, anonymous article, "De la composition originale."

233. Ibid., vol.26 (1829), p.118, article signed T. B. on Chateaubriand.

234. Sainte-Beuve, article on Jouffroy in 1833, *Portraits contemporains*, vol.1, p.318.

235. It called itself *Mercure de France au dix-neuvième siècle* after October 1827.

236. Sainte-Beuve, letter of 14 May 1862 to Guttinguer (*Correspondance*, ed. Bonnerot, vol.12, p.35).

237. Vigny, *Journal d'un poète*, in the edition of his works in the Bibliothèque de la Pléiade, vol.1, p.1233 (1845).

238. Evariste Boulay-Paty, "Le Charme," in *Odes* (Paris, 1844), p.17; this poem dates from 1827 (see Ségu, *L'Académie*, vol.2, p.269).

239. Victor Pavie, "A Victor Hugo," in *Oeuvres choisies*, ed. René Bazin, 2 vols. (Paris, 1887), vol.2, p.360. The poem, which is not dated, is most certainly from the time of the *cénacle*.

240. Victor Pavie, letter of 18 December 1826 to Hugo (*Correspondance*, edn. Imprimerie Nationale, vol.1, p.437, note 1); see also Alexandre Dumas, "A mon ami Sainte-Beuve," in the *Mercure de France au dix-neuvième siècle*, vol.25 (1829), p.53.

241. Lamartine, *discours de réception* at the Academy (1 April 1830), published in the *Revue de Paris* (April 1830), pp.118ff.

242. Sainte-Beuve, 1833 article on Musset, *Portraits contemporains*, vol.2, p.180.

243. Sainte-Beuve, 1855 article on Banville, *Causeries du lundi*, vol.14, p.76.

244. The 1825–30 movement is characterized, as is well known, by the presence of artists (Louis Boulanger, the Devérias, the Johannots, David d'Angers, Delacroix) alongside the poets.

245. Stendhal, *D'un nouveau complot contre les industriels* (1825), in Martineau's edition of the *Oeuvres* (Le Divan), vol.2 of *Mélanges de littérature*, pp.221ff., 227, 238–39.

246. On his scorn of the bourgeois, in 1831 as in 1811, see the *Vie de H. Brulard* (Pléiade edn. of his works, volume of the *Roman et nouvelles*, p.52: "I have always

and as if by instinct . . . deeply scorned the bourgeoisie"). The texts on the prosaic, tedious character of democratic morals are innumerable.

247. Fifteen years before the *Chroniques italiennes*, Mérimée had likewise had recourse, in his *Théâtre de Clara Gazul* (the two works resemble each other only in this, obviously), to the violence of the Spanish way of life.

248. On the superior charm of aristocrats, see an 1824 text (ed. Martineau, *Mélanges de politique et d'histoire*, pp.179–81); texts of this sort multiply after 1830: thus *Mémoires d'un touriste*, same edition of his works, vol.2, pp.182–84.

8. THE BEGINNINGS OF THE GREAT GENERATION

1. Emile Deschamps, preface to *Etudes françaises et étrangères* (1828), ed. Henri Girard (Paris, 1923), pp.12–13.

2. Ibid., p.13. The word *poème* designates at this time the narrative poem in particular; thus, among others, in Mme de Staël, *De l'Allemagne*, part III, ch.12, "On German Poems."

3. Published in vol.7, pp.230ff., of the *Continuation des mémoires de littérature et d'histoire* by Desmolets et Goujet.

4. Emile Deschamps, review of Creuzé de Lesser's *Romances du Cid*, in *La Muse française* of November 1823 (ed. Marsan, vol.1, p.243).

5. "Le Trappiste" appeared as a brochure in October 1822; "Moïse" appeared in 1826, in the collection *Poèmes antiques et modernes*; Vigny dates both from 1822 in the 1829 edition of the *Poèmes*.

6. *Poèmes antiques et modernes*, ed. Estève (Paris, 1914), p.5. "Dramatic" is an allusion to the presence of dialogue in certain poems — "La Prison," for example.

7. *Journal*, Pléiade edn. of the *Oeuvres*, vol.2, p.891 ("20 May" [1829]).

8. Estève edn., already cited, pp.6–7.

9. "Cain," "a mystery," is from 1821 and was translated into French in 1822; "Heaven and Earth," another mystery, is from 1823, and its translation from 1824. "Eloa," which Vigny dates from 1823, appeared for the first time in 1824.

10. See the Baldensperger edition of the *Poèmes*, pp.314ff. The editor believes he can date this sketch from 1819, and calls it "a mystery," without saying whether Vigny himself at this date so designated his poem, which would give him priority over Byron.

11. Ibid., p.315.

12. Ibid., pp.328–29; "L'Ange tombée" dates from 1823, according to the editor.

13. Cited ibid., p.406 (article in the *Annales de la littérature et des arts*, vol.16 [1824], p.16, signed "A country dweller").

14. Gautier, obituary article on Vigny, in the *Moniteur* of 28 September 1863, reprinted in his *Histoire du romantisme* (Paris, 1874), p.163.

15. Vigny, *Journal*, cited edn., p.962 ("24 August" [1832]); see also p.983 [March 1833].

16. See in the Baldensperger edition of the *Poèmes* what remains of "Satan,"

pp.317ff., and on the link between "Satan" and "Eloa" pp.327–28. "Eloa" having appeared in 1824, Vigny continues to speak of "Satan" in his later correspondence: see his letter to Hugo on 5 October 1824, in the *Correspondance*, ed. Baldensperger, vol.1 (the only one published) (Paris, 1933), p.83, and the letter from Hugo on 25 April 1825 in vol.1, p.400 of the *Correspondance* in the Imprimerie Nationale edition of Hugo's work, where the poem is called "your formidable Hell."

17. *Journal*, p.875: same trio of works in the letter to Hugo of 5 October 1824, but there the title is "Satan."

18. Ibid., p.878; see also, p.876, a plan of a "Christian theogony," "an immense poem."

19. Vigny entitles it, however, "Le Bal, poème."

20. They will be found in the Pléiade edition of the *Oeuvres*, vol.1, pp.229ff.; the great majority of them were written after 1830.

21. "Une âme devant Dieu" can be read ibid., p.298. This piece, which is from 1826, is curiously reminiscent in its tone and even in its versification of the *Harmonies* that Lamartine was undertaking at the same moment, but which would only be published four years later.

22. *Journal*, p.902.

23. The projected "elevation" that figures under the year 1835 in the Ratisbonne edition of the *Journal d'un poète* (1867) and that Baldensperger reproduced as such (edn. of the *Poèmes*, p.360) should not be taken into account here: this dialogue of a suicide with God does not bear the name "elevation" in the *Journal* as Baldensperger ultimately knew and published it, and is from 1853 (Pléiade edn., vol.2, p.1310).

24. *Journal*, p.885.

25. In the particular case of farsighted Tom Thumb, the transposition amounts to a misconception; and indeed, Vigny did not write such a poem.

26. *Journal*, p.1104.

27. Vigny, "Lettres à une puritaine" (Camilla Maunoir), published by Ph. Godet in the *Revue de Paris* (1897), vol.4 and 5: letter of 21 December 1838, vol.4, p.676.

28. They were published respectively in 1832 and 1831, then collected in the 1837 edition of the *Poèmes antiques et modernes*.

29. See the letters to Sainte-Beuve of 29 December 1829 and 15 October 1835 (*Correspondance*, ed. Baldensperger, pp.212 and 404).

30. Browsing in the *Journal* is enough to convince one of this. Thus, at the beginning of 1836, p.1038, the "fable" inspired by a contemporary news item that is, curiously, an account that anticipates the story of Jean Valjean in *Les Misérables*; in 1839, p.1116, "L'Opium"; in 1840, p.1140, "La Poudre de diamant"; in 1841, p.1156, the fragment "Poème à faire"; in 1844, p.1217, "L'Hyène," "Le Canon," etc.

31. This is the hypothesis suggested by Georges Bonnefoy (*La Pensée religieuse et morale d'Alfred de Vigny* [Paris, 1944], pp.147–48).

32. *Journal*, pp.879–80.

33. Ibid., p.880.

34. *Journal*, p.888 [1828].

35. Ibid., pp.972–73 (1 December [1832]).

36. Ibid., p.1144 [1840]; see similarly p.1149 [1841].

37. Ibid., p.1342 [1859].

38. "Réflexions sur la vérité dans l'art" (preface to the 4th edn. of *Cinq-Mars* [1829]), dated 1827 by Vigny, Pléiade edn. of the *Oeuvres*, vol.2, pp.19ff.

39. A text of Schiller's in his preface to *La Fiancée de Messine* (Barante's translation of the *Oeuvres dramatiques* [1821]; republished in 1841, p.476: ideal art is "truer than any reality and more factual than any experience") was available in France; one can also think of Michelet's translation of Vico (p.xxiv of his introduction to *Les Principes de la philosophie de l'histoire traduite de la Scienza nuova de Vico* [1827]).

40. Ibid., p.19.

41. This translation was published in 1830; the "Lettre" is there dated 1 November 1829.

42. Around the time of Hugo's "Odes et ballades" and *Les Orientales,* Vigny made efforts in picturesque and energetic poetry; only two poems resulted from this, "La Frégate la Sérieuse" and "Madame de Soubise," both dated 1828, both of little interest.

43. *Journal*, p.920 (30 September 1830).

44. "Lettre à Lord ***" (Pléiade edn. of the *Oeuvres*, vol.1, p.331); *Journal*, Pléiade edn., vol.2, p.931 [1830]; p.937 [1831]: "The theater is a puppet-play! Not enough room for the development of characters and philosophy!" ibid., p.1045 [1836].

45. *Journal*, p.958, 972 [1832].

46. *Journal*, p.880 [1824].

47. Ibid., p.930 (28 December [1830]).

48. Ibid., p.897 [1824].

49. Ibid., p.890 [1829]; the pure man of action, far from being superior to the man of thought, "is only a thinker *manqué*" (ibid.).

50. Sainte-Beuve, 1864 article on Vigny, *Nouveaux Lundis*, vol.6, pp.412ff., 423ff.

51. In the Bible (Judges 11:35) Jephthah says only: "Alas, my daughter, thou hast brought me very low"; in Byron's *Hebrew Melodies*, "Jephtha's Daughter" is the girl's song, fervently resigned to the sacrifice.

52. Magnin, review of Vigny's *Poèmes* in *Le Globe* of 21 October 1829; Sainte-Beuve (anonymous article, uncollected, in the *Revue des deux mondes* [14 May 1834]: Pléiade edn. of the *Oeuvres*, vol.1, p.561, and see Bonnerot, *Bibliographie de l'oeuvre de Sainte-Beuve*, vol.III-1, no.167; David d'Angers, *Carnets*, ed. Bruel, vol.1 (Paris, 1958), p.392; Balzac, *Béatrix* (1839), p.143 in the Conard edition of the *Oeuvres*.

53. Vigny, "Lettres à une puritaine," in *Revue de Paris*, vol.4, p.677 (letter of 27 December 1838).

54. This is what David d'Angers does, loc. cit.: Moses, having understood "what

the human race is worth," "must have groaned deeply at the ingratitude of men," etc. Nothing in the poem resembles this.

55. See to this effect the edition of the poem by Fernande Bartfeld in the *Archives des lettres modernes*, no.83 (1967), especially notes 2 and 45, and the study of the same author on *Vigny et la figure de Moïse* (Paris, 1968), part II, ch.2.

56. Vigny dated "La Prison" from 1821 and placed it among the *Poèmes* published in 1822; "Moïse," dated 1822, was included in the subsequent collection (*Poèmes antiques et modernes* [1826]).

57. Dated 1822, and published as a brochure in the same year.

58. The Trappist, a royalist leader, betrayed and faithful "anyway," relies on God, at the very moment when the Man in the Iron Mask is blaspheming: testimony to the fact that the arrangement of subjects matters more to poets than the logical coherence of ideas; the two poems are nonetheless constructed on the same underlying foundation.

59. The first drafts of "Satan," according to Baldensperger, go back to 1819: see his edition of the poems, p.317 *in fine*. Vigny writes on 8 May [1824] to Delprat (*Correspondance*, ed. Baldensperger, p.62): "I have finished the *Satan*, which has decided to carry the name of his victim. You will receive *Eloa*." However, the correspondence between Vigny and Hugo in 1824 and 1825 (see above, note 16) informs us that Vigny is continuing to work on his "Satan," given as distinct from "Eloa" and "Le Déluge."

60. See "Les Reproches de Satan" (a prose project) on pp.320ff. of the Baldensperger edition of the *Poèmes*; ibid., pp.326–27, two accusatory fragments in verse; and pp.327–28, in prose, the redemption of Satan. The title of "Satan sauvé," given by Ratisbonne (*Journal* [1867 edn.], p.274) to some of these fragments, is not Vigny's, as Milner notes (*Le Diable dans la littérature française de Cazotte à Baudelaire* [Paris, 1960], vol.I, p.377); we have, however, seen that the *Journal* mentions a "Satan racheté" among the poet's projects. The redemption of Satan was still haunting Vigny in 1837 (*Journal*, p.1073) and 1838 (pp.1108–9); see also "Le Nouveau Purgatoire," an undated plan for a poem in the *Mémoires inédits* of Vigny published by Jean Sangnier (Paris, 1958), pp.419–20. [These texts are collected on pp.235–57 of the Germain-Jarry edition of Vigny's poetry and theater in the new Pléiade edition of the *Oeuvres complètes*, vol.I (Paris, 1986). *Trans.*]

61. Letter of 7 September 1823, published by F. Germain, *L'Imagination d'Alfred de Vigny* (Paris, 1961), p.536.

62. I admit that Bonnefoy does not convince me when, in his quite remarkable book, he detects at the bottom of the heresy of "Satan" a protest against the union of the soul to a body; there is in *Satan* something of this "angelicism," but there is also the contrary: see the Baldensperger edition of the *Poèmes*, p.322 (horror of disembodied thought); Vigny's speculations pull him in different directions; the permanent element in him is man's quarrel with divine inhumanity.

63. *Cinq-Mars*, ed. Baldensperger (Paris, 1922), pp.189, 275, 478, 481–83.

64. On Vigny's adhesion to this theory, see J. A. Catala and R. Pomeau, "Vigny au Maine-Giraud en 1827 d'après un carnet inédit," in *Revue d'histoire littéraire de la France* (1964), pp.220–21.

65. *Journal*, p.1049.

66. This interpretation is confirmed by Vigny himself (*Journal*, p.1153), and see also the *Mémoires inédits* already cited, ed. Sangnier, p.378. It is generally accepted that "L'Almeh," which appeared in April and May 1831 in the *Revue des deux mondes*, was written several years earlier.

67. *Cinq-Mars*, cited edn., p.433.

68. *Cinq-Mars*, cited edn., p.534.

69. A few years earlier, Victor Hugo had used the same text as an epigraph to his ode on "Le Génie," in which he addresses Chateaubriand. The text is taken from the *Pensées diverses* that were published by Lamennais in 1819 at the end of a new edition of his *Réflexions sur l'état de l'Eglise*; it can be read in vol.6, p.433 of the *Oeuvres complètes* (12 vols., 1836–37). Lamennais continued: "Those kings who do not go by this name but who truly reign by force of character and greatness of thought are chosen by the events that they must command." It is obviously a question of leaders of peoples brought to the fore by necessity; perhaps the thought dates from the time of Napoleon. Hugo had correctly cited Lamennais, for in his apology for Chateaubriand he mingled his literary glory and his political activity. Vigny, in his epigraph, inserted an apocryphal expression; he writes: "[T]he royalty of genius, last resource of exhausted peoples. *Great writers* . . . those kings who do not go by this name," etc. This little falsification, or, if you prefer, gloss, is very significant.

70. *Journal*, p.975 (1832).

71. Letter to Emile Deschamps of 16 January 1825, published by F. Germain, op.cit., p.540.

72. *Journal*, pp.898 and 895, respectively (1829). In the case of the first fragment, there is no need to point out that, philologically, the last observation is a misinterpretation.

73. Letter to Théodore Carlier of 4 January 1830 (*Correspondance*, ed. Baldensperger, p.214).

74. "Lettre à Lord ***," in the Pléiade edition of the *Oeuvres*, vol.1, p.347. He nicely distinguishes, corresponding to the three hands of the dial, three levels of human thought: the crowd (the hour hand), the mass of enlightened people (the minute hand), and genius (the second hand); it is not clear where in this scale he would place governments: "Every government," he tells us elsewhere, "is merely the active symbol of outmoded thought" (*Journal*, p.1003 [1834]).

75. *Journal*, p.901 (1829). Baldensperger wonders if this last sentence, which contains in potentia all of "Le Mont des oliviers" (published in 1843), was not added later; but he does not say that he saw any indication whatever of this in the manuscript or elsewhere.

76. Amédée Guiard, *La Fonction du poète, étude sur Victor Hugo* (Paris, 1910), p.viii.

77. Ibid.

78. Saint-Valry, *Madame de Mably*, vol.2 (1836), pp.541ff. (text cited by E. Biré, *Victor Hugo après 1830* (Paris, 1891), vol.2, pp.181–82; reprinted by Charlier, *Une Amitié romantique*, pp.10–11 of the separate reprint.

79. See especially Bernard Guyon, *La Vocation Poétique de Victor Hugo, essai sur la signification originale des "Odes et ballades" et des "Orientales", 1818–1828*, Publications de la Faculté des Lettres d'Aix-en-Provence, new series, no.4 (1953); and Géraud Vanzac, *Les Origines religieuses de Victor Hugo* (Paris, 1955).

80. G. Vanzac, op.cit., pp.580, 583.

81. See a supplement of testimonies supporting this conclusion in abbé Pierre Dubois (*Victor Hugo, ses idées religieuses de 1802 à 1825* [Paris, 1913], pp.300ff., and in G. Vanzac, op.cit., p.476 and pp.503ff., n.2.

82. Letter to the editor of the *Moniteur universel*, dated 26 November 1822 (on Soumet's *Sahl*), reprinted in the Imprimerie Nationale edition of the *Oeuvres*, in the volume entitled *Littérature et philosophie mêlées*, p.435.

83. V. Hugo, *Odes*, I, 5; I, 9.

84. *Odes*, II, 2: "L'Histoire."

85. Review of the *Odes et ballades* of 1826 in the *Journal des débats* of 8 January 1827, signed J. V. (?)

86. *Odes*, III, 1: "A M. Alphonse de Lamartine."

87. *Odes*, Preface to the edition of 1823.

88. *Gazette de France* (15 September 1822); *La Quotidienne* (20 September 1822) (article signed M. J., that is, Mély-Janin): texts reprinted in the Imprimerie Nationale edition of the *Oeuvres*, in the volume entitled *Odes et ballades-Orientales*, pp.567–68.

89. This ode is already from 1825, which explains the vehemence of the passage.

90. *Odes*, preface to the 1822 edition.

91. Ibid.

92. *La Muse française* (May 1824) (ed. Marsan, vol.2, pp.249–50): article reprinted by Hugo in *Littérature et philosophie mêlées* (pp.136–37 of the Imprimerie Nationale edn.) and transformed, because of his quarrel with Vigny, into a eulogy of Milton's *Paradise Lost*.

93. Apropos of the French translation of the *Psaumes* of Boishuguet (*Le Conservateur littéraire* [August 1820]: ed. Marsan, vol.2, part II, p.199).

94. Hugo, review of Jules Lefèvre's *Le Parricide* in *Le Réveil* of 19 February 1823 (passage reprinted in *Littérature et philosophie mêlées*, ed. I. N., p.79; see the entire article, ibid., in an appendix, pp.345–46).

95. Hugo, review of Lamennais's *Essai sur l'indifférence*, in *La Muse française* of August 1823 (ed. Marsan, vol.1, p.75).

96. Hugo, "Sur Georges Gordon, lord Byron," in *La Muse française* of June 1824 (ed. Marsan, vol.2, p.301).

97. *Odes*, IV, 2: "La Lyre et la harpe" (piece dated 1822, published the same year).

98. Hugo, review of *Les Méditations* in *Le Conservateur littéraire* (April 1820) (ed. Marsan, vol.2, part 1, p.189).

99. Hugo, review of Walter Scott's *Quentin Durward*, in *La Muse française* of July 1823 (ed. Marsan, vol.1, pp.27–28).

100. *Odes*, II, 10: "Le Dernier Chant" (piece dated 1823, published in 1824).

101. *Odes*, I, 1: "Le Poète dans les révolutions" (dated 1821, published in 1822).

102. He offered, however, before Lamartine, some very striking examples of sacred or spiritual poetry of a hymnic cast (*Odes*: IV, 9, "L'Ame"; IV, 13, "L'Antéchrist"; IV, 18, "Jéhovah").

103. Hugo, review of Vigny's *Poèmes* in the *Etoile* of 24 March 1822 (reprinted in the I. N. edition of *Littérature et philosophie mêlées* in an appendix, p.341).

104. See *Odes*, II, 1: "A mes odes," poem dated 1823, which in 1824 opened the collection of *Nouvelles Odes*.

105. *Odes*, IV, 1: "Le Poète" (dated 1823, published in 1824).

106. *Odes*, V, 14: "Actions de grâces" (dated 1823, published in 1824).

107. Sainte-Beuve, preface to *Les Consolations* (dated December 1829) (Paris, 1830), pp.xxix–xxx.

108. V. Hugo, "Idées au hasard," in *Littérature et philosophie mêlées* (ed. I. N., pp.139, 134); these fragments are collectively dated "July 1824" by Hugo; those from which our citations are drawn were unpublished when Hugo issued this collection; given their vehemence, they do not seem to antedate 1826, the certain date of one of them.

109. Hugo, letter to the publishers at the beginning of *Le Sylphe, poésies de feu Ch. Dovalle* (1830) (text most certainly antedating the July Revolution); this passage is reprinted in *Littérature et philosophie mêlées* (ed. I. N., p.149).

110. Hugo, ibid., p.150.

111. Preface to the *Odes et ballades*, 1828 edn.

112. *Odes*, III, 8: "Fin" (poem dated 1828, published the same year).

113. *Odes*, V, 5 and 7: both pieces dated 1822.

114. These are the first three ballads of the definitive collection.

115. Thus "Les Deux Archers," "A un passant," "La Ronde du sabbat" (1825; respectively, *Ballades*, 8, 10, 15).

116. Thus "La Fée et la péri" (1824), "A Trilby" (1825), respectively *Ballades*, 15 and 4.

117. *Ballades*, 5 (1825): "Le Géant"; the entire poem could be cited.

118. See, for example, *Les Orientales*, 36 ("Rêverie") and 41 (*Novembre*).

119. *Les Orientales*, 34 (1828): "Mazeppa."

120. Preface to the *Les Orientales*, 4th paragraph.

121. Hugo, preface to *Cromwell*, ed. Maurice Souriau (Paris, n.d.), pp.176–77.

122. The book of Genesis is given as the type of the primitive lyrical poem; Greek tragedy is not drama; Pindar is not lyrical; Herodotus is not a historian; all the ancients are epic poets, etc.

123. The succession lyricism-epic-drama as the total explanation of the literary creations of humanity has provoked many discussions among critics. Hugo's sources for his idea have been sought. The first element in the model, in any event — namely the notion of a primitive lyricism — was everywhere, as we have seen sufficiently; for a century it had been the almost official accompaniment of scriptural commentary. The entire model, with its three terms, is found in a form strikingly similar to Hugo's, even in its nuances, in Eckstein, on the very eve of the preface to *Cromwell*: see *Le Catholique*, vol.4 (November 1826), pp.226ff. (primitive lyric or hymnic poetry — then heroic age and epic poetry — then dramatic poetry). Eckstein developed the ideas again in *Le Catholique* of October 1827 (vol.8, pp.108ff.), emphasizing the popular character of dramatic poetry. Let us recall that Hugo dated the preface to *Cromwell* October 1827, and that the volume containing the play and its preface appeared in December of the same year, bearing the date 1828.

124. Preface to *Cromwell*, cited edition, pp.183ff. Hugo, like Chateaubriand, also emphasizes the historical cataclysms that marked the first Christian centuries.

125. See Hugo, article on *Quentin Durward*, already cited, p.24.

126. Preface to *Cromwell*, pp.192–95, 222–23.

127. On this point, too, Eckstein should be mentioned, for he has "the power of the ugly" being born from the Fall (*Le Catholique*, vol.4 [December 1826], p.538).

128. See his answer, in the *Journal des débats* of 26 July 1824, in the review of Hoffman's *Nouvelles Odes* (reprinted in the I. N. edition of the *Oeuvres*, volume *Poésies*, pp.562ff.).

129. *Le Temple du romantisme en prose et en vers* (Paris, n.d.), p.7 (the work bears no date, but it is reviewed in vol.22 [1826], p.218 of the *Annales de la littérature et des arts*).

130. Ibid., p.4. Castelnau, op.cit., pp.212–17, wishing to define romanticism, finds himself unable to escape this difficulty.

131. J. M. V. Audin, *Du romantisme* (at the beginning of *Florence ou la Religieuse* [Paris, 1822]), pp.i–cxxiii.

132. Sainte-Beuve, review of the *Odes et ballades* in *Le Globe* of 2 January 1827 (article reprinted in the *Nouveaux Lundis*, vol.1, pp.164ff.).

133. Article in *Le Globe* (6 December 1827) (for the attribution to Sainte-Beuve, see Bonnerot, *Bibliographie de l'oeuvre de Sainte-Beuve*, vol.III-1, no.57); reprinted in Maxime Leroy's edition of the *Oeuvres* (Pléiade), vol.1, p.273.

134. Letter from a subscriber on *Vie, poésies et pensées de Joseph Delorme*, in *Le Globe* of 15 April 1829; for the identification of the author, see G. Antoine's edition of *Joseph Delorme* (Paris, 1956), p.cxxviii. The "subscriber" commented on a preceding review by Magnin (*Globe* [11 April 1829]), which also contained reservations on the point which interests us.

135. *Revue française* (January 1829), p.243. "De la nouvelle école poétique" (anonymous article); the author was L. de Guizard, one of the founders of the review (for the identification see the prospectus at the beginning of the thirteenth

installment). I do not cite the protests against the theory of the grotesque on the part of Chauvet and Héreau in the *Revue encyclopédique* (vol.40 [December 1828], pp.739ff.; vol.50 [April 1831], pp.81ff.) because these are by writers generally hostile to romanticism.

136. Preface to *Cromwell*, p.267.

137. Thus, p.260 of the preface, the allusion to "the timid partisans of romanticism" who confuse reality according to art and reality according to nature; the defense of verse, obviously against liberal advocates of historical drama in prose, follows this development immediately (see pp.267ff., and on the same subject, p.275, the allusion to "the error of several of our distinguished reformers").

138. Sainte-Beuve, *Portraits littéraires*, vol.3, p.545, no.15 (a sort of spiritual autobiography).

139. Review of Pichot's *Voyage littéraire et historique en Angleterre* (*Globe* [15 December 1829], article collected for the first time in Maxime Leroy's edition of the *Oeuvres* [Pléiade], vol.1, pp.134ff.).

140. Ibid. At this time Sainte-Beuve knew the Lake poets, he tells us, only through Pichot's volume; he actually read them only later; see on this subject Thomas G. S. Combe, *Sainte-Beuve poète et les poètes anglais* (Paris, 1937).

141. Review of Tissot's *Poésies érotiques* in *Le Globe* of 4 May 1826 (*Premiers lundis*, vol.1, p.119).

142. Review of Casimir Delavigne's *Sept Messéniennes* in *Le Globe* of 20 March 1827 (*Portraits contemporains*, vol.5, p.471).

143. "Songe charmant, douce espérance," final stanza: this poem, which Sainte-Beuve mentions in a letter of February 1827 (*Correspondance générale*, ed. Bonnerot, vol.1, p.56), is intercalated at the end of the *Vie* that opens the volume.

144. Autobiographical note already cited (*Portraits littéraires*, vol.3, p.545).

145. Already cited review of the *Odes et ballades*.

146. See *Causeries du lundi*, vol.19, p.82 and note.

147. See Baudelaire, letter of 15 March, in the *Correspondance*, ed. Crépet, vol.5, pp.64–65; and Sainte-Beuve, letter of 29 March 1865, in the *Correspondance*, ed. Bonnerot, vol.14, p.133.

148. The Academy held a competition on this subject in 1826 and 1827; Sainte-Beuve published his study as articles in *Le Globe* in 1827 and 1828, and then in a volume in 1828. On Sainte-Beuve's variations during the course of this work, see G. Michaut's Latin thesis (Paris, 1903).

149. Sainte-Beuve, *Tableau*, 1828 edn., vol.1, pp.366ff.

150. Notably apropos of the theater, *Tableau*, vol.1, p.331; and from a general point of view, p.365.

151. See *Les Cahiers de Sainte-Beuve*, ed. Troubat (Paris, 1876), p.42.

152. Sainte-Beuve makes the "conversion" of Joseph to artistic technique date from this poem.

153. See Victor Pavie's testimony, cited by Michaut (*Sainte-Beuve avant les Lundis* [Paris, 1903], p.73).

154. The collection, which appeared in March 1830, was composed in the second half of the preceding year.

155. Sainte-Beuve, letter of 6 December 1828 to Loudierre (in *Souvenirs et indiscrétions publiés par son dernier secrétaire* [Paris, 1872], p.162; reprinted in the *Correspondance*, ed. Bonnerot, vol.1, p.111).

156. *Vie, poésies et pensées de Joseph Delorme*, Pensées, no.15 (ed. G. Antoine [Paris, 1956] p.147).

157. Ibid., Pensées, no.3 (p.132).

158. Ibid., pp.132–33.

159. Sainte-Beuve, *Les Consolations* (Paris, 1830), pp.xxv–xxvi.

160. *Joseph Delorme*, Pensées, no.18 (p.150 of the Antoine edn.).

161. *Joseph Delorme*, piece entitled *Le Cénacle* (p.62 of the Antoine edn.; the editor dates the poem from 1828).

162. Sainte-Beuve, article on Jean-Baptiste Rousseau (1829), collected in *Portraits littéraires*, vol.1, p.131.

163. *Les Consolations*, "A mon ami Leroux" ("September 1829").

164. *Les Consolations*, "A Alfred de Vigny" ("November 1829").

165. *Les Consolations*, "A mon ami M. P. Mérimée" ("December 1829"). We know that in 1830 Sainte-Beuve was in contact with Ballanche (see *Correspondance*, ed. Bonnerot, vol.1, p.182, and *Portraits contemporains*, vol.2, p.32).

166. *Joseph Delorme*, in "Bonheur champêtre" (ed. Antoine, pp.58,59). See also, ibid., pp.36ff., "Le Suicide"; also in the *Consolations*, the poem "A Boulanger" ("When the heavenly voice . . .").

9. 1830 AND THE JEUNE-FRANCE

1. Sainte-Beuve, 1833 article on Jouffroy, collected in the *Portraits littéraires*, vol.1, pp.298–99.

2. To cite only the best known, Nanteuil and Maquet were born in 1813, O'Neddy in 1811, Gautier and Bouchardy in 1810, Borel in 1809, Nerval and Du Seigneur in 1808.

3. See s.v. "Artiste" (by Diderot) in vol.1 of the *Encyclopédie* (1751); he observes that the word is pejorative when it opposes the execution to the conception, the simple artist to the inventor.

4. *Dictionnaire de l'Académie*, s.v. "Artiste," 4th edn. (1762), and 5th edn. (1798).

5. Saint-Simon, *Lettres d'un habitant de Genève à ses contemporains*, reprinted in the *Oeuvres de Saint-Simon and d'Enfantin*, vol.1 (Paris, 1865), p.27.

6. See Sébastien Mercier in his *Néologie*, vol.1 (1801), p.50; reprinted and cited in an article in *Le Corsaire* (4 November 1823).

7. D'Hautel, *Dictionnaire du bas langage* (1803), cited by G. Matoré, *Le Vocabulaire de la prose littéraire de 1833 à 1845* (Geneva-Lille, 1951), p.236.

8. E. Jouy, *L'Hermite de la Chaussée d'Antin*, vol.5, p.116 (chronicle of 26 February 1814).

9. Mme de Staël, *Aspasie*, in *Oeuvres complètes*, octavo edn., vol.17, p.344. The word recurs frequently in the book *De l'Allemagne* as a noun or an adjective.

10. *Complément du Dictionnaire de l'Académie française* by Barré and Landais (Brussels, 1839), s.v. "Artiste."

11. F. Pyat, "Les Artistes," in *Nouveau Tableau de Paris au dix-neuvième siècle*, vol.4 (1834), pp.3–5. Pyat later notes the outward traits that accompany the mania of *artistism* (long hair, medieval style, Bohemian existence outside of society, special language) and the repertoire of insults peculiar to the band ("bourgeois," "rococo," "peer of France," "empire," "wig," "comme il faut," etc.) (ibid., pp.8–9, 18).

12. *Le Figaro* of 15 September 1833, anonymous article entitled "L'Artiste soi-disant." Here, too, a description of the attributes of the "artist" (dagger, Henri III beard, hair like Raphael, Robespierre vest, etc.) and of his lexical enthusiasms.

13. See *Dictionnaire de l'Académie*, 5th edn. (1798), under the word *art*.

14. Charles Deglény, "Le langage à la mode," in *Nouveau Tableau de Paris au dix-neuvième siècle*, vol.6 (1835), pp.308–9.

15. Cousin, *Du vrai, du beau, du bien*, pp.223 and 224.

16. Sainte-Beuve, *Correspondance*, ed. Bonnerot, vol.1, p.103, letter to Hugo of August 26, 1828.

17. Testimony of Juste Olivier (*Paris en 1830*, journal published by A. Delattre and M. Denkinger [Paris, 1951], p.77, under the date June 7).

18. Hugo, *Lettres à la fiancée* in the Imprimerie Nationale edition, pp.61, 92, 127 (letters from 1821–22). We must take into account the young Hugo's ferocious jealousy, but the texts remain indicative. The woman whose emancipatory influence he feared was Mlle Duvidal, Adèle's drawing teacher and future wife of Abel Hugo.

19. Lamartine, *Correspondance*, sextodecimo edn., vol.1, p.122, letter to Virieu dated "Lyons, 1810." See, in a similar tone, the journal of Crozet, Stendhal's friend (in Stendhal, *Oeuvres intimes*, Pléiade edn., p.1356, lines dated 1805); and Stendhal himself, *Pensées*, ed. Martineau, vol.1, p.69 (1803).

20. See the article "Les Jeunes-Frances" in *Le Figaro* of 30 August 1831.

21. Balzac, *Une Fille d'Eve* (1838–39), p.104 in the Bouteron-Longnon edition of the *Oeuvres* published by Conard; Vigny, *Mémoires inédits*, ed. Sangnier (Paris, 1958), p.358 (undated fragment).

22. See Ernest Legouvé, *Max* (Paris, 1833), pp.vii–viii; and Deglény, cited article, pp.310–11.

23. The second edition of the *Dictionnaire de l'Académie* (1718) gives as examples of the pejorative use of the word the expression "a bourgeois look [*mine bourgeoise*]."

24. In the society of antiquity, founded on the privilege of freemen, *liberalis*, like ἐλευθέριος, means "worthy," "generous," "frank"; in feudal Europe *noble* (or its equivalent in other languages), which is the name of the masters, is also that of the virtues.

25. *Le Corsaire-Satan*, editorial of 4 November 1844.

26. Henry Bulwer, *La France sociale, politique et littéraire*, 2 vols., p.118 (the English original is from the same year; the author was ambassador in Brussels and Paris). The enumeration of the "reigns" in this passage goes over the succession of political eras of France: the old royalty, the eighteenth-century encyclopedist, the Revolution, the Empire, the Restoration (priests and poor nobles), and finally the Revolution of 1830.

27. See in J. Marsan, *La Bataille romantique*, 2nd series (Paris, n.d. [1924]), the chapter entitled "The Bourgeois Reaction"; also R. Jasinski, *Les Années romantiques de Théophile Gautier* (Paris, 1929), pp.129ff., 175ff., 185ff.

28. We can only evoke here Henri Monnier and his Joseph Prudhomme, Traviès and his Mayeux, Daumier and his ferociously caricatured bourgeois. Monnier wrote a *Physiologie du bourgeois* (Paris, n.d. [around 1840]), in which we can read that "among artists . . . the word Bourgeois is no longer a denomination, a meaning, a qualification; it is an insult, the most obscene that the vocabulary of the studio can express" (p.9).

29. Sainte-Beuve, *Les Consolations*, preface to Victor Hugo.

30. Sainte-Beuve, *Pensées d'août* (1837), "A Madame Tastu," undated, but replying to a poem written by that lady in 1833.

31. Sainte-Beuve, *Premiers Lundis*, vol.2, p.181 (1 March 1833 article in the *Revue des deux mondes*).

32. Gautier, *Histoire du romantisme*, title of ch.2, and passim. On the group and its ideas and attitudes, see René Jasinski, op.cit.

33. Nerval, letter to Sainte-Beuve, no.11 of the correspondence in the Béguin-Richer edition of his works (Bibliothèque de la Pléiade); this letter is believed to be prior to October 1832; he praises to Sainte-Beuve the works of Du Seigneur, whom he has admired, he says, "for the two years I have known him and that I have been a member of the *petit cénacle*, to which he belongs." Gautier tells us that he joined the group rather late (op.cit., p.16).

34. *Histoire du romantisme*, p.64.

35. Jeunes-France, and even Jeunes-Frances, were also written.

36. In a series of satirical articles beginning on 30 August 1831 and running several months; they are attributed to Léon Gozlan; it is on 10 September 1831 that this contributor boasts of having coined the "epithet" *Jeune-France*.

37. On this question, see my article, "Jeune-France et bousingots," *Revue d'histoire littéraire de la France* (1971), pp.439–62. [This article appears in a different form in Paul Bénichou, *Variétés critiques* (Paris, 1996), pp.79–109. *Trans.*]

38. *Histoire du romantisme*, pp.86–87.

39. Letter mentioned above, reprinted in Gautier, *Histoire du romantisme*, pp.85–86.

40. *Histoire du romantisme*, pp.67–69. The banquet, Gautier tells us, was celebrating the nomination of Célestin Nanteuil to the direction of the Ecole de dessin in

Dijon; this nomination took place in 1867. O'Neddy had only published one volume of poems, *Feu et flamme*, in 1833; Gautier's question, thirty-four years later, may have been cruel; on the other hand the allusion to the mystery surrounding O'Neddy's life charitably mingles obscure affairs of the heart going back to his youth with his aborted literary destiny.

41. Gautier, *Emaux et camées*, "Le Château du souvenir."

42. Francis Dumont, introduction to the special number of *Les Cahiers du sud* on "Les Petits Romantiques français" (1949), p.8.

43. Armand Hoog, *La Révolte métaphysique et religieuse des petits romantiques*, same number of *Les Cahiers du sud*, p.13.

44. See Estève, op.cit., pp.219ff.

45. See Louis Maigron, *Le Romantisme et les moeurs* (Paris, 1910). The author draws on a mass of unpublished documents that have come to him from various sources: precious documents whose value is not at all lessened by his pejorative comments.

46. On this subject see contemporary testimonies in Jasinski, op.cit., pp.163–65. The meetings in the impasse du Doyenné, which came later (Gautier, Nerval, Houssaye, the painter Rogier), have a different character; the Jeune-France passion is no longer there.

47. See Jean-Daniel Maublanc, *Surréalisme romantique (bousingotisme et lycanthropie)* (Paris, 1934); *Ephémères II* (Paris, 1940); Jules Krieser, *Les Ascendances romantiques du surréalisme contemporain*, thesis at the Université de Paris (1942) (especially the introduction; this work was also published under the name of Francis Dumont and the title *Naissance du romantisme*); finally, the special number, already cited, of *Les Cahiers du sud* in 1949, on which several writers linked to surrealism collaborated, notably Tristan Tzara ("Les Bourgeois comme phénomène social," pp.56–61 of this number).

48. *Le Figaro* of 10 September 1831, article entitled "Le Festin des Jeunes-Frances."

49. *Le Figaro* of 30 August 1831, article "Les Jeunes-Frances."

50. Asselineau, *Mélanges tirés d'une petite bibliothèque romantique* (Paris, 1866), p.140.

51. Asselineau, p.xxi of the introduction to his edition of *Gaspard de la Nuit* (1868).

52. Baudelaire, article on Pétrus Borel, in the *Revue fantaisiste* of 15 July 1861, collected in *L'Art romantique*.

53. Th. Gautier, *Histoire du romantisme*, pp.19ff.

54. O'Neddy, "Lettre inédite" (posthumous) published by Asselineau (Paris, 1875), pp.9–10.

55. This variant had doubtless spread beyond the group as well. By chance I have read the works of André Imberdis, a lawyer from Ambert, who was among the defenders of the republicans accused in the great trial of 1835, later the author of

works on the history of Auvergne and magistrate in Riom and in Algiers. He was born in 1810, and although as far as I know he was from a milieu foreign to the *petit cénacle*, his republican novels of the 1830s are, in their themes and their tone, strongly marked by the Jeune-France spirit (*L'Habit d'Arlequin* [1832]; *Le Dernier Jour d'un suicidé* [1835]); see also his *Cri de l'âme*, a collection of poems (1835). He is, of course, enamored with the notion of the mission of poetry (see especially the preface to *L'Habit d'Arlequin*, pp.xii–xiii). Imberdis is only an example; others, I think, could be discovered.

56. This is his first work, published in 1831. He was born in 1809.

57. Borel indeed lived in the most dire need until the day in 1846 when he obtained a position as colonial functionary in Algeria, where he succeeded so badly that he was twice removed from his post. He died in 1859; it seems that he was, in this last period of his life, rather far removed from the revolutionary ideas of his youth (see especially on his life Enid Starkie's book, *Pétrus Borel, the Lycanthrope: His Life and Times* (London, 1954).

58. The "immoral tales" that make up the collection entitled *Champavert* (Paris, 1833) are supposed to be the posthumous work of a suicide (as they put it then), Champavert-Borel, and ends with the narration of his own death.

59. Thus in his novel about *Mme Putiphar* (2 vols. [Paris, 1839]).

60. *Champavert*, "Testament," p.357 of the A. Marie edn. (Paris, 1922).

61. Preface to the *Rhapsodies*, p.13 of the Marie edition. The name "lycanthrope" (werewolf) has remained associated with Pétrus Borel in literary history; see also in *Champavert*, p.171, what he says of his character Three-Fingered-Jack, also a "lycanthrope" and hard up in any society.

62. *Champavert*, p.357.

63. *Rhapsodies*, p.15 (*sic* for the last two words).

64. Gautier, *Histoire du romantisme*, p.21.

65. O'Neddy, *Feu et flamme* (Paris, 1833), ed. Marcel Hervier (Paris, 1926), p.12: O'Neddy makes Borel speak under the transparent anagram of Reblo.

66. Pétrus Borel, "Des artistes penseurs et des artistes creux," in *L'Artiste*, vol.5 (summer 1833), pp.253–54. Unfortunately, it is to be feared that the Spanish inscription, if it was really seen, is a glorification not of humanity but of the masculine sex.

67. Ibid., p.253.

68. Ibid., p.254.

69. Ibid., p.259.

70. See the note by Ernest Havet to O'Neddy's *Poésies posthumes*.

71. Philothée O'Neddy (Théophile Dondey), *Poésies posthumes* (Paris, 1877). His *Oeuvres en prose* were later collected in a volume (Paris, 1878).

72. See his correspondence with Ernest Havet at the end of Marcel Hervier's republication of *Feu et flamme* (Paris, 1926), pp.79–143.

73. Gautier, *Histoire du romantisme*, p.63. Havet's notice to the *Poésies posthumes* contains almost all the information that we possess on his life; see also a chapter on

him in Armand Silvestre, *Au pays des souvenirs* (Paris, 1892) (Silvestre had been his office colleague and the witness of this abortive destiny).

74. Note to the *Poésies posthumes*, p.7.

75. Valéry Larbaud, *Théophile Dondey de Santeny (1811–1875)* (Tunis, 1935), p.23.

76. *Feu et flamme*, ed. Hervier, pp.1–3.

77. Ibid., "Nuit 9ᵉ, Incantation," p.52.

78. O'Neddy, "Lettre inédite" already cited, p.14 (the letter is from 23 September 1862).

79. It is by this inner logic, which extends the poetic absolute to the totality of man, that the Jeune-France were able to interest the surrealists a hundred years later. In fact, O'Neddy is the only one in whom this logic is made even a little explicit. But it is latent in all of them.

80. *Feu et flamme*, "Nuit 1ʳᵉ, Pandémonium," p.14. See, in the same order of ideas, a sonnet in the collection *Mistica Biblion* (1834–46), published in the *Poésies posthumes*, p.203 and entitled "La Vraie Noblesse" (the title *Mistica Biblion* echoes the famous *Erotica Biblion* of Mirabeau).

81. *Feu et flamme*, same poem, p.16. "Calculator" [*chiffreur*] is a synonym for *bourgeois* in O'Neddy's writings.

82. Letter to Havet of 16 November 1862 (edn. Hervier of *Feu et flamme*, p.134).

83. "Lettre inédite," p.14.

84. *Feu et flamme*, foreword, p.3. "Many young people": doubtless an allusion to some recent Jeune-France recruits coming from republican ranks. We should like to know more about this, and more generally about the hearing that the Jeune-France were able to get among militant youth.

85. See in the *Poésies posthumes*, especially pp.410–16, the poem entitled "Les Visions d'un mort vivant," which dates from 1861–62.

86. *Feu et flamme*, p.4.

87. *Feu et flamme*, "Nuit 1ʳᵉ, Pandémonium," pp.9–10.

88. See ibid., "Nuit 10ᵉ, Trinité," pp.48ff.

89. Ibid., "Mosaïque," first fragment, "Spleen," pp.55–56 and 57–58.

90. *Poésies posthumes*, pp.274ff., "Epilogue général: Le Cul-de-jatte."

91. *Poésies posthumes*, p.135, "Preface-Dedication" to *Mistica Biblion*, dated November 1858.

92. Ibid., p.151, "Une Fièvre de l'époque."

93. *Poésies posthumes*, p.160, "Ode-Ballade" (composed between 1835 and 1843). In this poem it is love that is supposed to penetrate the essence of things, in that love is one of the forms of that essential *passion* or inspiration proper to Poets and that makes them capable of revelation. See also, from the same period, in "Les Trois Idylles," the sonnet that figures on p.176 of the *Poésies posthumes*.

94. The group did not last long, as we have seen, and in order to situate exactly the time spent in it by each of its members, it would be necessary to be able to trace its history month by month, which we are unable to do.

95. These poems, published as brochures or in periodicals, have been collected in vol.6 of the Lévy edition of the works. There is some controversy concerning the paternity of several pieces: see Jean Senelier, *Gérard de Nerval, Essai de bibliographie* (Paris, 1959).

96. O'Neddy, "Lettre inédite," p.10.

97. See *Oeuvres*, ed. Lévy, vol.6, and variants in J. Richer, "Documents concernant Nerval" in the *Revue des sciences humaines* (1958), pp.401ff.

98. The sheet is paginated 9 according to J. Richer, who published it (see the preceding note) and reproduced it in the Pléiade edition of the *Oeuvres* (1960), p.49. Nerval is going to lunch at his grandfather's after having visited the bibliophile Jacob, and — more curiously — having dropped by the home of "the venerable Laurentie," a friend of Martignac and Lamennais, who, he tells us, played a role in the fall of the Bourbons. This text must have been written a considerable time after the events, since Laurentie, whom Nerval could very well have gone to see in 1830 (he had just published in February, in his Bibliothèque choisie, Nerval's *Poésies allemandes*, and was going to publish in October in the same collection his *Choix des poésies de Ronsard, Dubellay, Baïf, Belleau, Dubartas, Chassignet, Desportes, Régnier*), was then only thirty-seven years old; with time he took on a "venerable air," as a veteran of Legitimism. We may be surprised that during the uprising, Nerval visited this immoderate royalist, who had, by your leave, fought Martignac in his time, and supported Polignac in his *Quotidienne* during the final crisis (see E. Biré, *Etudes et portraits* [Lyons-Paris, 1913], p.363).

99. "Mémoires d'un Parisien, Sainte-Pélagie en 1832," in *L'Artiste* of 11 April 1841 (reprinted in *La Bohème galante* of 1855 under the posthumous title "Mes Prisons"). It is probable that this imprisonment took place in reality in the fall of 1831 (see *Revue d'histoire littéraire de la France* [1971], p.488 n.92).

100. Letter to Auguste Lireux (May 1849) (no.135 of the correspondence in the Pléiade edition of the *Oeuvres*, vol.1), in response to an article by Champfleury in *Le Messager des théâtres et des arts* of May 11.

101. The last of the collection that bears the same title.

102. In the *Mercure de France au dix-neuvième siècle* of 7 May 1831; the poem is reprinted by Spoelberch de Lovenjoul (*Histoire des oeuvres de Théophile Gautier*, vol.1, pp.21–22), who believes that it is by Gautier, "in collaboration perhaps with Gérard de Nerval." But Pétrus ought to know about it.

103. Lovenjoul seems to take *extra* in the sense of *super* (as in *extra-fin*) and he is doubtless correct.

104. This is, of course, the passage that Borel chose for his epigraph.

105. *Choix de poésies de Ronsard*, etc. (Paris, 1830).

106. *Poésies allemandes . . . , morceaux choisis et traduit par M. Gérard* (Paris, 1830).

107. *Observations* at the beginning of his translation of *Faust* (1828) (Champion collection of the works, Baldensperger edn. of *Les Deux Faust* [Paris, 1932], p.6). He makes this remark apropos of the passage when the Spirit covers Faust with scorn.

108. Thus "Laisse-moi" (1831), "Une Allée du Luxembourg" (1832), "La Grand-mère" (doubtless 1831), "Fantaisie" (1832).

109. "Le Bonheur dans la maison," in the *Mercure de France au dix-neuvième siècle*, vol.33 (1831), pp.198–203; for the Nervalian paternity of this text, see Claude Pichois, *L'Image de Jean-Paul Richter dans les lettres françaises* (Paris, 1963), pp.144–45.

110. Nerval, translation of Hoffmann, "Les Aventures de la nuit de la Saint-Sylvestre," in the *Mercure de France au dix-neuvième siècle*, vol.34 (1831), p.546.

111. This concerns the shepherd Aubert-le-Flamenc, in "Le Prince des sots," ed. J. Richer (Paris, 1960), p.69 (a work of the 1830s, whose precise date is the subject of controversy).

112. Nerval, "Le Cabaret de la Mère Sagnet" (published 13 May 1830 in *Le Gastronome*; collected in the Pléiade edition of the *Oeuvres*, vol.1, pp.47–48).

113. Nerval knew well the German variant of the ministry of poetry, and this is visible in his translations (thus *Faust*, "Prologue sur le théâtre," ed. Baldensperger, p.17, and especially, in his 1830 collection, the poems of Schiller, "Puissance du chant," "Partage de la terre," "L'Idéal"). But his idealism, at this date, is ahead of that of his models, and is more disillusioned with the real, more secretly tragic, it would seem.

114. "Sylvie," 1. In the romantic avant-garde of 1830, this orientation and this character of being a harbinger do not belong to Nerval alone. We are considering here only the Jeune-France proper, but the literature of a group always emerges from a wider zone of analogous efforts. Thus Louis-Aloysius Bertrand, who did not belong to the little *cénacle*, is moving in the same direction as its members. And we know how much Baudelaire and Mallarmé admired him. His fantastico-gothic romanticism has too often led the deeper features of his work to be forgotten.

115. Remarks reported by Edmond de Goncourt in his preface to Bergerat's *Gautier* (1878), p.vi. (This concerns Gautier's purported red vest at the opening of *Hernani*, which had in reality been, according to him, a pink doublet.)

116. *Journal* of the Goncourts, ed. Ricatte, vol.6, p.77.

117. Gautier, *Poésies complètes*, new Jasinski edition (Paris, 1970), vol.1, p.113; and see Jasinski, *Les Années romantiques*, pp.80–81. This sonnet was supressed in the 1845 edition of the *Poésies complètes*.

118. Poem entitled "Paris," which appeared for the first time in the *Mercure de France au dix-neuvième siècle* of 11 June 1831; Jasinski edn., vol.1, p.115.

119. This follows from a quip by Gautier reported by Maxime Du Camp (*Souvenirs littéraires*, vol.2 [1883], p.27); Gautier, justifying in 1851 his refusal to serve in the national guard because of the ugliness of their uniform, declares that he renounced Saint-Simonianism for the same reason: "In 1832, I wanted to become Saint-Simonian, but when I saw that you had to wear white pants, a red vest, and a long blue frock-coat, I recoiled in horror and spontaneously renounced the worship of the god Father-and-Mother." What weight shall we give this remark? This may be a pure witticism without any real biographical significance.

120. See similarly the invectives of Philothée O'Neddy against the "calculators."

121. The manuscript of the poem is dated 2 October 1831; the poem appeared in 1834 (see Spoelberch de Lovenjoul, *Histoire des oeuvres de Th. Gautier*, vol.1, p.52); ed. Jasinski, vol.2, p.152.

122. "A Jehan Duseigneur, ode," poem published in the *Mercure de France au dix-neuvième siècle* of 22 October 1831; ed. Jasinski, vol.3, p.133.

123. Gautier, "De l'originalité en France," *Le Cabinet de lecture* (14 June 1832); article collected in 1880 in *Fusains et eaux-fortes*, p.16.

124. Thus, in the ode "A Jehan Duseigneur," the Italian Renaissance; in the article "De l'originalité en France," old Christian painting; in "Mélancholia" (*La France littéraire* [March 1834]; ed. Jasinski, vol.2, pp.83ff.), Dürer and German Catholic art.

125. "A Jehan Duseigneur," p.134.

126. "Mélancholia," pp.89 and 90. I give the 1834 text; the last two lines are different in 1838, without an appreciable change in meaning.

127. "Pensée de minuit," poem dated in the manuscript January 1832 (Spoelberch de Lovenjoul, op.cit., p.152); ed. Jasinski, vol.2, p.127.

128. Gautier, *Albertus*, stanzas 71 and 72.

129. The collection appeared in the summer of 1833.

130. "Elias Wilmanstadius ou l'homme moyen âge" appeared in the *Annales romantiques* of 1833 (published at the end of 1832) and in the *Le Cabinet de lectures* of 24 December 1832; "Onuphrius Wphly" in *La France littéraire* of September 1832 and *Le Cabinet de lecture* of 4 October 1832. It is only when publishing these in book form in the following year that Gautier turns his two heroes into Jeune-France, and the second into an admirer of Hoffmann.

131. This sermon is different in the text of the reviews and in that of the volume; from one year to the next Gautier deepened his critique of the life of the imagination.

132. See in "Daniel Jovard ou la conversion d'un classique" (*Les Jeunes-France*, Charpentier edn. of 1878, pp.80ff.) the speeches of Ferdinand de C. "a beau of the new school": pp.86ff., the lessons he gives to a neophyte and the latter's prodigious conversion, going over "to the most cannibalistic, ferocious Hugolatry."

133. *Les Jeunes-France*, cited edn., "Celle-ci et celle-là," pp.163, 199, 200.

134. *Les Jeunes-France*, p.xiv of the cited edition.

FINAL REFLECTIONS

1. It is not by chance that the literary genres to which romanticism gave new life in order to influence a vast public — drama and the novel — were able to develop in parallel popular variants — melodrama and the serial novel — that spread romantic themes and the romantic philosophy to a vast multitude, up to the very limits of uncultivated ignorance. An in-depth study of this literature (which we have not been able to treat in this book), of its diffusion and success, would be of the greatest interest as a way of illuminating the nature of Romanticism itself.

Index

The translator has added entries for selected subjects and themes to the index of names in the original. Included are names of real or legendary persons mentioned in the course of the work as well as the names of fictional characters (preceded by a dash) and titles of periodicals and anthologies that appeared during the period studied.